SPAIN UNDER FRANCO

Spain Under Franco

A HISTORY

by Max Gallo

Translated from the French by

Jean Stewart

NEW YORK

E. P. DUTTON & COMPANY, INC.

1974

CONTENTS

7

photographs follow pages 96, 194, and 294

PREFACE

The agony of the Spanish Civil War, the hope and courage and the death of the men who fought in it, will dwell forever in our hearts since Hemingway, Malraux, Picasso, Koestler, Sartre, Bernanos, Eluard, Orwell and so many more, confronting that tragedy, have made their sufferings our own.[1]

The Spanish war has thus become an important part of our culture, and accounts of the conflict are naturally rife. The history of Spain, for many people, means Guernica, Teruel, Guadalajara.

But there is no more fighting, nowadays, on the stony soil of the sierras. Since those days, violence has assumed fresh forms: we have seen the Second World War and other wars. If 'Spain is different', as the posters say, for her millions of holiday visitors, it is because sunshine is cheap there. Hemingway himself, revisiting the land of *For Whom the Bell Tolls*, told of toreros' rivalries and assessed the aggressiveness of bulls.

True, for the past few years Spain has been front page news again: there have been strikes and students' demonstrations in plenty; a pretender to the throne has appeared on television; the rate of Spain's industrial growth and economic development have been acclaimed as miraculous. Yet historic continuity seems to have been broken: there was the Civil War, and then a gap of darkness and silence, and now Franco's Spain, on the road to progress, facing the same problems as every other European country.

No doubt it is a matter for some surprise that thirty years after the end of the Civil War the country should still be in a state of emergency, and that the Head of State should be the same General Franco as in 1936, that discreet Caudillo who in his thirty years of power has never left Spanish soil except to visit occupied France for a talk with Hitler and a meeting with Mussolini and Pétain.

It is remarkable, too, that he should have been able to keep the political game in his hands to the point of authoritatively nominating his successor, Don Juan Carlos, on 22 July 1969, thus bestowing on Spain a king chosen by himself to prolong Francoism beyond the life of its founder.

But there remains a gulf between the present scene and the Civil War. There are few books on the subject, and people are ill acquainted with those that exist and with such young Spanish writers as Goytisolo, Antonio Ferres and López Salinas. And yet we feel inevitably that the Spain of today and tomorrow can be understood only if that thirty-year gap is filled; that in darkness and in silence, a nation has gone on living and has, perhaps, kept up its struggle; that 1939 was not the last act of the tragedy.

How could nothing have happened in Spain, after those three years of relentless fighting, in which more than 600,000 fell, when the vanquished were inexor-

[1] Aldo Garosci: *Gli intelletuali e la guerra di Spagna* (Milan, 1959).

9

ably handed over to the victors while the Germans of the Condor Legion and the Italian Black Arrows were triumphing everywhere?

How could nothing have happened in Spain, when in 1945, while Hitler was committing suicide in his bunker as the Soviet troops gathered round, and Mussolini was done to death by those who had fought in the International Brigade, the Franco regime survived and even in 1947, organized its first referendum?

Step by step, from the disappointed hopes of the opposition to the Caudillo's successes, the history of Franco Spain brings us to the present day. And now that Franco's choice of his successor has marked the end of a stage in that history, the time seems ripe to try to understand what took place during those thirty years of Francoism, which, as the Civil War fades into the past, have determined the present and the future of living Spain.

Indeed, to explore that history means, also, to learn what the victors made of their victory and the vanquished of their defeat, to learn, in short, what men were fighting for, what they slaughtered one another for. And gradually, as we reconstruct the story of Franco Spain – that of the Caudillo and his policy, and that of the Spanish people – one fact stands out: the heroism of the Spanish people did not die when the last man fell in the Civil War. The history of Spain under Franco, if it contains less bloodshed than the three years of conflict, is just as rich and possibly even more significant.

In a word, it is clear that ever since 1936, although in a different way, we have been and still are, whether we wish it or not, whether we are aware or unaware of it, confronted with the destiny of Spain and involved with it.

M.G.

He who receives the honour and the burden of being the Leader of a Nation cannot at any moment accept relief or rest. He must spend his whole life in the forefront of the fundamental enterprise to which he has been summoned by the voice and approval of his people, deepening the roots of the system he has established and bringing it to perfection.

FRANCO, 30 December 1960

We are neither a parenthesis nor a dictatorship between two periods . . . We constitute a veritable historic rectification.

FRANCO, 17 July 1958

The glorious epic of our liberation has cost Spain too much blood to be forgotten.

Nevertheless the struggle of Good against Evil is not ended. It would be puerile to believe that the Devil has yielded. He will invent new snares and new masks and he will take new forms in keeping with the times.

FRANCO, 1 April 1959

The army constitutes the backbone of the Fatherland. . . . The sacred mission of a nation's armies consists in maintaining order, and this is the mission which we have accomplished.

FRANCO, 28 April 1956

SPAIN UNDER FRANCO

BOOK I

VICTORY

1938–1942

CHAPTER I

FRANCISCO FRANCO
AND THE DEATH OF
THE SPANISH REPUBLIC

A hand of hatred, O my Spain – lying
like a broad lyre, seawards, between
two seas – has traced zones of war,
military ridges along your plains,
hills, slopes and mountains.
ANTONIO MACHADO

Spring 1938: that pitiless conflict, the Spanish Civil War, had been raging for nearly two years. Since 1936, Europe, having countenanced the crushing of independent Ethiopia by Fascist Italy, had seen war drawing closer. Hitler had remilitarized the left bank of the Rhine, and in defiance of the Treaty of Versailles had brought back compulsory military service. Mussolini, after his triumph over the Negus, Haile Selassie, envisaged with even greater arrogance Italian domination over the whole Mediterranean. And when, on 17 July 1936, the troops of the Spanish Legion of Morocco rose under the leadership of General Francisco Franco y Bahamonde, when the garrisons of the peninsula attempted, with varying degrees of success, to seize its cities, when Italian aircraft enabled the Moroccan *Regulares* to cross from Africa into Spain, when Fascist 'volunteers', side by side with Nationalist troops, openly attacked the democratic forces of the legal government, it became clear to all that war had come to European soil.

French tourists, visiting the Basque country thanks to the first holidays-with-pay granted by their Popular Front government, looked across into Spain at the explosions that marked the advance of an army defying its own *Frente Popular* (Popular Front) government, duly elected in February 1936. Through rented field-glasses, ensconced under leafy bowers or sunshades, they watched war going on, as though they were immune to its contagion.

In fact, from the first days of the fighting, Europe had been involved. Indeed, even before the opening of hostilities, before war broke out in all its cruel reality, Mussolini had given advice and financial aid to the Falangist and traditionalist elements which were preparing their onslaught on a Republic still unsure of itself, torn by internal contradiction – driven by a powerful urge towards social

15

revolution, and yet led by men of the bourgeois class, who, inhibited by their interests, their origins or their prudence, shrank from the necessary upheavals. Italian aircraft intervened from the start, followed by the German Condor Legion, then by Italian troops, some 60,000 strong.

Italian submarines torpedoed those neutral or Russian ships that ventured towards Spanish harbours, while the British and French Governments, paralysed by their pacifism and by the activity of Fascist sympathizers, and misled by the illusory hope of possible compromise, adopted and clung to a policy of non-intervention.

Meanwhile, however, volunteers from many countries had come to Spain to fight by the side of the Republican troops. They fired from the ruined buildings of the University City outside Madrid, and from November 1936 onwards they triumphantly resisted the assaults of Franco's forces, defeating the Italians on the Guadalajara in March 1937. It was a bloody prefiguring of the struggle which was to rend Europe a few years later; those who cried *Arriba España* and those who replied *No pasarán* were acting out the prologue to the Second World War.

The Spanish War Is a Charnel-House (Bernanos)

Spring 1938: the killing had been going on in Spain for two years.

Picasso has shown us that Spain, preyed on by monsters and shattered by explosives, with despairing women lifting up their arms and their eyes to heaven, from whence (as at Guernica on 26 April 1937) came death. But these victims of air attacks (they numbered almost 12,000 by 1938) were not the only casualties. There were wholesale massacres. In the bull-ring at Badajoz, in August 1936, 1,800 Republicans were executed in the space of twelve hours, and seven of their leaders were shot in the bull-pen before 3,000 spectators. At Málaga, which fell on 8 February 1937 into the hands of Roatta's Italian troops and the Nationalist forces, suspects were shot without trial from morning till night. In the other zone, priests, notables and landowners were being killed. Public squares, bull-rings, barracks yards, dirt roads in small villages and paved streets in cities, all were scenes of slaughter. The age of barbarism had begun. The murder of Federico García Lorca by the Nationalists is the image of Spain.

> 'Dead, Federico has fallen
> With blood on his brow and lead in his guts.
> Yes, the crime took place in Granada –
> Know that: poor Granada – his own Granada . . .'

wrote the poet Antonio Machado. 'The Spanish war is a charnel-house,' cried Bernanos.

'A civil war is not a war but a disease,' said Saint-Exupéry. 'In a civil war the enemy is within, one is as it were fighting against oneself. And that, no doubt, is why this war assumes so terrible a form; there is more shooting than fighting; death here is like a quarantine camp – germ-bearers are liquidated. . . . They shoot men as though they were deforesting the land.'

Arthur Koestler, taken prisoner and condemned to death by the Nationalists after the fall of Málaga, then rescued from the firing-squad, wrote in his *Spanish Testament* that other wars might be a series of battles, but this one was a series of tragedies.

There were battles too, where often the tragedy of civil strife was heightened by the horror of summary executions by the roadside or in a field: soldiers in blue overalls and rope-soled sandals, ill-trained Republican soldiers who for a long time rejected all organization, heroic undisciplined anarchists, leaving the trenches at night to sleep in town, together with international fighters, sometimes – as in the case of the Italians – facing their compatriots on the other side. Fierce Moroccans recruited for a crusade, raping, plundering and killing; pitiless battles where nobody expected pity, where every man was aware of his fate – for the vanquished, usually death. Nationalist officers deliberately sought to inspire a 'salutary horror', and it is well known that at a ceremony in the great amphitheatre of the University of Salamanca, on 12 October 1936, General Millán Astray aimed his revolver at the old Basque philosopher Unamuno (who had in fact supported Franco's enterprise during the first few months), with the cry '*i Abajo la Inteligencia! i Viva la muerte!*'[1] The words and the action reflect the tone of the war that had been ravaging Spain for two years. 'You will win,' Unamuno replied, 'because you possess more brute force than you need.'

The War (July 1936 – Spring 1938)

In fact, between July 1936 and the spring of 1938 the Nationalists strengthened their positions and the balance seemed likely to turn in their favour. True, their hope of a swift triumph had been shattered by the resistance of the people; true, Franco's troops advanced only thanks to the help of Fascist Italy and Nazi Germany, and thanks to the non-intervention of the democratic powers, which refused aid to the legal government in Madrid. Mexico remained loyal, the U.S.S.R. provided aircraft, tanks and men, but these two powers were remote; whatever the causes of Franco's successes, these were undeniable, and that was what mattered primarily.

Protected by Italian aircraft, Franco and his forces succeeded in crossing the Straits of Gibraltar, in spite of the fleet's loyalty to the Republic; but they failed to take Madrid, even with the help of German bombers, and meanwhile the Italians were defeated on the Guadalajara (March 1937). Although their advance was checked at the heart of Spain, the Nationalists took Málaga in the south (February 1937), and despite a Republican diversion at Brunete (6 July 1937) – the bloodshed was appalling, 25,000 Republicans and 1,000 Nationalists were killed – Franco's troops gained possession of the Basque country (summer to October 1937): here the Republican defeat not only led to the repression, the summary executions which crowned the work begun at Guernica, but furthermore provided Franco's army with rich industrial provinces and created a Nationalist zone running from the south to the north of Spain, covering the west

[1] According to A. Plen (*Les Temps Modernes*, May 1950), Franco's wife Carmen prevented Astray from firing at Unamuno.

side of the peninsula, bordering on Portugal and touching the Mediterranean and the Atlantic.

Meanwhile, the collapse of the north revealed the military weakness of the Republican government and released a considerable body of Nationalist troops to attack eastwards, threatening Madrid. The Republican commanders, seeking to take the initiative, launched an offensive in the Teruel region. The attack began on 15 December 1937. An icy wind blew from the near-by high sierras, sweeping over the plain and rushing down the Turia valley, at —20 °C sometimes. Teruel is built on a steep rocky prominence standing in the centre of a ring of hills nearly 6,000 feet high. It fell to the Republicans on 7 January. It was the only important town they were able to reconquer throughout the war.

This victory had undoubted psychological significance, but it was won at the cost of heavy losses and it did not prevent the Nationalists from resuming the offensive. On 22 February 1938 Teruel was retaken by Franco's troops; the battle of attrition, the long-drawn-out battle of Teruel may have saved Madrid, but it bled the Republicans white. The superior power of the Nationalists was becoming evident. The sky was theirs, too: at midday on 20 January 1938, as crowds were leaving offices and factories, Italian aircraft attacked Barcelona, repeating the Guernica exploit with the same aim – terrorization. On 16 March, at three in the afternoon, there began a series of seventeen raids on the Catalan capital which continued uninterruptedly for some ten hours, killing 1,300 and wounding 3,000. Spain was unmistakably a testing-ground for the Second World War.

During this same spring of 1938, Nationalist troops, together with Italians of the *Corpo Truppe Volontarie*, broke through the Republican lines all along the south bank of the Ebro. On 15 April the Nationalist troops of Alonso Vega reached the Mediterranean at Vinaroz: Republican Spain was cut in half. The central southern part was isolated from Catalonia. Nationalist and Italian soldiers might well shout for joy and throw their helmets in the air on the beach, while Moroccans went swimming; a decisive turning had been reached. Nationalists also attacked all along the Pyrenees, and refugees poured into France in their thousands; women, children and old men fled from Aragon, which was occupied by the troops of Generals Moscardo and Yagüe. Although the Republican soldiers reaching France were eager to go back to fight, fiercely raising clenched fists as they leaned out of the carriage windows, the Republic, now cut in half, was already faced with defeat.

Spring 1938: the fighting, the killing had been going on for two years, and the greatest battle was still to come, launched on 25 July by the Republicans, who with their surprise crossing of the Ebro broke up the enemy lines. 'The Italians have fallen into the Ebro, and only Republican flags now fly on its bridges'; so ran a popular song. The violence of the clash was something unparalleled in any civil war; and in fact this conflict had long been more than that. The Germans were there with their first Stukas, the Italians with their artillery, hundreds of tanks appeared, and opposite them the International Brigades under General Lister fought with relentless courage. 'The *tabors*', according to the report of the 13th Nationalist division, 'must advance and clear the trenches every ten metres, by means of hand grenades, of an enemy whom we have failed to dislodge either through repeated bombardment or by continued concentrations of artillery.' The Republicans fought with an energy that amazed the whole world, half-trained soldiers resisting the strongest units of the Spanish, Moroccan, German and Italian armies, civilian-soldiers who knew that death was the only outcome.

The Spanish Labyrinth

It has sometimes been asserted that this proud, despairing acceptance of blood-shed and death is something innate in the character of Spain, that arid land of violence and crusades, the home of the corrida, where scarlet and black, gold and steel whirl and flash amid tumultuous cries. In fact this colourful legend explains nothing, merely disguising a failure to understand the 'Spanish Labyrinth.'[2] As Karl Marx said, 'there is perhaps no country except Turkey so little known to, and so falsely judged by Europe as Spain'. Undoubtedly the difficulties encountered in an attempt to analyse the situation in Spain are due to the historical, social and economic peculiarities of that country, which are all connected with the factor of its backwardness, its archaism in relation to twentieth-century Europe.

From the point of view of political unity, Spain in fact displays powerful centrifugal tendencies which make the problem of the state and its coherence one of the crucial questions in her history. The centralizing, unifying heart of the country is Castile, but it is the peripheral coastal regions, from the Asturias to Catalonia, which have the greater wealth and dynamism, being open to commerce and industry, rich in coal and endowed with a spirit of initiative. And yet, historically and strategically, the co-ordinating centre is the high, windy plateau of Castile, over which run those sinuous walls of grey stone that form the enclosures where bulls graze. Under these conditions unification must inevitably assume an authoritarian and military character, that of a *reconquista* of the active periphery by Castile; while in Seville or Bilbao, but above all in Catalonia, the effort made to break the link is natural and enduring, an inherent factor in the economic and cultural development of the region. The separatist tendencies which in most European countries (even in those whose unification came late, such as Italy and Germany) have been crushed or canalized were still very much alive in twentieth-century Spain, a striking symptom of archaism. Like Turkey, but also like Greece or the Balkan countries, Spain lay on the fringe of Europe, although her past was bound up with the essential history of European civilization.

A Land Without Bread

Another sign of Spain's backwardness was the dramatic acuteness of her agrarian problem. *A Land without Bread*, Buñuel's film made between 1932 and 1937 in the region of Las Hurdes, not far from the Portuguese border, shows to what extreme inhumanity peasant destitution can lead; but pictures of savage creatures

[2] Gerald Brenan, *The Spanish Labyrinth* (Cambridge, 1943). A basic study. See also P. Vilar, *La Catalogne dans l'Espagne moderne* (Paris, 1960), a model of historical analysis.

living in dens do not tell the whole truth about the evil from which rural Spain was suffering: that evil can be identified as inequality in the distribution of land.

True, geographical conditions also played a part: Spain is a table-land of primary rocks whose average altitude is over 2,000 feet above sea-level. It suffers from aridity: lunar mountains, barren hills covered with sharp, white, broken rocks have gradually over the centuries created conditions of enhanced aridity, which in turn generate an insatiable erosion of the soil. The cycle erosion-aridity-erosion-desert thus covers ever larger areas; but underlying this 'geographical' disaster we can trace human history, man's methods of tilling the ground, irrigation giving place to grazing which, though more immediately remunerative, is ultimately destructive, since grass replaces crops of fruit trees and stone presently replaces grass. Thus a study of natural conditions brings us back to that of the agrarian system and the ownership of land.

Here we discover conditions that recall those of a bygone or disappearing Europe, of France in the first half of the eighteenth century, southern Italy, pre-Revolutionary Russia or Central Europe. For while 200,000 landowners or rich peasants owned some 40 per cent of the cultivated land, we find more than 3 million poor peasants and more than 2 million *braceros*, landless labourers. In that part of Spain which had been assessed in 1929, out of 1,062,412 tax-paying landowners or tenants 847,548 earned less than one peseta a day.

As always in an agrarian system of this type (which still survives in Latin America today) there existed side by side large estates, often uncultivated, latifundia that employed agricultural labourers at starvation wages, ready to accept anything since the supply of unemployed was inexhaustible; small plots of land, insufficient to provide for the poor peasant family, who were therefore forced to work on others' land or to emigrate to the outskirts of large towns, where they formed a sub-proletariat whose directly rural origins were reflected in violent and unstable behaviour; finally, farmers and share-croppers, often bound by short-term leases which the landlord was generally able to modify to his own advantage, owing to the large number of landless peasants who were ready to make any sort of concession. These three elements were differently combined according to region.

The central and northern regions (Galicia, Asturias, the Basque provinces, Navarre, Old Castile, León, Aragon, Catalonia) were mainly characterized by zones of small properties, sometimes leased out to tenant farmers or share-croppers (in Catalonia, for instance, the *rabassaires*, whose contract was based on the life of the vines). These regions enjoy an adequate rainfall, have their own strong peasant traditions and have been Christian since the tenth century. In the Levante region (particularly around Valencia), with its irrigated lands, the peasants managed to make a living from their smallholdings by dint of intense labour; while in the Granada region, also well watered, day-labourers and farmers were strongly enough organized to protect their living conditions. This group of regions (the poorest being Galicia, León and Old Castile) constituted what Gerald Brenan has called 'the fortunate districts of Spanish life, where the conditions can be compared not unfavourably with those in other parts of Europe'.

However, there is another Spain, which we find in Andalusia for instance, formerly a rich province with busy industrial towns set like gems in a vast, well-watered zone, but which was ruined when it was reconquered by the Castilian Spaniards, who drove out the Muslims, used the land to pasture their flocks and destroyed the political, demographic, religious and economic structure of the region. This is the Spain of latifundia and short leases which leave the tenant or share-cropper under permanent threat of eviction, the Spain of a destitute peasantry hopelessly indebted to the money-lender and at the mercy of an irregular climate that may entail long periods of drought. The figures speak for themselves: 7,000 landowners, for the most part not living on their estates, owned more than 6 million hectares in the provinces of Estremadura, Andalusia and La Mancha; in the Avila region of Castile, out of 13,530 inhabitants only 320, in 1929, earned more than five pesetas a day. The area of the latifundia covered 96 per cent of the land in the province of Cadiz; often these latifundia, sometimes consisting of excellent arable land, were devoted to stock-breeding. Here bulls or horses ranged over thousands of hectares, while elsewhere men were concentrated in infertile zones, owning nothing. Gerald Brenan quotes that impartial observer, the geographer E. H. G. Dobby:

'I recall an incident during a visit (in 1935) to an experimental pig farm in an out-of-the-way part of Andalusia. From the darkness at one end of the building came a red glow. I went along and found a labourer's family crouched on the floor round a twig fire with smoke so thick that breathing was difficult. The malodorous squalor contrasted with the carefully washed sties that I had been seeing. To my query an old woman mumbled: "Yes, we live here. Worse than the pigs." At which the owner beside me exclaimed indignantly: "You have a roof over your head. What more do you want?"'[3]

Demographic pressure, moreover, was such in many regions that, as the landlord's exclamation implies, to work, under any conditions whatsoever, was in itself a privilege. For Spain had not adapted herself to the growth of her population, which had risen from 11 million in 1808 to 18·5 million in 1900 and 24 million in 1935. This sharp, swift rise in the birthrate is yet another sign of primitivism in comparison with Europe, making Spain more akin to the under-developed countries. This, too, explains Spain.

Men less cared for than animals, inequalities and customs dating back to the Middle Ages; whole families at starvation level, endemic diseases (such as trachoma) due to nutritional deficiencies or lack of hygiene; insecurity. This was the lot of most of Spain's rural population on the eve of the Civil War, while thirty-eight great nobles owned between them more than half a million hectares for hunting: 79,146 hectares belonged to the Duke of Medinaceli, 51,015 to the Duke of Peñaranda, 47,202 to the Duke of Villahermosa, 34,455 to the Duke of Alba. .... This was the true cause of violence in Spain; the law on agrarian reform promulgated in September 1932, and the law on the revision of leases of 1933 were derisory palliatives for this age-old malady: on 31 December 1934,

[3] 'Agrarian Problems in Spain', in Geographical Review of the American Geographical Society (April 1936).

12,260 peasants were settled in 529 estates over a total area of 116,857 hectares! Under such conditions violence was bound to break out. By the end of 1932 the long-oppressed peasantry in many regions, particularly in Andalusia, rose and took possession of the land; the big landowners united in a solid block against this movement.

The savagery of the Civil War is not to be ascribed to any specifically Spanish characteristic; it was a result of the hostility which is deeply rooted in the agrarian question. It is a well-known fact that landed proprietors and poor peasants have never shown any mercy to one another, and the whole history of Western Europe throughout the Middle Ages is marked by risings and massacres and savage repressions – as in seventeenth-century Brittany, where the roasting of a child on a spit was witnessed and described by that refined lady, Madame de Sévigné.

This was what exploded in Spain, in the twentieth century, in the Civil War, because Spain was a backward country in which there had never been any redistribution of the land, and because for Nationalist officers whose fathers were landed proprietors a peasant was nothing better than a beast, to be hunted down like quarry and slaughtered when his sufferings drove him mad.

Consequences of the Agrarian Question

The agrarian question – that essential aspect of Spain's economic backwardness, of which it was at once a consequence and a cause – is crucial, moreover, for the understanding of most aspects of the Spanish situation. Anti-clericalism, which gained strength from the beginning of the twentieth century, and not in the bourgeoisie alone, can be partly explained by the fact that the Church was an important landowner (11,000 estates, valued at about 130,000,000 pesetas) and had formed, almost everywhere, a close alliance with the big landlords, symbolized by the way the massive church towered over the village as the castle had in medieval times.

The Spanish Church was a fighting, crusading institution, and in the south particularly, where peasant poverty was most extreme and widespread, the illiterate rural masses looked on it as an instrument of oppression. The phenomenon was less noticeable in the north, because there a settled rural economy existed, with small peasant proprietors or share-croppers, so that the Church had a close link with the people and a following among them, while reciprocally the clergy were less directly connected with the ruling class. The example of the Basque provinces is highly significant; here property or lease-held land was handed down from father to son, and the 'family community' system was the rule; in such a social context, clergy and peasantry were bound to one another, particularly as they shared a common culture and way of life.

On the one hand, therefore, we find such representatives of the Church as Mgr Segura, Archbishop of Toledo, or Mgr Goma, who took upon himself to send a letter on behalf of all the Spanish bishops, urging 'the bishops of the whole world to condemn the Republic'. On the other we find the bishops of Tarragona and Vitoria, both in exile, and above all those Basque priests whom

Franco's supporters persecuted, so that at least sixteen of them were shot. Of course the 'national' aspect of the problem plays a part: the victims included Father Aristimuno, a specialist in Basque civilization, but the example shows explicitly how a particular agrarian system provides a basis on which a vigorous sectionalism can flourish, bringing together Church and people in stubborn resistance.

Economic backwardness – which implies the agrarian system – is the factor which, together with specific historic circumstances (the representative of the First International in Spain was the Italian deputy Fanelli, a disciple of Bakunin rather than of Marx) explains the importance of anarchism in Spain. Independent peasants in the parcelled-out lands of the east and north, peasants ruined by debt, the large artisan population of a country not yet given over to industrialization, these form a social stratum susceptible to anarchism. That ideology, moreover, with its summons to violence, its generous and mystical utopianism, its nostalgia for a golden age, is readily adaptable to a country which is still essentially rural, where the proletariat are numerically weak and of immediate peasant origin, and where the Catholic faith has for a long time been the bearer of hope and consolation to humble folk. Anarchism is thus yet another form of primitivism, by which Spain differs, in this twentieth century, from the rest of Europe, and the Civil War made possible the outbreak of that primitive revolt[4] which was to intensify the violence of the clash and the scale of the repression, and also, in the Republican zone, to hinder the necessary organization of authority.

Thenceforward, while at the front the Republicans were resisting Franco's forces, they were fighting one another at the rear. Members of the *Confederación Nacional del Trabajo* and of the *Federación Anarquista Ibérica*, anarchist followers of Durruti (whose past history was one of violence – he had killed Cardinal Soldevila at Saragossa) were struggling against Socialists and their *Unión General de Trabajadores*, and above all against the Communists, who were few in number on the eve of the Civil War, though their decisive role in the resistance of Madrid in 1936, together with the help given to Spain by the u.s.s.r., soon brought them into the foreground.

Divisions Within the Republic

These dissensions within the Republican camp were inevitably a cause of weakness, and help to explain its ultimate defeat. The conflict in fact was not confined to Anarchists, Communists and Socialists: the bourgeoisie was also deeply involved.

Moreover, the nature and position of this bourgeoisie also reflect the backwardness, the archaism of Spain. Industry, which existed only in Catalonia and Asturias, remained a secondary factor; small-scale enterprise and cottage industry were the rule. The Spanish bourgeoisie, the product of this economic under-development, could not constitute a ruling class, particularly within the national framework that confronted it in Castile and among the large estates of the south; it

[4] E. J. Hobsbawm, *Primitive Rebels* (Manchester, 1959).

23

therefore favoured sectionalism, primarily in Catalonia, where it was the most powerful. At the same time, by reason of the manifold factors of backwardness in the economic and social evolution of the peninsula, the bourgeoisie had to face an accumulation of contradictions, both archaic (the agrarian problem with its feudal implications, the problem of industrial development, the role of the army, the Church and the nobility) and contemporary (the power of the revolutionary movement, of the peasant masses, of Anarchists and Socialists). In most European countries, these contradictions between different levels of development have been solved by degrees: witness the French Revolution. In Spain they were telescoped, so that they reacted on one another, leading to a situation homologous to that experienced in Russia. In other words, Spain was now ripe for a revolutionary explosion.[5] The Spanish bourgeoisie was thus in a position of weakness, incapable of holding the country, constantly threatened by the centralizing feudalism of landowners backed by the army, the Church, and the Castilian traditions of state control, but at the same time in danger of being swept away by a revolutionary wave.

In the early thirties, when the world was in the throes of economic crisis, the Spanish workers' movement intensified its activity, at the very moment when the agrarian question had become acute, following local peasant risings and seizures of land. The abdication of King Alfonso XIII on 14 April 1931, after the municipal elections, the creation of the Second Spanish Republic's provisional government, encouraged this revolutionary upsurge (of which, at the same time, they were the political consequence), giving the masses the impression that Spain's backwardness, the poverty, injustice and flagrant inequality in land tenure from which she suffered were about to disappear.

It might have seemed indeed that this Second Republic would make it possible to get rid of that political, social and economic archaism which kept Spain out of phase with other countries – France for instance – that had experienced a bourgeois revolution. But in fact, not one of the classes involved was in a position to impose its hegemony over the rest, and their mutual alliances were inevitably fragile, since within each class there were such divisions that no single group was capable of cementing the class to which it belonged.

The bourgeoisie was divided. The peasantry and the working masses were not homogeneous socially or ideologically: small property-owning peasants, sharecroppers, *braceros*, artisans, proletarians, the unemployed, Anarchists, Socialists, Communists, and before long the dissident Communists of the *Partido Obrero de Unificación Marxista* (P.O.U.M., a group founded in 1934 by Andrés Nin and other former Trotskyists), all these were at odds with one another. However, mass strikes (Seville, July 1931) and a succession of daring, if futile, anarchist *coups de main* (8 January 1933, in Barcelona, Madrid, Lérida) created a revolutionary atmosphere. Acts of violence and terrorism displayed not only the resolute spirit of the revolutionary and anarchist fighters, but also the archaic character of their ideology and the inadequate organization of their methods, all of which aspects were bound up with the economic and social situation in Spain.

[5] See the author's essay on the mechanics of revolution, "*Gauchisme, réformisme et révolution*," in the series *Contestation*, Robert Laffont (Paris, 1968).

The bourgeois Republic took fright; everywhere the Civil Guards intervened, repressing savagely, restoring order by gunfire. After the elections of 1933 the Republic was in the hands of the right wing, and the *Bienio negro*, the 'black two years', began, marked by repressive measures, by the annulment of such timid social reforms as had been initiated, by the reduction of wages, and consequently by a recrudescence of workers' and peasants' demonstrations and the creation of working-class alliances to combat the right wing organization *Confederación Española de Derechas Autónomas* (C.E.D.A.) of Gil Robles, whose Fascist sympathies were unmistakable. In September he had attended the Nuremberg rally.

The Struggle Intensifies

On 4 October 1934, a general strike was declared and an armed insurrection broke out in Asturias. It was crushed by Franco with his *Tercio* (Foreign Legion) and Moorish troops: at least 3,000 to 4,000 workers were killed, 7,000 wounded, 30,000 taken prisoner. This was civil war already: workers were fettered or slaughtered, while soldiers of the Legion stared down with indifference at the bodies of their victims; strikers were mown down by machine-gun fire or tortured by the Moroccan *Regulares* and the Legionaries. The fight had already proved an unequal one, and the army had won it. The success of the *Frente Popular* on 16 February 1936, with 268 deputies elected, of whom 158 were Republicans, 80 Socialists and 17 Communists, against 205 for the centre and right parties, was an answer to repression, confirming the existence of a popular upsurge, proving indeed that since the establishment of the Republic in 1931 that movement had grown in scope and power. In a few months, between February and July, important measures were taken: lands were confiscated and then distributed among poor peasants and *braceros*, and the autonomy of Galicia and Catalonia was proclaimed.

The problems and contradictions that had been exposed had by no means disappeared, rather the reverse. The success of the *Frente Popular*, and then the outbreak of civil war started by the Spanish army, carried revolutionary feelings to a fresh point of intensity. Yet the legal framework was still that of a 'democratic', 'bourgeois' government, led by President Azaña, who declared: 'We want no dangerous innovations. We want order and peace. We are moderates.'

A 'Democratic' Republic or a Social Revolution?

Henceforward it was clear that the essential problem confronting Franco's opponents could be summed up in a few questions: could victory be achieved without going beyond a 'bourgeois' republic, could it be achieved without a social revolution (in rural areas by giving land to the peasants, but also in the towns), or on the other hand, could it be achieved by severance from that wing of the bourgeoisie which had accepted the *Frente Popular* and was fighting for the Republic? This was the crux of the conflict between political groups behind the front line, in Madrid or in Barcelona.

And naturally the international situation affected attitudes directly. The

U.S.S.R. under Stalin, harrying the Trotskyists and organizing the bloody farce of its treason trials (1936–7), committed by fear of the Nazi threat but also as a result of Stalin's 'conservative' home policy to a rapprochement with the Western democracies, and haunted by the fear of a united hostile bloc of capitalist states (from France to Germany), was naturally in favour of stabilizing the situation in the Republican zone on the basis of a 'democratic' compromise with elements of the petty and middle bourgeoisie. Now the Spanish Republic could not do without Soviet aid, and Moscow's advice was therefore listened to with respect, particularly as it coincided with the objective organizational needs of a country involved in a struggle.

The Spanish Communists were the fervent, efficient and tenacious spokesmen for the line that sought to impose, by any means, discipline and order, and unity with the petty bourgeoisie on the basis of a 'democratic front'. They were further anxious to establish their control over the whole working-class and revolutionary movement. Thus an implacable struggle for hegemony went on behind the scenes in the civil war. In May 1937 the barricades went up in Barcelona, and the workers (among whom there were unquestionably some Francoist provocateurs) clashed with the reconstituted Republican police; the Anarchist leader Berberi, an Italian anti-Fascist exile, was murdered, as was also, soon afterwards, Andrés Nin, one of the founders of the P.O.U.M. The revolutionary masses were thus kept under control, the army reconstituted, property was preserved and the revolution was checked. All these conditions were necessary for the re-establishment of the Republic and for restoring the confidence of bourgeois elements; they were indispensable for the military struggle against Franco's armies. The Spanish Communist Party thus became, at all events in appearance, the dominant force, the organizing power, in association with the more moderate elements in the Socialist Party. Resistance had become possible; Anarchists and Trotskyists had been called to order; Durruti had fallen in battle, Berneri and Nin were dead. The Republican army was enabled to resist, to counter-attack at Teruel, to cross the Ebro. This discipline, this control, this consolidation also meant the death of a type of revolutionary activity that allowed the spontaneity and initiative of the masses to express itself: it meant an end to the revolutionary militia, to the committees, to collectivization in the countryside, to the taking-over of industrial concerns (it was not always clear by whom), as well as an end to pillaging, vandalism and summary executions.

'We cannot achieve the revolution unless we win the war; the first thing is to win the war', said José Díaz, secretary of the Spanish Communist Party. The anarchist Camillo Berneri, on the other hand, had written in 1936:

'The war must be won, yet we shall not win the war by confining the problem to the strictly military conditions of victory but by associating these with its political and social conditions. . . . The only dilemma is this: either victory over Franco by means of a revolutionary war, or defeat.'

The tendency represented by the Communist Party won the day, and one might say, quoting Saint-Just, that 'the revolution was frozen'. Nevertheless victory was to elude the Republic which, for its sake, had postponed revolution.

The Two Sides

For while the Spanish war had become the theatre of a trial of strength between European Powers, the international situation in that era of fascism and nazism was hardly favourable to a revolutionary upsurge. Moreover, the situation on the two sides was different. The 'Republican' side was, as we have seen, heterogeneous and its diversity reveals the different levels of development within Spain. The result of this was that no group could become dominant except as the result of a ruthless struggle against the groups closest to it (Communists against Anarchists and Trotskyists), and even so could not impose its hegemony over the 'Republican' whole. Communists collaborated with Socialists, representatives of the 'bourgeoisie' and of the traditional army. Negrín, the last leader of the Republican Government, was a member of the upper bourgeoisie with Socialist sympathies. This diversity might have been a source of strength had it maintained political coherence and led to real unity; in point of fact the antagonisms, being fundamental, subsisted and were further aggravated by military reverses.

On the other hand, despite rivalries, struggles for influence and differences in motivation, the Nationalist camp was far more effectively united. Its social constitution was more homogeneous (landed proprietors, financiers, the middle classes in general), being based on historically traditional structures to which many regions still clung. These structures were, by their very nature, those of the state, expressing the centralizing principle of Spain; above all, the Church and a nationalism of the most summary sort provided them with an ideological coherence that was simple but sufficient, and more effective than the concept of a Republic.

For the Nationalists, archaism was a source of strength, because it was bound up with the history and situation of Spain. Furthermore, Franco's followers had a single, hierarchized party, whose organization had proved its efficiency; this party, for which there was no equivalent on the Republican side, was simply the Spanish army. This was the body whose hegemony the Nationalist side accepted unquestioningly: a body that included such picked troops as the *Tercio Extranjero* (the Foreign Legion) and the Moroccan *Regulares*, fighters seasoned during the Rif war and above all during the repression of the workers' rising in Asturias in October 1934. The army, moreover, had already launched one pronunciamento, that of General Sanjurjo in August 1932. It was hostile to any thorough-going reform; it defended traditional Spain, the unchanging Spain of the big landowners and of the monarchy, 'Eternal Spain'. It formed the powerful cement that united the Nationalists, despite the mutual jealousy of their generals. Basically, together with the Catholic Church, it was the most powerful and best organized *political force* in Spain at that time. And these two forces were on the same side.

Moreover, a leading personality had gradually emerged – and this, too, was something the Republic lacked; after two years of civil war, he already occupied a dominant position.

27

General Francisco Franco y Bahamonde

This is not to say that by the spring of 1938 General Francisco Franco y Baha-monde had his partisans completely and unquestionably under control. Stohrer, the German Ambassador to the Generalissimo, notes for instance in a report of 19 May 1938, on *The political situation in Nationalist Spain*:

'Nationalist Spain still lacks unity and solidarity in many respects . . . persons who know the situation well estimate the number of politically unreliable people in White Spain at about 40 per cent. This fact is emphasized by a number of assassinations, attempts to destroy bridges . . . acts of incendiarism and guerrilla fighting . . . and although the war and the needs of the hour require unity in political opinion, one can often hear quite different opinions on this or that problem even in military and governmental circles.'[6]

However, such resistance or opposition was strongest when the military situa-tion was uncertain; and from the spring of 1938 onwards it evolved in Franco's favour. Above all, he could be relied on to surmount all obstacles and break any resistance.

Indeed, his whole past history reveals unquestionable qualities of prudence, obstinacy, determination, shrewdness, ambition, love of power, firmness in applying decisions and a lack of what might be called 'humanitarian prejudices'.

His life story epitomizes one aspect of the old Spain and its efforts to prevent the birth of a new Spain, and he is one of those men who, born in the last third of the nineteenth century (Mussolini 1883, Hitler 1889, Franco 1892) chose nationalism and had to face the revolutionary tide that rose in 1917, enduring and exploiting national grievances, in various degrees, in order to build up the state in opposition to liberals, democrats, and all other 'corrupting' elements within the nation.

Franco's individual destiny must therefore be considered in a wider historical context that covers the whole inter-war period, and that includes the conflict between liberal democracy, communism, nationalism and fascism. But whereas Mussolini and Hitler were 'outsiders' who had broken with society in order to identify themselves with, and assume leadership of, a particular group and ideology, Franco on the contrary is the finished product of a class, a caste and a life-history of 'classic' type. This difference between the future Caudillo and the Duce or the Führer, between the youngest general in the Spanish army and those ex-N.C.O.'s, ambitious upstarts climbing to power amidst tumult after irregular careers, unstable visionaries – this distance between the traditional career-man and those other adventurers measures the distance existing between Spain and Germany or Italy: Spain, where the archaic, traditional element still prevailed even in this reaction against twentieth-century innovation; Italy or Germany, where the opposition to communism took a radically new form. It was already obvious that the doctrines and methods of Franco were to evolve differ-

[6] *Documents on German Foreign Policy*, series D, vol. III, *Germany and the Spanish Civil War (1936–1939)* (London, 1951), p. 658.

28

ently from those of fascism or nazism, owing to that specific Spanish backwardness which is reflected in the life of the Spanish dictator.

Galician and Army Man

Francisco Paulino Hermengildo Teodulo Franco y Bahamonde is a native of Galicia. He was born on 3 December 1892 in the town of El Ferrol, in that province whose damp climate recalls Ireland's, where the widely scattered dwellings display the peasants' individualism, each family living in autarchy on its own plot of land, that Galicia so different from the rest of Spain, lying back to back with cold, stony Castile. Franco naturally looked seaward; as a boy, he hoped to be a sailor. His father, Nicolás Franco, was a naval paymaster. His mother, Pilar Baamonde,[7] bravely endured her husband's infidelities and bouts of drunkenness, and the petty provincial scandals provoked by his behaviour. A separation followed; in that Spanish middle-class milieu, narrow-minded, pretentious, vaunting its respectability, this was a bitter blow to the whole family, to the mother primarily but also to her three sons, Nicolás the eldest, Ramón the second son and Francisco, 'Franquito' as they called him, a lad with delicate, girlish features and an over-soft voice, who had just moved on from the College of the Sacred Heart to the Naval Preparatory Academy.

He came from a military family, he had been christened in a military parish. When the navy ceased to accept recruits, he became a cadet at the Military Academy of Toledo. By the age of fifteen Francisco Franco was already inseparably bound to the Spanish army. It was his family; he learned, before all else, to obey, to carry out orders, to submit, to command, to endure in silence. The army was a backwater, a sort of ghetto embittered by the humiliation of defeat (in 1898 Spain had lost Cuba at the end of her war with the United States), brooding over memories of past glory (Cortez, the glorious Spanish infantry, the Golden Century) and exalting military 'virtues' – obedience, courage in the face of death, the eternal spirit of Spain. It was a ghetto set apart from the Spain of its day, which witnessed the ambiguous intellectual regeneration of 1898 and the attempt to tackle the problems of development. For Franco this ghetto meant a refuge, it brought hopes of advancement, and like the rest of the officer caste he saw in it the true spirit of Spain, its physical and spiritual health.

On 13 July 1910, when he was only seventeen, Francisco Franco became a sub-lieutenant in the 8th Regiment of Zamora, garrisoning the naval base at El Ferrol. He was back in his native town: this meant all the petty resentment and the dreariness of barracks life, with a sense of frustration. Before long he demanded, resolutely and stubbornly, to be sent to Morocco.

Africa and Asturias

Africa represented a ghetto within the military ghetto; the colonial army was, as it were, the army in essence, its most extreme element, and Morocco was the last remaining theatre in which a soldier could display heroism and win rapid

[7] The 'h' was introduced later.

29

advancement. It was the happy hunting-ground for the ambitious, but it was yet a further stage removed from the other Spain, and Franco was to become a typical colonial army officer.

In July 1912 we find Franco at Melilla, lieutenant in charge of the *Regulares*, native mercenaries, violent and pugnacious. There was real fighting going on here, and Franco dedicated himself assiduously to his profession. He led his men forward at risk of his life. He was promoted captain in 1915; on 28 June the following year, during a fierce engagement, as he bent down to pick up a gun to fire, he was seriously wounded in the abdomen. Franco's ambition was proof against gunfire and his physical courage was undeniable. He was honoured with a medal and promoted major on 19 June 1916. He was then twenty-four.

On 13 May 1917, he resumed active service, at the heart of 'the other Spain', at Oviedo, the 'red' centre of the working-class mining province of Asturias. Here he met Carmen Polo y Martínez Valdés, the young daughter of a wealthy, old-established Oviedo family. In spite of some resistance from her people, for whom Franco was merely an unknown young officer, they were married in 1923 at Oviedo, and their witness was the military governor, representing King Alfonso XIII, for in the meantime Franco had gained distinction. Until 1917 he had merely been a brilliant young officer who had won promotion under fire, in the remote colonial adventure which was not wholly approved of in Spain, even in conservative circles. In Asturias in August 1917 he encountered the other Spain, and History, when the Asturian miners, carried away by that great revolutionary wave that was sweeping Europe from Petrograd to Turin, from Kiel to the factories of central France, joined in the movement for a general strike that was affecting the whole of Spain. Franco, at the head of a column of infantrymen and civil guards armed with machine-guns, was instructed to restore order and break the unlawful strike. He carried out his orders like a soldier accustomed to obey, like a member of the military caste convinced that he embodied the rule of truth and law in Spain, and like a colonial officer whose campaigns in Morocco had rid him of any tiresome scruples about human life: at least a hundred Spaniards were killed, while Largo Caballero and the founder of the Workers' Socialist Party, Pablo Iglesias, who was to confront Franco during the Civil War, were thrown into prison. Thus the army, strong in its twofold tradition as a repressive colonial force and a protector of the established social order, asserted its vocation to restrain the other Spain by force of arms; and thus Francisco Franco's historic destiny was made manifest, while he was still only twenty-five.

Viva la Muerte!

He went back to Africa. He had met Millán Astray who, fascinated by the role played by the Foreign Legion in the First World War, had succeeded in creating a Spanish unit of the same type. For the Spanish army numbered among its frustrations that of having taken no part in the great hecatomb; it longed to win by its African battles or its political interventions the glory it had not achieved on the Yser, at Verdun or on the Piave. Lieutenant-Colonel Millán Astray was authorized, in 1920, to create the Spanish Foreign Legion, the *Tercio de Extranjeros*. He canvassed Franco, who joined him without hesitation, leaving Oviedo and postponing his marriage. By 10 October he was at Ceuta. The legionaries, encouraged by Millán Astray to shout *'Viva la Muerte'* and taught a creed of which one article declared that 'the spirit of the Legion is one of blind and ferocious aggressiveness in face of the enemy', sang to the tune of *La Madelon*:

> *'El comandante Franco es un gran militar*
> *que aplazó su boda para ir a luchar.'*[8]

The *Tercio Extranjero*, which was made up of social outlaws, was an ideal unit for brave and ambitious officers of Franco's stamp. Here casualties were unimportant; what mattered was success. Spain herself, the other Spain, was not encouraging, and Franco wrote in his *Journal of the Legion*:

'The country is out of touch with the actions of the Protectorate and looks on with indifference at the self-sacrifice of the army and of those devoted officers who pay their daily tribute of blood amidst these scorching mountain peaks. What irresponsibility! ... Our hope of forming a vanguard is being gradually frustrated and our officers are depressed and thoughtful. ... The soldiers seem to share our vexation.'

These significant comments reveal the growing gulf between the aims of the colonial army and the aspirations, and policy, of the country. Naturally, since the army seemed the embodiment of Spain and the army's policy entailed glorious deaths, since self-sacrifice was needed, it was Spain that had to yield. The army's policy prevailed. In 1921 the Riffan war against Abd-el-Krim broke out at last and Franco, tanned and slender, in his open-necked shirt with a broad-brimmed hat shading his rather weak features, still youthful in spite of a thick dark moustache, was able to lead the forces of the Legion in the Spanish army's war – which, according to the officers, was Spain's own war.

The Most Successful Product of His Caste

Franco won distinction in this war, and for a while was acting commander of the whole *Tercio* while new troops were being raised. On the front he met all the officers who were to lead the 1936 crusade, first and foremost General Sanjurjo, later the leading spirit in the plot against the *Frente Popular*, who had come to prepare the *reconquista* operations. In Spain itself the Moroccan crisis aggravated a situation which economic difficulties had already made tense. The army incessantly demanded reinforcements and credits; the 'juntas' refused to take a decision; there were protests on all sides, and taking advantage of this state of affairs General Primo de Rivera, Captain-general of Catalonia, forced King Alfonso XIII to accept a Directory led by himself. Primo de Rivera's dictatorship was to last from 13 September 1923 to 30 January 1930. His success can be explained by a combination of factors: the power of the military caste, the colonial problem, and the propertied classes' fear of the Anarchists, Syndicalists and Socialists. The determining factors in the Spanish situation were already present.

[8] 'Major Franco is a great soldier who put off his wedding to go and fight.'

Meanwhile, however, Franco was pursuing his career. On 7 February 1925, at thirty-three, he became a colonel. General Saro recommended him to the Supreme Command, after a landing operation in the bay of Alhucemas:

'Special mention must be made of Colonel Franco who, by his brilliant action in this engagement, has further confirmed the opinion, held by everyone without exception, of his ability, his courage, his serenity and all the exceptional qualities which make of him a leader deserving all praise.'

On 3 February 1926, by royal decree, he was appointed brigadier at the age of thirty-four; he was the youngest general in the Spanish army, indeed in any European army. The perfect, brilliant product of an institution and a caste.

What Was to Be Done?

His rank, and above all his swift success, entailed duties, first and foremost towards himself. At this early stage in his life he had already reached a high level of military honour, so that, by contrast with this rapid series of promotions, what lay before him must inevitably seem like marking time. After the triumphant rise which, particularly in a man in his early thirties, not only bore witness to ambition but sharpened and intensified it, Franco returned to garrison life as commander of the First Brigade, First Division, in Madrid. His boredom turned him to intensive study. In a country where history had often been made by the army's intervention into public life, where a general – Primo de Rivera – was at present in power, how could Franco's thoughts fail to turn to politics, which alone would enable him to envisage a future commensurate with his early achievements?

Thus the whole history of Spain, the traditional role of the caste to which he belonged and the problems of his country led this young general, ineluctably, to play a part in the political game. Would it be a leading or a subsidiary role? It was still too soon to say, even if his past could vouch for his future. In 1927 Franco was appointed Director of the General Military Academy of Saragossa, recently re-established by Primo de Rivera. This implied control of the formation of future army cadres. He chose, as teachers, veterans of the African campaign; in his speeches to the cadets he praised the traditional military virtues. Maginot, the French Minister of War, having come to inspect the Academy and decorate Franco with the Legion of Honour for his prowess in Morocco, declared:

'This is no mere model organization but, in its way, the most modern centre in the world. ... General Franco, despite his youth, struck me as a mature leader and an experienced and clear-headed Director, versed in the psychology of leadership.'

As Director of the Academy, Franco was at the centre of the military institution, since he was responsible for maintaining its continuity and thus for guiding its attitude. His post offered further advantages. In the first place, he was able to exert influence through his students, the cadres of tomorrow, particularly as the more ambitious of them were fascinated by his rapid rise. Then, while Spain went through a troubled period (Primo de Rivera resigned in 1930) Franco stood apart, avoiding direct political activity, waiting in his military stronghold for the decisive moment. Others committed themselves too soon, wasting their efforts. Captains Galán and García Hernández attempted a rising against the King and tried to advance from Jaca to Saragossa; both were shot. Franco brought out his cadets against them, although his own brother, the aviator Ramón Franco, had had to escape abroad on account of his republican opinions. When the Republic was proclaimed on 14 April 1931 and Alfonso XIII driven into exile after the municipal elections, when there appeared to be no monarchists left on Spanish soil, Franco merely declared:

'The discipline and exact fulfilment of orders which has always prevailed in this centre are more necessary at this moment than ever before. The army, calm and united, must sacrifice all personal thought and all ideology for the good of the nation and the tranquillity of the motherland.'

The army must be preserved, such was the meaning of Franco's message, and it tells us further that he was a cautious man, with that typically Galician prudence, that *retranca* which means waiting for the right moment, lying low until it is time to leap. When, on 17 April, the press announced that the Republican Government was going to appoint him High Commissioner in Morocco, Franco denied this in a letter of the 18th to the Monarchist daily *A.B.C.*, an ambiguous and highly skilful letter in which he refused the offer before it had been officially made, and was thus able to avoid cutting himself off either from the Monarchists or from the new regime. The young general was an adept at strategic manoeuvres.

The Art of Waiting

The Republican Government, meanwhile, was seriously concerned about the attitude of the army. It attempted to solve the historic problem of the relation between state and army by the unsatisfactory method of offering to pension off, on full pay, all officers willing to give up their career. Ten thousand accepted, but these were by no means the ones most hostile to the new regime. There was, moreover, the Civil Guard, on which popular hatred was focused, and whose function was wholly repressive. The Republic dared not dissolve it. These measures were none the less sufficient to sharpen the resentment of the officers. Franco shared it, particularly as on 30 June 1931 the Academia General of Saragossa had been abolished. He declared: 'The machine is being dismantled, but its product remains; you, the seven hundred and twenty officers. . . .' But he had to wait. Military leaders were being arrested, subjected to inquiries about their past and their responsibilities. For the new Spain, in the course of its development, inevitably came into conflict with the military institution, that mainstay of the old Spain, the 'Black Spain' of the big landlords, of the Church and tradition. This was the Spain that the Republic seemed bent on destroying. Partial measures, such as the separation of Church and State ('Spain is no longer Catholic', declared Azaña, head of the government) and an attempt at agrarian reform, were however powerless to restrain the revolutionary and anarchistic upsurge; in a land where local life has always been intense, with its traditions of *cabildo* (open discussion between all members of a village) and *fuero* (local privileges), the state seemed to be breaking up not merely into regional units (such as Catalonia) but into villages (which proclaimed 'Libertarian Communism' and, at Casas Viejas for instance, attacked the Civil Guard).

Franco, military governor of Coruña, waited. He must have felt deep resentment; he had been given no new post for a whole year, and promotion on grounds of military merit had been abolished. He waited, none the less, prudently assessing risks; he stood aside while General Sanjurjo plotted a rising. Having been informed of the preparations, like the rest of the army, he made contact with the conspirators in Madrid, assessed the hazardous nature of the project, advised certain officers to withdraw or not to intervene, then returned to Coruña. On 10 August the rising was suppressed and Sanjurjo arrested.

Birth of 'National-Syndicalism'

General Francisco Franco thus remained in reserve while the Right formed its organizations: the C.E.D.A. under Gil Robles (hailed as *Jefe*, chief, at public meetings), and other even more extreme groups. On 14 April there appeared the first number of *La Conquista del Estado* (*The Conquest of the State*) by Ledesma Ramos and Giménez Caballero, in which the influence of Hitler's ideas is obvious. 'The new State will be constructive and creative', it declared. 'Its authority will replace that of individuals and of groups, and it will be the sole repository of national sovereignty. . . . We are in favour of a totalitarian State. . . . The State will organize and control production.' After this promise of a strong national and 'syndicalist' state comes an assertion which could not fail to appeal to the officer caste: 'We do not desire the backing of the majority, but the support of a few daring and courageous men. . . . We expect a politician to display a sense of responsibility and a combative spirit worthy of a soldier.' Furthermore, these officers responded to the mystique of Spain's imperial past, as expounded in *La Conquista del Estado*. At Valladolid, on 13 June 1931, the group *Libertad* was founded by Onesimo Redondo, son of a poor peasant family, who as Spanish teacher in a German university had come into contact with Nazi ideology. He spoke on behalf of the small farmers of Old Castile against the bourgeoisie and the capitalists. As paid official of a union of *remolacheros* (beetroot growers) he combined syndicalism with nationalism, proclaiming that '. . . the young must train for the struggle, must worship violence. In the young patriotic violence is just, necessary and desirable. We must whole-heartedly accept a moral code based on violence and a warlike spirit.'

This was almost word for word the ideal which the officers sought to defend and propagate. On 10 October 1931 the group in Madrid (*Conquista del Estado*) and that of Valladolid (*Libertad*) were merged to create the *Juntas de Ofensiva Nacional Sindicalista*. The symbol of the *Jonsists*, suggested by a student from Granada, Aparicio, was the yoke and arrows of the Catholic kings; Ledesma proposed watchwords which were to become those of all Spanish Nationalists –

Arriba and *España Una, Grande y Libre*. Their anti-Marxist and anti-Semitic programme stressed Spain's undying traditions and her national demands (Gibraltar, Tangier). On 19 October 1933 José Antonio Primo de Rivera, eldest son of the dictator, defined the aims of the *Falange Española*. He developed his ideas in the significantly-named journal *El Fascio* from 16 March until its suppression by the government. We find here the classic themes of fascism, claiming to be a 'third way' between capitalism and socialism; José Antonio declares: 'The fascist ideal is not an ideal of the right (for the right seeks to preserve everything, even what is bad) nor of the left (for the left seeks to destroy everything, even what is good), but an ideal valid for the whole nation.'[9]

A Decisive Political Action

Franco watched the blocs forming, Spain stirring, anxiety growing (as capital left the country at an increasing rate). He carried on his career meanwhile: in March 1933 he was appointed Commander-General of the Balearic Islands, but his ambition was still smouldering under a semblance of calm. He listened to those who invited him to stand as deputy for Madrid. The suggestion came to nothing, but it was significant: Franco was somebody who mattered, on whom political circles could count. This new young general, ambitious and yet prudent, was not to be ignored. The two years of reaction, 1934–6, the *Bienio Negro*, during which the Republic was in the hands of the right wing, were to make of him a figure on the national scale. In March 1934 he was promoted General in charge of a division; in October of that year he put down the revolutionary movement in Asturias by bringing out the *Regulares* and the *Tercio Extranjero*, seventeen years after his first encounter with the other Spain in 1917. The importance of the repression that followed is well known: it was Spain's 'Commune'. Franco reported on his action, specifying: 'The Moroccan war with the *Regulares* and the *Tercio* had something romantic about it, like a war of reconquest. This war is a frontier war waged against socialism and communism and the other forces that are attacking civilization in order to replace it with barbarism.'

Francisco Franco was no longer merely a young general: he had definitely proved his mettle, he had become the tough leader, the man who had unhesitatingly organized repression with his African troops, without any sentimental qualms. In Asturias, without departing from his soldierly role, Franco had achieved a decisive political action. He was now in the forefront, even if he did not yet play a personal and independent role.

Franco as Boss of the Spanish Army

The Lerroux government, after the successful Asturian campaign (the army lost 22 officers, 25 N.C.O.'s and 173 privates) lavished honours on him: he was awarded the Grand Cross for Military Merit and in February 1935 appointed

[9] We shall study below the development of the *Falange Española* and the personality of José Antonio.

Commander-in-Chief of the Moroccan army. He had obviously become the most important man in the service. General Sanjurjo, its other star, was in exile in Portugal, following his failed *coup d'état* of 1932.

In May 1935, when the *Jefe* Gil Robles, leader of the c.e.d.a., whose portraits covered four stories of the house-fronts of Madrid, became Minister of War, he chose Francisco Franco as General Chief of Staff. This last promotion made Franco the boss of the Spanish army. General Fanjul was appointed Under-Secretary for War and General Goded Head of the Air Ministry. The Ministry of War thus became the bastion of the most openly traditionalist military caste. Franco reorganized local commands, putting at the head of various units men whom he had known in Africa and who most fully represented the officer caste. General Mola was made commander of the Moroccan army, while Varela, who had been sentenced by the Republic, was amnestied and promoted General. The Military Academy at Saragossa was reopened.

Naturally, this reorganization of the army leadership had a precise political significance: the annulment of all the steps taken by the Azaña Government between 1931 and 1933 in its attempt to bring the army under government control and to crush that permanent threat of reaction that it represented. This reorganization was directed by the man who had put down the Asturian rising: decorations were generously bestowed on those who had taken part in that repression. The aim of Gil Robles and Francisco Franco was 'to restore the morale of the army' by emphasizing its traditional characteristics so as to ensure its loyalty to their policy. Generals Miaja and de Riquelme (future leaders of the Republican army) were dismissed. A special information service was set up to investigate the morale of soldiers and officers; it discovered 25 per cent of militant revolutionaries among conscripted men! Franco then envisaged strengthening the professional army by a systematic recruitment of volunteers. He also kept watch over arms factories, forbidding workers to join political organizations. Technical measures were adopted, such as the creation of mechanized divisions, the general use of steel helmets, increased production of cartridges and an order for twenty-five batteries of artillery. The Council of Ministers gave its approval to a special budget of 1,100 million pesetas to achieve this transformation of the Spanish army in a space of three years.

Now in the Spain of 1935–6 – since no danger threatened the nation, even Morocco having been pacified – this strengthening of the army under the leadership of Gil Robles and Franco could only be directed against the other Spain, the Spain of Asturias and Barcelona and of the land-hungry peasantry; this strengthened army could only be intended to maintain order – as it had shown in Asturias – and protect those Spanish grandees who had just been awarded the considerable idemnity of 230 million pesetas for the land which had been expropriated in 1932. The army that Franco had forged was a force making ready, if need be, to control the country and had acquired the means to do so, both in men and equipment. And one of Franco's tasks was to complete all preparations for the application of martial law and the transfer of power to the army, should the need arise. Franco thus played a vital role in the technical preparation of resistance to any political change which might mean the victory of the other

Spain and of 'all the forces that are attacking civilization in order to replace it with barbarism', as he had declared in 1934.

He assumed that role with due caution, never overstepping the limits of his functions as General Chief of Staff; he had been summoned to that post by the government and had acted with the approval of his Minister. In short, he had not compromised his traditional career; short of a radical upheaval, he would remain a great soldier. At the same time he had prepared the ground, placed his men, kept watch on the morale of his troops and strengthened their arms. He had consolidated his instrument; the nine months he had been in control had been enough. When Gil Robles was forced to resign after a Cabinet crisis, Franco further extended his influence in an army where many key posts were held by officers whom he had appointed precisely on account of their sense of caste and their loyalty to 'Eternal Spain'.

The speech addressed by Franco to Gil Robles on the latter's departure makes it clear that for him – and for the officer class – the only possible policy was that sponsored by the leader of the c.e.d.a. 'I can only say, at this point,' he declared, 'that our regrets are wholly sincere. Honour, discipline, all the fundamental concepts of the army have been restored and embodied by Your Excellency.'

Franco was still working at the Ministry of War, regularly and resolutely, present in his office from early morning until late at night. His only interruption was a visit to London to represent the Spanish Government at the funeral of King George v. He met Edward viii, stopped off in Paris for four days, then returned to Madrid, where the violent battle for the elections of February 1936 had begun. The victory of the *Frente Popular* (in Madrid the Socialist Besteiro won 40,000 more votes than Robles) immediately raised the question of the attitude of the army and that of Franco himself.

Franco and the Victory of the Popular Front

Even before the results were announced, Franco had made contact (through Lieutenant-Colonel González Badia) with General Mola, whom he had put in charge of the Moroccan army, warning him to be ready to send over to the mainland the largest possible contingent of *Regulares* and units of the *Tercio*. Franco had already envisaged the project which was to be carried out in July 1936. Mola was ready but, as usual, Franco's political prudence and shrewdness led him to act with the minimum of personal risk. He wanted to intervene as a saviour, but on a basis of 'formal legality'. What mattered, in a word, was the real pressure he could exert rather than any show of daring which might diminish his chances of success. He thus tried to persuade the Director-General of the Civil Guard, General Pozas, and the Minister of War, General Molero, to declare a state of martial law. The two men were reluctant and referred Franco to the Prime Minister, Portela Vallarades, who refused to take the initiative and suggested that the army act on its own account. Franco, despite pressure from a number of officers and right-wing personalities, refused to commit himself.

This attitude is wholly characteristic of the man. He was ready for a 'legal' intervention, although this would mean a *coup* in defiance of universal suffrage, but to venture, at short notice, on something so uncertain as a military pronuncia-mento, risking everything, when his whole life's achievement and his future were at stake, was not in keeping with General Franco's personality. He was a winner but not a gambler, ambitious but not rash, a hard-headed realist, interested not in gestures but in the success of his actions. What great politician, of the sort who *lasts*, ever acted on impulse?

So Franco gave way. Manuel Azaña formed the new Cabinet and hurriedly transferred the more dangerous generals: Mola was moved from Morocco to a post at the head of the Brigade of Infantry at Pamplona, capital of Navarre; Goded was sent to the Balearics. Franco, on 9 March, was posted to the Canaries as Commander-General. It was clearly a form of retirement, and was recognized as such by Franco and by public opinion.

The fact is that, since the Asturian business, since he had joined the General Staff, Franco's political character had become clearly defined. Some of his biographers have stressed the ambiguity of his attitudes. In fact the apparent ambiguity was merely a prudent endeavour not to declare himself formally, not to lay himself open to direct attack, but it was clear to partisans or opponents of the Popular Front that Franco had made his choice. Only he did not want to fall into a trap, he would not become involved in an operation of minor importance, leading nowhere, a pronunciamento like Sanjurjo's. Franco would intervene only for a decisive battle, undertaken under the most favourable conditions and waged to the bitter end, that is to say until the total defeat of one side; moreover an attack on Franco would imply that the Republic had decided to get rid of the traditional Spanish army, and the more clear-sighted Spanish statesmen were aware of this.

In May 1936, when there was talk of Franco's candidature in the second round of the elections, the Socialist leader Indalecio Prieto wrote: 'General Franco, being young, gifted, having a network of friends in the army, is the man who, at a given moment, has it in him to lead such a movement [of military insurrection] with maximum probable success because of the prestige he enjoys.' Prieto adds, however: 'I do not dare to attribute to General Franco any such designs', and he accuses the 'protectors' of the former Chief of Staff of seeking to induce him to intervene in political affairs. It is true that Franco was once more being urged to take action, but he was not the sort of man who lets himself be led: a rapid and brilliant career such as his is not achieved by chance. It implies that he knew how to take action, but in his own best interests, and his successes had only strengthened his determination to choose his own time. Franco's strength lay, perhaps, in his stubborn ambition and self-confidence: in the political conflict, his first concern was with his personal success, and this accounts for his prudence. As is so often the case, great ambition assumed the cloak of a great cause and made that cause triumph.

In order to choose one's time, one must be well informed. Moreover, Franco's position was such that it might perhaps be possible to act without him, but certainly not in opposition to him. Before returning to the Canaries, Franco attended a meeting at the home of the stock-broker José Delgado, where the leading generals (Mola, Varela, Franjul, Goded, Villegas, Orgaz) and the chief of the *Unión Militar Española*, Lieutenant-Colonel Galarza, discussed possible moves. These men represented no single trend of opinion: some were monarchist, others republican, but all were concerned with preserving the order of society and preventing by force of arms any evolution of their country towards liberalism, *a fortiori* towards socialism. Eternal Spain must be protected. The decision was taken to prepare the garrisons and organize the plot methodically (with Galarza as chief of staff of the conspiracy), while Franco was to be kept informed of their preparations.

His absence from Spain was not the only explanation for the subsidiary role that Franco played on this occasion: in point of fact, he could not and would not be a mere agent, he had to be the leader, but this would mean involving himself in an operation which by its very nature must remain uncertain until it was actually triggered off. Now prudence, personal interest, his very position required Franco to remain on the side-lines, standing back like the Commendatore's statue, ready to intervene or not to intervene, and this was the considerable advantage of his attitude of semi-involvement.

Despite his prudence, his *retranca*, his avoidance of front-rank activity, Franco's role was clearly recognized by both sides, as many facts prove.

When he left Madrid for the Canaries, officers of all arms and many generals came to bid him good-bye at the station and this demonstration clearly showed that the professional army stood solidly united around its former Chief of Staff, its symbolic representative. But there was another Spain: when Franco reached Tenerife a hostile crowd, mustered by *Frente Popular* organizations, shouted insults and hissed the 'butcher of the Asturias', the 'fascist general'. A general strike was even declared in protest against his nomination.

What nobody knew was when, and under what circumstances, Franco would come out into the open. As to which side he was on, there was no ambiguity, only that strategic skill which leaves the adversary in ignorance of the place and time of the attack, preventing him from anticipating it.

Crossing the Rubicon

Those on the left of the *Frente Popular* sensed the danger and gave warning of it. On 10 April Largo Caballero declared: 'The army must be reorganized on such a scale that generals become corporals and corporals generals.' Fascist groups used terrorist methods in the tradition of the *pistoleros*; civil guards were shot down by anarchists. In this pre-civil war atmosphere the military conspiracy took shape, and Franco was constantly kept informed of developments.

Mola, at Pampeluna, had the support of the Carlists, who had organized units of *Requetés* led by Manuel Fal Conde. These legitimists, opposed to the monarchy of Alfonso XIII, were in contact with Mussolini and with Generals Varela and Sanjurjo. General Queipo de Llano, Inspector of the *Carabineros*, although a Republican, joined the plot. Colonel Yagüe, who had directed the repression in Asturias, was one of its most active figures. The leaders of the conspiracy were men who had fought in Morocco or in Asturias and who had Franco's backing.

The new Prime Minister, Casares Quiroga, and the government were disturbed by the rumours that reached them. They set up inquiries and organized surveillance. It was at this moment, 23 June, that Franco wrote the Prime Minister a long letter that once again reveals his cunning. Speaking on behalf of his fellow officers, he set forward their grievances against the government, adding: 'I cannot conceal from Your Excellency the danger represented by this collective state of mind at the present juncture, when professional anxieties are added to those which any good Spaniard must feel about the great problems confronting our country.'

This move of Franco's served both as a camouflage behind which the preparation of the plot could go on and a shield which, in case the government should nip the attempt in the bud, would protect Franco himself; it was, moreover, an assertion of his special role as spokesman for the whole army. His letter confirms the fact that he was not merely 'an obscure African general', as has been said,[10] but that on the contrary he, the former Chief of Staff, who had been the youngest general in Europe, claimed to interpret the conscience of the army – which implied, in some people's view, the conscience of Spain herself.

General Mola, it is true, was the central figure of the plot, its director, responsible for bringing together the Republican supporters of 'order', Carlists, Monarchists, Christian Democrats and Falangists; while Sanjurjo, still in exile in Portugal, was chosen as leader of the rising, Franco being regarded only as chief of the Moroccan troops. The army's new man, however, its most powerful figure and the one most favourably placed, was undoubtedly Francisco Franco.

In July 1936 there were further political assassinations: on the 12th the leader of the opposition, Calvo Sotelo, was murdered. Two days later the diplomat José-Antonio de Sangróniz, one of the most important figures in the conspiracy because he ensured liaison between the army and political circles in Spain and abroad, appeared in Tenerife, a further indication of Franco's importance. On the 16th, pretexting the need to attend the funeral of General Balmes, Franco left for Las Palmas, with some relief, since he had become suspect to left-wing circles in Tenerife, hostile slogans had begun to appear everywhere and he had been obliged to set an armed guard around his house. Indeed, he left Tenerife in the middle of the night to avoid demonstrations.

On 17 July the Moroccan army rose. Franco returned to the Canaries and fiercely crushed the resistance of Popular Front supporters, unhesitatingly ordering his men to fire on the ill-armed crowd, determined to push home his advantage with the utmost speed.

From Tenerife he sent a message to the mainland garrisons, couched in authoritative language: 'Glory to the heroic African army. Spain above all. . . . Blind faith in our triumph. Long live Spain with honour.' A few hours later, in a long manifesto, he explained the reasons for the rising and his aims: 'We offer you justice and equality before the law, peace and mutual love among Spaniards, liberty and fraternity without licence or tyranny. Work for all. Social justice shall be achieved without hatred or violence. . . .'

On 18 July at 6.30 p.m., on board a specially chartered British aircraft piloted

[10] Luis Ramírez, *Vie de Francisco Franco* (Paris, 1965), p. 196. This is none the less an excellent biography.

by Captain Bebb, he left Las Palmas and touched down at Agadir and Casablanca, which enabled him to make a final assessment of the situation. He was travelling on Sangróniz's passport. At seven in the morning the aeroplane landed at Tetuan, where the *Tercio Extranjero* and the *Regulares* were in control. A few hours previously the rebels had shot the commandant of the aerodrome at Melilla, who had remained loyal to the legal government; he was Franco's own cousin, Major Lapuente. The Civil War had begun.

Favourable Circumstances

Thus, right at the outset, Franco had with him the best troops in the Spanish army, consisting of well-disciplined mercenaries. This further reinforced his personal position, which was already very strong, and circumstances were to be a considerable help to him.

In the towns the people were resisting; in Valencia, Barcelona and Seville the soldiers disobeyed their officers; the Civil Guard were hesitant; the pronunciamento had succeeded technically but failed politically, since the government did not capitulate, even though most army cadres had gone over to the rebels. What was needed, therefore, was a *reconquista* of Spain, and Franco possessed the most efficient instrument, the colonial army. This was his first piece of luck. The second was the difficulty encountered by General Mola, the director of the plot, in the north of Spain; whereas Morocco was safe ground. Finally, an all-important stroke of fate, General Sanjurjo, the proposed head of the new state, was killed in an aircraft accident on his way back to Spain.

Thus, by 20 July 1936, General Franco was clearly in a position to assume authority. His past career marked him out for it and circumstances favoured him; he still had to exploit them in order to establish himself unshakeably at the head of Nationalist Spain.

Generalissimo Franco

He took only two months to become Generalissimo and Head of State. Two months, even with all the trumps in his hand, was a short space of time, and he had to display much political skill and shrewdness as well as resolute, clear-cut ambition to reach the summit. He was favoured by his past, his authority over the army, the fact that chance liquidated his rivals, for Sanjurjo's death was followed by those of José Antonio Primo de Rivera and the other Falangist leader, Onesimo Redondo, who were shot by the Republicans in November 1936.

There were other generals left, all of whom had private ambitions; particularly General Mola, moving spirit of the conspiracy. Mola, however, expressed their common aim when he declared: 'Spain, true Spain, has laid the dragon low and made it bite the dust. . . . The army must govern now, because it alone has the authority required to maintain unity between the heterogeneous elements that make up Spain.' The army was indeed the mainstay of the Nationalist Spain that was emerging.

Now the army that Franco had brought from Morocco was gaining victories;

his troops entered Badajoz and massacred the population, they gained control of Southern Spain and Franco set up his headquarters at Seville, at the Yanduri palace. His brother Nicolás, who served as his political adviser, Colonel Yagüe and Millán Astray, his fellow-soldiers in the colonial wars, and the journalist Luis Bolín, former London correspondent of the newspaper *A.B.C.*, made up a team that campaigned for him in military and Falangist circles and, thanks to Bolín, abroad, particularly in Italy and Germany. Gradually, since the foreign press played an important part in building up the myth, Franco's name recurred like a leitmotiv.

He was, moreover, unquestionably the strongest personality on the Nationalist side. When he visited Burgos on 16 August to take part in the Junta of National Defence formed by Mola on 25 July, which included the chief military leaders, the crowd acclaimed him. He already occupied a place apart, like a victorious general.

From 26 August onward he established his staff headquarters near the front, at Cáceres, in the medieval castle of Los Golfines de Arriba. Here, he worked with his usual diligence, as the crucial battle for Madrid began. It was Mola who directed the offensive, and who had even threatened Colonel Yagüe with the firing-squad for having briefly had the same ambition. The fact is significant: whoever entered Madrid in triumph might hope to seize victory. Francisco Franco was well aware of this, and while the battle for Madrid was being waged he carried on his own battle for power.

The Battle for Power

Gaining support in Falangist circles, tending his popular fame, making direct contact with the Fascists and the Nazis, Franco first assumed power in the relations between Nationalist Spain and her allies. His most skilful manoeuvre was to make use of the resistance of the Alcázar of Toledo so as to appear as unquestioned leader. True, in order to relieve Moscardo's troops, which were being besieged in the ancient citadel, Franco was forced to put a stop to a brilliant offensive against Madrid which seemed likely to succeed; but is this to be considered as the blunder of a short-sighted strategist, a sentimental gesture, or, rather, as a master-stroke of political strategy? For by relieving the Alcazar just when the clash between the two Spains seemed to be concentrated in that struggle,[11] Franco shattered Mola's hopes (the war was to last a long time, and Mola did not conquer Madrid) and at the same time appeared as the saviour of the beleaguered men. Amid the ruins, Franco the Liberator stepped forward by Moscardo's side; the press of the whole world spoke of him as uncontested leader, and the army, whose 'boss' he had already been, recognized its representative in him. One high-ranking officer, Colonel Castejón, declared (and he seemed to speak for the 'technical' cadres): 'I follow Franco. That's all, and that's enough. Politics, at top level, isn't my business. . . . But I think that for a very

[11] For everything concerning the siege of the Alcazar of Toledo, see H. R. Southworth, *Le mythe de la croisade de Franco* (Paris, 1964), and Luis Quintanilla, *Los retrenes del Alcázar de Toledo* (Paris, 1968).

long time the role of supreme arbiter, unrivalled and impartial, must fall to the army.'

Franco symbolized the army. Thanks to the support of the royalist generals Kindelán and Orgaz – in whose view Franco, just because he was the Spanish army, could have no personal political ambition and was bound to restore the monarchy – thanks above all to the position he had held for many years at the head of the army, Franco was appointed sole leader on 12 September, despite objections from the president of the Junta, General Cabanellas. The news was still kept secret; the Junta might change its mind, but a decisive stage had been reached for Franco. The generals of the insurgent army had recognized the authority of their former Chief of Staff. Mola accepted the appointment because, like several other officers, he saw the choice of Franco as a purely technical matter. Apparently, Franco's rivals were not far-sighted.

Surrounded with glory, thanks to the relief of the Alcazar, backed by skilful propaganda, supported by the Falange and the Monarchists, encouraged by his family and his fellow-soldiers, and above all guided by his own lucid ambition, Franco was now close to seizing power. He was not the sort of man to rest content with being *primus inter pares*. On 29 September at Salamanca, in that splendid city where the golden beauty of the stone, the pattern of streets and squares remind one ceaselessly of Spain's past greatness and her people's genius, Nicolás Franco had organized for his brother's arrival a display of enthusiasm which was to decide the question. '*Franco, Franco, Franco Generalísimo*' was the cry that rang out in the streets. Falangists and Monarchists were in the forefront. Before the united Junta, Kindelán read Article 3 of the decree appointing Franco Generalissimo and – a further stage – Head of the Government. This time the political operation was obvious. The generals protested. The meeting broke up. The crowd was there, shouting 'Franco, Franco, Franco'. The past was there, reminding these officers that they had already recognized Franco as their 'boss'. Moreover, there seemed to be an urgent need for a government led by a strong personality capable of welding together the forces of Nationalist Spain. Finally, Mola and Cabanellas, who had been the most recalcitrant, agreed to sign. Franco was now Generalísimo and Head of the Government. At the last minute, when the decree was actually in the press, a message from Nicolás Franco altered his title to Head of State. He had reached his goal at last: he was at the very top. He was forty-three years old. He was bound by no constitution, master of the army and therefore master of the state without control by any assembly. The month of September 1936 was thus decisive for the history of Spain.

I Will ...

Before the assembled dignitaries – confronted to their surprise with a Head of State instead of the mere governmental head they thought they had appointed – Franco addressed Cabanellas and the members of the Junta. 'You can be justly proud', he told them. 'You took over a broken Spain. You hand over to me a Spain united in a single great ideal.' These words surely betray Franco's feeling that men and events were mere instruments guiding Spain into his hands. 'You have handed over Spain to me,' he went on, 'and I promise you that my wrist will not tremble, that I will maintain a firm hand. I shall take the Motherland to her summit or die in the attempt.' 'I ... I ... I ...', the tone is that of a leader who brooks no rival, whose self-confidence was not born overnight but formed gradually after a series of successes and promotions in the course of years. He might indeed declare: 'I want your collaboration. The National Defence Junta will stay by my side. Long live Spain!' What claims one's attention is not the formal declaration of intent, but that 'I shall, I want ...' which is the key to his past history, his personality, his success, and the future of Spain.

These simple words tell us more than the long speech pronounced by Franco at his investiture at Burgos on the same occasion. Here the Generalissimo asserted that 'Labour will enjoy an absolute guarantee; it will neither be enslaved to capital nor, organized as an advanced class, will it adopt an aggressive and embittered attitude'. He announced:

'Spain's internal organization is to be based on a broad totalitarian conception, through its natural institutions ... and the establishment of a hierarchical regime. ... The national will shall be displayed, in due time, through technical organizations and corporations. ... Associations and individuals will enjoy the greatest freedom, within the framework of the sovereign interest of the State.'

In this first speech Franco seems to withdraw, to stand aside behind classic themes (the end of the class struggle, a hierarchized and totalitarian state, corporatism, the state as supreme value) derived from Fascist experiments and propaganda and which had spread from Rome over the whole of Europe with growing success from 1930 onwards. To know and understand the Generalissimo we should note above all that expression of personal will, without neglecting the ideology expressed in his programme, which shows that Franco was acquainted with fascism, or at all events that he expressed as his own the ideas that the Falange was trying to propagate in Spain.

Franco and the Falange

It was not by accident that Franco thus committed himself. The Falange had, in fact, become a force to be reckoned with. In 1934 the F.E.T. (*Falange Española Tradicionalista*) had formulated a twenty-six point programme (echoed in the Generalissimo's speech) which, directly inspired by fascism, extolled the spirit of Spain, paid respect to the Catholic Church, and above all denounced Marxism, the class struggle and capitalism, while proposing certain agrarian reforms and the nationalization of banks and railways *inter alia*. The Falange had been involved in the preparation of the rising; and despite the loss of its leader, José Antonio Primo de Rivera, its numbers had grown rapidly. In conquered areas it assumed para-military administrative and police functions; above all, it aimed at becoming a mass party able, through the revolutionary aspects of its programme – as had been the case with the Nazi and Fascist Parties – to appeal to social strata hitherto influenced by socialism. Moreover, for reasons of personal safety, many

Republicans supported the Falange in zones under Franco's control. The movement was in fact the only one with any pretension to a coherent ideology, claiming to provide a contemporary solution to Spanish problems. In this sense it appealed to the young and all those who, seduced by the examples of Italy and Germany, sought to restore Spain's greatness by means of a new order. By becoming the *Caudillo* and proclaiming a Fascist ideology, Francisco Franco satisfied those Spaniards who demanded a Duce or a Führer. He thus brought his movement, originally a traditionalist one, into line with the atmosphere and the international problems of the day.

Furthermore, in the nationalist camp the Monarchists were powerful too, well organized and strongly rooted in Navarre, Aragon and Castile. They had co-operated with Mola in preparing the rising and as early as 1934 the *Comunión Tradicionalista* had established contact with Mussolini. Now the Carlist *Requetés* were engaged in a fanatical battle with the Republicans and provided the major part of General Mola's army. Their leader, Fal Conde, favoured the immediate restoration of the monarchy. This was a real threat to the Caudillo. On receiving the German Ambassador, Faupel, on 11 April 1937, Franco accused Fal Conde of having 'not long ago taken a number of measures for the reintroduction of the monarchy which he, Franco, could not but regard as directed against him and his government. . . .' 'Franco told me,' adds Faupel in his letter of 14 April 1937, 'that he had been on the point of deciding to have Fal Conde executed immediately for high treason, but had refrained from doing so since that would have produced a bad impression among the *Requetés* at the front, who were fighting bravely there.'[12]

Unlike these Monarchist movements, the Falange, which had been without a leader since the death of José Antonio, and which had no such precise aims as an immediate restoration, could prove useful to Franco. His brother-in-law, Serrano Suñer, who had joined him in February 1937, advised him to this effect, and the Generalissimo therefore proceeded to develop a skilful political strategy, characteristic of the man, which consisted in using the Falange and its vaguely innovatory aspects against traditionalists whose well-defined ambitions were dangerous to his personal power. This, however, did not imply destroying the Monarchists, but merely bringing them under control with the help of the Falange, and preserving them in order, if need be, to control the Falangists. Franco thus strove to neutralize the two groups in his own interests, becoming the keystone, the resultant in which two antagonistic forces, added together, cancelled one another out. This was why from February 1937 onwards the Generalissimo set about preparing the formation of a single party of which, of course, he was to be the head, and which – to all appearances at least – would provide Spain with a system identical with that to be found in Fascist Italy or Nazi Germany.

The Single Party

On the evening of 19 April 1937 Franco spoke over the radio, discussing at length the decree that founded the new Party.

[12] *Documents on German Foreign Policy*, op. cit., p. 268.

'The Falange and its programme bring us the mass support of the young, a new style of propaganda, a political form of heroic character befitting our own day; the *Requetés* have brought us the sacred trust of the Spanish tradition, tenaciously preserved, with its Catholic spirituality.'

The decree included three articles which were the basis on which Franco's Spain was to be built up. They were set forth in military style.[13]

Article I stipulates:

'The Spanish Falange and the *Requetés* . . . are integrated *under my command* into a single nation-wide political authority to be named *Falange Española Tradicionalista y de las Juntas de Ofensivas Nacional Sindicalista*.[14] This organization will be the intermediary between society and the State, its principal purpose will be to inform the State of the opinions of the people and to disseminate among the people the thought of the State; by means of the political and moral virtues of service, hierarchy and fraternity . . . All other political organizations and parties are dissolved.'

Article II specifies: 'The direction of the new political organization will be in the hands of the Head of the State, a political Junta or secretariat and the National Council.' Franco, Generalissimo and Caudillo, was thus the leader of the *Movimiento* as well. The programme of the Falange could now repeat the twenty-six points defined in 1934, glorifying Spain's 'unity of destiny within the universal', together with an apologia for the state as a 'totalitarian instrument in the service of the integrity of the Fatherland' and a repudiation of 'the capitalist system which disregards the needs of the people and dehumanizes property', as well as a condemnation of Marxism. What really mattered was that the party was to become a tool in the hands of Franco, who had power to appoint directly all the members of the first National Council. At the same time, the Caudillo was also Chief of the National Militia.

Fortune favoured him still further when the death of General Mola delivered him of his dangerous rival. Of course, all sorts of rumours were current about the lucky coincidences which had cleared the field for Franco, but the facts remained. He was easily able to crush an attempted plot hatched against him by a few *Camisas viejas* of the Falange, led by Hedilla and the sister of José Antonio, who had remained loyal to the original spirit of the Falange. To defeat these he did not even need a 'night of the long knives';[15] a tribunal served the purpose.

Thus by the spring of 1937 Franco had at his disposal a political instrument which, since as Caudillo he was sole master of the army, finally made him master

[13] See *Notes et études documentaires*, no. 1368 (Paris, August 1950).

[14] See list of abbreviations (p. 370) for an explanation of the nature of this organization.

[15] In Italy and in Germany, the Fascist and Nazi Parties, once established in power around a leading personality (Mussolini, Hitler), had to get rid of their left-wing elements, and there were many plots in the first few years which were invariably crushed. In Germany it took the murder of several hundred S.A. during the 'night of the long knives' to liquidate the opposition to Hitler within the Nazi Party itself.

of all Nationalist Spain. On 1 February 1938 a new government was formed. Its seat was at Salamanca, and its moving spirit was Serrano Suñer, who was at once Minister of the Interior, of the Press and of Propaganda. Five generals (including General Jordana, Minister of Foreign Affairs) were included in this government, which, since it excluded the chief Falangist and Monarchist leaders, served unquestionably as an instrument for Franco's policy. A decree passed on 19 July 1938 conferred on the Generalísimo a dignity hitherto the sole prerogative of the kings of Spain: that of Captain-General of the army and navy. On 5 February 1938 the new regime had already adopted the armorial bearings of the Catholic kings. Franco had indeed become the heir to the sovereigns of Spain. And yet in order to achieve his aims he must win not only dignities but also, since Spain was Catholic and the role of the clergy all-important, the support of the Church.

Franco and the Church

The Church did not disappoint his expectations. On 1 July 1937 the Collective Letter of the Spanish bishops had described the campaign being waged by the Nationalists as a crusade. On 1 October 1937 the representative of the Vatican, the nuncio Antoniutti, presented his letters of credit to the Caudillo. Henceforward the regime and the Church drew ever closer to one another, particularly as Serrano Suñer was an ex-pupil of the Jesuits and, as Stohrer, the German Ambassador, notes, 'well known as an ardently religious man'. And Suñer exercised continuous influence over the Caudillo.

Stohrer wrote to Berlin in a dispatch of 19 May 1938:

'The influence of the Catholic Church has greatly increased in the last few months. . . . A proof of this that is publicly evident is the release of the decree according to which the Society of Jesus is again permitted in Spain, its former rights restored (3 May 1938). . . . It is certain that the Vatican is attempting to exert a strong influence on Franco's entourage and thus on the Generalísimo himself. . . . Spanish dominicans – Padre Menéndez Reigada . . . is one of the Generalísimo's advisers – and other churchmen, among others Mgr Luzurika (who by the way is considered an enemy of the Jews and Freemasons) have access to the very pious family of the Generalísimo and have the possibility of exerting a strong influence there. . . . The religious atmosphere of Franco's home is clearly characterized by the recent solemn initiation of the young daughter of the Generalísimo into a Catholic youth organization of the Falange.'[16]

This does not imply that the Church handed over its independence to the Caudillo, nor that the Caudillo became the tool of the Vatican. In fact each of the two forces considered it indispensable to support the other and strengthen it against the common enemy. Point 25 of the Falange's programme had stated: 'Church and State must reconcile their respective powers so as to admit of no

[16] *Documents on German Foreign Policy*, p. 661. See also microfilms of National Archives in Washington, T. 586, R. 434, 018813.

intrusion or activity threatening the dignity of the State or the integral character of the nation.' For the time being the hierarchy of the Spanish Church required only that Franco's state should protect it, restore its ancient prerogatives and extirpate from Spanish soil that 'destructive communism', that latter-day Islam which could legitimately be combated with Moorish aid.

Conversely, the advantage that Franco found in the Church's help was considerable: it sanctified his task, providing for the state he was building up deep roots in the history of the Spain of the Catholic kings. Soon one of the Generalissimo's biographers could write: 'Franco's life has been guided by the hand of God, with special signs of election.'[17] This meant, too, that to choose the opposite side meant consenting to fight against the Church, even if worship was re-established in the Republican zone, even if Franco's soldiers occasionally shot priests.

Traditionalists, Falangists, landowners, Church dignitaries, capitalists (Juan March and all those who had an interest in the Moroccan and Asturian mines), and military men – Franco succeeded in banding together all these forces *to his own advantage*.

He succeeded, moreover, in impressing his importance on international opinion, primarily on his allies, Fascist Italy and Nazi Germany. From this point of view the support granted him by the Catholic Church was of considerable value, in view of the connections maintained by the Vatican with the most diverse milieux throughout the world. Franco's selection of certain of the Falange's principles furthermore enabled him to represent his actions as forming part of the current of international fascism, so powerful in 1936-7. For there were old-established links between the Falange and fascism.

The Truth About the Falange and José Antonio Primo de Rivera[18]

These were not solely ideological links, which are well known; it can furthermore be revealed, on the basis of documents photographed by the Americans in Rome in 1944 and at present in the United States National Archives in Washington, that the Italian propaganda services regularly financed the leader of the Falange, José Antonio Primo de Rivera, as early as the beginning of 1934. Thus the man who was to become the John the Baptist of Franco Spain, whose name was to be blazoned on all her churches, was literally a paid agent of the Italian Embassy in Paris (he was No 2, No 1 being a French politician), earning 50,000 lire a month – a sum which was reduced to 25,000 at the end of 1935.

In exchange for this regular remuneration José Antonio Primo de Rivera provided detailed reports on the Spanish situation. For instance, on 24 August 1935 the Italian information service in Paris communicated to Rome a statement in which the head of the Falange, under the title *The Assault on Power*, pointed

[17] Luis de Galinsoga and Franco Salgado, *Centinela de Occidente* (*Semblanza biográfica de Francisco Franco*) (Barcelona, 1956).

[18] The reader is referred to the author's as yet unpublished thesis, 'Contribution à l'étude de l'information et de la propagande de l'Italie fasciste dans l' immédiat avant-guerre'.

out that if things happened quickly 'the Falange might soon be able to attempt to seize power, unlikely as this seems at the moment'. He added, further on – and it should be remembered that the elections that brought the *Frente Popular* to power were held in February 1936:

'If a left-wing government of Socialist tendencies were to attain power the whole army, so long as it was commanded by its present leaders, would willingly follow the first man to give the word for a national rebellion. . . . For the time being the task of the Falangist organizers is to strive untiringly to strengthen all its agents; in October we shall be able to consider a complete plan and calculate the elements needed to realize it.'[19]

This document, which is of the highest importance in proving how far the pronunciamento of 17 July 1936 was planned in advance of that year's events (elections, acts of violence, etc.), also reveals the closeness of the financial and political links that bound José Antonio to Fascist Italy. And when Francisco Franco, in turn, assumed the role of hero of the Falange, he was able to make use of the advantages of collaboration.

Franco, Italy and Germany

Moreover, from the very first months of the conflict, Italians and Germans were well aware of the international significance of the battle that had begun. Meeting the Nazi minister Frank at the Palazzo Venezia in Rome on 23 September 1936, Mussolini asserted that

'in Spain two fronts have already been formed: on one side the Germans and Italians, on the other the French, Belgians and Russians. . . . Italy has helped the Spaniards and at the present moment numerous acts of help are being performed without conditions, although much Italian blood has been shed. . . . Our actions in Spain are an effective proof of our participation in the anti-Bolshevist struggle.'[20]

Very soon both Italy and Germany came to realize that there were also Spaniards in Spain and that they had to reckon with the Caudillo who, as early as 1936, sought not so much to satisfy the ambitions or the political and ideo-logical projects of Fascists and Nazis as to ensure his personal power. Thus, in spite of a secret Italo–Spanish agreement of 28 November 1936, which stipulated that the two countries should 'lend one another mutual assistance with a view to defending their reciprocal interests', by 1937, on a visit to Germany, Mussolini told the Chief of Protocol, von Bülow-Schwante, that 'the Spanish adventure had cost him nearly 3,000 million lire. . . . He was determined to recoup the capital he had invested and thought this perfectly possible owing to the large stock of raw material to be found in Spain. . . . Finally, he banked on the loyalty

[19] Document 45 in the author's thesis.
[20] Ciano's *Diplomatic Papers* (ed. Malcolm Muggeridge, translated Stuart Hood), p. 45.

of the Spaniards, *although he did not expect much from General Franco himself.*[21]
These reservations about Franco recur in the dispatches sent to Berlin by
Ambassador Stohrer. In July 1938, at San Sebastian, the summer seat of the
Spanish Government, he also attempted to secure concessions of raw materials.

'It would be understandable,' he told Franco and his minister Jordana, 'that in
view of this new delivery of war material for Spain we had a justified interest
in a friendly and co-operative attitude on Spain's part to insure our own
supply, since it would be recognized that Germany was a country relatively
poor in raw materials. . . . I told him [Franco]', adds the Ambassador, 'we had
regretted that the new mining law just published [on 8 June] had been drafted
without any confidential exchange of views with me or my Government.'[22]

In the rest of his report Stohrer makes further complaints about General Franco
and his policy.

These texts are important because they show to what extent, in the midst of
the Civil War, the Caudillo managed to remain independent of the allies whose
help was essential for his victory. We have here yet another illustration of his
political skill, and a foreshadowing of the friction which in 1940–1 marked the
relations between Franco's Spain and the Axis powers: fresh light is shed,
moreover, on the diplomatic *volte-faces* of the years 1943–4.

This does not mean that the Italians and Germans failed to get a firm footing
in Spain. The Nazis, for instance, created a transport company, the *Hispano
Marroquí de Transportes* (HISMA), and an export company, ROWAK, for the
purpose of controlling the exchange of goods between Germany and Spain and,
naturally, of securing a share in various economic sectors, from mines to agricultural undertakings, from the radio network to the provision of war material. The
Italians, with less powerful means at their disposal, pursued a similar policy,
while the growing influence of Germany caused them some concern. They
sought to influence the press, and the Italian Embassy at Salamanca tried to
secure control over broadcasting. Similarly, Italian services attempted to spread
their propaganda by 'buying' certain journalists, or else, as the Press Attaché to
the Embassy wrote in a letter to Rome, 'to remind these Spanish circles – the
National Council of the Falange – of the corporative achievements of fascism,
and as far as possible to influence the members of their Committee towards the
adoption of our system in preference to that of other countries'.[23]

Franco and his regime were thus subjected, by the very fact that they needed
foreign support to conquer Republican Spain, to pressure from the two great
Axis Powers, but the Caudillo retained his freedom to manoeuvre, as the Munich
crisis clearly shows.

[21] *Documents Secrets du ministère des Affaires étrangères d'Allemagne,* p. 21.
Author's italics.
[22] *Documents on German Foreign Policy,* vol. III, p. 716.
[23] The author's thesis, document of 12 April 1937.

Franco and Munich

The crisis was, moreover, a crucial moment in the history of the Spanish war and a test of Franco's skill at manoeuvring. The Republicans, in fact, were banking on the resistance of the democracies to German ambitions, and reckoning that if war broke out between the democratic and Fascist Powers, French troops would move in from Morocco and the Pyrenees, and that such action would be amply justified by the fact that Italian and German contingents were assisting Franco. The Caudillo, on the contrary, was afraid of such an event, for the military balance of forces might easily be upset, the Nationalist camp being short of reserves. He was also apprehensive of a general bargaining in which the Italians and Germans would abandon Spain in return for concessions made by the democracies in Central Europe.

At the Council of Ministers on 20 September 1938 the Caudillo 'expressed grave fears that a speedy and peaceful solution of the Sudeten question might be accomplished at the expense of Spain, i.e. through undesirable and unfavourable intervention by the powers'.[24] He thus endeavoured to keep Spain out of any negotiation between the great powers and also out of any possible conflict. He therefore opted for neutrality, anticipating the wishes of the French and British Governments which were not at all anxious, from a strictly military point of view, to become involved with a new front in the south. After thus negotiating with the democratic powers and obtaining their consent, Franco turned towards Berlin, pointing out that Spain had not been kept informed of German intentions. On 26 September the Spanish Ambassador in Berlin declared that 'Spain intended to remain neutral in the event of a European conflict and wished to enter into negotiations with the British and French Governments. The reason he gave for this step was that Spain would not be in a position as long as the Civil War lasted to intervene actively on the side of friendly powers.' In point of fact, these negotiations had already taken place.

When Ciano learnt of Franco's diplomatic manoeuvres which resulted in neutrality, when he discovered that Franco's primary aim was to defend his own personal interests without unduly troubling to discuss matters with those who were still assisting him, he declared: 'Our dead must be turning in their graves.' As for Stohrer, the German Ambassador, he noted:

'In Berlin, the dissatisfaction with Generalissimo Franco appears to be growing. It is founded less on the fact that during the Czech crisis Franco assured France and England of his neutrality in the case of a European war than ... that he informed us belatedly of his negotiations with the above-mentioned powers and allegedly even promised them that the Condor Legion would be interned as proof of his good will.'[25]

In any case, Franco's attitude was quite clear: solidarity with his Italian and German allies in so far as this strengthened his own position; disengagement as

[24] *D.G.F.P.*, III, p. 746.
[25] *D.G.F.P.*, III, p. 746.

soon as the risks seemed excessive; a constant prudence which led him only to play his hand when the game was actually won (as, here, the disclosure to Germany of his neutrality). Franco's diplomatic procedure reflects the characteristics which, at every stage in his career, contributed to his strength.

In September 1938, however, the primary source of the Caudillo's strength was the weakness of the democratic powers, which yielded to Hitler's pressure and deserted the Sudetenland and thus, in the end, the whole of Czechoslovakia. Munich also dealt the death blow to Republican Spain because, after so many other capitulations, it proved that the democracies were less than ever ready to intervene in Spain. In the Republican camp discouragement and defeatism became more marked. The Nationalists, on the contrary, flaunted their certainty of victory. On 1 October 1938, the 'Caudillo's day', Franco declared at Burgos: 'This dawn of peace sounds the knell of Red tyranny. The efforts of our armies will soon lead to a victorious peace.' Jordana, Minister of Foreign Affairs, told Stohrer that 'the peaceful solution of the Czech conflict by the four great European powers without Russia, which had been entirely in accordance with German demands, meant that the Civil War would now have to be prosecuted by the Nationalists with redoubled energy in order to bring about the capitulation of the Reds.'[26] Autumn 1938 thus sealed the doom of Republican Spain. Democratic Europe had already let her fight alone, now she would have to die alone.

The End of the International Brigades

Moreover, Negrín, anxious to display the goodwill of Republican Spain, had requested the Assembly of the League of Nations (21 September) to set up a commission of inquiry to control the withdrawal of foreign volunteers who had fought by the side of Spaniards in both camps. Whereas Italy and Germany withdrew only men who were no longer involved in direct fighting (10,000 Italians, sick and wounded, etc.), Negrín's decision entailed the departure of the International Brigades, which were one of the strongest units in the Republican army. On 23 September they were withdrawn from the front. On 9 October, a few days after Munich, Negrín made his farewell speech: 'You are leaving with bruised hearts. I have seen you shed tears at the thought of abandoning the front. But you can go away with the conviction that our firmness will remain unshaken.' One month after Munich, on 28 October, their farewell parade took place in Barcelona, amid songs and flowers and flags, while crowds rushed to meet them and women to embrace them. La Pasionaria exclaimed: 'Banners of Spain, greet this crowd of heroes! Bow down before so many martyrs! . . . We shall not forget you.' Although some of the volunteers (notably the anti-Fascist exiles) remained in Spain, this departure was a significant event. After Munich, it marks another stage in the desertion of the Republic. Franco, on the contrary, obtained fresh supplies of material from the Germans in exchange for a majority interest in five important mines, and he was thus enabled to launch his offensive on Catalonia.

[26] *D.G.F.P.*, III, p. 760.

The Fall of Barcelona (26 January 1939)

This offensive, begun on 23 December, was crowned with success. The Segre front gave way. The Republican troops were exhausted, their air force was non-existent or ineffective, and they were short of arms. Day after day Barcelona was bombed by Italian aircraft; the Fascist volunteers under Gambara advanced successfully. 'In Spain things are going ahead full sail', noted Ciano in his Diary. In ravaged Barcelona, amid its charred and ruined homes, morale was at a low ebb. It was January, and there was no more coal and only 300 grammes of bread a day. The streets were empty and the shops shut. With Nazis and Fascists triumphing all around, Barcelona was unable to fight in January 1939 as Madrid had fought in 1936; on the 26th the city was occupied without a struggle.

This meant total psychological defeat for the Republican side, apart from the strategic importance of the Catalan capital: tens of thousands of refugees, women and children, the old and the disabled, and also some fighting men, deserters, fled into France, crossing the frontier huddled in blankets, with the drawn, begrimed, unhappy faces of the vanquished. Regrouped and interned by the French authorities, they were crowded into camps behind barbed-wire fences, in wooden huts, at Argelès, Prats de Mollo and Saint-Cyprien.

Meanwhile Navarrese battalions paraded past on the Paseo de Gracia with arms outstretched in the Fascist salute; the co-operative stores of the various political parties were thrown open to plunderers, and a solemn mass was celebrated on the Plaza de Cataluña. The *Auxilio Social*, organizing relief for war victims on the Francoist side, began its distributions of bread and soup to the proud, heroic population, so noble-hearted, so ardent, so politically conscious and so brutally shattered. Crowning his victory, on 21 February 1939, the Caudillo inspected 80,000 men in the Catalan capital, before an enthusiastic crowd. Already the leading nations of the world were sending representatives to Burgos. Léon Bérard, Daladier's unofficial envoy, negotiated France's recognition of Franco's government. The end was near.

On 7 February President Azaña took refuge in France; on the 24th he tendered his resignation. Churchill wrote clear-sightedly on 23 February:

'Although General Miaja and the Madrid army may perhaps be capable of maintaining a solid resistance for several months, they cannot prevent the ultimate victory of General Franco and the Nationalists. . . . General Franco's triumph opens to him only a vista of difficulties. He cannot live by terror. Half a nation cannot exterminate or subjugate the other half. He must come to terms with the rest of his fellow-countrymen. It is in his profound interest to do so.'[27]

Churchill might have been mistaken on this point. Indeed, the most alarming rumours as to the future were already current by the end of 1938 in diplomatic circles. Stohrer, in a dispatch to Berlin of 19 November 1938, wrote:

[27] Winston Churchill, *Step by Step*, pp. 331–4.

'Franco is supposed to have said recently that he had a list of 2 million (according to other reports 2½ million) names of Spanish Reds who have been guilty of some crime or other and who would receive their punishment. When I asked Foreign Minister Jordana whether this statement had really been made he answered evasively that he did not know whether the Generalísimo had made such a statement. It was a fact, however, that they had a long list of Red criminals who had to be given their just punishment.'[28]

In fact the persecution of 'Reds' had already begun in territories recently 'liberated' by the Nationalists. In Barcelona, executions followed fast on one another, and the exodus of refugees tells us clearly enough what they dreaded.

What restraining force, indeed, could prevent Franco's justice from taking its course? True, Churchill implies that Britain might show her gratitude, and even offer assistance, provided there was no terror: 'We seek a united, independent Spain, making the best of itself apart from Europe. For this purpose it is above all things important that no cruel retribution should be exacted from the vanquished.'

The Prime Minister was Neville Chamberlain; and the power-relations in Europe were such that Franco, for the time being, could do as he pleased. The day following the fall of Barcelona (27 January), about which Ciano remarked that 'victory in Spain is signed with a single name, that of Mussolini', the Duce received the British Ambassador, Lord Perth, who conveyed to him the text of the speech which Chamberlain was to make in the House of Commons. 'I believe', Mussolini said to Ciano, 'that this is the first time that the head of the British Government has submitted to a foreign government the outline of one of his speeches. It is a bad sign for them.'[29] It was against this background that the death-agony of the Spanish Republic took place. Franco had his hands free. And his first aim was to strengthen his own power.

The Caudillo's Power on the Eve of His Victory

Praise and advice for Franco poured in from every side. The Spanish papers of the Nationalist zone lavished their flatteries in the style of Fascist and Nazi publications. 'Franco, Caudillo and father', one of them writes, 'always succeeds in what he attempts and accomplishes what he has promised.' Another proclaims:

'A new year, a happy year. ... It will be a happy one. For Spain and her Caudillo and her government; for the men and the land of Spain. For you, our Christian, Spanish reader. Not in vain do our victorious standard-bearers tread the soil of Catalonia. And Franco, who has won such difficult victories, is at work during the long day and the deep night. Above him the heavens, before him the sea, and around him, close-knit and unanimous, Spain. ...'[30]

[28] *D.G.F.P.*, III, p. 801.
[29] Ciano, *Journal politique, 1939–1943* (Geneva, 1948), vol. I, p. 27. See Bibliography, section v, for details of English and American editions.
[30] Quoted by L. Ramírez, *Franco*, p. 251.

The unanimity that surrounded Franco was both the fruit of coming victory, of ruthless military victory, and the result of implacable repression.

Ciano notes on 22 February 1939: 'The situation in Catalonia is good. Franco improved it with a very thorough and drastic purge.' And he adds this revealing phrase, which needs no further comment: 'Many Italians, anarchist and communist, were also taken prisoner. I informed the Duce about this, and he ordered them all to be shot, adding: "Dead men tell no tales".'[31] Moreover, legal justification was claimed for this repression which was quite openly an act of political vengeance, an attempt to crush a hostile ideology by the physical liquidation of its defenders. Thus a commission of jurists had been sitting since 21 December 1938, attempting to prove the illegality of the Republican government of July 1936. According to its findings, the elections of February 1936 were 'an electoral deception'; consequently 'the glorious national uprising cannot in any case be called a rebellion in the juridical sense of the word; it was on the contrary a supreme recourse to the legitimate use of force, which offered the only means of restoring justice and right, which had been ignored and often violated'. Under these circumstances, even the officials of the Republican Government – those of them who had remained at their posts – became suspect, if not actually guilty, and a wide field was thrown open to repressive action. On 9 February 1939 the law on Political Responsibilities was passed. All those who had been members of any party, trade union or masonic lodge *during the period prior to the Civil War*, who at any time from 1 October 1934 were 'held to have helped to undermine public order, or after 18 July 1936 to have impeded the national Movimiento . . . by definite acts or by being grievously passive . . .' were to be judged by a 'National Tribunal on Political Responsibilities'.

Protected by terrorism, delivered from his enemies, defended by a Press law (22 April 1938) which regulated the number of publications and the profession of journalism, Franco saw his power firmly established by the beginning of 1939. Since the decree of 30 January 1938, the Caudillo was officially head of the state, head of the government, head of the single party, generalísimo of the army; in fact he possessed complete executive, legislative and judiciary powers. Thus even before acquiring doctrinal formulation, the *caudillaje* which made the Caudillo (Captain-General in July 1938) the central figure, the keystone of the regime, had become an indisputable fact.

Such a development, in keeping with Franco's personality and ambition, was inevitably furthered by the situation of the Duce and of the Führer in 1939. Mussolini, for instance, constantly exhorted the Caudillo to keep the reins in his own hands. On 9 January 1939 Ciano wrote in his Diary:

'The Duce has answered with a cordial letter to Franco, urging him to proceed with caution until the war is virtually ended, without accepting compromises or mediations of any kind. Also as regards the restoration of the monarchy, the Duce suggested that Franco should go slow. He prefers a united and pacified Spain under the guidance of the Caudillo, head of the country and of the Party.

[31] Ciano, op. cit., vol. I, p. 43.

It will be easy for Franco to govern if he first achieves full military success. The prestige of a leader victorious in war is never questioned.'[32]

On 5 March, Mussolini instructed General Gambara, leader of the Italian volunteers in Spain, to tell Franco of his distinct aversion to the restoration of the monarchy. 'The return of the monarchy would be equivalent to plunging Spain into a new civil war within three years. The King is entirely discredited, and the best that can be said of his sons is that they are morons, completely at the service of Britain and France.'[33]

His advice, of course, coincided with Franco's wishes. Gambara reported back to Mussolini that 'Franco expressed himself in clearly anti-monarchical terms, and he insisted that even if it should be necessary to countenance a restoration it would be a matter of waiting for many years'.[34]

The Caudillo's attitude is understandable. His position was more secure than ever. Stohrer indicates in a report of 19 February that the internal dissensions within Nationalist Spain had abated, and that Franco's successive victories had rapidly increased his prestige. The enhanced authority of the '*cuñadisimo*' (brother-in-law-in-chief) Serrano Suñer contributed, moreover, to the consolidation of Franco's power, in so far as the Caudillo could rely on his brother-in-law. Stohrer notes that Suñer, Minister of the Interior, was now [February 1939]

'indisputably the leading and most important adviser of the Chief of State and Generalissimo. ... But he is a fanatic who inclines towards mysticism and whose actions it will be difficult to predict. ... He is Jesuit-trained and has strong Church leanings. This permits the assumption that he is open to suggestions from the Vatican, although . . . he seems so far to have preserved a somewhat independent conception of future Spanish policy with reference to the Church.'[35]

In any case, Suñer acted primarily on behalf of the Caudillo, who made use of the Falange in the same way.

The Falange on the Eve of Franco's Victory

In fact Franco, ever prudent and suspicious, took great care to exclude from that organization all those sincere Falangists who dreamed of making the F.E.T. into the great national party of the totalitarian state. For he was well aware that such a structure might prove a counterpoise to his own power, a political force liable to outweigh his own in Spanish opinion. Now the personal power of the Caudillo depended on his being the sole authority, and consequently the Falange, though it had to exist, must be a mere framework without real autonomy, subject to the Caudillo and his final decisions. Falangists such as Aznar and González Vélez, who sought to influence the government from within, were arrested and then

[32] Ciano, op. cit., I, p. 19.
[33] Ciano, I, p. 48.
[34] Ciano, I, p. 51.
[35] *D.G.F.P.*, III, p. 848.

exiled to distant provinces. Moreover Franco, with considerable skill, while unhesitatingly combating any assertion or suggestion of political independence, was quite ready to accept theoretical declarations which, without modifying the content of his power or disturbing the economic and social structure of a Spain now more than ever dominated by the landowning class, protected by a victorious army and a Church reinstated in all its privileges, might serve to give formal satisfaction to the Falangists and to maintain the illusion of a revolution.

The Labour Charter

Thus the Labour Charter,[36] which was proclaimed on 9 March 1939, implemented the concept of a National-Syndicalist state, dear to the Falangist Fernandez Cuesta. Central to the system was the 'vertical syndicate' (as opposed to the Fascist-type corporation which the Falangists criticized as 'class syndicates'); this was 'both a point of departure and a point of arrival'. The Charter condensed all the themes of the new regime, seeking to show that the principles of the Falange, somewhat edulcorated, were in the direct line of Spain's historic evolution, It asserted that

'by renewing the Catholic tradition of social justice and the lofty sense of humanity which have inspired our legislation of the Empire, the National State . . . in reaction against liberal capitalism and Marxist materialism, undertakes to realize – in a military, constructive and gravely religious form – the revolution pending in Spain, which shall restore to Spaniards once and for all their Fatherland, Bread and Justice.'

Labour was defined as 'man's participation in production', and 'because it is an essentially personal and human thing, labour cannot be reduced to a material concept of commodities'. The state must stress the dignity of labour, 'that fertile experience of the creative spirit', and also make it compulsory as being 'a social duty . . . an obligatory contribution to the National Heritage; and also to celebrate it. Thus 18 July, the anniversary of the uprising, became a national holiday 'in honour of labour'. Naturally capital, private initiative and enterprise were recognized as essential elements in production, and the state undertook to protect private property: the family being defined as 'the primary moral institution'.

The Charter, of obvious Catholic inspiration, thus sought deliberately – in spite of its denunciation of liberal capitalism – to replace any analysis of Spain's economic reality, however vague, by a rhetoric bearing no relation to the facts. Unemployment was rife in Spain at the beginning of 1939, yet the Charter proclaimed that 'the right to work is the consequence of the duty imposed on man by God'. Stohrer, analysing for Berlin's benefit (19 February 1939) the characteristics of the Nationalist regime then gradually taking shape, notes ironically: 'A German who has been active in Spain for decades recently answered the question: "how do you find the new Spain?" by saying: "When I find it, I shall tell you about it".'[37]

[36] Notes et études documentaires, no. 1368 (Paris, August 1950).
[37] D.G.F.P., III, p. 848.

In point of fact, there were certain new elements. The Labour Charter for instance denied the right to strike. Since 'national production constitutes a single economic unit in the service of the Fatherland, individual or collective acts liable to interfere in any way with the regularity of production, or to affront it adversely, shall be considered offences against the Fatherland'. The workers were thus deprived of any weapon against their employers. In exchange, 'the company must educate its personnel so as to strengthen their awareness of responsibility'. The Charter, moreover, openly asserts that 'the vertical syndicate is an instrument in the service of the state, the chief means by which the latter will carry out its economic policy', and at a time when the Fascist powers were triumphing in Europe, the Franco government could proclaim that 'the national-syndicalist organization of the state shall be inspired by the principles of Unity, Totality and Hierarchy'.

The Charter furthermore makes clear the fusion, and the balance, achieved by Franco between Falangist principles and the traditional, Catholic trend. However, if on the theoretical plane the ratio between the two forces seemed to have been preserved, in fact all the measures taken strengthened the influence of the Catholic Church. From 1938 onwards clerical laws established the Church's hold on the educational system and made Catholicism into a state religion. As Stohrer wrote in February 1939:

'The decree revoking the separation of Church and State which was issued not long ago and was certainly proclaimed with Suñer's consent if not at his instigation is another relapse into the former subjugation of the State to the Church, which is now, at the end of the war, at least as strong as prior to the proclamation of the Republic.'[38]

José Antonio, Patron Saint of the Regime

The Church's triumph provoked some resistance from the Falangists, but this was soon broken, since they had no real power. By way of compensation Franco skilfully offered them the cult (organized by himself) of José Antonio Primo de Rivera. This was no more than a rhetorical advantage, which moreover was of use to the Franco regime since the Caudillo, by giving it official sanction, annexed the myth of José Antonio to his own, while at the same time handing over the memory of the Falangist hero to the Catholic Church, which honoured him as the purest of its martyrs.

The anniversary of José Antonio's execution, 20 November, became a day of national mourning: huge letters in relief spelt out his name on the walls of every church in Spain, facing the parvis; in school, teachers devoted a whole lesson to the work and achievements of the 'absent one'; chairs of political science bearing his name were founded in Madrid and in Barcelona; his writings were collected, his speeches edited, and Franco encouraged this enthusiasm the more readily since it was posthumous and since it contributed to his own glory. In a speech made on 18 July 1938 he declared that in 1934 José Antonio had been prepared

[38] *D.G.F.P.*, III, p. 848.

to hand over to him the direction of the Falange.[39] Thus from 1938 onwards the man whom the Italian propaganda services in Paris had known as Agent No 2, at a salary of 50,000 lire per month, became the consecrated hero and the symbol of the new Spain.[40]

The Caudillo, thus cleverly turning to good account the age-old power of the Spanish Church, together with the appealing myths of the Falange and its leader, by means of terror, repression, armed force and the international situation, kept a firm control over the new Spain which, by the beginning of 1939, knew that its victory was assured. Europe knew it too.

Europe and Franco on the Eve of Franco's Victory

Britain and France, involved in the policy of appeasing Nazism of which Munich marked the most important stage, made an increasing number of approaches to the Caudillo. One of the most significant documents, as regards the attitude of the French government, is a note from the German diplomat Campe, counsellor to the legation in Paris, written on 1 February 1939 with reference to *a possible Franco–German collaboration for the reconstruction of Spain*.[41] Campe writes:

'The question now arises whether an attempt should be made to suggest at this point such co-operation in the reconstruction of Spain as well' (i.e. practical co-operation of German and French economic groups in large-scale undertakings in third countries). '... Since the fall of Barcelona French economic circles had been pressing more and more for a speedy restoration of normal relations with Franco. The country's economic and financial elements are only waiting to play the part in building up Spain which, in their opinion, is of necessity bound to fall to them in view of the fluidity of the French capital market and their close personal and kindred connections across the frontier. In the meantime the Government hesitates to make another sudden *volte-face*, but is only seeking as a last resort a good excuse to be able to resume relations with Franco without too great a loss of prestige.'

The British Government, for its part, spared no efforts to bring the war to a speedy close. Thus, British mediation secured the surrender of Minorca to the Nationalist forces on 8 February 1939; obviously, to intervene as mediator at that date could only mean hastening the acceptance of a *de facto* situation: the victory of Franco.

On 27 February the decisive step was taken: France and Great Britain recognized the Caudillo's government. Marshal Pétain was the French Ambassador to Burgos. On 24 March, in full dress and escorted by the Caudillo's Moorish guard, he proceeded, through streets where all traffic was prohibited and where the shutters were closed on every house, to the *Capitanería* to present his letters of credit. The brief audience was a moment of triumph for Franco and must

[39] cf. Stanley G. Payne, *Phalange* (Paris, Ruedo Ibérico, 1965).
[40] cf. above and the author's thesis, op. cit.
[41] *D.G.F.P.*, IV, p. 501.

surely have whetted the ambitions of the French Marshal, who had already often dreamed of power.[42]

France's recognition of Franco aroused concern in Fascist Italy. Ciano writes in his diary: 'We sent a telegram to Berlin, urging them to reach a conclusion quickly on the agreement with Spain in order to counteract the rapprochement between Burgos and Paris. We shall then make it known that we have had an agreement with Spain since November 1936.'[43] The Munich experience had in fact revealed to the Italians the independent character of Spanish diplomacy. The Nazis were also trying, at the same period, to associate Franco with the policy of the Axis, while the Spaniards prudently sought to evade involvement. Weizsäcker, head of the political section at the Wilhelmstrasse, intensified pressure to win Spain's adherence to the Anti-Comintern Pact. The Spanish Ambassador, on 9 February, merely repeated that his government felt that 'weapon in hand, it was doing more than any other in the spirit of the Anti-Comintern Pact ... that his government was naturally entirely in favour of joining the Anti-Comintern Pact but thought that a better time for it would be after the end of the Civil War'. The German diplomat concludes: 'I again gave the Ambassador to understand how much importance we attach to having Spain accede as soon as possible.'[44] Franco displayed his usual prudence, trying to ensure a way out for himself, to postpone choice until the last minute and above all to preserve his autonomy of decision. On 20 February his government finally decided to join the Pact. Stohrer wrote to Berlin: 'The Spanish Government is prepared to sign at any time, but urgently requests that the accession itself be treated with strict secrecy until the end of the war.' Once the Pact had been signed – on 27 March, the day before the fall of Madrid – Spain postponed publishing the news, while Germany put increased pressure on her to do so without delay.

Mussolini expressed great satisfaction at Franco's decision. Ciano reports his words:

'The event is of great importance and will influence all future happenings in Europe. After three centuries of inactivity Spain thus again becomes a living and dynamic factor, and, what is more important, an anti-French factor. Those silly people who tried so hard to criticize our intervention in Spain will one day perhaps understand that on the Ebro, at Barcelona and at Malaga the foundations of the Roman Mediterranean Empire were laid.'[45]

Knowing Franco's habitual secretiveness and the prudence which he had already displayed in his diplomatic dealings, we can reasonably wonder whether Mussolini was not, once again, seriously deluding himself.

One thing is certain, on the other hand: the end of the Spanish Republic and the fall of Madrid represented a defeat for the democracies.

[42] cf. author's thesis, op. cit., Laval's confidential remarks to an Italian diplomat in March 1938.
[43] vol. I (8 February 1939).
[44] D.G.F.P., III, pp. 834, 852.
[45] op. cit. (22 February 1939).

The Fall of Madrid (28 March 1939)

Franco, pursuing his usual tactics, refused to attack Madrid immediately after the collapse of Catalonia. He would leave his Republican opponents to rot; Madrid, unconquered in 1936, Madrid the *trinchera romántica de todos los hombres libres* to die a lingering death. His calculations proved even more accurate than he could have hoped. In defeat, old antagonisms revived and disillusionment found expression. The Negrín government, Álvarez del Vayo and the Communists were determined to resist, even if Madrid should fall, if only to cover the escape of all those tens of thousands doomed to the firing squad or the *garrote* should they fall into the hands of Franco's troops. Some hoped, moreover, that the European war would bring help to the dying Republic.

The people themselves were exhausted; they endured daily bombardment, years of privation had worn them out and the shattering of their hopes had broken their spirit. Meanwhile the Anarchists and Socialists hostile to the Third International sought revenge against the Communists; they rebelled against Negrín's appointment of Communist officers to key posts, particularly in the seaports. Professional officers such as Colonel Casado sought to end the war as quickly as possible by negotiating with Franco on terms of a reasonable compromise. British agents acted as intermediaries, trying to bring the fighting to an end at all costs. And throughout the Republican zone, in Madrid first of all, while the governmental authority was breaking up, the fifth column, the Francoists, reappeared.

On 3 March, at Cartagena, the Republican fleet gave up the struggle and took refuge at Tunisia. Violent clashes took place between Communist-led troops and a section of the garrison. In Madrid, on 6 March, Colonel Casado formed a Junta demanding the resignation of the Negrín government. For a whole week there was fighting in the capital between Casado's partisans (an Anarchist division was even withdrawn from the front to bring him support) and Communists: 2,000 were killed. Well might Nenni write in the *Nuovo Avanti*: 'Before the barricades put up in the autumn of 1936 were overthrown by enemy tanks, Madrid was conquered, crushed, humiliated by internal discord ... the hour of defeat is always cruel, but it becomes unbearable when it is accompanied by treachery.'[46]

Franco, however, refused to negotiate with Casado, demanding unconditional surrender. Then followed the swift disintegration of what was left of the Spanish Republican Government. There was a race to escape. Leaders of political parties and army generals left for exile in various ways, the chief Communist leaders for instance leaving by air on 25 March.

Meanwhile Franco's troops met with no resistance as they made for Madrid in armoured trucks, in driving rain. The advance guard entered the city on 28 March 1939. At 11.30 a.m. the Nationalist flag, red, yellow and red, flew over the deserted government building.

Everywhere in the Republican zone there was total collapse. At Alicante the

[46] Pietro Nenni, *La Guerre d'Espagne* (Paris, 1959), p. 289 (article of 11 March 1939).

hopes of 20,000 waiting men and women were centred on two small ships flying the British flag, the *Maritima* and the *Stambroock*. The latter weighed anchor with over 3,600 passengers on board, mostly Socialist leaders and fighters from the International Brigade. The captain of the *Maritima* took on only seventy-four members of the Casado Junta, who had been authorized by Franco to leave the country. Then Italian aircraft appeared, dropping bombs and firing machine-guns: there were suicides among the soldiers; and soon, less than an hour after the *Stambroock* had sailed, Italian tanks drove in. Then repression began.

In half-ruined Madrid the streets were unlighted; broken shop windows were filled in with sacks; flags, cloths, coloured rugs were hung out in sign of surrender. Young men wearing the Nationalist emblem shouted Franco's name. All day an aimless crowd filled the streets: Republican soldiers, unarmed, grimy, bearded; refugees from the countryside, homeless and destitute. They were starving. The reporter of the French weekly *L'Illustration* stated that 'the need for food is so great that everyone has lost all sense of dignity.' The people clustered round the places where the *Auxilio Social* distributed scraps of bread and smoked fish. A Nationalist soldier eating in the street was immediately surrounded by a horde of starving children.

On 1 April 1939 Generalísimo Franco entered Madrid. The previous day, 31 March, he had signed at Burgos the Spanish–German Friendship Treaty whereby the two states, 'considering the community of interests of their governments, the likeness between their political concepts and the bonds of close sympathy uniting their peoples . . . were happy to see that their friendly alliance had already borne fruit'.

Ciano writes enthusiastically on learning of the fall of Madrid: 'Madrid has fallen, and with the capital all the other cities of Red Spain. The war is over. It is a new, formidable victory for Fascism, perhaps the greatest so far. . . . Demonstrations in the Piazza Venezia because of the fall of Madrid. The Duce is overjoyed. On pointing to the atlas open at the map of Spain he said: "It has been open in this way for almost three years, and that is enough. But I know already that I must open it at another page". He has Albania in mind.'[47]

Thus the fall of Madrid gave a fresh impetus to the forces of fascism in that spring of 1939. Yet another Italian, Nenni, who had fought in the International Brigade, answers Ciano's triumphant assertion:

'Something has been wounded to the heart, something that goes even beyond Madrid, beyond the fate of that magnificent city which, for two whole years, lit up the world with the imperishable light of its heroism . . . (but) life goes on and other men will arise from the heart of the people, from the proletariat, to take up and bear forward the flag of revolution.'[48]

Seen from the international stage, the fall of Madrid, the end of the Spanish War, were thus recognized as the conclusion – fortunate or dramatic – of the first battle in a long conflict which was only just beginning. But for Spain?

[47] op. cit. (28 March 1939).
[48] Nenni, op. cit., p. 290.

On Saturday, 1 April, there was broadcast from the Radio-Nacional station the last communiqué issued by the Nationalist headquarters: 'Today after capturing and disarming the Red army, the national troops have reached their last objective. The war is ended.' The fall of Madrid, the end of the war, the victory of the Nationalists: one Spain, it seemed, had taken captive and disarmed *the other Spain*.

CHAPTER II

THE FIRST FRUITS OF VICTORY
APRIL–SEPTEMBER 1939

For three years, Spain had been front-page news in the world's papers. The name of Spain had been a rallying-cry in the streets of great cities; it had served as a banner to intellectuals everywhere; it was a symbol of hope. Then, when Madrid had fallen, Spain faded out: just a few articles remained on a back page describing some ceremony or military parade.

Silence

Silence submerged Spain. The fire had broken out elsewhere; on 15 March Hitler occupied Czechoslovakia and Prague became the capital of the German protectorate of Bohemia-Moravia. On 7 April, Good Friday, Mussolini's troops attacked tiny Albania. And the flames were spreading; on 31 March Neville Chamberlain had given Britain's guarantee for Poland's safety; on 28 April Hitler denounced both the Anglo–German naval agreement and the German agreement with Poland.

Silence lay over Spain, as though the curtain had fallen on the first act of a tragedy which democratic Europe was anxious to forget, her eyes being turned elsewhere. Silence over Spain, leaving the victors free to act as they chose.

Victory could not, in the space of a few hours, change Spain, which for three years had been waging an unequal struggle against Franco's forces. After the Republican defeat, 'weeping women could be seen, by night, slowly tearing up, as though rending their own flesh, photographs of their sons and husbands in military uniform, their anti-Fascist cards, their propaganda leaflets'.[1]

Republican Spain did not change, but it suddenly learned to keep silence. In the streets of Madrid, which was still not completely occupied, 'gentlemen' with the insignia of the Falange or the inscription *Arriba España* embroidered on their coats began to enforce order and, before long, to denounce suspects. For days on end, long lines of Republican prisoners, soldiers in tattered dungarees, barefoot or in rope-soled sandals, streamed down city streets and country roads, under escort, towards some enclosure or football ground (that of Vallecas for instance) which was to serve as their concentration camp.

Europe's silence over Spain was what made repression possible.

[1] Jesús Hernández, *La grande trahison* (Paris, 1953).

64

Repression

There were purges and denunciations, arrests, sometimes torture and death. Teams of Falangists combed villages and city neighbourhoods, hunting out all who had made their mark under the Republic. When anyone was arrested away from home, his name and all relevant details were immediately forwarded to the place where he was known so that vengeance might take its course. The principle was carried to the utmost limits: the sons of men shot by the Republicans were often chosen to join firing squads, or serve as jailers of the prisons in which Republicans were herded together. No classic scenes of national reconciliation for these victors: the vanquished[2] must pay the full penalty. Humble folk every-where were further humiliated. We hear of gangs of arrogant young Falangists driving peasants along by the side of some road on which they had scrawled slogans in praise of Franco and their party; of workers being forced to eat their U.G.T. cards; of unarmed soldiers being stripped. For the end of the war had caught hundreds of thousands of men far from their homes. They were obliged to keep on the move, always liable to a random check, to be arrested or released, beaten or shot at their captors' discretion. *Requetés*, legionaries, Moroccans and Italians robbed them of such things as watches and fountain pens. Sometimes these men would resist: had not Franco promised that 'those whose hands were not stained with blood had nothing to fear'? But resistance meant death on the spot; their lives counted for nothing.

In the concentration camps they waited, lying on the bare ground, under the rain that fell in torrents that spring of 1939, and the still icy wind that blew down from the sierras. In the Puente de Vallecas stadium they crowded on to the tiered seats, huddling close together for warmth. The sentries forbade the use of the highest tiers, since some prisoners had already committed suicide by throwing themselves down.[3]

Sometimes they were transferred from one camp to another. The loud-speaker would slowly call out the names, and from the dark mass a grey figure would emerge, a man wrapped in his sodden cloak, walking with difficulty, his legs and ankles swollen through extreme undernourishment; a defeated man, making his way to the sorting-office. Long queues formed at the tables where *Requeté* officers or army chaplains studied lists of names. Inclusion in a list often led to the firing squad. Sometimes the sentries were ordered to 'liquidate' a prisoner who had attempted to escape; and then a single shot would ring out in the night. At Orihuela camp, close to the great palm grove, the Socialist deputy Mairal was thus put to death. Despair and fear, or desperate anger, demoralized many prisoners. There was apprehension, too; every day 'commissions' of Falangists arrived from some particular district or village, demanding their contingent of

[2] *Les Vaincus* is the title of an admirable, restrained novel by Antonio Ferres (Paris, 1964). See also the prison journal of *El Mexicano*, a Spanish peasant: a unique document, published by Robert Laffont (Paris, 1969).

[3] Armando López Salinas, *Chaque jour compte en Espagne* (Paris, 1965); cf. also *El Mexicano*.

prisoners for the sake of revenge. Generally the men thus handed over were killed before reaching home. The waiting was endless. At dawn, if cold had not already woken the prisoners, a bugle call would rouse them from sleep; a corporal accompanied by two soldiers distributed one tin of sardines and a loaf of Italian bread to each five men. Then more waiting. And even if one of these prisoners were to be set free, he was always liable to be recaptured at another checkpoint.

A Nation of Suspects

The fact is that all inhabitants of the Republican zone were more or less suspect. Some were known, avowed enemies, those who had been militant, who had held responsible posts in the administration, in politics, trade unions or the Republican army; these were executed without trial or else condemned to death or given prison sentences ranging from twenty years to life. Those who had merely been sympathizers, voting for the left, demonstrating with the crowd, were subjected to brutality and humiliation and given sentences ranging from six months to twenty years. Those, finally, who had been drafted into the Republican army with their age group, without enthusiasm, officials who had accepted the 1936 regime as they had its predecessors, might be released from the camps and avoid re-arrest on condition that they produced two guarantors who declared them 'loyal' to Franco's regime. Yet since vindictiveness and self-interest were the order of the day and denunciations were rife, since everyone felt the need to play safe, and since not every village had its Falangist representatives, these unwilling Republicans might well have to spend several months or even years in the camps. Sometimes they were drafted into forced labour gangs – which also included men under conditional arrest – employed on reconstruction projects. It occasionally happened that right-wing sympathizers who had been forced to serve the Republic were also imprisoned and had to wait several months to be released.

Naturally, if this whole population was suspect and deserved punishment, it must have sinned grievously: 7,937 members of the clergy had been shot or assassinated (including 12 bishops, 283 nuns and 192 monks) in the Republican zone; then there had been the executions of Falangists (in the first place, that of José Antonio Primo de Rivera) and the crimes committed in the name of anarchism, socialism or communism. There must obviously have been a 'Red terror', often uncontrolled, which, because it was aimed at the upper classes, assumed an excessive psychological significance, particularly when amplified by Franco's skilful propaganda.

The Greatest Mercy

The repression which had already been raging in the Nationalist zone and which now, since victory was won, swept over the former Republican zone was on quite another scale. Seeking to punish not merely acts of violence but the political resistance of the whole population, it was aimed effectively against masses of men and women. In 1939, according to the evidence of Father Martin Torrent, the *Prisión Celular* of Barcelona, where he was chaplain, contained 8,000 prisoners. This was the largest prison population in Spain. There were daily executions, and Father Martin Torrent writes: 'The only man who has the incomparable good fortune to be able to reply to this question (when shall I die?) is the man who has been condemned to death. . . . Can any greater mercy be granted to a soul which has gone through life separated from God?'[4] In point of fact such 'mercy' was seldom granted.

The liquidation of opponents was moreover carried on with meticulous diligence: in 1942, at the *Cárcel Modelo*, there began a new, leisurely investigation of events having taken place in 1937, which were to entail the death penalty for those involved in them. The English journalist A. V. Philips reported in 1940, after spending 132 days in prison in Madrid, that 'death sentences are pronounced in Madrid at the rate of about 1,000 a month' and that in eleven months (March 1939 to March 1940) almost 100,000 Republicans were executed there.[5]

According to the official figures of the Ministry of Justice (in a statement made to C. Foltz, correspondent of the Associated Press), between April 1939 and 30 June 1944, 192,684 persons were executed or died in prison. These official figures naturally do not include the summary liquidations of the first few months, but who can affirm that they cover all the executions, when the sole fact of having been an officer in the Republican army meant immediate death, and when 6,000 school teachers and 100 out of 430 university teachers had been shot in this way?

Ciano's Evidence

Ciano, officially visiting Spain in mid-July 1939, bears witness to the scale of the repression, and he can hardly be suspected of bias. In the report he sent to Mussolini after his interview with Franco he writes:

'The problems which face the new regime are many and serious; first of all there is the so-called question of the Reds. Of them there are already 200,000 under arrest in the various Spanish prisons. Trials are going on every day at a speed which I would almost describe as summary. . . . Those condemned may however redeem themselves and shorten their sentences by working on reconstruction projects; each working day equals two days of their sentence. . . . The sons of Reds executed or killed in the war are treated with a spirit of great humanity; they are mixed with the sons of Nationalists in the youth organizations of the Falange.'

After this optimistic note the Italian Foreign Minister goes on: 'It would be useless to deny that all this still causes a gloomy air of tragedy to hang over Spain. *There are still a great number of shootings. In Madrid alone between 200 and 500 a day, in Barcelona 150; in Seville, a town which was never in the hands of the Reds,*

[4] Martin Torrent, *Qué me dice usted de los presos? Contestación por* . . . (Alcalá de Henares, 1942), quoted by H. R. Southworth, *Le mythe de la croisade de Franco*, p. 288.

[5] *Spain under Franco* (London, 1940), quoted by Southworth, p. 292.

80.'[6] Which gives a minimum of 6,000 executions a month in Madrid, a figure not so far removed from that of A. V. Philips.

According to Ciano, however, the new regime was not to blame.

'This must be judged in terms of the Spanish mentality, and one must add that even in the face of these events, the populace maintains an impressive spirit of calm coolness. During my stay in Spain, while more than 10,000 men already condemned to death awaited in the prisons the inevitable moment of their execution, only two, I repeat two, appeals for pardon were addressed to me by families. I may add that the Caudillo granted them forthwith.'

In point of fact, the explanation must be sought not by reference to 'the Spanish mentality', but through an analysis of political and social conditions, which shows how in a country which is still archaic the traditionally dominant classes and castes take their revenge for the fear they have experienced by methods already used on a smaller scale in the past (as for instance when a landowner, supreme authority over his estate, punished his labourers) but now extended to a whole country and its population. The terrorist repression which crushed the Spanish people after Franco's victory revealed the backwardness of social and human relations, a backwardness hailed as a virtue in those days of triumphant fascism and nazism. Two barbaric systems, that of the past and that of the present, combined and encouraged one another.

As for the 'calm coolness' of the people, this was to be explained as much by the fatalism of the vanquished, their spirit broken after three years of struggle, as by the conviction – based on experience – that in that spring of 1939 there was nothing that could be attempted and that it was useless to hope for justice.

Lawcourts, Prisons and Camps

Confessions wrung by torture, military tribunals with specially appointed officers as counsel, trials that took three minutes, with sentences printed beforehand and filled in in a few seconds, where penalties were carried out even when a reprieve had been granted, and prisoners were released only to be picked up again and shot down outside the city gates (as in the case of the Rector of the University of Granada, Dr Ernesto Vila): such was Spanish justice in 1939 – a ruthless machine for dealing death.

In the prisons, hundreds of thousands of prisoners were herded together; thirty were crammed into a room just big enough for two. Cold and hunger (the diet consisted mainly of vegetable peelings), neglect and lack of hygiene completed the work of the firing squads. Condemned men were sometimes kept waiting for death, left for months or even years in daily anguished expectation, then, as their turn came inexorably, dragged from the death row and finally executed after that long period of mental torture, unbearable to many. The chaplains attempted, with every kind of pressure and blackmail, with threats and promises, to win last-minute conversions; their efforts were for the most part useless. Neither women nor adolescents were spared.

[6] Ciano, *Diplomatic Papers (1936–1942)*, p. 293.

In the concentration camps the situation was no better. Prisoners had to work on a diet of a few cabbage leaves a day. Sometimes they were so enfeebled as to be incapable of the least physical effort, and even had to extract one another's excrement by means of tin-opener keys. They were reduced to eating grass or the bark of trees. Needless to say there were a great many deaths: more than thirty a day, for instance, in the del Dueso prison. Thus perished tens of thousands of Spaniards, including some of the greatest.

Miguel Hernández

The poet Miguel Hernández was one of these, and his fate is typical of that time when sickness and death, hope brutally shattered, anguish and courage were the daily experience of tens of thousands. Having fought for the Republic, Miguel Hernández managed to cross into Portugal, but Salazar's police handed him back to the Spanish authorities. On 18 May he was imprisoned in the Torrijos jail in Madrid. However, as he had not been sentenced and his name was on no list, he was released. He went to his home in Orinhuela, where he was recognized, denounced and arrested again, and this time condemned to death; after some months of waiting, his sentence was commuted to thirty years' imprisonment. He was sent from jail to jail and finally imprisoned at Alicante. Some Francoist intellectuals tried to persuade him to recant: freedom in exchange for a slight degree of collaboration. Miguel Hernández refused. Before very long he fell ill through privations and lack of hygiene, and died in prison. As the poet Léon Felipe wrote:

> 'Spain, Spain!
> Everyone thought
> – man, History, Legend –
> everyone thought
> that you would end in a flame . . .
> You have ended in a slough.
> See: nothing is left.
> On the edge of the muddy waters . . . a sword
> and in the distance . . . the exodus:
> a starving hunted people
> fleeing.'[7]

How many Spaniards endured such experiences, in prisons and camps? In the province of Madrid the *auditorial de guerra* recorded more than 130,000 cases, in the province of Badajoz more than 100,000. There may perhaps have been more than a million and a half prisoners in Spain.[8]

The price exacted by the victors was a heavy one, all the heavier in that war had already scarred the country with a deep and cruel wound.

[7] '*Elle est morte. Regardez-la*' in *Romancero de la résistance espagnole*, vol. II, p. 17 (Paris, 1967).

[8] cf. *Les Temps Modernes*, no. 55 (May 1950) (article by F. Ferrandiz Alborz).

The Toll of War

One million dead: that is the figure most frequently quoted when the casualties of the Civil War are assessed. In relation to the truth, it is too high and yet too low, even if its huge brutality expresses clearly enough the feeling – experienced in Spain and outside Spain, by everyone and above all by every Spaniard – that these three years of furious fighting were a long-drawn-out butchery.

In fact, demographic calculations enable us to assess the loss in the Spanish population due to the war as around 560,000 dead, including combatants and victims of bombing raids. No doubt this total includes about 320,000 men killed in battle (200,000 Republicans) and about 100,000 summarily executed, but this figure of 560,000 does not give us the real cost of the war in human lives. We should further take into account not only the demographic deficit, the loss to the birth rate, due to the death in their prime of so many of the country's best men and women, but also the results of repression and, of course, exile. Some 350,000 Spaniards left their country: many at the time of Franco's offensive against Catalonia, a motley crowd crawling through the snow – children with frozen feet, wounded fighters, poor peasants, workers and intellectuals mingled. Among them was Antonio Machado, one of the greatest of Spanish poets, who had joined the Republican side from the start and had written to Colonel Lister: 'If my pen could equal your army pistol I would die content.' Machado, like tens of thousands of other Spaniards, succeeded in reaching France, but he did not survive exile and died at Collioure on 22 February 1939. Others held out, in the camps set up by the French government; some made for the U.S.S.R., where the icy atmosphere of Stalinism bred bitter disappointment; others, again, reached Mexico. Spain was thus deprived of many of her bravest and most capable sons, driven by defeat into foreign lands. Thus the demographic loss due to the war and its consequences must be assessed at nearly 1,500,000 inhabitants; for a country with a population of 26,000,000 this meant a deep gash that bled it white.

A Ruined Country

Furthermore, to this immense loss of life must be added the boundless destruction of property which is the ruinous heritage of any war. According to recent reckoning, the economic cost of the war amounted to a million million pesetas (1953 value);[9] 183 towns were devastated, among them Madrid, Barcelona and Málaga, and also hundreds of villages, some razed to the ground like Brunete or Guernica, others partially destroyed; over 500,000 houses were rendered more or less uninhabitable; 75 per cent of Spain's bridges were unusable, 61 per cent of passenger trains, 22 per cent of goods trains, 27 per cent of locomotives had been destroyed by air raids and shells, or worn out by excessive use. Agriculture suffered severely from the conflict; compared to the 1953 figures, there was a drop of 30 per cent in the production of wheat, of 35 per cent in the production

[9] H. Paris Equllaz, *El desarrollo económico español, 1906–1964.*

of barley, tobacco and olives, 65 per cent in that of beetroot. A large proportion of the country's livestock was decimated: 40 per cent of horses, 25 per cent of mules and of cattle. Although the Asturian mines and the industry of Bilbao were unaffected, the production of cast-iron and steel dropped almost 50 per cent in comparison with 1929. Moreover, Spain was in debt to her German and Italian allies, and also to Standard Oil, which had granted Franco long-term credits to enable him to provide his army with petrol. The Republicans, on their side, in order to pay for their purchase of arms, had sent most of the gold in the Bank of Spain into the U.S.S.R.; the rest had gone to Mexico and France. Only the latter power consented to refund this gold to the Nationalist Government. The immediate consequence of this financial and economic situation was the sharp drop in revenue to a level below that of 1900. Above all, the ruin of Spain affected the physical existence of the poorest men and women, for whom the end of the war did not mean the end of suffering, rather the reverse.

Spain's Destitution

Food supplies were exhausted. The overpopulated towns were starving. *Hambre*, hunger, is one of the key words of that year, 1939, a word which every Spaniard was to feel in his stomach for years to come. In Madrid the Falangist *Auxilio Social* distributed 780,000 rations on 2 April, 750,000 on 3 April. But charity has never yet solved any social or economic problem. Industries were slow to resume production, and unemployment was rife; here again a 'sponsor' was needed to secure a job. Yet one had to eat; food was the constant preoccupation of most Spaniards at that time. They lived on lentils ('Dr Negrín's pills'), on 'San Antonio purée', consisting largely of potato peelings, on sliced tomato with salt, on dried figs or onions. When his wife wrote in September 1939 that she could get nothing to feed her son with but a little bread and a few onions, Miguel Hernández, imprisoned in Torrijos, wrote for the child a lullaby which expressed the misery of that time:

'Cradled in hunger
my child lies sleeping
The blood of the onion
is what feeds him.
But it is your blood
frosted with onion-sugar,
with hunger.
A dark-haired woman
– her body – all moon
sucked dry, drop by drop,
over the cradle.'

Children orphaned by the storm, their parents dead or exiled; disabled soldiers, granted a meagre pension if they had fought for the Nationalists, none at all if they were Republicans; unemployed workers; women who, having secured some scanty provisions, deprived themselves in order to convey these to the prisoners in transit from one camp to another, or managing by some miracle and by dint of endless plotting to meet their man in a station waiting-room, between trains, and under the lack-lustre gaze of the Guardia Civil slip him a piece of bread; a whole nation of destitute, gaunt and hungry Spaniards, often in rags, yet almost always dignified, roaming listlessly about city streets and country roads. There was the inevitable increase in delinquency, prostitution and mendicancy, and petty illegal traffic – the sale of water, of cigarettes or half-cigarettes. Physiological distress and deficiency diseases, hitherto confined to certain regions of rural Spain, spread over the whole country. The towns, thronged with workless refugees, were perhaps even worse affected than the countryside. Here people lived in the promiscuity of poverty, several to a room, and moreover in perpetual fear of denunciation and arrest. From the earliest days of Franco's victory, in large cities, concierges acted as informers: sometimes they were actually police officers who managed to stave off poverty by fulfilling a dual function. Everywhere things were hard for the poor; in the countryside the landed proprietors, after punishing those of their tenants who had come to terms with the Republic or occupied lands, had recovered their power and their pride. The Civil Guards kept watch over the fields and orange groves in the south and opened fire on anyone who tried to take a little fruit.[10] The wages of workers (and those who had work were fortunate) were reduced to the level of 1936. There was a general reaction in every sphere against the achievements of the Popular Front, and no attempt was made, once victory had been won, to implement the ambitious programme set forth in the Labour *Fuero* of 1938. The distribution of rations by the *Auxilio social*, the voluntary work of Falangist girls in the hostels for abandoned children, or those whose parents had been imprisoned or shot, were the most notable achievements of the regime during these first months of 1939.

Apart from this, the government had to establish a system of rationing essential foodstuffs (bread, meat, coffee, sugar, oil, rice, potatoes, dried vegetables) and above all it allowed the cancerous growth of the black market, *el estraperlo*, that classic reaction to scarcity which promotes corruption and unfairness and enables the wealthiest, and a few opportunists, to live in comfort. The spread of the black market, the destitution and hunger that generate all kinds of anti-social behaviour from theft to prostitution, are all indications of the moral and political cost of the war.

The Moral and Political Cost of the War

This is hard to assess, but obviously it was extremely high. A whole generation of intellectuals and political men, who had taken up arms for the Republic, had been cut off (by death, imprisonment or exile) from playing any part in social life. No society can gain by thus depriving itself of a large number of its potential leaders. Furthermore, all those members of the working class, the militant

[10] See the vivid documentary account of El Cordobés' life by D. Lapierre and L. Collins . . . *ou tu porteras mon deuil* (Paris, 1967).

element in political parties and trade unions, who formed a grass-roots *élite* and might thus have contributed to the development of Spain, had also been eliminated.

For another thing, the Civil War and the victory of Francoism marked the triumph of violence and the rejection of political action in favour of the use of armed force. The reprisals and executions which went on long after victory had been won mark an undeniable retrogression for any civil society governed by traditional norms of law. From now onwards, that confrontation between men and between ideas which makes so important a contribution to social development ceased to exist. Officially, as we have seen, it had been decided as early as 1937 to establish a regime akin to fascism and nazism. Franco, in an interview of July 1937, told the United Press: 'Spain will have the structure of a totalitarian regime such as Italy and Germany. ... Its regime will include corporative structures, many of which already exist in our country, and it will put an end to the liberal institutions which have poisoned our people.' This explicit reference to totalitarian systems whose madness was revealed by the Second World War enables us to gauge the political cost of the Civil War to Spain.

Moreover, the acceptance of violence as the means whereby society functions (remember the significant cry of Millán Astray, the Francoist hero, *Viva la muerte*), the consolidation of social inequality, the oppression by the traditional 'Black Spain', brought about a general corruption of Spanish society, encouraging stagnation and even retrogression. The moral and political cost of the war, in 1939, can be measured by the existence of two kinds of Spaniard in Spain. There were those who queued in front of shops and those who were promptly served when they showed their Falange Party card, or identified themselves as policemen or ex-Nationalist soldiers; there were those who had the right to live free, and hundreds of thousands who died in jail; there were those who dared not raise their eyes and those who paraded down the streets; there was not one kind of Spaniard, but a set of men who had succeeded in imposing on others their laws and their ideas, their prejudices and their privileges; there were the victors and the vanquished. On 20 April Churchill wrote: 'One side has triumphed by foreign aid, and the vanquished, at least half the nation, are for the moment crushed and impotent.'[11]

The Victory Parade

Yet the triumph took some time to organize. The country must first be taken in hand, which meant controlling, administrating, purging, sentencing and shooting. Madrid fell at the end of March and the victory celebrations took place only in May.

Undoubtedly the refractoriness of the population and the technical problems involved in the maintenance of public order were partially responsible for this delay. Stohrer wrote to Berlin on 14 April that 'the greater part of the Spanish people even now secretly favours the Reds'. Then there were the susceptibilities of Franco's allies to be considered. Mussolini and Hitler had both sent

[11] *Step by step*, p. 355.

congratulations on his victory; to the former the Caudillo replied that 'the Spanish people remember with emotion the sister nation which helped and encouraged them at difficult times. The blood shed by your soldiers on the soil of Spain has created indissoluble bonds between our two nations.' To the Führer Franco expressed 'his gratitude and that of the Spanish nation', assuring him of 'the friendship of a people who in their hardest hours discovered their true friends'. After this exchange of messages, there still remained the rivalry between Italians and Germans to be coped with: on 21 April Ciano, in an interview with Viola, the Italian Ambassador to Spain, expressed his concern that his visit to Spain should precede Goering's: 'It would make a bad impression on the Italians if that fellow should get there first.'[12] Goering meanwhile was taking all possible steps to make sure he did get there first. 'Field-Marshal Goering,' wrote the German Ambassador on 2 May, 'is considering the idea of arriving in Spain from San Remo about 13 May and participating in the parade if an invitation is extended by General Franco.'[13]

This situation enabled Franco to avoid issuing such an invitation, and Goering had to content himself with cruising up and down the Spanish coast and exchanging friendly telegrams with the Caudillo, who thus showed, once again, that he meant to keep victory in his own hands and was not prepared to share his glory with anyone. For the victory was his own, and it must serve to consecrate the Caudillo, saviour of Spain, equal to the greatest of her kings, chosen by God to conquer and to reign. Pius XII addressed a wireless message to the new Spain which unequivocally greeted the victorious regime and its leader. 'It is with immense joy,' declared the new Supreme Pontiff, 'that we turn towards you, very dear children of Catholic Spain, to express our paternal congratulations on the boon of peace and victory with which God has deigned to crown the Christian heroism of your faith and charity, tested in so many sufferings so generously borne.' The victory celebrations organized on 19, 20 and 21 May in Madrid emphasized, moreover, this identification of the destiny of the man they honoured with those of the monarchical tradition which he claimed to inherit, and of the Church which he professed to serve and protect.

The 19 May was the army's day. Franco, having received from General Varela the Grand Silver Ribbon of San Fernando, stood alone on a high narrow rostrum in front of a broad platform packed with dignitaries. Behind, two massive rectangular columns in Italian Fascist style bore his name, thrice repeated, and in the centre, above a huge shield bearing the arms of Spain, the word *Victoria*. A fine drizzle was falling and the spring-time scent of acacia blossom filled the air. Franco was alone. He had put on weight during the years of war and responsibility, and his face under the red beret of the *Requetés* was round and smooth, unlined, almost debonair, expressing with half-smiling lips immense self-satisfaction, pride in having attained his goal, and the deliberate savouring of delight in being at the top; while, close beside him, but a couple of yards behind, stood the Primate Cardinal of Spain and the Grand Vizier of Morocco. If Franco raised his arm in the Fascist salute, it was not with Hitlerian rigidity nor the haughty

[12] Ciano's Diary.
[13] *D.G.F.P.*, III, p. 902.

air of Mussolini, but in the controlled, assured gesture of a man of forty-seven who had succeeded, year by year, in overcoming obstacles with prudent stubbornness, a man who knew what he wanted and who got it.

The troops filed past the Caudillo, the plump little man with hooded eyes, master of a bruised, ruined and still bleeding country. Flowers had been strewn on the Paseo Castellano, carnations and roses to be trampled by the soldiers. Every balcony was decked with flags and splendid tapestries, or with bed linen and quilts ('the poor brought out their festive rags', wrote a French journalist), hung out under the fine rain by frightened people because a display of joy had been decreed. There was a huge crowd. The Moorish standard-bearers, mounting guard at the foot of the rostrum, were much admired. The troops paraded past: a battalion of Italian Blackshirts led the procession, followed by the motorized units of General Gambara, then, for five solid hours, the Spanish troops: the Navarrese army corps led by General Solchaga, the nimble men of the Zaragoza battalion, marching to the sound of fifes playing a *jota* and preceded by four huge crucifixes. Then came the Legionaries in pale blue shirts, the Moroccan troops, lads of the Falangist Youth in their red berets, and the Falange itself, preceded by its fetish, a huge beribboned merino ram with a monkey on its back. Overhead, flights of heavy aircraft darkened the sky above Madrid, that city which their bombs had shattered. German troops and the Condor Legion brought up the rear. They had Guernica to their credit.

The 20 May was the day consecrated to the Lord. At the church of Santa Barbara, after a Te Deum, Cardinal Goma, Primate of Spain, bestowed his blessing on the victorious general. In his pastoral letter *Catholicism and Fatherland*, on 5 February 1939, when victory was imminent, the Cardinal had explained the significance of his support for the Caudillo's regime:

'We expect the revival of Catholicism in our country,' he wrote. 'We can already behold the promise of it in the firm will of the Head of the State, who has repeatedly declared that, following the necessary course of our history, and through his own personal conviction, Catholicism must provide the sinews of the Spain that is to be. ... Spain is what she is thanks to Catholicism. The powers of State, the Supreme Pontiff was saying to me not long ago, do what they like with nations nowadays; let us thank God that those at the summit of power are willing to make of Spain a Catholic country.'

And Franco, on 20 May 1939, removing his sword from his belt, handed it to the prelate, who laid it on the altar, while the Caudillo declared in his light gentle voice: 'O Lord, graciously accept the effort of this people which was always Thine, and which with me and in Thy name has with heroism defeated the enemy of truth in this age. ... Lend me Thy help to lead this people to the full liberty of dominion for Thy glory and that of Thy Church.' The Church received the reward of the Crusade, and Franco, on behalf of the people and through the Church, the support of God.

That afternoon the Caudillo appropriated Spanish history. He made his way to the Escorial, along the slow uphill road, while Moorish horsemen, posted on rocks, kept watch. He remained for a long while in meditation over the tomb of

Charles v, clearly revealing thereby what tradition – that of Imperial Spain – he sought to inherit, and in what lineage he took his place. During this time, in the beautiful gardens of the cloister, where Moors in red cloaks, with drawn swords, mounted guard, the diplomatic corps were waiting. The reception took place in the Pavilion of the Apostles, and Franco might well feel that his consecration was being confirmed as he received the ambassadors of most of the great powers: the representatives of Germany and Italy, of course, but also of Great Britain, while Marshal Pétain, advancing bare-headed and smiling, greeted him with a wave of the hand, representing that French Republic which for so long had withheld approval and now was constrained, like Spain, like the rest of the world, to accept the victory of Francoism.

That evening in Madrid – where all the cafés had to remain closed, although the day should have been given over to popular rejoicing – bands of young Falangists roamed through the streets shouting 'Franco, Franco, Franco'; then about two in the morning the town became silent once more. Thus, after a six-hour march past, in which Italian Fascists and German Nazis, symbolically enough, led the parade and brought up the rear, after a religious ceremony in which the sword joined the Cross on the altar, after a visit to the Escorial, New Spain was officially born. The Caudillo was its unquestioned master. During these first months, he had nothing more to fear from the vanquished.

Opposition to Franco During the First Few Months

True, isolated groups went on fighting up in the mountains. But they were cut off, hunted by the Guardia Civil, denounced, and short of arms, munitions and provisions. Some of these *guerrilleros* managed to cross over into France, others got killed, a few went underground and escaped capture, while others took to banditry. In the countryside, resistance took the primitive form of private revenge: barns, haystacks, cornfields were set on fire, cattle slaughtered. Almost always the labourers who had committed such actions were arrested and condemned to twenty or thirty years in jail, often indeed to death.

However, the chief obstacle to the continuance of the struggle was not so much the fear of repression as the terrible gaps left in the ranks of the resistance movement by that repression (and by war and exile before it). Above all, the sense of despair at defeat after three years of struggle had sapped men's energies. Food was short and work scarce; police and informers were on the watch. Under such conditions, a man's primary aim is to save his own life.

Moreover, political organizations had been unable or unwilling to set up a clandestine network. Even the Spanish Communist Party, which seemed best fitted to do so, was helpless. Jesús Hernández tells us that when he proposed setting up a clandestine organization, Togliatti, the Comintern representative, accused him of being 'obsessed with a sense of collapse'. Furthermore, the very circumstances of their defeat, the open dissension that had brought Communists into conflict with Anarchists and Casadists in the streets of Madrid, prevented the immediate formation of any united front. Indeed, the different groups within the resistance movement were divided by mutual hatred; they had no sort of political line with which to face their triumphant enemy. The few Communist cells, which were the first to be set up, did indeed attempt to analyse the circumstances of defeat and the prospects of the struggle, but there was no sort of liaison between them. The two members of the Central Committee present in Spain had been assassinated. A minor party official, Heriberto Quinones, Communist organizer in Catalonia, tried to establish some sort of contact by means of hand-written leaflets. On the whole the Communists, during these first few months, stressed the need to reconstitute their organization, for, even if the battle had been lost, the imminent world war might make possible the revival of armed struggle in Spain. At no moment did these groups achieve any contact with the masses; they were a mere handful of men.

Early in April, nevertheless, in Barcelona a group of thirty-five young people of between fifteen and seventeen years of age, members of the Unified Socialist Youth, attacked and killed a military judge. They were promptly arrested; thirteen girls (dressed in white and singing *The Young Guard*) and nineteen boys were executed. In Madrid some students formed a Lenin Club. Its members were arrested and tortured in a semi-secret police station near the race-course; the death sentence was imposed, then commuted.

The chief political activity of the opposition centred around and within Franco's jails. There were attempts at solidarity involving the families of those who had been imprisoned or shot. Inside the prisons, Communists, Socialists and Anarchists formed groups whose first object was to prevent suicides. In Jaen prison members kept watch every night to see that those who had been condemned to death did not hang themselves. One night the watchers themselves committed suicide in despair, for the struggle was hard and frightful. To keep up the morale of men who every day saw dozens of their comrades struck down by hunger, sickness or the executioner was a task almost beyond human power, and yet it was achieved. In some places the prisoners organized discussion groups and studied political questions. Everywhere the more responsible members tried to weld the prisoners together by sharing out rations. In some cases prisoners rejected the material advantages to be gained by a confession to the chaplain. Occasionally the struggle sharpened when collective action was engaged for the improvement of their diet. Such actions were very rare in the early months and had to be paid for by death, or by solitary confinement, which often meant death too. These battles, fought at the lowest levels, and the small cells of resistance formed outside the prisons (at first in the Levante, then in Catalonia, in central Spain, and in the regions of Bilbao, Santander and the Basque country) had no direct or immediate political importance. Nevertheless, they represented a form of struggle against despair, they asserted the existence of something enduring, and while Franco's forces swept over the country they enabled a few men to remain upright, and others, some of them young, to realize, even in April 1939, that another Spain existed. This was essential, even if it bore little weight and even if the Caudillo was able to go on organizing his regime as he chose.

Franco's Regime after Victory

In the declarations he made after his triumph Franco repeatedly stressed the social aspect of the new Spain. At Valencia, on 4 May, he declared to the cheering crowd: 'I promise you that I will achieve the healthy and constructive revolution, which shall remove your anxieties about bread and the morrow.' The official slogan of the regime was, moreover, *Por la Patria, el pan y la justicia*. On 5 June, at Burgos, presiding over a meeting of the National Council, Franco asserted once again that the essential need was for 'production, production, production'. He declared, when receiving Ciano on 19 July, that he was 'determined to carry out a policy of great social reforms' and wished, 'to use Mussolini's formula, to go out to the people's wishes'.[14]

There was of course in these appeals and affirmations some sense of the realities of the Spanish situation, combined with the usual demagogy, but also a desire to fulfil, at least verbally, the expectations of those who had chosen the Nationalist side, and primarily of the Falangists. True, the single party was already under Franco's control, but he was not the sort of man to neglect any problem, and in the summer of 1939, once the Republicans had been eliminated, the Caudillo's principal concern was to secure his power on a firm basis, and therefore to assess the situation of the various political forces.

From the different Monarchist groups which enjoyed the support of certain generals (Kindelán, Vigón) Franco had little to fear. They were uninfluential and divided in their allegiance (partisans of Alfonso XIII, living in exile in Rome, of Don Juan, his younger son, or Carlists). Referring to these, the Caudillo told Ciano 'with unequivocal frankness that Spain cannot now return to old formulas of the past; the country is breathing new air, it intends to move towards material and spiritual reconstruction. Any person or institution from the past would act as a brake and would perhaps halt its march.' According to Ciano, moreover, 'an absolute majority' of the population were 'strongly anti-monarchist', and the Italian Foreign Minister deduced somewhat over-hastily from Franco's declarations and his own observations at the time that the Falange, 'a party which is still only beginning to build up its formations and activity but ... already has grouped around it the youth, the most active elements and in particular the women' was 'the central factor in the country'.

This was an error of judgement: for one thing, Franco still mistrusted the Falangists. For instance, no sooner was the war ended than he suppressed the Militia and regrouped its veterans in ex-soldiers' associations. General Franco was not going to tolerate the existence of armed forces, even though they claimed to be his supporters, outside the army. Another significant event was a decree on 31 July, fixing the statutes of the *Falange Española Tradicionalista y de las* J.O.N.S. Naturally, these enabled Franco to control the party, the F.E.T. They define the F.E.T. as

'a militant movement, the inspiration and basis of the Spanish State, which in communion of will and belief assumes the task of giving Spain the profound

[14] Ciano, *Diplomatic Papers*, p. 292.

sense of an indestructible unity of destiny and the faith resulting from its Catholic and Imperial mission as protagonist of history, of establishing an economic regime overriding the interests of individuals, groups and classes, with the purpose of increasing goods, in the service of the power of the State, of social justice and the Christian liberty of the individual.'

Affiliated members, local Falanges, provincial authorities, general inspections, regional inspections, departments of social, moral and economic activity, militia and syndicates, national inspections formed a hierarchized framework strictly subordinate to the national delegates appointed by the Chief of the Falange. The general secretary of the Falange was *de jure* a member of the government. A political Junta, a National Council summoned at least once a year *by* the Caudillo, completed the edifice, entirely dominated by the Caudillo as national Chief of the Falange, whose role is thus defined in Article XII: 'As author of the historic epoch in which Spain has achieved the possibility of fulfilling her historic destiny and at the same time attaining the goals of the Movement, the Chief exercises the fullest and most absolute authority. *The Chief is responsible before God and before History.*' No clearer assertion could be found of the doctrine of *caudillaje*, no more evident demonstration that after 1939, irreversibly, Franco had control of the Falange.

Moreover, the Falange itself altered swiftly once victory was won. The year 1939 was the first in which it lost supporters. War-weary men, disappointed men, tended to abandon all political activity, including that Falange which had embodied some of their hopes for the renewal of Spain, for the Falange, losing all real life, had become a structure composed of bureaucrats. Its militants occupied posts of authority in trade unions, and they controlled local political life by doubling the functions of civil provincial governor and provincial Falange chief. By the summer of 1939 it had become obvious that the Falange, which had never been a mass‚party, would never become one, that it formed merely an extra caste in the life of Spain, and one which included many members of the traditional castes.

On 9 August 1939 a Cabinet reshuffle showed that Franco's sole aim was to strengthen his personal power and not to favour the Falange, of which he was head. The party theoretician, Fernández Cuesta, was appointed Ambassador to Rio de Janeiro, and General Muñoz Grandes, a professional soldier who had fought at Franco's side in Morocco, was made Secretary-General of the party. Pedro Gamero del Castillo, a friend of Serrano Suñer, became Minister without portfolio and Under-Secretary General of the F.E.T. Above all Serrano Suñer, the *cuñadísimo*, asserted his omnipotence as Minister of the Interior and also president of the political Junta. Moreover, a certain number of Falangists (Manuel Valdés, José María Alfaro, etc.) released from Republican prisons, were raised to key positions by Franco and Suñer, over the heads of the few *camisos viejos* still in office (only one of these members, Ridruejo, was a member of the political Junta). These new men, who owed everything (their freedom, for a start) to Franco and Suñer, were reliable allies. Thus, by a clever use of institutions and a cunning policy of maintaining forms while destroying their content, by the creation of clan loyalties and the use of promotions which were actually demotions (Queipo de Llano, who had displayed too much independence at Seville, was appointed head of the Spanish military mission to Rome), by the power over men that he achieved by pitting them against one another, by controlling them and making use of them, and by a constant habit of compromise, playing off one force against another, Franco was more than ever before, by the summer of 1939, the only political power in Spain.

A mass organization (an attempt made in August to organize youth into the *Frente de Juventudes* had soon been abandoned) would be more of a danger than an asset to him. The only bodies he tolerated, because in one way or another he was sure of them, were the army (and its appendage the Guardia Civil), the State and the Church. These were all he needed to hold the country firmly within his grasp. In a long conversation held in early June 1939 in Berlin between General Aranda and Colonel Kramer who, as superior officer of the security services, reported it to the German High Command,[15] we find the echo of these realities. The Spanish general asserts that 'the Falange is not capable of realizing these aims', namely of defining the national ideal. Aranda adds that 'the overwhelming majority of the population of great cities such as Madrid are still Red'. According to Kramer, 'apart from a sense of admiration for the Caudillo ... only the Catholic Church constitutes, to any extent, a unifying factor'. Aranda asserts his view that 'there is still a shortage of outstanding personalities in Spain ... in consequence of which the whole burden lies on Franco's shoulders, even in the sphere of internal politics'.

On 8 August 1939, a series of provisions on the central administration of the state conferred, *de jure*, on the Caudillo full executive, legislative and judiciary powers, which he already held *de facto*. As Spain had been ruined by the war, as the intermediary bodies had disintegrated, as exhaustion was widespread and opposition non-existent, as he had control over the armed forces and had beaten the people to their knees, the Caudillo's power was absolute. In other words, he had become what he had openly expressed his wish to be: the equal of his allies Hitler and Mussolini.

Franco's Spain, Mussolini, Hitler and the European War

This apparent identity of situation, the demonstrations of mutual friendship, and Franco's explicit references to the Fascist and Nazi regimes obviously aroused fears, in the democratic countries, that in the event of a European war – the threat of which loomed large in the spring of 1939 – Spain would side with the Axis Powers; this seemed the more likely since the signature of the German–Spanish friendship treaty on 31 March 1939 and Spain's adherence to the Anti-Comintern Pact.

Churchill expressed concern (20 April): 'Now that all Republican resistance has been crushed, he [Franco] may feel himself less held by local necessities, and at the same time more gripped in Nazi and Fascist hands.' He notes that

[15] *Documents secrets du ministère des Affaires étrangères d'Allemagne. Espagne (1939–1943)* (Paris, 1946) pp. 64–5.

'there is no doubt that all kinds of potentially hostile preparations are being made opposite to Gibraltar. German pocket battleships ... would be well placed at Cadiz to strike at all the trade reaching the British Isles from the Atlantic'.[16] At the beginning of the following month (8 May) another disturbing sign occurred: Franco Spain left the League of Nations, as Japan, Germany and Italy had already done. General Kindelán, Spanish Minister for Air, had already declared at Genoa: 'The union of our two air forces, Spain's and Italy's, has made the Mediterranean into a lake which the enemy cannot cross.' The anxiety felt by France and Britain, the powers directly concerned, was understandable.

Nevertheless, there were a number of signs to be set against these facts which reveal Franco's prudence in the conduct of foreign politics. Reluctance to allow the publication of the Anti-Comintern agreement continued even after victory had been won, and Ribbentrop protested violently. 'We fail to understand,' he telegraphed on 3 April, 'how the Spanish Foreign Minister can raise any new objection to the announcement of Spain's accession to the Anti-Comintern Pact.' The cause was simply Franco's prudence, together with a desire for independence from his allies. Impressive ceremonies honoured the Italians and the Germans, but they were ceremonies of farewell: on 11 May at Logroño for the Italians, and on 22 May at León, in presence of the Caudillo and all the Spanish generals, the Condor Legion held its farewell parade. True, economic influence – particularly that of Germany – grew considerably after the negotiations that took place at Burgos between 12 June and 5 July 1939, and led to the strengthening of the *Hisma* and *Sofindus* companies; and no doubt the Germans emphasized their propaganda by increasing donations (a million pesetas offered by Dr Ley on 22 May for the families of Spaniards who fell in battle), exhibitions, inaugurations, publications (*Signal, Aspa*), town-twinning; but the troops left.

Moreover, Stohrer reported to Berlin on 13 March the remarks made by the Caudillo to General Gambara on Spain's attitude in the event of a European conflict. Spain, Franco, declared, 'would absolutely have to have a period of quiet in order to recover from the effects of the war and to build up a strong defence force. If an armed conflict should develop in Europe in the foreseeable future, *Spain would have to remain neutral*'.[17]

These unmistakable reservations were, naturally, dictated by the objective situation; Spain was impoverished, dependent for her supplies on communication by sea and thus having necessarily to reckon with the United Kingdom. Churchill, moreover, with imperturbable logic and frankness, put the problem clearly when he wrote:

'Unless immediate overwhelming victory rewarded the totalitarian states, and Hitler with perhaps Mussolini at his tail became the master of the world, General Franco's government would never be able to send another ship to sea, nor receive a salt-water cargo. They and their island possessions would be a target for powerful and indignant combatants.'[18]

[16] *Step by Step*, p. 353.
[17] *D.G.F.P.*, III, p. 865 (Author's italics).
[18] *Step by Step*.

Now in the summer of 1939 the victory of the Nazis seemed by no means assured; so we can understand that these facts were appreciated by the Caudillo's government, and further reinforced his prudence. To deduce from this attitude that as early as 1939 Franco had chosen a definite policy would evidently be a mistake. As a practical man, he adapted his attitude to circumstances, his only constant principle being the protection of his personal position as Head of State, which coincided, in his opinion, with the protection of Spain's interests. His sympathies, however, were never in doubt. General Aranda thus declared to Kramer on 5 June 1939, while Hitler was inspecting the volunteers of the Condor Legion on their return to Germany: 'Franco is deeply and firmly convinced that his path lies by the side of Germany and Italy. He openly detests the French and he does not love the British. He believes that in case of war the British will be unable to keep Gibraltar.'[19]

Certain military men went much further. For General García Valino, who was also a member of the Spanish delegation in Berlin, 'nothing can henceforward destroy the union of the Spanish and German armed forces'. 'In case of war', he estimated, his task as Commander in Morocco would be 'to gain ground as rapidly as possible, through a general advance made by means of offensive operations.' The General was 'convinced that Spain would dominate the straits of Gibraltar from bases in Morocco. The British would be unable to offer any serious opposition.'[20]

Thus, in the summer of 1939, even before the outbreak of war, we find Franco's regime caught in a dilemma that was hard to solve because it depended on the relative strength of the Axis and the democratic powers; and this was difficult to gauge, being continually variable. On the one hand we see Franco's real solidarity with Berlin and Rome, and certain Spanish interests, such as Gibraltar; on the other, Spain's weakness, her exhaustion, her needs. Serrano Suñer, accompanying the Italian 'Black Arrows' on their homeward journey, with an escort of over 3,000 Spanish legionaries, was given a triumphant welcome by the Italian Fascists; in conversation with Ciano, he set forth clearly the situation of his country. 'His *bête noire* is France', Ciano reports. But

'Spain fears a war in the near future because she is today at the end of her resources. In certain regions there is famine. If she can have two or preferably three years, she can reconstitute herself and complete her military preparations. Spain will be at the side of the Axis, because she will be guided by feeling and by reason. A neutral Spain would, in any event, be destined to a future of poverty and humiliation. Furthermore, Franco's Spain intends to solve the problem of Gibraltar.'

Suñer stressed this issue:

'As long as the British flag flies on Gibraltar, Spain will not be a completely free and sovereign nation. The youth of Spain lives in the desire and hope of

[19] *Documents secrets* . . , pp 64–5.
[20] idem.

pushing the British into the sea, and is getting ready to do so. Spain also has accounts to settle with France, that "dishonest and dishonourable France", and these accounts are called Morocco and political and economic independence. . . .'

Suñer was 'very glad to learn' from Ciano, who had been deceived by Ribbentrop, that 'we and the Germans also wish to postpone the conflict for some years'.[21]

In this euphoric atmosphere – the war seemed remote, one merely had to be prepared for it – Suñer was treated to victory celebrations in plenty. A grand military parade in Rome, when Spanish legionaries marched past before Alfonso XIII; conversations with the Duce, who lavished advice, condemned the monarchy, praised the one-party system and promised to organize a visit to Italy for Franco; official banquets, and to crown the visit a reception by the Pope himself. Pius XII, while trumpets played the Spanish Royal March, received in audience, as an exceptional favour, not only Suñer and his generals but also the Spanish soldiers, who fell on their knees to receive his blessing. The Pope told them: 'You have sacrificed yourselves heroically to defend the imprescriptible rights of God and Religion. . . . Our thoughts turn, first of all, towards those of your companions who fell on the field of honour.' The Civil War had indeed been a crusade.

In July it was Galeazzo Ciano's turn to be greeted by cheering crowds when he visited Spain. Tens of thousands of Falangists from all over the country welcomed the Minister at Barcelona, when he arrived on the cruiser *Eugenio di Savoia*, with cries of 'Franco-Ciano', '*Viva el Duce*', with flowers and tumultuous enthusiasm. Ciano notes: 'In all the cities I have passed through, except in the suburbs of Madrid where the attitude of the population aroused strong doubts as to their sentiments, support of the regime seems full and complete.'[22]

The climax of the visit was Ciano's meeting with Franco at San Sebastian. The two men did not know each other: one young and vain, all smiling self-importance, aware of his good social standing and his relationship with the Duce, the other self-controlled, silent and watchful, having built up his career step by step and now reached the summit, and intending to remain there. To Franco, Ciano was Mussolini's mouthpiece and the way to Mussolini's ear, and so his speech covered a wide field, beginning with an expression of gratitude to the Duce. But the essential part of their conversation was devoted to foreign policy. Franco reasserted 'his firm intention to follow more and more definitely the line of the Rome–Berlin axis, while awaiting the day when Spain's general conditions and military preparations would allow him to identify himself with the political system of the totalitarian countries'.[22] But like Suñer (and Ciano), Franco congratulated himself on the assurances given him by Ciano and the Duce (in all innocence, since they were unaware of Hitler's plans) as to the 'period of peace now opening'. Franco, with his usual prudence, indicated that for Spain such a period must go beyond the two or three years suggested. 'Franco considers that a period of peace of at least five years is necessary, and even this figure seems to many observers optimistic.'[22]

[21] Ciano's Diary.
[22] Ciano, *Diplomatic Papers.*

Was this duplicity on the Caudillo's part, a skilful diplomatic manoeuvre enabling him to promise without giving anything away, or an example of the delaying tactics of the strategist? In fact, and indeed more precisely under the weight of facts – Spain's condition of famine and her vulnerability – Franco, within the general framework of solidarity, on principle, with the Axis powers, was reserving his decision. This attitude was in conformity with all previous actions of the Caudillo, who, like any gambler who is bent on winning, only staked his money when he held a good hand. Moreover, he did not conceal from Ciano that 'if in spite of what is foreseen and in spite of goodwill, a new and unexpected fact should hasten on the testing time, Spain repeats her intention of maintaining a very favourable – even more than very favourable – neutrality towards Italy.'[23]

The Caudillo, with characteristic skill and flexibility, after thus unmistakably advancing, drew back, declaring that neutrality could only be maintained for a short while, since, if the totalitarian states should win, a neutral Spain would 'have only a wretched future'. On the alternative hypothesis, that of 'a victory of the democracies ... the survival of the Franco regime after the defeat of the other and older totalitarian regimes is out of the question'.[24] And the Caudillo then stressed the necessity of speeding up Spain's armaments programme; he demanded the design of the latest Italian cruisers, asked for the help of Italian aircraft, and announced that the Pyrenean frontier must be fortified.

It is clear, in short, that Franco retained the same sang-froid in dealing with his powerful allies as he had done at the time of Munich. Was this due to the force of circumstances, or to his own political intelligence? The Caudillo, to give him his due, did at least know how to weigh circumstances.

Nevertheless, like Mussolini and Ciano, Franco and his regime were taken aback by the *coup de théâtre* of the German–Soviet pact of 23 August 1939. The news caught all Spain's propaganda – praise of nazism, denunciation of communism as the incarnation of all evil – on the wrong foot. It increased the aversion of many Francoists – particularly those in Catholic circles – to a too close involvement with Hitler the adventurer, and thus confirmed Franco's conviction that decisions on Spanish policy must be taken at Burgos or in Madrid, by himself alone, since it was evident that Berlin's first concern was with the interests of the Reich. Thus the Caudillo's tendencies towards prudence and a wait-and-see policy became even stronger, particularly as the same tendencies were marked in Fascist Italy. The news in any case heralded imminent war. The defeated Spaniards, above all the Communists, who had hoped for so much from its outbreak, could no longer rejoice. The German–Soviet pact meant, yet again, the end of hope for prisoners, the birth of new hatreds between Franco's opponents, between Communists and Socialists in particular, as though after betrayal, defeat, repression, a new proof – the most unexpected, the most absurd – had been given that nothing could now reverse the course of Spain's history.

[23] Ciano, *Diplomatic Papers*.
[24] This observation, made in 1939, must be borne in mind if one is to understand Franco's policy after 1942, particularly in 1944.

CHAPTER III

SPAIN AND THE SECOND WORLD WAR
SEPTEMBER 1939–JULY 1940

Neutral Spain

On 1 September 1939 Hitler invaded Poland. On 3 September Britain and France declared war on Germany. The same day the Caudillo broadcast from Radio Burgos an appeal for peace, and in a note to the belligerents he begged them to 'localize the conflict'. He spoke as a man of experience, almost as if he represented the 'conscience' of Europe. 'With the authority of one who has borne the weight, for three years, of a war to free our country,' he said, 'I speak to the nations whose hands could unleash a catastrophe unprecedented in history. . . .' On 5 September the press published the text of a decree in which Franco, 'considering the official state of war that unfortunately exists . . . imposes the strictest neutrality on all Spanish subjects'.

This attitude is unequivocal: the war had broken out too soon and was raging in the West, leaving the U.S.S.R. to calculate its moves, acquire booty and divide up Catholic Poland with Germany. Franco's regime, caught between apparently contradictory sympathies, incapable of intervening in view of its weakness, chose a propaganda theme that seemed likely to consolidate and vindicate it: that of anti-Bolshevism, which in an interview with Manuel Aznar the Caudillo skilfully, and in orthodox fashion, expounded. 'The irruption of Russia into Europe is of very deep gravity,' he declared. 'It is necessary to act quickly so that new and yet graver perils for the European spirit do not come from Eastern Europe. And this cannot be done unless peace is restored in the West.'

Spanish diplomats acted accordingly. On 3 October Admiral Magaz, Ambassador in Berlin, and on 10 October Colonel Beigbeder, Foreign Minister, offered Spain's good offices to Germany as mediator, being 'completely and utterly at [Germany's] disposal in respect to the peace question'. Warsaw had fallen, crushed under the bombs of a German air force whose best pilots had done their training over Spanish cities, and Hitler had just pronounced (8 October), at the Reichstag, one of those classic appeals for peace which he infallibly made after every fresh conquest. 'Why this war in the West?' exclaimed the Führer, 'Millions of human lives will be sacrificed in vain. . . . This war in the West can solve no problem.' For their part, the Spanish Ambassadors in Paris and in London reported to the Wilhelmstrasse on the conciliatory state of mind that prevailed in certain circles, particularly in Paris. Thus Franco's diplomacy, while expressing a genuinely Spanish point of view, was none the less in line with the German political offensive as the 'phony war' began in the West, that autumn of 1939.

Moreover the Spanish press – frequently infiltrated by the German and Spanish secret services – left no doubt as to the sympathies of the regime. In the Madrid papers we read, for instance, that 'apart from Germany, Italy, Portugal, Spain and Japan, the rest of the world consists of freemasons and Communists, mere scum'. When the U.S.S.R. attacked Finland in November 1939, a fierce propaganda campaign was unleashed against the 'Reds', and in December the Caudillo in a violent speech denounced the Soviet Union as 'the common enemy'. The political line of Francoism was clear: in principle, active solidarity with Germany within the framework of a favourable neutrality, and a desire for the constitution of a united front in the West against the atheistic Soviet East. Franco thus, from the very beginning of the war, set forth the theme of a New Europe's crusade against Bolshevism. This was in fact only an extension of his interpretation of the Civil War and of his own aim: the building of a *new* Spain.

A New Spain

In Spain, that summer, since the bulk of the Republicans were in jail – according to an official estimate 250,719 in December 1939 – and the situation had been stabilized, life should have resumed its normal course. The regime was anxious to keep up appearances: episcopal palaces issued decency regulations; short sleeves and skirts and low-necked dresses were banned, at any rate in church; priests were entitled, and in duty bound, to call to order those who, in the streets or other public places, offended against propriety; dancing was frowned upon, if not actually forbidden. Bathers who undressed on the beach, instead of actually at the water's edge, were liable to a heavy fine; the Civil Guard kept watch, for the Provincial Governor was responsible for upholding the episcopal decrees. Moral order seemed triumphant, but at the same time bull-fighting recovered all its glory (the first corrida took place in Madrid on 24 May) and the *toreros* Domingo Ortega, Pepe Bienvenida, Juan Belmonte, and above all the new star Manolete of Cordoba, were acclaimed by enthusiastic crowds. Football matches were revived; bull rings and sports grounds were thronged. There were *circenses* at any rate.

Bread was still scarce, rationed, greyish. The threat of famine – in the strictest sense – was admitted in official speeches; Spain was short not only of a quarter, at least, of her wheat supply, but of oil and rice too. Poverty was widespread, further accentuated by the arrival of the first rains, the lack of fuel, the dilapidation of dwellings. Meanwhile a minimum of 500,000 Spaniards were completely unemployed; and the level of pay was still that of 1936, whereas the cost of living index had doubled since that date.

Naturally the situation was highly favourable to landed proprietors, who not only promoted an actual agrarian counter-reform in their own interests but also took advantage of the scarcity of agricultural products and the corruption rife at every level of society to run the black market, *estraperlo*. At the same time, the more important of them began to invest their surplus profits in industrial enterprises, and thus, by the end of 1939, big landowners and business men formed a solid bloc with the state, the Church and the army. Meanwhile destitution prevailed, with wages below subsistence level, children in rags in the southern villages, town children reduced by hunger to thieving in gangs or begging for a crust of bread, squalid rooms let at a rent of 150 pesetas to an office worker whose salary, if he was lucky, might be 500, breakfasts consisting of a glass of darkened warm water and dinner of a mush of turnips or starches, while men in grey patrolled the streets, whip in hand, ready to lash out at any signs of a scuffle, manhandling anyone who dared protest, and civil guards armed with rifles stood at every street corner; yet all this was not enough to provoke a popular uprising.

The prisons were still full; the shootings and torture went on there, and raping, for instance, in the women's prison at Ventas. Above all, the internal rifts had widened, for after the occupation of part of Poland by the U.S.S.R. Communist parties everywhere had declared that the war was one between imperialist powers and did not concern the working class. Now for many Spaniards there was an obvious difference between France and Hitler's Germany. Consequently the propaganda of the small, self-enclosed Communist cells, heroic and sectarian, lost all influence. When at the end of 1939 six members of the Central Committee of the Spanish Communist Party tried to return into Spain via Portugal, they were handed over to the Francoist police and executed. Meanwhile abroad, in Mexico, Cuba and Russia, exiles misled by false news of strikes, resistance and demonstrations elaborated their political strategy, issued slogans (the Communists, for instance, urging a single united proletarian front) – whose only result, by and large, was to multiply animosity between groups of exiles without ever succeeding in mobilizing the Spanish masses.

The fact is that during this period Franco's power was growing daily. He felt more secure than ever, guided by God, praised by men, upheld by history; he had become that tubby figure with deep-set, hooded eyes, small mouth and receding chin who so often wore a look of feigned surprise. Great thoroughfares now bore his name; many Spanish cities had their *avenida del Generalísimo Franco*.

On 18 October 1939 conditions being more normal, the Caudillo left Burgos for Madrid, where he settled, not in the Royal Palace, which was to be kept for solemn receptions, but at the palace of El Pardo, built by Charles v. This had been the home of Philip II before he retired to the Escorial: another link, for Franco, with the greatest Spanish traditions. He lived there at a distance of sixteen miles from Madrid, in a palace surrounded by ilex-covered hills, enjoying his power in quietness. The Moorish guard kept watch over the estate; further afield, the Guardia Civil. Franco could safely go for long rides on horseback or play tennis. His wife, Doña Carmen Polo de Franco, and his daughter lived the same kind of life. Days and weeks were governed by a strict time-table. On Tuesdays he went to Mass and confession and received visitors; on Wednesdays he went hunting; on Fridays from 10 a.m. there was a lengthy Cabinet meeting which, with a break between two and five in the afternoon, went on until two or three next morning, and at which Franco never really expressed his thoughts, letting others speak, listening, knowing how to take decisions, but in a quiet, unobtrusive way, with the calm certainty of always having been right, of belonging to a higher plane than hectic humanity, among the elect; sure, in the words of the official documents that set forth his functions, of being responsible only 'before God and before history'.

This conviction gave Franco that untroubled conscience which, with its constant references to religion, became the official style of Franco Spain. Addressing his people on 31 December 1939, while the greater number of them were suffering from cold and hunger, and while, in his prisons, women who had just given birth were being shot, Franco proclaimed:

'What we need is a united, responsible Spain. It is necessary to liquidate the hatred and the passions left us by our past war. But this liquidation must not be accomplished in the liberal manner, with enormous and disastrous amnesties, which are a deception rather than a gesture of forgiveness. It must be Christian, achieved by means of redemption through work accompanied by repentance and penitence. The man who thinks otherwise is irresponsible or a traitor.'

A realistic, skilful and suspicious policy of repression prevented any 'irresponsible or treacherous' elements from influencing the life of the country.

Controlling the Country

Towards the Falangists,[1] some of whom brooded resentfully over their disappointed hopes, the regime generally acted with a clemency that was often bribery in disguise. The party was under Suñer's control; since the resignation, on 15 March 1940, of Muñoz Grandes, considered too 'military', it had been run by the assistant Secretary-General, Pedro Gamero del Castillo. Now certain veterans who considered themselves cheated by the new regime had established contact with one another to form a clandestine political Junta in Madrid, at the end of 1939; their leaders, Patricio Canales and López Cotevilla, tried to involve the ambitious General Yagüe in a plot. At the same time they tried to win the aid of the German Nazi chief in Madrid, Thomson, holding out the bright prospect of a *truly* National-Socialist regime in Spain. In fact these men represented nothing but themselves, their ambitions, their dreams and their grudges. Their conspiracies were packed with informers; when they actually envisaged killing not only Suñer but the Caudillo, they came to realize how closely they were bound up with the regime and its leader. Yagüe was betrayed and summoned to the Caudillo's presence; he burst into tears and ... was granted promotion. As for the veterans, they were allotted 20 per cent of all the posts in all Civil Service competitions. Henceforward the plots died out of their own accord, and their liquidation became, as their development had been, a form of settling accounts between factions: the Falangist José Pérez de Cabo was shot for black-marketeering because the army (represented by the Carlist General Valera) was anxious to discredit the Falange. These waves died down at the feet of Franco, and merely reinforced his personal power.

Doctrinal justification for that power was the mission of an Institute of Political

[1] See S. G. Payne, *Phalange*.

Studies, founded on 9 September 1939 and directed by one of the founders of the Falange, Alfonso Garcia Valdecasas. Juan Beneyto Perez, with his books *El Partido* and *Genio y figura del Movimiento* (1939 and 1940), was the declared theoretician of the F.E.T. He propounded the idea that 'a new concept, issuing directly from the revolution, requires one man to become the leader and embodiment of a national community'. Under these circumstances, 'the supreme task of the Party is therefore to select the Chief'. Now in Spain this had already been done. Nothing was therefore left to the party but subordinate administrative tasks. Only one of these was still politically important: the control of the *sindicatos*, the trade unions. On 9 September 1939 this task was entrusted to Gerardo Salvador Merino, a sincere National-Syndicalist, anxious to develop a controlled but powerful working-class movement which could strengthen his own position and play the part of a pressure group. Merino tried to make use of the Law on Syndical Unity of 26 January 1940 to make the unions into the most powerful organization in the country. However, while at first his movement promised to be of use to Franco and Suñer as a counterpoise to other forces, as soon as it began to develop, when Merino tried to get thousands of workers marching through Madrid, when his anti-capitalist demagogy threatened to become a little too realistic, he encountered relentless opposition, notably from financial and business circles and their representative on the Falange National Council, Demetrio Carceller, who had financed José Antonio Primo de Rivera and whose fortune had kept pace with Franco's power. In July 1941 Merino was accused of being a freemason, dismissed from office and exiled to the Balearics: yet another proof that the function of Falangist unions was to control and discipline the working masses, not to provide them with autonomous representation, even in the spirit of National-Syndicalism. A similar function was allotted to education.

Education and the Opus Dei

For with the return to normal life there arose the question of reopening schools and universities. At the end of September 'patriotic examinations' were held in every faculty; all former fighters on the Nationalist side passed automatically and were welcomed with shouts of *Arriba España*. Now somebody had to begin to teach. There was a great shortage of teachers, 60 per cent having been dismissed in the provinces of Asturias, Aragon and Salamanca; indeed, 50 per cent of them had been shot! From the two most famous universities, Madrid and Barcelona, almost the entire teaching staff had left Spain. This disastrous situation, however, was propitious to a reorganization of the educational system, the more necessary in that, according to the supporters of the *Movimiento* and according to the Church, teachers in the past had been responsible, through their liberal and atheistic views, for all the misfortunes that Spain had endured.

Primary education – blatantly inadequate – was now put under the control of the Catholic Church. Curricula were reformed, and devotional exercises made compulsory; pupils and teachers must attend Mass or New Testament readings every Saturday, when each pupil must hand in a written account of his good deeds for the week. Parish priests, particularly in the villages, kept constant watch over the teaching staff, and candidates to the profession were, of course, strictly selected in accordance with religious criteria. But political aspects were not neglected: the programme of studies laid down (22 July 1940) for prospective teachers gave prominence to the following: the war of liberation, its military leaders, the Caudillo (a complete study of his eminent personality). As for the children, every morning, with arms outstretched in the Fascist salute, they attended the raising of the colours and sang the Falangist hymn, 'Cara al sol'.

This collaboration between Church and Falange in the educational field, with the Church in an unquestionably privileged position, was presided over by the Minister of National Education, Professor José Ibáñez Martín, who was to retain the post for twelve years and who thus played a decisive role. A former Deputy for Gil Robles' C.E.D.A. who had joined Franco's party, he was an uncompromising Catholic, a clever and ambitious man. During the war, having taken refuge in the Chilean embassy in Madrid, he had made the acquaintance of José María Albareda, another refugee. He too was a professor; but above all, he was the friend of a priest who was to become an important figure in contemporary Spain, José María Escriva de Balaguer, born in 1902. All three were Aragonese.

It happened that Father Escriva, in reaction against the liberal climate of opinion in the University of Madrid, where he had studied after being ordained priest in 1925, had (on 2 October 1928) gathered together a few Catholics in a group which assumed the name of *Opus Dei*. José María Albareda was one of its members. The influence of the Opus Dei was, to begin with, restricted to university circles, even if, from its inception, a universal mission had been allotted to it by its founder, an immensely gifted man with a powerful and inspiring personality. Little by little his movement spread; settling at Burgos during the Civil War, Father Escriva there composed what was to be the spiritual breviary of the Opus Dei, *Camino* (the Path), which was published at Burgos in 1939 in an edition of 2,000 copies. It tells us that the Opus Dei

'is an association of the faithful who, through their specific vocation, devote themselves to seeking Christian perfection and exercising the apostolate in their own sphere, each in the exercise of his profession or worldly task, to bear witness to Jesus Christ and thus to be in the service of the Church, the Supreme Pontiff and all souls.'

The end of the war was to mark the rise of the Opus Dei. The best elements in the younger generation of bourgeois intellectuals, concerned with self-sacrifice and effective action, found in it a framework and a mystique more appealing than that of the Jesuits or the Falange. The first members were highly gifted men, chiefly from the universities. Soon (March 1941) the Opus was officially recognized as a diocesan association by the Bishop of Madrid-Alcalá, whose links with the regime were well known. The government was no doubt delighted to see the development and growing influence of the Opus Dei, a specifically Spanish creation. In October 1943 the Holy See conferred on it the status of 'community institute'. In the meantime the Opus Dei, thanks to the Minister Ibáñez Martín, had secured for itself a strategic position which would enable it to control a major part of the intellectual elite of Spain. On 24 November 1939, there was set up by law the *Consejo Superior de Investigaciones Científicas* (C.S.I.C.). The preamble to the act states unequivocally: 'It is necessary to impose on the order of culture the essential ideas which have inspired our glorious movement, ideas which combine the purest teachings of the universal Catholic tradition with the needs of our time.' Stress was laid on the need to 'restore the traditional Christian unity of the sciences, destroyed in the seventeenth century'. Now the head of the Consejo, from 1939 until his death in 1966, was José María Albareda. This function involved, in practice, administering a considerable budget, deciding the direction of research, encouraging careers by grants and appointments, and through the medium of the *patronatos* (corresponding to the eight branches of learning, including theology) and the *Institutos* (some twenty to start with, 180 by 1963), running higher education by securing control over professorial appointments, by allotting grants and favours and by inspiring journals (*Arbor* from 1943 onwards). In short the Opus Dei, as early as 1939, with the support of the authorities – and primarily that of Ibáñez Martín – strove to influence and subjugate the Spanish intelligentsia by dominating the universities in which the elite and the leaders of the country were trained.

For the masses other methods were used. They might simply be left uneducated, through lack of primary schools: from 1945 to 1960 the credits granted to the C.S.I.C. were six times those allotted for the building of primary schools. That traditional resource, repression, was not neglected, but use was also made of festivals, sports and ritual.

Thus, for instance, patriotic and religious excitement found vent for eleven days following 20 November 1939, when the coffin of José Antonio was carried in procession from Alicante to its resting place in the Escorial, by way of Albacete – the town of the International Brigades – and Madrid. At every village there was a halt before the altar, mass was said and fires lit on the hillsides to mark the progress of the funeral cortège; simultaneously there was an increase in the number of executions of political prisoners. At the Escorial, under the swastika banners sent by the Führer and Mussolini's Fascist *gagliardetti*, in the presence of the entire diplomatic corps – Marshal Pétain being the last to pay homage – the body was interred. 'May God grant thee eternal rest, and to us may he grant none till we have harvested for Spain the seed sown by thy death', the Caudillo was to declare. A harvest sown by death – the expression is crucial for the understanding of Spain at that time. On 2 April 1940, for the first anniversary of victory, the sound of explosions announced that work had begun on a vast construction, a unique monument to the dead, *El Valle de los Caídos*, the Valley of the Fallen. Outside Spain, too, death was the order of the day, for the war was spreading and Franco's regime was once again obliged to define its attitude.

Spain Confronted with the Evolution of the War

The Spanish press had not waited. It vaunted the military successes of Germany and reverted constantly to the question of Gibraltar. In January 1940, organized demonstrations of young Falangists shouted *i Gibraltar para España*! In the same month Spain was driven by necessity to conclude commercial agreements with

France and Great Britain, by which she received foodstuffs and non-ferrous metals. The German invasion of Scandinavia and its success (April), the feeling that the war was nearing its turning-point, the evolution of Fascist Italy, where propaganda in favour of entering the war was being intensified, gradually affected the climate of opinion within Spain. Stohrer notes on 16 April, in a report to Berlin:

'Serrano Suñer, who is today the authoritative man in Spain, told me frankly a few days ago that he was convinced that with an entry of Italy into the war Spain would also have to decide on her attitude. The complete confidence which the Minister of the Interior has in our victory, which is shared by Franco, and his strong stand against England . . . are the guarantee that they are on our side.'[2]

The Foreign Minister, Beigbeder, expressed the same feeling, but emphasized Spain's 'poor economic situation' (shortage of gasoline and bread grain). Stohrer adds: 'The hope of driving the English out of Gibraltar plays a special part with two leading Spanish personalities, namely Franco and Serrano Suñer, as well as in military circles. The acquisition of Tangier is also hoped for.'

Spanish deeds went further than words. Refuelling facilities *as early as April 1940* were granted to German submarines in the port of Vigo, and as Colonel Kramer pointed out to Goering on 8 May, 'German meteorological aircraft could fly under Spanish ensigns and the radio station of Corunna operates for the Luftwaffe.'[3] Goering, however, protested violently to the Spanish Air Minister General Barrón, then on a visit to Berlin, that 'Spain's behaviour is super-neutral . . . he was disillusioned and indignant over the attitude of Spain' and, while he was confident of General Yagüe's attitude, 'he would like to learn what the attitude of the Chief of State, General Franco, and the other leaders of Spain was'. Barrón replied by pleading famine and Spain's continued dependence on imports.[4]

In point of fact, the Caudillo was as usual playing safe, and at the date of this conversation (8 May 1940) nothing decisive had yet happened; the balance of forces had not yet tipped in Germany's favour. On 3 May Ciano notes in his diary: 'Franco sends a colourless message to the Duce, in which he confirms the absolute and unavoidable neutrality of a Spain preparing to bind up her wounds.'

On 10 May the German offensive broke out: Belgium and Holland were invaded and the French front broken at Sedan on the 14th. Franco was delighted: 'The Germans have a good eye. They always pick the right time and place.'[5] Yet he preferred to keep on waiting: on 12 May the Madrid Government re-affirmed Spain's neutrality. However, Franco meanwhile refused a credit of $100 million offered by the United States, and at the same time signed a commercial treaty with Rome which was very much to Italy's advantage. But – still showing prudence – the Foreign Minister emphasized to Stohrer the disastrous conditions

[2] *D.G.F.P.*, VIII, p. 191.
[3] *D.G.F.P.*, VIII.
[4] idem.
[5] *D.G.F.P.*, IX, p. 395.

prevailing in Spain and also the danger of 'a revolution in Portugal induced by England . . . which could lead to a catastrophe for Spain'.

All these confidential statements reveal the Spanish Government's perplexity in face of the speed with which things were happening and the complex nature of the situation, while all its sympathies went to the Reich, and Spain itself was on the verge of famine, but the Nazi victories were so brilliant that gradually even Franco's prudence slackened and the temptation to join the war grew stronger.

On the Brink

On 3 June 1940 Franco wrote to Adolf Hitler:

'Dear Führer, at the moment when the German armies, under your leadership, are bringing the greatest battle in history to a victorious close, I would like to express to you my admiration and enthusiasm and that of my people, who are watching with deep emotion the glorious course of a struggle which they regard as their own, and which is realizing the hopes that already burned in Spain when your soldiers shared with us in the war against the same, though concealed, enemies. The great upheavals which Spain underwent in the three years of war . . . have put us in a difficult position . . . have forced us to make our official attitude a neutral one.'

And after these congratulations and this explanation, Franco promises rather vaguely:

'I do not need to assure you how great is my desire not to remain aloof from your cares, and how great is my satisfaction in rendering to you at all times those services which you regard as most valuable. With my best wishes for the future and greatness of Germany, and with the expression of my unchanging friendship and regard.'[6]

It was inevitable under these circumstances that the visit to Madrid, on 1 June, of Sir Samuel Hoare as British Ambassador on an extraordinary mission took place in a difficult atmosphere. The Ritz in Madrid was 'filled with very aggressive Germans. . . .' He writes to Halifax:[7]

'The Germans and Italians are deeply entrenched in every department of the government and in every walk of life. The day to day conditions of life are impossible. Food is very short and daily more expensive, ordinary life is dislocated and everyone is living on their nerves. . . . The streets are filled with soldiers, Falangists and police, the roads are heavily patrolled with guards of all kinds . . . the machine of government does not work, whilst in daily life there is every kind of difficulty owing to the breakdown of communications and the fact that most of the skilled workmen of the country are either dead or in prison! . . . The whole of Spain is already suffering from something very near famine.'

[6] D.G.F.P., VIII.
[7] Ambassador on Special Mission (London, 1946).

Hoare realized that under these circumstances Britain might be able to buy Spain's neutrality by promising Franco that nothing would be done against his government, indeed quite the reverse. Moreover, for Hoare, a British Conservative whose claim to fame lay in the pro-Mussolini policy he had pursued with Laval, 'if Franco's Government fell tomorrow, there is not the least chance of a stable government of the left'. Hoare therefore set to work, but his task was a difficult one. He was met with hostile Falangist cries of *i Gibraltar para España!* Contrary to diplomatic custom, he was refused a private audience with the Caudillo. He was even afraid of being kidnapped, in a town where the Nazis had complete freedom of action, and he would only travel about under the protection of an armed British detective.

In particular, the evolution of the military situation told against Hoare. On 10 June Italy entered the war, and at Mussolini's request Franco, on 13 June, transformed Spain's neutrality into *non-belligerency*, 'the conflict having spread to the Mediterranean, and in order to give Spain greater freedom of action', according to the text of the decree. On the 14th Paris fell, and headlines in the Madrid journal *Informaciones* proclaimed: 'We salute the fall of Paris as a mortal blow dealt to the democratic regime.' That same day – possibly as a preface to more extensive undertakings – Spanish troops under Colonel Yuste occupied Tangier. The swastika flew over the French frontier post at Hendaye, occupied by German panzer divisions, while Marshal Pétain, new head of the French Government, through the intermediary of the Spanish Embassy requested an armistice. On 16 June, during these days of triumph, General Vigón, received by the Führer in the castle of Acoz, discussed with him Spain's 'desire to take the whole of Morocco under her protection'.

Was Spain going to join in the conflict? There were some in Madrid who were strongly in favour: Suñer, who had been described by Ciano in 1939 as an extremist whose francophobia was almost pathological, and by Hoare as a 'fanatic in bad health' with 'prematurely white hair, a chronic cough and a nervous twitch', was to speak later in his memoirs of the 'historic occasion of Dunkirk', the moment when Spain was to occupy the North African coast. But Franco, Beigbeder, and Jordana still hesitated. Britain was a power to be reckoned with, so was America; and it is curious to discover in these twentieth-century Spanish rulers, confined though they were within their narrow conservatism and their avowed sympathy for fascism, a sense of the realities of the world situation, an attitude towards Britain and America that seemed the true national tradition of the heirs to the Conquistadores, statesmen whose vision was not parochial but included the Atlantic – a quality in which men like Mussolini and even Hitler were notably lacking.

The Caudillo pursued his plan. On 22 June he received Hoare in his country palace. Hoare, like a true Briton, had noted the poverty and dirt in the village of El Pardo. On the Caudillo's desk were signed photographs of Hitler and Mussolini. 'Why,' he asked, 'do you not bring the war to an end now? You can never win it. All that will happen, if the war is allowed to continue, will be the destruction of European civilization.'

Franco knew that he would have to reckon with the United States, which provided oil, and its powerful ally, Britain; for Britain had wheat, controlled exports from the Argentine and Canada, and granted the navicerts indispensable for the transport of goods. The British Government played a cunning game, without regard for the problems of Spain's internal policy – and anyhow, when had Britain ever been well disposed towards the Spanish Republic? On 4 July 1940 the Duke of Alba, Franco's ambassador in London and a strong anglophile, stated in an important telegram that the British Government was ready to 'recognize its mistakes and to consider later our aspirations and our problems, including Gibraltar'; its sole wish was to see a strong and independent Spain.

Franco's Spain was seething. Nazi successes seemed to be opening up all sorts of possibilities; the army was talking of imperial conquests; on the walls, in huge letters, their claims were set forth: 'Algiers and Oran for Spain.'

On 18 July, the anniversary of his uprising, Franco seemed ready to commit himself too, with talk of 'two million young men in arms' and the need to 'create the real unity of the nation and forge an empire for it. . . .' 'Our duty and our mission,' he declared, 'are clearly marked out for us: to regain mastery over Gibraltar and deepen our influence in Africa.' The following day, when the great military parade took place, cries of *Gibraltar para España* rang out once more. Had Franco, then, made his choice? Yet, on 24 July, a new commercial agreement was signed with Great Britain, completing those made in March and April.

For Franco's regime the contradiction between what was wished for and what was possible remained.

CHAPTER IV

THE CRUCIAL MONTHS

JULY–DECEMBER 1940

In the summer of 1940 the triumph of nazism extended from Warsaw to Oslo, from Brussels to Hendaye. In Spain that July the heat was appalling; towns and villages were short of water, and hunger was still rife. An agreement was reached with Portugal for the transit through that country of imported wheat and crude oil; this indicated a diplomatic rapprochement between the two Iberian powers, already bound by a pact of friendship signed on 17 March 1939. On 19 July, one day after the anniversary of the uprising, the Eucharistic Congress was held in El Ferrol, Franco's home town, in presence of the Apostolic Nuncio, Mgr Cicognani – a religious event, pregnant with political symbolism, which had no effect in relaxing an atmosphere still dominated by the question of war. On 2 July a law had been passed organizing the Falange militia into a home army which, divided into a permanent force and pre-military militia (front line and second class), took in all Falangists between the ages of eighteen and fifty-five. In August, military service was raised to two years; works had been started in the neighbourhood of Gibraltar. These convergent signs, as well as an intense diplomatic activity, confirmed that Spain was on the eve of grave decisions.

Spain's Negotiations with Germany and Italy

The Caudillo was no Mussolini; he was not the sort of man to commit himself unprofitably, and very soon Spain's immense ambitions were made clear. On 8 August Baron von Stohrer, in a Memorandum to Berlin entitled *Operation Gibraltar*, wrote that one of the conditions laid down for Spain's entry into the war was 'the fulfilment of a number of national territorial demands: Gibraltar, French Morocco, that part of Algeria colonized and inhabited by Spaniards (Oran), and furthermore, the enlargement of Rio de Oro and of the colonies in the Gulf of Guinea.' Now such demands conflicted with Germany's policy which, taking into account the part that might be played by France's navy and her African troops if left intact, was anxious to secure the collaboration of the Pétain government in order to prevent these French possessions and forces from joining the British side. It was therefore imperative to avoid directly offending France, at this juncture, by dismembering her Empire for the benefit of Spain or Italy. Hitler had already made this clear to the Duce, who had given in; but Franco was stubborn, and sought support for his negotiations.

Following the victory of the Popular Front in the Spanish elections of 1936, a military conspiracy undertook to "reconquer" the country. General Francisco Franco y Bahamonde quickly assumed the leadership of this uprising. *Upper photo:* Franco in 1936. *Lower photo:* After overrunning a ridge defended by Republican militia, Nationalist troops lead their prisoners down the slope at gunpoint. *(Photos: Keystone)*

On both sides, massacres and summary executions *(Roger-Viollet)*

José Antonio Primo de Rivera, founder of the Falange, who was executed by the Republicans in November 1936 *(Keystone)*

A leftist detachment leaving for the Saragossa front *(Roger-Viollet)*

The victorious General Franco, accompanied by General Mola, entering Burgos. There, on 1 October 1936, in the course of a ceremony of investiture, Franco announced the internal reorganization of Spain "based on a broad totalitarian conception." *(Keystone)*

Units of the Condor Legion arriving from Nazi Germany to fight alongside the Nationalists *(Keystone)*

Republican prisoners. After the Civil War, some 200,000 persons were executed. *(Keystone)*

Nationalist victory parade at Valencia, 4 May 1939. Henceforth Franco was Chief of State, chief of the sole recognized political party, and generalissimo of the armed forces. *(Keystone)*

Franco and Hitler meeting at Hendaye, 23 October 1940. Was Spain about to enter the war on the side of the Axis? *(Keystone)*

Would the Allied victory in World War II sound the knell of Francoism? Within Spain guerrilla bands attempted to assault the regime. And at the United Nations, José Giral *(left)*, Prime Minister of the Spanish Government-in-Exile, submitted to Secretary General Trygve Lie a massive document denouncing Franco's activities during the war. *(Keystone)*

On 13 December 1946 the General Assembly of the United Nations denounced the Franco regime as being of fascist character. *Above:* Following this news Franco, surrounded by his ministers, harangues a government-organized mass meeting, appealing to wounded national pride. *(Wide World Photos)*

Opponents of the regime continued to be lodged in 150 large Spanish prisons such as that of Barcelona. *(Keystone)*

On 16 August he sent a long letter to Mussolini: 'Since the beginning of the present conflict,' he writes, 'it has always been part of my intention to hasten our preparations with a view to entering the war at a propitious moment. . . .' He recalls 'the part played by Spain in the establishment of the new order' and announces that 'once again she can give proof of her loyalty to the European cause by preparing to take her place in the struggle against the common enemy'. The end of the letter is unequivocal: 'It was urgently necessary for me to write to you to request the support of your solidarity in order to assert our safety and our greatness.'

Franco needed precise assurances, real support; he was no hot-headed ideologist or mythomaniac to be satisfied with the sort of declarations lavished by Mussolini in his reply of 25 August, according to which 'Spain, if she did not participate in the conflict, would put herself outside the history of Europe. . . . It is the duty of a triumphant revolution to pursue its external objectives.' Spain, the Duce concludes, if she remained neutral, would 'lose all moral claim to solve her problems'. Now Franco could not be satisfied with 'moral claims'. His regime was still too fragile to engage in a war without sure profits, and he could not accept the equivocal Italian reply, which furthermore betrayed unwillingness to let another claimant share the spoils. Franco's regime needed clear and precise answers, and needed them quickly, for by now (end of August – beginning of September 1940) the economic crisis and the food shortage had become its predominant preoccupation. The wheat supply was 130,000 tons short, and since cotton stocks were only sufficient for two days' work a week in the factories, it was feared that the blast furnaces might have to close down. Spain had to survive, if Franco's regime was to survive. Now credits, as well as wheat and petroleum, were in Anglo–American hands. On 7 September, the financier Carceller asked United States Ambassador, Alexander W. Weddell, for a credit of $100 million. The same day, an agreement was reached for the provision of petroleum between Texaco and the Spanish firm Campsa, which promised that the fuel would be consumed solely on Spanish soil. One can see what a part these vital realities must have played, during those hungry months, in the line taken by Spanish diplomacy. And yet meanwhile Suñer visited Berlin and Rome, because Franco was anxious to know what he could hope to gain by entering the war.

Suñer was happy. The *Ehren Kompanie* saluted him at Hendaye, Abetz received him in Paris. He visited the battlefields of France and Belgium and gave interviews to the *Völkischer Beobachter*: 'Gibraltar belongs to us,' he declared; 'I assert our intention to extend our influence as far as Spanish America. . . .' Finally he met Hitler and Ribbentrop on 17 September, to clarify the conditions under which Spain was prepared to take part in the war by the side of Germany.

Mutual congratulations went on, in the heavily imposing setting of the new Reich Chancellery. Suñer proclaimed that 'Germany had won the war and can claim the leadership of the New Order'. Hitler recognized Spain's rights over Morocco but, as Ribbentrop was to tell Mussolini on 19 September, 'the Führer is, in principle, in favour of making these concessions for the sake of ensuring

Spain's entry into the war, which would have as its immediate object the occupation of Gibraltar'. 'Suñer,' Ciano adds, 'did not lay down the date for entering the war. Military circles think that Spain's entry into the war may take place in four weeks' time.' In a letter to Hitler dated 22 September Suñer seemed to conform with Hitler's wishes concerning Gibraltar. He writes: 'We have been preparing the operation secretly for a long time. We began mobilization some months ago.' And he concludes that he hopes to be able to 'renew the old bonds of comradeship existing between our two armies'.

Was it to be war, then? Suñer, received on 1 October at the Palazzo Venezia by the Duce and Ciano, gave them his assurance that 'Spain is preparing to take up arms to settle her age-old dispute with Great Britain'. At the same time in Madrid, Foreign Minister Beigbeder declared to Weddell (26 September) that Suñer had undertaken this visit on his own initiative to satisfy his personal vanity, and that nothing would come of it. Better still, on 30 September, Beigbeder emphasized that, although he could not make any public statement, he could promise that Spain would enter the war only if she were attacked. On 3 October he urged Weddell to get Washington to send a cable announcing the dispatch of wheat, and he had already asked Hoare 'to start immediately a steady and constant campaign upon the B.B.C. about the economic help you are giving to Spain'. There were thus at least two trends within the Spanish government. Franco, for the time being, as was his habit, let others venture, anxious to choose, at the right moment, whichever line would be most advantageous to himself.

The British Government kept a close watch over Spain's attitude and made generous promises in an effort to retain her friendship. On 14 September the Duke of Alba informed Madrid, by telegram, that the British Colonial Minister was strongly in favour of Spain's controlling the French zone of Morocco. On 8 October, in the House of Commons, Churchill declared: 'We look forward to see her take her rightful place both as a great Mediterranean power and as a leading and famous member of the family of Europe and of Christendom.' The Prime Minister had chosen the very terms that could best please Franco! It is true that Britain was facing the enemy alone.

Now while Britain was making these diplomatic advances, Germany and Italy were holding back. On 28 September Ciano, received by Hitler in Berlin in the gloomy atmosphere of a city preparing for a long war, exchanged embittered comments on the Spaniards and their insatiable demands. Yet the Führer concluded, 'without the aid of our two countries there would be no Franco today'. When the Duce and the Führer met at the Brenner Pass on 4 October they soon reached an understanding about the importance of securing the collaboration of Vichy France against England, and agreed that 'any action must be avoided which may not be absolutely necessary for the struggle', and that it would not be right to 'assume undertakings like the Spanish government's requests concerning Morocco'. In short, as Ciano points out in his diary, Hitler was opposed to Spanish intervention 'because it would cost more than it is worth'.[1] These contradictory factors – London's friendly advances and the cautious attitude of Rome and Berlin – led the Caudillo to assume that he had nothing to fear from

[1] 28 Sept. 1940.

the British, that the Reich and Italy had as good as won the war already, and that he must therefore endeavour to wrest a few favours from them by taking one more step towards intervention.

One More Step

In the first place, the advocates of prudence must be got rid of. On 17 October Beigbeder learnt through the press of his own dismissal. Serrano Suñer, who was still Minister of the Interior, replaced him at Foreign Affairs, and Demetrio Carceller, who had accompanied him to Berlin (but who also negotiated with the Americans) became Minister of Commerce and Industry. Suñer's appointment meant the triumph of the pro-war party. On the walls of the capital posters displayed a soldier standing upright against a starry sky, with the caption: 'Dawn is here, I feel it from the joy in my inmost being!' The inscription 'For the Empire! Towards God!' appeared everywhere, and the newspapers repeated that Spain would want *lo que quiera el Caudillo* – whatever the Caudillo wants. On 20 October Madrid was decked with Nazi flags: Himmler, who had arrived the previous day, met the Caudillo. Already on 18 September, in Berlin, Suñer had been taken by Himmler and Heydrich round the central offices of the Gestapo. He had waxed enthusiastic about their perfection, and the paper *Arriba* had demanded for Spain 'a police system as severe and as solid as that which exists in the third Reich.'

In Madrid, in October, deeds followed words. Himmler initiated collaboration between the two police forces, and officials of the Gestapo moved in to police headquarters in Madrid, having been granted every facility to circulate freely in Spanish territory. Already, in the Pyrenees, political exiles were being sent back into Spain by the Gestapo and sometimes by the Vichy police. A present from Himmler: thus Companys and Zugazoitia were handed back to the Spanish authorities and shot on the spot. Himmler also urged the speeding up of repression, and in fact this period witnessed an increase in the number of executions. If there was to be a war, Franco and the Nazis wanted to ensure the safety of their rear. Thus, in the cold dawn of Franco's prisons, died the first victims of a potential war. In the streets of Madrid, cars blazoned with swastikas and uniformed Gestapo agents became a familiar sight. Military co-operation was intensified through the espionage services of the German and Italian intelligence organizations. The aviator Ansaldo, who had been invited to England, was entrusted with a mission by the German intelligence service, and on his return was interrogated by Admiral Canaris in person. Units of the *Falange Exterior* set up by Suñer in various Latin–American countries provided the best support for Nazi activities there. German propaganda meanwhile took on increased vigour in Spain.

The Italian Embassy in Madrid drew up, on 28 November, an impressive statement of this day-to-day activity, which was heavily subsidized and based on a German community led by the Nazi Party.[2] All kinds of means were used: it

[2] See National Archives, Washington D.C., reports from the Italian Embassy in Madrid, T. 586. R. 434.

was proposed to endow chairs of German in Spanish universities, Himmler presented a hundred radio sets to the *Auxilio Social*, twenty-eight tons of religious objects were sent to the Spanish clergy, while exhibitions of German products, books and so forth were organized. A press agency, Transocean, extended its activities and signed an agreement with the Spanish news agency. Spanish journalists were given presents: the head of the photographic department of *La Vanguardia*, for instance, received a Contax III camera, while, according to the same Italian sources, the editor of *Informaciones*, Victor de la Serna, was granted a partnership in a commercial enterprise which, with the backing of the Embassy, obtained preferential import licences, acquiring thereby considerable financial advantages in a country where everything was rationed. The German authorities bought 50,000 copies of a certain journalist's book entitled *Poruqé Lucha Alemania* (Why Germany is Fighting).

Germans were everywhere; they seemed to take an interest in everything. Thus they offered a whole set of equipment to the Anti-Tuberculosis Institute of Barcelona, they inaugurated and sponsored right and left, and at the same time were active in the economic field: the *Banco Alemán Transatlántico* had tripled its German, and doubled its Spanish personnel since 1939. The economic plan drawn up by Funk enabled the Germans to intervene in the Bilbao zone, where they hoped to supplant Anglo–French interests. Basically the Nazis sought to restrain industrial development, asserting that once the war was over Germany would provide all industrial needs, while Spain was to specialize in agriculture. This propaganda was so blatant and so unbridled as to provoke resistance among the clergy and members of the teaching profession. It was ironically whispered in Church circles that the objects of worship presented by the Reich probably came from Poland. Above all, many Spaniards were afraid lest their country should be reduced to the status of an agricultural and mining colony of a victorious Germany.[3]

However, in this atmosphere, when on 24 October the Spanish papers appeared with huge front-page photographs showing Franco smiling radiantly as Hitler met him at Hendaye station on the 23rd, when the Caudillo and the Führer, side by side, inspected an s.s. guard of honour, it seemed that the next act must inevitably be war. Yet, in spite of smiles, the result of the Hendaye meeting was ambiguous. Hitler and Franco did not take to one another. Franco's train arrived an hour late, and this portly little black-eyed man with his calm, monotonous, sing-song voice exasperated Hitler who, at one point in a nine-hour interview, sprang up, unable any longer to put up with a Caudillo whom he described to Mussolini as 'a brave spirit, but a man who has become leader only by chance and is not cut out to be a politician or an organizer'. For Franco, the Führer was 'an affected man, lacking naturalness and play-acting in a questionable fashion'. However, that is not the essential point. Hitler, who had just had his meeting with Laval and was preparing to discuss things with Pétain at Montoire (24 October), refused to commit himself as regards the French colonies, meanwhile inciting the Spanish to take action against Gibraltar. The special German troops who had seized the Belgian fortress of Eben-Emael could attack the Rock on

[3] idem.

10 January 1941. Franco, for his part, while proclaiming his happiness at fighting by Germany's side, demanded foodstuffs, aircraft, and guns. He drove such a hard bargain Hitler declared that 'he would rather have four teeth pulled out' than deal with such a man again. Dinner in Hitler's dining-car did not help to relax the atmosphere.

The meeting, none the less, was not wholly negative. Two protocols were drawn up – with difficulty, it must be admitted – between Ribbentrop and the man he called 'that Jesuit Suñer'. Mussolini was to say, in Florence, that they represented Spain's 'secret adherence to the Tripartite Pact'; Madrid undertook to enter the war at a date to be agreed on, and to receive material and food supplies from Germany, and later, colonial territories from France. Stohrer indicates in a telegram (25 October) that the Spanish Government had accepted Article 5 of the protocol hitherto under discussion, and on 3 and 4 November Ciano, meeting Ribbentrop and Schönhof in the Sudetenland, signed it on behalf of Italy.

There must therefore have been an agreement reached at Hendaye, stated in terms so precise, weighty and clear that Hitler could launch Operation Felix and Isabella for the conquest of Gibraltar. In Spain, too, many signs showed that a choice had been made; the press spoke enthusiastically of the historic moment. On 2 November a Council of *Hispanidad* was created to ensure the continuity of the Spanish genius. On 4 November the occupation of Tangier was announced; Franco intervened in person, with a speech (6 November) in which he praised 'the cordiality of German friendship' and the 'battle for social revolution taking place in the skies and on the seas of Europe, and for which we have struggled together'. And yet uncertainty remained, for Franco had retained a way out for himself – no definite date had been fixed. In short, he had gone as far as possible towards committing himself to join the war, while preserving his freedom of action until the last moment, just as when, as an ambitious general, he had watched the preparation of the plot in 1936 and joined in only at the last moment. But contrary to what happened then, the situation at the end of 1940 forced the Caudillo to withdraw.

Withdrawal (November–December 1940)

In a letter written by Hitler to Mussolini on 27 December 1944, we find the bitter echo of that moment at the end of 1940 when for the first time the Axis was in difficulties. Hitler writes:

'I had decided to close the western door of the Mediterranean (Gibraltar). My meeting with the head of the Spanish Government had this aim in view. The agreement reached on this occasion should have been carried out. But we suddenly learned, to our consternation, that Italy intended to declare war on Greece.'

For on 28 October the Duce had blindly flung himself into this venture.

In the course of a few days Italian defeats followed in quick succession, the Germans were forced to intervene, and the centre of strategic gravity shifted to the eastern Mediterranean. The balance of the Axis was, still only temporarily, broken: the Italian fleet was crushed at Taranto on 11 November, Graziani was held up in Libya, and General Wavell launched a general counter-offensive which led to the rout of the Italian forces. The Germans were thus, willy-nilly, bogged down in the Balkans and in Africa.

Franco, hesitant and cautious as ever, immediately reassessed the balance of forces in the Mediterranean. As Suñer was due to meet Hitler, the Caudillo called a meeting of a reduced cabinet, consisting of the military members of his government plus Suñer. They agreed that 'Spain could not and must not take part in the war'. On 18 November Suñer was entertained at Berchtesgaden, in the Berghof, where the whole setting was calculated to enhance the prestige of the Führer and condition his interlocutor; he told Hitler, who urged him to organize the assault on Gibraltar, that Spain was short of provisions. The Führer promised wheat, but he had understood. In Madrid, on 7 December, Admiral Canaris tried to get Franco to guarantee German troops free passage through the peninsula to attack the British Rock on 10 January 1941. In vain. 'After the conquest of Gibraltar, Spain would prove a heavy burden for the Axis Powers,' Franco told him, and went on to describe the hunger that was racking his country, the inadequacy of her railways, the lack of coal and the shortage of shipping. All these things, of course, had already existed in September and October, but the general situation had changed and Franco had changed with it.

This ability to change one's line in order to preserve what is essential – power, one's own power – is one of Franco's gifts, and it presupposes a gift for distinguishing the important from the accessory and for always keeping one's escape-route open; it presupposes, too, a supply of men to act as screens (Beigbeder, Suñer, etc.), whom one can allow to take risks the better to safeguard one's personal freedom of action and of withdrawal. Spain thus stayed out of the war, after those months of indecision during which the regime really came as near as possible to joining in. For a time the unwillingness of the Germans and Italians to yield French territories, then Britain's resistance and first successes, which could only mean that the war would be a long one, the dissensions between Spanish leaders and their interests (for instance their involvement with Anglo-Saxon capitalism), the terrible situation of Spain in the grip of *los años del hambre*, the years of hunger, and finally the Spanish people themselves, all this – and Franco's ability to see it – explains the withdrawal of the Caudillo, a withdrawal which proved decisive since in the long run it saved the regime from the disastrous fate of the Nazis and Fascists.

The Spanish people counted for something too, since in those winter months, while long queues formed for coal – which was scarce and prohibitively expensive – Hoare could note, on 20 December 1940: 'National feeling is steadily growing in the hearts of this ravaged nation.' He witnessed a number of brawls with Germans. Some young men vowed, if German troops entered Spain, to try to rouse up the people, to lead a guerrilla war against the Germans like that of 1808–9. They listened to the B.B.C., and despite the violence of repression their will to fight revived.[4] According to one witness, nails were often thrown into the

[4] Juan Hermanos, *La fin de l'espoir, Témoignage* (Paris, 1950).

streets to burst car tyres. In Franco's eyes, Spain was not yet secure enough for him to venture on a risky policy, and it is not the least of Spain's visible paradoxes that the gagged and persecuted opposition influenced, by its shadow, the external policy of the regime and thus contributed to saving it.

December 1940: hunger and cold prevailed. A *Frente de Juventudes* (Youth Front) was formed on 6 December and marches were held. A financial agreement was signed with Britain. Christmas in Madrid: late night suppers in the restaurants were officially forbidden; families must forgather by the crib, the *nacimiento*. The press inveighed against the pagan custom of Christmas trees. It announced, too, that Marshal Pétain, in token of friendship, was sending the Little Singers of the Wooden Cross to visit Madrid and sing at the midnight mass in San Francisco el Grande.

CHAPTER V

THE LAST TEMPTATIONS
AND THE FINAL CHOICE
1941–1942

For several months a rumour was current in Madrid which the press had frequently echoed: at the end of 1940 Franco himself mentioned it in confidence to Lequerica, his ambassador in France: 'Can you believe it, I've got hold of an inventor of genius who can make petrol from plants, wild flowers and water, together with a product which, out of pure personal friendship, he is reserving exclusively for me!¹ A model factory was even to be built in the neighbourhood of Madrid, near the Jarama or the Henares, whose waters might some day be transformed into fuel! This 'petrol fever', which possessed the Spanish press between the autumn of 1939 and the winter of 1940, and the astonishing naïveté of the Caudillo – like that of some Great Dictator imagined by Chaplin – can be explained by the dream of an independent Spain, rich in oil or in wheat and thus able to decide her own foreign policy. The dream did not last, the inventor of genius had to be shut up, and in January 1941 Spain signed a fresh agreement with Britain for the import of Canadian grain.

Colonel Donovan, Roosevelt's special envoy, received by Suñer in February, was able to take a firm line because he was well aware that the United States had the oil that Spain needed. These realities – and the military reality of the relation of forces – frustrated all Axis attempts to draw Spain into the war.

Hitler and Mussolini Put Pressure on Franco²

Hitler, in fact, had not given up his efforts, despite the failure of Admiral Canaris's mission. True, he was under no illusion. On 12 December 1940 he wrote to Mussolini: 'Franco has refused to collaborate with the Axis.' Ribbentrop, receiving Ciano at the Berghof on 19 January, was equally realistic: 'The Spaniards are moving closer to England so as to derive from her immediate advantages of an economic and material nature. . . .' He did not however 'consider that Spain intends to intervene in the war before the British collapse has begun'.

¹ Juan Antonio Ansaldo, *Mémoires d'un monarchiste espagnol (1931–1952)* (Monaco, 1953).
² Quotations are taken mainly from Ciano's *Diplomatic Papers* and the *Documents on German Foreign Policy*.

That same day, in the vast conference room at the Berghof, looking out over a panorama of snowy mountain peaks, the Führer and the Duce once again discussed the Spanish question. Hitler spoke bitterly, relating 'with a wealth of detail the preparations made by Germany for the occupation of Gibraltar, preparations which have since been frustrated by the . . . hesitant and faithless attitude assumed by Spain'. He laid the blame on Serrano Suñer and the influence of the Church on the Spanish Government. Gibraltar was well worth a few *démarches*, and so Ribbentrop and Hitler stressed the importance which 'a personal move by Mussolini might have in making Franco decide on intervention'. The Duce as usual gave way to Hitler, and Ciano, on 22 January, in an official yet friendly letter to his 'Dear Ramón' (Suñer) paved the way for a meeting between Duce and Caudillo. On 6 February, in support of Italy's pressure, Hitler wrote a fresh letter to Franco, pressing and flattering; Franco, however, delayed his answer until he had first met Mussolini.

It was at Bordighera, on the Italian Riviera, that Franco and Serrano Suñer stayed in the sumptuous villa of ex-Queen Margherita, where at the time of the March on Rome the Fascist chiefs had settled the final details of their action. The two dictators exchanged compliments, and inspected a parade of Sardinian grenadiers: two short, portly men, Mussolini displaying the gravity of an elder statesman, Franco acting the part of an attentive disciple. The conversation was a long one: it went on all day on 12 February. The Duce spoke with pompous eloquence of the Axis victory, and declared that 'the present meeting is an anticipation of the visit which Franco will pay to Rome, and which will be the first visit after the end of the war'. Franco listened and assented. Mussolini spoke as a military leader, giving details about current operations and the number of prisoners; of course, he admitted, 'I am led to think that the English resistance will still be long, but Germany will do everything possible to end it in 1941. She has prepared everything for the landing in England.'

Nevertheless, Mussolini was well aware that all this was debatable and uncertain, so he produced his final argument: 'If tomorrow,' he said, 'to put forward an absurd and inadmissible hypothesis, the democracies were to emerge victorious, the first nation to be hit would be Spain.' Then he could not resist adding a final touch: 'Hitler has a great personal sympathy for the Caudillo.' Franco replied with that calm deliberation which had irritated the Führer at Hendaye, 'speaking with complete frankness' since the Duce was 'a great and proved friend of the Spanish people'. He, too, produced details: 'When the European war broke out, Spain experienced the bitterness of not being able to participate in it.' The Germans preferred the French, he complained. 'In the summer [of 1940] the Spanish Government had offered to join; it repeated this offer last November; but Germany did not seem to lay much store by Spain's intervention.' Now, the Caudillo implied, it was too late, the Spanish people were hungry: 'Only eight of the Spanish provinces have three months' grain, the others are entirely, or almost entirely, without it.' Mussolini was not taken in. He interrupted brusquely: 'If suspicion should have arisen among the Germans that Spain does not wish to enter the war because of the failure to effect a landing in England and Italian reverses in Libya, can he (Franco) assure the Führer of the contrary?' The Caudillo raised his voice: 'Absolutely. Spanish faith in the success of the Axis is the same as on the first day.'

What could Mussolini add? After a renewed exchange of compliments, the meeting ended. Making his report to Berlin, the Duce pointed out that 'Spain is not in a state to enter the war. . . . Under these conditions the programme of German–Italian relations should confine itself to preserving Spain as a political ally of the Axis.' A modest but realistic programme. Spain's attitude was in fact to depend on the evolution in the balance of forces.

On their way home Franco and Suñer stopped at Montpellier, where Marshal Pétain and Admiral Darlan were expecting them. General Delattre de Tassigny presided over the great military parade that took place in front of the Prefecture. The Caudillo could thus assess, yet again, what a long way he – and Europe – had come; it seemed a long time ago (and yet it was only five years) since Popular Front Paris had considered him as a factious general backed up by mercenaries. . . Vichy France, on its knees, paid homage to him.

Back in Madrid, the Caudillo could send a calm reply to the Führer's letter. It opened with grandiloquent declarations: 'I stand ready by your side today, entirely and firmly at your disposal, united with you in a common historic destiny, to desert which would mean my suicide and that of the cause which I represent in Spain.' Then came the reality: 'The development of facts has to a large extent left behind the circumstances which, in October, were taken into consideration.' Which amounted to saying that Spain no longer considered herself bound by the Hendaye protocol. However, this did not mean that collaboration with the Axis was going to cease, or that the situation in Spain had improved.

The Situation in Spain

Repression, restriction, poverty had indeed become even harsher. Refugees poured in, sent back from France, rejected by Pétain's government. A friendly witness notes this comment by a member of the reception committee: 'There have been unbelievable scenes with the women. They scream, roll on the ground, bite the Civil Guards. In France, you see, they've got used to being fed without doing anything. So they don't like the thought of beginning to work again. Particularly as these women are obviously not the best we can produce.'[3]

The *Auxilio Social* continued to take in the children of victims of the repression in its *hogares* (homes), and Don Carlos Croocke, head of the *Informaciones e Investigaciones* (the Falange police), revealed in a conversation with the same witness the intentions of this institution, and also certain psychological and moral aspects of Franco's regime during the years 1941–2, when he declared:

'You understand . . . these children are not responsible. And they represent the Spain of the future. We want to teach them to say some day: true, Falangist Spain shot our fathers, but it was because they deserved it. On the other hand it gave us care and comfort in our childhood. Those who in spite of everything might still hate us at twenty would be the worthless ones. The dregs.'[4]

[3] A. Corthis, *L'Espagne de la Victoire* (Paris, 1941).
[4] idem.

And these orphaned children, in their uniform overalls, before their meal, had to give the Fascist salute to the great photographs of the Caudillo that adorned the refectory walls in the *hogares*. Of course, the shooting had not stopped. According to the Law on State Security (March 1941) the death penalty was imposed in almost every case. It was inflicted the more readily in that priority in the appointment to judiciary posts went to men wounded or disabled in the war, to those who had been prisoners of the Republicans, to war orphans or the relatives of those who had been shot. Vengeance was still the order of the day.

Outside Spain, the Gestapo tracked down anti-Francoists to hand them over or else deport them to Germany. In France more than 40,000 exiles were sent to German labour camps, with the more or less explicit consent of the Spanish authorities. Moreover, in April 1941 the national delegate of the trade unions, Salvador Merino, concluded an agreement in Berlin by which 100,000 Spanish workers were to be deported. Thus Spain, even if she was not at war, was an active collaborator. From the end of 1940 until, at any rate, 1943 she also provided a military collaboration which was not confined to the facilities granted to German intelligence services.

There was, in the first place, the export of non-ferrous metals (wolfram, lead, etc.) which Germany badly needed. Spanish factories in Valencia, Barcelona and Seville made cartridges, submarine engines, pieces of artillery, uniforms and parachutes for the Reich. Above all, bases and observation posts were provided for the Luftwaffe and the Kriegsmarine. Aircraft bases at Badajoz, Vigo and Seville, in the Basque country and in Galicia; radio and meteorological observation posts along the coasts and near Gibraltar. There were six of them (with 400 men) between Melilla and Tangier. During the summer of 1943 the post at Cape Spartel enabled the Germans to sink 50,000 tons of shipping. The Canaries were an important base for equipment. At Las Palmas, in the buildings of the German company Bloom und Voss, spare parts for submarines were stored. In the autumn of 1942 the Spanish cruiser *Canarias* took to sea to rescue a German vessel. There was a secret arsenal in the island of Tenerife. Submarines, after their raids, refuelled and rearmed in the ports of Gijón, Vigo and El Ferrol among others. The Kriegsmarine thus enjoyed a considerable strategic advantage, since its units were safe from shelling while within reach of their hunting ground. Crews could go ashore to rest while officers were entertained in Falangist families and from Spain could travel to Germany on leave, then rejoin their units. Lieutenant-General Krappe, German Military Attaché in Madrid, declared in a note to Berlin (with perhaps some slight exaggeration) that Spain was more use as a neutral than as a belligerent, since she provided a breach through the blockade.

The visible presence of the Germans could only arouse spontaneous forms of disapproval: street fights, chalked-up slogans, muttered conversations, grumbled protests when some train passed through a station loaded with oil and rice and inscribed: '*Surplus goods, destination Germany*', for the mass of the population were still living in conditions of extreme penury.

True, there were the privileged few. New and rapid fortunes had been made, with the complicity of those in power since, for instance, one needed only official authorization to import and monopolize some scarce product to accumulate immense profits. Naturally, such authorization was not granted free. There was almost a standard rate for bribes: passports, patents, certificates could all be bought. Specialized agencies were set up for this purpose and advertised in the press, giving details of the possibilities they offered. Certain indispensable certificates could only be obtained by these means. In the central streets of Madrid this new wealth was flaunted, proud, powerful and arrogant, since protest was unimaginable. In middle-sized towns or villages it was even more oppressive, since its power was enhanced by the ancient traditions of feudalism and provincial custom.

The bulk of the Spanish people had to go on trying to survive: peasants herded together in the new zones that had begun to proliferate around the cities, day labourers waiting in village squares for a gracious summons from the landowner, silent workers accepting wretched wages meekly because jobs were scarce and the police were watching. To secure a little money people would sell all they had, down to their household furniture or an occasional piece of jewellery, even wedding-rings. Professional men (school and university teachers) who had been dismissed from their posts although not imprisoned, could find no work, and tried to subsist as best they could – of what use is an intellectual? The degrading signs of poverty were everywhere. Workers wore threadbare clothes or old military uniforms. In Madrid, at the rush hour, this drab crowd thronged the underground and the dilapidated trams. Near the Plaza Cuatro Caminos street stalls were set up, selling figs, sunflower seeds, almonds, pancakes made of lupin flour. On the steps of the Metro women proffered cigarettes or bread. In the evening prostitutes of every age came out.

All these people lived in terror of the 'rubber syndicate' – the police with their truncheons. Housefronts bore huge inscriptions like 'No hearth without a fire, no Spaniard without bread', or the Falangist emblem (the 'Crab', people called it). On Sundays tipsy workers roamed the streets and truckloads of Falangists from the Youth Front drove past singing and waving their red berets. Couples who dared not clasp each other too closely, since Franco's Spain was still prudish, would seek out the shelter of some garden, only to incur a fine of five pesetas, plus insults, if they were caught embracing. Dark cafés provided a refuge where you could play *mus*, a favourite card game, and discuss the problems of the future – lodgings, money, jobs. Franco said that same year: 'Poverty is our title of nobility.' A title paid for dearly by some Spaniards for in the spring of 1941, in the poor quarters of Madrid, an epidemic of exanthematic typhus caused by under-nourishment and lack of hygiene (shortage of water, slum housing and so forth) claimed a large number of victims. A further agreement for the import of 380,000 tons of wheat from the Argentine did not suffice to improve the situation.

While these living conditions failed to provoke any organized protest, political circles, under the safeguard of the army and police, could go on settling the problems of rivalry between factions and personalities which had always been characteristic of the regime.

The conflict was once again confined within the triangle Falange-Army-Caudillo, the latter, as usual, acting as arbiter and eventually benefiting from the clash of opinions. A group of old Falangists still gathered, in the hope of exerting influence, around their priestess, Pilar Primo de Rivera, who 'had sacrificed herself body and soul to the doctrine and ideal of her lost brother'.[5] Suñer, in whom the whole country saw the embodiment of pro-Axis policy (Franco had cleverly allotted him that risky role) and who was seeking to strengthen his position, somewhat compromised by the evolution of relations with Germany, sought to use the Falange to create a totalitarian state in which he would be the leading personality. Franco, however, mistrusted him. He had no desire to play Victor-Emmanuel III to Suñer's Duce. On 5 May he appointed General Galarza Minister of the Interior instead of the Cuñadísimo. The General was a notorious anti-Falangist and his appointment entailed reshuffles and resignations.

The journal *Arriba* published an article against the new Minister under the title *El Hombre y el Currinche* (The Man and the Runt). Franco promptly made amends to the military faction, who had protested violently, by dismissing the two Falangists, Ridruejo and Tovar, who had been in charge of press and propaganda. He was killing two birds with one stone: they were protégés of Suñer. The Caudillo did not intend, for all that, to become the tool of the generals. He therefore sought in his own fashion to restore the balance. Two ministerial posts, Labour and Agriculture, were offered to the Falangists José Antonio Girón and Miguel Primo de Rivera.

To all appearances the Falange now carried some weight in the government. In fact, the power of the ministers was limited; and above all, by accepting these posts from Franco, the Falange finally relinquished all its independence, and Suñer lost all possibility of relying upon it. The Caudillo concluded his brilliant political manoeuvre by appointing to the still vacant post of Party Secretary a veteran relative of José Antonio, José Luis Arrese. A staunch supporter of the Caudillo, trained by him for this responsible function, a convinced Nationalist and an intransigent Catholic whose motto was 'we believe in God, our country and Franco', Arrese became Suñer's opponent. The latter felt the ground give way beneath his feet. He tried to extend his powers as president of the political Junta, but in fact Arrese, backed by the Caudillo, blocked all his decisions. May 1941 thus witnessed the beginning of the end of the Cuñadísimo's political career. With Arrese at its head and its two ministers, the Falange no longer had even a semblance of autonomy. On 28 November 1941 a decree suppressed the dozen national services set up in 1938 which had given the F.E.T. a structure parallel with that of the administration, and hence a certain power. Now the F.E.T. had nothing but its propaganda and its syndicates. In 1942, out of 106 members of the National Council only some forty could be considered as Falangists.[6] The Caudillo, once again, had secured and strengthened his position, the more so in view of the important military successes won by the Axis during the spring of 1941.

[5] According to Serrano Suñer.
[6] S. G. Payne, *Phalange*.

Revival of Pro-war Feeling (April–May 1941)

From 6 March onwards, in less than three weeks, the German army had occupied Yugoslavia and Greece (Athens fell on 27 March), then the Peloponnese and Crete (21 May). In Cyrenaica Rommel's troops drove forward towards the Nile, after taking Benghazi (3 April). The balance of forces seemed once again tipped in favour of the Axis, and an intense propaganda campaign throughout Europe proclaimed the definitive success of the New Order.

In Spain, the consequences of this altered situation were quickly felt, and the pro-war party became vocal once more. Of course Serrano Suñer – the 'Axis Minister' – whose future was at stake, led the movement. On 2 May he inveighed against the 'plutocratic democracies. . . . It is Spain's duty to take into account the realities of our time and in a warlike spirit to march towards a new destiny.' A few days later, he took a further step in this direction by suppressing the international administration of customs at Tangier, but Suñer was not alone. *Arriba* declared that 'Spain must listen to the voice, and follow the wishes, of her dead'. The Caudillo – and this is a more serious sign, since Franco never took any step lightly – on inaugurating the new Staff College in Madrid on 17 April 1941 declared to the senior officers: 'Peace does not exist, peace is a ceaseless preparation for war. I have faith in you, in this generation which will raise up Spain and guide her on the road to Empire.' The atmosphere in Spain was reminiscent of that of 1940; in fact, Madrid had just obtained credits of £2,500,000 from London for the purchase of foodstuffs and raw materials, but the surge of pro-war feeling indicates the influence of the military situation.

Furthermore, the war seemed at that time to offer a means of unifying the different Nationalist factions. Thus military circles quite seriously considered a war against Portugal. Radio Valladolid (partially under German control) issued warnings to Salazar's regime to 'renounce an unnatural alliance' with Great Britain. Stohrer and the Air Attaché of the Reich, Colonel Kramer, emphasize the bellicose spirit of the generals. Kramer writes on 7 May 1941: 'Military circles are now seeking an opportunity to make Spain take part in the war; the initiative comes from the Spanish and no longer from the German side. It is certain that our victories in the Balkans have played a determining part in strengthening this tendency.'[7]

Kramer reports hearing Commander Navarro, the Generalísimo's aide-de-camp, declare:

'War is a necessity for Spain, for reasons of internal politics. It is the only way to make all her internal quarrels recede into the background and to unite the whole of Spain in the struggle against the external enemy. The result of a war against Portugal would be to restore control of the nation into the hands of its natural leaders (the generals). . . . Spain would then really become a totalitarian State, in conformity with the European system of Adolf Hitler.'

[7] *Documents secrets. . . .*

It was in this atmosphere of excitement aroused by the successes of the Axis that the news of the German attack on the U.S.S.R. broke on 22 June 1941; the war, to Franco and his followers, had at last revealed its true meaning.

The Last Temptation (Summer 1941)

The press reacted with unbounded enthusiasm to the lightning advance through Russia of the Reich armies. In the streets demonstrations of solidarity were organized, and on 27 June *Arriba* announced that the Falange leaders had decided to enlist volunteers for a Legion. The first recruits – young Falangists whose enthusiasm had been disappointed by the regime (among them Dioniso Ridruejo and Enrique Sotomayor) – formed the nucleus of the *División Azul,* which was to fight from October 1941 to November 1943 before Novgorod and Leningrad, and which comprised some 50,000 men, not all of whom were, strictly speaking, volunteers, many being officers and soldiers who had been urgently requested to volunteer. The division, which left Madrid at the end of July, was commanded by General Muñoz Grandes.

The speed with which the departure of these men, who were to fight in German uniform, was organized is clear evidence of political intention. As early as 28 June Stohrer telegraphed to Berlin that

'the moves of Serrano Suñer in the last few days show even more clearly than hitherto that he is with clear aim preparing Spain's entrance into the war. The sending of Spanish volunteers against Russia. which must bring Spain into sharper opposition to our foes, is to be attributed to his initiative.'

In Stohrer's view, Suñer 'had won Franco over for this plan, which was immediately explained to us in order to bind the easily influenced Chief of State'. Suñer went even further. Identifying his own political destiny with Spain's entry into the war, he realized that the opportunity once missed had recurred. He exaggerated minor incidents with Great Britain, 'he consciously exaggerated matters', the German Ambassador notes, 'in order to sharpen antagonism towards England and to stir up public feeling'. He was anxious to 'make Spain's entry into the war unavoidable'. According to Suñer, 'a provocation on the part of the English was necessary for bringing about Spanish unity. . . .' And Stohrer, like a good diplomat, adds: 'If necessary, such a provocation had itself to be provoked.'[8]

During the whole of August, propaganda was stepped up. On 3 July *Arriba* published Suñer's declarations to the correspondent of the *Deutsche Allgemeine Zeitung*: 'In face of the German–Russian war, Spain will adopt a position of moral belligerency and she seeks to play an effective part in the conflict.' It must be emphasized that the war against the U.S.S.R. restored to the international situation, in the eyes of all supporters of the regime, a coherence which the Soviet–German pact had destroyed. Now the crusade against *los rojos*, the Reds, revived. The Francoist themes of the Civil War reappeared, enlarged to world dimensions, as if the faith of the Spanish Nationalist fighters had finally spread

[8] *Documents secrets. . . .*

to the whole world. On 17 July 1941, in his traditional anniversary speech, the Caudillo referred to 'these anxious moments when the fate of our nation is struggling in the balance, together with the fate of Europe'. Speaking to the National Council of the Falange, he announced that 'the destruction of Russian communism, that terrible nightmare of our generation, is henceforward inevitable'. He advised America not to intervene, he denounced Great Britain's 'inhuman blockade', and his peroration, in a would-be mystical vein, conveys the atmosphere of a time when even Sweden allowed a division of the Wehrmacht to pass through her territory.

'At this moment, when the German armies are waging the battle so long awaited by all Europe and all Christendom, and when the blood of our sons is about to mingle with that of our Axis comrades, as a living expression of solidarity, let us renew our faith in the destiny of our country, over which, closely united, our armies and the Falange are watching.'

The speech is unmistakably that of an ally of the Axis, of the national leader of a signatory to the Anti-Comintern Pact, and of the representative of a caste which, since 1917, in Asturias, on the Guadalajara and in Madrid, had been relentlessly harrying that 'terrible nightmare', Communism.

At the same time, Franco read his speech in his habitual unimpassioned way, implying that he believed in the words and principles but could, if need be, forget them. London's reaction to the speech followed promptly. On 24 July 1941, in the House of Commons, Eden pointed out in a few incisive words that the success of the economic agreements depended on the goodwill of Spain. London thus reminded the Caudillo that economic assistance might be broken off. Now Spain was still hungry. For Suñer and the Falangists Eden's speech was the pretext they were looking for. A huge demonstration marched from the Falange headquarters in the Calle de Alcalá to the British Embassy. Carts filled with paving-stones were waiting near by. German newsreel men were already on the spot. The Falangists hurled stones at the Embassy and tried to break in the doors, but the staff, reinforced by refugees from outside, succeeded in repulsing them. The provocation failed. Suñer and Franco were forced to receive the British diplomats who came in a body to protest. Moreover, Britain's resolution to go on fighting was so manifest that Francoist circles once more began to hesitate, particularly as the Soviet Union, although gravely wounded, did not seem on the point of collapsing either. When the first snows fell in Russia on 6 October, and above all at the beginning of winter outside Moscow, it was clear that the Wehrmacht was becoming exhausted, that losses were heavy (as they also were in the *División Azul*) and that the Red Army had not disintegrated. This new international situation aroused fresh hopes in the hearts of anti-Francoists who had gone on stubbornly fighting amid the darkness of their long defeat.

The Opposition

The Soviet Union's entry into the war played a decisive role in this respect. For the opposition, as for the Francoists, the conflict had now recovered the logic of the Civil War, and the divisions born of the Soviet–German pact and the ambiguous policy of the U.S.S.R. could perhaps be healed. Unity was no longer unthinkable. The Communists, who had remained the most active and best organized of Franco's opponents, issued in August 1941 an appeal for the formation of a 'national anti-Francoist bloc' as a first step towards the *Unión Nacional de todos los Españoles*. Its realization remained highly problematical. There was inadequate liaison between the leaders of the exiled Spanish Communist Party and the groups within the country which, under the leadership of Heriberto Quiñones, were carrying on the fight in isolation: militants who, now that the U.S.S.R. was at war, pinned all their hopes on the Red Army and did not realize the need for unity. Moreover, the repression was still highly efficient, and a number of police spies had infiltrated clandestine organizations. Almost all the Communist militants were captured by the end of 1941 and Quiñones, after being horribly tortured, was shot, propped up on a chair because his spine was broken. When Jesûs Carreras was sent from France by the leaders of the Spanish Communist Party to try to revive the organization, he too was captured and executed.

Meanwhile, independent of any party, groups of young students got together to listen to the B.B.C., planned and prepared an insurrection in Madrid, and tried to find a thousand men ready to rise and stand firm for twenty-four hours, until the people should decide to join them. Tense and courageous, they slipped leaflets into letter-boxes and forgathered in cafés; by the end of 1941, and during the winter of 1942, their numbers grew – and repression was intensified. The battle for Moscow and the United States' entry into the war strengthened this movement, in spite of Pearl Harbor and the setbacks inflicted on the British Navy by the Japanese. Italian reports even mention the success of British propaganda among the Spanish clergy, thanks to the Catholic journal *The Tablet* and the broadcasts that stressed the persecution of the Catholic Church in Germany by the Nazis.

Some Spaniards ventured to visit the British Embassy to collect its bulletin, which twice a day published the B.B.C.'s communiqués. And yet this meant risking persecution and frequently imprisonment. The Spanish staff at the Embassy was subjected to constant pressure: Lady Hoare's masseuse was sentenced to eighteen months' jail without being charged. In spite of this, however, the bulletins were widely read, and were resold at 20 pesetas a copy. In Franco's Spain, where all information was strictly controlled and to a large extent in German hands (the Madrid paper *Informaciones* for instance) this bulletin offered a loophole for hope.

Abroad, the exiles began to organize. In France the first groups of Spanish resisters were formed at the end of 1941, and early the next year began their illegal activity, often within the framework of such organizations as *Main d'Oeuvre Immigrée, Francs-Tireurs et Partisans Français*; the initials M.O.I., however, were in Spanish circles frequently interpreted as *Milicias Obreras Internacionales*. Hundreds of *Unión Nacional* committees were set up among Spaniards, and at Grenoble in November 1942 a first meeting of representatives of all democratic tendencies, including Catholics, took place with the aim of creating a broadly based National Union government, which even some of those who had followed Franco in 1936 could support. In September the Central Committee of the Spanish Communist Party issued a manifesto to this intent, and in Moscow Dimitrov tried to convince Jesús Hernández that controversy between left and right must be forgotten and that what mattered now was national unity against Franco. But many sections of the opposition, the Socialist Party and the C.N.T. for instance, were still suspicious of the Communists and rejected the idea of a National Union, considering it as yet another disguise for Moscow.

In America, Generals Miaja and José Asensio of the Republican army made contact with the Allied services, and on 25 July 1941, we find in a Spanish journal published in New York, *España Libre*, the suggestion of an attack on the Canaries.

However, while the opposition thus struggled to revive, the regime was by no means enfeebled, and its powers of reaction and manoeuvre remained practically intact, even though its doubts as to the line it should adopt were real ones.

Uncertainties of Franco's Policy

The Madrid Government remained, at first, subject to pressure from the Axis. Ciano writes on 3 June 1941 to his 'dear Ramón': 'In a few days Croatia will become a part of the Tripartite system. . . . Why does Spain not do the same?' The Duce adds a postcript, in his own hand, to Ciano's letter: 'Spain must *at least* adhere to the Tripartite Pact.' Hitler in all his talks with Mussolini 'employed bitter terms against Spain and affirmed that this country has proved a real disappointment to him' (25 August 1941, at his headquarters), and when Serrano Suñer visited Berlin on 25 November for the renewal of the Anti-Comintern Pact, the Führer 'complained at not having been able to attack Gibraltar last winter', which 'gave Suñer the clue to tell of all the difficulties with which his government is struggling, beset as it is by monarchists, seditious militarists and by dormant Reds. He ended by saying that Spain will intervene because she cannot do otherwise.'[9]

In fact Spain *could* do otherwise. The attitude of the United Kingdom – its economic assistance, its promises – made clear that London had no wish to overthrow Franco's regime nor to exploit the difficulties he might encounter. It was simply trying to keep Spain out of the conflict. In other respects, as in 1936, which the Caudillo could not have forgotten, it declared, in advance, its nonintervention in Spain's affairs. It thus offered Franco an implicit post-war guarantee. As the German army was retreating before Moscow and the United States was now involved in the conflict, it is easy to understand why the Caudillo reaffirmed, by decree, his country's non-belligerency. Not, as yet, neutrality, but a definite withdrawal from the position held in June and July 1941. In January 1942 a fresh agreement was signed with the Argentine for the import of wheat.

A meeting between Franco and Oliveira Salazar at Badajoz, on 12 February 1942, marks a further important development, considering the warlike declarations made in May 1941. The Portuguese President, who had many links with

[9] All these quotations are from Ciano, *Diplomatic Papers*.

Great Britain, reassured Franco: 'There is no need to overestimate the danger of bolshevism', he said. 'England and the United States would in fact oppose its extension on purely selfish grounds.' Franco, according to Suñer's report to von Stohrer, convinced Salazar of the inevitability of a German victory. In fact, Franco's advances to Salazar masked an approach to Britain and the United States. When Franco and Suñer confided their fears of an Anglo–American landing in the Portuguese islands, when Suñer pointed out to Salazar that the British were preparing to overthrow the Portuguese regime with Communist aid, they were hinting at questions that concerned Spain: would the Anglo–American forces land in Spain, did the British want to overthrow the Caudillo? Salazar replied – referring to Portugal – that he was convinced that there was no threat, and that Sir Samuel Hoare had entirely reassured him. Franco, knowing all the similarities between the regimes of Spain and Portugal, could not fail to gather from this valuable indications as to the Anglo–Saxon attitude towards himself.

On leaving Salazar, Franco undertook his first public journey since the end of the Civil War. He travelled through Andalusia; all the houses along his route had been searched. Large reinforcements of police had been brought from Madrid. All suspects had been jailed. Franco, duly protected and acclaimed, made a number of speeches. In Seville he addressed the officers of the garrison in terms which contrast sharply with all that had happened since December: 'We shall remain faithful', he said, 'to our traditional policy, to our loyalty towards the peoples who shared our suffering. If one day', he concluded, 'the road to Berlin lay open, it would not be a mere division of volunteers but a million men who would offer themselves to defend it against the Red hordes.' Next morning the press headlined these remarks, which appeared to Sir Samuel Hoare as a fresh proof of 'Franco's tortuous intelligence'. Coming after his interview with Salazar, they do indeed suggest that the Caudillo was anxious to conceal the line he was evolving, in order to protect himself against the pro-war party and at the same time to prove to Britain that he was fully in control of the game and could play it as he chose. The young anti-Francoists who risked their lives distributing leaflets in the university buildings, in defiance of the Falange, were mistaken when, on reading the press reports of Franco's speech, they reassured one another by saying: 'Britain won't forget this; after such a speech, it's as if we had been given the key to our prison.'[10] In fact, Britain had already, as we have seen, chosen her policy, and so had Franco.

The Choice

The Caudillo was acting with characteristic prudence, and the pro-Nazi speech made at Seville was part of his general policy of flexibility, dissimulation and tergiversation. For he had to reckon with the political groups that formed the basis of his power. Now, with the weakening of the Falange and the evolution of the general situation, there had been a revival of monarchist feeling. Alfonso XIII, whose rights had been fully restored by a decree of 12 December 1939,

[10] J. Hermanos, *La fin de l'espoir*.

had abdicated on 5 January 1941 in favour of his third son,[11] Don Juan de Borbón, Count of Barcelona, who assumed the name of Juan III. A few weeks later Alfonso XIII died and Franco organized great mourning ceremonies in Spain. This did not mean, however, that the Caudillo favoured a restoration. Since 1936, as we know, he had kept the Monarchists out of power because he intended to remain sole master. He had won control over the Falange away from Suñer, thanks to Arrese, and now he had to keep an eye on the Monarchists because, as Stohrer observed, on 8 May 1942, the Foreign Minister seemed to be seeking their support. The Cuñadísimo, in fact, deprived of his Falange backing and incapable of imposing his foreign policy, sought to cling to power by encouraging certain generals (Yagüe, Muñoz Grandes, Vigón) who were pressing for a restoration of the monarchy, with support from Goering and other Nazis.

This was really Suñer's last desperate bid. In June he went to Rome. 'All Madrid is talking about this visit . . . the purpose of which is to discuss the question of the monarchy with Italian statesmen.' In Rome Suñer met Victor-Emmanuel III, Ciano and Mussolini, who warned him that a Spanish king would promptly suppress Falangism. Suñer was pre-occupied less with the fate of the Falange than with his own personal future, and in his talks with Ciano he declared that the British had adopted a favourable attitude towards the restoration and that the Axis should show greater friendliness towards the Pretender. Marshal Badoglio was in favour of bringing to the throne Don Juan's 6-year-old son, which would enable Franco to remain Regent. Then Suñer saw the Pope, with whom he had a friendly and 'absolutely frank' interview. Suñer, in short, had explored the ground. His efforts were in vain: on 30 April 1942, during one of their regular meetings, held this time at Salzburg, Ciano and Ribbentrop decided that 'Spain in the present phase of the conflict seems to have become a factor of secondary importance'. Above all, Franco was now encouraged to take the offensive by the fact that both in the U.S.S.R. and in the deserts of Cyrenaica the German attacks were halted before Stalingrad and El Alamein. When on 17 July 1942 the Caudillo spoke before the National Council, who would have dared recall his violent declarations of the previous year? His present speech was a vague and cautious one, thus dissociating himself henceforward from Suñer, and at the same time he announced the creation of the Cortes, thus presenting the Monarchists with the *fait accompli* of a totalitarian institution of corporative type. The Caudillo retained complete authority over this body, in which the *Procuradores* (deputies) were not elected, but were members by right, nominated by the government or appointed by municipalities or corporations. Moreover, the Caudillo and his government were entitled to propose laws, and all bills had to be approved by the Caudillo. Franco thus ran no risks; but he had taken the initiative.

To deal the final blow, he waited for Suñer to betray himself or for some incident to provide the opportunity. Meanwhile Hoare was travelling over Spain, making contact with business circles, which were almost exclusively

[11] The eldest, Don Alfonso de Borbón, had died. The second, Don Jaime, was a deaf-mute and therefore renounced his claim.

anglophile, or with Catholic circles, for instance with Cardinal Segura, Primate of Spain, in Seville. An unmistakable indication of a change of policy was the fact that the Madrid government began to show more leniency towards the thousands of Frenchmen or other Allies who, having escaped over the Pyrenees without proper papers, had been imprisoned at Pampeluna, Gerona or Figueras before being sent to the concentration camp of Mirando del Ebro in Vitoria province; there was now less brutality. It took a hunger strike by the prisoners to secure their release, through the intermediary of the British Ambassador, after which they were enabled to rejoin the Allied forces. We witness here the gradual weakening of open commitment to the Axis side and the threat of Spain's direct military participation in the conflict. Serrano Suñer, the man who symbolized that policy, was still Foreign Minister. Franco was watching for the opportunity to have done with him.

Now on 16 August 1942 the Carlists of Vizcaya, who had just been celebrating Mass in the sanctuary of the Virgin of Begona at Bilbao, sang a satirical verse as they came out:

> Tres cosas hay en España
> Que no aprueba mi conciencia
> El subsidio
> La Falange
> Y el cuñado de su excelencia.[12]

A fight broke out with some young Falangists, one of whom threw a grenade which wounded some of the Carlists. Was there a real plot, was it a case of provocation; were German agents involved? At all events, General Varela, Minister of War, who had been attending Mass, and who was both a Carlist and an anglophile, very hostile to the Falange, presented the affair as an attempted outrage against the army and the Monarchists. Not only was the guilty Falangist condemned to death, but Varela and General Galarza, Minister of the Interior, without consulting Franco, summoned the Captains-General of Spain to react against the Falange. In so doing they were attempting an act of insubordination, thereby proving dangerous to Franco, who now that they had rashly come into the open felt entitled to take action. According to his usual tactics, he attacked both parties, and from the summit called to his side certain newcomers who, whatever their original allegiance, owed their advancement to him, and who, for a time (until they had served their purpose) reinforced his power. A classic procedure, and one which on 3 September 1942 marked the end of an epoch: Generals Varela and Galarza, Ministers of War and of the Interior (*Gobernación*) were replaced by two 'Falangists' who were, in fact, liegemen of the Caudillo's: General Asensio and Blas Pérez Gonzalez. Meanwhile, attacking from another angle, he replaced Serrano Suñer, the Cuñadísimo, the 'Axis minister', by General Jordana, who had already been Foreign Minister during the Civil War and whose pro-British sympathies were well known.

[12] 'There are three things in Spain of which my conscience does not approve: the subsidy to the Bourbons, the Falange, and His Excellency's brother-in-law'.

Hoare was exultant. He had always considered Suñer as a sort of Spanish Ribbentrop; and Ciano had no illusions about Jordana, who 'has always been a sympathizer with France and Great Britain, not whole-heartedly with the Axis'.[13] Thus, in the autumn of 1942, the turning-point had been reached and the choice made. For instance, the regular Italian broadcasts were practically banned by the censor's insistence on prior knowledge of all the spoken parts of their programmes, and above all – we recognize Franco's characteristically insidious policy – the prohibition of all broadcasts of music with words in a foreign language. Now the Italian programmes consisted mainly of songs. These orders, the Italian Embassy notes, 'kill our broadcasts'.[14] Such details are revealing.

A few days after Suñer's dismissal an agreement was reached with the Argentine for the purchase of a million tons of grain. Gradually, thanks to such imports, the economic situation eased; Spain was no longer on the verge of famine.

Franco in Control

This crisis gave yet a further proof of Franco's mastery of the political game. He could afford to declare to the National Council of the Falange on 7 October, that 'the German, Italian and Spanish revolutions are phases of the same general movement', the choice lying between 'the barbaric formula of totalitarian bolshevism and the patriotic and spiritual formula that Spain and a few other Fascist peoples offered to the world'. He put forward Francoist Spain as a model to other nations, and we can well imagine that the constant success of *his* policy – namely the strengthening and preservation of his power – must have established and confirmed his conception of himself as the man of destiny.

This did not preclude a patient and stubborn realism. After having extolled universal fascism, he received the British Ambassador, Hoare, on 10 October, and had a very long conversation with him. They discussed supplies, of course, but also talked of the future. Franco and Jordana expatiated on the rumoured plots to invade Spain or the Canaries being hatched by 'Red exiles' with American support. (Madrid had even applied to the Reich for arms for self-defence in this eventuality, which was a clever move to clear itself in German eyes.) Meanwhile, Franco sought for reassurances from Hoare and from the new American Ambassador, Carlton Hayes, who both promised that the Allies had no intention of violating Spanish neutrality in any way. None the less, anxiety persisted. It was only to be completely allayed on 8 November 1942, when Hayes came to wake up Jordana at 1 a.m. with a message for Franco from Roosevelt, assuring him that the Allied landing then taking place was aimed solely at French North Africa. Franco's regime had nothing to fear. The Caudillo could now afford to receive Hayes at nine o'clock in his room decorated with autographed portraits of Hitler and Mussolini.[15] Roosevelt, in his letter, appealed to the Caudillo's 'vast military experience' to explain the necessity of the Allied intervention. And he declared

[13] Diary, 4 September 1942.
[14] Washington National Archives, T. 586, R. 427.
[15] Carlton J. H. Hayes, *Wartime Mission in Spain* (New York, 1946).

that this movement was in no wise directed against the government or the people of Spain or of Spanish Morocco. Appreciating Spain's desire to remain neutral, he reassured Franco that she had nothing to fear from the United Nations, and signed himself cordially 'Your good friend, Franklin D. Roosevelt'.

For so many anti-Francoist Spaniards who were then pinning their hopes to the Allied nations, the letter was obviously a bitter blow. Their confidence was restored as the Axis suffered setbacks. At Stalingrad a great battle was being waged, the apparent endlessness of which revealed its crucial and uncertain character. The idea took root that Mussolini and Hitler would one day be swept away, and many people felt sure that Franco would go with them. What already surprised certain perspicacious observers was the self-confidence of the Caudillo and of his official entourage. The Spaniards were, of course, unaware of the dispatches being sent from London by the Duke of Alba to his government. On 26 November he informed Franco that Churchill, full of confidence in victory, had repeated that 'his sole desire is to make of Spain a strong, prosperous and happy power. In his view, France and Italy will emerge weakened from the war; Spain will be able to fill a place which has not been hers for centuries.'

Even more specifically, Eden declared to the Duke of Alba on 4 December 1942 that he and Churchill would take advantage of the first opportunity to declare their sympathetic attitude towards Spain, and their firm decision not to interfere in her internal politics.

It is understandable that, having received all these assurances and promises, the Caudillo felt free, in spite of Montgomery's successes at El Alamein, the American landing in North Africa and the German fiasco at Stalingrad, to let his press refer to 'Spain's just demands in Africa', repeat his praise of National Socialism on 7 December and, in his estate of El Pardo, indulge in his favourite pastime, hunting.

BOOK II

SURVIVAL AND A SECOND VICTORY

CHAPTER I

FRANCISCO FRANCO'S GREAT PLAN

1943

In January 1943 the soldiers of the Wehrmacht fighting in front of Stalingrad had as their daily ration 150 grammes of bread and 30 grammes of fat. The last attempt at a breakthrough had failed. Von Paulus's men were doomed, and the shock of their death-agony – they were to capitulate on 2 February – was felt as far afield as Franco's Spain.

The Caudillo now saw spreading over Europe the shadow of that Bolshevism which he had denounced in 1939, during the phony war; and in the early months of 1943 he attempted, with the firmness, obstinacy and passion of a man who feels himself personally threatened, to realize a great diplomatic plan which might protect him and save the West, imperilled by the advance of Stalin's troops.

Franco's Diplomatic Offensive

He directed his offensive at London, judging the ground there to be particularly favourable. Already on 4 December 1942, his Ambassador, the Duke of Alba, the day after a speech by Eden which was friendly towards the Soviet Union, had cabled to Madrid that he had warned Eden of the bad impression this speech might produce in Spain. Eden replied, the Duke goes on, 'that he understood my point of view and that moreover his opinions had not changed, but that the conditions arising from the war obliged him from time to time to say things that would be agreeable to the Eastern Ally.'[1] On several occasions the Spanish diplomatic services reported that leading British personalities, including a member of the Cabinet, were disturbed by the Russian advance. It must therefore be possible to make such men see reason. On 6 January, the feast of the Epiphany, the Caudillo traditionally received the diplomatic corps. Protocol required that the representatives of the Axis and those of the Allied Powers should be entertained together, although at different tables; Pietri, representing Vichy France, notes with satisfaction in his Memoirs that he was placed at the Allied table. The atmosphere among the British and Americans was euphoric, among the Axis ambassadors it was one of gloom. Stohrer had recently been recalled to Berlin, a sign that the Wilhelmstrasse considered he had failed; and his successor, Moltke, had not yet presented his credentials. The cold wind from Stalingrad could be felt.

[1] Quotations from *Documents secrets.* . . .

The Caudillo, who on previous occasions had avoided the British Ambassador, now, to everyone's surprise, began a long conversation with Sir Samuel Hoare. Franco went straight to the heart of the matter: 'I consider,' he said, 'that England is making the greatest mistake in continuing to support Soviet Russia.' He referred to information received about the Stalin–Churchill negotiations and to the possibility that the Russians might advance as far as the Rhine: 'Leaving aside Spain and her own possibilities of defence, I have no doubt but that Holland and Belgium at least will be immediately submerged by the Bolshevist troops and that communism will spread as far as the English Channel.' Hoare listened; Franco even had 'the impression that personally Hoare shared his opinion on the Russian danger, but that in the absence of instructions from London he could not express his point of view in a more definite fashion'. Then the Caudillo continued: 'My feelings of solidarity with Europe lead me to see the only solution in an attempt by Britain to reach a compromise peace with Germany; she will thus succeed in averting the danger of communism not only to Europe but to herself.' In a single conversation, Franco had set forth his whole project. This consisted in an attempt at mediation, aimed at arousing, or making use of, the anti-Communist feelings of the British ruling class, in order to restrict the success of the U.S.S.R. or, better still, to prepare a reversal of alliances, and in any case to prevent the collapse of National Socialism. The British Ambassador replied that Franco's 'declarations seemed to him of the highest interest and that it was desirable that conversations to this end should be pursued'.[2] Once again, the Caudillo could feel that he had successfully chosen the theme and ground for his action.

Parallel with this exploratory conversation with the British representative, close relations were being maintained with the Reich. Moltke, the new Ambassador, was received by Jordana 'in a particularly friendly atmosphere' on 13 January. Next day Arrese, Secretary-General of the Falange, was in Berlin to discuss problems of party organization with the Nazis, experts in this field. Hitler made a last, though not very hopeful, attempt to persuade Spain to enter the war, but Arrese, in accordance with the Caudillo's instructions, replied that Spain felt committed solely to the war against Bolshevism and could not possibly fight, *at the same time*, against the Anglo–Saxons. Thus in Berlin too the Caudillo was pressing for a compromise peace with the West, so as to strengthen the fight against the Red peril. Meanwhile he continued to give the Nazis proof of his loyal support: in February an agreement was probably signed by which Spain engaged to repel by force of arms any attempt at invasion of Spanish territory by the British and American armies. Jordana could under the circumstances refuse to send 50,000 workers into Germany, while continuing to receive commodities from the Reich.

Berlin, in any case, was perfectly well aware of Franco's intentions. The German counter-espionage service transmitted the dispatches sent from Madrid to the Spanish Ambassador in London. This was in fact superfluous, in so far as the Caudillo imparted his plans to Moltke when the latter called on 24 January to present his credentials. Their meeting was an extremely cordial one, lasting a

[2] *Documents secrets.* . . . See also Hoare, *Ambassador on Special Mission*, p. 185.

whole hour instead of the regulation fifteen minutes; in this way Franco could display his 'particular attention to the representative of Germany' with 'very friendly declarations of a personal character'. From the outset Franco stressed that Germany was the friend of Spain; England, America and Bolshevism were her enemies. He specified that Spain wanted to help the Reich 'in the struggle which fate has imposed on that country.' He proceeded to set forth his plan: 'One might, for example,' he said, 'envisage action on the part of Spain aimed at deepening the contradictions between Britain and the Soviet Union, or between Britain and America.' This was not merely a skilful attempt to get the Germans to admit the information provided by their agents about his approaches to London, but expressed the real purpose of his manoeuvre. He went on: 'The longer the war lasts, the more uncertain does victory become. That is why we should be thinking, right now, about the possibility of ending the war.' Naturally, Moltke reaffirmed his certainty of success, but Franco persisted: even if the psychological requirements for his plan were not as yet all present, Spain could 'help her friends' in this direction.

A Neutral Bloc for a United Front

Spanish diplomacy during the ensuing weeks sought to back up the project se forth by the Caudillo. On 24 February Moltke informed Berlin that 'a memorandum submitted to the ministers of Ireland, Sweden and Switzerland proposed the creation of a group of states ... to intervene at the opportune moment ... with an appeal in favour of the cessation of hostilities for a common defence against the Bolshevist danger.' Portugal was cast for a leading role in this project, which Jordana expounded to Hoare on 18, 19 and 22 February. 'The conclusion of these talks,' Moltke reports, 'was a pressing appeal from Spain to England to move away from Russia in the interest of the preservation of European civilization, and not to let slip *the chance of creating a single front against Bolshevism.*'

Jordana's approaches to neutral powers and to the United Kingdom prove that the Caudillo's project did in fact correspond to a very far-reaching political idea, unquestionably looking ahead of the immediate situation, which in a memorandum communicated to Hoare on 21 February stressed 'the great danger of a sovietized Germany', appealing to the good sense of the British people. By prophesying that 'if Russia were victorious we consider England, too, would certainly have to take up this attitude', the Caudillo showed that he had grasped one aspect, perhaps the fundamental aspect, of the war and its sequel, but that on the other hand he attempted through the argument of anti-communism – in his view logically unanswerable – to deny another aspect, the struggle of the democracies against Nazism.

It is difficult to imagine that Franco, invariably so prudent in all his actions, should in 1943 have carried so far an attempt which anticipated the chimerical hopes of certain Nazis in 1945. One may hazard the guess that he was encouraged, at least tacitly, by Mussolini's Italy (where a trend in favour of compromise peace was very strong at the beginning of 1943),[3] by certain German circles and perhaps

[3] cf. the present author's *Italie de Mussolini, vingt ans d'ère fasciste* (pub. Marabout, no. 109, Verviers).

by the Catholic Church, whose role in Spain is well known. It is true that this diplomatic démarche of the Caudillo's was too consistent with his own interests (if successful, it would have satisfied 'his heart and his reason') and his past as a crusader against Bolshevism not to have been attempted. It had, above all, the immense advantage of allowing him, if it succeeded, to consolidate his regime for an unlimited period. So, despite the rebuffs he met with from Hoare, who was convinced that the post-war period would witness the establishment of a vast British Empire in Europe, Franco remained 'subjugated by this idea'. Jordana untiringly reminded Hoare that 'a Russian victory would make all Europe Communist – the result ... would be the destruction of European civilization and Christian culture ... Germany,' Jordana added, 'is the only existing force in the centre of Europe capable of realizing the great universal work of containing and even destroying communism.'

Franco's effort was brought to nothing by the Anglo–Saxon powers' insistence on the unconditional surrender of the Reich, and the conviction of the Germans that victory was still within their power; nevertheless it was too vital a part of his creed to be completely dropped. So his great design, so rich in hope, remained present in his mind until the outbreak of the cold war, which he had been anticipating and praying for since 1943.

For the time being he had to reckon with realities, with the ever-increasing influence of General de Gaulle, for example. Thus on 3 March 1943 the representatives of Free France took up their posts in Madrid. Spain already recognized the Red Cross documents issued to 'dissident Frenchmen' as identity papers. In May a further step was taken: Madrid accepted the passports issued by the Provisional Government in Algiers, and authorized the Free French delegation to use the diplomatic bag and code, like any normal mission. A few weeks later Franco sent an official representative, de Sangróniz, to General de Gaulle's Government: an unusual step to be taken by the friend and admirer of Marshal Pétain, the old soldier who was still nominally head of the French Government. The Caudillo knew how to bow to facts.

Thus when on 1 May a new German Ambassador, Hans Dickhoff,[4] presented his credentials in the former Royal Palace after a ceremony of mingled Castilian and African splendour, Franco, having first expressed admiration for the Führer and his achievement, did not conceal the fact that he had ceased to believe in the possibility of completely crushing the u.s.s.r. During their conversation, which was an exceedingly long one, Dickhoff had to listen to the Caudillo's description of the immense resources of the British Empire and the United States, and the German Ambassador writes: 'I was left with the feeling that ideas which would be difficult to eliminate had become firmly rooted in his mind.'

Only Axis successes could, in fact, have uprooted these ideas, and in the spring of 1943 these were out of the question. Franco had one moment of hope, when the troops of the Afrika Korps clung to the Mareth line, and he spoke of a standstill, a point of equilibrium reached in the military operations; but on 29 March German resistance was at an end, and rescuing aircraft carried off the defeated officers of the Reich.

4 Moltke had died in April.

Franco thus had to revert to diplomacy, issuing appeals for peace. For the 450th anniversary of Christopher Columbus's return to Spain, in March, Jordana made a great speech in Barcelona, once more warning the belligerent powers against the menace of communism. Evidently such an appeal could only have been made to the West. In May Franco took over from his Foreign Minister. He travelled round southern Spain, surrounded as usual by a huge bodyguard, preceded by lorries loaded with Falangists, who drove from town to town and gathered the platform set up in each public square to acclaim the Caudillo. At Almería, on 9 May, in his final speech, he addressed the whole world with an appeal for peace: 'In these days when the world is submerged in a sea of blood and hatred, Spain raises her voice and joins the Supreme Pontiff in making an appeal to the conscience of the nations.'

The Caudillo's venture, even if it deliberately followed those made by Pius XII, was not disinterested. Franco did not want peace at any price. 'We consider it insensate to delay peace,' he went on, 'and I say this because behind the façade there is something worse: communism.' In the Allied capitals the speech had a poor reception. London and Washington felt surprised at Franco's making his appeal so late, when the fortunes of the Axis were shaky. Even in Berlin the situation was not considered desperate enough for a compromise peace (an idea wholly foreign to the Führer at this stage of his life) to seem desirable.

The Caudillo, together with certain other allies of Germany, was thus proving more far-sighted than the rulers of the Reich, more realistic and a shrewder politician, as he had always been. In June 1943 it was clear that his appeal would not be listened to by the belligerents. The Allies were making ready to assail the 'fortress of Europe', the Soviet armies were preparing fresh offensives. Thus in early summer a new situation was taking shape.

Monarchist Activities

This evolution of the war inevitably had its repercussions within Spain itself.

Monarchist circles did not consider the question of the regime settled by the solemn inauguration of the Cortes, on 17 March, by the Caudillo; the institution was devoid of any real power or representative character. Some of the most ardent Monarchists proposed that the King (Don Juan) should march into the Pardo Palace, surrounded by high-ranking officers, and that the Caudillo would then be obliged to give way. Most Monarchists hoped that the Caudillo would of his own accord ask for the return of a monarchy which he had always respected and never repudiated. So in June 1943 a group of twenty-five personalities, among them the Duke of Alba, García Valdecasas, General Ponte and Admiral Moreu, addressed a petition to Franco in favour of a restoration. The Monarchist Party also had its representatives in business circles, which were strongly pro-British and had begun to envisage the post-war situation; they had repeatedly made contact with Hoare, showing that they believed – and, for the most part, always had believed – in a victory for the Anglo–Saxon forces. Moreover, the British Ambassador gave clear support to Monarchist circles, and the Duke of Alba was known to be an Anglophile. As for Don Juan himself, if at the beginning of the war he had expressed openly pro-German feelings, he now lived in Lausanne and remembered that he had served in the Royal Navy; while the Queen Mother, Doña Victoria, had always proclaimed her confidence in British victory.

In their petition, the signatories suggested to the Caudillo that the only way to avoid an Allied intervention at the time of the Axis defeat, or even before it, was to promote the return of the Bourbons, which would prevent the left from coming to power. For Franco, this was the most direct attack since the Civil War, and also the most explicit, for the meaning of the petition was clear: the Caudillo was no longer considered – taking into account the general evolution of things – as the strong point of traditional, ruling-class Spain, but as its weak point: he was no longer its shield and buckler, but the wound through which the disease – the Reds – might infiltrate into Spain.

The threat was a grave one. If this point of view was adopted by the bulk of Franco's supporters he would find himself set aside in favour of another great figure, King Juan III, behind whom traditional Spain would be united. He therefore had to prove that Spain had no alternative but to trust him; that he alone, although he had shaken hands with Hitler and Mussolini and praised national-socialism and fascism, could hold together the forces that ranged from Falangists to Monarchists, from the army to the Church and landed proprietors, that he was the only bulwark of social order against *los rojos*. It was a life and death struggle for Franco, and he was to carry it on for years, confronted by classes and political groups who were equally afraid of deserting him and finding themselves defenceless, or of staying loyal to him and being involved in his fall. By his political skill, by his manoeuvres, Franco constrained these classes and these men to support him, sometimes against their will, and to feel their fate linked with his.

The first step to be taken was to make it clear that he would brook no opposition. To this end he hit out: the signatories to the petition were excluded from the National Council of the Falange and dismissed from their posts. He also took clandestine action: he got the Falange to subsidize a movement in favour of the legitimate pretender supported by the Carlists, solely in order to show that no Monarchist solution could replace Francoism, since the Monarchists were divided. To abandon the Caudillo therefore meant choosing uncertainty and chaos, and inevitably, as a Falangist pointed out, 'a Communist reaction'. Franco's manoeuvre succeeded, and the representatives of the propertied classes renounced monarchy yet again, trusting their Caudillo to protect them while he protected himself. Franco could then declare on 17 July, before the National Council of the Falange, that any action taken against his regime was the result of 'foreign propaganda and machinations'. He further asserted in private that monarchy was *lo parcial*, whereas his regime was *lo total*. 'I represent victory and *la integridad española*. I am here,' he finally declared, 'to fulfil a divine mission and any manoeuvre opposing this is directed against Spain herself.'

The Caudillo's success, that summer of 1943, was the more important in that a series of events occurred during July which reversed the situation in the Mediterranean and which *might have been the preface* to a restoration in Spain. On 10 July, Allied troops landed in Sicily. On 25 July King Victor Emmanuel III ordered the arrest of Mussolini and on the 28th the dissolution of the Fascist Party. The fall of the Duce, who had done more than anyone else for Franco's success, the end of fascism, which had been his model and inspiration (so soon after the inauguration of the Cortes, direct descendant of Mussolini's Fascist Chamber and the Italian Corporations), the rout of the Italian army and of the Black Arrow contingent which had fought in the Civil War and had paraded through Madrid, all this *might* have dealt a fatal blow to Franco's regime and opened the way (as in Italy) for its replacement by the monarchy – particularly since in both peninsulas the Monarchist parties enjoyed British support. This whole complex of events, from the petition of the Spanish Monarchists to the collapse of Italian fascism, suggests the dangers threatening Franco. True, Spain was not in the same disastrous situation as Italy, where power had disintegrated as a result of the war, but on the other hand the fact that the forces of order were powerful and well controlled, and opposition from the left and extreme left still badly organized, meant that the transfer of power from Caudillo to King could be envisaged without any danger of a breakthrough from the left. In short, but for the Caudillo's skill, and above all the incapacity of his Monarchist opponents and their disunity, which the regime naturally encouraged, the Monarchist venture would have stood a chance of succeeding; indeed, this was the moment when it stood the greatest chance of doing so.

From Non-belligerency to Neutrality

To strengthen his internal position, as against the Monarchists who seemed the *alternative* solution, Franco was obliged to show the Allies, now unquestioned victors in the Mediterranean, that he was capable of *changing*, of providing, in short, what a future monarch might have offered. On 29 July (four days after Mussolini's arrest, remember) he received Carlton Hayes, the United States ambassador, at El Pardo; Hayes had come to transmit his government's objections to the attitude of the Spanish press and radio, which systematically favoured the Axis, and to the presence in Russia of the *División Azul*. Franco replied quite calmly (he realized what a shrewd interlocutor he had in Hayes) that he would issue instructions for the press to remain strictly neutral henceforward; then he expounded his argument that two wars were taking place simultaneously, the war between the Western Powers and the Reich, in which Franco was neutral, and the war against communism waged by the Reich on behalf of Western civilization, in which Spain could not be neutral. The Caudillo stood by his original analysis.

Nevertheless, in view of the insistence of the Allies, he considered withdrawing the *División Azul* from the Eastern front. He was also forced to have two interviews with the British Ambassador, who came armed with proofs that contradicted Franco's declarations. In July, Hoare presented the Caudillo with a *grande remontrance*: he enumerated the Spanish ports that served as bases for German submarines, the airports where German planes landed after sinking British ships, he spoke of the facilities offered for espionage, the bogus travel agency *Alemania* with its office in the Calle de Alcalá in Madrid; all of which implied not a war against the Reds, but support given by Spain to Germany's war against Western nations. Franco denied nothing, but merely listened, replied evasively and protested about the flight of British aircraft over Spanish territory. His undeniable sang-froid was obviously based on the conviction that, the Monarchist menace having been averted, the only policy open to the British Government was to come to terms with him, since it would not use the only real and effective political weapon at its disposal – the overthrow of Francoism by the left. The Caudillo was well aware of this. Furthermore, the failure of the Monarchists, and Franco's ability to control the internal political situation, considerably strengthened his position with regard to London: he seemed the only alternative to chaos and revolution. It thus appeared possible to negotiate. On 20 August, after a long and wearisome journey by air and by car, Hoare arrived at the estate of Pazo de Meiras, near Coruña, where the Caudillo was spending his vacation.

It was a small fortified manor 'situated on a wooded slope and approached by a drive bordered on each side by blue hydrangeas', as Hoare describes it in his memoirs. Hoare and Franco held a lengthy conversation. They discussed the future of Europe. The Caudillo

'expressed his fear of a defeated Germany throwing itself into the arms of a victorious Russia. His complacency was almost overpowering. . . . My strong words,' Hoare goes on, 'so far from setting off explosives, fizzled out in cotton wool . . . I began to wonder whether I should ever be able to penetrate the heavy mist of self-complacency that protected the Caudillo, this small, quiet fat Gallego . . . self-possessed, complacent and seemingly confident of his own future. . . .'

However, negotiations proceeded. 'The Spanish Embassy in Washington . . . issued a statement that the talk had been friendly and satisfactory, and implied that relations were excellent between Spain and Great Britain.' This unilateral and calculated indiscretion of Madrid's was evidently aimed at making London face up to its responsibilities, and recognize that a more or less formal agreement existed between the two capitals. It clearly implies that London must have given some kind of guarantee for the future of Franco's regime in exchange for Spain's 'disengagement' from her actively pro-Axis sympathies.

On 3 August the Vice-Secretary for Popular Education informed the United States Embassy that, in accordance with Hayes's request, a note had been communicated to the press requiring it to observe neutrality. The satisfaction thus granted was purely formal, for a secret note meanwhile encouraged the press to go on as in the past. In fact, there was so much propaganda in favour of Germany (no doubt because the Germans had financial control over newspapers and journalists) that a favourite joke among Madrileños in 1943 was the whispered comment: 'The situation in Berlin is much better than Hitler admits.'

Yet the facts were there: on 8 September Italy signed an armistice, and the release of Mussolini by German commandos, the foundation of the Social Republic on 23 September, could not, despite newspaper rejoicings at a revival of fascism, wipe out the gravity of the event. Spaniards, when they met, would whisper delightedly 'Guadalajara', recalling the earlier defeat of fascism. It was not by chance that Arrese, on 9 September, emphatically dissociated the Falange from any connection with Mussolini's Italy: 'The Falange,' declared the Secretary-General of that party, 'is in no way a totalitarian system and is not the subsidiary of any foreign regime.' We can gauge from this the pragmatism, not to say opportunism, of the Spanish leaders and the extent to which they were willing to readjust their attitude. Arrese goes on to assert that the Falange 'is not, and has no intention of being, a political programme. It is a state of mind and a tendency, both supported by national and social feeling, and which can always prove flexible and adapt themselves to contingencies and events.'

Franco directed and assumed this new attitude with the same tranquillity that led him earlier to assert quite contrary positions. On 1 October, in the great reception rooms of the Royal Palace, when he entertained the diplomatic corps on the occasion of the anniversary of his accession to power, he spoke of Spain's *neutrality* instead of *non-belligerency*, and like Arrese he declared that the Falange was a purely Spanish movement owing nothing to foreign ideologies. His reference to the massacres carried out by *los rojos* during the Civil War, his denunciation of the danger of communism, were not really likely to offend Hayes, Hoare or their governments. The weight of arms had enabled them to obtain satisfaction. On 12 October, the very day when in the Azores Portugal granted facilities to Britain, men of the *División Azul* began to be relieved by German troops. By 3 November none were left but the unyielding few who, convinced of the rightness of their cause, refused to abjure their faith and formed a *Legión Azul* which was to go on fighting until the total collapse of the Reich; the Madrid government, however, deprived them of their Spanish nationality. Principles were unseasonable now, and taking risks had never been in Franco's nature.

The withdrawal of these men from the Russian front did not imply that Franco had given up anti-communism. It merely meant that since the great diplomatic plan had proved unrealizable for the time being, he had to try to neutralize the Anglo–Saxon powers by showing that Francoism was still the best bulwark against a Bolshevist threat in Spain. Jordana wrote to Carlton Hayes on 21 October 1943, pointing out that the United States and Great Britain, by maintaining trade relations with Spain, were contributing effectively to avoid the creation of conditions which might favour a recrudescence of communism. This, although an obvious manoeuvre, was a skilful way of committing these powers to a policy of support for Franco, at any rate in the economic field. Another way in which the Caudillo consolidated his regime and obviated its openly Fascist aspects consisted in emphasizing its typically Spanish qualities. It now owed nothing, so he claimed, to fascism.

A further stage in this disengagement could be reached by increasing the advantages granted to the Catholic Church (to the detriment of falangism which, despite all assertions to the contrary, still bore the marks of its links with totalitarianism), by allowing the Church a greater share in the state and making of it the sacred, traditional, unassailable shield of the regime.

The Church and Francoism (1943): National Catholicism

Ever since the beginning of the Civil War, the relations between Francoism and the Catholic Church had been excellent; and now they were strengthened even further. Thus on 16 June 1941, an agreement was concluded between Madrid and the Holy See fixing the procedure for the appointment of the clergy; its terms show the complete mutual trust between Rome and Madrid. The Caudillo carried even further the close collaboration of his regime with the Church, since, despite the existence of a Vice-Secretariat at the Ministry of Popular Education which was dependent on the Falange, education at all levels was in actual fact placed under the control of religious authorities. Now this influence over the young was a point of capital importance for the Church, the touchstone by which a regime could be judged. It was in this connection that the Church had come into conflict with fascism and nazism. In Franco's Spain nothing of the sort occurred. The Caudillo left the Church in sole control over the young, and this indicates, indeed it almost demonstrates, that Francoism was not a Fascist regime anxious to secure a mass basis (particularly among the young), but an extreme form of traditional Spanish reaction, which owing to the circumstances of the time borrowed certain features of fascism.

Thus the important *Ley de Ordenación de la Universidad española* of 29 July 1943, laid down that 'The university shall adapt its teaching to Catholic dogma and morality and to the norms of canonic law in force'.

Meanwhile, however, students were obliged to belong to the S.E.U. (*Sindicato Español Universitario*), the university branch of the Falangist unions, while according to Article 40 of the *Ley*, rectors of universities appointed by the government 'must be active militant members of the Falange'. Article 56 of the *Ley* laid down, moreover, that 'in order to be a teacher in the university or any other branch of education, it is necessary to prove one's firm adherence to the fundamental principles of the movement, which adherence must be attested by a certificate issued by the General Secretariat of the Falange'. Furthermore, all second-year students had to belong to the Militia, or else do three years' military service in the ranks; and they must follow a course of military and civic training under army officers and Falangist leaders, with theoretical and practical exercises every Saturday.

All these arrangements clearly show that the university had to be at the service of the state, that teaching staff and students had to form part of the Francoist set-up, show loyalty to the Caudillo and support the system. A few intellectuals, in fact, tried to provide an ideological justification for the regime, but from 1943 onwards the main concern was to stress the special destiny of Spain in order to detach Francoism from its Fascist and Nazi associations. Arrese set the tone in his speech of September 1943; he reverted to it in his book *El estado totalitario en el pensamiento de José Antonio* (1944). University teachers followed suit. Under these circumstances the doctrine of the Falange could only consist of a glorification of Spain, *destino en lo universal*, and of the forces that embodied this: the Caudillo, the army and the Church. Thus the evolution of the war and the imminent defeat of the Fascist Powers led to Spain's being dominated, from 1943 onwards, by a sort of National Catholicism.

The Role of the Opus Dei[5]

It was thus no accident that in spite of the existence of the S.E.U. Spanish universities became, in fact, Catholic universities, where there prevailed 'an atmosphere of piety contributing to the development of spiritual education in every act of the student's life'. Religious teaching – with a check on that teaching by means of examinations – was obligatory at every level of higher education. Students lived in communities, the *colegios mayores* set up by the *Ley* of 1943, where their lives were controlled and supervised by priests and indoctrinators. Some of these houses were in the hands of the S.E.U. and thus of the Falange, but very soon the Opus Dei founded its own *colegios mayores*, to which it attracted the best students and trained them as future cadres. It also introduced its own men into the *colegios* which it did not control, in order gradually to influence the minds of the whole group. Naturally the Opus Dei continued to enjoy the support of the Minister of Education, Ibañez Martin. This is clearly shown, for instance, as regards the appointment of university professors. The title of *catedrático* (chair-holder) was awarded after a public debate, the *oposiciones*, between a candidate and the jury. Now Ibañez Martin claimed the right to appoint the five members of the jury (including three professors in the same discipline as the candidate), which changed the whole point of the institution, making it into a process of co-optation and selection on political and religious grounds. It has been asserted that from 1943 onwards the Opus Dei set out to secure university chairs,[5] an offensive which it found the easier in that it already controlled the *Consejo Superior de Investigaciones Científicas*.

Moreover, the central idea of the Opus, as expressed in *Camino*, encouraged this quest for the top places, which was motivated not only by a secret or sordid desire to gain control over the whole of society by a judicious placing of men, but also by a will to perfection, a mystique of social aspiration combined with individual disinterestedness and submission to higher ends. Thus Article 16 of *Camino* declares: 'What, reduce yourself to the common level, form part of the vulgar herd? But you are born to be a leader! Amongst us there is no room for the lukewarm. Humble yourself, and Christ will set you ablaze with the fire of love.' In Article 345 we read: 'Culture! culture! well and good. Let no one outdo us in our ambition to seek it and possess it. But culture is a means, not an end.' And Article 836 adds: 'To serve as mouthpiece for the enemy is a supreme error. And if the enemy is God's enemy, a great sin. That is why, in the professional field, I shall never praise the learning of one who uses it as a platform for attacking the Church.'

Backed by those in power, maintained by the ambition of some of its members, the mysticism of others, the opportunism of the majority, the Opus Dei thus secured (during the period 1931–51) almost one quarter of university chairs. By its means, within the framework of a university system and a political regime

[5] Daniel Artigues, *L'Opus Dei en Espagne*, I, 1928–57 (Paris, Ruedo Ibérico, 1968).

that were already Catholic by definition, a religious spirit asserted itself which was deeply concerned with action within, and on, secular society, even though, at the same period, Father Escriva warned his followers against too close an involvement in political affairs. The ideal of the Opus was *political* in the strongest and noblest sense of the word, namely to gain control of the *polis*, of the body civic as a whole, by taking over the means of directing opinion and the place (the university) where ideology is shaped. It is significant that the Opus sought in the first place to take over the Chairs of History and Philosophy, and after these of Law and Science. Through the men it placed, through the positions it won, through the ideas it diffused, the Opus Dei contributed to the interpenetration of religion with politics with the university, and thus tended to make of Catholicism the factor that bound Spanish society together, while seeking to ensure for itself, within that society – and soon, some thought, within the Church – a position of hegemony.

The Wonderful Legend of Spain

University life, however, and the general intellectual climate of Spain, suffered gravely from this political and religious pressure. The first generation of the Opus Dei, composed of men of real merit, was by 1943 being replaced by ambitious opportunists seeking to become *catedráticos*.

Orthodoxy prevailed everywhere; by plundering untranslated foreign works, Spanish scholars built up reputations that were unassailable, since there was no free discussion of ideas. Students, at their examinations, had to reproduce their teachers' lessons word for word. Praise of Francoism, or of the thirteenth century, considered as the golden age of Western civilization, had to be accepted without argument. Tracts were even distributed in certain universities demanding the restoration of death by fire, as under the Inquisition. In crucial subjects such as history and philosophy, the systematic distortion of facts was the rule, and whole sectors of these disciplines disappeared or were condemned in the name of Spanish Catholicism and its traditions. The period was one of intellectual asphyxia. Yet the student body did not react. Compulsory attendance at lectures had kept out of it all those who had to earn their living, and the others were the more easily controlled, from childhood onwards, in that they came from the wealthier social strata which supported Franco. Besides, they had their careers to consider: silence and approval were the best policy. Their topics of conversation were football, films and women. The better pupils learnt what they were taught; their gift was for repetition rather than for invention or criticism. Those in opposition were a tiny minority.

Higher education was only one aspect of this mind-conditioning process. Its target was the whole of youth. We need only consult, for instance, the book by Ernesto Giménez Caballero, *España nuestra, el libro de las Juventudes españolas* (*Our Spain, the Book of Spanish Youth*), published in Madrid in 1943 by the Vice-Secretariat of Popular Education, to recognize the dominant ideological themes. Caballero, dedicating his book to the teaching profession, urges the inculcation of two basic emotions, '*el religioso y el heroico*' (Religion and Heroism), summed up in the slogan '*¡ Padre nuestro! ¡ España nuestra!*' (Our Father! Our Spain!) In the chapter entitled 'Founders of Spain', he studies successively: (1) the saints, (2) the heroes – the last of these being the new, and yet traditional, Caudillo, (3) the crowd (mothers, soldiers, bourgeois, farm workers, artisans). The epilogue is significantly entitled 'The wonderful legend of Spain':

'Spain was a princess . . .' [the story begins. Misfortunes overwhelmed her] '. . . until a certain summer's day – under the sign of the Lion – when there appeared on the horizon a rider on a white horse. In his hand he held a flaming sword. . . . Spain gradually opened her eyes . . . and the bells rang out. . . . Spain, freed from the poison distilled by envy . . . married her rescuer the Caudillo. They lived happily for many years, to the greater glory of heaven and earth. The End. Praise be to God.'

This was how they taught children Spanish history in 1943, in the form of the Sleeping Beauty's story. It is easy to imagine how such an intellectual atmosphere gave many people the sense of retrogression towards past centuries and that, stifled morally, politically and physically, they tried to keep up a basic opposition to Francoism in spite of difficulties. And 1943, the year of Stalingrad and of Mussolini's fall, revived their hopes.

The Revival of Hope

The regime had extended its repressive powers still further. The law of 2 March 1943, which forms part of the Code of Military Justice, was so imprecise that it allowed all dissidents to be brought before the *Consejos de guerra*, whatever their offence. It stipulated, in fact, that

'the following are held guilty of the crime of military rebellion, and shall be penalized accordingly: those who propagate false or tendentious news with intent to disturb the public peace, to provoke international conflicts, to injure the prestige of the state, of the army or of the authorities; those who commit acts liable to interrupt or disturb the functioning of public services, means of communication or transport. . . .'

More serious, however, is the extension and generalization of these notions contained in the brief phrase (implying the threat of arrest, imprisonment and torture) which says, 'this shall also be taken to include strikes, sabotage, workers' unions and all similar actions, when the aim pursued is political and liable to cause serious disturbances to public order'.

Henceforward everyone was liable to prosecution. And yet some men went on fighting. Grenades were thrown in Falangist clubs. It was sometimes difficult to know who was responsible. When on 15 February 1943, a bomb went off in the offices of the Vice-Secretariat of Popular Education, in the Calle Genova, the Communists claimed responsibility for the action, whereas it was probably due either to a Falangist provocateur or to a feud between rival Falangist groups. Militants were tracked down and denounced. Sometimes a girl who had engaged in the clandestine struggle might betray her comrades, under pressure from her confessor, and then withdraw into a convent; or else the police, warned by an informer, might surprise some students printing leaflets and shoot them down as they tried to escape. These men were under constant tension; they lived in isolation, meeting only in cafés, wary of their neighbours and always concealing their activities.

And yet in 1943 they were still borne up by hope. They would speak in excited whispers about the latest news from the battle-fronts; some indulged in day-dreams – Franco would commit suicide on the day the Allies won the war. American films were already being shown; after a showing of *Gone with the Wind*, spectators found their car tyres slashed by Falangists. When the first film in the series *In Which We Serve* appeared, shouts and hisses drowned the commentary, but these displays of resentment could not prevent the expression of popular feeling. Hoare reports that during an exchange of British and German wounded in Barcelona, the British men were greeted with demonstrations of enthusiastic sympathy.

Many people, however, merely went on hoping and waiting in silence. The victory of the Allies seemed inevitable, repression was efficient, the memory of the Civil War still cruel; surely the best thing was not to commit oneself but to trust the Allies, who would infallibly overthrow Franco after Mussolini and Hitler. Old leaders of Socialist and Anarchist organizations, convinced that the balance of forces in Spain was still extremely unfavourable to them, took refuge in a wait-and-see attitude.

On the other hand, the Communists kept up their activity and sponsored in France, and in Spain, a *Junta suprema de Unión nacional* whose programme (adherence to the Atlantic Charter, a state purge, amnesty for political prisoners, restoration of liberties, a general election for a constituent assembly) sought to rally the whole range of democratic opinion. Suspicion of the Communists lingered. Left-wingers had not forgotten certain episodes of the Civil War, and feared lest the Communist Party should seize control of the future Spanish state; the end of 1943 witnessed a regrouping of the parties of the non-Communist left. In November there was set up in Mexico a *Junta española de Liberación* which comprised the *Partido Obrero Español*, the *Izquierda* (left) *republicana*, the *Esquerra republicana de Cataluña*, and the *Accio republicana de Cataluña*. Its leader was Martínez Barrio.

Within the country the Communists – and isolated groups of anarchists and young militants – were the most firmly rooted. They were strong in Catalonia; towards the end of 1942, in Barcelona, a city being gradually disfigured by new buildings in neo-Classical style, proud and imposing, typical of totalitarian periods and of rapidly-acquired wealth, they published the first clandestine leaflets in Catalan, asserting that the Catalan national spirit, stifled under Franco's regime, could and must be revived in support of the democratic movement. In France, in the middle of 1943, there were at least 3,000 Spanish *maquisards*, and in Spain itself small cells of determined men already envisaged forming guerrilla groups. Yet the opposition to Franco remained divided, and above all it failed to win over the masses. Hunger, poverty, fear, bereavement, the cost of the Civil War and the memory of it, the subsequent executions and the harshness of an ever watchful repression, all this kept workers and peasants in a state of passivity, where their hostility to the government remained unexpressed. There was, more-over, the sense that it was safer to wait till the Allies had won and the opposition was united. As always happens, in short, the mass of the people would not act until an immediate concrete issue presented itself.

At the end of 1943, in spite of their hopes, this issue seemed remote and Franco's regime as solid as in the days of Axis triumph.

The Caudillo's Pride

As in the past, Spain went on sending wolfram to the Reich (2,770 tons for the year 1943), in spite of the démarches undertaken by the United States Government. Receiving the German Ambassador on 3 December, the Caudillo declared with satisfaction: 'A neutral Spain providing wolfram and other products is more useful to Germany at the present moment than a Spain at war would be.' This was no longer a mere pretext, for the Reich was in no position to intervene in Spain. Indeed, Franco firmly refused to stop the dispatch of wolfram to Germany. The United States threatened to put an embargo on petroleum, yet Franco would not give way. Through the intermediary of his minister Jordana, he continued to admonish the Allied ambassadors. Carlton Hayes, demanding the inclusion of Soviet communiqués in the press, was treated to a long anti-Communist tirade, and the assertion that Spain would never give up her campaign against bolshevism. On 20 December, the conclusion of the treaty between Spain and Portugal which constituted the Iberian bloc provided a fresh opportunity to declare not only the neutrality of the two nations but the need for defence against communism. This was in fact the leitmotiv and the grand plan of the year 1943.

Sir Samuel Hoare could write, on 11 December 1943, without analysing the causes of the phenomenon: 'During the two months that I have been in Spain I have noted a definite consolidation of the Franco regime and a growing complacency on the part of Franco himself.'

Doubtless the fact of having safely rounded the cape of such a crucial year, from the fall of Stalingrad to that of the Duce, was enough to reassure the regime and its leader. At home, the forces of order had the country well under control, and the Monarchists were for the time being out of action; as for London and Washington, they might reject the advice of Madrid but at any rate they allowed it to be offered and they listened to it. Was this not already a sure sign – and one further supported by guarantees – that the future would not be as dark as it might seem to some naïve opponents?

CHAPTER II

THE *NOCHE NEGRA* OF FRANCOISM
1944–1945

In January 1944 a red poster was displayed on the walls of French towns. It showed, inset, the faces of ten men wanted as criminals by the German occupying authorities. They belonged to the Manouchian group, composed of foreigners and including one described here as 'Alfonso, Spanish Red, 7 criminal attempts', for as the notice specifies, 'these acts are always committed by foreigners . . . unemployed workers and professional criminals'. Celestino Alfonso, condemned to death, was executed on 21 February 1944; his last letter runs: 'Dear wife, dear son, I am going to be shot at three o'clock this afternoon. I do not repudiate my past. If it had to be done again I should be the first. . . . Let my son get a good education. . . . I am dying for France.'

Spaniards died in France, and others – still a great many of them – in Spanish prisons: there were at least 1,000 executions in 1944 (an average of three a day); sometimes the condemned men had been awaiting their death since 1940 and when, on visiting day, their relatives arrived with parcels, the jailer would refuse admission without saying why; then the black-clad women would be hurried away before the noise of their weeping could entail the general prohibition of visits for all these people who had often come from very far away. In orange groves where the trees were so heavily laden that their branches touched the ground, in sierras and caves, survivors from the Civil War went on living clandestinely in rags, making an occasional foray, marauding or kept supplied by the peasants, clutching their revolvers, some of them sleeping in shell-holes for months on end, always on the watch. Now that victory had changed sides, they began to hope.

Don Juan, Petroleum and Wolfram: a New Political Success

Don Juan, the claimant to the throne, also thought the time was near when Franco would have to hand over his power. At the beginning of 1944 circumstances seemed favourable, as in June and July 1943. For the Caudillo, apparently abandoning his customary prudence, stubbornly resisted the Allies on the question of Spain's continuing to supply wolfram to Germany. At the same time, although he refused to yield to German requests that he should recognize Monreale, Consul for the new Italian Fascist republic of Salo, as Ambassador, he allowed Monreale to open a passport office in Madrid. When the Allies protested, the Spanish Foreign Minister implied that the situation was the same as for the French Provisional Government, whose seat was in Algiers. Relations grew tense: Eden declared in the House of Commons on 19 January that he had warned the Spanish government of the extreme gravity of its decision to keep up the supply of strategic products to Germany. At the same time rumours were rife about a landing of Allied forces in Spain, and the Caudillo transferred a number of Spanish troops to the Atlantic coast, presumed to be the chosen point (a second Sicily) where the Allies could get a foothold in Europe with a view to opening a second front. In a final interview on 27 January Hoare attempted to persuade the Caudillo to stop the dispatch of wolfram. 'There in the Prado was the little Generalísimo, fat, smug, complacent, apparently unworried by his past, undoubting as to his future, as confident of his indispensability as of his own wisdom.' In fact Franco did not give way; so on 28 January Great Britain and the United States called off their supplies of petroleum to Spain *sine die*.

The situation had taken a grave turn, and it was during this tense period that Don Juan, from Lausanne, sent Franco a telegram which was the first public expression of his claims. The text is clear: 'Only two solutions possible. Maintenance Your Excellency's regime at all costs or revenge with foreign aid by those defeated in Civil War Stop. . . . Should thus be better able defend principles which we upheld against *Frente Popular* Stop Tomorrow may be too late Stop.'

Don Juan thus stood as candidate for the succession, and offered himself to the social and political bloc of traditionalist Spain as a means whereby the Francoist victory of 1939 could be saved in spite of the defeat of the Axis. This conjunction of circumstances – Don Juan's démarche, Franco's resistance to the Allied request and the Anglo–American action with regard to petroleum – was clearly no accident. The Caudillo wanted to show yet once more that he had full control of his country, that he alone could call the tune. The assurances he had already received (particularly in 1943) convinced him that London and Washington were only trying to put pressure on him. Resistance, even temporary, to the Allied demands concerning wolfram, meant forcing them to recognize that they must deal with no one but himself, since only he was capable of imposing fresh sufferings on his country while still maintaining order. Under these circumstances, if they chose to reject Franco's regime and to support Don Juan, the Allies would risk disturbing the political and social order that prevailed in Spain.

The Order Prevailing in Spain

Order did, in fact, prevail during those early months of 1944. Yet the privations resulting from the cutting off of oil supplies hit the country hard: industrial activity was partly paralysed, so was transport; unemployment grew and poverty was widespread. Order prevailed, because hundreds of thousands of men were in prison, because arrests and shootings still went on, and the information services were entirely controlled by the regime. Don Juan's telegram was not published, the true reasons for the shortage of petroleum remained unknown, and of course news from the front was distorted. One cannot, moreover, reject the idea that Franco's stubbornness also entailed a wish to help the Reich to hold out as long as possible in the hope of fomenting disagreements between the U.S.S.R. and the Western Allies and bringing about that compromise peace in the West which had been, and still was, Franco's grand design. Essentially Franco's resistance can be explained by his anxiety to show the groups who supported him that he could stand up to the Allies and oblige them to have dealings with himself alone.

Now, in addition to the landed gentry, the Church, the business circles and high ranking army officers who enjoyed considerable freedom of action, the regime had introduced a whole network of accomplices into the lower strata of the population: former Falangists owing their jobs solely to their political past, concierges, museum attendants, petty officials, bound to the establishment through the general corruption from which they benefited to some small extent. They supported Francoism, moreover, out of *fear*, lest the defeated Republicans should some day take their revenge; and they were all the readier to defend the Caudillo when they had themselves been responsible for exacting vengeance on the vanquished, when they were high up in the hierarchy and therefore feared reprisals proportionate to their deeds. When a Republican fell, pierced by the bullets from a firing squad, Francoism did not merely kill a disarmed enemy, an already defeated political prisoner; it also bound closer to itself all those who, having given active or passive consent, must now consider themselves as its accomplices: judges, prison warders, lawcourt officials, men in the firing squad, officers who had taken part in the repression to any degree or had simply allowed the execution to take place. A great deal of killing had gone on in Spain, and executions were still taking place, so there were a great many accomplices who were, in a way, victims.[1]

This was how the Caudillo controlled Spain in 1944. The army, the police, all those who, in one way or another, were bound up with the regime, enjoyed real material advantages: passports, priorities, special food rations for soldiers and the forces of order. With the absence of news that then prevailed in Spain, an intense propaganda campaign was able to present the Caudillo's policy as one of resistance to foreign threats. In his reply to Don Juan, Franco deliberately notes:

'Your declaration evidently made with an eye fixed on foreign countries has aroused unease in Spain even among men attached to monarchy Stop. It is a discordant note in the concert of unity which all non-Red Spaniards strive to preserve both inside and outside Spain Stop. ... Spain not disposed to lose advantage our victorious Crusade on account world war Stop. ... The restoration of the monarchy is our ultimate aim.'

Thus Franco resisted both Allied pressure and the latest Monarchist move. On 21 February the United States had indeed drawn up an indictment of Franco's regime, but the Caudillo was well aware that Churchill was opposed to any action, indeed that the Prime Minister had put pressure on Washington to resume exports of petroleum and that Britain was already preparing to import agricultural produce from Spain. Moreover, Moscow had announced in a communiqué of 7 February that the U.S.S.R. 'was not for the time being interested

[1] The most powerful and impassioned account of this situation is the film *El Verdugo* (The Executioner) by L. Berlanga (1964).

in the Iberian peninsula, which was merely a passage where the Allies might be halted as they had been in Italy, but rather on the basic attack to be launched against the Reich in its Atlantic fortress'.

Formal Capitulation and Basic Victory

All these facts (in the first place, the maintenance of order within the country, from which everything else followed, the Monarchist setback, the disagreement between the United States and Great Britain) now made possible a *formal capitulation* by Franco on the issue of wolfram and of the export of products to the Reich, which was at the same time a *basic victory* on the essential point: the survival of Franco's regime and its recognition as an interlocutor by the Anglo–Saxon Allies at this new stage of the war. On 2 May 1944, economic agreements were concluded: Spain would export to Germany only insignificant quantities of wolfram (twenty tons, then forty); in the political field, she even consented to close the German consulate at Tangier and to expel the Nazi intelligence agents. In exchange she was to receive the oil she needed. The real importance and significance of the agreement were conveyed by Winston Churchill's speech to the House of Commons on 24 May. In a single sentence, he absolved Franco's Spain from its past non-belligerent support of the Axis by declaring, with reference to the dangerous moments of summer 1940 and the landing in North Africa: 'I shall always consider a service was rendered at this time not only to the United Kingdom and to the British Empire and Commonwealth, but to the cause of the United Nations.' Coming from the man who was the embodiment of resistance to Nazi Germany, this tribute, with its implied consequences, was of fundamental importance politically. Churchill added a warning: 'I have therefore no sympathy with those who think it clever, and even funny, to insult and abuse the Government of Spain whenever occasion serves. . . .' And since Franco's regime had been so helpful to the warring Allies, Churchill's conclusion, also pregnant with meaning, can hardly have come as a surprise:

'As I am here today speaking kindly words about Spain, let me add that I hope she will be a strong influence for the peace of the Mediterranean after the war. Internal political problems in Spain are a matter for the Spaniards themselves. It is not for us to meddle in such affairs. . . .'

Never before had British policy been so clearly defined in public.

The Spanish press naturally welcomed Churchill's speech with enthusiasm. It proved that there was no immediate threat to the regime: the Caudillo – as the early months of 1944 had once again shown – knew very well that he was strong enough to fear nothing, after five years of uninterrupted and ruthless repression, from the 'Spaniards themselves' of whom Churchill spoke. The British Premier was explicitly telling Franco: keep control of your country, we shall not intervene or let anyone else intervene in the internal affairs of Spain. A number of statements by leading Francoist personalities show, moreover, that the regime, well protected by the *Guardia Civil*, the army, the police and the fear it had inspired, was in fact afraid of nothing but some action from outside which, by forcing an issue, would upset Spain's internal political conditions. At the end of May, meeting François Pietri, the Ambassador from Vichy France, Franco inveighed against France's failure to fight against those 'eleventh-hour patriots, the Communists', and above all he stressed his concern lest Red Spaniards, concentrated in southern France, should venture an attack on Catalonia.

The Regime Threatened

The Caudillo's fears were not unjustified. It was all very well for Churchill, from the rostrum of the House of Commons, to re-write history and define his policy; other men had very different experiences during that period, which witnessed the success of the Normandy landing on 6 June and the retreat northward (abandoning southern France and the Pyrenean frontier) of the German troops, harried by the *maquisards*, who included several thousand exiled Spaniards – as many as 60,000 according to some authors. Henceforward the F.F.I. (*Forces Françaises de l'Intérieur*), French gendarmes, customs officers and regular troops guarded Pyrenean passes and valleys. Often in towns or villages, during the parades under arms that marked the liberation, units composed solely of Spaniards marched past under their own banners, and at Bordeaux, in 1944, General de Gaulle saluted the flags of the Spanish Republic and the Basque flag of the *Guernica* and *Libertad* battalions. These exiles in arms, fresh from doing battle with the German troops, were moved by a single passion: the liberation of Spain, which seemed to them the logical sequel to the fight begun in 1936 when the airmen of the Condor Legion, men of the now routed Reich, had given support to their opponents. In August there was formed at Toulouse the *Junta Española de Liberación* comprising Republicans and members of the non-Communist left-wing *Partido Socialista Obrero Español*, who had already united under that name in Mexico in November 1943; this time, however, they were joined by the *Movimiento Libertario Español*. The aim of these political groups was to be ready to return to Spain when, as they confidently expected, the Allies should intervene.

In Spain itself, the Allied landing, then the liberation of Paris in August, even though the news was delayed and distorted, aroused wild excitement in those who were waiting. Groups would form, in Franco's jails, around some prisoner who had managed to collect scraps of news which were passed from one yard to another, scribbled on bits of paper, whispered in corridors. The prisoner would read out in a low voice: 'Comrades, Paris is free. The Americans have crossed the Marne. Spaniards are carrying on the struggle everywhere in France. The Republican flag is flying over Hendaye. *¡Salud!*'[2] The confident conviction spread that the long martyrdom was about to end, that 'They' would come, since only a bridge separated Hendaye from Spain. Prison officers grew nervous, and intensified repression in an effort to forestall revolt. Meanwhile, *guerrilleros* who had never given up their weapons went off into the mountains; militants who had gone underground came out of their hiding places; daring deeds were attempted, bombs were thrown. For the first time since the end of the Civil War (and the

[2] Antonio Ferres, *Les Vaincus*.

phenomenon was to continue into 1945) underground anti-Francoist organizations won a number of recruits, and were able to reconstitute themselves in many towns and factories, particularly in Catalonia: the Socialist and Communist Parties and the Anarchist C.N.T. came to life again. The Communists, the moving spirit of the *Junta Suprema de Unión Nacional,* were in favour of armed struggle. They aimed at a radical upheaval; they hoped to combine internal action by small groups of partisans with a broad mass movement, and also with the activities of *maquisards* who, coming over from France, would form a *cintura armada* in the Pyrenees, a plague-spot for the military and political authorities; thus facing the Allies with the necessity of making a choice, and also obliging the Republican forces to acknowledge the Communists. In short, they sought to bring Spain's future into the open, out of the corridors of politics and diplomacy, and make it depend, now that fascism was in retreat throughout Europe, on guerrilla warfare in the mountains and fighting in the streets. The non-Communist Parties of the opposition were clearly mistrustful of these prospects which, apart from their hazardous character, were likely to lead to a situation in which the Communist Party played the leading role. According to their interpretation, Spain, being an integral part of the Western world, should wait for its liberation by the Allies, which would result in a parliamentary democracy in Western style. In October 1944, as a counterpart to the J.S.U.N., there was set up the *Alianza Nacional de Fuerzas Democráticas,* in which the various Republican, Socialist and Liberal movements were united.

The fight was already on. In Asturias, in León, in Galicia, in the southern provinces, in Catalonia, in Aragon, by the end of 1944 guerrilla groups, sometimes consisting of men who had been fighting ever since 1939, took to action. They cut off roads, shot down Civil Guards, and they were constantly hunted down, often betrayed because the country was strictly controlled and civil war seemed a terrible nightmare that must not recur. The Asturias were once more in a state of siege, while in mines and factories militant groups tried to organize strike action. These groups were chiefly composed of Communists or Anarchists, members of the J.S.U.N., as also were the *maquisards* who, during the summer, gathered on the French frontier under the guise of peasants or of workers in the timber firm of Fernández, Vallador y Cía. While their original plans envisaged guerrilla warfare, inspired and directed by a small number of mobile groups, the atmosphere of the time, which encouraged illusions and revolutionary optimism, together with the lack of reliable information on the state of opinion in Spain and on the stability of Franco's power, and with a natural impatience, led to the creation of an *Agrupación de Guerrilleros* comprising between ten and fifteen thousand men, well armed with weapons taken from the Wehrmacht. In September 1944 they attempted to invade the region of the Col de l'Hospitalet and the Val d'Aran as far as Viella, and succeeded in holding a zone of Spanish territory for about ten days. In fact the attempt was doomed to failure; the Spanish army had assembled some 45,000 troops whose superiority in arms, equipment and logistics was overwhelming. Moreover, political conditions were not conducive to a frontal operation of this type: no co-ordination was possible with groups acting within Spain itself. Driven back, encircled, fighting vigorously but outflanked, the Republicans were forced to retreat, leaving three to four thousand prisoners in Francoist hands. Men who had eluded death and capture between 1936 and 1939, men who had kept on fighting but had managed to avoid Nazi concentration camps, were caught now, in 1944, condemned to death or to thirty years in jail. General Yagüe was in command of the Francoist forces: the adversary and the victor were still the same.

This unhappy episode, when looked at with hindsight, displays sources of weakness in the opposition to Francoism which had already been revealed during the Civil War. Impatience, lack of co-ordination, heroism, division into rival political factions, led to a waste of energy and of human lives; the fighting spirit was unimpaired, but at the same time it proved powerless.

Franco's opportunities for action were still very considerable in 1944, so long as his army had the upper hand within Spain. Now there was an overwhelming disproportion between the repressive apparatus of the Franco regime and the forces that opposed it. The Caudillo therefore had merely to make sure that no political development at home or abroad should disturb the military balance of forces, repression being the final argument of a regime born of military action. To this end Franco had to manoeuvre, and at this he was a past master.

Franco's Manoeuvres

When, shortly after the successful landing in Normandy, the American Ambassador, Carlton Hayes, was received by the Caudillo, he observed that in the reception room of the Pardo Palace the photographs of Mussolini and Hitler had been removed and only that of Pope Pius XII remained. The conversation was to last more than an hour, and the Caudillo declared himself ready to collaborate with the Allies. He proffered advice: in order to avoid civil war in Europe, he said, occupying troops must be maintained there for at least five years, and he hoped that the Anglo–Saxons would protect his country from Russian interference. He arranged for Spain to co-operate with U.N.R.R.A. (United Nations Relief and Rehabilitation Administration), the body which brought aid to the populations of liberated areas; considering the poverty and undernourishment of certain regions of Andalusia, this was less a token of great devotion on the part of Francoist Spain than a political move, proving the Caudillo's determination to join the Allied side without delay. Meanwhile, basically, the ground on which he chose to manoeuvre was that of anti-bolshevism, the Communist danger and the threat from Russia. On 18 July 1944, speaking to the National Council of the Falange, he reiterated his 'appeal for peace, not to render service to any belligerent but in order to avoid the spread of communism throughout Europe'.

This classic theme was to be employed again by the Caudillo in the letter he sent on 8 October, through the Duke of Alba, to 'our good friend the British Prime Minister', Winston Churchill: a letter which quickly became famous. He declared that the 'noble words' uttered by Churchill on 24 May were 'a guarantee that Spain's pre-occupations would arouse a sympathetic echo in his heart'. Churchill had enjoyed a good press in Spain even before 24 May. He was said to be a realist, aware of the danger of communism, quite unlike Roosevelt, who had become a tool of the U.S.S.R. and whose wife, according to some Francoists, was an agent of international communism. Franco foresaw a strengthening of Russia and the United States as a result of the war, with consequent disastrous results for Europe. As a spokesman for European interests, he declared: 'We cannot trust Communist Russia . . . and we know the insidious power of bolshevism.' The Western powers must get together. In fact, there were only three countries that counted: England, Spain and Germany, the only nations to have shown themselves 'strong and virile'. Germany was now destroyed; France and Italy were 'corrupted from within'; and according to the Caudillo, 'the mutual friendship of England and Spain was desirable . . . in order to lay the foundations for common action in the future'. He set forth the advantages of Spain, 'a country of great strategic importance, healthy, virile and chivalrous'. Then came a warning: abroad, there were bad Spaniards who wanted to change things within the country . . . such changes could only serve the interests of Russia. Thus, logically, his argument closed with this basic theme, considered as most apt to protect his own regime and to convince Churchill. It was audacious of him to seek to win Churchill over and make him take a stand, and the Prime Minister could only reassert his loyalty to the Anglo–Soviet alliance, the framework for the world organization of the future. Churchill also requested Franco to remove the final obstacles to collaboration with the Allies.

Franco's advances had met with a refusal, but one accompanied by advice and respect, which lessened the affront. In any case, what else could he have expected? His Foreign Minister, since Jordana's death on 3 August, had been José Félix de Lequerica, formerly Ambassador to Vichy France, whom the Monarchist Ansaldo had described as 'more German than the Germans'. There was nothing naïve about either Franco or Lequerica. The Caudillo's letter must be considered less as a specific invitation to open immediate negotiations on the questions raised than as a suggested programme which, once it had been received and 'studied with great interest', as Churchill wrote, had fulfilled its purpose.

At the same time, in the realm of facts, Franco's attitude remained unaltered. The *guerrilleros* were harshly and efficiently put down; torture was usual. A stern note was sent to the French Provisional Government demanding an end to the activities of groups of Spanish exiles. On 25 October, at a press conference held at the Ministry of War in Paris, General de Gaulle showed little anxiety on this issue. When a journalist asked him what he thought about civil war in Spain, the General replied that there were no signs of civil war in Spanish territory at the moment. He admitted his concern at the fact that many Germans had taken refuge in Spain, but when someone remarked: 'They say that there are 40,000 Germans in Spain and that Franco has threatened to set France in order . . .' he simply replied: 'They say all sorts of things!' In answer to another question he reaffirmed that regular diplomatic relations existed between Madrid and Paris.[3]

Spain, for the time being, had nothing to fear from the French Provisional Government. It seemed as though she could take her place in the new community of nations. On 3 November 1944, the Caudillo, in an interview with the correspondent of the United Press, specifically declared that Spain had never been

[3] Charles de Gaulle, *Discours de guerre*, III (Paris, 1945).

Fascist or Nazi. 'Spain is now prepared to intervene in all the political decisions of the moment; which gives her the right to collaborate on all international planes for the organization of the post-war world. Moreover,' he concluded, 'Spain and the other neutral countries must participate in the negotiations for the peace treaty.' Thus, according to the Caudillo, Francoist Spain must without let or hindrance make her voice heard, now that the Axis was shattered, just as she would have done if the Axis had won, taking her share of the spoils of the democracies.

December 1944

On 23 December 1944, a new penal code was promulgated, which contained clauses very restrictive on personal liberty, but abrogated the earlier provisions of the vague law of 2 March 1943.[4] This seemed to mark a progress which would put Spain on a level with the victorious powers; however, the law of 2 March continued to be applied. Such was the state of things in Spain at the end of 1944. When the Germans launched their offensive in the Ardennes, the press began once more to hail Germany's imminent victory, due to her secret weapons; Falangists greeted the news with shouts of triumph. Amid the flood of rumours, and in spite of the B.B.C., anti-Francoists were in despair. Then towards Christmas Hitler's last desperate attempt was broken and the Spanish press forgot the war; but at the same time British troops were clearing out Athens and Attica, thus proving that Churchill was not the sort of man to let communism and disorder prevail in Britain's Mediterranean preserves.

Franco looked on calmly. Those around him may have been uneasy about the future, but he, the Caudillo, sure of the rightness of his cause, prudent, holding back his trump cards, would take no risks, convinced (because he had heard and seen and understood) that the future would inevitably bring about that Western coalition against the Red, barbarian East, which he longed for and foresaw and which would give him his chance. How could he feel anxious, since as a soldier he had known from boyhood onward that a human being is nothing more than flesh and blood and that by piercing that flesh, shedding that blood one can kill his ideas – *for a time* only, of course, but a time that may last as long as another man's life, his, Franco's, life for instance? Sir Samuel Hoare describes him thus, harshly, in 1944: 'At the top of this chaos was Franco, a dictator who flourished upon division and inaction, an almost inaccessible Buddha without whose detailed approval no Minister was willing to take an important decision.' By December 1944 Mussolini and Hitler, the big men who had once helped him, who had treated him with condescending kindness, were in desperate straits. He, the Caudillo, was calmly reigning.

However, the evolution of the international situation, the disintegration of the Reich, and above all the general swing to the left throughout Europe, the immense prestige enjoyed by Stalin's Russia which, in the early days of 1945, embodied victorious communism in the eyes of millions of men, could not fail to have repercussions in Spain and on the relations between Spain and the Allied

[4] See above.

countries. The Yalta meeting (4 to 12 February 1945), which displayed the understanding between the Big Three, confirmed the failure, even if only for the time being, of Franco's grand plan. In spite of Churchill's reservations, Roosevelt and Stalin concluded an agreement, favourable to the U.S.S.R., to which Great Britain, henceforward a second-rank world power, was forced to subscribe. For Franco's regime, this marked the beginning of a year that seemed as perilous as a *noche negra*, a black night which it would have to try to survive.

New Dangers for the Caudillo

Within the country, now that the fears and hopes aroused by the Ardennes offensive had died down, men prepared for a fresh struggle. Groups were organized: young men went off into the mountains; others prepared for possible mass uprisings. Former militiamen or Republican officers constituted, by means of individual contacts, an *Agrupación de Fuerzas Armadas Republicanas Españolas* (A.F.A.R.E.) which sought to re-create a Republican army with the support of guerrilla groups, a kind of adaptation to the Spanish situation of French resistance organizations such as the F.F.I. or secret army. The A.F.A.R.E. was directed by a committee consisting of Republican ex-professional soldiers, and it made contact with the Republican Government in exile. Even though the armed activity of this group was limited in scope, the fact of its constitution indicates the way the situation had developed. Moreover, a small number of strikes broke out; they were soon suppressed, but they implied a possible intervention by the working masses and the peasantry in the political battle which, for the time being, was restricted to a few groups.

Faced with this deterioration of the atmosphere within the country, the Caudillo reacted. Even though his press and certain broadcasting stations (such as Radio Valladolid, on 4 February 1945) extolled Germany, 'confident in her destiny, ready to save herself and to save Europe', Franco deliberately drew closer to Britain and the United States, and trade relations were intensified. Even more significantly, in February American planes of the Air Transport Command were granted the right to land in Spain, and then the United States Air Force was authorized to fly over Spain and to establish aerodromes which, before the end of 1945, had become American bases. Finally France allowed the United States to establish direct radio contact. These important advantages reveal the Caudillo's awareness that the United States had assumed the leadership of the coalition, and that his diplomatic efforts must be directed towards that power. Moreover, encouraging signs proved that certain circles on the other side of the Atlantic appreciated the potential role of Spain. 'With the imminent collapse of Germany,' wrote the *New York American* on 14 February 1945, 'and its destruction as bulwark against communism, Spain and Portugal assume the role of barrier against the Red flood.' *Stars and Stripes*, the journal of the American armed forces, asserted (on 14 March) that American policy was based on the realization that Franco's regime could not be replaced.

These positive factors in the American attitude were still only *potential*. In

1945 there was a strong anti-fascist flavour about many of the decisions taken by Washington under the leadership of President Roosevelt, who was firmly loyal to the Grand Alliance of the anti-Nazi war. Thus, factors disturbing to the Caudillo accumulated. The gravest was undoubtedly the letter addressed by Roosevelt on 10 March 1945, to the new Ambassador in Spain, Norman Armour. The President declared curtly that the fact that the American Government maintained formal diplomatic relations with the present Spanish regime should not be interpreted by anyone as implying approval of that regime and its single party, the Falange, which had been openly hostile to the United States and had sought to propagate its Fascist ideas in the Western hemisphere. The letter concluded with an open threat: the Allied victory over Germany would entail the extermination of Nazi ideology and others like it ... there was no place in the community of the United Nations for a government founded on Fascist principles. Roosevelt repeated insistently: 'We shall never forget. ... The present Spanish regime has in the past identified itself with our enemies. ...' Coming from the head of the world's most powerful nation, whose troops then occupied a large part of Europe, these words stirred up the hopes of all those who were fighting Franco's regime and strengthened their belief that Germany's surrender would result directly either in the entry of Allied troops into Spain or, without that even being necessary, in the collapse of a regime and a man now proved anachronistic and condemned accordingly.

It was hardly by coincidence that Don Juan-de-Borbón now put forward for the second time his Monarchist solution, speaking no longer to Franco but to the Spanish people themselves: a clear indication that the regime was in difficulties.

Don Juan's Manifesto

This document, written in Lausanne on 19 March, is severely worded. Don Juan declares that

> 'six years after the Civil War, the regime instituted by General Franco and inspired from the beginning by the totalitarian systems of the Axis Powers, so contrary to the character and tradition of our people, is basically incompatible with the circumstances now being created in the world as a result of the war. ... Spain runs the risk of finding herself involved in a new fratricidal conflict and isolated from the rest of the world. ... Her present regime exposes her to this twofold peril.'

Naturally, for Don Juan, 'only the traditional monarchy can prove an instrument for peace and can reconcile Spaniards'.

Don Juan proposed a set of measures (a political constitution determined by vote, recognition of individual human rights, the guarantee of political liberties, a legislative assembly elected by the nation, recognition of regional differences, amnesty, a fairer distribution of wealth which, if applied, might have provided Spain with the basis for democratic development, but the time for a monarchy was past. The two sides were now clearly defined; and in the context of 1945, unlike that of 1943, the Republican opposition seemed so strong that the risk of the extreme left outflanking the monarchists with a consequent upheaval in the social order inevitably appeared as the greatest danger in any political change. True, Don Juan declared: 'I am not raising the standard of revolt, nor encouraging sedition.' The propertied classes preferred to these assertions the real, tested and effective guarantee of the Caudillo. As for the latter, he was not inclined to listen to Don Juan's appeal from exile: 'I call on General Franco to recognize the failure of his totalitarian endeavour and to renounce power, thus making possible the restoration of the traditional regime in Spain, which alone is capable of guaranteeing religion, order and liberty.'

In fact, the Caudillo was perfectly capable of guaranteeing order and religion. After the Manifesto, the number of those enjoying liberty was merely cut down a little further. Certain Monarchists were dismissed or demoted. The Duke of Alba, Ambassador to London, resigned. The regime was not really weakened thereby because the Monarchist threat existed only in terms of the pressure from without and within. Intrinsically, the Monarchist-Francoist battle was an inter-tribal conflict. The fate of Franco's regime was being decided elsewhere.

The Death of Roosevelt

In spite of Roosevelt's letter, Spain's reception of the American Ambassador, Norman Armour, took the form of a demonstration of Spanish–American friendship, and on 11 April 1945, after a violent press campaign, the Madrid government broke off diplomatic relations with Japan. Franco obviously realized that there were several trends in the United States and that the trend represented by Roosevelt was not necessarily the most important one for the future. He therefore played skilfully on the theme of American friendship, and when Roosevelt died on 12 April the Falangists felt a real sense of release and joy, while Hitler and Mussolini congratulated each other, taking the event for a propitious omen.

Nothing but despair, on the other hand, was felt by Franco's opponents, particularly those who had expected so much, if not everything, from Allied intervention. One of them describes how, on learning the news from a friend, 'I felt in my throat and in my breast my old companion, anguish. And once again the impression that it was useless, that everything was useless, that fate had it in for us.'[5]

Yet the struggle had to go on, in spite of the increasing efficiency of the police, who during this tense period undertook a great many 'preventive' arrests.

The balance of forces was still disproportionately in favour of Franco's regime; this is proved by events in Madrid at the time of Roosevelt's death. A Falangist club at Cuatro-Caminos was attacked, its files removed, some of its members killed. This called forth savage reaction from the authorities, determined to display the superior power of the Franco regime precisely because it might have seemed weakened. The whole Falangist body, armed and blue-shirted, assembled in the centre of the city. Shops and schools were closed by order; the procession moved to the working-class district of Ventas, where the Falangists struck down

[5] J. Hermanos, *La Fin de l'Espoir*.

all those – workers or passers-by – who were not wearing blue shirts. They broke in the doors of houses, plundered them and attacked the inhabitants, terrorizing the whole city. Their opponents were roused to such a pitch of fury that in spite of their numerical inferiority, in spite of certain failure, they fought back, tackling Falangists and policemen, repeatedly defending the Republican flag they had unfurled. These premature acts of spontaneous bravery disorganized the resistance network that had been constituted and helped to maintain that atmosphere of civil war on which Francoism flourished. Once again the lack of co-ordination revealed the technical and political weakness of the opposition.

True, on 1 April 1945, at Toulouse, Santiago Carrillo, representing the leadership of the Spanish Communist Party, appealed for the unity of all democratic forces, asking them to prepare a general political strike in support of national insurrection. Unity could as yet be only a remote objective; national insurrection, or a general political strike, were goals which twenty years later would still seem maximalistic, a scarcely attainable ideal.

In fact the differences in the degree of opposition to Francoism shown in various regions, which characterized the situation in 1936–9, persisted. The under-development of certain southern regions was such, their poverty so crushing, the physiological weakness of their inhabitants so universal that social relations remained feudal, and after the flare-up of 1936 the age-old discouragement had overwhelmed them once more. There remained the cities, Asturias, Catalonia and the Basque country, traditionally lively regions where national feeling backed up the opposition. Thus in March 1945, after the Bayonne declaration, all the Basque parties supported the exiled Euzkadi government and formed an executive council. The authorities concentrated armed forces in these regions, setting up a regular state of siege. Strikes were broken from the start, and the 'ringleaders' arrested, tortured, exiled to the south. At Almería a model prison, built of white stone by labour gangs and finished in 1944, was quickly filled. When a troop of soldiers confronted strikers or surrounded a factory they obeyed orders because they sensed that the group facing them was isolated, powerless for all its courage. Thus although the 1945 resistance movement involved a great number of men, it did not arouse the whole country; the exhausted masses waited resignedly. Whole generations of active men had experienced defeat in 1939 and then repression, which had left on them an indelible imprint; the cadres of the working class had been systematically hunted down. The new generations had not yet reached manhood; they were not old enough in 1945 to fight. True, we can trace the emergence of a new spirit among intellectuals, notably among the group who founded, in 1945, the Union of Free Intellectuals: this underground organization brought out its weekly, *Democrito*, almost regularly for two years. The atmosphere of the time, reflecting the weakness of working-class action, is more truly conveyed by Carmen Laforet's novel *Nada*, which won the Nadal prize in 1945. *Nada* (Nothing or Nothingness), while others hoped and fought; this was the attitude of many people, clear-sighted and sceptical members of the middle strata, who chose to wait and see, disillusioned by Franco's regime but reluctant to commit themselves against it. It was also the more confused feeling of large sections of the population, instinctively aware that this regime, which went on functioning with apparent confidence, could not be overthrown.

Furthermore, despite all appeals for unity, the opposition continued to split up. In Paris, at the first congress of the two anarchist movements in May 1945, two trends emerged: one favouring political action within the *Alianza Nacional de Fuerzas Democráticas*, had a majority in Spain but a minority in France; the other, arguing for ruthless and independent direct action, had a majority in France but a minority in Spain. The division into two factions, clearly marked in May, became official at the full meeting in August. These sectional struggles, these rivalries between political trends, this patchwork of groups had become a permanently frustrating feature of the opposition. And this, even though the details of division and controversy were not generally known, reinforced the apathy of the masses. They were victims of hunger and want, of harsh exploitation by employers or landlords, and they found no echo of their day-to-day preoccupations (the need to survive; to eat; to work a little less hard; to earn a little more money; to find a home; not to see one's children blinded by trachoma or reduced to theft and mendicancy) in programmes and aims that were too exclusively political, or that failed to show clearly the connection between political issues and daily life. Thus the attitudes of the working-class masses, and above all of the peasants, lost all flexibility under the strict control of the regime's repressive forces; and the chances of that regime's survival grew ever greater. By mid-April 1945, while French troops were subduing the last pockets on the Atlantic coast, the Madrid government felt strong enough to allow Spanish ships to provision the encircled Germans, which called forth protest from the British and French governments. At the beginning of the same month an important agreement was signed between the Spanish news agency E.F.E. and the United Press. It marked the collaboration between the two agencies and thenceforward the development of their common interests, which, since E.F.E. was an instrument of the Francoist government, meant the diffusion of strictly controlled news from Spain – and that on a world scale, owing to the power of the United Press. At a time when world opinion was a decisive factor in settling the fate of Franco's government, this seemingly anodyne agreement was of great importance. The Caudillo, in an interview with A. L. Bradford, head of the United Press, had no scruples about declaring: 'Whatever opinion one may have of General Franco's government, one must admit without a shadow of hesitation that Spain is an example of a tranquillity and progress that are remarkable in the Europe of today.'

The Death of Hitler

This atmosphere of self-satisfaction, of reiterated praise, was not broken by the death of Hitler or by Germany's unconditional surrender, signed on 8 May. When the Führer's suicide was announced, masses were said in his honour. A notice sent out by the town of Santander, adorned with a photograph of Hitler, declared: 'To perpetuate the memory of one who continued until his death to defend the civilization of the Christian West, the friends of Great Germany

dedicate this souvenir to him and beg you to pray for his soul.' The journal
Informaciones covered its front page with the headlines: 'Facing the enemy in the
place of honour, Adolf Hitler dies defending the Chancellery', and the article
continues:

'An immense *Present Arms*! spreads over the whole of Europe because Adolf
Hitler, a son of the Catholic Church, died defending Christianity. On his tomb,
on the huge funeral pyre in Berlin, might be inscribed the Spanish epitaph: "He
who lies here did not die. His death was the beginning of life. . . ." The secret
soul of Germany, the colossal bomb which was to ensure the victory of an
ideology lay within the heart of Adolf Hitler. Now it has burst. The war against
bolshevism has entered on its victorious phase. . . . And in Heaven there is much
rejoicing. On earth, men of good will envy his death.'

Such a lack of moderation, of prudence and decency, even if the men and the
journals that displayed it were more closely connected with Germany than the
rest of the Francoist establishment, is none the less a sign of the strength of
the regime that permitted it. It is, moreover, a feature of the psychological battle
then taking place in Spain. Unquestionably Francoists and Falangists were
frightened, but to show it, to admit mistakes, would mean beginning to give way
and hence beginning to lose. To hold out all along the line, to proclaim – even
while contradicting oneself, yielding in point of fact, reversing one's whole
policy – that the Caudillo and his regime had always been right, was not merely
a sign of self-satisfaction, it was a process of political indoctrination.

On the day of Germany's surrender the news broke about three in the afternoon. Members of resistance groups called one another up; the streets emptied,
the Falangists took fright. There was talk of immediate action by Franco's
opponents and by the Allies. At Bilbao and San Sebastian the Basques became
active, clashes with the Civil Guard and, being unarmed, were quickly arrested,
dispersed or hunted down. In Madrid the prisoners in the Yeserias jail demonstrated. No one else took any public action in the capital on V-Day. Then, when
that day was over, the government reacted. It gave orders for flags to fly on
public buildings. The papers published huge photographs of Generalissimo
Franco with large captions: *Caudillo of Peace*, or *Caudillo of Neutrality*. According to *Arriba*: 'For Spain, the proclamation of peace in Europe confirms the
success of a magnificent *tour de force*: the preservation of neutrality'; and
according to *Juventud*: 'Spain has been saved because she has had a Caudillo
and a Falange, and History, which judges dispassionately, will proclaim that the
day of peace is the day of Falangist victory.' To be sure, these antics did not
convince those who had their own opinions and some political judgement. Thus,
few people in fact hung out flags for victory; even the Falangists felt genuinely
embarrassed. Such declarations were not aimed at the opposition; they were
intended to maintain, however artificially, the coalition between all who dreaded
change, disorder, civil war.

These articles, these unexpected assertions, reassured supporters; and all these
actions were not the result of passionate feeling in particular circles, but the
expression of a political necessity at a time when the battle was reaching its crisis.

There must be no apparent weakening. That May, speaking at Valladolid, cradle of the Falange movement, while attending some ceremony in company of José Luis Arrese, the Caudillo declared: 'Recent world events confirm the clear-sightedness of the Spanish movement. . . . Spain has prepared for this moment, she can await events with serenity.'

Behind this necessary immutability, there were adaptations and changes of front, which were incorporated into the façade of permanence. The international situation was now worsening, as far as Franco's regime was concerned.

The Noche Negra

On 19 June 1945, during the conference of the United Nations at San Francisco, the Mexican delegation, amid general applause, gained approval for a motion refusing Spain a seat in the future United Nations Organization. On 30 June Panama broke off diplomatic relations with Spain. These were only minor facts, but on 7 July the elections in Great Britain brought in a Labour Government, and Clement Attlee, who had visited Republican Spain during the Civil War, became Prime Minister on 27 July, with Ernest Bevin as Foreign Minister. The swing to the left was felt all over the European continent. Already in France, on 29 April, municipal elections had favoured the left and even the extreme left. The British Labour Party had moreover focused its electoral campaign on a criticism of Conservative policy in Greece and Spain, and had engaged to restore democracy in both these countries. Churchill's defeat and departure might mean a dangerous turning for Madrid.

Even more disturbing: the Potsdam conference, which brought together the Big Three from 17 July to 2 August proclaimed, in its final communiqué, that

'The three governments feel bound . . . to make it clear that they would not favour any application for membership [of the United Nations] put forward by the present Spanish Government, which, having been founded with the support of the Axis Powers, does not, in view of its origins, its nature, its record, and its close association with the aggressor states, possess the qualifications necessary to justify such membership.'

This communiqué, by reason of the importance of its signatories and the pre-cision and vigour of its terms, aroused bitter resentment in Falangist circles. The Monarchist Ansaldo, recalling the atmosphere in Madrid when it was first announced, speaks of 'the demoralization of Gestapists and Falangists'.

On the other hand, it gave fresh confidence to Franco's opponents. Some went off into the maquis, others – in Bilbao, Barcelona – went on strike. Hopefully, they waited; only the continuation of the war against Japan could have prevented the Allies from intervening. Preparations went on, in spite of the repression that affected not only strikers but their whole families, in spite of the leaden curtain of the censorship which paralysed solidarity. A strike only became known in a town after it had been repressed. There were indeed foreign broadcasts – from Britain and Russia – and lately a 'free' wireless station, *Radio Pirenaica*, had sprung up; but their news was inadequate, and moreover only a minority in

Spain had radio sets. There were many attempts at public demonstration, but these remained isolated. Yet hope was stubborn, in that early summer of 1945.

In July the leader of the Carlist movement, 'Fal Conde,' who before his exile had been one of the great figures of the 1936 'Crusade', issued a manifesto in which he declared his opposition to 'Fascism and the myth created by Franco according to which the Carlists had shed their blood in order to maintain the ideology of the (Falangist) *Movimiento*.' The regime thus seemed threatened with disintegration and with isolation, and to be sunk in that *noche negra* which would lead to its overthrow.

For the Caudillo, such a situation could not be prolonged: every day counted. He must regain the initiative on the psychological plane, by proving the vigour of his regime, and at the same time he must disarm the great powers, the only real threat, by depriving them of any formal pretext for intervention. To this end he must give pledges, and since in every country – and primarily in England, where the Labour Party had just come to power – there was talk of democracy and constitutionalism, the Caudillo realized that the cleverest line would be to proceed of his own accord to an apparent transformation of his regime. This would provide a rallying-point for Spain's defenders, enabling them to fight the supporters of intervention not only on the ground that order must be maintained, or that national sovereignty must be respected, but also on the ground that order must be allowed to evolve.

Transformations: July 1945. El Fuero de los Españoles

July was the decisive period. The Labour Party took power; the Potsdam negotiations might involve the fate of Spain. Franco had to act quickly.

On 13 July the *Fuero de los Españoles* was promulgated. The word *fuero* suggests the liberties and rights secured of old by various Spanish communities. This 'basic text' claimed to define the rights of Spaniards, their duties, the guarantees to which they were entitled. They must serve their country and their Caudillo, obey the law, acquire instruction, fulfil some useful task. In exchange 'the Spanish State proclaims, as the guiding principle of its acts, respect for the dignity, the integrity and the liberty of the individual'. Spanish citizens were entitled to correspond freely, to live where they chose, and they must not be detained for more than seventy-two hours without appearing before an examining magistrate. These liberal principles seemed broad enough, but they were already restricted by Article 12 which declared that 'any Spaniard may freely express his ideas so long as they do not interfere with the basic principles of the State', and Article 33 which stipulated that 'the exercise of the rights recognized by this charter must not in any case interfere with the spiritual, national and social unity of the country'.

Above all, the individual liberties thus granted and proclaimed might be, thanks to Article 25, 'temporarily suspended by the Government'. The *Fuero* in short recognized all these rights (thereby representing an important step forward, due to international pressure) but guaranteed none of them. Even more serious, it failed to modify the everyday practice of the police and of the authorities.

Similarly, on 17 July, a municipal law established the principles of municipal elections, but the Minister of the Gobernación assumed the right to appoint the mayors of all communes of over ten thousand inhabitants.

Thus, while the real state of things was practically unaltered and as strictly controlled as ever, the Caudillo disguised it with a new façade. The divergence between words and reality is clearly revealed in the amnesty proclaimed on 17 July 1945, for the ninth anniversary of the Glorious National Movement. This specifically excluded 'those who have committed actions repugnant to any honourable conscience' and did not apply to any accessory penalties which had been superadded to the principal sentence. In other words, it was left, as always in the past, to the entire discretion of the Caudillo, and it affected only a tiny minority of prisoners, although at that very moment a large number of new prisoners were being taken to their cells.

The Caudillo could, none the less, make use of all these measures to proclaim before the National Council of the Falange that his regime – which, he pointed out incidentally, had been recognized by the leading Great Powers at the end of the Civil War – was very much alive. He also asserted, in order to paralyse his Monarchist critics, that 'monarchy is the traditional system of Spain', then, returning to the provisions of the *Fuero de los Españoles*, concluded that the *Movimiento* was basically popular and democratic in content.

Principal Line of Defence: the Church

Franco's regime had thus set up a first, 'democratic' line of defence; it was perhaps not the most important. At the same time, in fact, the Caudillo changed his government. On 21 July Lequerica learned that he was no longer Foreign Minister; Arrese, Secretary-General of the Falange, Carceller, Minister of Trade, and the Ministers of War, the Navy and the Air were also replaced. The Minister of Labour, José Antonio Girón, kept his place. One of the founders of the Falange, Raimundo Fernández Cuesta, reappeared on the scene; Suances replaced Carceller as Minister for Trade and Industry, but the name that explained the significance of the reshuffle was that of Martin Artajo, now Foreign Minister. He was a lawyer from a family closely linked to the Church, and a very active member of the *Acción Católica*; a leader-writer on the Christian-Democratic paper *El Debate*, he had consulted the Cardinal Primate of Toledo before accepting his new post. His entry into the government thus implied that the Church, at this critical phase, offered its full support to the regime and that the Caudillo had chosen, as his main line of defence, to stress the Catholic aspect of his regime.

The Falange was thereby diminished: it had only two representatives in the new cabinet, and the Caudillo, in one of his speeches, went so far as to specify that the Falange (now more frequently called the *Movimiento*) was not a state party but an 'instrument of national unity'. On 27 July the Under-Secretariat for Popular Education, which was dependent on the Falange and responsible for propaganda, became a department of the Ministry of Education, the head of which was still Ibáñez Martín, well known for his connections with the Church and the Opus Dei.

On the international plane the Caudillo's choice had been clever and effective. The Christian-Democrats played a leading role in France and Italy; the Catholic Church was increasingly influential in America, and Pius XII was permanently preoccupied with stemming the Communist tide at all costs, with the support of the United States. The National Catholicism which the new government represented was an effective bulwark for Franco's regime. It presupposed an even greater subordination of state to Church.

Already, the *Fuero de los Españoles* had proclaimed that marriage was 'one and indissoluble', and that the family was the foundation of society. It defined Catholicism as the state religion, protected by the state, and its services the only form of public worship allowed. Moreover, the law of 17 July declared that primary education must be inspired by Catholicism and Spanish tradition, and conform to the creed and dogmas of the Church and the considerations of canonic law. By decree, the Church now had the right to open training schools for teachers, and degrees from Catholic universities were equally valid with those of the state. The Church had definitely scored a victory, for which she paid by granting her protection to the Caudillo's regime. On assuming his functions on 21 July, Martin Artajo stressed the significance of this orientation: 'This new government, presided over by the Caudillo, marks a stage on the road to our country's spiritual and material reconstruction.'

After this, declarations in support of the Caudillo followed thick and fast, and while his regime met with general international censure and its partisans abroad kept silence, the Church spoke out loudly in its defence. On 2 September the Cardinal Primate issued a pastoral letter confirming the position taken by the Church in 1937 and adding: 'We must acknowledge that for many centuries the independence of the Church has never been so well recognized as by the present government, both *de jure* and *de facto*.' In a pastoral letter of 14 September Mgr Blanco Najera, Bishop of Orense, eulogized Francoism as 'the bulwark of the Catholic faith . . . the only one to have resisted and defeated the hordes of the godless'.

So the Church unhesitatingly sided with the regime during this critical phase. For many prelates, Spain seemed one of the bastions of Catholicism against the tide of modern heresies. Now that the Church controlled education there, she could combat these heresies openly. The seventeenth edition of the *Nuevo Ripalda*, a catechism published at the end of 1944 (its author was the Revd. Father Ripalda) declares: 'The principal errors condemned by the Church are thirteen in number: materialism, Darwinism, atheism, pantheism, deism, rationalism, protestantism, socialism, communism, syndicalism, liberalism, modernism and freemasonry.' The freedom of the press is condemned as evil; and to the question: 'Are other forms of freedom evil?' the author replies: 'Yes, freedom of teaching, freedom of propaganda and freedom of assembly.'

Thus the regime stood firm behind its new constitutional façade and its alliance with the Church, which entailed submission. It took no unnecessary risks. Pierre Laval, who had taken refuge in Spain at the beginning of May, sure of the protection he would receive from his friend Lequerica and his friend General Franco, from whom he had a letter dated 1936 thanking him for his efforts in favour of non-intervention, was turned out of Spain on 30 July. Prudence had prevailed again. On 11 September a decree was published abrogating the law of 1937 which made the Fascist salute obligatory.

Franco, however, did not dissolve the Falange as some of his advisers proposed; emptied of its substance, it was no longer a danger, and moreover to suppress it would be to repudiate the past, whereas he needed to show the present as being the natural development of that past, independent of circumstances. Thus the *Fuero de los Españoles* was only one landmark in a long straight road. An official publication declared:

'There exists in Spain an open constitutional process, begun in 1938 and consisting of a series of laws which, by reason of their normative character, are called fundamental. This process began with the Labour Charter of 9 March 1938, and was later completed by the law constituting the Cortes of 17 July 1942 ... and the *Fuero de los Españoles* on 17 July 1945.'[6]

This integration of all the various 'turning-points' was necessary for the assertion of continuity, and in fact it expresses a truth: the changes made in 1945 were, in practice, a matter of pure form. The Falange therefore had to be preserved as a useful structure which at any moment might once again serve as counterpoise to some other group; the *Movimiento* had become a mere coterie in the service of the Caudillo.

Faced with this flood of apparent innovations, Spaniards watched and waited, aware that the situation was unstable but, at the same time, that Franco's Government still controlled it, being active and inventive, and that, far from disintegrating, it still enjoyed the support and praise of the Church, that new Ministers had appeared, while the *Guardia Civil* was still there and arrests and executions still went on. Those who were involved in the struggle clenched their fists. Summer, with its torrid heat, increased their exasperation and anxiety. When the atomic bombs were dropped on Japan on 6 and 9 August, and the war came to an end, there were more tense moments, followed once again by waiting, with isolated actions doomed to failure; thus defeatism gradually crept in, because now the war was over and yet the regime remained unshaken, as in the past. Abroad, however, a different feeling prevailed among Spaniards in exile; the situation seemed to be coming to a head and heralding the fall of Francoism.

The Caudillo in Danger?

In the first place, the opposition seemed to be achieving unity: the Communists, anxious to have their existence recognized by other groups, considered dropping the *Junta Suprema de Unión Nacional* and asking for admission to the *Alianza Nacional de Fuerzas Democráticas*. In Mexico, a meeting of the republican Cortes on 17 August brought together some hundred exiled deputies and the diplomatic representatives of several countries, including Czechoslovakia, France and the Soviet Union. Martínez Barrio was elected President of the Republic. On

[6] *Fundamental Laws of the State* (Madrid, 1968).

21 August a government was formed, led by José Giral: it was recognized some days later by Mexico. President Truman declared: 'None of us likes Franco or his government.' On 4 September the Big Four, meeting in Paris, called on Spain to evacuate Tangier.

Yet weaknesses remained, grave and profound, even if still only in the background. Bevin emphasized, in the House of Commons, that the Spanish people alone had the right to determine their own political regime. This was a fine democratic principle, but the decisive question of how to realize it was never asked. Moreover, the *Alianza Nacional* was already split into opposing trends: supporters of a wait-and-see policy, or of mass action (i.e. the Communists). In any case, it was not in touch with the reality of the Spanish situation. What could Giral and his government and the Cortes meeting in Mexico City, a lingering echo of 1936, mean to the Spanish people? The gulf dividing these exiles from their homeland was a deep one, and the realities of life had changed. Naturally, the regime fought back. An informer – the Socialist Alfaro – was on the executive body of the *Alianza Nacional*; a fresh wave of arrests followed, and when the police saw fit, all the leaders were rounded up. On 25 August two exiles who had crossed the frontier illegally, Sebastián Zapirán and Santiago Álvarez, were caught in Madrid; the police asserted that they had been sent by the Communist Party to organize a campaign of violence, and discovered plans and secret stores of weapons. The two prisoners were condemned to death. Public opinion all over the world was shocked; there were protests, primarily but not only from the left. Bevin announced in the House of Commons on 10 October that the British Government had made representations to Madrid on the subject. This did not put a stop to the repression; on the contrary, more executions took place than before, including, early in November, that of Sigfrido Catala. London and Washington protested; Bevin stormed in the House of Commons, 'We detest this regime,' he exclaimed on 5 December.

Repression was not the regime's only means of defence. When the writer Ortega y Gasset went back to Spain in August he was given a triumphant welcome, to show that his return was seen, rightly or wrongly, as a sign of approval of the regime. The support of the Church was, as ever, invaluable. On 30 September the leading Catholic paper, *Ya*, bore the headlines: 'Tomorrow the Caudillo's day: A Catholic Head of State. Franco, Knight in the Service of the Apostolic Roman Catholic Church.' The article declares that 'his life, his doctrine and his work are in conformity with the principles and standards of the Church. This has just been solemnly affirmed by the Catholic hierarchy.' Meanwhile, the other line of defence was kept up: on 22 October a law was promulgated establishing the legality of a national referendum, and leaving it to the Head of the State to decide the occasion and the grounds on which it should be held. The referendum, this decree declared, was the means whereby all Spaniards could collaborate in the work of the state; it would give 'greater spontaneity to popular representation in the framework of a Christian regime of community life'.

Meanwhile, in France the elections to the Constituent Assembly proved the strength of the swing to the left; Socialists and Communists won 50 per cent of the votes. On 19 December the Foreign Affairs Committee of the Constituent Assembly called on the government – whose Foreign Minister was the Christian-Democrat Georges Bidault – to break off relations with Madrid; on 14 December Paris had already had consultations with London and Washington on the matter, and on the 21st the American Ambassador, Norman Armour, left Spain, the United States being now represented in Madrid only by a chargé d'affaires.

International opinion, and French opinion particularly, was by now highly hostile to Franco's regime. Serrano Suñer, letting fly a vindictive dart at the Caudillo, declared in an interview with *Paris-Presse*:

'Yes, I was pro-German and Spain was pro-German. . . . I blame Spain for refusing to admit this today. Nationalist Spain has Fascist origins. . . . Franco and I, and Nationalist Spain behind us, not only banked on Berlin's victory but wished for it with all our hearts. My plan was to enter the war at the moment of Germany's victory. . . .'

One can imagine the effect of such declarations, coinciding with the opening, on 20 October 1945, of the Nuremberg trials, which for the general public were to put beyond the pale of humanity those who became known as 'war criminals', including Ribbentrop and Goering. These men had known Franco well and had often exchanged congratulations with him. Diplomatic documents were published (notably in the American *White Book*) which revealed the close relations between Madrid and Berlin. Copious evidence was produced both about Nazi crimes and about the secret history of the pre-war period, particularly of the Spanish war, and hence of the conditions of Franco's rise to power. The moral and political isolation of the Francoist regime had probably never been so great, because public opinion throughout the world was, on the occasion of the trial of the Nazi chiefs, both well informed and passionately aroused.

This was indeed the *Noche Negra*. The Caudillo had to hold on at all costs. He had come safely through the war; the attacks of the *maquisards* had been crushed, and part of the internal opposition was by now perceptibly demoralized. He had to hold on. The Caudillo was not one to neglect public opinion, but he knew by experience that public opinion counts for nothing unless it is organized into *forces* and unless these forces act. Holding on implied waiting. Now in November 1945 one fact did not escape the notice of Franco's diplomats: on 15 November the United States, Great Britain and Canada refused to communicate the secret of the atomic bomb. This was important because it meant that the understanding between the victors was not as complete as was generally believed, and that therefore Spain might once more make her voice heard. The Caudillo was probably inclined to believe, in more political terms, what Mgr Blanco Najera prophesied to his flock on 23 December 1945: 'Spain, which has always been the bulwark of Christian civilization, will be the star towards which one day all the nations of Europe will turn their eyes, as they have done in the past.'

CHAPTER III

FROM SURVIVAL TO INITIATIVE

JANUARY 1946–JULY 1947

Through the fog that clung round the Asturian coast, one January day in 1946, there approached from France a boat loaded with armed men, former members of the Maquis and exiles from Latin America. They had been fighting since 1944, and hoped to join the fifteen to twenty thousand *guerrilleros* who, scattered through the country from Catalonia to Asturias, from the mountains of the Escorial to the Levante region, were opposing the Guardia Civil and preparing to support the general uprising which was to mark the Allied entry into Spain. The boat drew near, the men landed, keeping their craft steady despite the undertow, and as they stood waist high in water gunfire broke out: most of them fell dead, the rest were taken prisoner. The Guardia Civil had prepared a successful ambush.

This scene was often to be repeated in Spain in 1945 and 1946: at the mill where a dozen hunted *guerrilleros* had taken refuge, resisting the assault of a company of Civil Guards a whole night long[1]; on the famous Plaza de Catalunya in Barcelona, where shots were ruthlessly fired into the crowd and the hunted men fled; in Vizcaya, where a whole series of explosions rang out. *Guerrilleros* lived in caves in the Guadarrama; they occupied whole sections of the Sierra Morena, where they even organized road checks. In March 1946 the Civil Guards of Andalusia were attacked two or three times a day and the government had to set up operational zones with local authorities to organize repression. One of these, directed by General Pizarro, had its headquarters at Teruel – crucial scene of a civil war which was still going on. Lister, the former Republican general, declared: 'The struggle has not ended with our temporary defeat in 1939.' Others merely noted that *todavía hay guerra en España* (the war is still going on in Spain). Franco had already won the civil war in 1939 and after seven years in power, the military strength of his regime had increased considerably.

The Power of Francoism

Franco's police, while retaining all its original brutality, had now perfected its methods. Guided by German experts, trained in the school of Hitler's Gestapo, it had acquired all the techniques which had formed the strength of the Nazi

[1] J. Hermanos, *La Fin de l'Espoir* and J. Izcaray, *Las Guerrillas de Levante*, preface by E. Lister (Paris, 1949).

repressive organizations. It had learnt the art of infiltration into underground networks, of waiting before pouncing, of setting traps, and it had adopted many of the techniques of interrogation after arrest, with graduated degrees of violence, which might lead a prisoner to break down and confess, or to commit suicide. Former members of the German police or the French militia had been more or less officially engaged by Spanish police organizations, which could take their pick among the many refugees who had come into Spain. By routes that led from southern Germany to northern Italy, they had managed to reach the Iberian peninsula and from there some of them had left for South America. In Madrid there were to be seen s.s. men or *oustachis* under their leader Ante Pavelitch; the famous Otto Skorzeny, who was soon to set up his engineering firm, with offices in the Calle Montera; a great many French veterans of the Legion of French Volunteers against Bolshevism (Rodolphe Bibé, the Abbé Jean-Marie Perrot, Captain Koptev), some former Vichy ministers such as Abel Bonnard, who had come over with Laval but had been granted permission to reside in Spain; and such men as Bodiguet, head of the Perpignan *Milice*, Baron Darquier de Pellepoix, who had exercised control over sequestrated Jewish firms, and the Belgian Léon Degrelle, whose presence drew a protest from Foreign Minister Spaak on 3 May 1946. Franco felt strong enough to refuse extradition.

At the same time that it welcomed, and sometimes brought in, former Nazis, militiamen and collaborators, the regime did not hesitate to condemn and execute members of the resistance movement who had returned to Spain and were leading guerrilla groups. In the context of the time, this inevitably appeared as a flouting of international opinion. At the end of January ten prisoners, captured by the *Guardia Civil*, were executed in Madrid jail. The British Government protested vigorously, and also denounced the trial of thirty-seven Socialists, while the press of the whole world stigmatized Madrid's attitude; the regime, however, maintained its harshness, since with each execution it gave further proof of its own strength and the weakness of the Allies, demoralized its opponents and at the same time, as we have seen, created accomplices. Its procedure, of course, was irregular, to say the least; men arrested in the provinces were not even inscribed on any prison register, so that a prisoner would gain greatly if he could manage, after manifold approaches which were invariably costly, to be transferred to Madrid. Here, at least, his existence would be recognized.

In point of fact a prisoner was never safe. Manuel Castro Rodríguez, for instance, who was executed at Carabanchel in February 1946, had been arrested shortly after crossing the frontier, when he could not possibly have carried out any of the actions attributed to him. For thirteen days he had been severely beaten three times a day. A man could be charged with having served in the French Resistance or, it goes without saying, in the Republican army; he could be indicted with offences, such as plunder, which he could not possibly have committed since he was already in jail. The die was cast before judgement, and the subsequent stages of procedure were pure formality: Cristino García, who had fought with the *Forces Françaises de l'Intérieur*, was executed at Barcelona in February before his dossier had been sent back from Madrid. One might spend months in prison without appearing before a court, one might be granted a period of freedom under surveillance and then be re-arrested. The police took their time. If the man they were after was not at home, they would not keep watch for him, but would allow him to remain in hiding for a while and when, reassured by a lull in police activity, he re-emerged, they would arrest him, detain him, release him and, before long, re-arrest him. Many a Spaniard who had been in prison from 1939 to 1943 might be condemned to death, reprieved, released under surveillance and re-arrested five times between 1944 and 1949. For such men this meant sleepless nights and anxious days, and above all the impossibility of doing a job.

All the jails were full, although new ones had been built everywhere. There were about 150 big prisons in Spain in 1946, and about 200,000 prisoners, not counting those who had been provisionally released and were in *libertad vigilada* (freedom under surveillance). Seven thousand men were crammed into the provincial prison of Carabanchel, 5,000 in that of Yserias where they had barely forty centimetres sleeping space each. There were 10,000 in Barcelona, 2,000 at Tarragona, 10,000 in Valencia, 20,000 in the Asturias, of whom over 8,000 were in the Cote prison. Two thousand women were held in each of the jails of Ventas, Claudio Coello and Quiñones. There were overcrowded prisons at Alcalá, Getafe, Torryos, Santa Rita, San Antón, Ventas Comendadores, Vallecas and Tetuan. Tuberculosis, exanthematic typhus, hunger and brutal treatment took their toll. There were the 10,000 people in seven labour battalions, numbered 91 to 97 (three stationed in Morocco), who worked from seven in the morning till eleven at night on road-making or prison building, or on the railway between Burgos and Madrid. There were the 300,000 people whose liberty was restricted and who had to present themselves to the police every week; and all those who kept quiet because they were afraid of being caught uttering subversive remarks, and knew that plain clothes detectives were stationed in all public places. The whole of Spain was in *libertad vigilada* in that post-war period, when in most neighbouring countries, after years of silence and fear, people were experiencing the joy of being able to talk aloud of anything to anyone.

Such surveillance exercised over a whole country required a large personnel and a considerable outlay. In 1946 the expenditure on the armed forces represented 62 per cent of the national budget; the army consisted of 500,000 men, together with 150,000 foreign volunteers, 50,000 native troops and 40,000 Foreign Legionaries, on all of whom the regime could rely. The *Guardia Civil* numbered 112,500 equally staunch supporters. The armed figures of these Civil Guards standing motionless by the roadside, pacing through the city streets or keeping watch over the fields, symbolized Spain. The credits allocated to the police force in 1946 were higher than those assigned to the three Ministries of Agriculture, Industry and Trade put together. The *Dirección General de la Guardia Civil* was granted the equivalent of $50,000,000 for its surveillance over villages and rural districts. These traditional bodies were supported by political police forces subordinate to the *Comisaría General de Orden Público*, or the *Sección de Política Interna*, or the *Dirección General de Seguridad*. The latter organization, directed by Lieutenant-Colonel F. Rodríguez Martínez, was the best known; its headquarters, a brick building five storeys high, stood by the Puerta del Sol in Madrid, and every Spaniard knew that underneath the building there were a large number of cells in which detainees were 'prepared' for interrogation.

Professional soldiers and policemen enjoyed direct advantages which bound them to the regime. True, policemen were poorly paid (an average of less than 800 pesetas), but there were bonuses to whet their zeal: supplementary rations of food (oil, for instance), a privilege in that hungry land – on a small scale indeed, but enough to bind them to the social order that conferred authority on them, and which they embodied with arrogance and pride and that boundless self-confidence that most men feel who acquire the right to dispose of others' lives almost as they choose. There was swift promotion in the army, and the chance of using discretionary powers to obtain important advantages. In the rich region of Castellón, market gardeners who brought vegetables and fruit to the city were stopped at the gates and obliged to sell their produce immediately, at set rates, to a tradesman who would then sell it again in town at seven or eight times the price, sharing out the profit with the authorities responsible for price control, officers or policemen who thus used their power with the dual aim of maintaining their personal power and that of the regime which ensured it and which they protected by protecting themselves.

If in the last resort Francoism derived its strength from these military and police forces and the repression **they** exercised, it is also clear that the very existence of these forces, their capacity to maintain cohesion and achieve efficiency, their loyalty to the man and the regime reveal that Francoism was *something other* than the ephemeral dictatorship of a group or a man, was in fact the political expression of the economic and social situation in Spain. Now this basic fact about Francoism raised political problems which, in 1946, the opposition did not always grasp or analyse correctly.

Political Analysis of Francoism in 1946: the Choice Before the Opposition

To large sectors of the opposition, in fact, the Caudillo's regime appeared as a Fascist regime in the direct line of those of Hitler and Mussolini. The international conditions that had prevailed during the Civil War, the aid given by Italy and Germany to the Nationalists, then the world conflict and the many bonds forged by Franco with Mussolini and Hitler, finally the creation of a united front of the democracies and the Soviet Union against the dictators seemed to many exiles to confirm the identity of Francoism and fascism.

Yet Francoism, if examined closely – as we have already noted – as regards its appeal as a mass party, the role of youth, the attitude of the Church and the career of the Leader himself – reveals certain peculiar characteristics which, under a façade of fascism due to the period, make of it rather a *reactionary movement of classic type*, expressing the interests of *all* the traditionally dominant strata. True, elements of the petty and middle bourgeoisie joined, and led, the Republican side, but in traditional backward Spain, with its landlords and its feudalism, they were only a minority, and a geographically restricted one, being found chiefly in Catalonia. Once the political representatives of these social categories had been liquidated – by exile, imprisonment or death – two forces remained face to face in Franco's Spain. On one side were the propertied classes (the new bourgeoisie who had grown suddenly rich through illicit trading and corruption, together with the big landowners), a middle bourgeoisie linked to the regime (civil servants and army men), and a stratum associated with authority (the police and so forth). On the other side was the mass of peasants and workers, suffering severely from poverty and totally deprived of political cadres after seven years of repression. A few groups of intellectuals and liberals, in isolation, had striven to survive ever since 1939, oppressed and despairing.

Now in 1946 this social structure and its political implications could not have led to a 'democratic' solution, such as had followed fascism in Italy. There was literally no social stratum capable of envisaging the replacement of Francoism by a democracy of Western type, uniting political and public liberties, parliamentary government and capitalism.

The propertied classes were petrified with fear lest any change in the regime should lead to revenge by those defeated in 1939 and to social revolution. At the same time the groups in opposition, misled by the 'Fascist' appearances of Francoism, clamoured for *democracy*, which, we must repeat, presupposed the existence of social strata other than the peasantry and the proletariat to support it. Now such strata did not exist. The opposition was thus in a hopeless situation unless it sought Socialist revolution, that is to say the overthrow not of Francoism but of the social bloc which supported it; but this path, already suggested by some people in 1936, was a blind alley in 1946. Spain, through her geographical situation, was in the Western camp; moreover, who in Spain was going to bring about the Socialist revolution? The Republican and Socialist Parties wanted a parliamentary democracy in the line of that Second Republic which they were trying to keep alive in Mexico City or in Paris. The Communist Party line now, as in 1936, was for unity of all democratic forces, on the model of what was happening in France and in Italy. The Spanish situation was radically different. Moreover, even the most determined Spanish revolutionaries were perfectly well aware that the watchword of Socialist revolution would make little appeal in their exhausted country, except as the starting point for a highly problematical 'long march'.

Thus the international context and the national situation combined, once more, to thwart Franco's opponents. They could not propose the only path which, in view of Spain's socio-economic structure, was *theoretically* possible – namely that of Socialist revolution, which was an impasse *in practice*. Thus they were confined to other impasses, theoretical and practical: either a democratic regime to replace Franco's, or a change of regime which might be Francoism without Franco. For the time being, now that fascism stood condemned by all and Franco, whom most people identified with fascism, shared in the opprobrium, opponents in exile and within Spain could not but hope, striving day after day to make ready to take over the succession of that regime which seemed near its end.

Anticipation

The Monarchists considered themselves the most favourably placed. After having tried to convince Franco (in 1943) and his supporters (in 1944) of the necessity for the restoration, they now turned towards Franco's opponents, who were united in the *Alianza Nacional de Fuerzas Democráticas*.

These Monarchists came from the groups which were the least committed to Francoism: from the former *Liga Regionalista Catalana* or the magazine *Acción Española*, which had been the focus for a number of intellectuals and writers, and they constituted a *Confederación de Fuerzas Monárquicas*. Their aim was, with the aid of the *Alianza*, to constitute a *Frente antifranquista*, which should prepare the restoration of the monarchy in the person of Don Juan. A plebiscite would give popular sanction to the project. This proposed solution was accepted only by the libertarian movement. Socialists and Republicans rejected it; it would oblige them to repudiate the Republican government in exile, heir to the pre-war Republic and, in their view, the sole legitimate government. The Communists, who had just joined the *Alianza*, had renounced the *Junta de Unión Nacional*, the moving spirit behind the guerrillas, and this indicates that their party, like those of the Socialists and Republicans, envisaged the fall of Franco as a result of intervention by the Allies.

On 9 February 1946, in fact, the General Assembly of the United Nations declared itself convinced that the government of General Franco, imposed by force with the aid of the Axis powers, did not represent the Spanish people and rendered impossible the participation of the latter in international affairs. The French government, in a diplomatic note to the Big Three on 27 February, stated that Franco's government represented a menace to European peace, declared itself ready to bring the matter before the Security Council, and announced the closure of the Pyrenean frontier as from 1 March 1946.

A new step had thus been taken. Among Spanish exiles, excitement was at fever pitch, and rumours, conversations and bargaining with diplomats had never been so continual or so lively. There was talk of a transference of power from Franco to Don Juan. The latter had settled in Portugal, a few hours' journey by road from Madrid. He was living there at Belver, on the Estoril heights, constantly visited by messengers and go-betweens. José Maria de Oriol tried to bring together Don Juan and the Caudillo. Others, including the secretary of the *Alianza Nacional de Fuerzas Democráticas* – who was also political secretary of the C.N.T. – tried to put forward a coherent transitional programme which went so far as to admit that each group should accept the result of a plebiscite, whether this favoured monarchy or a republic. Meanwhile Don Juan was sailing about in his yacht, the *Saltillo*, making use of the talks held by certain Monarchists with the Republicans as a new (although classic) means of putting pressure on Franco, but the latter did not give way. Far from it, he maintained his firm grasp on the country. In spite of protests from London, arrests and executions went on without remission. Franco's traditional backers did not fail him. On 27 February, the very day when France sent her diplomatic Note, the Vatican announced that the Primate of Spain had been admitted to the College of Cardinals. This, of course, was an internal affair of the Church, but the Primate declared: 'We must let the voice of our crusade ring out. . . . In presence of such a fact as our crusade, we cannot deny today what we asserted yesterday.'

On 1 March 1946, the French government did in fact close the Pyrenean frontier. Was this a decisive step towards intervention and stern measures or, as had happened in 1935–9 with sanctions against Fascist Italy,[2] a futile gesture, a mere pretence of action?

From Churchill's Speech to the Declaration by the Big Three

It may be that Largo Caballero, who died in Paris that month as a result of his experiences in Nazi concentration camps, believed – like many other exiles, like most readers of those newspapers that showed French gendarmes and Civil Guards confronting one another across a lowered barrier – that Franco, once he was shut up with the Spanish people, was bound to succumb. In fact the blockade could not be a total one. Even apart from exchanges kept up with Britain and the United States, there was always the frontier with Portugal, and Salazar's Portugal was a loyal ally, a regime whose legitimacy nobody disputed and which therefore had every facility for trading with the world and with Spain.

Above all, barely four days after the closure of the frontier, an event took place which seemed quite unrelated to the Spanish situation, yet which proved to the Caudillo that he had made no mistake, that whatever the exiles in Mexico or Paris or the Monarchists in Estoril might think, all was not lost. This was the famous speech made by Winston Churchill at Fulton on 5 March, in which he warned the world against the Communist danger, which must be contained behind an 'iron curtain'. True, Churchill no longer had any governmental responsibilities; but by speaking thus to the United States he showed himself yet again a prophet of things to come. That speech, triggering off the cold war, was more important for the future of Spain than was the closing of the Pyrenean frontier. How could the Caudillo be driven out, when he had been foretelling for years – to Churchill himself, in 1944 – that the time would come when the West must unite against the Red peril? After the Fulton speech, the Madrid papers, which reported it fully, stressed the fact that the British statesman had echoed the Caudillo's ideas.

On 1 April 1946, Franco celebrated with even greater pomp and ceremony than on previous years the Day of Glorious Victory, with a grand military march past in Madrid, on the Avenida de la Castellana, where the Black Arrow Fascists and the Germans of the Condor Legion had paraded in 1939. Today, only Spanish detachments marched past. The Falange itself, for the first time since 1939, took no part in the parade; but the essential thing was that the regime still stood, that Franco – somewhat stouter and squatter, no longer saluting with out-stretched arm but standing on the dais, surrounded by the dignitaries of the Church, the army and civic bodies – was still the Caudillo.

He had recently, on 6 March, settled the composition of the Cortes, which

[2] M. Gallo, *L'Affaire d'Ethiopie aux origines de la guerre mondiale* (Paris, 1967).

comprised his nominees (members by right, or 'elected'), the representatives of all the hierarchies of traditional Spain: prelates, generals, landed proprietors. This was the Spain on which he could rely, as also on the troops that marched past. True, the Norwegian Parliament on 6 March expressed its disapproval of his regime; true, on 8 March the U.S.S.R. agreed to have the Spanish question brought before the United Nations, while France asked the United States and Britain to declare an embargo on oil for Spain. After the gloomy summer of 1943, after the *noche negra* of 1944 and 1945, now that Churchill had spoken and the American press referred with increasing unanimity and frequency to the danger of communism, how could the Caudillo lose heart? On the contrary, within the country, and for the first time since 1939, despair seemed to grip those who, even after the fall of Madrid and that of Paris, had held firm, those who had gone on fighting and had taken fresh heart after 1943.

The Caudillo could salute his parading troops with confidence. Next day, 2 April, the paper *Arriba* headlined over a whole page: 'Franco's Catholic Victory. Magnificent religious unanimity of the crowd. The Catholic voice speaks out loud and free. Increased vitality and progress towards the achievement of an integrally Catholic life.'

Yet official hostility to Francoism did not abate. On 4 April 1946, the British, French and American governments published a common declaration on the subject of Spain. It showed no indulgence towards the Caudillo. It referred to the absolute lack of freedom and the use of harsh repressive measures preventing all normal political activity in Spain. It condemned the Spanish government for obstinately seeking to perpetuate intolerable rules. At the same time the three ministers – Bidault, Bevin and Byrnes – clearly indicated their hope that leading patriots and liberals should find some means to secure Franco's peaceful withdrawal; following which they envisaged a provisional government under which the Spanish people could freely define the political regime that seemed to them best, and elect their own representatives. This was a firm, uncompromising declaration, condemning Franco's regime as well as the activities of the *guerrilleros*, inviting all opposition groups, from Republicans to Monarchists, to unite to form a transitional government, and clearly implying that there was to be no Allied intervention in Spain. It was up to the Spaniards themselves to settle the problem of Francoism in a *peaceful* fashion.

How? And what if the Caudillo refused to retire? The declaration gave no answer to these two vital questions. It assumed that Franco would retire of his own accord, unable to face the world-wide disapproval represented by the Great Powers and the United Nations.

Diplomatic pressure was undeniably strong. On 5 April Rumania broke off relations with Spain. On the 6th Poland recognized Giral's Republican Government as the only one representing Spain. In fact, with the significant entry of the Communist Santiago Carrillo into Giral's cabinet, the latter now represented all the opposition forces (except the Monarchists) united and thus corresponding to the wishes of the three Western Powers.

On 13 April Yugoslavia, in her turn, broke off diplomatic relations with Spain; on the 27th Bulgaria followed suit. Moreover, since 17 April the Security Council had been considering the Spanish question. The Polish delegate, Oscar Lange, denounced the Caudillo's regime as a threat to peace: German scientists, he said, were working in Spain on the atomic bomb. The discussion was abortive, because obviously – as the declaration of the Big Three made quite clear – none of the major Western Powers was anxious to intervene in Spain. In a highly traditional fashion, harking back to the old habits of the League of Nations, the Security Council set up a sub-committee to deal with the Spanish question (29 April); which, in the language of international conferences, invariably means the more or less prolonged shelving of a problem which they are unable or unwilling to solve. This sub-committee had to present its solution by the autumn. The problem remained, since the Caudillo seemed less than ever ready to retire. Inaugurating the electrified Madrid–Avilá–Segovia railway line, he declared: 'If our goodwill is misunderstood and if we cannot live looking outward from Spain, we will live looking inward.' The press – like that of Mussolini at the time of the 1936 sanctions – extolled Spain's proud isolation, her courage in the face of international pressure, and began a great campaign on the theme of nationalism.

However, little by little, as time elapsed – a year had already gone by since the end of the war in Europe – the Spaniards became convinced that nothing could change. For some, this strengthened their attachment to the regime which protected them without exposing them; for others it meant a mounting tide of scepticism and discouragement, proportionate to the height of their earlier hopes.

The regime, moreover, seemed never to have been so sure of itself. Speaking on 14 May 1946, the Caudillo proudly asserted the violent sources of his power: 'Revolutions and civil wars', he said, 'are the creators of history and the origin of the majority of states.' Furthermore, and this gives some idea of his self-assurance, he replied to all those – the United Nations and the Big Three – who had accused him of having conquered Spain with the help of the Axis that this was precisely what was happening throughout Europe: that 'the states now being constituted in the invaded regions owed their existence to foreign victory and to the protection of the forces that had liberated them.'

This was not the speech of a defendant, of a leader threatened with collapse, but on the contrary the proclamation of a man aware that time was on his side, observing that, whether over the question of Trieste or that of Poland or Czecho-slovakia, tension between East and West had been mounting ever since the Fulton speech. He had to hold firm, so he went on speechifying, declaring that Spain had nothing in common with the totalitarian states and that she was being attacked, not by other nations but by the 'two fronts of Western sectarianism and Asiatic communism'. Nevertheless, added the Caudillo, echoing the pious and prophetic language of Mgr Blanco Najera, 'Spain will always be where truth and reason are'. Hostility to Spain came from 'the sectarian policy of the groups that have taken possession of the news media'; it was 'the permanent achievement of Pharisees, the Barrabas of a deceived multitude'.

The Caudillo thus counterattacked vigorously; and who could have prevented him, now that the *guerrilleros* – abandoned, isolated, hunted down – had been gradually exterminated, and his political opponents had become bogged down in fruitless negotiations? These negotiations, in fact, were all directed towards post-Franco Spain, neglecting the crucial stage of the Caudillo's fall, which it was assumed must inevitably follow from the pressure of the Great Powers, whereas these refused to use any weapons other than moral ones.

Moreover, Franco had nothing to fear from the real Spain which, under his surveillance, lived for the most part from day to day, incapable of exerting any influence on political issues.

Spain 1946–1947

True, hunger was less acute in Spain now, but in some regions, and in parts of the cities, men were still eating acorns and carobs; at least 17 per cent of the people were still illiterate, and moreover, this national average is misleading, since the percentage in the south was enormously higher. At least 50 per cent of the working population were still peasants, and that always meant poor peasants; 5 million farms out of just over 6 million were less than one hectare in area. The product of a hectare varied, according to the degree of irrigation, between 750 and 150 pesetas per annum. There were still those rural masses (almost 40 per cent) who owned nothing at all: day labourers begging for jobs from the 9,000 big landowners who possessed more than 20 per cent of the cultivated land, the best in Spain; agricultural workers, recruited every morning by the bailiff who came to inspect them in the village square and choose the strongest and most docile, earned two pesetas for twelve hours' work, while a peasant who worked his own land might get from it less than one peseta per day. In cities, a brewery worker earned five pesetas per day, workers employed on the construction of a dam ten pesetas for a ten-hour day. Here nobody complained: employers did not require one to produce papers, and men who had been in prison or who were wanted by the police, and therefore found it hard to get work, accepted this wretched wage. In any case, if they protested, there were truckloads of peasants from Almería who earned nothing at all at home and for whom these ten pesetas were a fortune. A skilled workman, a mechanic for instance, might earn up to twenty pesetas. The police were better off, although their 500 to 800 pesetas a month was not a princely wage. Bread cost 12 to 17 pesetas a kilo, oil 27, sugar 60, coffee 80, lentils 20, maize flour 14. True, there were trade unions, which had even been organized in detail on 20 June 1946, but being by law officially in the hands of the Falangists they had no power. Men survived by plying various trades at once, sometimes by illicit trafficking. Poverty and the day's worries were too burdensome, surveillance was too close, the repression had been too strong and the need to work was too great, for political action to be envisaged, when no result was foreseeable, especially after the heroic but vain attempts of 1945. Sometimes the employees of a particular firm might attempt a protest, or a trade guild – the road sweepers of Barcelona for instance – might start to take action, but repression followed immediately. The simplest punishment, and the severest, was dismissal. There was always somebody starving, ready to take up the job.

The peasants went on crowding into the city suburbs to escape from the destitution of the overpopulated countryside and the paralysis of their age-old oppression. Wooden shanties sprang up in the waste ground around Madrid; families crowded into caves in the hillside, such as the Calle Cea Bermúdez, where refuse from the markets was frequently discharged. Other cities besides Madrid – Pampeluna, Barcelona, Granada, Seville and Valencia – were afflicted by this leprous growth, so revealing of the state of things. The extent of the country's poverty can be measured by the fact that the cost of living had almost quadrupled between 1936 and 1946 whereas wages had only doubled. Often, during this post-war period, factories would stop for lack of electricity, and wages would be reduced to two days' pay a week.

This was not the whole of Spain. There were corridas, too: Manolete could earn his 100,000 pesetas a day, firing the imagination of the excitable young peasants who, at peril of their lives, tried to prove their courage on cattle ranches, driven by hunger to seek that *moment of truth*[3] that would bring fortune or death. Crowds flocked to watch Manolete or the Mexican matador Arruza. Religious fiestas were still held in 1946 as they had always been, in Seville and Toledo; while in the sunbaked city streets water-vendors went to and fro, and street-urchins, *pilletes*, peddled their wares and ran away from the police. For the regime, determined to impose morality, had recruited policemen who received no wages but who were entitled to keep back one half of the goods they confiscated or the fines they imposed. The black market, hitherto anarchical, was now concentrated in a few hands. In some places, swimming pools were closed down because public bathing was considered indecent; elsewhere others were opened under the supervision of the clergy. Cinema showings were suddenly interrupted so that the police might surprise lovers embracing under cover of the darkness; a young man would be rebuked for putting an arm round his girl friend's shoulders, *a fortiori* round her waist – Spanish decorum must be maintained; morality must prevail, like order, in the Spain of 1946. Stendhal's *The Charterhouse of Parma* and Flaubert's *Salammbô* were banned, because they were liable to disturb both order and morality; the press, still heavily censored, reported only anodyne or edifying news and sports results.

In point of fact, during the years 1945 to 1947 Spain combined the typical features of economic underdevelopment with the authoritarian political forms by which its social consequences were intensified to the advantage of the privileged classes. Within the order thus maintained, a rapid accumulation of capital took place, investments increased and so did the profits of many firms. The export of agricultural products from hungry Spain to Europe, where everything was in short supply, enabled big landowners to swell their revenues. In 1940 there had been 434 firms with a capital of 1,119 million pesetas; in 1945 there were over 900, with almost 3,000 million. Moreover these businesses had benefited by German investments which, according to the United States government, represented $95 million, over $80 million of these being placed in Spanish firms (45 million in private concerns, 35 million in *Sofindus*, the official German company), and 15 million in various official sectors. On 15 May 1946, the

[3] The title of a remarkable film by Francesco Rosi (1965) which gives a fascinating analysis of Spain.

Caudillo decided to block all German credits in order to avoid action by the Allies, but a collaboration was soon established between Spanish organizations and the Joint Trusteeship.

These aspects of economic life explain the increased social preponderance, and the political loyalty to the regime, of the Spanish propertied classes, which were wholly unaffected by the destitution that surrounded them. Indeed, the bonds between political power and economic power were such that political authority contributed, directly or indirectly, to increasing wealth. When the National Institute of Colonization bought up the estates of great landowners, it was not unusual for the latter to make a profit both on the selling price to the government and on the purchase price, since, through different middlemen or simply by means of usurious loans to peasants who were constrained to purchase, the same landowners immediately, or after a few years, recovered the lands they had just sold.

For these privileged classes, the political regime then in force was the best possible, now that the risk of its collapse had diminished. They leaned on it, and at the same time they supported it; there was no real reason why they should cease to identify themselves with it.

Under the circumstances, the man who was still sometimes described as 'Franco the African' could sit back and wait for the end of the international crisis, in his palace of El Pardo, chatting with his few intimate friends, Father Leopold María de Castro (his confessor) or Dr Cabestán, his private physician. Sheltered by the strictest etiquette, protected by 4,000 men of the Moorish Guard, he could indulge in his favourite pastimes, painting and hunting. He even wrote the scenario of a film, *Raza*, and visited the studio regularly to watch the shooting. Reigning in untroubled sovereignty, maintaining control over all those Spaniards who had, or who had ever had, political ambitions, he could make or unmake their careers, and condemn them to gilded but irrevocable oblivion. He must have read with a certain irony, in the memoirs of Serrano Suñer, published in Switzerland in 1947 under the title *Between the Pyrenees and Gibraltar*, the account of a conversation between the then all-powerful Foreign Minister and the late Duce. 'What preoccupies me in regimes of Fascist type', Suñer had said, being consumed with personal ambition, 'is the problem of succession. ... I assure you that I cannot envisage this prospect without real anxiety and a certain curiosity.' 'If the system is really powerful, it will engender its own successor,' the Duce had replied. In Spain, in 1946 and 1947, it seemed that the Caudillo's successor could only be the Caudillo.

Yet some people still believed that an ultimatum from the Allies would be enough to overthrow the whole regime. Suñer himself wrote, about 1946: 'At the present moment – and for how much longer? ... [the regime] is a mere scaffolding of power, a powerful *de facto* set-up which, confronted with disorder and catastrophe, keeps a whole people clinging to its traditions and its hopes, but whose political form is still non-existent and undeveloped.'

If Francoism was a mere scaffolding, it was difficult not to believe that the hostility of the Great Powers would overthrow it. Once again, during the summer and autumn of 1946, Franco's opponents were over-sanguine.

Negotiations Over the Succession

The crucial conversations were those that took place between the Monarchists of the *Confederación de Fuerzas Monárquicas* and the Republicans, now all united in the *Alianza Nacional de Fuerzas Democráticas*. Their problem was to define the characteristics of a transitional government, since the Allies, without whom they were powerless, recommended this formula. In this case what would become of Giral's Republican Government, the only legitimate one? There was sharp tension between the *Alianza* and the Giral Government. Finally the *Alianza* accepted the idea of a plebiscite, to define the future regime, and also expressed its hostility to any attempt to restore the monarchy without obtaining the nation's approval (December 1946). Thus, in point of fact, the opposition gave up the Republican *sine qua non* and, without explicitly saying so, accepted all the recommendations (which were demands) of the Western Big Three. The Communist Party itself took up the same position, or did not openly repudiate it; the fall of Francoism was the essential thing, and it seemed imminent.

By accepting participation – even with reservations, and retaining its own objectives – in the Giral Government, the Communist Party cancelled out all its overt efforts to promote armed struggle within Spain itself. The party's organization, though still more powerful than any other, was affected by a fresh crisis. Leaders outside the country directed the political line, which was all the harder to follow because the conditions of underground work made discussion impossible, and in the name of Marxism–Leninism issued denunciations of past errors which might be tomorrow's truths. Thus for instance the new leader of the organization inside Spain, Jesús Monzón, was accused of failing to understand the role of the masses in the people's struggle. Actually these crises, these shifts of policy, these accusations were evidence of the general impotence of the opposition confronting Francoism.

This opposition, moreover, must inevitably suffer from the change in the international situation, which was to Franco's advantage. On 4 June Perón was elected President of the Argentine Republic, and on 30 October an important agreement was signed between his country and Spain: Perón granted Madrid a credit of 350 million Argentine pesos and dispatched large quantities of wheat. For hungry Spain, suffering from a partial blockade, this was an important success, which triggered off a press campaign of nationalistic type about Hispanic solidarity and the acknowledged greatness of Spain. During the summer, while Christian-Democrats triumphed in the Italian elections, while atomic bombs exploded at Bikini, and while in the Soviet Union Zhdanov called the intellectuals to order, civil war broke out again in Greece (1 September) with sporadic armed clashes between the two sides. On 23 November in Indo-China French troops bombarded Haiphong. On 25 December, fighting between Communists and Nationalists broke out again in China. All these convergent facts affected Spain indirectly. Coming a few months after Churchill's Fulton speech, they heralded the opening of the cold war between the Western world and the Communist world; and they strengthened Franco's position.

The development thus clearly initiated had not yet revealed all its consequences in every sector of international life. Thus at the United Nations, after many delays, the Spanish question was at last to be discussed, and some people believed that this was the start of a process which must lead to action against the Caudillo. In fact, despite appearances, it was the close of a long period of illusions which had opened during the years 1942–3.

The Last Scene: the Resolution of the General Assembly of the United Nations (13 December 1946)

In Spain, the meeting of the United Nations was awaited with tense anxiety. Some Falangists were panic-stricken; those who were too closely involved with the regime talked of escaping to Portugal or the Argentine. Conversely, the hopes of the opposition rose to fever pitch. Through the foreign radio it was learnt that Tom Connally, the United States delegate, had stigmatized Franco's Government, 'imposed by force' and of Fascist character. He recommended that General Franco should hand over power to a provisional government respectful of democratic liberties. His tone was violent, his conclusion weak (what if Franco refused to hand over?), but at that time in Spain the tension was too great for these nuances to be perceptible. Franco's opponents had waited too long not to clutch at this last chance. News from the United Nations was expected about midnight on 13 December. City streets had emptied; in Madrid, the Gran Vía was deserted, and moreover darkened because of lighting restrictions.[4] The regime had taken its precautions; the city was in an unofficial state of siege. Machine-guns were at the ready, embassies were guarded, public buildings occupied. The Caudillo was a prudent soldier, and even when there was nothing to fear he acted as though danger were imminent. On the Avenida de la Castellana, soldiers and policemen were posted in every doorway. Everyone waited for the United Nations communiqué. Franco told one of his ministers: 'I spent the afternoon painting. Really, I enjoy painting more every day.'

Those who nourished hopes and illusions were in a different frame of mind. Gathering in groups at some friend's home, they waited for the news. At last the communiqué came. It censured Franco severely:

'In origin, nature, structure and general conduct, the Franco regime is a Fascist regime patterned on, and established largely as a result of aid from Hitler's Nazi Germany and Mussolini's Fascist Italy. . . . Incontrovertible documentary evidence establishes that Franco was a guilty party with Hitler and Mussolini in the conspiracy to wage war against those countries which eventually in the course of the World War became banded together as the United Nations.'

The General Assembly 'recommends that if within a reasonable time there is not established a government which derives its authority from the consent of the governed . . . the Security Council consider that adequate measures to be taken in order to remedy the situation.'

Meanwhile it recommended member nations to withdraw their ambassadors from Madrid. This measure had its symbolic and moral importance, but for those, who for years, had been expecting an ultimatum, it seemed a trivial

[4] J. Hermanos, op. cit.

gesture. For them, this 'reasonable time' was a cruelly ironic phrase which told them harshly what they had not dared admit to themselves, that they had to face Francoism alone. Most of them gave up the struggle, absorbing themselves in the affairs of daily life if they were not too heavily compromised to be able to pursue them; others chose to carry on the struggle till death. On the underground press of the students' organization U.F.E.H. they produced an anonymous book of poetry, *Pueblo Cautivo*, which contains the lines:

> *Un día más transcurre.*
> *Aún podemos seguir llamándonos esclavos.*[5]

Discouragement affected not only the small groups of militants, but also all those who had believed that the United Nations Assembly might bring new life to Spain. That belief made their disappointment all the harder to bear. The regime, meanwhile, was stronger than ever.

Very skilfully, that December, it appealed exclusively to national pride, mortified by the way foreign nations had sought to dictate to Spain what course she should follow. Its propaganda found an echo outside the circles traditionally loyal to the regime. Falangists went round recruiting signatures; and they got them. Leaflets and posters proclaimed that Spain would never be a colony. A mass demonstration was arranged in Madrid, and this fact alone shows that the regime felt strong enough to assemble several hundred thousand people in the streets for a purpose other than to watch a military march-past. It proves that Franco's propaganda had achieved its aim. Of course, the demonstration was well organized. Everyone had to go to his place of employment and thence, under the guidance of a Falangist delegate, to the Plaza de Colón. Then the crowd would move in procession towards the Royal Palace, where Franco was to make a speech. Some two or three hundred thousand people – some convinced and enthusiastic, some reluctant, driven by fear or discouragement or national pride – assembled and acclaimed Franco in one of the very few great public ceremonies in which he had been willing to take part. 'We should need the whole land of Spain,' he said, 'for this immense demonstration of enthusiasm. ... It is the most categorical answer to those who, from outside, are speculating clumsily on your loyalty and on our internal peace. ...' He denounced Red domination, yesterday over Spain and today over a dozen nations. 'The world situation,' he concluded, 'and its shames give even more meaning to our glorious crusade. We must think of what would have happened without it. ... To the great strength of our reason let us join the strength of our unity. With these and with God's protection nobody, nothing can sabotage our victory.' Newspapers and films made the most of the demonstrations; in every provincial town similar ceremonies were organized. In Seville, Queipo de Llano urged all Spaniards to prepare to transform their country into 'a second Numantium' should foreigners seek to invade it.

There had never been any question of this and, like Mussolini at the time of the purely formal sanctions imposed by the League of Nations, Franco encountered an insignificant danger with a show of resistance intended primarily to

[5] 'Another day goes by, and we can call ourselves slaves'.

unite in his support, on the basis of nationalism, the largest possible number of Spaniards. Thus, while the ambassadors of various countries were leaving Madrid – all except the Papal Nuncio and the representatives of Portugal and Switzerland – when Franco's regime had apparently never been so isolated, it was in fact nearing the end of a difficult period. It had survived. Now it could once again take the initiative.

Disintegration of the Opposition

In the first place, because the opposition was disintegrating, men who had stood firm since the end of the Civil War suddenly gave up and turned their thoughts towards emigration. The police – many of whom had experienced a fear as great as the hopes of their adversaries – intensified their violence. The regime realized that it had weathered a dangerous cape and could now act as it pleased. In the Plaza de Cuatro Caminos and the Plaza de la Cibeles, in the Plaza de Cataluña in Barcelona, raids and arrests were made, houses were forcibly entered, affrays and manhunts took place. During the last few days before the United Nations decision some people had been rash; now they paid for it. The regime was determined to crush the opposition, once and for all, to have done with these stubborn cells of resistance. At the same time the authorities felt themselves strong enough to allow a certain number of conditional releases. Trials and executions went on unremittingly. On 9 January 1947, there began in Madrid the trial of fourteen persons accused of belonging to the *Alianza Nacional de Fuerzas Democráticas*. It was a political trial, publicly announced if not held in public, since the regime now had no hesitation about facing world opinion. When some witness seemed likely to prove an embarrassment – such as the Francoist General Aranda, a Monarchist charged with having maintained political contact with the accused – he was prevented from giving evidence and exiled to Majorca. In the sierras, the army set about liquidating the last groups of *guerrilleros*, mainly anarchist. In March several of them, including Amador Franco and Antonio Lopez, were shot. In April the whole of the underground committee of the *Federación Universitaria Española* (F.U.E.), which had been reconstituted by a group of very young men, were rounded up as the result of an act of betrayal. The police did not hesitate to search the premises of the Lycée Français in Madrid, although its status, while not actually conferring diplomatic immunity, did provide a certain *de facto* independence. The police disregarded this, for circumstances were largely in their favour.

That same April, indeed, the division of the world became a *fait accompli*. The Moscow talks (10 to 24 April), which were to have discussed the peace treaty with reference to Germany, broke down. Already in March, Belgian Communists had been excluded from the government. In April the Communist Party was banned in New York State; in France, on 4 May, Communist ministers were dismissed. On 5 June came the proposals for the Marshall Plan; then, in another sector of the United States, the Taft-Hartley anti-strike law.

Spain could now proclaim herself justified, which her press did not fail to do. All these were cruel blows struck at an already enfeebled opposition, whose collapse coincided with the break-up of the wartime coalition. In February Giral had handed over to Llopis the leadership of the Republican Government in exile. This still included representatives of all tendencies, from Republicans to Communists, from Socialists to the Anarchists of the C.N.T.; but it was committed to opening negotiations with the *Confederación de Fuerzas Monárquicas*. The Big Three had thus obtained satisfaction. However, the talks led by the Socialist Trifón Gómez between March and May 1947 broke down. The Monarchists were now in a strong position. They envisaged the nascent cold war as favourable to their cause. They assumed that the great Anglo–Saxon allies would inevitably support them against a 'unitarian', and now anachronistic, government. So they went a step further in their demands, and refused to deal with the exiled Republican Government, now settled in Paris, although that government had made a considerable concession by initiating preliminary talks. On the other hand, the Monarchists made it known that they would be willing to discuss matters with the Socialists, which would in fact imply the end of the Republican Government in exile. In the spring of 1947 the Socialists were still reluctant to take this step.

Now, as the world fronts became more clearly outlined, the Communists, who were still represented in the exiled government, began to say out loud what they had always thought in secret. Their policy took a new turn. In a report presented to the third Plenum of the Party, held in Paris from 19 to 22 March 1947, Dolores Ibarruri declared:

'Neither the British imperialists nor the North American reactionaries wish for the re-establishment of the Republic in Spain, even of a moderate republic. They want to keep Spain in a particular situation of weakness and instability, with Franco or without Franco but with Francoism intact; with a king or a regency, or a military directory or a hybrid government; but without democracy, without liberty, without sovereignty.'

In certain sectors, in Spain, the Communists attempted to revive the guerrilla movement, and Lister, in his preface to the book *Las Guerrillas de Levante*,[6] writes that 'it is not by imploring the Chancelleries of London or Washington that an end can be brought to the horrible tragedy of the Spanish people'. Then he indicts those armchair strategists who think that the Francoist forces are too powerful for guerrilla warfare to develop, and gives as example the struggle against Napoleon in 1809, when the conqueror of all Europe was defeated in Spain. A further proof, if one was needed, of the political uncertainty of the opposition and of its incapacity in 1947, faced with the failure of its whole post-war strategy, to invent another, this appeal for guerrilla warfare when Francoism, as East–West hostility flared up, had never been so sure of its support, could lead only to fresh defeats.

Yet during the same period an event of capital importance took place, showing that opposition to Francoism could find wide support provided it retained contact with the realities of Spain. For the first time since the Civil War a strike broke out in Vizcaya. Starting in Bilbao on 1 May 1947, it lasted until 11 May, affecting almost 75 per cent of the workers in that vital mining and metallurgical

[6] Published in 1949.

region. The movement inaugurated by the *Consejo Vasco de la Resistencia* proved that the workers' fighting spirit was still alive. For the conditions of the struggle were extremely harsh. Hundreds of workers were arrested, some tortured, and countless police searches went on; the whole region was in a state of siege. Eventually 14,000 workers were dismissed. The fact remains that the strike did take place, the men had stood firm, and there was much to be learnt from it. It proved that when 'regional' (or Basque national) feeling combines with social demands (the workers' situation, as we have seen, was shocking) the political struggle against Francoism might succeed; but – and for the opposition this was the negative side of the event – the conflict was confined to one social group (the industrial workers) and one region (the Basque country), and hence was doomed to failure, or at best to partial success, without much general political significance.

Through the example of this 1947 strike we grasp how far the unequal development of Spain (the preponderance of agriculture, the localized character of industry) and above all the force of sectional interests (such as Basque national feeling) can thwart a united struggle against the central power, particularly as the opposition lacked any co-ordinating centre, any unity of views and aims. Thus, the regime could settle, one after the other, whatever problems might arise, and inflict certain defeat on adversaries who advanced in such disunity. So the Caudillo retained the initiative.

Franco's Initiative

His capacity for manoeuvring and his political skill were to be displayed in the spring of 1947 over the draft law on the succession.

On 1 April 1947, the anniversary of the Victory, Franco announced his intention of setting before the Cortes a declaration that Spain 'as a political unit was a Catholic state, social and representative', and that, in keeping with its tradition, it constituted a kingdom. This first article disarmed the Monarchists; but Article 2, immediately following, specified that the leadership of the state belonged to 'the Caudillo of Spain and of the Crusade, Generalísimo of the Armies, Francisco Franco y Bahamonde'.

In other words, the Caudillo was to remain absolute master until his death, while the restoration was postponed to an unspecified future. Furthermore, the Caudillo laid down the composition of a Council of the Realm which limited the powers of the future sovereign, and above all, he reserved the right to propose his successor to the Cortes, 'with the title of King or Regent', and having nominated him, to dismiss him at will. In short, the Caudillo remained the real sovereign for the present and also, so he hoped, for the future. Since he could choose and dismiss his successor he held an effective weapon to force claimants to bow to his will. A Council of Regency, consisting of the President of the Cortes, the highest ranking prelate in the Cortes, and the Captain General of the army, would substitute for the Caudillo should his position become vacant, and could propose his successor to the Cortes if he had not done so himself. This law was to be submitted to referendum, and here was the final stroke of skill: while paralysing the Monarchists and ensuring his own power, Franco would secure the people's support for it, thus disarming his opponents in the United Nations. Henceforward, it mattered little that Spain was excluded from the International Organization of Civil Aviation (14 May) or of Telecommunications (22 June); a unanimous vote by the whole country must command acceptance.

Of course, the Monarchists saw the danger of a law which recognized them only to deprive them of political significance. On 7 April Don Juan de Borbón, at Estoril, attacked Franco's proposal in a violent manifesto. The rules proposed for the succession to the crown, he wrote, were 'in formal contradiction with history. ... Let no one ask me to agree to actions totally contrary to my sacred duty, which is to safeguard rights that are not only the rights of the Crown but part of the spiritual heritage of our country.' However, there was little Don Juan could do; and on 13 April, in an interview with the *Observer*, he declared himself ready to come to an agreement with Franco, but with the sole purpose of ensuring a peaceful and unconditional transmission of power.

At the very moment when everything confirmed his triumph, the Caudillo was hardly likely to enter into negotiations with Don Juan. On 7 June the Cortes unanimously approved his project and an enthusiastic press announced the forthcoming plebiscite. The presence of Eva Perón in Spain (8 to 25 June) was made the occasion for great demonstrations, intended not only to thank the Argentine for sending wheat but also to show how the Caudillo's influence had spread to Spanish-speaking America. In Madrid, on the Plaza de Oriente, a mass demonstration was organized in honour of the wife of the Argentinian dictator: the Caudillo, naturally, standing by the side of the ex-actress. At the same time (22 June 1947) a decree specified the measures to be taken against anyone who abstained, under a law of 1907 stating that a certificate could be obtained from the polling station attesting that one had fulfilled one's electoral duties. Every Spaniard understood that a check would be made at the time of voting and that it would be difficult to evade doing one's duty. The referendum was fixed for 6 July. On the 4th the Caudillo broadcast an important speech. 'The law on the succession is not in the interest of any one faction,' he declared. 'It is a law in the service of the nation and in the general interest of all Spaniards.' He appealed to his people in emotional terms: 'I urge all Spaniards to vote for this law. ... Although the present of our fatherland is in my hands, I cannot serve it beyond death, its future thus rests in your hands. May God enlighten you at this hour!'

The Referendum of 6 July 1947

Governmental pressure for the referendum was vigorous and unremitting. The streets were strewn with leaflets calling on people to vote, the walls covered with posters. A pastoral letter to the same effect was published, and according to the Monarchist Ansaldo, the threat of refusal of absolution to those who said 'No' was frequently brandished. Everyone very quickly realized that, at the time of voting, each elector would have to present his ration card to be stamped, failing which the card would be invalid and not renewable. Then it was announced that civil servants who did not vote would get no pay, and furthermore that voting papers were to be filled up at home, which meant that on the day of the referendum it would be easy to pick out, either in the street or actually in the polling-booth, those who had decided to vote 'No'. Yet Anarchist organizations circulated leaflets pointing out:

> *Si votas SI votas por Franco*
> *Si votas NO votas por Franco*
> *Si NO votas votarán por ti*
> *pero no obtendrán tu voto*
> *No Votes!*[7]

Falangist veterans also urged people to abstain or to vote 'No', but their influence was negligible.

There was an enormous poll. Out of 17,178,812 electors 15,219,565 voted. In some polling-stations everyone who had voted was issued with a stamped certificate which had to be shown on pay-day. Long queues formed in front of the ballot boxes and the journalists of the whole world's press could watch, photograph and film the scene. Social pressure was felt everywhere, together with a general anxiety as to the personal consequences of a hostile vote. The weightiest factor was the feeling that there was nothing else to be done, that it was impossible to fight or to abstain either individually or collectively. This sense was particularly strong in the smaller localities, where the risk of discovery was greater. In large cities it was possible to vote 'No'; but this meant keeping the voting-paper folded in one's pocket while queuing at the ballot-box, resisting panic while those staunch supporters of the regime who had voted 'Yes' displayed their papers to all and sundry. There were thus 14,145,163 votes in favour, 722,656 against, and 336,592 spoilt papers; naturally, only supporters of the regime had been allowed to count the votes. The law on the succession was proclaimed on 20 July.

Eleven years almost to the day after the start of the Civil War, eight years after his victory, Franco had now given proof that the regime retained technical and political power over the country. International opinion as expressed through the Great Powers at the United Nations must take that reality into account: the Caudillo, whatever the conditions of his referendum may have been, had secured popular sanction. What did it matter if immediately afterwards, whereas the press and the radio waxed enthusiastic about the results, many Spaniards rashly admitted, as though to redeem themselves, that they had voted 'Yes' out of fear? The police did not bother about them, because the result was an enduring fact. History takes note of troubled consciences only when they are embodied in active political forces.

Thus, after its victory of 6 July 1947, Francoism was able to offer a useful democratic façade to those who desired one.

---

[7] 'If you vote YES you vote for Franco
If you vote NO you vote for Franco
If you don't vote they will vote for you
Yet they will not have had your vote
Don't vote!'

179

CHAPTER IV

THE SECOND VICTORY, AND ABSOLUTION

JULY 1947–1950

Franco's government had thus succeeded in securing the votes of 92 per cent of the Spanish people. Observers and adversaries were not taken in; but the fact remained. For those in opposition, and for the broad masses, it meant discouragement and disgust, or the confirmation of a conviction felt, though never expressed, by the very poor: politics could not alter their living conditions, their starvation wages, that confined existence which was the lot of most Spaniards. They buried themselves in their personal problems, which were too grave and exacting to be dispersed or modified by these political battles that never ended in victory but only made bitterer the defeat of 1939. If the opposition wanted the backing of the working masses, it would have to seek them out and speak to them of their crushing afflictions. That summer of 1947, republican Spain both at home and in exile was undergoing a crisis.

Crisis of the Republican Government in Exile; Franco's Game

It was clearer than ever, after the referendum, that the collapse of Franco's government, considered as an imminent goal, could be achieved only through the help and intervention of the Allies. Now the latter wanted a union of all 'liberal' anti-Francoists, which implied the inclusion of the Monarchists in the political plans of the exiled Republican government. Before the referendum, the Socialists had been hesitant. Now they took the decisive step; in July the *Partido Socialista Obrero Español* (P.S.O.E.) withdrew from that government in order to negotiate with the Monarchists and come to some agreement. This 'realistic' policy was an unquestionable surrender to the Monarchist demands, and it sealed the death of the Republican government. Anarchists, Communists, the *Partido Nacionalista Vasco* and the *Esquerra Republicana* also abandoned the government. Now, even though it still carried on under the presidency of the Republican Alvaro de Albornoz, it represented nothing; the Civil War era was at its end, and another Spain, with other problems, was gradually emerging.

Indalecio Prieto, Secretary-General of the P.S.O.E., represented a policy that attached importance to practical possibilities, and hence to the attitude of the Anglo–Saxon powers and to the cold war. Speaking on 7 August over the French radio he declared categorically: 'My solution to the Spanish problem consists in uniting all anti-Francoist Spaniards, both of the right and of the left, with two exceptions: Falangist totalitarianism and Communist totalitarianism. Only thus can we offer the United Nations the government they wish to see.' In September the P.S.O.E. issued an appeal to all opposition forces to renounce all *sine qua non* conditions, as he himself had done regarding Republican institutions. The Monarchists were thus invited to give up their demands for 'legitimacy'. This 'realistic' policy in fact neglected the essential factor: what interest could the Anglo–Saxon powers, now involved in the cold war, have in overthrowing Franco, since his departure would only entail upheavals which, once initiated, might prove difficult to control? We know by experience that morality, even on an international scale, weighs little on political decisions. Now the Franco government controlled Spain, ensured order, and above all was making ever more numerous advances to Washington.

The Caudillo, indeed, neglected nothing that might encourage the United States to adopt an equally realistic policy, one that would take Francoism seriously as the leading anti-Communist regime. In an interview with the correspondent of the Hearst press, that August, Franco demanded that Spain be treated on an equal footing with 'other countries, some of which were quite recently [America's] enemies', and added: 'If our country is small in size and in population, these characteristics are compensated by its strategic position in the world, the nobility and loyalty which our people have displayed throughout our history, and by the quality and sobriety of our men.' The approach was unmistakable: Franco was banking on the strategic and economic interests of the United Nations. He had the country in his grasp, he could afford to wait.

Meanwhile, Spanish exiles and hundreds of French intellectuals could celebrate, with fervent reverence, the fourth centenary of the birth of Cervantes, in the great amphitheatre of the Sorbonne, showing thereby that Spain still lived outside Spain; while in London the Labour leader Ernest Bevin endeavoured, from October 1947 onwards, to set on foot negotiations between Indalecio Prieto and the Monarchist Gil Robles. Such happenings had no genuine political significance. Don Juan moreover soon hinted that he was not really committed by the talks going on in London: this was a 'realistic' point of view, since the actual strength of Prieto's Socialists was negligible. It was a manoeuvre too, one which Don Juan had already tried out and was to use again, consisting in making use of the opposition without committing himself, in order to influence Franco's choice.

How could the Caudillo fail to feel that time was working for him, when each international event was another blow dealt to his adversaries? The creation of the Cominform, on 9 October, brought clear evidence of Communist pressure, and on 19 November – a further proof of the general political trend – the Communists were excluded from the Italian Government.

At the United Nations Assembly, too, the political situation had evolved in favour of Franco Spain. In November the minority opposed to anti-Franco measures rose from six to sixteen votes, including the highly significant vote of the United States, as well as those of Canada and Australia. Skilfully, the Caudillo encouraged the development of this trend. In a statement made in

November to the Brazilian daily *O Jornal* he hinted that Spain was ready to engage in a struggle against Bolshevism and that she was highly experienced in this respect.

In Spain itself the evolution of the international situation contributed in no small degree to the consolidation of Francoism. The Caudillo was seen by the various social strata and groups which supported him as the man who had succeeded in weathering a difficult cape without damage to himself or to those whom he symbolized. The anti-Bolshevism which had gradually come to pervade international life seemed to confirm the policy of the regime, and the press recalled that crusading Spain had been the first to wage war against Slav communism, that her leader had warned the West against that peril. In Barcelona in 1950, on the Ramblas and in the Plaza de Cataluña, great posters advertised the sale, in bookshops, of *Mein Kampf* and of Skorzeny's Memoirs.[1] The papers tirelessly quoted articles from the Anglo–Saxon (chiefly American) press stressing the importance of Franco for the Western world. On 6 November 1947, for instance, they reproduced an article from the *Washington Times Herald* which recalled that long before the rest of Europe and the United States had decided to oppose Stalin, the Spaniards had faced the problems of a terrible and devastating civil war. Stalin, it was said, had marked out Spain as a dependency of his domain, but fortunately for the world a great number of Spaniards had opposed communism so that Stalin should not succeed in having a doorway on to the Atlantic. 'Franco has fought for our cause. . . . If the United States have billions to put at the disposal of Britain's Socialists, billions for France, Germany, Italy, Greece, Turkey, etc., why should there not be a few millions for Spain?'

The Caudillo could afford to wait, and to go on ruling Spain as in the past, while conceding a few formal readjustments. Having reaffirmed that Spain was a kingdom, he could attend to the promulgation of a law (16 October) on titles and honours within that kingdom, a method of distributing titles of nobility to holders of office within the state and thereby binding them even closer to his power and to his person. He could, also, for the first time hold a public trial in Madrid, before a military tribunal (December 1947): the accused were twelve students and two members of the teaching staff of the French Lycée in Madrid, leaders of the *Federación Universitaria Española*, all young Spaniards of good social standing. The sentences were light: six months to three years in prison.[2] The regime could afford to show clemency in a public trial.

The stubborn *guerrilleros* who went on fighting, however, were mown down on the spot, and the Anarchists taken prisoner were executed without pity. In November 1948 the death sentence was passed on the C.N.T. militants José López and José González Puig; the former was shot immediately. Other members of the C.N.T. were court-martialled in January and February 1949: Marcos Nadal was condemned to death; the following November, López Penedo was condemned and executed in Barcelona, and Cruz Navarro in Saragossa. On 24 February 1950, Manuel Sabater Llopart was executed by *garrote* in the Barcelona jail for having

[1] Jacques Laurent Bost, *L'Espagne au jour le jour* (Paris, 1951).

[2] Three of those sentenced, Sánchez Albornoz, Manuel Lamana and Ignacio Faure Logarón, succeeded in escaping from the Cuelgamuros prison in 1948.

crossed the frontier clandestinely in order to join the *guerrilleros*. When it felt threatened, the Franco regime did not hesitate to strike hard.

It was able to do so the more easily in that Anarchist groups persisted in carrying on their violent activities. The police hunted them, but they fought back. In November 1949 there was a violent clash in Barcelona; one policeman and six Anarchists were killed; the same month, in the neighbourhood of Corunna, seven Anarchists were shot down. In March 1949 *guerrilleros* and Civil Guards met in fierce conflict in the province of Orense. Once again, Anarchists were shot down. The police did not attempt to make arrests, but to kill, and the Anarchists knew what to expect. When, on 26 June 1948, the Argentinian Anarchist Raúl Carballería, leader of the militants of the C.N.T., was surrounded at Montjuich, he committed suicide.

Nevertheless, these violent and desperate acts on the part of men who refused to give up their particular form of action did not shake the regime, and therefore failed to move world opinion. On the contrary, this was gradually evolving in favour of resuming normal relations with Spain, that is, towards the official and definite recognition of Franco's regime.

Towards the Normalization of Relations with Spain

As early as 5 January 1948, the French government announced its intention of reopening the Pyrenean frontier, 'to the satisfaction of diplomatic circles in Washington', as the French press reported. The journal *United States News*, explaining the reasons for this change of policy, wrote that Spain governed by Franco had an increasing strategic importance. On 10 February the frontier was reopened. Georges Bidault pointed out in the Chamber of Deputies: 'The whole world now has relations with Spain, except France. . . . Only those who have a special interest in promoting Anglo–Saxon interests in the peninsula can refuse the re-establishment of diplomatic relations with Spain.'

In fact, while the Western world displayed its indignation at the 'Prague coup' (20 February 1948), discussions had begun between American bankers and the Madrid government. There was now open talk of including Spain among the countries to benefit by the Marshall Plan for Economic Aid, which was to take effect from 1 April.

The Spanish papers *Pueblo* and *A.B.C.* emphasized Spain's pre-eminent position, her urgent need for aid and the extent of the communist menace. On 2 March *Pueblo* wrote: 'The Marshall Plan, European unity can save Europe economically, but she must also be saved from a military point of view. . . . Hence the necessity for a military alliance.' *A.B.C.* on 6 March described Spain in enthusiastic terms as 'representing in the world today an incontestable position because she has been the first, and hitherto the only, European nation which, in an open war with Russia, the treacherous aggressor, had joined battle with communism and defeated it'.

With great shrewdness, the Caudillo made contact with a number of American public figures, invited by official Spanish bodies to visit Spain and meet its ruler. Congressman A. E. O'Konski, the Republican representative for Wisconsin, the Republican Senator Chan Gurney of South Dakota, political men such as James Farley, journalists, academics, all who were 'opinion leaders' and as such might influence Washington's decisions, were warmly welcomed in Madrid. The Caudillo – and hence the American press – insisted on each occasion on Spain's role as primary bastion against communism, and on the order that prevailed in his country. At a time when France and Italy were being disturbed by violent strikes, and when the Russians were preparing to blockade Berlin (24 June 1948), these arguments bore weight. The *Consejo Superior de Investigaciones Científicas* (in which the influence of the Opus Dei was preponderant) invited visitors from foreign universities, and naturally the political significance of these visits was obvious: in 1950 twelve Nobel prizewinners and a large number of scholars attended the ceremonies at the tenth anniversary of the foundation of the C.S.I.C.

This served to break down the last barriers that had confined Franco Spain, and furthermore to transform these academics, who were given a magnificent reception, into possibly unconscious propagandists for the regime.

Students belonging to the F.U.E. or the U.F.E.H., underground movements harried by the police, tried to distribute leaflets that protested:

'Foreign scholars who have come to Spain: the Spain they want to show you is not the true Spain. Those who are responsible for showing you our monuments are merely intruders. . . . They open the doors of our universities to you, whereas we are forbidden to enter them. . . . Are you going to bear witness to the supposed virtues of this regime? For it is solely with this aim in view that the expenses involved by your visit are included in the budget of a cunningly organized propaganda. . . .'

These efforts were in vain, for the police were keeping watch and official propaganda had powerful means at its disposal. The *Consejo de Hispanidad* relayed the efforts of the C.S.I.C. to Latin America and the theme of 'Spanishness', tirelessly reiterated on the occasion of the agreements signed with Perón's Argentine, became one of the regime's chief ideological weapons. This propaganda, moreover, served a double purpose: intended primarily to convince foreigners, its successes were also exploited within Spain to strengthen the Caudillo's regime, if only by discouraging its opponents.

On 30 March 1948, the United States House of Representatives voted by a huge majority (149 votes to 52) for the amendment proposed by O'Konski, the Representative for Wisconsin, for the inclusion of Spain in the Marshall Plan. This called forth shocked reactions in Europe: there were protests from exiles everywhere, from Prieto to his British friends, from Italian Social-Democrats who, in the person of Saragat, Vice-President of the Council, formed part of the government, and from Paris where the socialist Vincent Auriol was President of the Republic. Madrid was triumphant, and the vote of the American representatives did in fact imply an important success, showing that for the majority of American politicians, that is to say of the American ruling class, Spain had to be readmitted, with her regime, to full membership of the community of Western nations. Thenceforward, even if, under pressure from President Truman, who was aware of the reaction in European circles, themselves affected by the hostile attitude of public opinion, the Joint Committee of the Senate and the House of Representatives rejected the O'Konski amendment (1 April) and thus denied Spain the advantages of the Marshall Plan, Franco could rest assured that the United States *could no longer* remain unfavourable to him. It was just that they *could not yet* show their favour openly. Thus Truman, at the very time when he was opposing Spain's inclusion in the Marshall Plan, hinted to Martin Artajo, the Spanish Foreign Minister, that the American government had no objection to a loan from private American banks to Spain. Once again, it was just a question of waiting, of relying on the military men in the Pentagon, on Catholic circles, on the racist Southern Democrats and Republicans who constituted that Spanish lobby which acted in the name of strategic, religious or ideological necessities. In April the Caudillo's envoy to Washington was José Félix de Lequerica; the continuity of Spanish policy was thereby demonstrated, and we can imagine Franco's sense of quiet triumph as the White House welcomed his former Ambassador to Vichy, whose anti-American feelings had been so strong at that time that he forbade the diplomats on his staff to meet their American colleagues. Martin Artajo, a few months later, could proudly assert: 'We see that the greater part of world opinion has come, even if it will not admit it explicitly, to adopt an ideological line which Spain has been maintaining for thirteen years.'

The Spanish papers could register fresh successes. On 3 April – two days after the refusal to include Spain in the Marshall Plan – Spain and the Argentine signed an important economic agreement: Perón offered credits of 1,750 million pesos at a rate of 2·75 per cent, 30 million cwt of wheat, 10 million cwt of maize, 8,000 tons of oil. Spain was to provide industrial material. At a time when the country was still suffering from hunger, when long and disastrous droughts had diminished her harvests, this Argentine aid was vital. When one realizes the financial and economic links that bound the Argentine – even under Perón's dictatorship – to the Anglo–Saxon countries, one may well ask whether this was not the indirect means whereby Washington and London came to Spain's rescue.

Moreover, Franco on 8 May and England on 13 May 1948 signed important commercial treaties with Madrid: the Paris–Madrid agreement involved more than a milliard and a half pesetas.

The time was long past when, in the euphoria of the Liberation, Spaniards from the French *maquis* had set forth confidently to storm Franco Spain. Now, trucks loaded with oranges were crossing the Pyrenees. An anti-Francoist wrote bitterly, in 1948 or 1949, in an anonymous manuscript which he sent abroad, like a bottle in the sea: 'They have bought the conscience of the nations with tons of oil and tons of oranges.'[3] True, the reality was more complex, but for many Spaniards this was how it appeared, irremediable, past hope. Others, on the contrary, saw here a confirmation of success, of victory, the vindication of their policy. On 27 July 1948, 150 million peseta pieces were issued in Spain, bearing the image of the Caudillo and the superscription: '*Francisco Franco Caudillo de España por la G. de Dios.*'

Yet the Caudillo was not the sort of man to let success go to his head. He kept

[3] J. Hermanos, op. cit.

watch over the efforts of his exiled opponents, who were attempting one last manoeuvre.

Last Efforts by the Opposition in Exile

If there was still a chance for the opposition, it lay in the agreement between Socialists and Monarchists. Prieto, in London, was stubbornly persisting, under Bevin's sponsorship, in his talks with Gil Robles, who represented the *Confederación de Fuerzas Monárquicas*. In late August came the surprising news that the Caudillo and Don Juan had met off San Sebastian, in Franco's yacht *Azor*. The talk lasted several hours, after which Don Juan had returned to his own boat, the *Saltillo*. In theory the conversation had dealt with the education of the Pretender's son, Don Juan Carlos, who by his ancestry united the two rival branches of the House of Borbón, and who had Franco's permission to study in Spain. There was bitter resentment in some Monarchist circles, while the Socialists realized that they had been duped, or at any rate out-manoeuvred. Franco had pursued his usual tactics, dividing his opponents, creating rivalries and meanwhile retaining sole command. By his approach to Don Juan, he had caused difficulties for the latter's supporters, who were negotiating with the Socialists: the double game played by the Monarchists was now fully revealed. Franco succeeded, moreover, in complicating the trends within the Monarchist movement by letting it be understood that a restoration under Don Juan Carlos might be possible. By thus thwarting the efforts of the opposition, he strengthened his personal position in the eyes of the American and British governments. Don Juan attempted to clear up this ambiguous situation and gain some advantage from an encounter which had in fact benefited only the Caudillo. A note from Don Juan's secretariat on 15 November indicated that

'the interview which took place between the King and General Franco . . . and the discussions that followed it had as their sole aim the evolution of the present Spanish regime towards peaceful liquidation. The King is convinced that he has thus rendered a great service to democracy and to the peace of the world and that he has made possible the adherence of Spain to the anti-Communist bloc of the Western nations, which is out of the question so long as General Franco remains in power. . . .'

A few days later – on 24 November – there was published the London agreement between Monarchists and Socialists, known as the 'Saint-Jean-de-Luz Agreement': it recognized the rights of Spaniards to the principal individual liberties and anticipated a plebiscite to determine the nature of the future regime. At the same time – and we can assess thereby the contradictory character of the opposition and of its policy – the Monarchist note of 15 November clearly implies the existence of the King and of his personal strategy, thus giving a merely formal value to the 'Saint-Jean-de-Luz agreement'. Moreover, the powerlessness of this whole 'realistic' political line is clearly expressed in the closing words of the royal communiqué: 'We can be sure that it depends today on the United States whether Franco abandons or retains his power.'

Which raises once again the question: why should the United States and the Western Powers in general, engaged in a difficult struggle against the Communist world, take the risk of overthrowing the Franco regime, so long as that regime ensured order in Spain and gave proof of its goodwill towards the aims of the American government?

The Caudillo did, in fact, untiringly display his goodwill on every possible occasion. In an interview with C. L. Sulzberger, Chief Correspondent of the *New York Times*, at the end of 1948, he stated that 'for Spain an agreement with the United States would be an excellent thing. Spain would thereby recover more rapidly and would be sooner in a position to co-operate in the rebirth of Europe.' Meanwhile, he continued to ensure order – against the members of the c.n.t., the u.g.t., the Communists, and also against the supporters of Don Juan. A young Monarchist died in jail; when the Duchess of Valencia, Luisa Maria Narvaez, protested, she was arrested and condemned to a year's imprisonment. The regime never relaxed its hold, and brutality was only in abeyance. In December 1949 a partial amnesty was proclaimed: it affected only 13,000 prisoners, less than 3,000 of whom were in fact released. Thousands more remained in jail. And they had been there since the end of the Civil War, many of them condemned to up to thirty years' imprisonment.

Franco's opponents of every colour had to face defeat, to assess the situation and to seek new routes.

The Opposition Admits its Bankruptcy

The first of them to face the bitter fact of bankruptcy was the head of the exiled Republican government, Álvaro de Albornoz. Speaking at the *Centre de politique étrangère* in Paris on 30 October 1948, he recalled the hope that had inspired thousands of Spaniards in 1944–5, and stressed that

'they had never thought that those who had been the first to stand up against tyranny and had given a million dead to the cause of the free peoples would be denied their share of the common victory. Franco himself, transforming his former insolence into mendicancy, believed his last hour had come. To overthrow him it needed only one breath from the new Europe, the slightest gesture by the victors. But, by a cruel irony of history, the longed-for triumph of the democracies served to uphold the usurper and only tightened the fetters of our people.'

Such was the sombre vision of the Spanish exiles, a simplified version of history due to disappointment and despair, for Franco had been confident of his future ever since 1943, and, as we have seen, had never lost control of the situation.

The Communists meanwhile, that same October 1948, now that the cold war was in full swing, gathered together their leading militants and those of the kindred *Partido Socialista Unificado de Cataluña*. After all the concessions made for the sake of unity, they had found themselves isolated, described by Indalecio Prieto and the Socialists as totalitarian, excluded from the common cause. They had reacted to political isolation in the traditional fashion, with sporadic revivals of an armed struggle which had in fact never really ceased. Everywhere the *guerrilleros*, generally confused with anarchists, were being defeated and massacred. Those of the old leaders who had survived since 1939 now disappeared, some imprisoned and executed, others overtaken by despair or by death. The new leaders fell too: Zoroa was shot, Sánchez Viesma murdered by the police. When armed action became impossible, they had to seek fresh forms of struggle. In October 1948 the party decided on a drastic change of policy: an attempt to infiltrate into existing mass organizations such as the Falangist vertical syndicates, to carry on a legal struggle among the people; this implied a tactical and circumstantial reduction of their objectives in order, through partial battles, to raise the political level of the masses by involving them in struggles that concerned them directly. This was unquestionably the end of one policy and the inauguration of a new form of strategy, based on the lessons learnt from the failure of armed struggle. Its success could only be a long-term prospect. It presupposed dispersed underground action preceding open conflict. A factor in its favour was that the Communist Party was the one most firmly rooted in Spain, and that by the 1950s a new strata of the working class had been formed from those who had only been children at the time of the Civil War, who had never directly experienced defeat. Ten years old in 1939, twenty in 1949: perhaps the hope for Franco's adversaries lay simply in the biological transformation of the working class, which, reinforced by the influx of thousands of peasants, was gradually recovering from the ordeal of civil war and repression.

This could only be a long and exacting process, and it met with obstacles in the international field. In Paris, in October 1948 General George C. Marshall, the American Secretary of State, officially requested the United Nations to annul their condemnation of Spain. At the same time, an American military commission, led by Senator Chan Gurney, visited Madrid. Gurney had long talks with the Caudillo and with General Vigón, Minister of War. Back in Washington, Gurney declared: 'All those who are resisting communism must understand that it is in their interest to bring Spain into the United Nations.'

The logical sequel to this assessment of the situation was direct aid to the Franco regime. And this the Americans, being realistic, now proceeded to organize.

American Aid for Franco Spain (1949–1950)

Truman, re-elected on 2 November 1948, and Dean Acheson, Secretary of State, continued none the less to criticize the Franco regime severely in public. In May 1949 Dean Acheson once again denounced Spain as 'a symbol of fascism'. However, there was no option. On 4 April 1949, the North Atlantic Treaty was signed. On 13 July the Holy Office published its decree excommunicating Communists and left-wingers. One can guess what repercussions this had in Spain. Next day the first Soviet atomic bomb exploded. The threat of war thus seemed an imminent reality and the conflict became an internal one in every country. On 21 February 1949, the *New York Herald Tribune* described Franco Spain as a country of law and order in happy contrast with strike-ridden Italy and France. The same month, the Chase National Bank granted Madrid a loan of $25 million for the purchase of foodstuffs. This was little enough, but in the difficult economic situation that prevailed in Spain – the inadequate harvests, the low level of power production – it would stop the gap and enable the country to hold on until more substantial sums could be released. Above all, this initial credit was the sign that Spanish–American relations had entered a new phase: on 3 September 1949, a squadron of the United States Navy visited the port of El Ferrol. Franco had indeed declared in May, still harping on the theme of national pride: 'To hope for gifts is immoral and is not in the Spaniards' nature. We shall not disdain foreign aid because it would speed up the rhythm of our reconstruction. But if that help were conditioned by blackmail, we should refuse it and pursue our unchanging aims alone, although more slowly.'

In fact, in exchange for credits, the Caudillo offered strategic opportunities, and even if his declaration was aimed at resisting economic pressure from the United States which demanded considerable shares in Spanish undertakings and a reorganization of the country's economic structure, Spain needed help too badly to be able to reject it. As for the United States, it needed Spain. And on 18 January 1950, in a letter to Tom Connally, Dean Acheson wrote that the United States was ready to put before the General Assembly of the United Nations a resolution inviting member nations to appoint ambassadors to Spain, which would be admitted to the specialized organizations of the United Nations; and that as regards economic relations, the policy of North America was determined not by political but by economic considerations; that Spain, finally, was free to apply to the Import–Export Bank on the same terms as any other country.

This unambiguous declaration showed that a new stage had been reached. Moreover, on 21 October 1949, the leaders of the American Communist Party had been sentenced; and on 26 June 1950, the Korean war broke out. Franco's regime, which had pointed to the cold war as the vindication of its own existence, did not hesitate to commit itself, and on 1 August 1950, the Spanish Embassy in Washington published a communiqué which declared: 'Spain wishes to help the United States to check communism by sending forces to Korea.' A few days later the United States Congress voted an amendment to the law allocating credits for 1951 to include Spain, which was to be granted a loan of up to $62,500,000. This time the Caudillo had definitely won his postwar battle and this victory duly strengthened his power over Spain during the 1950s.

Spain in the 1950s: the Power of Franco

The Caudillo now ruled with ever greater confidence in his own skill and in the rightness of his cause and his policy: had not the Pope excommunicated Communists and left-wingers? The reins of power were firmly in his hand; addressing the Cortes on 18 May 1949, he declared: 'As regards the future and the eventuality, which thanks to God still seems remote, of the exhaustion of my energies and the end of my existence, the law of succession stands.'

Stouter, more blandly authoritarian than he had ever been, the very embodiment of an easy conscience, he went on playing on the rivalries between factions,
using rewards, secrecy, the art of manoeuvring to stifle any slight show of political
independence. A hint of the revival of Monarchist ambitions brought the sudden
announcement, on 6 December 1949, that Don Jaime, the Pretender's elder
brother, a deaf-mute who had renounced all his rights in favour of Don Juan, had
changed his mind and was now asserting his claims. The Caudillo also revived
the Falange, because he needed a counterpoise, and Fernández Cuesta recovered
his ministerial post, becoming Secretary-General of the *Movimiento*. The
Ministry of Labour was still held by José Antonio Girón, who was also a Falangist, and who in spite of some opposition managed to initiate some sort of
rudimentary social legislation.

The Falange thus provided the Caudillo with an alternative political personnel
with which to confront Monarchists and military men. For at any moment any
man's career might be broken if Franco considered him dangerous. General
García Valino, for instance, was dismissed (March 1950) from his post as Chief
of Staff of the army, and appointed Captain-General of the military region of
Valladolid, because he was suspected of Monarchist sympathies and had clashed
with the Minister of War. Franco knew how to make use of rivalries between
those about him so as to remain supreme arbiter.

This atmosphere of uncertainty and intrigue pervaded the whole country. It
was impossible to ascertain the true causes of events, since the police and the
censorship were all-powerful. When in March 1949 the secretary of the *Frente de
Juventudes*, Pinol Ballester, was assassinated, it might well have been a case of
inter faction vendetta. Again, in June 1949, when a dozen bombs exploded during
a visit of Franco's to Barcelona, could one tell whether this was an outrage
organized by the C.N.T. or, on the contrary, as the underground Communist
news-sheet *Mundo Obrero* suggested, an act of provocation by the police?

Concealed by this veil of secrecy, this dearth of information, political rivalries
and struggles for influence proliferated. Occasionally, when an affair was too big
to be hidden, something would come to the surface, suggesting the scale of the
activities going on behind the suave declarations. Thus, for instance, the corruption which was universal and never admitted was suddenly revealed in the affair
of those millions of bushels of Argentine wheat which were sold by those in
charge to foreign purchasers before they had ever been unloaded in Spain. The
Argentinians disclosed the scandal, and punitive measures had perforce to be
taken. The Falange, encouraged by the authorities, organized demonstrations
demanding the punishment of those responsible. The minister Girón promised
justice to the students who had been incited to clamour for it, and members of the
consortium which had been formed to sell the wheat were arrested on a charge of
illicit trading. Then, when the affair had served its purpose – to display the virtues
of Franco's justice – it was damped down and most of the accused were set free.

The smooth surface closed over again; nothing had been expressed save self-
satisfaction. Franco lost no opportunity of extolling his policy and his Spain. On 18
May 1949, he told the Cortes: 'Many of those foreigners who were against us only
yesterday are now beginning to recognize in the stability and order of our regime

a sheet-anchor against possible disaster for our continent.' Spain was presented as the last outlying island of the West, battered by the Red tide which had fortunately been driven out of Spain. 'Imagine what the Western world would be today if we had lost the battle,' Franco went on. 'Spain anticipated by several years the battle which the world has begun to wage today.' For the 1950s might, according to Franco, be considered as a pre-war period. All around Spain, as he was to assert in another speech at the end of 1949, reigned injustice and materialism; the Spaniards, on the contrary, 'march in the way of truth because Spain is so closely knit to Holy Mother Church that she enjoys the special blessing of God'.

Fortunate Spaniards! After praise of Spain came praise of Franco. According to *Arriba* (21 October 1950), 'Franco is the leader and star of the whole world.' On 4 December 1949, the Falangist organ offered birthday greetings to

'the man with the invincible sword who belongs to the advance guard of Providence ... the man of God. ... Who can dispute his right to the laurels of victory, the most fruitful, just and honourable victory? ... It is thanks to Franco that the Vatican and Washington and the whole world are now on a war footing. ... And as if all this were not enough, the Caudillo, the monarch, the prince, the lord of armies is also a simple, affable man, home-loving and human, deeply human.'[4]

On 10 April 1950, Spain's father-figure married his daughter Carmen to Cristóbal Martínez Bordiu, Marquis of Villaverde. The latter was a doctor and also a big landowner; thus, even in this domestic relationship, we can recognize a significant social aspect of the regime, namely the bonds being formed between military families, landed proprietors – often provided with aristocratic titles – and bankers and industrialists. For Franco's family had increased its wealth since his seizure of power. Not so much the Caudillo himself or his wife – who was fond of antiques and old jewellery – as his close relatives. His brother Nicolás Franco y Bahamonde was connected through his wife with Manuel Coca García, member of a wealthy family from Salamanca that controlled the Coca Bank. He was on the board of a number of firms and his fortune increased after 1950 with the rise of Spanish industry, His son, Franco's nephew, Nicolás Franco Pascual de Pobil, was a leading figure in business circles, as also were Franco's brothers-in-law, including Serrano Suñer, and the relatives of his son-in-law Martínez Bordiu, whose opportunities increased after marriage to the Caudillo's daughter. Most of these men combined political activity with an economic role – they were deputies in the Cortes, Inspectors-General in some ministry or other, high-up officials in the world of finance – and it was precisely because they were so close to power – were, in fact, power – that they became influential business men and that their wealth increased. Indeed, they held all the control levers (they issued authorizations, modified the laws in favour of such and such a firm, were warned before-hand of any political event which might have financial or economic repercussions) and were thus in a position to manipulate these levers to their own advantage or that of the firms which, prudently, offered them directorships. Thus, at the summit, in the Caudillo's own entourage, the close links between

---

[4] L. Ramírez, *Franco*.

power and wealth were further strengthened; so the Franco clan were directly involved in his domination over Spain, in the economic as well as in the political field.

In view of his successes in the realm of international politics, and the powerlessness of his opponents, Franco was obviously disinclined to modify that domination in any respect. In an interview with *Le Monde* in March 1950, when asked whether he intended to alter the constitution of the Spanish Cortes, Franco replied sharply: 'That is out of the question.' Again, he was not at all disturbed by the formation in Paris, on 28 April 1950, of a 'Spanish Federal Council of the European Movement', an indirect way of putting before Europe (the E.C.S.C. having been set up on 9 May) the question of the Franco regime and the need to democratize it. The Socialists, Republicans and Monarchists of whom it consisted wished to prevent the integration of Spain into European organizations until a free referendum had been held. Since conditions had not changed, why should this project succeed at a time when countries of the Arab League were clamouring for the restoration of normal diplomatic relations with Madrid?

Confirming this favourable trend of circumstances, on 7 September 1950, the French police took action against the representatives of the Spanish Communist Party. Their premises were occupied, militants put under house arrest and the P.C.E. decreed illegal, its publications forbidden. A few days later, 28 September, General Omar Bradley, Chairman of the United States Joint Chiefs of Staff, indicated that from a strategic point of view, military bases in Spain would strengthen the frontiers of the Atlantic bloc.

Franco had nothing to fear from what was happening outside Spain. Everything depended on the country itself.

Spain in the 1950s: the Country

It had clearly changed little since the immediate post-war years, 1945–7. Towns still suffered from electricity cuts, due to the inadequate supplies of power, but also to the severe drought of 1949. In Madrid the current in all districts was restricted to three days a week from 10 a.m. to 1 p.m. and from 2 p.m. to 5 p.m. During the winter of 1948–9 Madrid ran disastrously short of water. The serious inadequacy of the road and railway systems was one of the main obstacles to the development of an economy in which the agricultural sector was still predominant. Now the latter had not altered: cereal production during the period 1945–54 stood at 32·8 million cwt as against 32·7 million for the years 1904–13. Livestock production was lower than it had been in 1933. It is true that drought contributed to this, but its effects were enhanced by the wretchedness of social and economic conditions. The peasants had grown poorer, and the drift to the towns accelerated. The *Instituto Nacional de Industria*, set up on 25 September 1941, which had originally been endowed with 50 million pesetas and intended to bring about economic self-sufficiency according to Fascist ideas, had not been able to promote industrial development. The index for industrial production in 1949 was 133 per cent of what it had been in 1929. It was only after 1949, when the first American loans were received, that industry began to develop (index in 1950: 152). The consequence of this stagnation was that the standard of living remained unchanged, or changed for the worse. Thus the index of income per head of the working population sank from 100 in 1935 to 70 in 1945 and 82 in 1950. At the same time the rapid inflation of the years 1947–9 entailed rising prices and lessened the purchasing power of money.

The Falangist trade unions, the *sindicatos*, could not really protect wage-earners. A few innovations were made, sponsored by Girón: for instance, the creation of company committees on 18 August 1947; but this 'syndical democratization', this transformation of the company from an authoritarian unity to a communal unity, this attempt to involve the workers as 'participants' had little or no effect, in the early fifties, on their living conditions. On the contrary, never in the whole history of Spain had the gulf between wages and prices been as great, and consequently never had surplus value been so high. Franco's regime, while maintaining social order, thus achieved that accumulation of capital which is indispensable for investment and industrial development, and Spain, several decades behind the great powers, created – as it had done in the nineteenth century – its wealth out of the poverty of workers and peasants.

For poverty was present everywhere in Spain in the 1950s. In the Catholic periodical *Ecclesia* (4 July 1950) Mgr Olaneta pointed out that 42 per cent of Spanish workers, at least, lived in impossible conditions, and he added: 'The immense mass of the workers are not for the Church, indeed they hate the Church. But they are even less for their employers They hate them even more.' Discontent clearly existed, and it gained strength as the younger generation matured, even if it could not yet express itself in collective action.

It was in the cities that poverty was most glaringly evident. The country regions of the south were at an even lower level, that of total destitution, but in Madrid and Barcelona (1,618,000 and 1,280,000 inhabitants respectively in 1950) overcrowding made the sight of this poverty even more shocking. Not only in the Barrio Chino in Barcelona, where Civil Guards, armed with tommy-guns, moved through the crowds of ragged children, blind men, beggars and prostitutes, and where a pregnant woman with a child in her arms might be seen selling white bread[5], but all around Madrid, in the belt of slums that was constantly spreading – the hovels of the Paseo de Extremadura and Manzanares, the shanties of the Abronigal, the districts of Cerro Negro and La Plata and Las Latas, the area round the cemetery of Nuestra Señora de la Almudena. From one year to another the population was swollen by peasants from Jaen – known as 'croakers' because of their accent – and agricultural labourers from Cuenca or Toledo, pouring into the capital to escape from their wretched condition, further worsened by drought.[6]

True, the whole of Spain was not like this: people still went on living, under conditions of varying hardship. There were still corridas and football matches, and music hall shows featuring the famous star of the fifties, Pepe Blanco. Yet extreme poverty was the dominant feature, mortifying to many Spaniards, such

[5] The Barrio Chino is vividly depicted by A. P. de Mandiargues in *La Marge* (Paris, 1967).

[6] Armando López Salinas, *Chaque jour compte en Espagne* (Paris, 1965).

as the student who confided to a journalist in 1950: 'Like most Spaniards, I am in an intolerable position which I have given up all hope of ever changing, because I feel incapable of doing so, and that's humiliating.'[7]

This was an exaggeration, no doubt, since not all Spaniards shared this feeling; yet it reveals an unease that had begun to find an echo in intellectual circles.

Spain in the 1950s: towards a New Generation of Intellectuals

The censorship, of course, was still all-powerful; and the educational level was still deplorable. In 1950, attendance at primary schools was just over 58 per cent and at secondary schools only 8·2 per cent. Under these circumstances, obviously, the influence of intellectuals outside their own social group was very limited. Moreover, that group was still dominated by the Opus Dei. This body, which had become a secular institution on 24 February 1947, had adopted as its aim 'to spread throughout all classes of civil society and particularly among intellectuals the quest for evangelical perfection within the world'. Discreet, hierarchized (*numerarii*, all equipped with university degrees and capable of becoming priests some day, *oblates* without degrees, and members with diplomas suffering from some physical handicap), the Opus played an increasingly important role. Each member was obliged to submit to constant spiritual direction, and *Camino*, now published in an edition of several thousand, taught such maxims as: 'Your duty is to be an instrument', or 'Blind obedience to one's superior . . . the path to holiness'. At the same time members were urged to succeed in their professions, where they enjoyed complete freedom of action.

The influence of the Opus Dei and its role in university circles provoked reactions which represent protest against its assumption of hegemony and also the rebirth of a spirit of criticism in the new generation of Spanish intellectuals. Now several members of the Opus Dei were associated with Monarchist circles. Calvo Serer, one of its most eminent thinkers, favoured an agreement between Franco and Don Juan to restore the monarchy, and thus prevent any period of unrest or uncertainty should the question of the succession have to be settled at a moment of crisis, such as the death of the Caudillo.

We can see why, under these circumstances, the Falange was the official structure around which the opponents of the Opus Dei grouped themselves. Moreover, the Falangist ideology, through its demagogical character, gave scope for a critical attitude towards traditional conservatism, and for attempts at innovation. Thus in the *Revista de Estudios Políticos*, edited by Francisco Javier Conde, we find expressed a desire for liberalization on a basis of National-Syndicalism. On the other hand the Opus Dei journal, *Arbor*, edited by Calvo Serer, defended a traditional point of view. When Pedro Laín Entralgo published (in 1948) his book *España como problema*, in which this Falangist writer tries to show the need to go beyond the quarrel between progressives and traditionalists, and asserts that today's heritage comprises both these formerly antagonistic trends, Calvo Serer replied in 1949 by a work entitled *España sin problema*. Here he proclaimed that Spain had found her right way: since 1936, the nation's duty

[7] J. L. Bost, *L'Espagne au jour le jour.*

A village in Castile. In the years after the Civil War thousands of peasants deserted the poverty-stricken countryside to flock into the suburbs of the cities. *(Keystone)*

The regime exalts its heroes: members of the Falange paying homage to the memory of its founder, José Antonio Primo de Rivera. *(Keystone)*

Spring 1951: a general strike paralyzes Barcelona as the masses come into the streets for the first time since the Civil War. *(Wide World Photos)*

In view of the Cold War the Franco regime, champion of anti-communism, is granted absolution. Franco looks triumphant after receiving the letters of accreditation of Stanton Griffis *(right)* as United States Ambassador to Spain at the National Palace in Madrid, 2 March 1951. *(Wide World Photos)*

Weary of sufferings and sterile struggles, the nation seemed numbed. Men sat apathetically around the fountains adorning Madrid's Plaza Mayor. The opposition sought new tactics. Would the younger generation take up the struggle? (*Belga*)

October 1954: General Franco, accompanied by high officers, is the guest of Vice Admiral Combs, Commander of the United States Sixth Fleet, aboard the aircraft carrier U.S.S. *Coral Sea*. *(Belga)*

At the requiem mass celebrated annually in memory of the kings of Spain, at the church of the monastery of San Lorenzo at El Escorial, north of Madrid *(Wide World Photos)*

General Franco receives President Dwight D. Eisenhower in Madrid, 21 December 1959. *(Belga)*

Miners on strike in Catalonia in 1962. This was a year of conflict. Despite the declaration of a state of emergency in several provinces, the movement for social reforms gathered force and flowed over into the political area. *(Parimage)*

New governmental reshuffling: on 13 July 1962 Captain-General of the Army Muñoz Grandes takes the oath of office as Vice-President. More than ever the Army was the backbone of the regime. Tending to counterbalance Grandes' appointment, younger officials leaning toward "liberalization" were named to various posts. *(Keystone)*

was no longer a matter for discussion. History had decided in favour of a tradition in which Catholicism alone could provide Spain with a framework.

Naturally the ecclesiastical hierarchy supported him. In May 1949 the Bishop of Astorga wrote:

'It has been said that the Catholic conscience ought to have entirely repudiated the legal privileges enjoyed by Catholics, and that the ideal was for men of all religions and even of no religion to live together, not only in a common existence imbued with charity, but in absolute juridical equality within the nation, and it has been concluded that any social or political difference in favour of the Church is more liable to jeopardize than to promote her spiritual mission. This doctrine is entirely contrary to the teaching of the Church.'[8]

This intransigent position, which had already been rejected in *España como problema*, came under an attack from various directions. In little reviews such as *La Hora* (Madrid) or *Revista* (Barcelona) we sense that the younger generation of intellectuals could no longer accept the idea that Spanish history had begun in 1936 or 1939. They discovered that *before* the Crusade there had been another Spain, which could not be rejected or denied. As they thus retraced their own history they learned to criticize the present, the intellectual atmosphere of contemporary Spain with its censorship and its blacklisting of the greatest names in literature, art and philosophy. Young writers, too, began to appear: in 1949 Alfonso Sastre wrote his first play (*Death Squadron*), in 1950 Blas de Otero published his first book of poems, *Angel fieramente humano*. These writers discovered the way to realism: they looked at Spain. Eugenio de Nora, after *Songs of Destiny* (1941–5) and *Contemplation of Time* (1945–7) published *Spain, passion of life*, written between 1945 and 1950 and whose very title reveals its orientation,

> 'I feast my eyes on your presence
> my lovely Spain my joy,
> but you grieve me, my country with your mutilated breasts,
> and your pale mouth,
> because the sons whom you cherish equally
> hate one another and hate you.'

And the poet sets those who are with him, *we*, against the others, *they*, official Spain.

This upsurge, coinciding with the biological reconstitution of a whole generation (Nora was born in 1923) is important: it tells of an independent, critical activity which the regime had tried to strangle. The threat implied by these early poems was realized, for the review *Espadaña* founded in 1944 by Eugenio de Nora and Lama y Cremer was banned in 1950. This action clearly shows that the regime was not prepared to liberalize itself, that it was on the watch for any danger, however slight, since what harm could a literary journal do at a time when the regime was receiving absolution from the highest international authorities?

[8] Quoted by Father J.-María González Ruiz in the magazine *Frères du Monde*, no. 42.

Absolution and a Second Victory

Indeed, the United States and most of the great powers involved in a cold war which was becoming daily more savage were determined to secure the annulment of diplomatic sanctions against Spain. On 3 November 1950, Chinese troops intervened in Korea, which suggests the climate of international affairs at the time. On the 4th the General Assembly of the United Nations annulled by thirty-eight votes (including that of the United States) against ten (those of the Communist bloc), with twelve abstentions (including France) its 1946 resolution, and thus authorized the powers to resume diplomatic relations with Madrid. A few days later Spain was admitted to the United Nations Food and Agriculture Organization and began to co-operate fully with other international organizations.

This meant absolution, and a second victory, for Francoism, following that of 1939. Soon Stanton Griffis was appointed United States Ambassador in Madrid and Lequerica was officially sent to Washington. The United States went further than this 'normalization'. Senator Robert A. Taft, raising the question of the credits promised to Madrid, urged President Truman to 'follow the evident wishes of the American people', in other words to come swiftly to the aid of Spain.

Dismay struck the hearts of Spaniards in exile. This time, without a shadow of doubt or a glimpse of hope, the 1936 Republic and the plans of Socialists and Monarchists had been crushed. Defeat was total and irremediable. A whole political class had lost for the second time what it had already lost in 1936–9 and what the 1945 situation had seemed to offer a chance to recover.

The leaders did not conceal their bitterness. 'My failure is complete,' declared Indalecio Prieto. 'I am responsible for having induced our party to rely on powerful democratic governments which did not deserve our trust, as they have shown now. Through my fault, my party has been the victim of an illusion which had dazzled me.' The illusion was that of political realism. And Prieto gave in his resignation as president of the P.S.O.E. Rodolfo Llopis, Secretary-General of that party, declared: 'Europe has spoken at the United Nations Organization and has abstained. . . . Not a single European country led by Socialists voted against Franco, not one.'

Franco had indeed won a second victory. 'We are very weary,' an anti-Franco-ist wrote from Spain. 'We've had enough of it. It's almost too late already. Who can go on fighting here?'

It is clear indeed that a whole generation of Franco's adversaries had been crushed, some for the second time. 'The best of us have only one thought: to emigrate. The others are indifferent to that too.' Indifference, fear, and also disgust and humiliation: 'This is what they have made of us all, those swine, democrats and blueshirts together. That's what they have made of us today: cowards.'[9]

Defeat, bitterness, despair and flight. The year 1950 unquestionably marked the ultimate and symbolic end of the Civil War era. Prieto, Llopis and that speaker from within Spain were all men of the 1936–9 period. They were

[1] J. Hermanos, op. cit.

exhausted. They had no voice left. They could not know yet that their time was irrevocably over, (some of them took months and years to understand it), because their enemy was still in Madrid in the Pardo Palace, because *the war was over*,[10] having ended in that year 1950 which witnessed the absolution of Franco's regime, the liquidation of its international debit. Even if the Caudillo still symbolized Francoist Spain, another epoch had begun because new generations were springing up. In this sense, the second victory of Francoism in 1950 was indeed an absolution; it was valid only for the past.

[10] *La guerre est finie*, title of Alain Resnais's film about Spain, scenario by J. Semprun (1965–6).

BOOK III

THE BIRTH OF A NEW SPAIN
1951–1959

CHAPTER I

THE BEGINNING
1951

In those small cafés in Paris or Rome where Spanish exiles met, where they retraced the past of their Republic or dreamed up its future over a glass of wine, in the Spanish bookshops of every capital, kept by intellectuals who had grown old with their hopes, bookshops crammed with pamphlets and leaflets and the badly-printed little magazines that every opposition movement produces, where-ever – in Rome or Paris or Mexico City – another Spain still lived, uprooted and unyielding, the United Nations' annulment of the measures against Madrid came as a cruel blow. Despairing or bitterly resentful, Spaniards in exile knew, or could no longer refuse to admit, that they stood alone; while General Franco's regime, absolved by the United Nations, prepared to exploit its second victory. There was nothing modest about its triumph.

Spain's Generous Forgiveness

Martín Artajo, the Foreign Minister, addressing the Cortes on 14 December 1950, extolled the success of 'the country's foreign policy with its heroic watch-word, resistance to foreign interference'; that policy had enabled Spain to tri-umph, despite the 'insensate' action of the Great Powers and the manoeuvres of international communism; Spain remained unmoved and the world returned to where it should always have been.' Reversing roles, Martín Artajo concluded amidst the enthusiastic cheers of the *Procuradores*:

'Gentlemen, Spain, which has been so grievously offended and which has paradoxically paid for its neutrality more dearly than the vanquished nations paid for their defeat; which in return for its heroic crusade against Communist barbarism has been isolated from the rest of the world ... this Spain of ours, Gentlemen, which loves Christian peace and which serves the cause of Western civilization, in this solemn historic moment grants an amnesty to the nations which are willing to come to an understanding, and is prepared to forget the injuries done her ... for the sake of the common cause, so gravely jeopardized.'

Franco's Spain thus generously offered to forgive the world.

At the same time, the Minister praised Catholics the world over who had supported and defended Spain, and pointed out the decisive part played by the

United States in favour of Madrid; thus confirming the orientation of Spanish foreign policy under its two protectors, the Vatican, symbol of the Spirit, and Washington, representing sword and shield and horn of plenty.

Henceforward, on every possible occasion the Spanish press expatiated on these themes, or on that of the anti-Communist crusade to be undertaken by the West under the leadership of the United States. Madrid was in fact trying to become Washington's best European ally. According to *A.B.C.* (29 December), 'Spain is one of the poles around which revolves the colossal struggle of the Christian world against the Communist world.' France and Britain represented only out-of-date conceptions, and the editorial of *Arriba* (30 December) proclaimed: 'It is in Spain that the role of the United States in the world, since the fall of Germany, has best been understood and appreciated. . . . It is in Spain that the importance of the Marshall Plan and the American action in Korea have best been understood. . . .' The consequence is clear: 'A Europe whose structure is that of Charlemagne's ideal needs, at the beginning of this Atlantic era, a strong Spain, restored to her proper rank.'

The Defence of the West

The Spanish government continued to exploit the strategic and political situation of the country in order, in the harsh atmosphere of the cold war, to obtain economic and political advantages from the Western Powers (and primarily from the United States). The Madrid press did not fail to report any declaration by a foreign personality that showed the importance of Spain in the Western defence plans. 'No exclusions!' General de Gaulle had exclaimed, during his speech at Lille on 12 December 1950. The Spanish press headlined: 'De Gaulle recommends incorporation of Spain in Western defence.'

An alarmist campaign (not, of course, peculiar to Spain, but developed in Madrid with particular vigour) repeated that Europe and the world were on the brink of war. On 31 December the Caudillo in his New Year's Eve broadcast message, after asserting that his regime 'played a forerunner's role in history', referred to Spain's military preparedness, the strength of her navy, and added: 'We must thank providence for having allotted us a favoured geographical situation, in this Western spur with its powerful barriers.' Spain was ready: 'The heroic fibre of our Crusade has not slackened.' Spain was 'united with unanimous fervour to her Mother Church'. She could follow her path, sure that 'the destiny of nations is in the hand of God'. More concretely, the Caudillo proceeded to display for Washington's benefit the unquestionable advantages of an alliance. The newspapers carried on a violent campaign against the French army, accusing it of being ill prepared, undermined by the gangrene of communism, weakened by purges, having at its disposal only obsolete equipment, and reservists who had had no military training or 'who are the very soldiers who refused to fight in the last war' (*A.B.C.*, 12 January 1951).

The Caudillo, every time he gave an interview to American press agencies, stressed the decadence of certain European nations and the moral health of Spain. He warned the United States, in a declaration broadcast by C.B.S. on 4 January

1951: 'It is not possible to avoid being affected by war merely by refusing war ... It is useless to want to obtain peace and security without sacrifices.'

Since international tension was at its height, Madrid scored points. On 16 January 1951, General Dwight D. Eisenhower, coming from London, landed at Portela airport in Lisbon to examine the practical consequences of the mutual defence agreement signed on 6 January between Portugal and the United States. True, Eisenhower did not visit Spain, but it is quite obvious that there had been talks between the two Iberian capitals before the arrival of the Commander-in-Chief of the Supreme Headquarters of the Allied Powers in Europe. The Caudillo knew that he could rely on Oliveira Salazar to defend the Spanish point of view, particularly since according to Spain – as *Arriba* emphasized on 19 January – the problem of Western defence was less a question of manpower than of getting rid of the fifth column from which most countries suffered, except two: Spain and Portugal. This point of view was bound to prevail in Washington in the long run, and there were many indications that this might happen soon. Eisenhower declared on 15 March that he would welcome anyone who was really against the enemy. Madrid echoed this theme, dilating on the importance of Spain for the defence of the Mediterranean and stressing the urgent need for an alliance; and since Britain, under a Labour government, and France seemed reluctant to admit Spain directly into the Atlantic Pact, Franco declared (to Karl von Wiegand, representing the Hearst Press, on 13 February) that 'a direct agreement to collaborate with the United States would be less complicated than the inclusion of Spain into the Atlantic Pact'.

Thus, taking advantage of the international situation, the Caudillo played a clever game: having quickly discerned the dominant role of the United States, he used the cold war to consolidate his regime, stressing the nature of that regime in order to win a support which strengthened it still further. Of course, it would be a mistake to ascribe these political victories to Franco's personality alone. The logic of the cold war entailed the support of the adversaries of communism everywhere, whatever the special characteristics of the regimes they represented. This logic worked for other countries besides Spain. None the less we must attribute to the Madrid government, and thus to the Caudillo himself, the coherence and resolution of a policy pursued with a single aim in view, and succeeding, despite the twists and turns in international affairs, in preserving the power of Franco and the social groups supporting him.

When on 9 January 1951, units of the sixth squadron of the United States Sixth Fleet, under Vice-Admiral John J. Ballentine, put in at the port of Barcelona, the series of receptions at which Spanish military and civilian authorities and American officers entertained one another illustrated the new state reached in relations between Spain and the United States and this was not to be the last.

His success in gaining United States support encouraged the Caudillo to display towards those lesser members of the Atlantic Alliance, Great Britain and France, an arrogance which was intensified by the fact that it allowed him to foster nationalist feeling within his own country. While Madrid was wooing Washington it could profitably assert, loud and clear, its independence of London and Paris.

Spanish Declarations and Claims

France and Great Britain had already incurred its censure on many occasions. When London demurred at the proposal to admit Spain into the Atlantic Pact, the Spanish press fulminated. 'The obtuse policy' of the Labour government was condemned with lofty contempt. *Arriba* calmly and frankly declared (1 March 1951): 'No government need tremble today at the passionate hostility of an English Under-Secretary of State, since there are other great nations and other parties in the world, thanks to which one can do without British friendship when that friendship is withheld.' 'The opinion of the British Labour Party is of very little interest to Spaniards', asserted *La Hoja* on 26 February.

Madrid's attitude towards France was also highly contemptuous. Commenting on an unfavourable decision by the Foreign Affairs Commission of the French Chamber of Deputies, the Spanish papers see this as proof of 'the pathological state of permanent inconsistency and hesitation which afflicts France today'. When certain French deputies paid an official visit to Spain, the press pointed out that 'there have always been two Frances: real France and legal France, to quote one of her great men, Charles Maurras, now in jail'.

The papers did not fail, moreover, to insist on the excesses of the French Liberation, when 'Communist bandits' hoped to seize the country. In February, on the occasion of the thirty-fifth anniversary of the battle of Verdun, they ran a campaign in favour of Marshal Pétain, which was surely a form of intervention in a foreign country's affairs. Luis Calvo, Paris correspondent of *A.B.C.*, wrote for instance that 'the same sword that won the war under the walls of Verdun strove to save the peace and honour of France'. *Arriba* went even further. On 25 February its front page featured two huge portraits of the Caudillo and the Marshal. It published an interview with Franco about Pétain which is exceptionally unambiguous, considering that it expresses the verdict of one Head of State on a politician belonging to, and condemned by, another country, with which the speaker's state had diplomatic relations. Franco did not hide his feelings. Pétain 'was a magnificent soldier . . . essentially patriotic and chivalrous . . . a true knight. . . . Guided by his spirit of chivalry, he served France in the first place by sparing her a third frontier for the future'. Finally Franco offered Pétain, 'should the need arise, the hospitality of our marvellous Mediterranean climate, where, pending the cooling of passions, he could spend the last years of his life, cherished and respected'. Early in March, Maître Isorni arrived in Spain at the invitation of Señor Rocamora, President of the Ateneo and Director-General of Propaganda. The Parisian lawyer gave a lecture on 'Justice in France'; he was granted an interview and then entertained by the Caudillo; Francoist Spain was not afraid of offending liberated, Republican France – it had long since chosen its own France.

Franco went even further. After December 1950 Spanish claims on Gibraltar were once more pressed vigorously. The Under-Secretary of State himself wrote, under the pseudonym Juan de la Cosa, a series of articles in *Arriba*. Was this a way of exerting pressure to secure Spain's admission to the Atlantic Pact, or the return of a Nationalist theme? Both, probably, but the accent was placed primarily on Spanish sovereignty, on Spanish pride. 'We, the Spaniards,' wrote *Arriba* on 13 December 1950, 'know that Gibraltar cannot be sold . . . because Gibraltar is the honour of Spain, and the honour of our people cannot be bought or sold.'

Henceforward the name of Gibraltar recurs constantly in the press to remind everyone that the Rock was Spanish. Countless journalists repeated its story and, to crown the campaign, on 15 February 1951, the Youth Front instituted a 'Gibraltar Day' (4 August) to be celebrated every year, 'to remind all our comrades and all Spaniards of the grief caused to Spain by foreign occupation of the Peñon'. Gibraltar, 'whose name alone arouses a passionate desire to claim our legal right', thus became, at the start of 1951 – now that Spain was out of quarantine – one of the goals proposed to national feeling. This was a further proof that Franco's regime now considered itself in a position of strength with respect to the nations of Western Europe.

Beyond Gibraltar lay Africa. Repeatedly the Spanish press put forward the idea that there were 'many injustices to be repaired'. In other words, Madrid demanded a redistribution of African colonies to its own advantage and to the detriment of Britain and France.

Clearly, the evolution of the international situation and the support of the United States had restored all its early boldness to Franco's regime.

The Ambassadors' Return

The Caudillo had nothing to fear. The West needed Spain; Western capitalism could not risk a change of regime in Madrid. In vain did Salvador de Madariaga, President of the Spanish Federal Council of the European Movement, speaking in Paris on 8 February to the Council of Europe, describe the danger of 'any alliance with the present totalitarian regime in Spain', declaring that 'the defence of Europe demands the disappearance of the Francoist regime. Europe must act. . . . The Council of Europe must immediately initiate European intervention to bring about the evolution of Spain towards democracy.' None the less, the ambassadors went back to Madrid.

When Stanton Griffis, United States Ambassador, reached the Spanish capital on 20 February after landing at Cadiz, the papers displayed his photograph with the caption: 'Welcome, Señor Ambassador'. On 2 March, with great ceremony, he presented his credentials to the Caudillo. Crowds, 'demonstrating sympathy and affection' according to the Madrid press, lined the streets along which he passed in a coach drawn by six horses with blue and white plumes. There was a cordial interview with the Caudillo, with handshakings for the benefit of photographers; from the window of his residence, Stanton Griffis greeted the cheering crowd. That same evening he held a press conference. He began by telling the throng of journalists:

'When I was Ambassador in Poland, behind the Iron Curtain, I realized perfectly clearly that the Catholic Church was one of the most powerful bulwarks against the Communist ideology. Spain is a great Catholic country and she has a host of Catholic brothers in the United States. The United States and Spain, standing side by side once more ... will strengthen the cause of Christian civilization which we both cherish equally.'

This declaration obviously told strongly in favour of the Caudillo's policy, which aimed at initiating a new Axis in international politics – the Vatican–Madrid–Washington Axis. Naturally, one journalist questioned the Ambassador about his impression of General Franco. Stanton Griffis replied that the General had 'reacted with great vivacity and spoken with great sagacity on all questions. He constantly gave me the impression of being a great head of state, capable and alert, always at his post, with the swift precise speech of a well-informed man.'

The Caudillo thus reaped the first fruits of his policy. It was the United States which, through the intermediary of its delegate, secured the admission of Spanish observers to the UNESCO conference to be held in June in Paris. Franco had banked on the United States and he had won.

His supporters could now freely display, in the streets of Madrid, their contempt for the Ambassadors of Great Britain and France. On 5 March 1951, just as in the dark days of 1940 when Sir Samuel Hoare arrived in Madrid, Sir John Balfour, His Majesty's Ambassador, was greeted with ... broken glass: Falangists had smashed the windows of the British European Airways office in the Calle de Alcala. On 15 March the British Ambassador's presentation of credentials was not announced in the press; this avoided any risk of a sympathetic demonstration, but allowed a gang of young men to accompany the coach with shouts of protest.

During the same period – the first fortnight in March – the entire press of Madrid reiterated its eulogies of Marshal Pétain. Calderon Fonte, who had been correspondent of the journal *Madrid* in Paris during the Occupation, and had been famous for his articles on 'the crimes and treacheries of the *maquis*', sketched for *Pueblo*, the trade union journal, a portrait of 'Philippe Pétain, the oldest prisoner in the world'. The resumption of this campaign was occasioned by the arrival in Madrid of the new French Ambassador, Bernard Hardion, who presented his credentials on 17 March. *Arriba* illustrated the ceremony with two photographs: one showing the Caudillo, listening stiffly to the Ambassador's address, with the caption, *France, too*; the other showing some doughnut vendors, a few uninterested loungers and a coach in the distance, with the caption, *The new ambassador drives past*. For the United States, a triumphal reception; for France and Britain, neglect. The Caudillo had always known how to recognize the real relation of forces.

He played upon this relation, whether because he thought – like most responsible circles in Madrid – that war would break out between 1952 and 1956, or because his regime needed the credits and the economic aid which only the United States could give him. At the same time he was able to appease his resentment and satisfy the Falangists' national self-esteem a little at the expense of the British and French Ambassadors. He did not lose sight of his political aim. He was sure of Washington's support; he had already won that of the Church, but this had to be codified. In March 1951 the Caudillo requested Ruiz Jiménez, Ambassador to the Holy See, to take the first steps towards the establishment of a Concordat.

Naturally the primary object of these moves in foreign policy was to strengthen the power of Francoism over Spain. For in spite of the successes gained in the international field, Spain still had her problems, and they were primarily economic and social ones.

Spain's Social and Economic Problems (1951)

During the year 1950 inflation had intensified and sent prices soaring. Wages lagged behind, and in 1951 the situation worsened. At the same time the development of investments and the contribution of American credits made possible a rapid rise of industrial production, even if this took place under archaic conditions, with a predominance of small firms, while the road and rail network and the production of power were still inadequate. Poor harvests and the rising price of raw materials on the international market increased tension. The government was thus compelled to tolerate inflation. Paper currency, originally fixed (in October 1950) at 28 milliard pesetas, reached 25 milliard by December. Industrial development, investments, and the quest for maximum profits in a land where social order was ensured by the government with exemplary firmness, led to the steep rise of prices.

At first the government assumed a *laissez-faire* attitude, but this inevitably led to social difficulties; so on 17 February 1951, price control was restored for certain products. However, this control was only partially exercised. Prices went on rising. Corruption, the lack of any real enforcement, inevitable economic factors (scarcity of products, the desire to make a profit, the workers' reaction, held in check by the government) encouraged the continuing rise of prices and the lowering of the purchasing power of the working class. Spain was experiencing the first upheavals of postwar industrial development. Because of the political regime, Spanish workers and peasants – who had already paid once for this development by making possible the accumulation of capital – paid for it a second time by enduring soaring prices, long hours of work and harsh living conditions.

At the same time, as social contrasts were intensified – the rich growing richer, the poor poorer – the working class increased in number, because industrial development in this first phase entailed an increase in employment, particularly as the mechanization of production was still inadequate. Moreover, this working class was renewing itself (reconstituting itself *biologically*, as we have pointed out): the children born in 1936 were now fifteen years old. True, it was still politically subjugated, but it was becoming aware of its exploitation, and its reactions in the spring of 1951 showed that something was *beginning* in Spain.

Boycott in Barcelona

8 February 1951: leaflets began to circulate in Barcelona, type-written leaflets in

Catalan and Castilian. They said:

'If you are a good citizen, from 1 March onward, in order that the fares on the Barcelona Tramways Company should be in line with those of the capital, go on foot to your daily occupations, and in your own interest, as quickly as possible, make four copies of this chain-letter and send them to four different friends. If you want to be an honourable citizen, make eight more. *One* Spain? Then *equal* for all.'

These leaflets were stuck on housefronts and on factory doors, and strewn about cars. The word spread: 'Don't take the tram on March 1st.' At the end of February students demonstrated, handing out leaflets, putting firecrackers under the wheels of street cars, and flinging stones at their windows. Soon young workmen joined the students, and demonstrations were held in spite of the patrolling *policía armada*. On 25 and 27 February, communiqués were issued by the Civil Governor, Don Eduardo Baeza Alegría, and by the head of the police. On the 26th students were hunted down, even in the libraries. On the 27th some medical students were charged by the police.

From early morning on 1 March groups of workers set out on foot, carrying baskets of provisions so as to save a journey. They were in high spirits, calling out messages from one party to another, grouped according to districts, then for the last stage of the journey according to their place of employment. A few windows were smashed, but on the whole things were quiet. The boycott was carried on until 6 March, in spite of torrential rain. On 3 March the Civil Governor expressed his bewilderment at 'the reaction thus displayed two months after the introduction of the new fares'. On the morning of the 6th, after various approaches had been made by leading officials, the Minister of Public Works authorized the Civil Governor of Barcelona to suspend the fares. On 8 March the Mayor of Barcelona resigned. The people of Barcelona had won a victory, but the event had repercussion far beyond the Catalan capital.[1]

In fact, for the first time since the Civil War, *the masses* had come out into the streets and had invented a new, powerful form of action, confined to precise objectives but bearing an unmistakable political significance.

The Franco regime had been forced to retreat before popular pressure, and by this very fact had proved that this form of action, directly bound up with the lives of the majority, might be crowned with success. The Civil War was indeed over.

Second National Congress of Spanish workers: the Pope, and the General Strike

The importance of the event was quickly assessed by Franco and his supporters, and also by the workers. On 6 March, in fact, there opened at Madrid the Second National Congress of Workers, and the happenings at Barcelona formed the background for discussions on 'the transformation of the socio-economic system in industry', of improvements in working conditions. An echo, albeit stifled, of the workers' demands sounded in the sanctum of official syndicalism.

When the Caudillo, standing at the head of the great staircase in the Palacio de

[1] Juan Goytisolo, *Pièces d'identité* (Paris, 1968), p. 88.

Oriente, addressed all the members of the Congress who had come to display their loyalty, he declared – and the admission is significant even if the blame is laid on ancient history:

'I recognize, with you, the existence of a series of social injustices accumulated through the centuries. Yet there are many more due to speculation. . . . This is why I understand how the tone of your comments, and your unrestrained indignation, have gone beyond that serenity which is required for the study of these problems.'

On 11 March the trade union organization summoned all workers to the Plaza Almería, where they were to hear a message from Pius XII. The Pope's support of the Franco regime was clearly expressed. He concluded his speech by saying that 'he felt bound to address a few words of paternal praise to the institutions which you have created, and which you are still creating, to educate young workers'. He prayed for God's blessing, and bestowed his own, on the leaders of the country, pointing out that in the world concert of nations, Spain, its leader and its institutions enjoyed his special concern and fatherly affection. All the press enthusiastically emphasized the event. *Arriba* wrote on 13 March that 'what took place on Sunday was possible because a state and a political doctrine had accomplished the miracle, after bloody and heroic sacrifices, of imposing on history the teachings of the Catholic Church as the supreme formula for social activity'.

This commentary deliberately concealed the fact that after the Pope's speech, on Monday, 12 March, a general strike, the first of such importance since 1939, had paralysed the city of Barcelona.

Three hundred thousand workers in Barcelona had downed tools to protest against the rising cost of living. The news shattered the calm of Franco's regime. On the morning of the 12th the men gathered in front of the factories, refusing to work, and then the various groups converged towards the city centre. The Ramblas and the Plaza de Cataluña were black with people. Towards the end of the day the street cars attempted to set off, forcing their way through the crowd. One was set on fire in the Calle Rosellón. Workers and women and children demonstrated before the town hall; some groups sang the Internationale. Private cars were set on fire. The armed police and cavalry charged and then fired, chiefly into the air. At midday civil guards arrived by special train; by two o'clock they were parading, rifle or tommy-gun in hand, along the walls of the Plaza de Cataluña and the Paseo de Gracia. Night fell on a deserted city, while in the suburbs and industrial quarters of the region, which were also affected by the strike, the police rounded up groups of stragglers. Public buildings were put under military guard and the radio repeated an appeal by the Governor denouncing 'the work of Communist agitators' belonging to the P.S.U.C. The evening papers had reported the strike as a Communist outrage, a sequel to 'the lamentable events taking place throughout the world in execution of the terrorist orders of the Communists, propagated by agitators. . . . Traitors had attempted to disturb the peace of the Catalan capital.'

In point of fact, the strike was primarily the result of poverty. Textile workers, for instance, had for months been condemned to semi-unemployment, and earned an average of 15 to 30 pesetas. Meat, which should have cost 35 pesetas, was being sold at 50 or 60. In Barcelona a storm of indignation had been brewing for ten years and now broke out – like the boycott the previous week – on a specific economic issue, since it was obvious in the spring of 1951 that the Franco regime was not likely to be overthrown easily. True, militant Communists from the P.O.U.M. and the C.N.T. had been involved, but not alone; and if the strike assumed such considerable proportions, it was because *Catalán* industrialists (the national factor was obviously influential) promoted its development, thus asserting greater freedom of action in face of an archaic, corrupt and inefficient administration. By 13 March the city was more or less quiet again; reinforcements of police and marines brought by several destroyers were standing by.

The authorities had been badly frightened. They reacted with harsh repression (there were several hundreds of arrests), but at the same time, under pressure from the Bishop of Barcelona (Mgr G. Modrego) and probably from the United States Ambassador, they lifted the penalties imposed for striking. There were dismissals – the Civil Governor and the regional delegate of the *Sindicatos*. There were speeches. Fernández Cuesta, Secretary-General of the *Movimiento*, denounced (20 March) 'the immoral speculation, the frantic desire to acquire wealth which affect many individuals and many sectors of Spanish society and economy'. Referring to his movement, he stressed: 'To be a Falangist and not to obey is a contradiction in terms. The Falangist must have blind faith in whoever gives him orders.' As a political and social programme he promised 'austerity, discipline and unity'. Thenceforward the press dwelt tirelessly on the need to fight against speculation, the black market, rising prices, illicit profits; and on 2 April a special council met under the chairmanship of the Caudillo to examine these questions.

The Barcelona strike had been a sign, because the Civil War was long past, because the working class was regaining its cohesion and increasing numerically, because it was being harshly exploited, because it was daily discovering the need to fight and taking over the historic traditions of the struggle, because it had set itself concrete aims, the regime began to understand that this class was a force to be reckoned with, and could not be strangled and conquered by repression alone. The spring of 1951 does indeed mark the opening of a new period.

The Movement Spreads

The proof of this is that the protest movement born in Catalonia soon spread. Press campaigns, speeches by Franco, official statements that 'the rise of prices is a world phenomenon', the announcement of consignments of cereals did not allay the unrest. On 2 April the students of Madrid protested with street demonstrations against increased fares in urban transport. In Catalonia some factories (those of Mansera for instance) were paralysed by strikes: the workers demanded a weekly increase to offset the rising cost of living.

The gravest disturbances arose in the Basque provinces. As in the case of

Catalonia, the oppression endured by this national minority since the end of the Civil War was a further factor explaining the vigour of the demonstrations. On the morning of 23 April, after leaflets calling to action had been distributed on previous days, the workers downed tools in Viscaya (at Bilbao) and in Guipuzcoa (at San Sebastian). In spite of the governor's threats and of police violence, the strike lasted forty-eight hours and affected almost 250,000 workers. According to *Arriba* this was 'a conspiracy against the political unity of the country and against national security'. In fact, it was an expression of protest against harsh living conditions, and it continued in spite of 2,000 arrests. A few days later fresh strikes broke out at Vitoria and at Pampeluna. In the latter town, housewives demonstrated against a rise in the price of eggs. Shots were fired in front of a shoe factory; one woman was severely injured. Faced with the spread of the movement, the authorities intensified their repression. Hundreds of workers were arrested. On 16 May at Barcelona the police announced that they had taken fifteen members of the C.N.T., instigators of the March strikes. 'They were trying,' the statement runs, 'to provoke clashes of a revolutionary character under cover of peaceful protest against the rising cost of living.' Basque Nationalists and members of the Socialist U.G.T. were arrested, as was also one member of the Catholic Action group: this was a new phenomenon, heralding important developments. All were threatened with court martial.

The press let fly. *Arriba* spoke of an external conspiracy between freemasons and Communists, and denounced 'the blindness of certain Spanish political groups, particularly Catholics, whose irresponsibility verges on treachery ... the unsavoury alliance between Socialists, Communists, separatists and certain pseudo-Catholics'. It is in a headline in *A.B.C.* on 20 May that we see the clearest indication of the government's future strategy. The paper writes that social disturbances are 'a manoeuvre by enemies defeated yesterday who are trying to raise their heads today'. The Minister of the Interior went even further: 'Some of the heads of the old revolutionary hydra, crushed in 1936, are being lifted again in the shadows to try to destroy the tranquillity and peace of Spain.' In short, the old bogies of civil war, anarchy, separatism and communism had to be revived if the regime was to retain the support of the Spanish bourgeoisie and the propertied classes and all those who by tradition, ideology, belief, interest or prejudice felt themselves bound to it. They had to be scared. The manoeuvre succeeded: for instance, when in Madrid on 22 May the boycott of public transport was organized, when the streets from early morning onward were crowded with workers whistling cheerfully as they marched, despite the presence of large numbers of police the wealthier districts remained unaffected. In the districts of Vallecas, Legazpi, Cuatro Caminos or Tetuan, in factories, the leaflets and the clandestine issues of *Mundo Obrero*, the slogans on walls, the conversations during meal-breaks or in cafés had their effect, had carried conviction. The movement did not affect *all* Spaniards. On the contrary, the traditional social groups gathered closer around the regime and its leader the Caudillo, thus enabling them to take action.

Governmental Reactions

They reacted with repression and intimidation: they manoeuvred. The Caudillo himself took part in the battle. Addressing a congress of agricultural guilds on 15 May he spoke with a violence that reveals his awareness of the serious social phenomenon implied by the strikes. He declared:

'The country is a fortress besieged by the enemy. Strikes are only lawful, and can only be accepted as such, when the principle of the class struggle is legally accepted. . . . But when class warfare is proscribed because it means the ruin of the fatherland . . . striking is a criminal offence . . . a revolutionary weapon, a crime.'

Loud applause. The tone was set. The papers warned the Spanish people that 'any demonstration, even harmless, leads sooner or later to sedition' (*Ya*, 20 May). They praised the achievements of the regime which, as the Caudillo said in June on his visit to those regions of Andalusia which were the poorest in Europe, 'is hated by rapacious men within and rapacious nations without'. Fernández Cuesta addressed the workers of the Basque country and spoke to them 'like a comrade taking on a task to help Franco, the best defender the workers have ever had in Spain'. The weaknesses of the economy and social injustices were made out to be a legacy from the past, or the result of international communism or vindictive nationalism, whereas the new regime promised industrialization, thanks to such bodies as the *Instituto Nacional de Industrias* (I.N.I.), created in 1941.

In fact, if industrialization was indeed advancing (communications, electrical power stations, dams connected with the irrigation system), it was thanks primarily to American funds. On 26 July Dean Acheson announced the release of credits in the order of $100 million 'within the framework of the bill for economic and military aid to foreign countries'.

Obviously, the price paid for American support was Spain's military and political commitment to the cause of the United States. For Franco this had a twofold advantage. American dollars enabled him to promote industrialization, and the military alliance strengthened his regime. Not a day passed but some Spanish or American personality proclaimed either Spain's determination to fight against communism, or the strategic necessity of gaining Spain's alliance. Lequerica, in Washington, vaunted 'the experienced Spanish army which has shown its mettle in combat and which is partially mobilized'. General Galarza, Air Minister, stressed the advantages which would accrue to the Western defence system by the admission of Spain; members of the American Senatorial Committee on Foreign Affairs visited Madrid, making various contacts and declarations, and finally on 17 July Admiral Forrest P. Sherman, Chief of Naval Operations of the American fleet, landed at Barajas airport with his staff. He had a couple of interviews with the Caudillo. Their talks, lasting six hours, turned on the conclusion of a bilateral military agreement and the possibility, within this framework, of the United States using military bases in Spanish territory. The discussion was highly concrete, and above all highly significant.

18 July 1936–18 July 1951: Fifteen years between the start of the military rising and Franco's interview with the American Admiral. Spain and the Caudillo had been involved in the cruel pageant of world events: Ciano had visited Barcelona and Madrid, Franco had met Hitler at Hendaye and Mussolini at Bordighera. The world had witnessed the rapid rise and fall of the figures that sought to embody its future, dictators swept away, ambitious policies crumbling; over Europe armies ebbed and flowed, alternately victorious and defeated. The Caudillo and his regime stood firm, and the most powerful nation in the world now offered its support to Francoism. The greatest capitalist power offered its far from disinterested help to Spain's frail capitalism, still fettered and held back by the economic mediocrity and corruption, the inadequacy and feudalism of its recent past. The Spanish press might well sing Franco's praises, and the paper *Informaciones*, which throughout the war had upheld the most intransigent Nazi point of view, wrote on the anniversary of the rising: 'Fifteen years of Franco's government have happily and profoundly transformed Spain. . . . Our nation has risen from the rank of a forgotten nation to that of a nation sought after and welcomed, and this change is directly due to Franco. . . . The cycle closes with this anniversary.'

Once again, Franco had the widest possible scope for manoeuvring, despite the workers' unrest in the spring. As usual he made the best possible use of it. On 20 July 1951, a series of decrees brought reorganization of the central administration and promised an important Cabinet reshuffle. A skilful redistribution of posts enabled the Caudillo to control power, as in the past, while bringing into his government the different groups which supported his regime. The position of the Falange was reinforced by the entry of Cuesta, Secretary-General of the *Movimiento*; the cold war allowed Franco to use the movement once again against the Monarchists, who were represented by Count Vallellano (Public Works) and Iturmendo (Justice). The Catholics, with Martin Artajo, retained Foreign Affairs, and as a further brake on the Falange Education was entrusted to the former Ambassador to the Vatican, Ruiz Jiménez. The latter was, quite rightly, held to be a broad-minded man; in order to control him and diminish his influence, the ministries of Education and Information were now separated, and a new Minister of Information and Tourism appointed: Gabriel Arias Salgado, a loyal supporter of the Caudillo. The army was fully represented. Admiral Moreno Fernández, another faithful Francoist, was appointed to the Admiralty; Captain Carrero Blanco, a relative of the Caudillo's, was Minister to the *Presidencia*, and finally Lieutenant-General Augustín Muñoz Grandes was Minister of War. He had been responsible, in 1941, for organizing the Blue Division, and he still flaunted the Iron Cross he had won in 1943 on the Russian front.

The Caudillo could thus rely on a wide range of trends and personalities. Backed by the United States, helped by the cold war, maintaining order in the country by means of powerful military and police forces, enjoying the support of the 'bourgeoisie', in the widest sense of the word, with all information media under its control and the Church behind it, the regime seemed about to enter on a new phase. What could the opposition do against it?

The Opposition (1951)

The Monarchists were increasingly committed to collaboration with the authorities, particularly since the Caudillo repeatedly declared that the regime was moving towards constitutional monarchy. Moreover, for Don Juan the problem was still the same: on whom could he rely? He therefore wrote . . . to Franco on 10 July 1951, asserting that he was bound to no party, that his hands were free, that if some Monarchists had negotiated with anti-Communist workers' parties it was entirely on their own responsibility, and . . . in order to prevent these workers becoming revolutionaries. Needless to say, Don Juan declared that the time had come for a Restoration, failing which Spain's peace would be imperilled by 'needy masses driven to extreme despair'. He proposed an agreement with Franco to establish a stable regime in Spain. Surely Franco's regime was stable enough? Why should Franco have responded favourably to such an appeal?

The only result of Don Juan's letter was to oblige the Socialists to break off their pact with the Monarchists officially. Their sole hope now lay in trying to persuade the new organizations of United Europe to condemn Francoism and put pressure on Spain. Why should a plea to the United Nations which had proved ineffective in 1944–6, when Spain was condemned in principle, succeed in 1951, in the very midst of the cold war?

As for the Communists, they were indubitably the group most closely in touch with the Spanish masses. Their militants had taken part in strikes and boycotts, organizing them, fomenting them, and the Party had suffered cruelly under Government repression. One result of the cold war had been to isolate Spanish Communists from the rest of the anti-Francoist forces. In December 1950 they proposed the constitution of a National Republican and Democratic Front; in October 1951 their leaders explicitly set forth the new political line: unity of all Spaniards in the struggle for democracy. 'To fight for the development of democracy is not a question of propaganda but a fundamental task!' It was the road to socialism. Nevertheless this policy of national reconciliation of all Spaniards against a Francoist hard core (if need be against Franco alone) hides the fact, already apparent in the events of spring 1951, that the country was still *divided*; and that the propertied classes in their struggle against the economic demands of workers and peasants stood, whatever their particular political preference might be, on the side of Franco's government. In so far as the latter was not only the expression of a single personality or a limited group but the manifestation of a given social structure and the guarantee that a certain social order would be maintained, the Communist programme of reconciliation between *all* Spaniards remained a goal so remote as to be inaccessible. Naturally the signs that something was stirring in Spain, in the spring of 1951, were greeted with enthusiasm in left-wing circles. 'The Spanish people can stand no more,' we read; and Barcelona's 'glorious, heroic gesture' was widely acclaimed. Some people interpreted it as a sign of the disintegration of the Francoist regime, or a presage of its

214

imminent collapse, thus losing sight of the fact that these achievements, important though they were, remained limited in aim and short-lived. They confirmed, indeed, the existence of potentialities for mass action within Spain; but between these and the overthrow of Francoism there lay an enormous gulf, and one not readily to be crossed, considering the manifold support enjoyed by Franco inside and outside Spain, the rifts within the opposition, the still intact strength of the state and the skill of the Caudillo.

Francoist Optimism: a Perfect, Unchangeable Regime

Under these circumstances, it is easy to see why optimism prevailed among Francoists, from the Caudillo himself to the humblest of his journalists. It was accompanied by haughty self-assurance. 'Fifteen years before other European nations we faced the political, social and economic problem of our time,' Franco declared on 24 August to the correspondent of *Newsweek*. 'We are therefore closer to solving it than they are.' On 30 September the Caudillo's Day was celebrated with great pomp. Condemned strikers were amnestied: 'Only the strong can pardon,' commented *Arriba*, adding 'Today we shall inaugurate the establishment of a regime of political power which is perfect and, in our opinion, unchangeable.'

Hispanidad, Spanishness, was extolled on every possible occasion: the arrival in October of the President of the Philippine Republic, or the meeting of the Ibero-American Congress of International Law. 12 October was the *Fiesta de la Hispanidad*. Institutes and art exhibitions were opened. Thus the regime celebrated its own achievements, while at the same time playing upon the national and imperial theme.

International events still worked in its favour: on 31 October, the Conservatives won the British election and Churchill returned to power. There was general satisfaction in the Spanish press and on the Madrid Stock Exchange. The new British Premier was relied on to facilitate Spain's entry into the United Nations, and that November Madrid officially applied to join UNESCO. New trade agreements were signed with London and Paris. The new French Resident-General in Morocco, General Guillaume, met his Spanish opposite number. On every side there were signs of the complete normalization of Spain's relations with the Free World. The regime moved from triumph to triumph.

Tourists began to flock in: 35,000 French visitors in Madrid during the summer months. Some newspapers welcomed the invasion, but on the whole the press was hostile, not having, as yet, discovered the profit to be got from what was described as 'this herd on the move, enjoying its holidays with pay' (*A.B.C.*, 4 September). *Ya* and *Ecclesia* denounced the 'impudence and Tarzanism' of this 'grotesque cavalcade'; *Ecclesia* went so far as to call for 'Christ's scourge on these desecrators'. But the process had begun, and on this plane, too, 1951 marked a new beginning, pregnant with profound changes.

So optimism prevailed. On 14 November seventy-five members of the C.N.T. were given long prison sentences (eight to thirty years) and two condemned to death; but this fact went unmentioned. At the same moment the Caudillo had an interview with the *Sunday Times* in which he criticized the ineffectiveness of the United Nations. A scandal was disclosed, involving certain high-placed personalities: illicit trading in shares, to the sum of 100 million pesetas. The Caudillo in his end-of-the-year address spoke of the moral ideal of the movement he led, 'the nobility and grandeur of the Spanish crusade', and added: 'We must convince all Spaniards that in a poor country the population is inevitably poor.' He promised a rapid improvement of the situation, since, as he concluded, 'God, guiding our steps, enables us to deliver Spain from the tribulations through which other nations are passing. *¡ Arriba España!*'

So time passed; by December, the spring-time happenings in Barcelona seemed a long way off. Salvador Dali himself, visiting Madrid, made a speech in honour of Franco, as a leader 'who has established clarity, truth and order in the country at the most anarchical moments of the world. This seems to me a sign of great originality.' Amid applause, he secured approval for a telegram to . . . Pablo Picasso: 'Spain's spiritual nature is at the furthest extreme from Russian materialism. . . . We believe in the absolute, Catholic freedom of the human soul. Know then that despite your communism we consider your anarchical genius as the inseparable patrimony of our spiritual empire and your work as one of the glories of Spanish painting. God keep you. Madrid, 11 November 1951. Salvador Dali.'

Spaniards were invited to sign the message, the significance of which was explained by Dali himself at Barcelona: 'We must recover Picasso, just as we must recover Gibraltar, for Picasso and Gibraltar are Spanish.'

Less than fifteen years after Guernica, under Franco's regime, Dali's venture was both daring and piquant. And it aroused a number of protests in Falangist and Catholic circles. Petitions from 'Spanish artists having fought in Franco's army' circulated, supporting Dali and 'modern' tendencies in art, and attacking conservatism. Here again, something was stirring in Spain in 1951.

As for the Caudillo, he did not interfere. A painter himself, he knew no doubt that pictures by themselves never brought down a government, and that the regime might find it useful to 'recover' artists and their works, even when these indicted it.

CHAPTER II

NEW SUCCESSES AND NEW PERILS
1952–1955

In 1951–2 a young man of barely twenty wrote his first novel, *Juegos de Manos*.[1] The young author had already won the *Joven Literatura* prize in 1949 with a novella which the censor had banned, but it was his novel that made his name famous: Juan Goytisolo. He belonged, as he himself said in 1954, to

'those young novelists of today who were only children during the Civil War. With their childish eyes, they watched atrocious things happening, unmoved. They forgot them, but as they grew up, a time came when they remembered. The recollection became sharper as their bones hardened and their blood grew richer. Then, not in order to forget these things – that would have been impossible – but to get free of them, they began to write novels.'

Juegos de Manos, then, is a beginning; and also a statement about those young Spaniards sprung from the petty or middle bourgeoisie who, having grown up under the Franco regime, had broken with it and with their families, seeking oblivion in drink or with prostitutes. 'Nothing binds us to the past,' one of his characters says. 'Not even the future. We live from day to day.' They want to protest against the world, and this is more than play, for their actions acquire political significance even though their resolution is mingled with, and based on, the impulse of youth seeking to assert itself through action. One of the students in *Juegos de Manos* agrees to undertake the assassination of a politician, but at the last moment, when the man welcomes him, he is incapable of killing him and runs away. His personal failure is also the symbolic failure of a whole young generation, whose violence is turned back on itself: the failed executioner is put to death by one of his companions. For a number of years to come this generation was to prove powerless to break cleanly, violently if need be, with its father-figure (paternal authority, the regime, social class or career).

This father-figure, moreover, seemed stronger than ever: in February 1952, the Barcelona court martial was still judging and sentencing. This time thirty militants, members of the C.N.T., Anarchists who had already been two years in detention, received prison sentences of up to the traditional thirty years. Eleven were condemned to death, and five were actually executed. Franco could not forgive the *Juegos de Manos*. This repression did not, however, prevent the regime

[1] Translated into English as *The Young Assassins*.

217

from winning important diplomatic victories, including, in the first place, admission to UNESCO.

Spain enters UNESCO (November 1952)

Protests from anti-Francoists in exile had no effect. *Batalla*, the organ of the P.O.U.M., published caricatures in plenty: in one number, a smiling Franco offering 'My Lady UNESCO' a model of her future palace, which was patently a prison; in another, Franco busily wiping away traces of blood. This was merely the indignation of unyielding opponents. Governments took a different view. Forty-five countries voted on Spain's admission (18 November); only three opposed it (Mexico, Uruguay, Yugoslavia), and seven abstained. France voted for admission. A few individuals resigned from national delegations; some intellectuals protested. Pablo Casals withdrew from the musical commission of UNESCO. These were ripples of little consequence in practice, and the regime could justifiably congratulate itself. The papers proclaimed the defeat of international socialism, since the Socialist Congress held in Milan had recommended a hostile vote, and the Paris correspondent of *Arriba* had nothing but contempt for the 'pygmies ... the homeless intellectuals ... who, faced with Spain's diplomatic triumph, sought somewhere to hide, like rats in a leaking ship.'

For the Madrid government, the vote was a precious sign; it confirmed that the way to the United Nations was open. It further emphasized the fact that the United States, most of the Latin American countries and the Arab delegations as a body provided reliable support for Spanish diplomacy. The latter, clearly, was in no way embarrassed – indeed quite the reverse – by the situation within Spain and the character of its government. Except by émigré circles and left-wing groups, whose influence was fast decreasing in various European countries, the Spanish regime was completely accepted. This situation favoured Madrid's foreign policy, which in return (as we have already stressed) strengthened the regime.

Franco and the Great Powers

Franco's government, moreover, continued to benefit by the cold war. The West was strengthening its defences on every side. General Ridgway (whom the Communists accused of having used bacteriological weapons in Korea) had become head of North Atlantic Treaty Organization in place of Eisenhower, who was running as candidate for the United States Presidency. With the Bonn agreement, in May 1952, West Germany was officially admitted into the Atlantic coalition. All these facts told in favour of Franco's policy, which posed increasingly as a *model* for the West.

Spain, moreover, used her most authoritative voices in an attempt to create a state of mind, to inspire the West with the will to undertake a crusade of liberation. The Caudillo had set the tone in his speech at the end of 1951. He had vehemently indicated 'the cowardice of leaving to their fate the peoples under the sway of Russian Communism'. The idea was reiterated indefatigably. On 10

January 1952, Martín Artajo, the Foreign Minister, published an article in *Ya* in which he spoke even more categorically than his leader: 'Spain considers that the acts of aggression already perpetrated by Russian communism . . . demand justice. Consequently the primordial aim of all military plans, in free Christendom, must be the *deliverance and liberation*[2] of these brother nations subject to the most appalling of oppressions.' Nothing could be clearer: in the Spanish view, a war of liberation must be undertaken without waiting for further aggression: 'A great alliance,' Artajo goes on, 'cannot neglect the plea for liberty of the countries shamefully subjected to bondage and Red imperialism.' Referring to the history of the Crusades, the press (*Ya* in particular) upheld this extreme argument, which had the advantage of postulating that the national crusade begun in 1936 had initiated the forthcoming campaign of liberation.

This policy, the danger of which scarcely needs emphasizing, anticipated the most fanatical American support for the 'roll-back' policy, and showed that Francoism was indeed a model of its kind. The armed forces had already begun to collaborate. Spanish officers on board the aircraft carrier *Roosevelt* watched the manoeuvres of the United States Navy, whose ships put into Spanish ports and were greeted with salvoes from coastal batteries. Asserting relentless support for the crusade was also a way of securing, as soon as possible, that treaty of alliance with the United States which throughout 1952 and the early months of 1953 was being prepared for by meetings between politicians and military men from both countries. Lieutenant-General Muñoz Grandes, Minister of War, in an interview with the *New York Times*, spoke as one with long experience of war in the East. The Caudillo himself granted increasingly frequent audiences to American journalists. The aim was still the same: to convince American opinion, to speed up negotiations, to show that the Franco regime was a model to be followed. On 3 January 1952, through the intermediary of the representative of the *New York Times*, Franco invited the delegates of American trade unions to 'visit Spain in order to study the social evolution of the nation and the progress achieved by the workers' in a country where strikes were 'forbidden as an outdated form of action'.

Another favourite method of promoting Francoism was to insist on the danger for the United States of depending on countries like France or even Great Britain. France, in particular, was the object of Spanish invective: it was called an unreliable country, corrupted and infiltrated by Red fifth-columnists, a feeble pawn, a source of discord. In February 1952 Madrid issued a pressing request that 'Paris should not obstinately refuse to recognize the reality of the rebirth of Germany'. *Ya* notes with satisfaction that 'Germany is once again in a position to lay down conditions to its conquerors'. The violent Communist demonstrations that greeted Ridgway's arrival in France in May 1952 enabled Madrid to insist on the risk that American installations ran in France. For such demonstrations were merely the beginning of 'a vast programme of sabotage and outrages against United States troops' (*Pueblo*, 28 May).

French manners and morals, French tourists, the mental, political and religious attitudes of the French all aroused shocked disapproval. José María

[2] Author's italics.

219

Gironella, who, a few years later, was to produce a would-be objective chronicle of the Civil War in novel form,[3] expressed himself (in *A.B.C.*) stupefied by the variety and eclecticism of the French mind, which could allow a representative of freemasonry to broadcast over the national radio, followed immediately by a Roman Catholic priest. He concluded: 'The variety of French radio programmes . . . is sheer madness.'

Obviously a similar situation was unlikely to occur in Spain where the radio and the press continued to transmit only official opinion. The newspapers were so jejune that their circulation dropped regularly. *A.B.C.*, a paper of Monarchist tendency but closely associated with the regime, sold barely 100,000 copies; *La Vanguardia* of Barcelona 80,000 and *Arriba*, the Falangist organ, less than 10,000. On the other hand *Marca*, the sporting paper, sold over 200,000. It is easy to see why one *A.B.C.* journalist felt 'an indescribable unease' when he considered France.

Naturally, it needed only a favourable declaration by a French statesman or public figure to alter this attitude towards the French. When in October 1952 Marshal Juin told the review *Destino* that 'there could be no true Europe without Spain or without North Africa', the Spanish press was unstinting of praise. Trade agreements and the creation of a Franco–Spanish Commission for Economic Liaison were also greeted with enthusiasm.

Much the same attitude was adopted towards Great Britain, with, from time to time, a renewal of verbal violence to remind readers that the Rock was Spanish, or an incidental philippic against democratic principles.

Franco Spain's happiest relations, in Europe, were those with the kindred regime in Portugal. It was with great pomp that the President of the Portuguese Republic, General Craveiro López, was welcomed in Madrid on 15 May 1953. Much stress was laid on the strategic unity of the Iberian peninsula, on the identity of attitude of the two regimes, 'united like brothers in the defence of their sacred spiritual heritage'.

Another nation was entitled to respect: Germany. Its rebirth was greeted as the pledge of a new balance of power in Europe. Franz von Papen, former Reich Chancellor, and Dr Hjalmar Schacht were welcomed in Madrid. German engineers collaborated in the arms industry, Willy Messerschmitt directed the manufacture of a new type of aircraft in Spain. At times one even has the impression that the war had never taken place, or rather that it had ended differently. 'German virtues' were contrasted with French 'pettiness, resentment and ambition'. The Rome correspondent of *A.B.C.* reported on 26 September 1952 that De Gasperi and Adenauer were about to inaugurate a new Axis. 'Practically, the Rome–Bonn Axis, if not the Rome–Berlin Axis, is being resuscitated,' the journalist notes with satisfaction.

The press – and naturally in Spain this initiative was government-inspired – undertook a campaign in favour of the 'so-called war criminals', denouncing the 'infamy' of the Nuremberg trials, in which the Western Powers, France particularly, were 'slaking their thirst for revenge'. *Arriba* even suggested that 'the

[3] J. M. Gironella, *Les Cyprès croient en Dieu*; *Un Million de morts*; *Quand la paix éclata* (Paris, 1964–8).

rehabilitation of the German generals logically involves that of the Third Reich'
(30 September 1952).

Franco's Foreign Policy

The foreign policy of Franco's regime is thus perfectly clear; it can be accused of
everything except incoherence. Its aim was to wipe out the consequences of
Germany's defeat and to revive Franco's grand plan of 1943 for a Western
alliance in a crusade against bolshevism. In this campaign on behalf of Christianity Franco's regime had been the forerunner. The crusade of the 1950s aimed to
justify its permanence, to justify all the deaths of the Civil War years and the
continuance of repression. Any increase in international tension promoted anti-
communism and strengthened Franco's regime. It therefore fomented hostility
as far as it could, as a means to win American support and ensure its own survival. Franco's diplomatic game involved approaches to the new Germany and
to the Arab states, to the Holy See as usual, and, as for a number of years past, to
Washington.

Now, far from seeking to forget the past, Franco Spain boasted of its experiences. The memory of the *División Azul* had never been more revered. On 9
June 1952, a decree set up a group of schools in Granada which bore its name.
'The soldiers of the Blue Division,' wrote *Arriba* next day, 'have fought two
battles during the past eleven years. The first was waged from Volkov to the
outskirts of Leningrad; the second ... against oblivion.' Now the time had
come to do justice to these heroic fighters, whose leader was now Minister of
War. On 15 July the same paper greeted the memory of Spaniards who had died
fighting by the side of Hitler's men 'for the defence of Christian civilization'.
The battle was still going on.

Of course, any attempt to lessen tension was greeted with a sarcasm that
betrayed profound anxiety. Francoism would be less necessary, the alliance with
the United States less certain, if normal relations were established between East
and West. Marshal Tito's visit to London in March 1953 called forth the harshest
comments on Great Britain's shameless alliance with 'a criminal who had persecuted the Yugoslav clergy'. The Soviet peace offensive which followed the
death of Stalin was also denounced with violence and disquiet. *Arriba* did not
hesitate to write, on 9 April: 'Moscow's vast manoeuvre heralds imminent war.'
When Churchill declared his willingness to open negotiations with the U.S.S.R.
(11 May), Madrid reacted: 'The wind blowing from London ... is a wind of
surrender.'

The cold war at any price, tension and the crusade were the principles of
Franco Spain's foreign policy at a time when the threat of a new world cataclysm
seemed to be retreating for the first time since 1947. On 16 May the Caudillo,
after attending a corrida on the Plaza Monumental, with the Portuguese President
by his side, at the close of a sumptuous banquet, uttered a new appeal, which
amounted to a rejection of any sort of peaceful coexistence:[4] 'We rebel against

[4] On 28 May, in Lisbon, Salazar replied indirectly to Franco by declaring that
peaceful coexistence was possible between the West and the U.S.S.R.

the idea that a precarious peace might be bought at the cost of permanent slavery for captive nations, handed over defenceless to the cruel despotism of Soviet communism.'

The Caudillo was being true to himself: he had been saying the same thing ever since 1936. This fierce indictment of *détente*, this fomenting of antagonism were due to the fact that peaceful coexistence might prevent Franco's diplomacy from obtaining the triumph for which it had been waiting for years, an agreement with the United States.

Concordat with the Holy See (27 August 1953) and the Madrid Pact (26 September 1953)

Madrid need have felt no anxiety. In the summer of 1953 Francoism scored two resounding successes: the Concordat with the Holy See on 27 August and the Madrid Pact (an agreement on military defence and economic aid) with the United States on 26 September. Thus, at an interval of one month, Spain had attained two important objectives. A few weeks later, the Cardinal-Archbishop of Toledo, His Eminence Reverendissimo Pla y Daniel could write in *Ecclesia* (31 October 1953): 'It is due to Divine Providence that one month after the signing by Spain of a Concordat with the Holy See, through which Catholic unity is established, this country has been enabled to sign agreements of an economic and military order with the United States.'

Providence had been assisted by lengthy negotiations; and furthermore by the Republican success in the American elections of November 1952. Franco's government could get on better with General Eisenhower as President and John Foster Dulles as Secretary of State than with a Democratic administration. The negotiations for the Concordat had taken place between Mgr Tardini and Ambassador Fernando Castiella in Rome, and between the Nuncio, Mgr Cicognani, and Martín Artajo in Madrid. The Catholic Church and the Francoist state had together produced a text which satisfied both parties and aimed at strengthening each of them. The Church gained considerable advantages: Catholicism became the official state religion in Spain; canonical marriage acquired legal validity; education must conform with Church dogma; the censorship was in the hands of the bishops, who could ban any unorthodox work; religious instruction at all levels was obligatory. The state undertook to use all its propaganda media to spread the faith. Economic aspects were not forgotten: the state must provide for the support of the clergy by creating an ecclesiastical fund. As for the state, its gains were by no means negligible. It had the right to put forward candidates for Church appointments, while Spanish became one of the canonical languages. Above all, apart from such opportunities for intervention in the life of the Spanish Church through the Tribunal de la Rota, the Francoist state benefited organically from the Concordat by winning the open support of the Church. The Caudillo was made a proto-canon of the Basilica Santa-Maria-Maggiore; every year three masses were said in his name, and Article 6 declares: 'In conformity with the concessions of the Supreme Pontiffs Pius V and Gregory XIII, Spanish priests will offer up each day their prayers for Spain and for the Head of the State, according to the traditional formula and the prescriptions of the sacred Liturgy.'

The bishops, meanwhile, took oath before General Franco: 'Before God and the Holy Gospels,' they declared, 'I vow and promise, as befits a bishop, loyalty to the Spanish State. I vow and promise to respect and to make my clergy respect the Head of the Spanish State and the government established according to Spanish law.' Every day, in every church in Spain, priests prayed for the Caudillo. Understandably, the Spanish press stressed this fact, for it marked the *political* victory which the Concordat implied for Franco. True, youth and education had been handed over to the Church, and the state paid a high price – literally – for the support obtained; but the Caudillo had secured *recognition*.

One month later, on Saturday, 26 September, at 3.45 p.m. American and Spanish negotiators assembled at the Palace of Santa Cruz. The Madrid Pact was signed at 4.07 p.m. in the Ambassadors' Hall. Its terms, briefly summarized, amounted to the provision of military bases, chiefly airfields, in exchange for a grant of $226 million for the fiscal year 1954. The United States also promised to provide military material and equipment.

It was a triumph for the regime. The news was headlined over every front page. The papers stressed the preservation of Spanish independence, included in the military clauses, and the economic advantages of the agreement. On 1 October the Caudillo addressed the Cortes, expressing complete satisfaction. 'This is the honour of fulfilment of our foreign policy,' he declared, and proudly recalled how in 1943–4 he had warned Great Britain of the dangers of communism. No one then had listened to Spain. *Arriba*, on 2 October, boasted: 'We have become the decisive axis of world policy.' This overstatement reflects the boundless self-satisfaction of the regime and its supporters.

The Caudillo's Day, 1 October 1953. Fulfilment

For Franco's supporters, Thursday, 1 October 1953 was surely the happiest of all 'Caudillo's Days'. The regime was triumphant. Opponents were silent, defeated or enfeebled. The anxious days of 1951 were forgotten, the line taken during the Second World War justified. The press recalled 9 December 1946, when on the Plaza de Oriente the crowd had protested against the United Nations' vote of censure. Today, Franco's Spain had a seat in UNESCO, today and every day prayers were being said for Spain and for the Caudillo, today the first American military missions had arrived and the investment of dollars had begun. ¡ *Arriba España*!

On that 1 October work stopped everywhere between 11 a.m. and 4 p.m. The Caudillo, lifting one white-gloved hand, looked down from the balcony of the Palazo de Oriente to greet the crowd that filled the square. Overhead, placards proclaimed: 'Franco, we vow to follow you.' The Grand Cross of San Fernando glittering on his chest, Franco reappeared five times on the balcony in response to the clamours of the crowd, who waved handkerchiefs and sang the Falange hymn, *Cara al Sol*. That morning a Te Deum had been celebrated in the church of San Francisco el Grande. Now, after his acclamation by the crowd, Franco could withdraw to his Pardo Palace, knowing that his control of Spain was secure. Underground realities could be discounted so long as the facade held good, and his successes – UNESCO, the Concordat, the Madrid Pact – demonstrated to the propertied classes that the Francoist regime, which had so skilfully won for itself the support of such widely different, but equally powerful forces as the Holy See and the United States, was still the best of bucklers. 'Yesterday', *Arriba* asserted, 'the Spanish people gave a perfect demonstration of their unity ... telling Franco this is what we are, we are Spain, we are Spain's decision. Another era has begun.' In fact, it was not the Spanish people who had spoken. In one sense, what did that matter? Tomas Centeno Sierra, a member of the underground executive committee of the Spanish Socialist Party, who had been arrested, died, probably under torture, in his cell in the *Dirección General de Seguridad* in February 1953. Franco's Spain carried on. Many Spaniards imagined, in 1953, that their living conditions would improve.

Economic Development

Bienvenida Mr Marshall! The two young Spanish film producers, L. G. Berlanga and Juan A. Bardem, who made this film in 1952–3, showed clearly what most Spaniards were hoping for from a *rapprochement* with the United States: the transformation of their country, symbolized by one wretchedly poor Castilian village expecting miracles from Mr Marshall – who sped past in a cloud of dust without stopping, leaving the village and its peasants as poor as before.

The reality, in fact, was not as simple as the story invented by these two producers, whose work shows that the cinema, too, was stirring – for Berlanga and Bardem had ventured, like novelists or poets, to seize Spanish life in its tragical or comical everyday reality. If the cinema, and literature, and men's minds were stirring, it was because reality was stirring too.

The signing of agreements with the United States could indeed only accelerate the trend towards industrialization which had already begun. The Spanish propertied classes trusted in the stability of the regime. They went on investing. American capital, too, had begun to flow in. Naturally, the structural weaknesses of this economic development remained, the gravest being undoubtedly the deficit in the balance of payments. Spain imported industrial products, machines, raw materials essential to the rise of industry which in turn involved an increasingly rapid inflation. From 1955 onward, difficulties (bottlenecks, with respect to coke and scrap iron for instance, and inflation, created a potential economic crisis. Yet this had not been caused as in the past by stagnation but by the tumultuous, anarchical development promoted by an avid bourgeoisie, acquiring rapid wealth and enjoying state protection against possible demands from the workers. The period, moreover, witnessed the growth of state capitalism resulting, for instance, from the investments of the *Instituto Nacional de Industrias*.

Franco was personally involved; he inaugurated dams in the Valencia region (one of which was christened *Generalísimo*) and industrial installations in the Levante region. Visiting the industrial complex of Puertollano on 20 May 1952, Franco extolled state intervention. He declared that private initiative was now inadequate, since investments and projects were vast and benefits insubstantial. Amid applause, he proclaimed: 'We should conceive of an instrument capable of carrying out these plans, an instrument which without killing private initiative but, on the contrary, stimulating it, completes it by achieving what the Fatherland requires. . . . We have created that instrument, the I.N.I.' In fact the whole process was a classic one: the economic infrastructure was made the responsibility of the country, and the more fruitful sectors left as a field of action to private enterprise.

Another classic factor was foreign investment. In 1953 at Aviles in Asturias there was launched the *Empresa Nacional Siderúrgica S.A.* (ENSIDESA), with a capital of 1,400 million pesetas, 400 million of them subscribed by the Spanish state, the rest by four great British iron and steel groups, backed by the Lloyds and Lazard banks. As in the past, Britain thus played an important role in the Spanish economy. With one important difference, however: she was no longer alone. The United States had taken first place, while Germany and France were also involved.

As a result of all these factors some development undoubtedly took place, although it was uneven, ill balanced and unhealthy because threatened by inflation. None the less, the production of steel between 1953 and 1956 was multiplied by 1·4, that of cement by 1·8; the electrical industry and aircraft construction made progress. The index of industrial production (basis 100 in 1942) had risen to 128 by 1951 and to 198 by 1956. The national income was multiplied by 1·5 between 1951 and 1956, but during the same period the individual income of the working population had remained unchanged: a sign of the stagnation of the standard of living.

The reason for this was that development had been largely based on a demand for labour. The period 1951–6 therefore witnessed a speeding up of the rural exodus. The Minister of Agriculture, speaking in Madrid on 18 July 1955, declared: 'We must convince those who live in such poverty in the countryside that their condition will never improve unless a number of those who are in such a situation leave.'

Convince them? Words alone never yet drove peasants from their lands. The rise of prices could do so, together with the worsening condition of wage-earners and small-holding peasants. An agrarian reform promulgated on 3 December 1953 did nothing to change the situation. The solution to Spain's agrarian problem, according to the government, was for the countryside to become depopulated. Peasants from Murcia, Jaen and Castile crowded into the huts, hovels and caves around Madrid and Barcelona; they provided manpower for industry and often proved, as expected, passive, docile and undemanding. Each year between 1951 and 1956 at least 250,000 peasants left the countryside for the cities. Many began to envisage emigration, and hoped for visas which would enable them to reach those countries, France or Germany, where life seemed easy and there was work for everyone. Day after day, whole families saved up the few thousand pesetas which would make the journey possible. Between 1951 and 1956 the number of workers who settled permanently in France was multiplied tenfold. It was still only 9,000. By 1962 there were almost a hundred times as many as in 1950: at least 65,000, for there were many temporary workers and others who had emigrated illegally.

Social Consequences

Spain's economic reality thus changed gradually between 1950 and 1956. Tourists, whose number increased daily (after 1950, the whole of Europe was experiencing an economic revolution, and up to a point Spain followed the same pattern) became aware of these changes. Roads and railways had improved; dams and new buildings had appeared. Some farsighted people bought the first dwellings for sale on the Costa Brava, that still intact paradise.

The social consequences of these economic upheavals were considerable, even though, between 1951 and 1955, they were often only potential. In any case, the bourgeoisie were growing stronger, wealthier, more numerous. True, this new wealth and power were related to function and technical expertise; none the less, new strata were merging which had never been very numerous in Spain. They characterized the new state of economic development which the country had now reached.

It was no accident that, during this period, the atmosphere of the universities altered and improved under the direction of the 'liberal' Ruiz Jiménez, owing partly no doubt to his personal policy, but also to technical necessity; the economy needed a large body of competent experts, lawyers, economists, engineers and technicians. These must be sought among the sons of the petty and middle bourgeoisie and even among the most gifted of the working class. They must acquire practical and *effective* knowledge of their problems. It was realized that the university must *of necessity* enjoy a certain liberty, and that at the same time, for that very reason and because of the increased number of students, it was liable to become a field of action for the opposition. Thus, beside the 'hundred families' that ran the country, certain middle class strata gradually emerged. Would the regime integrate them, or would the opposition win them to its cause? This was already one of the basic questions facing the new Spain.

It held new dangers for Francoism, particularly as the proletariat was now becoming stronger. According to the 1950 census the working population, in the industrial sector, comprised 2,754,162 persons. By 1955 there were 4,481,000; and living conditions had not improved, because wages, when they had risen at all, had not kept pace with the very rapid rise of prices due to inflation. On the other hand, the profits of the six largest Spanish banks had risen between 1950 and 1954 from 489·5 million pesetas to 832·5, and those of the six most powerful firms from 231·9 to 525·4 million pesetas.[5] The workers were aware of these differences, but between 1951 and 1955, owing to the increase in the number of jobs and the fact that the new workers were of recent peasant origin, and also to certain improvements in living standards (ration cards were abolished in 1952), as well as to the success of Francosim in the international field, there was no large scale protest. A few strikes in Vizcaya (December 1953) were swiftly and harshly repressed. Here, too, fresh perils were accumulating.

[5] Manuel Tunón de Lara, *Variaciones del nivel de vida en España* (Madrid, 1965).

The only sector in which the future held no threats for the regime was the rural one. The exodus from the countryside had in fact gradually dispersed that potentially revolutionary mass – which had throughout Spain's history been a revolutionary force – comprised by the poor peasantry and the agricultural labourers. The security thus gained by the regime in the countryside might be forfeited in the cities.

Thus despite the apparent calm of a land which seemed to be enjoying social peace after the fierce industrial conflicts of 1951, despite the successes of a regime wooed and supported by the most powerful country in the world and the strongest spiritual organization, the years 1951–5 witnessed the accumulation of new problems born of the economic and social changes transforming Spain. The future might depend on the attitude of the various political forces.

The Catholic Church

In Spain the Church was a political force, more particularly since the Concordat had provided Catholicism with increased possibilities for interference in social life. Apparently, the regime had nothing to fear from the Catholic Church. True, the Church knew when to take a stand on certain issues. On 15 June 1952, the Archbishop of Seville, Mgr Segura, had no hesitation in criticizing a speech of the Caudillo's addressed to the Arab nations, in which the head of the state compared the Islamic and Christian religions. This was a dangerous confusion, the prelate declared. The same Mgr Segura warned the Spanish people, in a pastoral letter of March 1953 (at the time of the negotiations with the United States) against the Protestant heresy. 'In no case may Protestants be allowed the same rights as Catholics,' he wrote.

These were only minor difficulties, which the Concordat smoothed over. The Cardinal Primate, in a decree of 19 October 1953, urged priests to add 'to the prayer *Et Famulos* the words *Ducem nostrum Franciscum*'. Thus the ecclesiastical hierarchy and the Franco regime were at one.

Barcelona had already (May 1952) been the seat of the thirty-fifth International Eucharistic Congress. The city, temporarily purged of its prostitutes, who had been packed off to near-by towns to the great satisfaction of their inhabitants,[6] witnessed demonstrations whose significance was unmistakable: Franco Spain had the full support of the Church. Ruiz Jiménez, speaking as Minister of Education, declared: 'Lord, may the whole Spanish university be like a monstrance making possible every excess for Thy sake.' The papers spoke of the Caudillo's 'eucharistic devoutness' and Franco, greeting the Papal legate, was able to 'consecrate Spain to the Eucharist'.

This openly displayed support, with the march-past of young Falangists during the Congress, offended the convictions of certain Catholics. The compulsory prayers for the Caudillo caused self-questioning among some young priests, for instance in the Basque country where the clergy were anti-Francoist and in close contact with the population. The wretched poverty of workers and peasants, the arrogant wealth of Franco's supporters also led many priests and

[6] cf. a story by Juan Goytisolo in *Pour vivre ici* (Paris, 1962).

believers to ask themselves whether the path chosen by the Church was the best way to win the hearts of the Spanish people. Inquiries showed, on the contrary, that a majority of the poorest class, even when they accepted the Church's principal sacraments, were fiercely anti-clerical. Henceforward in those sections of the Church where the priests were in close contact with their flock, or where for historic reasons (as in the Basque country) there was hostility to Francoism, and in groups concerned with the conversion of the poor (*Acción Católica*) or the workers (*Hermandad Obrera de Acción Católica*: H.O.A.C.), anxiety was felt about official Church policy, and the idea began to emerge that in order to save the Church it must be detached from Francoism, and even committed to opposition. Thus, the very triumph that Franco seemed to have scored with the Concordat and the open support won from the Church entailed fresh dangers for him.

This threat to his power was naturally strengthened by the progress, in working-class circles, of Socialist or Communist ideas – which the Church was bound to combat – and by the tendency, now that the universities had been liberalized by Ruiz Jiménez, for students and teachers to reconsider the whole culture of Spain without concern for the disapproval of the Church.

The Church fought back. For instance, when the University of Salamanca wished to celebrate its seventh centenary by recalling Unamuno, Mgr Antonio Pildaín, Bishop of the Canaries, expressed shocked astonishment, describing the philosopher as 'a major heretic and a master of heresy' (October 1953, in *Ecclesia*). This combative attitude could not satisfy the whole of the Church, and on this cultural plane too many young Catholics chose a different reaction: comprehension rather than condemnation.

Thus between 1951 and 1955, while the Concordat completed, crowned, emphasized and glorified the collaboration between the Church and Francoism, new ferments had begun to work within the Catholic community itself.

The Opus Dei, the Third Force and the Falange

This potentially dangerous development was noted by many groups within the hierarchy and also in the Opus Dei. The Concordat, reasserting the Catholic character of the Spanish state, was considered by members of the Opus Dei as the triumph of their own theses, and they became increasingly critical of such Catholics as Ruiz Jiménez who, under pretext of liberalism, seemed to make concessions to ideologies which they considered anti-Christian. The leader of this movement was Calvo Serer, who, in an article entitled *The Internal Policy of Franco's Spain*, published by the French journal *Les Ecrits de Paris* in September 1953, took up his stand against the 'Christian Democrats'. This term included men like Martín Artajo, Foreign Minister, as well as Ruiz Jiménez and the writers on the journal *Ya*. Also under attack were left-wing Falangists, Syndicalists and Alfredo Sanchez Bella, Director of the Institute of Hispanic Culture. Then Calvo Serer set forth the programme of a 'Third Force' consisting of his disciples. In the political field, the Caudillo must be asked to prepare for a restoration of the monarchy; in the economic field, Calvo Serer demanded the auditing of public expenditure, the reorganization of the administration and the assurance of economic freedom. In 1954, in another article, *España después de los tratados*, Calvo Serer developed his ideas with even greater precision.

Serer's attitude had considerable repercussions throughout Spain. On 29 October 1953, a mass meeting of the Falange was held in Madrid; it was in fact the first national Congress of the *Movimiento*. In the great hall of Madrid University a succession of speeches inveighed against the 'Third Force', against the '*camarillas*' attacking the Falange, when the Falange was needed not by Spain alone by but the entire West to provide its 'new and constructive solutions'. Franco himself took the chair at a giant demonstration in the Chamartin Stadium near Madrid, attended by some 150,000 persons from all over Spain. Here again time seemed to have stopped short: tens of thousands of men raised their arms in Fascist salute to a Caudillo in black uniform and red beret, shouting 'Franco, Franco, *Arriba España*.' Mass was celebrated. Then at 12.40 p.m. Franco addressed the crowd, praising the work of the Falange, which had united Spain and created 'a type of complete man'.

Thus, once again, the Caudillo backed the Falange, this time against the pretensions of Calvo Serer and the Opus Dei. The fact was that Serer's attitude had revealed the existence of a coherent group who had set themselves up as *successors* to the team then in power. The existence and importance of the Falange were essential if the Caudillo, confronted with this new clique, was to retain his role as indispensable arbiter, hence, this ceremonial honouring of a movement which had seemed dead. If for the Caudillo, personally, the line taken by Serer and the Opus Dei seemed to hold a threat, it was because it did not challenge the essence of Francoism, namely government by the propertied classes. On the contrary, their programme aimed at thwarting any evolution towards liberalism (the Christian Democrats), or republicanism (the Falangists), or revolution (certain left-wing Falangists), while encouraging the progress of economic development.

Calvo Serer, then, upheld economic freedom against the Falangist supporters of autarchy and of state preponderance. His aim, as early as 1953, could be defined as *the taking-over by a new team*, though a highly conservative and traditionalist one, of the new Spain that was emerging. From this point of view, the Caudillo would prove a hindrance only if he clung to the Spain of the past or to the Falange. On the other hand, he would be a valuable ally if he remained the arbiter on whom everything depended. The skill with which Franco manoeuvred suggests that he quickly understood on what conditions he could prolong his personal power. However, the attitude assumed by Serer and that section of the Opus Dei which he represented shows clearly that the years 1951-5 heralded further changes for Spain.

Monarchists and Falangists

The Caudillo prepared to face these. He had encouraged the Falange as a means of countering the Third Force. Now he welcomed the manoeuvres of the Monarchists, which could help him to withstand both the Falange and the Third

Force. In his interviews he never failed to emphasize that Spain was, constitutionally, a kingdom, 'in conformity with her traditions' (5 December 1954) and that his regime, with its 'open and flexible constitution' (31 December 1955) had 'defined the institutional process of the kingdom'. He thus kept the Pretender on a leash. When in November 1954, at the municipal elections (at which only 25 per cent of the electorate voted) in the constituency of Madrid the Monarchist candidate Joaquin Calvo Sotelo polled 28 per cent of the votes, Don Juan's partisans claimed a victory: they had ventured to put forward a candidate, and despite adverse pressure he had won a not inconsiderable number of votes.

The Caudillo had more than one trick up his sleeve. He resorted to that well-tried manoeuvre, a meeting with Don Juan. This took place in December 1954 at Caceres. The *Sunday Times* announced that the Caudillo would resign in 1964 and that Juan Carlos, son of Don Juan, would be proclaimed King of Spain. Such promises won over the Monarchists. Don Juan in June 1955 declared to *A.B.C.* that he supported the spirit of the *Movimiento* and the Falange. Franco, once again, was master of the field: by allying themselves with him, the Monarchists made the restoration dependent on his goodwill . . . which, if one knew Franco, meant postponing it until his disappearance from the scene. What else could they do?

The Caudillo had encouraged the Falange to lift up its head again, and its demagogical appeal attracted a number of young men. At that time of growing social unease due to inflation, they inevitably conflicted with the Monarchists . . . to the advantage of the Caudillo, who saw the factions neutralize one another. In May 1955, while Roberto Cantalupo was holding a conference in the Ateneo in Madrid, Falangist students burst in and beat up the assembled Monarchists. In November 1955, at the close of a ceremony organized at the Teatro de la Comedia to commemorate the foundation of the Falange, a procession formed and marched past with shouts of '*No queremos reyes idiotas*' (We don't want idiot kings.)

The young Falangists assembled at the Escorial flung their red *boinas* (berets) to the ground before Franco shouting '*¡ Abajo el capital!*' (Down with Capital) and 'Gibraltar!'

These shouts and clashes inevitably proved useful, almost necessary to Franco. The 'revolutionary' violence of the Falangist anti-capitalists aroused anxiety in business circles, which were demanding more economic freedom, less bureaucracy or autarchy. Franco once again appeared to these circles as their sole protection against a new, uncompromising Falange, some members of which had gone so far as to demand the nationalization of the banks. What a useful part the Caudillo played in canalizing and containing these energies! He was the man on whom the Monarchists relied to counter the republican tendencies of the Falange, and whom the Falangists expected to restrain the ambitions of capitalists and Monarchists, the man who might bring about the new social order. True, in all these groups, in each faction, there were some who experienced increasingly bitter disillusionment, but Franco remained the only point of junction between the different groups when they all feared the triumph of their common enemy:

the partisans of the left-wing opposition. Thus he was still the indispensable *shield* and the *keystone* of the different sections of the propertied classes.

The Left-Wing Opposition

Yet the threat from the left did not seem very weighty. If the right felt anxious, it was rather about the future, from a sense that an unseen reorganization was taking place. The new generations had joined in the struggle; 1951 had shown this. Each year that passed inevitably brought in new young men who were not paralysed by the memory of defeat in 1939, nor by fear. New fighters, who emerged first in the universities, now that some degree of intellectual freedom had been restored there; new groups, their eyes turned towards their own country rather than to foreign lands; trends already emerging from Catholicism and even from the Falange. The relation of forces changed, moreover, within this opposition. Anarchists and Socialists gradually lost ground to the Communists, who were better organized and enjoyed the support of an effective international structure – dedicated men in close contact with the masses. Moreover, the international situation was now in their favour; the United States, since its rapprochement with Franco, had become discredited in the eyes of his opponents. One of the leaders of the Spanish Communist Party, Fernando Claudín, could thus declare in October 1953: 'For years the leaders of the right-wing Socialists, Anarchists and Republicans cherished the notion . . . that our only hope of liberation lay in the intervention of the democratic powers, primarily the United States. Reality has shattered these illusions and vindicated the policy of the Communist Party.' Many of the younger generation supported him, hoping that the new strategy clearly formulated at the Fifth Congress (November 1954) would succeed. This implied the development of the line laid down after 1950, aiming at regrouping all national forces from the bourgeoisie to the proletariat against Francoism, which was leading the country to bankruptcy. The national anti-Franco front would make it possible, once Franco's regime was brought down, to establish a democratic regime. This over-simplified vision of the course of history assumed that there was no alternative between bankruptcy and democracy. It left out of account both the interests of the bourgeoisie and those of the increasingly numerous middle strata connected with it, who were fearful of any alliance with the Communists. In any case, this line implied a patient process of explanation and propaganda by Communist militants who were, as ever, relentlessly pursued by the police. The Socialists also took part in the struggle, but, as before, they still hoped that Europe's evolution towards unity would bring an end to Francoism. In November 1954 Llopis, as Secretary of the P.S.O.E., asserted that Franco had played his cards badly by allying himself with the United States, since Great Britain was the dominant power in Western Europe. Facts were soon to dissipate this fresh illusion: in December 1955 Spain was admitted to the United Nations by ten votes, with a single abstention: yet another proof, for the opposition, that the fate of Franco's regime must be decided primarily in Spain itself.

Death of a Cyclist

Spain's admission to the United Nations, coming after her entry into UNESCO, the Concordat and the Madrid Pact, seemed to crown Madrid's diplomatic efforts. Ten years after the death of Hitler and the end of the war, Francoism was triumphant in the international field. Internally, industry was developing with hectic speed, and prices rising. On the labour front, all seemed quiet. But the university world was stirring. Small groups of students were studying Marxism. Others took advantage of official demonstrations in favour of the liberation of Gibraltar to proclaim their hatred of Francoism. The atmosphere was changing. In October 1955, on the occasion of the funeral of the philosopher Ortega y Gasset, liberal sympathizers from the university marched in the streets of Madrid. There was political discussion in university circles; leaflets were circulated; magazines such as *La Hora* and *Alculá* stressed this rebirth of political feeling, which was obviously connected with the change in the student population and in the character of university life. At the end of 1955 there was launched the idea of a congress of young writers: *El Primo Congreso Nacional Universitario de Jóvenes Escritores*. This was announced in a leaflet which included a eulogy of Ortega y Gasset. Posters were printed. The government did not interfere at first, but eventually reacted by arresting a large number of students, members of the university and writers, and the organizers, including Mugica Hertzog and Lopez Campilla. This act finally aroused an important sector of the academic world to political awareness, and behind the façade of Francoism, even more resplendent since Spain's admission to the United Nations, a new danger had arisen.

Bardem's film *Muerte de un ciclista (Death of a Cyclist, 1955)* gives a true picture of Spain at that time, with its shocking contrasts, where big bourgeois and profiteers, selfish and corrupt, lived side by side with an impoverished and suffering working class. Between the two, the film portrays a university teacher from Madrid, the lover of a rich woman, wife of an industrialist. A car accident in which these two are responsible for the death of a cyclist, a worker, enlightens the teacher and makes him see Spain as she really is. It did indeed seem at times that only a minor incident was needed to bring to a head the contradictions and problems underlying the outward successes of Franco Spain.

CHAPTER III

THE CRISIS BEGINS
1956 – SPRING 1957

'In streets and lecture halls
I learned the hated lesson
Of injustice and its laws.'[1]

These lines echoed the feeling of many Spanish students in the early days of 1956. In the universities discussions proliferated, debates were organized and pamphlets circulated. Hostility to Francoism grew. A questionnaire circulated among students showed that over 70 per cent of them were critical of the regime, and the Rector of the university, Pedro Laín Entralgo, wrote a report on the unease prevalent in university circles. He submitted this to the Caudillo, and proffered his resignation, which was not accepted. This did not mean that Franco underestimated the danger: far from it.

Warnings

The leading figures in the government repeated their optimistic speeches and their warnings. Muñoz Grandes and Girón spoke of 'social justice'. 'Comrades, Workers,' declared Girón at the end of 1956, 'justice shall reign, Franco has always kept his word. . . . Have faith in Franco and in this new year which will complete twenty years of our revolution. . . . Let us cry: *i Viva Franco! i Arriba España!*' The Caudillo meanwhile spoke to his country's youth, denouncing the facile power of the communication media, radio, cinema and television through which 'the poison of materialism and discontent threaten to invade our homes.'[1] He sought to give the alarm to 'all those who serve as guides to the new generations' which, although 'having attained the age of reason amid the splendours of victory' were in danger of being corrupted and led astray. In face of 'Red barbarism', discipline and unbroken unity must be maintained.

The warning was clear. Yet agitation went on. In the *Tiempo Nuevo*, a students' club which had opened in Madrid thanks to the liberal policy of Ruiz Jiménez, proposals were made for a national congress of students which could discuss university problems, notably that of the censorship, and those arising from the existence of an official Falangist syndicate, the S.E.U. Former Falangists such as

[1] José Augustín Goytisolo (brother of the novelist Juan), *'Autobiographie'*, in *Psaumes au vent* (1958).

233

Dioniso Ridruejo, sons of important personalities of the regime, took part in these discussions, which aroused concern in Francoist circles and particularly in those of the military hierarchy. Pressure was put on the Caudillo to act swiftly and crush this unrest before it overflowed from the academic world into that of the workers, whose harsh living conditions were aggravated by the ceaseless rise in prices. Franco waited. He had grasped the problem, as his speech at the end of 1956 clearly indicates, but as usual he preferred to wait until the situation had matured and the adversary had deployed his forces, a well-tried strategy which he had always found successful and which was based on the conviction that the regime, despite temporary setbacks, remained firm because *it was irreplaceable.*

No doubt Franco's conviction was confirmed by the new attitude now taken up by Calvo Serer. True, the representative of the Opus Dei still asserted in *A.B.C.* (12 and 21 January) that 'monarchy, social and popular' must be the ultimate achievement of the Spanish political process. At the same time he endorsed the message of the head of the state, and emphasized the need of 'loyalty to the Victory'. He extolled the principles defended by the *Requetés* and the Falangists; what was needed, he declared, was unity between persons rather than any alteration of principles. This must have reassured the Caudillo. The Monarchist Third Force, closely associated with the Opus Dei, had declared its readiness to support him in exchange for 'unity between persons', in other words to govern *under the Caudillo's guidance and in his name.* Thus, at the start of 1956, Franco was offered *an alternative solution,* the possibility of *widening* the circle of governmental personalities to include men of the Opus Dei.

The incidents occurring in Spanish universities could only accelerate the *rapprochement* between the *homines novi* of the Opus Dei and the Caudillo.

The Events of February 1956

On 1 February a duplicated leaflet was distributed in Madrid; it proposed to convoke a meeting of the National Congress of Students the following April. Students' representatives were to be freely elected. On Saturday 4 February, at the election held by the law students of Madrid University, the Falangist candidates of the s.e.u. were beaten. On the 7th the Falangists reacted and tried to impose their candidates by force. In the streets, the students demonstrated with shouts of 's.e.u. no! Free Unions!' On the 8th, groups from the s.e.u. armed with cudgels tried to prevent students from entering the lecture rooms. There were clashes in the Calle San Bernardo, which spread as far as the Plaza de Callao in the very heart of the city. Falangists and anti-Falangists marched in two processions to the Ministry of Education, demanding to see the Minister; he was out of Madrid. The processions streamed back; at the main university buildings, anti-Falangists stormed and ransacked the premises of the s.e.u. Armed police drove up in vans and turned their hose-pipes on to the students, who responded by flinging stones. On the following day a Falangist ceremony was held in honour of Matias Montero, who had been killed by the Republicans in 1933. It was attended by a number of prominent people, and the Falangists with raised arms sang their *Cara al Sol* before marching to the centre of the city.

Meanwhile, students from the Law Faculty, whose ages ranged between 16 and 25, made their way along secondary streets to the Institute of Arts and Crafts, still shouting 'Down with the s.e.u.! Free Unions!' They hurled stones at the Institute, which was run by the Jesuits, and at an annexe of the s.e.u. buildings. They were taking their revenge, for troops of the *Guardia de Franco* had pursued them within the university precincts and were still hunting them down through the city.

The first clashes broke out in the Calle de Aguilera. Policemen in jeeps were rushed up; but they did not succeed in restoring order. Suddenly a shot was fired; on a raised space at a crossroads, held by Falangists, a student was seriously wounded in the head and carried away. In spite of this, fighting went on for over half an hour more. Not until the afternoon was calm restored, after several students had been arrested.

These incidents shocked public opinion in Madrid and throughout the country. In Seville, the students marched in protest, demanding that lectures be called off as a sign of solidarity with their comrades in Madrid. On 10 February the government decided to cancel all teaching for three days. Emergency measures were taken. Articles 14 and 18 of the Spaniards' Charter were suspended: henceforward any Spaniard could be put under house arrest or detained for over seventy-two hours by the police, without trial. The *Seguridad* published a list of those accused: there were seven Falangists, including Dioniso Ridruejo, Miguel Sánchez Mazas, son of a former minister, and Ramón Tamames, son of a well-known Madrid surgeon. The film producer Juan Bardem, who was shooting on location his new film *Calle mayor*, was arrested on 12 February at four in the morning.

There was a ferment of excitement in intellectual circles. The Falange circulated a list of a hundred anti-Falangist intellectuals whom it threatened with assassination if the wounded student did not recover. The chosen victims included such men as G. Marañón and Laín Entralgo, as well as a number of Monarchists.

A wind of panic blew through Madrid. Chaos had reigned for a few hours in the capital, and those responsible were the sons of the bourgeoisie, privileged members of Franco's Spain who had grown up remote from the temptations of liberalism. The events both shocked and disturbed 'right-thinking' circles, which moreover disapproved of the actions of the thugs of the Falange, the *pistoleros* of the militia, such as the *Guardia de Franco*; these were trouble-makers, in many people's opinion. How could one rely on men who, while proclaiming their loyalty to Franco, also used words with disturbing implications such as 'comrades' (addressed to the workers), 'nationalization', or sometimes even 'revolution'? Moreover, had not certain Falangists such as Dioniso Ridruejo, or Tovar, Rector of the university, gone over to the liberal side?

It was such feelings of concern for the 'civil peace' of the Franco regime that led some military leaders to appeal to the Caudillo. Twenty years after the pronunciamento, the Spanish army still stood with arms at the ready, a force of order and conservatism, prepared to play its part as guardian of that order – its own order – which it identified with the welfare of Spain. Muñoz Grandes,

Minister of War, and Rodrigo, Captain-General of Madrid, visited the Caudillo to remind him that the army was ready, if need be, to replace the ineffective forces of the police.

The Caudillo had kept his head. Falangists and anti-Falangists had clashed, order had been restored, and he, Franco, remained alone on the battlefield. On 16 February he took a political measure which, as usual, had *two aspects and a single aim*: to strengthen his role as arbiter and hence his power. Ruiz Jiménez was removed from his post as Minister of Education, and Fernández Cuesta, Secretary-General of the Falange, suffered the same fate. Nevertheless the Caudillo did not crush the Falange, which could still be of use to him against the Monarchists or the army. José Luis Arrese, one of the leading theoreticians of 'National Syndicalism', who had already held office and had written treatises on *The Mission of the Falange*, now replaced Cuesta, while a technician, Jesús Rubio, was placed at the head of the university.

The new ministers made their solemn vows to the Caudillo, at the Pardo Palace. Franco's Spain had survived.

The Depth of the Crisis, and the Opposition

In fact, it had been profoundly shaken by the events of February. Their principal significance was to emerge with increased force during all the year 1956. Quite evidently, Francoism had proved incapable of absorbing the younger generation, more particularly the young intellectuals. This failure was serious, for the events of February had led many students not to 'settle down' but to become more radical. They had opposed the censorship and the monopoly of the s.e.u.; now they were turning anti-Francoist. Official propaganda, which repeated day after day that the February disturbances had been the result of 'Communist man-oeuvres' trying to make use of 'progressives . . . as a third order of communism', had the same effect. *A.B.C.* on 12 February, for instance, inveighed against 'those literary magazines published by progressives, such as *Observador*, which reveal the existence of a Spanish writer whom none of us had ever heard of . . . a recruit for the third order of communism'. The immoderate tone of such articles turned many students, hitherto undecided, towards the extreme left.

Communist activity now became livelier and found a ready response in these circles. *Mundo Obrero* advised student party members to combine legal and illegal forms of action, and to work out, 'for students of various tendencies, a minimum programme which would combine the aspirations common to the various groups'. These flexible tactics in the interests of unity bore fruit.

They must of course be viewed in relation to happenings in the Communist world. On 14 February 1956, the Twentieth Congress of the Communist Party of the u.s.s.r. opened, and on the 25th heard Khrushchev's report on Stalin's crimes. Published in Washington on 4 June, this had shocked Communist Parties throughout the world, including the Spanish c.p., which now intensified the *revision* of its strategy. Vicente Uribe, who had been the leader of the under-ground organization, was demoted. In April the Executive Committee published a clear statement of its policy: 'There are growing possibilities of understanding, in the struggle against dictatorship, between forces which fought on opposite sides during the Civil War.' Santiago Carrillo carried this policy to its extreme conclusion when he declared that 'the responsibilities of the Civil War, on both sides, must be forgotten'. Unquestionably this policy of consistent national reconciliation gained results: contacts were made with Christian-Democrats and even with representatives of right-wing groups, all concerned to relegate the Civil War to history and avoid any renewal of bloodshed. These *rapprochements*, this conciliatory strategy held potential threats for the Franco regime.

Moreover, 1956 witnessed the emergence of new centres of opposition, representing most sectors of Spanish opinion. These took shape as the *Agrupación Socialista Universitaria* (A.S.U.), the *Izquierda Demócrata Cristiana* (I.D.C.), which aimed at putting into practice the strictest Christian principles, and the *Partido Social de Acción Democrática* (P.S.A.D.), which, while prepared to accept a restoration of the monarchy, was anxious for the transformation of Spanish society. Finally, since Communist policy was highly exacting and at the same time lacking in glamour, coherent and realistic and yet liable to seem utopian, some young militants rejected it as too moderate and conciliatory, and initiated the *Frente de Liberación Popular* (F.L.P.). They declared in the first number of *Revolución Socialista*

'that there is in Spain an objectively revolutionary situation of which the traditional parties are unable or unwilling to make use. Our mission is to take over their task and to work without delay, in the secrecy imposed on us by Francoism, for our aim: a Socialist revolution, that is, the violent seizure of power by the worker.'

This strategy was radically opposite to that of the Communists, and it revealed not only the breadth of the movement of ideas in 1956 and the scale on which the opposition had developed, but also the uncertainty and powerlessness of that opposition, since the birth of the F.L.P., while reflecting the impatience of youth, also proves the failure of Communist strategy to yield decisive results.

The Anarchists, too, acquired renewed vigour from the events of 1956, but not on the scale of their former influence over the Spanish masses. In December 1956 the C.N.T. issued an appeal for active resistance against Francoism. Anarchist militants were still being shot down by the police; among them was José Lluis Facerías, known as the indomitable *luchador* (wrestler), who had been fighting Francoism for the past twenty years. At the crossroads between Calle Urrutia and Calle Verdun he fell into an ambush. In spite of individual acts of courage, anarchism does not seem to have made a deep appeal to the younger generation. The same is true of the P.S.O.E. and Republican groups committed to political projects which, having been conceived in exile without regard to the real evolution of the country, met with no echo there.

It seems clear that in Spain, as in other European countries, a regrouping of forces took place from 1956 onward: the Communist Party playing a preponderant role in the opposition, Catholic groups taking an active part, small revolutionary sects gradually becoming more clearly defined, and the consequent elimination of former influences derived from nineteenth-century liberalism, such as the Social-Democratic and Republican groups. The year 1956 was the starting point of this evolution and at the same time marks the unquestionable growth of the opposition movement, which attracted many young people to whom life and experience were bringing political consciousness.

One unmistakable sign was the daily increasing output of protest poetry. After the arrest of students in Madrid a song became widely known in the capital, written in the traditional form of verses sung alternately by the imprisoned students, guarded by the Social Brigade, and the chorus of mothers or of free students.

> ' Prison of Carabanchel
> our new school
> where we must learn lessons
> that must never offend
> our fatherland Spain
> nor its immortal Caudillo'.

José Augustin Goytisolo describes, in his *Search Warrant*, one of the scenes so common in university circles from 1956 onwards:

> 'Don't look over here,
> these are only books. I think
> you are making a mistake.
> ... these are merely poems,
> a few little verses, dead letters.'

The authorities harried these young poets because youth had become the focus and the starting-point of a movement which seemed dangerous; and they sought to arrest all those who in any way – by merely handing out leaflets, perhaps – had dared to oppose the regime. For instance, in the spring of 1956 they succeeded in identifying the authors of certain anti-Francoist pamphlets circulated in Madrid, who were brought to trial on 23 and 24 April. Four men were accused: Vicente Girbau, an official in the Ministry of Foreign affairs, Jesús Ibáñez, a lecturer in the School of Journalism, one civil servant and one clerk. A far more significant figure than the men in the dock was their defence counsel: Gil Robles. The former leader of the right-wing C.E.D.A., who had returned from exile two years previously, had undertaken to defend the accused. This caused a sensation, for the spectacular reappearance of this great ghost from the past proved that the whole political situation of the Franco regime was shifting: the right wing seemed to have split up into a multiplicity of trends. The accused and all witnesses (including Laín Entralgo, Dean Torres of the Faculty of Law and D. Ridruejo) agreed in laying the blame for the disturbances on armed groups from outside the university (the Falangist militia), and all stressed the disquiet prevailing in Spanish universities. The accused, of course, were condemned, but the trial had been held in public and Gil Robles had uttered his warning 'against the worship of the state'. 'It is lawful,' he had exclaimed, 'to criticize the authorities when injustices have been committed in their name.' Something was indeed stirring in Spain.

Even more symbolically: on 30 April, in the crowded hall of the Provincial Court in Madrid, there was held the public trial of four law students accused of having published a leaflet inciting students to a forty-eight hour strike on the occasion of the meeting of the Executive Council of UNESCO in Madrid. They, too, were condemned. Among the four young men – by one of those significant chances which history sometimes presents – were Manuel Fernández Montesinos, nephew of the poet Federico García Lorca, murdered by the Nationalists, and Francisco Bustelo, nephew of José Calvo Sotelo, the Monarchist leader, killed in July 1936 by Republicans. They stood side by side in the dock, so long after the Civil War, both enemies of Francoism.

The crisis begun in 1956 was thus a serious one. What made it even more dangerous for Francoism was the fact that it was not confined to student activities. It was in fact a manifestation of the changes taking place in the whole economic and social structure of Spain.[2] In that field the situation was very serious.

A Catastrophic Economic and Social Situation

Industrial production had indeed risen, but its rhythm was already slower than in the period 1954–5, and development was hampered by the restrictions on power, which still existed in 1957. Agriculture remained backward; indeed it now lagged even further behind other European countries: in 1956 one tractor served 605 hectares, as against 1 for 50 in France, which was by no means in the lead as regards the modernization of agriculture. Natural disasters had further aggravated the situation: frosts in 1956, catastrophic floods in the Valencia region, hurricanes over the Canaries which destroyed the banana plantations in 1957. Efforts at renovation affected only a few regions (Badajoz, Jaen) and barely 65,000 hectares of land. Under these conditions, agricultural production rose very slowly, and consequently agricultural exports tended to decrease.

This aggravated the cancer devouring Spain's economy, the deficit in the balance of payments: in 1956 it was two and a half times higher than in 1955; in 1957 it rose by 10 per cent above the 1956 level. American aid, though still on a considerable scale, could not solve the problem, since the United States was still the biggest buyer from Spain and its help only intensified the deficit in currency. As public – and private – investment increased, so did the total amount of money in circulation, and inflation assumed catastrophic proportions: 47 million pesetas in circulation at the beginning of 1965, 51 million by the end of the year. The value of Spanish money decreased daily on foreign exchanges, the rate in relation to the dollar shifting from 43 to 50. The gold holding now represented only 1 per cent of the notes in circulation. A general rise in prices ensued, intensifying social inequalities: in less than a year it reached 20 per cent. One solution would have been to reduce investments and the state budget, in short to return to stagnation. One of the laws of economics is the impossibility of reverting to an earlier situation. The working class, an increasingly important section of the population, would resent the reintroduction of rationing, and the peasants who had recently come to live in the cities would be unwilling to return to their arid, stony fields.

[2] cf. preceding chapter.

239

This was proved when, in the spring of 1956, as the standard of living worsened, a tense social situation arose throughout the country.

There were many unmistakable signs of this. Mgr Herrera, in a pastoral letter early in January, denounced 'the lack of social conscience among Spanish Catholics', condemned the distribution of wealth in the country, and echoed the disquiet aroused among industrial workers, peasants and intellectuals by the shocking way of life of the privileged classes. The government reiterated its declarations on the need to establish social justice, and set on foot a national housing scheme; on 13 January, joint production committees were set up in all firms employing 500 or more workers. *Pueblo*, the journal of the *Sindicatos*, put it quite simply: 'The policy of the national-syndicalist state is aimed at avoiding class warfare by closely associating the workers with the interests and control of firms.' Finally on 3 March the Cabinet decided to increase wages by 27 per cent (in two stages, on 1 April and 1 October), but the government assumed responsibility for part of the employers' contributions to national insurance . . . so that costs hitherto borne by the employers now fell on the mass of the Spanish people. The increase in wages was not, in the end, paid for by the employers, who on the contrary took advantage of it to speed up the rise in prices. The workers could reply only by going on strike.

This happened in April in the provinces of Navarre, Guipuzcoa, Viscaya, Alava and finally in Barcelona. On 13 April, in spite of appeals from the Civil Governor, several thousands of workers downed tools, demanding action against the rise of prices. In Barcelona, the men of the *Maquinista Terrestre y Maritima* went on strike; in Vizcaya, those of Babcock and Wilcox and General Electric. The Civil Governor countered with a lock-out. The movement spread none the less, despite a large number of arrests, particularly in Asturias. The government, meeting on 28 April in Seville with Franco presiding, realized that it would have to concede fresh wage claims. In the end, the workers secured an increase of 25 to 70 per cent, depending on the sector concerned. This did not halt the inflationary process: quite the reverse.

On 18 December 1956, panic rumours were rife in Madrid. A report by the Minister of Trade, M. Arburua, had been circulated to the various ministers before a Cabinet meeting. It consisted of sixteen typed pages, and it pointed out out that Spain's gold reserves had fallen to $40 million. Public investment had exceeded the nation's savings. Thus the minister conjured up the spectre of bankruptcy. He recommended a harshly austere policy as the only alternative to 'the flight of capital, the depreciation of money, the shortage of currency, the impossibility of accepting fresh credits . . . perhaps even a return to rationing'.

This reveals the gravity of the economic situation, (and the failure of Franco's policy), which took on particular importance in the political atmosphere of 1956. Things were definitely going badly for the Franco regime; the upsurge of intellectual youth had coincided with conditions favourable to mass action by the working class, at the very moment when the economic difficulties that threatened expansion were causing deep uneasiness to the coalition which, for the past twenty years, had supported the Caudillo. Now, to this already considerable burden, there were added two factors which *might* prove adverse to the regime:

the problem of Morocco and the political rivalry between various Francoist factions.

The Problem of Morocco

The Caudillo, 'Franco Africanus', whose military career had started on the hills of the Rif, had always attributed the greatest importance to Spain's presence on African soil. Moreover, Spanish diplomacy, anxious to secure allies who would vote with Spain in international assemblies, flattered Arab nationalism – which, needless to say, retained the traditional forms that expressed its immutable social, political and religious structure. Franco, for his part, extolled 'unchanging Islam', and all his speeches reflect the wish to provide Spain with an important role, that of tutor, representative and intermediary for the Arab world, Britain and France having lost all authority there. His policy was to supplant these countries and ensure for Spain and for himself the prestige of a grand imperialist enterprise: the classic ambition of a would-be 'great power'.

The failure of this ambitious aim is clearly demonstrated in Franco's dealings with Morocco. In order to secure the support of Moroccan Nationalists, Franco backed them in their conflict with France. He refused to recognize the Sultan Mohammed Ben Arafa, and in the Spanish zone Mohammed Ben Youssef, whom the French had deported, was the only leader for whom prayers were said in the mosques. Furthermore, the Spanish zone provided a refuge, a point of departure and assembly and an arms base for all Moroccans hostile to French policy. General Rafael García Valino, Governor of the Spanish zone of Morocco, was one of France's fiercest opponents. On 21 January 1954, Moroccan notabilities assembled in the race-course at Tetuan to hear a formal denunciation of French policy by the Spanish general. Entertaining these same notabilities in Madrid, the Caudillo promised 'to defend Moroccan unity resolutely', and thanked 'his Moroccan brothers' for the trust they had placed in him.

Unfortunately for Spain, Edgar Faure's government was to restore Mohammed V to the throne on 5 November 1955. The Caudillo was trapped by his own generous declarations. He resorted to a series of warnings against the dangers of too rapid an evolution in Morocco. Above all, the 'spiteful intestine conflicts of European political parties' must not be introduced into Africa. On 2 March 1956, France granted Morocco its independence. The Caudillo had to act quickly, for already the first skirmishes had broken out in the Spanish zone.

On 4 April 1956, therefore, he welcomed Mohammed V at the airport of Barajas. On order from the trade unions, all work stopped in the town from ten in the morning to allow the population to greet the Sultan. The two heads of state drove into Madrid in Franco's black Rolls-Royce, escorted by a score of horsemen from his Moorish guard. Behind the acclamations and friendly speeches, some hard bargaining went on, which lasted until 6 a.m. on 7 April, inevitably with the recognition of Moroccan independence. Spain, however, retained the Presidio of Melilla and that of Ceuta, and the region of Ifni.

The press, of course, acclaimed the event, attacking 'France's devious policy' and 'the efforts of Soviet Russia to penetrate Africa'; the fact remained that

'Franco Africanus', who had planned to build a greater Spain, had abandoned Morocco. In some military circles there was bitter disappointment. For the benefit of the general public, the press extolled the wisdom of Franco's policy, his friendship towards the Arabs. In May 1956 the Queen Mother of Jordan and King Feisal of Iraq visited Madrid. The Algerian war had already begun, poisoning France's relations with the whole Arab world, and Franco once again cherished the hope of playing a great international role. Feisal attended the grand military parade, the 'march past of victory', then he toured the countryside, visiting Toledo, Seville, Granada. Television, then a novelty in Spain, showed the victory celebrations and the mutual accolades of King and Caudillo. The press made much of the event, and *Informaciones* wrote of 'the increased possibilities of mediation that Spain could offer the free countries . . . friendship with Spain can provide reliable support for the North African and Middle Eastern nations.' Ceremonies, an ambitious diplomatic plan: so, perhaps, people might forget that Morocco had won its independence, and that Spain was still in the throes of a crisis.

To disguise that fact, moreover, it was always possible to stress the Red peril or the important part played by Spain in the defence of the West in the Mediterranean. When it came to finding scapegoats for the economic and financial crisis, much play was made of the fact that Juan Negrin, former Republican Premier, who died on 15 November 1956, left to the Madrid government the receipts from the U.S.S.R. for the Spanish gold he had transferred there; the fact was authentic, but it was not by publishing communiqués, or filling the front pages of newspapers with great photographs of Martin Artajo handing over to the Deputy Governor of the Bank of Spain thcse precious receipts (representing 15 to 20 milliard notes and 1,734 million pesetas in gold) that the economic and financial situation in Spain could be transformed.

That gold belonged to the past; and every day in Spain, as new generations emerged, the past was dying. It was a sign of changing times that discreet diplomatic talks were being begun with Moscow. A number of Soviet diplomats stationed in Europe visited Spain; Russian scholars and technicians attended congresses there. Time had passed. On 24 November the ship *Crimea* called at the port of Castellón de la Plana, bringing back 273 Spaniards from the U.S.S.R. They had left as children, they were men now: twenty years had gone by. It was clearly impossible for the Caudillo to lay the blame for the 1956 crisis on the outside world, it was impossible for him to conceal it by means of more or less fictitious international successes or to pretend that it was simply the result of a civil war now so remote that many Spaniards knew it only through vague childhood memories or their parents' stories. The crisis of 1956 was Francoist Spain's own sickness. It was a test for the Caudillo, the more dangerous because it was set him by a new Spain.

The Caudillo, the Crisis and the Falange

The Caudillo faced it skilfully. He paid visits to certain regions of the country: Andalusia in April 1956, Estremadura in October. He inaugurated improvements, he made speeches in praise of the regime and the work of the National Institute of Colonization, and called on the farmers around Toledo to bear witness to the transformation of their lands. The themes of unity, stability and discipline recurred constantly, concluding with the inevitable '*Arriba España*' to which local Falangists, led by the team that followed the Caudillo around on his journeys, replied with '*i Viva Franco!*'

These speeches had their effect, even if they only seem to fill the pages of newspapers which many Spaniards never read. In point of fact, they created a political atmosphere which, amplified by press, radio, television and news reels, was intended not so much to convince people as to display the enduring strength of the regime and its leader. The Caudillo's speeches and his visits to the poorest provinces of Spain did not arouse political awareness, on the contrary they increased political indifference; they were an expression of the political monopoly of the Caudillo and his supporters. However, speeches alone would have little effect on the Spanish exchequer, as Franco was well aware. Once again his tactics consisted in observing, and utilizing, the rivalry between factions.

After the February incidents, the Falange once again believed that its hour had struck. The Caudillo appeared to rely on Arrese and to have accepted, at last, the application of Falangist principles. He even entrusted the minister who was Secretary-General of the Party with the task of preparing the new fundamental laws which would provide Francoism with popular support, since they would initiate a regime of social justice, outside the capitalist system. The Falangist leaders, some of them in all good faith, undertook to prepare these documents. The *Movimiento*, benefiting by the uncertainties of the political situation and the social atmosphere, recruited new adherents for the first time in many years: several tens of thousands of young men without political education were attracted by its demagogy and its promises.

During the whole of 1956 Falangist activity was hectic. There were speeches, writings, confabulations and reorganizations: on 12 July, for instance, the S.E.U., whose authority the students had challenged, became a National Delegation of the Falange. There were also divisions among the Falangists, during these months which seemed to offer their movement its last chance. Some feared that once again the Caudillo was making use of them in the interests of his own power, without concern for the future of the movement. Luis González Vicén, former chief of the Valladolid militia, protested against the fact that the Falange leaders still relied on Franco's authority to establish the new system, although the power of a single man was always fragile and 'since, alas, if all men are naturally capricious, men in power are particularly so, and however highly placed he may be, a single man must not impose his whims on a whole country'. Such language was unacceptable to the Falangists. In fact, they were all bound to Franco, and depended on his recognition of their movement and their principles. They were even less able in 1956 than they had been previously to act autonomously without prejudicing their personal careers and their organization. Vicén had to resign.

The Caudillo moreover deliberately reassured and flattered the Falange. On 17 July 1956 (twenty years after the outbreak of the Civil War) we find him, clad in the uniform of National Chief of the *Movimiento*, wearing the Grand Cross of San Fernando, entering the former Palace of the Senate to address the 144 national councillors of the Falange. In a speech which took up fifteen columns in the newspapers he extolled the Movement in vague and obscure phrases, which did not commit him but suggested that he was ready to follow the Falangists as far as they could wish: 'I have unceasingly repeated, without always being under-stood,' he declared, 'that the continuity of the National Movement lay in the Movement itself.'

On the following day, 18 July, the anniversary of the Glorious Uprising, these themes were reiterated. The Caudillo inaugurated a housing scheme in Madrid (822 dwellings); he received the diplomatic corps at the Granja palace and confer-red decorations. *Arriba* asserted: 'Since its foundation, the Falange has been the keystone of Spanish policy' – an untruth which the Falangists were endeavouring to convert into a fact. The new fundamental laws, hectically prepared by Arrese, were at last going to transform Spain. On 29 September 1956, a huge assembly was held at Salamanca for the twentieth anniversary of the uprising. Arrese appealed with mystical fervour to the shade of the martyr José Antonio: 'You have no cause to be pleased with us, José Antonio,' he exclaimed. 'If you look down on us, on this twentieth anniversary of your death, it can only be with sorrow mingled with scorn. You cannot approve of the mediocrity and material-ism that prevail among us today.'

Now everything was going to be changed, thanks to the Falange and the Caudillo and the new laws.

Franco let them talk away. His speeches and actions implied that he approved. In fact he was observing and calculating. When the Falange inveighed against the liberal trends at work within the Church, when it attacked the Opus Dei, the army itself, or the Monarchists, Franco's power was enhanced as he stood arbiter, mediator between all these groups, the keystone of the system. It was a classic strategy which he had often employed with success. At the end of 1956, however, the choice before him was more crucial. To support the Falange, revive the spirit of José Antonio, give the men of the *Movimiento* a free hand, meant obstructing Spain's development, or at any rate letting it take an individual course which was not, or was no longer, that of Western Europe. On the economic plane it meant state control, a sort of interventionist planning, the reverse of the general tendency of capitalism towards the interpenetration of the state *by* big business.

In any case, Franco had no freedom of choice. The crisis – economic, financial, political and social – that existed at the end of 1956 showed that Spain could not continue to combine the tumultuous pressures of industrial growth with the burdensome constraint of archaic state control. The proof of Franco's realism, his opportunism, his political awareness, is that he understood the impossibility of retrogression or immobilization. He knew that to save the regime – and his personal power – the Falange could be made use of as a political force, a faction to set against another faction, but that he could not entrust it with the leadership of the country. It was a pawn, to be played against other pawns. It did not lay down the rules of the game. The Caudillo had long since understood the need to accept the rules dictated by the relations between forces due to economic development.

Relations Between Forces in Spain: the Role of the Army

Franco's expert intelligence enabled him to discern those relations clearly and to recognize where the real power lay.

On the one hand, there was the industrial working class – Asturian miners, factory hands of Barcelona – which had recently re-emerged from obscurity and was pressing its claims with demonstrations and strikes; and there was the world of intellectuals and students, a turbulent group clamouring for freedom of expression and seizing any pretext to show its opposition to the regime. On Monday 29 November 1956, a demonstration in Barcelona in support of the Hungarian rising developed into a display of hostility to Francoism. Students marched through the streets carrying posters that declared in huge letters: 'We students demand liberty, we are against dictatorship' – and below, in tiny illegible letters: 'for Hungary'. The police were obliged to intervene and clear the students out of the university buildings; a number of arrests were made. The most distinguished intellectuals, moreover, gave their support to this student protest movement. It was learnt at the end of November 1956 that a collective letter had been sent, on 2 November, to the Minister of National Education, signed by such men as Menéndez Pidal, José María Pemán, Marañón, etc., urging the release of the imprisoned students. Within the common front of workers and intellectuals there were various political trends which often conflicted: the events in Hungary, for instance, were scarcely likely to promote co-operation with the Communists, whose aim – to become the unifying and dominant force within the whole opposition movement – seemed remote from realization.

The conclusion was obvious: opposition from workers and intellectuals was a force which had many flaws. The existence of a superior force would bring out these flaws and reveal the powerlessness of the opposition to overthrow the regime. Now such a force existed, and the Caudillo knew it well, having sprung from it himself; it was the pride and joy of the regime – the Spanish army, together, of course, with the police force and Guardia Civil, with their specific attributes.

So long as he could count on the army, the Caudillo knew that his regime ran no risk. If the Falange was a useful pawn in political manoeuvres, enabling him to eliminate some particular faction or personality, the army could range over the whole chessboard.

Throughout 1956 therefore Franco strengthened his contacts with military circles. He had reassured Muñoz Grandes who, in February, had pressed for military intervention. On 28 April, during his tour of Andalusia, he visited the headquarters of military institutions in the Heliopolis district of Seville. Muñoz Grandes was with him. The Captain-General of the Second Region expressed the loyalty of all the armed forces: 'May God protect you, *mi General*,' he concluded, 'and may we always be at your orders. *¡ Viva Franco! ¡ Vive España!*' Franco answered with a speech which is of considerable importance, proving that he had already analysed the Spanish situation perfectly and assessed the various forces. The representatives of the army, navy and air force were assembled there to demonstrate their solidarity with the Caudillo. 'The army is the backbone of the Fatherland,' Franco began. 'Its forces, which are responsible for the external defence of the nation, must also protect its internal peace and order.' His conclusion was clear and positive: 'The sacred mission of a nation's armies consists in maintaining order, and that is the mission which we have fulfilled.'

A soldier and a realist, having come to power at the end of a civil war, the Caudillo knew that arms are the final argument in political conflicts, and these were in the hands of the army. True, in 1956 the Caudillo was not alone in his concern about the attitude of the army. Monarchist circles in particular were eagerly seeking contact with military men. Ministers, bankers, bishops and industrialists started talks with generals, forming what were described, in political circles in Madrid, as 'independent groups'. *Ya*, the organ of *Acción católica*, went so far as to write that 'the army is the institution which, in case of a crisis, can provide the best solution and take the necessary initiative for the nation, since it has a sense of historical continuity'.

The army meanwhile made quite clear that its officers were aware of the power they controlled. Military juntas were formed in Valencia, Seville, Valladolid and Barcelona. They comprised captains, majors, sometimes colonels, openly discussing political problems. Student demonstrations and strikes were severely censured and the abandonment of the Moroccan protectorate was also criticized.

Franco was the only man who really had the military institution under his control. He was its most perfect representative; he had lavished favours on it. Now the agreements with the United States provided officers with possibilities of promotion. In the Ateneo in Madrid, that March, General Carrasco Verde organized a series of discussions on the theme 'The officer in Spanish society', at which he asserted that on 18 July 1936, the army had finally been reintegrated into the nation.

Furthermore, the Caudillo had a hold over the Monarchists not only thanks to the 'succession', but also through his many personal contacts with military and monarchist circles. Thus the tutor of the Infante Carlos at the Military School at Saragossa, General Martínez Campos, Duke de la Torre, was a loyal supporter both of the Caudillo and of Don Juan. Even the Moroccan situation had finally been accepted; the army thus had no reason to oppose Franco, since he was prepared to let it retain the leading place which it had occupied in the country's life ever since 1936.

Sure of military support, the Caudillo could be sure of the future: order would be maintained. Now he could declare his choice.

The Caudillo's Choice : the Favourable Moment

On 15 June 1956, 'United States Day', the American Ambassador to Madrid, John Davis Lodge, visited the Barcelona Fair in the company of various local authorities. At the United States pavilion he made a speech to the assembled notabilities, the importance of which was quickly realized. He spoke of Spanish–

American trade, declaring that he was well aware that post-war problems had forced the Spanish government to impose certain restrictions; but, he went on,

'I am certain that Spain in her upward march will find a way to diminish the obstacles that hinder the entry of foreign capital, which might be of such use to her. American capital will then, if certain liberalizing measures are taken, bring effective help to Spanish capital for the economic development of the country.'

Washington had spoken: the past must be dropped, and more help would be provided. Spain must choose the Western way of development and reject an archaic form of state control. This was just what men like Calvo Serer, and the Opus Dei, had proposed. Moreover, as we have already noted, industrial development had already reached such a high point, and the importance and political combativeness of the working class had increased so much, that retrogression was impossible.

In December 1956 the Caudillo made his choice. He bowed to reality. Captain Luis Carrero Blanco, a minister in the Presidencio del Gobernio, who had all that year kept the Caudillo informed as to the intentions of the Opus Dei's political team, introduced into government circles a young professor of administrative law, Lopez Rodo, born in 1920, son of an industrialist and a minor figure in the Opus, who had attracted interest with an article on administrative reform. Lopez Rodo became *Secretario Técnico de la Presidencia del Gobernio*. Thus political power was almost within the grasp of the Opus Dei. Moreover the government had begun to show some concern for modernization, for a rational development of the economy.

However, the choice had been made. On 29 December Arrese presented his report on the new fundamental laws to the National Council of the Falange. This immediately aroused sharp opposition from the Catholic hierarchy, from financial and economic circles, from Monarchists and generals. Franco, however, took no action as yet. In his end-of-the-year speech he merely proffered generalities, declaring that 'the Spanish state is a Catholic state in conformity with the doctrine recently set forth by the Supreme Pontiff', and that 'the Spanish state has succeeded in reconciling social and national interests'. Meanwhile he was waiting for a favourable moment to make his choice known.

The economic and financial situation had deteriorated; social tension was growing. On 14 January 1957, there was trouble in Barcelona: a boycott of the tramways led to student demonstrations in which stones were flung at cars and some policemen were injured; the police then pursued the students into the university buildings. On 18 January, at La Pasarela, in the Calle San Fernando, some youths overturned a trolley bus; effigies of Franco and of José Antonio were thrown down from the top of the university tower. On 20 January all public entertainments were boycotted. Lawyers and teachers were arrested. The statue of Victory in the Avenida del General Franco was damaged; a bomb exploded and windows were broken. Next day the police organized a massive search.

There was talk, once more, of underground activity. Anxiety increased. In Madrid, unrest came to a head in February. An almost total boycott of the city's transport services was organized in sympathy with the workers of Barcelona.

Groups of students stoned cars on the Plaza de la Cibeles and beside the Toledo bridge. Hundreds of them rallied in front of the former Law Faculty building in the Calle San Fernando, shouting '*i Barcelona! i Viva la libertad!*' At the Gran Via crossroads the police charged and dispersed the crowd. The crowning audacity was an attempt by students to overturn a tram at the Puerta del Sol, almost immediately in front of the sinister buildings of the Dirección de la Seguridad. Policemen rushed out and pursued them. Arrests were made. On 11 February the University of Barcelona, which had been closed down, reopened, but students were allowed in only on showing their university cards, while police officers stood around. By the 18th trouble had broken out again. On the 21st students assembled in the main amphitheatre of the university and turned the lecture into a mass meeting. Deans of faculties forgathered hastily; ushers confiscated students' cards, and the Vice-Rector, García Valdecasas, called in two companies of Policía Armada. Some students who refused to leave the amphitheatre were arrested by the police.

Thus the early months of 1957 were full of unrest: street violence, mass demonstrations in Barcelona and Madrid, militant student action, and arrests, while the press denounced communism and the 'dupes, liberals, Christian-Democrats, don't-knows and grudge-bearers' who played the Communist Party's game (*A.B.C.*, 22 February). The atmosphere was one of uncertainty and unease, even though these events had evidently been confined to certain areas and social groups. Nevertheless it was a propitious moment for the Caudillo, since under these circumstances who, among the groups upholding the regime, could oppose his decisions without siding with the disturbers of order?

On 26 February 1957 press headlines announced a decree on the reorganization of the central administration of the state, and an important Cabinet reshuffle. Franco's Spain was starting out on a new path.

The Government of February 1957: Soldiers, Unconditional Supporters and Technocrats

The new government, in fact, represented considerably more than a change of team. Its composition implied an actual change of policy.

To begin with, it meant the end of the Falange's ambitions. Arrese, whose projects had been set aside, went so far as to circulate a leaflet in which he declared that 'Spain is once more in the hands of soldiers and priests. . . . The Falange is not responsible for the country's present situation.' Arrese was then made Minister of Housing! The Falange remained a pawn in the hands of the Caudillo; he simply replaced the 'doctrinaire' Falangist ministers (Girón in charge of labour and Arrese at the head of the *Movimiento*) by more insignificant and docile figureheads. The six Falangist ministers in the new Cabinet would give Franco no trouble: they were useful pawns to be played against other factions.

The army was back in full force with six ministers: in charge of the Interior was tough General Alonso Vega, an unconditional supporter and childhood friend of Franco's, while Muñoz Grandes, who had displayed too much independence, was replaced by General Barroso, another loyal supporter of the Caudillo. The latter thus had the army under his thumb, and by this means was assured of keeping order in the country.

The essential sign of the new direction that Franco's Spain was now taking was the inclusion of the technocrats connected with the Opus Dei: Planell, already Minister for Industry, Cánovas, who took over Agriculture, General Jorge Vigón at Public Works, and Navarro Rubio at Finance – all experienced technicians, many of them youngish men, who thus controlled the economic orientation of the country. The President of the National Economic Council, Villalbi, was appointed Minister without Portfolio; he was known to be connected with Catalan industry and a devotee of planning.

The first announcements by this new team made clear its intentions: 'The government's desire is to achieve without delay a greater degree of freedom in foreign trade,' a government spokesman declared on the evening of the first Cabinet meeting. On 1 March Planell asserted: 'The task of developing industrialization in Spain devolves in the first place on private initiative.' The long-term project of the new team was to secure an opening for Spain on to the outside world, in the first place on to Western Europe, to promote the play of economic forces, in short to *adopt the model of developed capitalist countries*. The government had inherited a difficult situation which it would have to remedy. There were the financial problems and the weakness due to the chaotic economic development during the period 1950 to 1957, there were social tensions caused by poverty and the low standard of living. The crisis begun in 1956 was thus not solved by the constitution of a new government. Supported as he was by the army, ready to repress any disorder, and by the team of Opus Dei technocrats capable of recognizing economic problems and anxious to solve them, the Caudillo could feel secure, and continue unconcernedly his lavish entertainment of such foreign potentates as Sultan Mohammed v and King Ibn Saoud of Saudi Arabia.

Spain: Spring 1957

The miners in the Oviedo collieries were on strike; leaflets circulated in Madrid urging the population to keep away from victory celebrations, to buy no newspapers, to boycott entertainments and public transport. In Barcelona, too, leaflets were distributed; the officers of the Seguridad hunted down the militants responsible, who were mostly Communists. Fourteen of them were caught in a hotel in the Calle Arturo Soria, where a secret printing press had been set up. Twenty more were arrested in Barcelona. In Salamanca the students demonstrated their solidarity with those of Madrid and Barcelona. One hundred intellectuals sent a fresh petition to the Minister of Public Instruction pleading for leniency in the sentences on students. This was Spain in the spring of 1957.

Forty thousand soldiers paraded in Madrid on 1 April, the anniversary of Franco's victory. Thousands of spectators watched the march-past, which lasted for two whole hours, and was accompanied overhead by a flight of some hundred aircraft. This, too, was Spain in the spring of 1957.

A leaflet distributed in Madrid reproduced an appeal from the Vatican to the Hungarian people. It declared: 'History proves that no army, no regime can indefinitely resist the clash with the most deep-rooted natural values of the human mind.' 'The people of Spain must say No,' the leaflet concluded.

But the troops marched past.

On 18 March the *New York Times* published a long interview with the Caudillo. 'Many countries,' General Franco declared, 'would be glad to have before them the potential future which is open to Spain.'

CHAPTER IV

A RENOVATED FRANCOISM VERSUS
THE NEW SPAIN

SPRING 1957–1959

Twenty Years After: Everyday Francoism

Twenty years previously the Civil War had been raging, with the visible hell of bloodshed and bombing – Guernica, Teruel, the Ebro. Twenty years ago. Now new Spain was visible everywhere: in the streets, in the universities, on the tiers of the bull ring, embodied in those lean, dark lads noisily displaying their contempt for some unskilful torero.

Spain was the cheerful crowd enjoying *ferias* in Valencia, Seville, Jerez, Madrid, Cordoba and Granada, waiting in the cold Easter-tide evenings to watch the processions pass, led by units of the *Guardia Civil* marching stiffly to the sharp beat of drums. Tourists poured in, for the rate of exchange was in their favour; Frenchmen, Germans, Belgians and Anglo-Saxons mingled with the crowd of poor Spaniards. Their cameras, their cars, their mere presence told of the miraculous advantages of the consumer society. They were propagandists for the new capitalism. They settled on the coast, bought land, dwellings, goatskins. They expressed surprise: so this is Francoism? They had imagined (the French in particular) something akin to an enemy-occupied country, as though the Francoists had been a foreign army in Spain. They had a momentary shudder when they saw the Civil Guards, then they got used to them. The *tertulias* (cafés) were full, the crowd lively and bustling, and wine was cheap. Granted, there were poor children begging in the streets; and in the south destitution was more glaring than the sunshine on the whitewashed walls. In Sicily and Naples, too, beggars followed you in the street. So what was Francoism? It seemed somehow to have become anodyne. The present government was one in which technicians predominated. Year after year, as one victory parade followed another, Francoism by its sheer staying power had become, to European eyes, the normal condition of Spain.

True, there had been unrest in the country since 1951, but crises and violence, strikes and police brutality are to be found everywhere; in May 1957 the Madrid papers, *Ya* and the Falangist organs in particular, voiced loud protest against French methods of maintaining order in Algeria. The special correspondent of the journal *Madrid*, Padilla, who had been expelled from Algiers, told of the use of torture and the suicide of the lawyer Ali Bounendjel. Official Spain had a perfectly quiet conscience in 1957, and to Europe Francoism was just an everyday phenomenon.

Tourists could visit Spain; Spanish workers could emigrate; and in this respect the country did not conform to the pattern of dictatorships inherited from the Second World War. Between 1956 and 1960 the number of tourists increased fourfold, and that of emigrant workers threefold. Spain was no longer a closed country: twenty years after the Civil War, the people were circulating freely throughout Spain.

There was much that the tourist never saw in Spain, all the facts relegated by most European newspapers to their foreign news items, tedious to the reader because they seemed to reiterate the same story periodically: police in jeeps breaking up student demonstrations, young men flinging stones as they escaped through the streets alongside the university buildings; protests from teachers; strikes breaking out, almost invariably in Asturias or at Barcelona; for a day or two, in Madrid or the Catalan capital, people would walk to work to demonstrate their disapproval; and then life would resume its normal course. Franco was still Caudillo; he made speeches, presided over ceremonies – military parades, ambassadorial visits. Months might pass without fresh troubles breaking out. Months, or a few days; in any case, seen from the outside they seemed, twenty years after the Civil War, only a few more incidents in the life of Spain, minor incidents since the Caudillo always came back in all his glory to greet his troops or the crowd. Sometimes conjecture ran riot: Don Juan or his son Juan Carlos were going to meet Franco and might soon succeed him. Some minister would make a pronouncement which could be interpreted as pro-Monarchist; some Falangist would accuse the Monarchists of plotting; and then everything would seem to be restored to order.

No doubt, for those who endured Franco's Spain day after day, the reality was somewhat different. *Para vivir aquí* (*To Live Here*), many Spaniards said – 'in order to live here you have to be unable to live anywhere else'. So they dreamed of leaving for France or Germany or Switzerland, the lands from which those tourists came whose wives exhibited themselves so shamelessly.

Living here, in Spain, meant consuming on an average – according to F.A.O. statistics – only 14 kilograms of meat per year, and accepting the fact that Spain ranked lower than Greece and Portugal in this respect, taking thirty-seventh place (1959). Living in Spain meant, for a Spaniard, working harder for less food. It meant working three times more than a Frenchman to earn one kilo of bread or of rice; five times more for one kilo of coffee; four times more for a litre of wine; or twice as hard to buy a newspaper.[1]

Life in Spain was easy for the tourist, hard for the Spaniard. 'Everyday Francoism' was invisible to the foreigner passing through rapidly or holidaying in the summer sun, but always present for the Spaniard. A boycott of public transport meant two or three columns in the newspapers of Brussels, Paris or New York, but it meant risk, excitement and fear for hundreds of young Spaniards.

[1] In *Spanish–American Trade* (Nov.-Dec. 1959).

'The rhythm of the city had suddenly altered', writes Goytisolo, 'and the faces of the men and women who crowded the pavements revealed firm and hopeful resolutions. An unspoken solidarity united us all. We had discovered that we were not alone and, after so many years of shame, this seemed to us a miracle. ... People performed their familiar journey in silence, and this silence on the part of hundreds of thousands of people was more eloquent than any words.'[2]

This concerted silence of ordinary people boycotting public transport was the cry of protest against everyday Francoism. To hear it, to measure its scope, it was necessary to be living here in Spain in those years 1957 to 1959 when everything was stirring, and a renovated form of Francoism was confronted, everywhere, with the challenge of a new Spain.

Repression

This entailed, primarily, repression: surveillance and police searches to forestall 'incidents', strikes and boycotts and so on; and afterwards, the pursuit of those involved in such demonstrations, arrests, fresh searches, dismissals. It was as though a storm were raging over the heads of Franco's opponents; some militants went abroad to wait for the situation to return to normal, when the Social Brigade would resume its routine activities, those sporadic checks and arrests and interrogation that filled the days when nothing much was happening in Spain.

The regime furthermore strengthened its legal arsenal. Faced with the increased number of strikes, the law of 22 March 1957 stipulated that in cases where those responsible for a collective movement could not be found, 'the most outstanding members of the accused or, where all seemed equal, the oldest of them would be held responsible'. In other words, hostages would be taken from among the strikers. A series of decrees reinforced this provision. Early in 1958, in order to crush any attempt to give a broad political trend to unrest, a court martial procedure was instituted which still further reduced the rights of the defence. A 'special jurisdiction over extremist activity' was established, and on 24 January a decree made one officer's name notorious throughout Spain. Article 1 read: 'Colonel Henrique Eymar Fernández of the Infantry is appointed special military judge with jurisdiction over the entire national territory, as regards the procedure to be applied to recently discovered extremist activities.' Then there was the procedure known as *sumarísimo de urgencia*, by which the defence counsel (a specially appointed officer) was allowed only four hours to prepare his speech!

Violence seems to have been habitual. Prisoners could be beaten or hung up by their feet or hands during the long periods spent without trial in the Jefatura de Policía or the Seguridad. Colonel Eymar travelled through Spain, going from one prison to the next, questioning detainees in police premises. Prison sentences fell thick and fast: four, eight, twelve years' imprisonment for having organized a

[2] *Pour vivre ici.*

strike or distributed leaflets. Fifteen years for Miguel Núñez, twenty for Simón Sánchez Montero, both Communists; almost a hundred Socialists, including Antonio Amat, their chief organizer, were imprisoned, a death-blow to the party; Christian-Democrats were also arrested and given harsh sentences. Thus on 9 November 1959, there began the trial of Julio Cerón, leader of the L.F.P., a Catholic diplomat accused of having prepared the abortive strike of 18 June (see below). Gil Robles was counsel for the defence, an air force colonel for the prosecution; the sentence was eight years in jail. Intellectuals and workers were the social categories most seriously affected. In April 1957 a document denouncing by name a number of intellectuals engaged in opposition to the regime was circulated in Madrid: arrests followed. Who were the anonymous informers? Members of the Opus Dei? That organization denied it, but the fact was typical of the atmosphere in Spain and the repressive methods of the authorities. In March 1959 leaflets were circulated in Barcelona urging the population to write on the city walls the letter P for *Protestar*. This was the work of Christian groups, the *Partido Democrático Cristiano* and the *Alianza de Trabajadores Cristianos*. The letter P appeared on a number of walls along railway lines and by the side of waste spaces; then the police came and obliterated them. Some dozen students were arrested.

The press presented all these facts in the darkest light: an international conspiracy against Spain, the sinister activities of men who blackmailed Spaniards into helping them undermine society, such as one Emilión Fabrego Arroyo, arrested on 12 April 1958 in Barcelona and supposedly employed by the Communist Party to 'inveigle the fiancés of girls whose fathers had died in exile'.

It was more difficult to present the facts when the accused was a man like Dioniso Ridruejo, former member of the *División Azul* and Director-General of Propaganda, who had moved so far left from his original Falangist position that he could tell the Cuban journal *Bohemia*: 'After so many years, many of us who were the victors feel ourselves defeated,' and declare himself to be a liberal and a Socialist. He had already been arrested in February 1956 and was now indicted again on a charge of having 'expressed extreme opinions'. The press could scarcely headline this arrest, for Ridruejo had been one of the founders of the Falange and, moreover, the author of the official party hymn, *¡Cara al Sol*! Now he was in jail, actually accused of having helped to found a *Partido Social de Acción Democrática*!

Ridruejo's evolution and arrest bear witness both to the growing strength of the opposition and to the severity with which it was being repressed. According to an incomplete survey, in 1958 Spanish courts condemned 104 people to a total of 541 years of imprisonment.

October 1958 witnessed the death of Pope Pius XII, who, according to Castiella, Minister of Foreign Affairs, had represented 'a new epiphany of the Church and of the Papacy in the modern world'. Official Spain went into mourning (*A.B.C.* declared on 9 October: 'We have a new intercessor in Heaven'). Then the coronation of John XXIII was celebrated, and an amnesty was proclaimed in honour of the new Pope. The press then revealed that 16,800 people were being detained

in jail and commented on the decree: 'Generosity and strength, joy and satisfaction for those amnestied, and for all Spaniards: such are the terms that
sum up Spanish policy today. The same terms synthesize the development
of an excellent governmental task: strength and generosity on the part of
those in power, and a happy and satisfied population' (*Pueblo*, 7 November
1958).

Less than a month after the proclamation of this generous amnesty, a fresh
wave of arrests swept the whole of Spain, affecting all the big towns: Madrid,
Barcelona, Bilbao, Granada, Seville, and also San Sebastian, Vitoria and Saragossa. The politico-social brigade that dealt with subversive activities, under
Colonel Eymar, carried out the operation. Doctors and engineers, academics,
relatives of diplomats were among its victims. They were accused of having
sought to reconstitute the Socialist Party. There was no mention in the press of
these arrests. This explains the incompleteness of official statistics, according to
which, for instance, fifty-two persons were sentenced in 1959 to a total of 202
years' imprisonment, and one to death, for subversive activities; but the real
number must have been far greater. Colonel Eymar was not idle. Repression
remained one of the basic aspects of Franco's policy. On this point there was little
difference between renovated Francoism and the original version. To be sure,
the firing squads were no longer kept busy, as they had been twenty years previously, but this was more as a result of a deliberate act of 'good will', or greater
skill in repression, or the absence of immediate necessity, or tactical impossibility,
than of any recognition of democratic rights. A Spaniard's freedom hung constantly by a slender thread which the police, like Fate, could cut at will or leave
dangling until the next arbitrary interruption. One was not inevitably, or even
usually, arrested, but one knew that one might be arrested and that other people
were. So one had to keep quiet and avoid attracting notice, on pain of experiencing that oppressive feeling of fear and uncertainty. 'From my room,' Goytisolo
writes, 'I listened to the sound of the elevator and my heart beat faster every time
the bell rang.'[3] Every Spaniard knew only too well that it might not be just the
milkman.

Strategy of the Opposition

Franco's opponents had to reckon with this repression, the atmosphere which it
generated and the conditions it imposed. They were forced to go on working
underground, and yet, in order to overcome the oppressive weight of fear, some
men had got to come gradually into the open, and assert their political commitment in a court of law, using the dock as a platform. The Communist Miguel
Núñez, for instance, had his counsel cross-question him before the judges in
such a way as to enable him to expound his party's political programme. Julio
Cerón and certain priests took the same line. So in the period 1956–60 Franco's
opponents were already emerging from the shadows, at whatever cost to themselves. Liberal intellectuals signed petitions; others sent articles to foreign papers.
This was a conscious and spontaneous movement which, through its daring, had

[3] *Pour vivre ici.*

the practical effect of securing freedom of expression: fear was gradually brought under control, it was no longer self-generating. Such an attitude was made possible by that of the masses, large numbers of whom, for instance, responded to the appeals for a boycott. A high price was paid for militancy: imprisonment, dismissal from university or employment; but the issue at stake was of overriding importance. Alfonso Sastre has expressed the clear-sighted resolution and the political intentions of certain Spaniards during these years, in his poem 'Manifesto' (written in July and August 1960):

> I sign everything.
> But it's not enough to sign. We've got to write.
> But it's not enough to write. We've got
> To read out loud. But that's not enough; we must also
> go out into the streets.
> But it's not enough
> just to go out into the streets; we must
> shout aloud on the pavements.
> But shouting is not enough. We've got
> to get together at last, all of us, for justice;
> for peace.
> But not only to get together;
> to sing too.
> But not only to sing; also
> to begin marching.
> But not only to begin marching; we've got
> to reach the end too, step by step;
> and (fall who must) to overthrow
> those who restrict and degrade us.
> But not only to reach the end, to overthrow: we've also got
> to build up Spain within Spain.
> And not only that. . . .[4]

This effort, and the situation of opponents within Spain, were not always understood by those outside. When young university Socialists, addressing the P.S.O.E., declared that the new generation no longer took the Civil War as its point of reference, when in August 1958, at the Seventh Congress of the P.S.O.E. at Toulouse, militants from inside Spain demanded common action with all forces of the opposition, in particular with the communists, they were ignored. The different parties (excluding the Communists, the P.O.U.M. and part of the C.N.T.) gave their approval to a document, the Paris Agreement (April 1957) which merely repeated that a provisional government should be set up without power to decide subsequent institutions; these would only be defined after a plebiscite. This document, which was signed by the former leading parties (P.S.O.E. under Llopis, the Republican parties, etc.) aroused bitter disappointment among members of that internal opposition which was in fact the only live opposition, the only one in contact with Francoism and with the Spanish people. It was difficult for anti-Francoists outside Spain to understand how the defenders

[4] In F. López and R. Marrast, *La poésie ibérique de combat* (Paris, 1966).

of the Communist Nunez included the lawyer Agustin de Semir, a leading member of the Barcelona City Council; and how another defending counsel declared that 'twenty years after the Civil War it was time to put an end to that factious spirit which was so alien to the feeling of the Spanish people'.

Movements such as the *Agrupación Socialista Universitaria* (A.S.U.) or the *Unión Democrática de Estudiantes*, comprising Christian-Democrats and liberals, appealed to the various opposing forces to join in common action; the *Movimiento Socialista de Cataluña*, at its congress held at Perpignan in August 1958, asserted the necessity of organizing the co-ordination of all democratic forces in Catalonia. Obstacles, indeed, abounded. At the seventh congress of the Socialist Party, Prieto declared that Franco granted the Communists facilities for action, to which Dolores Ibarruri retorted that 'prison and torture were the facilities he offered them'. What made the controversy so bitter was the way past antagonisms were fostered by present powerlessness and by future projects. Many people within the opposition imagined (and particularly after spring 1959) that 'the little world of Don Caudillo' was going to be swept away by history. Franco was growing old, and the Socialist Congress appealed to different parties within the Socialist International to ensure that in the event of his death the Western Powers would recognize only a legally elected Spanish government.

Once again, a great many quarrels raged over the disposal of the bear's skin before the bear was killed. On 19 January 1959 the *Unión Española*, a monarchist opposition party, was officially constituted, at a banquet attended by various important personalities, some followers of Gil Robles, some liberal Monarchists, and a number of generals. The police interrogated the participants, but released them immediately, and the left-wing opposition interpreted the formation of the new party and the leniency of the authorities as tokens of a weakening of Franco-ism and the disintegration of its social bases.

The Communist Party, whose central committee met from 7 to 9 September 1957, was almost alone in attempting to analyse the situation as a whole, and to define its strategy in relation to this. According to Dolores Ibarruri, the decisive factor in the Spanish situation was the contraction between the mass of the people (from the working class to the non-monopolist bourgeoisie) and the mono-polist oligarchy which was the chief support of Franco's dictatorship. The evolution of such Falangists as Ridruejo, the movements stirring in Catholic circles and in the petty bourgeoisie, and of course the big strikes, were all inter-preted as convergent signs of this situation. The party must therefore facilitate unity between all sections of the population; it was decided, in order to exorcise the spectre of civil war, which Franco used as a blackmail weapon, to organize a *Jornada de Reconciliación Nacional*, a sort of peaceful plebiscite excluding any violent confrontation. This would be the first step towards the *Huelga Nacional Pacífica*, or peaceful national strike, a higher stage in the people's fight against Francoism, in which, once again, any direct clash with the army must be avoided, since this would be pointless and indeed suicidal.

The Communists therefore embarked on these ambitious schemes, encouraged by their conviction that Francoism was now *a decaying Fascist regime*. Their projects obviously had much in common with the various trends within the country, ranging from Christian to Socialist, which sought unity in the struggle against the regime.

The prospect envisaged by the Communists depended on an analysis which from the start, even before any action was undertaken, was open to question. It was certainly true that the Francoist regime had undergone a process of decay between 1957 and 1959, but this process affected only its secondary political forms, and its weakness was thus only apparent, since side by side with that decay (which was in any case superficial, the military apparatus being, as we have seen, left intact) there was taking place a process of consolidation through economic change, being prepared (in difficult circumstances, it is true) under the aegis of the Opus Dei technocrats. Their project was to incorporate Spain into the capitalist system in its most advanced forms, obliterating its archaic characteristics. What the opposition took for the decay of the regime was merely the adaptation of Francoist power to the problems posed by economic development. In so far as that development was possible (and successful), and while the regime kept control of the armed forces, the opposition could achieve nothing decisive.

The adversaries of Francoism had, moreover, to face the problems that confront all opposition movements attempting to overthrow a regime by means that are unavoidably extra-parliamentary. The problem, first, of achieving *convergence* between all actions against the regime at a given moment; that of obtaining a fusion between the various opposition movements by transforming them into a radical political struggle against the regime. The strategy outlined by the Spanish Communist Party was clearly an attempt to realize this fusion in a national political strike. This presupposed a *co-ordination* of all the actions undertaken, that is to say the control of social categories throughout the nation, by such means as trade unions. In 1957–9 such a politico-syndicalist framework had not been achieved, since the opposition was still subject to repression and most of its cadres had to work illegally.

Among further obstacles which the opposition was incapable of removing were the regional disparities within Spain, and the safeguard that Franco had secured through his alliance with the United States. On 20 December 1958, John Foster Dulles, in an aircraft of the United States Air Force, landed on the American air base of Torrejos de Ardoz. Several Spanish ministers welcomed him, while units of the Spanish and American armies presented arms. In reply to a speech by Castiella, Dulles described his landing as symbolic of the close relations between the two countries and their resolution to 'defend together their independence and Western civilization against the threat of materialistic and atheist despotism'.

The Caudillo could still count on support from the United States. Meanwhile the return to power in France of General de Gaulle was welcomed by Madrid. Somewhat prematurely, it was interpreted as a proof that (in the words of the journal *Informaciones*) 'in 1958 the Cross of Lorraine is the symbol of the struggle of the aristocratic culture of the south against the north-eastern world represented by communism' (30 May 1958). In any case, it was certain that Franco's regime would not be hindered in its efforts against the opposition by the evolution of the situation in Europe and in the world.

The Fight Within Spain: Workers and Students (Spring 1958)

Spaniards hostile to the regime faced it alone. The struggle continued on the university front, but in an endemic fashion. The repression that followed the report attributed to the Opus Dei, which had denounced the four main opposition groups in university circles which were considered 'dangerous: communists, Socialists, Syndicalists and Liberals', the number of arrests made (among those taken was the brother of the Bishop of Málaga) seemed to drive the militant students underground for a few months.

A crisis broke out among the workers. On 4 March 1958, the miners of the María Luisa pit in the Asturias went on strike; seven men had been dismissed for insufficient production. The strike soon spread to other pits: Fondón, Sotón, Santa Eulalia and Duro Felguera. On 12 March the men from the collieries in the Langreo valley near Oviedo came out in sympathy. They demanded a reduction of the working day from eight to seven hours. The movement soon affected 15,000 workers.

Spain was unaware of the strike until on 15 March a government decree announced that in the provinces concerned, certain articles of the Spaniards' Charter were to be suspended for no less than four months. Once again, there was nothing, not even the precarious articles of a charter which had been unwillingly granted and never fully applied, to protect Spaniards from police action. The press inveighed against 'the disloyalty of a minority of malcontents', the Seguridad could denounce the strike as a result of 'Communist subversion' in which the miners, according to *Arriba*, had been 'used as cannon fodder'.

Once again the Asturian miners, with their grave faces and powerful hands, pulling their berets over their brows and turning up the collars of their shabby jackets, had to go back into the pits. Nevertheless their action had started off another movement. From 25 March until 9 April 1958 five major industries in Barcelona were affected by the strike. The governor immediately ordered them to be closed down. There were at least 25,000 strikers in the Catalan capital, including those at the S.E.A.T. motor works (a branch of Fiat) and the E.N.A.S.A. which built trucks. Three thousand workers in another factory downed tools out of sympathy. On 26 March the Basque country, the blast furnaces of Vizcaya and Guipuzcoa were also affected. Unrest was reported from the Valencia region. These movements encouraged action in the universities. In Madrid, Barcelona, Seville and Saragossa students boycotted lectures, and a number of faculties closed down, particularly the medical schools. Then, in April, industrial and academic peace seemed to be restored.

The lesson of these happenings was clear: militant workers in the underground unions which existed alongside the official *sindicatos* had an increasing hold on the whole working class. Miners from the Asturias, industrial workers in Barcelona unhesitatingly opted for strike action which, despite the law, had become a *normal* form of protest. This was unquestionably a victory for the opposition. At the same time its customary weaknesses were revealed: these movements were incomplete, geographically localized, badly co-ordinated, *limited* in time and in

259

their aims. In Franco's Spain they undoubtedly represented a considerable achievement, due to the tenacious efforts of hundreds of men and the courage of tens of thousands more: they proved that the days of fear and submission were over. The working class had recovered its strength: it was fighting back. Yet what a gulf lay between the nature and quality of these movements and the requirements implicit in their political objective: the overthrow, or isolation, of Francoism! These *partial* struggles, which helped to promote the fighting spirit and political consciousness of the working class, also rendered considerable sections of it ineffective by a series of sporadic acts. This ambiguous result was the inevitable fruit of the situation in Spain; it reflects the *superficial weakness* of Francoism, which was incapable of completely repressing any movement, and its *deep-seated strength*: it still controlled the country.

The 'Jornada de Reconciliación Nacional': 5 May 1958

The Communist Party's attempt to mobilize the whole nation in an intensified struggle against Francoism took the form of a 'Day of National Reconciliation', fixed for 5 May 1958. The project met with a first setback in that other opposition groups failed to join in the preparations for the *Jornada*, despite the claims of unanimous agreement made by *Radio Pyrénées* from Prague. Thousands of letters sent from abroad made the date of the event widely known, without specifying the origin of the appeal. Within Spain, militants worked with tireless devotion: dozens of them were arrested. The authorities were worried. The police were fully mobilized everywhere, and preventive measures were taken. The American fleet docked in the ports of Barcelona and Valencia. A forged issue of *Mundo Obrero* threatened the use of violence.

Plans for 5 May included the stoppage of work and the boycott of public transport. In Madrid and in Barcelona police and army forces were posted at crossroads and at bus and tramway stops. Jeeps patrolled the streets. Only working class districts were, in fact, affected by the boycott: the metro was only a quarter full. Stoppage of work was widespread, but not, as hoped, general: the *Jornada* was not a failure, but hardly a success.

According to the political bureau of the Communist Party, 'the *Jornada* of 5 May and the activities leading up to it constituted the first political movement of a national character organized against Francoism'. It is true, indeed, that nobody demonstrated in favour of the regime that day. In fact the demonstration was *incomplete*; it revealed the increased influence in Spain of the Communists and their ability to organize mass action, but at the same time the power of the Franco regime. A few days after the *Jornada* it was learnt that the Catalan Communist Juan Comorera Soler, condemned to thirty years' solitary confinement by the Council of War in Barcelona in 1957, had just died in jail at Burgos. The regime was strong, and its strength or weakness could not be measured by its capacity or failure to organize public demonstrations.

Addressing the Cortes on 16 May, the Caudillo referred to 'communism and its fellow-travellers who have tried yet again to attack the Spanish fortress, inaccessible to intrigue and to their manoeuvres'. 'All this,' he declared, 'justifies our ceaseless concern to disarm Communist attempts at infiltration and to prevent the organs of opinion from being influenced by Communist agents.' In Franco's Spain today silence no longer prevailed, the silence of a country bled white and broken by three years of civil war, kept under by repression, imprisonment and the firing squad, a land of starvation; today a new and vigorous generation had arisen and had begun to demonstrate. Spain's social and political problems had been brought to light.

Their emergence did not mean that the regime, as many of its opponents believed or asserted, had lost control of the situation; even when it was forced to retreat, as, for instance, when confronted with Catalan protests.

The Catalan Problem

For gradually, as Spain came back to life, the problems of the Basque and Catalan nationalist movements were revived, particularly as these industrialized regions were the first to be affected by any social movement. The Franco regime had sought to eradicate their strong separatist traditions and their unmistakable national characteristics. In Catalonia the *Partit Socialista Unificat de Cataluña* (the Communist P.S.U.C.) had intensified its underground activities. At the trade union elections it had put up a number of candidates against the official delegates, and had got them elected. The influence of the opposition was strong in such large industries as *Fabra y Coats* and *Maquinista Terrestre y Maritima*. Yet although there were successful strikes for specifically economic objectives, or to demonstrate workers' solidarity, the *Jornada* gained only meagre support. The Catalan *national* movement, however, developed irresistibly. The big bourgeois of the port approached the municipal authorities to protect the rights of Catalans. There was even a *catalañismo franquista*, represented in the government by Gual Villalbí; this gives further proof of the regime's resources and its ability to find answers to the various problems confronting it; and it shows moreover that the national movement was not necessarily anti-Francoist, and that one cannot consider Catalonia as a single whole. Thanks to economic development the big bourgeoisie of Catalonia (and Villalbí was their man) were prepared to deal with Francoism, new style. As for the Caudillo, under these circumstances he was ready to give way partially on the question of Catalan nationalism, particularly as popular pressure demanded both an understanding with the Catalan bourgeoisie and some concessions to *catalañismo*.

On 8 October 1957 the cruiser *Canarias* entered the harbour at Barcelona with the Caudillo on board. He stayed in the Catalan capital until the 24th, and showed the importance he ascribed to the great city by a series of speeches at inaugural ceremonies, a reception given to all the mayors of Catalonia by the Minister of the Interior, and a meeting of the Provincial Council of the Falange where he made a fresh appeal for unity. On the 20th Franco, opening the students' hostel for the sons of soldiers, thanked 'the workers and the employers of Catalonia for their collaboration in their country's progress'. The same month, also in Barcelona, was held the fourth Assembly of Workers' Delegates. The people of Catalonia must be shown that their country had not been forgotten, but on the contrary was the object of the state's deep concern. The Caudillo was ready to make concessions.

There was a great sensation in Barcelona when it was learnt that Luis de Galinsoga, editor of a leading newspaper, *La Vanguardia,* had interrupted a sermon preached in Catalan by shouting out in church: '*Todos les catalanes son una m . . .*' (All Catalans are s. . . .). The *Vanguardia* lost a great many subscribers; thousands of leaflets were circulated urging people to stop buying the paper, and its sales fell sharply. Tradesmen and business firms withdrew their advertisements. This united campaign by the whole population, in which all classes joined, won the day. Luis de Galinsoga, although a personal friend of the Caudillo, was dismissed from his post. The Catalans had triumphed, and their national movement showed that after twenty years it had recovered its full vigour, and that, where its aims were limited, it could force the authorities to retreat – provided, that is, that the political aspect of its action was indirect and of secondary importance, and that there was no open political opposition to the regime. This was clearly apparent in the *Huelga Nacional Pacífica* organized by the Communists.

The 'Huelga Nacional Pacífica' (18 June 1959)

The demonstration had been elaborately prepared. As early as February 1959 most of the organizations representing the various trends of the opposition within Spain distributed leaflets calling for a non-violent national strike. A committee for *Coordinación Universitario* (ranging from Communists to Socialists from the A.S.U., left-wing Christian-Democrats and members of the *Frente de Liberación Popular* had been formed, which acted in co-operation with the C.P., the P.S.U.C., the F.L.P., the *Grupos Demócratas Cristianos*, the *Movimiento Socialista Catalan*, and the *Partido Demócrata Cristiano de Cataluña*. This was the first time unity had been achieved on such a broad front, and there had been endless talks and difficult negotiations before an agreement was finally reached. The *Huelga* was a sort of test of the new opposition's strength and of the strategy worked out by the C.P., and also of the fighting qualities of the Spanish people.

The militants mobilized their forces in outstanding fashion: tens of thousands of leaflets were printed and distributed. Barcelona was swamped with them during the days preceding the strike; every other large town was the scene of similar efforts. An atmosphere of unease and expectation prevailed during the second week in June. Then suddenly the weaknesses of the opposition and the strength of Francoism became glaringly apparent. Unity was shattered when the *Izquierda Democrática Cristiana* (Christian-Democratic Left) accused the Communists of trying to dominate the strike. The call to action was to have been launched in common, but the Communists were said to have broadcast it on their own, in advance: the Socialists split on the attitude to be adopted, and the police moved in.

They arrested members of the new organizations, the F.L.P., the A.S.U., potentially dangerous since though non-Communist they were relentless in their hostility to Francoism and might perhaps attract new strata to which Communists did not, or did no longer, appeal. Everywhere the police proved efficient and generally well informed. On 18 June, the day of the *Huelga Nacional Pacífica*, the failure of the movement was patent everywhere, indeed spectacular if one considers the efforts that had been made and the hopes involved. The strike met with a very limited response. The regime had triumphed. It was a hard blow for the opposition, a bitter disappointment, a return to the depressing darkness of day-to-day tasks after the exacting tension of the preceding days. The authorities promulgated the *Ley de Orden Publico* (June 1959), further restricting the rights of the Spanish people. 'The new law,' declared General Camillo Alonso Vega, Minister of the Interior, 'with the help of the Almighty, must become the tutelary guide for many generations towards an honourable life.'

So the Caudillo remained master of the field. Moreover, the failure of the *Huelga* triggered off a number of crises or conflicts within the opposition. Had it been planned by émigrés, who were cut off from the real state of things in contemporary Spain, thrusting their doctrinaire schemes on a country which was not – or not yet, or no longer – what they imagined? Had these militants overestimated the possibilities of political action in Spain? The failure lay there. The Communists defended their line. 'We were conscious of the problematic character of its success,' writes Santiago Carrillo. 'But it had not been initiated by émigrés. It was based on the efforts of militants within the country, and on those of other groups whose strength we had no doubt overestimated. . . . It did not attain its objectives . . . but it provided the opportunity for mass agitation.'[5]

In any case, the opposition remained incapable of involving the whole country in a general, non-violent political struggle against Francoism. Industrial unrest and student rebellion, Catalan nationalism, a display of opposition from new strata, the dissidence of the younger generation, were all displayed in successive waves, and between each wave the tide would ebb; and the *Huelga* which had attempted to gather together all these protests into a nationwide movement against the regime had, on the contrary, proved void of strength. The inevitable conclusion was that the Spanish people were controlled and held together *not by opposition to Franco but by renovated Francoism*. In 1959 no alternative had yet been found for Spain to the path chosen by the regime, which, promoting as it did the continuous economic and social transformation of the country, proved that despite appearances it still held the initiative in this field, as in that of politics.

Political Initiatives of the Regime

The official mass demonstrations of the regime consisted of military parades and various festivals which all, on some historic pretext or other, were aimed at glorifying Francoist Spain and its leader. Thus, on 2 May 1958 there was an official commemoration of the 150th anniversary of the rising of the people of Madrid against Napoleon's armies. This was followed on 4 May by the Victory parade: parachutists who had fought against Moroccan nationalists in the Ifni

[5] S. Carrillo, *Après Franco quoi?* (Paris, 1966), p. 19.

zone marched past followed by American artillery pieces capable of firing shells with atomic war heads. The crowd cheered; there were still two Spains, the Spain that had planned the *Jornada de Reconciliación Nacional* for the following day, and the other which stood on the sidewalks to acclaim the Spanish army.

The Caudillo's regular visits to Spanish provinces also wore a ceremonial character, as did the speeches he made at the end of the year, in which he invariably set Spain 'under the tutelary shade of the victorious banners of the Crusade' (30 December 1958). The interviews granted to foreign newspapermen also contributed to this constant effort at self-glorification, since they were reproduced in the whole world's press, and as reported in foreign papers they acquired indisputable authority, strengthening the Caudillo's position by the mere fact that he was listened to with respect in New York or in Paris.

On 12 and 13 June 1958 Serge Groussard of the *Figaro* had a long interview with Franco. 'Have you come under any ideological influences in your career as statesman?' asked Groussard. 'No.' 'Not even that of Mussolini?' 'Not even that. . . .' Then the conversation went on (and this was one of the most important interviews ever granted by the Caudillo), raising all manner of problems: 'Did you never at any moment in the war,' Groussard asked 'consider joining in on the side of the Axis?' The reply was an unequivocal 'Never'.

Franco's constant concern was to remain in the centre of the political scene in Spain. He was well aware, for instance, that within what was left of the Falange underground cells were forming which sought a return to the strictness of the original movement. Thus at the start of 1959 some 25,000 extremists, mostly young people, took Manuel Hedilla for their hero, writing *Hedilla-JONS* on the walls in the streets of Madrid and handing out leaflets in the Atocha railway station. Then the Caudillo reverted to his old game of making successive advances to one group or the other in order to neutralize them both. Thus in October 1958 he invited to the Pardo Palace those Falangist leaders who had just celebrated the twenty-fifth anniversary of the foundation of their movement at the Comedy Theatre at Valladolid. Once again he extolled the Falange: 'I feel myself at one with you' he declared and the press sang the praises of the *Movimiento* and of General Franco. He had lost none of his skill in using the Falange as pawn, and in making that body, now a mere skeleton, into an apparent force in the interests of his own strategy.

Whether presiding over the Cortes, or – as at Castellón de la Plana on 13 June 1958 – indicting 'the Spain of political cliques, clubs of idlers and a few grumbling wire-pullers' – Franco remained the keystone of Spain's political organization.

This was obvious moreover, when on 17 May 1958, after reading his address to the Cortes, Franco rose and, facing the assembled *Procuradores*, all standing, promulgated the Principles of the National Movement. His voice rang out in the heavily decorated hall: 'I, Francisco Franco Bahamonde, Caudillo of Spain, conscious of my responsibility before God and before History . . . promulgate as Principles of the National Movement, implying the communion of all Spaniards in the ideals which gave rise to the Crusade, the following points. . . .' The twelve points which followed asserted 'Spain's unity of destiny within the Universal.

... May the Spanish nation consider obedience to God's law as a title of honour.
... Work is recognized as the basis of the hierarchy.'

When the Caudillo concluded, the *Procuradores* shouted 'Franco! Franco! Franco!' So, twenty years after the Civil War, the principles which had guided it were defined, and the law of Succession was reaffirmed in Point VII.

It was certainly far-fetched to declare, as the newspapers did, that the Spanish constitution was being built up step by step and that each item, coming several years after the previous one, fell into place through a pre-established plan so as to provide fundamental laws. The promulgation of the Principles is evidence of Franco's concern to provide a stable, institutional framework for his regime. On 17 July 1958 he stated his aim: to prove that 'our regime lives its own life, expects nothing from outside itself, is its own successor and is not preparing for any other. We are neither a parenthesis nor an interim dictatorship. ... *We constitute a real readjustment of history*.' This effort to provide laws was an attempt at consolidation and normalization (after twenty years), and it corresponded to the new economic and social path that had been chosen.

The New Economic Path: the Stabilization Plan (1959)

Here the technocrats of the Opus Dei were at work. Young and efficient, they produced a *coherent project* which had the backing of the banks and to which the Caudillo allowed full freedom of action. These technocrats, in power since 1957, faced with the social crisis and the continual inflation that provoked a rise in prices, had decided to opt for association with an increasingly united Europe. A few days after the Cabinet reshuffle in Madrid, the Rome treaties on the Common Market and on Euratom were signed (5 March 1957). Castiella, former Ambassador to the Vatican, and a keen supporter of the concept of United Europe, was now Foreign Minister. The men of the Opus Dei were in control of economic affairs: the line chosen by Spain was in keeping with that of all Western Europe. Spain was abandoning her national self-sufficiency. She now had to improve her economic situation so as to provide guarantees to foreign investors and at the same time to prepare for possible entry into the Common Market. In every sector, appropriate measures were taken: the rate of exchange was stabilized in April 1957 at 42 pesetas to the dollar; in December, new fiscal regulations were laid down: wages were frozen and the bank rate raised from 4·5 per cent to 5 per cent. These measures slowed down production, but their deflationary effect was intended to restore internal stability.

Wage-earners suffered, of course; but the state was capable of ensuring order.

The year 1958, moreover, witnessed the entry of Spain into the European community; she became an associate member of the Organization for European Economic Co-operation (O.E.E.C.), member of the International Monetary Fund, of the International Bank of Reconstruction and Development (January–September–November 1958). In other words, she became closely involved economically with Western capitalism. One revealing sign of this was the passing of a law, late in 1958, authorizing foreign oil firms to invest 100 per cent of the capital of subsidiaries they established in Spain. At the same time, legislation on collective labour agreements provided another means of controlling the working class.

In March 1959 the O.E.E.C. published its *First Report of Spanish Economy*, in which European experts sketched the broad lines of a policy of stabilization. On 30 June the Spanish government addressed to the O.E.E.C. and the International Monetary Fund a memorandum in which it set forth the measures it was preparing to take. The United States and Spain's creditor countries undertook to support these efforts. On 20 and 21 July the government announced by decree its new economic orders. The peseta was devalued, the rate of exchange controlled, wages frozen; the hope of increasing exports seemed justified, for the country's reserves had risen to $200 million by the end of the year.

The crucial point was that the regime, faced with a real impasse, had succeeded, while controlling (and indeed *because it controlled*) the social sector, in changing its economic course. Franco had definitely *associated himself with the economic system of the West*. Technical collaboration was established with European organizations (the Common Market had been functioning since 1 January 1959). Above all the Caudillo had realized that the support of the great powers had not failed him. Once again they had enabled him to extricate himself from a difficult situation. In July 1959 the United States opened a credit of $5,400,000 for the construction of bases in Spain, and the Export–Import Bank of Washington granted a loan of $17 million to Spanish firms. As Franco declared in his message of profuse thanks to Eisenhower, conveyed by Castiella in August 1959: 'Spain has received unceasing support from the United States.'

Yet another dangerous cape had been weathered: Spain had now embarked on economic stabilization. Franco could afford to wait calmly for its effects, while celebrating the twentieth anniversary of the end of the Civil War.

Spain 1959: Santa-Cruz del Valle de los Caídos

A concrete cross 153 metres high, weighing over 200,000 tons; a hollow cross, the arms of which, each 46 metres wide, were reached by means of lifts; an immense crypt dug out of the rock Risco de la Nava; a total cost of 1,000 million pesetas and twenty years' work: such was the giant graveyard thirty miles from Madrid and nine miles from the Escorial in the harsh stony valley of the Sierra de la Guardarrama, now being inaugurated on the twentieth anniversary of Franco's victory.

'This monument', the decree declared, 'must be the monument of those who have fallen and over whose sacrifice the peace-making arms of the Cross are spread in triumph.' During the spring of 1959 bodies were being exhumed in all the graveyards of Spain: for a start, the remains of José Antonio, which had been placed in the Escorial. *A.B.C.* wrote on 31 March 1959: 'At 20.05 hours the tombstone, weighing 305 kg, was raised to enable a workman to go in. . . . The bottom of José Antonio's coffin had rotted away, but the rest, as well as the Falange flag covering the coffin, was intact.' Exhumations went on all over Spain, despite protests from the relatives of the dead of both sides, unwilling to lose the privilege of visiting their graves in near-by cemeteries. According to the weekly *Blanco y Negro* (4 April 1959) 'a strict and accurate check on the transfer (of bodies) has been kept. Archives show that the work has been done with meticulous completeness. The arrangements have been undertaken by the Ministry of the Interior, who has informed the families of those whose place of interment is known.'

Death presided, that spring of 1959, over the twentieth anniversary of the Civil War, as though official Spain were fascinated by those thousands of corpses and sought, by calling up the spectre of that war, to remind people of the price it had been ready to exact and to pay for the conquest of the country and the triumph of its Crusade. *Blanco y Negro*'s reporter describes the scene: 'Trucks and cars, hearses and ambulances drove up uninterruptedly to the doors of the basilica, bringing the bones of Spaniards. . . .'

The first day of April witnessed the inaugural ceremony. Eight thousand temporary subalterns of the Nationalist army, who had recently formed a guild, the *Hermandad de Alfereces Provisionales*, together with thousands of children from the Youth Front, awaited the Caudillo's arrival. He appeared shortly after eleven, and was greeted with cheers. There was a huge crowd; the Cardinal Primate of Spain officiated. Señora Carmen Polo de Franco accompanied her husband. Ex-servicemen in serried ranks stood on the esplanade, and Franco addressed them: 'Our war,' he said, 'was clearly not a civil war but a real Crusade, as the reigning Supreme Pontiff described it at the time. . . .' Somewhat later, at the opening of the Seminary for Social Studies adjoining the basilica, he defined his regime as 'uniting the national and the social, under the sway of the universal'. In both these speeches he warned against the influence of communism and 'its power to subvert and exploit the movement'. Vigilance must never be relaxed, for 'Soviet gold and propaganda are servilely seconded by the traditional servants of anti-Spain'. '*¡ Arriba España! ¡ Viva Franco!*' reiterated the crowd.

Thus the twentieth anniversary of the Civil War was celebrated by the inauguration of an immense charnel-house, under the huge concrete cross whose shadow seemed to spread over the whole of Spain. Nobody must be allowed to forget the dead. 'The glorious epic of our liberation,' the Caudillo declared, 'has cost Spain too much blood to be forgotten. Nevertheless the battle of Good against Evil is not yet finished. . . . It would be childish to believe that the Devil is crushed. He can invent new snares and new masks and will take new forms in keeping with the times.'

Valle de los Caídos, the valley of the fallen: only the dead may be reconciled. For the living, good and evil remain.

Twentieth anniversary of the Civil War: in December 1959 Madrid gave a triumphant welcome to Dwight D. Eisenhower, President of the United States. The day of his arrival – 21 December – was declared a public holiday. The mayor of Madrid, Conde de Mayalde, uttered an inspired appeal:

'People of Madrid, the time of General Eisenhower's arrival is drawing near, and we must meditate on the significance of this amazing journey, which reminds us of St Paul's travels and the days when the Spanish Hadrian visited on foot the cities and villages of the Roman Empire. The most powerful man

on earth has travelled through so many lands on a humble mission of peace.
. . .'

Franco himself welcomed Eisenhower when he alighted from the presidential
Boeing. Then amidst a wildly excited crowd, the procession travelled the eighteen
kilometres from Torrejón de Ardoz to Madrid. The Paseo de la Castellana,
through which the two leaders drove in an open car, was black with people.
Spectators clung in clusters to the trees to watch the procession pass. It was a
triumph for the United States and for Franco. Next day, when Eisenhower left,
the two generals – the former chief of the Allied Armies and the other, on whose
desk had stood portraits of Hitler and Mussolini – embraced, to thunderous
applause. A triumph for Franco.

Soon afterwards, two exhibitions of Picasso's work were organized in Barcelona, and the anti-Francoist painter consented to the foundation of a museum
in the Calle de Mondaca devoted to his work. Undoubtedly Picasso was anxious
to speak to the Catalan people over the heads of the authorities and to establish
brotherly contact with them. Many Spaniards, who had experienced a sense of
despair at Eisenhower's visit, resented Picasso's acceptance, of which the regime
could make use in its efforts to present a new image of itself while constantly
recalling the victims and the hatreds of that war which had brought it to power.

The twentieth anniversary of the Civil War revealed the contradictory realities
of Spain and of the regime. Its leader, with tranquil self-confidence, speaking in
the chapter-house of the Benedictine monastery built close to the basilica of the
Valley of the Fallen, announced that, symbolically, this monastery was to be
devoted to the study of the evolution of social thought in the contemporary
world, and concluded with the words – unhesitatingly reported by the journal
A.B.C. on 2 April 1959: 'The Centre of Social Studies of the Valley of the Fallen
has now been inaugurated.'

BOOK IV

THE TURNING-POINT
1960–1963
From the Stabilization Plan to the *Desarrollo* Plan

CHAPTER I

THE PRICE OF STABILIZATION
1960

At the frontier posts of the Pyrenees and along the winding roads a line of cars, several kilometres long, stand waiting in the sun. Spanish customs officers and policemen, haughty and impassive, let through the hordes of travellers whose cheerful high spirits are somewhat tempered by awe of the Civil Guard.

In 1960, in fact, Spain was invaded by holiday-makers as never before. Everything coincided to feed the influx: the increase in car-ownership in Western Europe (in France particularly), the rising standard of living, the desire for sunshine and also the devaluation of the peseta. Spain, for Europe, became a synonym for holidays. The regime, which benefited by the spread of this image of the country, did everything it could to enhance its credibility. Roads were improved, hotels – *Paradores* – more or less luxurious, built on suitable sites. The tourist trade represented a safe investment: it promoted the growth of a category of wage-earners (hotel employees etc.) who were bound to the existing order because their incomes, although irregular owing to the seasonal nature of their employment, were often above the average of Spanish earnings. From 1960 onwards, therefore, tourism served chiefly to provide support for the government's economic policy, and, in one sense, to help maintain public order. It did of course open up Spain to the outside world, but at the same time it made the Franco regime an integral part of Europe. This had been precisely the aim of Franco's policy since 1957. The year of the great leap forward from this point of view was 1960, with an increase of almost 50 per cent on the previous year. A total of 6,113,255 tourists brought in almost $300 million in currency.[1] This influx, however, did not affect the whole of Spain, but barely 20 per cent of the land, chiefly the coast and the typical cities. Around the walls of the citadels that tourists visited lay the countryside, often desolate, and the roads over which their cars sped were but one more frontier, one further rift dividing Spain.

Spanish 'Islands', 1960

The Costa Brava and Majorca were transformed. Blocks of flats had sprung up; posters advertising them disfigured the Spanish landscape. Little by little the tide spread southwards towards Málaga. It reached Torremolinos, a small port

[1] Statistical appendix to *L'Espagne à l'heure du développement, Tiers Monde* (Paris, Oct.-Dec. 1967).

now become an international resort, where fishermen could watch the goings-on of the new Spanish bourgeoisie and the local lads – taxi-drivers, fishermen or out-of-work – could try their luck with the foreign women whom sun and sea had lured to Spain.[2] Bands of youths rushed about on Vespas or in sports cars, and in the bars middle-class Spaniards looked like Saint-Tropez holiday-makers. Ultra-modern hotels and luxury restaurants were built; such was the new look of Torremolinos and its sister villages all along the Mediterranean coast of Spain. Girls in bikinis strolled about freely; gone were the days when one had to undress at the water's edge and when Civil Guards kept stern watch on indecent exposure. A few years had brought about the change. Now even clerical threats went unheard. The new movement had transformed these villages, which history had left untouched.

In fact they were so many islands in the midst of a country which had changed little by 1960. True, the rural exodus continued, yet this did not imply any improvement in the cultivation of the land; on the contrary, particularly in the south, it became more and more of a desert. Mixed Spanish and foreign firms bought up the beaches, and some Spaniards (often the richest landowners in the region, who had been quick to discern the profits to be made) increased their fortunes in a few days; but a few kilometres inland the soil was still arid and stony. Men so sunburnt and toil-worn that it was hard to guess their age tried to earn a few pesetas by selling prickly pears; others waited by the roadside, offering tourists objects of woven straw or pottery, such as that of Nijar[3] which was famous throughout the south. The huge inscriptions FRANCO FRANCO FRANCO painted on the fences and walls of the wretched dwellings, the official exhortations to produce *more trees, more water,* reiterated along the roadsides, were insufficient to transform this southern landscape. Eddies of greyish sand still rose from the soil; men were poor, and the gulf had deepened between them and the coastal region, now swamped by tourists. That coast itself had its hidden side; behind the new districts lay neglected zones, the overcrowded homes of the poor, of workers driven from the sea-fronts by speculative building, the result of the tourist industry. At Almería for instance, the district of La Chanca contained some 20,000 people (the total population of the town was 80,000, of whom 17,179 were in want and 10,000 completely destitute, a poverty rate of 34 per cent) living in shanties and caves, without water or electricity. Seventy per cent of the poor were illiterate and lived by pilfering, or stealing from the Barranquilla fish market. Extreme poverty brought its usual consequences: prostitution, disease, a high rate of infant mortality. While at La Chanca these 20,000 Spaniards existed thus, clinging to the side of the great rock of Almería, in the enclosed gardens on its summit concerts were being given for the enjoyment of tourists.[4]

The truth about Spain in 1960 was not to be learnt from the impressions of tourists. And if things were particularly black in the south because of its special

[2] Juan Goytisolo, *Chronique d'une île* (Paris, 1961).
[3] Juan Goytisolo, *Terres de Nijar, la Chanca* (Paris, 1964).
[4] J. Maria Pérez Lozano, 'A Parish in Hell', in *Incunable* (Salamanca, Sept. 1960). Quoted by Goytisolo in *La Chanca*.

geographical characteristics, its erosion and aridity, together with the high birth rate typical of an underdeveloped region, the whole of Spain was experiencing hardship during the period when the Stabilization Plan was taking effect.

The Consequences of the Stabilization Plan

By the closing months of 1959 the effort to check inflation had resulted in stagnation. Coal mines and engineering works, textile and paper factories were affected. Unemployment rose, wages dropped rapidly, and for the first time for years consumer spending dropped in 1959 and 1960, which intensified economic stagnation still further. Incomes were considerably reduced, sometimes as much as 50 per cent owing to the suppression of overtime. The drop of the national income was reckoned at 3·6 per cent. Tens of thousands of workers left the country for France or Germany.

In the social field, the precariousness of employment and the return of poverty prevented strike action on any scale. Some firms shut down, while the process of economic concentration was speeded up, and the banks, owing to the steep increase in the rate of interest, realized high profits in 1960.

Foreign investors were encouraged by this combination of social quiet, a more stable financial situation and a high rate of interest: the International Monetary Fund and the O.E.E.C. granted credits of 220 million pesetas, and the banks and government of the United States 327 million. Thus the Spanish economy became increasingly integrated with the advanced capitalist bloc. The O.E.E.C. moreover closely followed the evolution of the situation in Spain. On 12 February it published the official report of its mission in Spain, which stressed that 'the application of the programme of stabilization has so far produced remarkable results, considerably above what might have been hoped for six months ago. The principal conditions necessary for stabilization are in a fair way to coexisting.' In August, in a new report, the O.E.E.C. once again expresses satisfaction at the results, but points out that investment must be stimulated, that 'the principal sector of any healthy expansion of the economy must be the development of productive private investment'. In short, by the autumn of 1960 the order of the day was no longer stabilization but revival.

The work of the Opus technocrats thus seemed to have been successful: productivity had risen, the deficit of the balance of payments had been wiped out, and part of the surplus manpower had found its way abroad. This dehumanized vision of the results of the Stabilization Plan conceals the cruel social reality. Families were broken up, because sons, brothers or husbands had gone to Ugine, Frankfurt, Essen or Denain; poverty and unemployment were widespread and even the necessities of life were being purchased in decreasing quantities. The tension that prevailed in the labour market helped the wage-freeze, but at the cost of increased social injustice and hardship. The Falangist unions, although officially controlled, echoed the anxiety and distress of the workers. Their journal, *Pueblo*, repeatedly protested against the instability of employment, a euphemism for the unemployment and the dismissals that occurred everywhere since the competitive atmosphere forced firms to cut down on costs.

273

These protests were ineffective, for one thing because the Falangist unions were seeking not so much to protect the workers or to impose a political line as to score over the Opus Dei, thanks to social difficulties. Unemployment merely served as another weapon in a contest between Francoist factions. On 17 March it was learnt that the Minister of Housing, the Falangist José Luis Arrese, had resigned. There was talk in Madrid of a clash over economic policy between opposing trends: Arrese wrote to Navarro Rubio, Finance Minister, that his harsh administration tended 'to aggravate the most severe economic depression which the regime has experienced during its twenty years of existence'.

The Caudillo's government was wholly committed to its new policy. It was staking its survival on economic transformation, and all it could do was to increase unemployment benefit and ... sign an emigration agreement with West Germany. The number of workers thus driven out of Spain by their living conditions increased by 50 per cent in 1960.

A Section of the Church Opposes Franco

A number of churchmen rose up in defence of these humble victims of implacable economic laws, and unhesitatingly defied the regime in so doing. The year 1960 witnessed the emergence of a whole section of the Catholic Church hostile to Francoism.

Dignitaries themselves were obliged to speak out. On 6 February the entire press publicized the joint declaration of Spanish archbishops who, discussing the Stabilization Plan, made a direct appeal to the authorities, pleading 'now, more than ever', for social justice. 'While taking measures for stabilization and economic development, the authorities must require immediate sacrifices from all classes in the country. The state has a particular responsibility towards its workers.' The archbishops protested against the rate of unemployment and the reduction of overtime: 'What we assert,' they emphasized, 'is the right to work, a consequence of the right to live in human dignity.'

This was an unmistakable reprimand, restrained but precise. It must be accounted for by the dramatic situation of many working-class homes, but also by the changes that were taking place within the Church. In Rome, John XXIII was striving to bring the Church into harmony with the problems of the time. In Spain, 1960 witnessed the appearance of a new generation of priests[5] who brought into the Church the attitudes of the post-Civil War generation. Finally, the work of militants in the *Hermandad Obrera de Acción Católica* (Workers' Brotherhood of Catholic Action) in contact with the working class had made even the upper ranges of the hierarchy aware of apostolic preoccupations very different from those of the Crusade and Civil War. Naturally, there were many contradictions within the bosom of the Church. Some priests were ready, in 1960, to commit themselves to active opposition, while many prelates remained faithful to the spirit of the Crusade. For them, Franco's regime was still the model regime of the Concordat, the bulwark of Catholicism.

As always in Spain, all problems were intensified by national characteristics. It

[5] 'Le drame du clergé espagnol', in *Études* (April 1968).

274

was the Basque clergy, which had always been opposed to Franco, which on 30 May 1960 brought to light the contradictions within the Spanish Church. On that day 339 Basque priests sent a letter, several pages long, to the Archbishop of Pampeluna and the Bishops of Vitoria, San Sebastian and Bilbao. It bore, by way of epigraph, these lines by Cardinal Salièges: 'To resign oneself to injustice without protesting is unworthy of a man and of a Christian.' Then it spoke with eloquence of 'man's natural rights, freedom of conscience, truth, self-determination. . . .' The priests criticized 'the lack of freedom of opinion and organization, the methods used by the police, state control, the doctrine of the Leader's infallibility, blind conformity and the system of official trade unions'. And, to crown their diatribe, they demanded autonomy for the oppressed Basque people.

This was a real indictment of the Franco regime, signed by priests and correspondingly sensational. The authors were Basque, and during the Civil War some Basque priests had been shot; so that the document shows at once the ineradicable national feeling of the Basques and the vigour of the opposition movement among the younger clergy.

Faced with this direct attack on the form of political and social life in Spain, the hierarchy reacted sharply. The Apostolic Nuncio emphasized that 'opposition to one's Bishop meant opposition to Christ'. The Basque bishops, in an official declaration, began by implying that the document 'offered no guarantee of authenticity', then they strenuously rejected its contents: 'This letter is totally inacceptable, both on account of the evident untruths it contains and because of its political character. Neither can we understand how political passion can have blinded certain priests to such an extent.'

The manifold reactions of the press and of the hierarchy reveal the anxiety of the regime and of the dignitaries of the Church; their whole policy since 1936 was being challenged. What they were defending was not so much obedience to the Bishops, or respect for the Concordat, as the general line followed by the Church of Spain. The Papal Nuncio, speaking on 8 July 1960 at the Pontifical University of Comillas, admitted this openly. He was presiding over the World Congress of the Catholic press, and addressing the assembled journalists he reminded them of 'the martyrdom of the Church of Spain . . . and how, on the ruins of war, a stronger and more stable Church had been rebuilt'.

None the less, for the Caudillo the Church was no longer the monolithic block on which he could rely. He would have to reckon with priests who were determined to fight his regime, and with a hierarchy which, while supporting it, did not wish to be identified with it. The Church was well aware that all men are mortal, and that the Caudillo was a man nearing the end of his life. The Church, being in contact with all levels of Spanish society, had grasped more quickly than the Francoist leaders the changes which were taking place. It knew that the regime could survive only by adapting itself to them. The technocrats of the Opus Dei were already working along this line. Now the hierarchy itself addressed the secular authorities. On 15 November 1960, Mgr Pla y Daniel, Primate of Spain, wrote to Don José Solis, the minister who was secretary of the *Movimiento*, in defence of the H.O.A.C. and of those Catholics who were in contact with the working class and often supported the workers' claims against the official Falangist unions. The prelate gave the minister a lesson in political realism which clearly defines the attitude of the Catholic hierarchy, aware of the changes which had affected Spain, its Church and the entire world.

'Your Excellency must recognize *the reality of the facts* and realize that in Spain, in 1960, *it is impossible to go on acting as in 1940.*[6] In 1940, Spain was emerging from a war in which the Nationalists' Crusade had been supported by nations with a totalitarian regime; even in 1943, in the Cortes, when many Spaniards believed that these nations were going to be victorious, the superiority of the totalitarian regimes was officially upheld. Today nobody dares assert this in the West, in Spain or elsewhere. There is nothing totalitarian about the *Fuero de los Españoles* which was published in 1945. . . .'

Thus, the Church had definitely opted for prudent evolution, and said so openly; it did not, however, tolerate the activities of priests undertaken against the government. The hierarchy's concern was to help the latter to adapt itself, rather than to oppose it as an enemy.

From this point of view the Church's attitude was akin to that of the more clear-sighted members of the government, whom, moreover, she influenced directly. The Caudillo himself accepted the path of controlled evolution of the regime, even though, unfortunately for a number of people, his control remained unshakeable.

The Return of Terrorism: Repression. The Opposition

Once again, bombs were exploding in Spain. The prevailing poverty, the drop in wages, the renewed passivity of the Spanish masses, the failure of recent strikes and of the Communist Party's efforts towards a peaceful solution, together with the way in which, despite all the vicissitudes of history, the power of the regime seemed to survive unchanged, made some men break out into violent action. They were *desperados* – the word expresses the despair which must have motivated them – anarchists, young men trusting in the effectiveness of acts of terrorism (by way of protest, example or appeal) or indomitable old-time militants who, having tried all other means in vain, reverted to violence. Some of them were former anarchists whose breach with society had never been healed, who had lived on its fringe, reduced to acting in isolation and seeing no alternative but death: for instance Francisco Sabater Llopart, known to many Spaniards as *El Quico*, who had fought Francoism ever since 1936, when he had served in the Republican army. In 1945, after fighting in the French *maquis*, he returned to Spain; here he became involved in acts of violence, hold-ups, clashes with the police, and the placing of bombs in the embassies of those countries which had supported Madrid in the United Nations. Hunted but elusive, he escaped into France, then in 1956 returned to Spain where he renewed his activity; back in France, he was arrested by the police, then once again crossed over into Spain, where, at dawn on 4 January 1960, he and a small band of followers clashed with the *Guardia Civil* near Gerona. Llopart was wounded, and though he managed

[6] Author's italics.

to escape he died the following day at San Celoni. Four of his companions and one lieutenant of the Civil Guard died in the skirmish. On 5 January all the newspapers talked of him as a *bandolero*, a gangster, and sharply criticized the French press for being too soft about this new Al Capone. In point of fact, the authorities were well aware that Spain was fascinated by Francisco Sabater, recognizing him not as a bloodthirsty assassin but as heir to the traditions of Spanish history. He had been admired or feared, and if he had few followers, yet he was not considered an unscrupulous criminal.

The death of Sabater and his comrades, at all events, served as a reminder that some men had chosen to fight Francoism, in 1960, with bombs or guns in their hands. On 18 February two bombs exploded in Madrid, one about two in the morning at the City Hall, the other at the Falange Club in Calle de Toledo. Three others were discovered and defused in time. In the street, close by the Falange Club, a man was picked up, fatally injured: he was twenty-seven, his name was José Ramón Pérez Jurado and he was a member of the *Directorio Revolucionario Ibérico de Liberación* (Iberian Revolutionary Liberation Council), which claimed responsibility for the incidents. According to the Spanish press the campaign was directed by a Cuban; but this was denied by the D.R.I.L., the leading spirit of which seems to have been Alberto Bayo, a former captain in the Republican army now resident in Mexico.

The fact remains that the whole opposition movement was keenly conscious of the example of Fidel Castro. Since his triumphal entry into Havana on 1 January 1959, guerrilla warfare and insurrection had found an increasing number of partisans in Spain, particularly among students. The cultural and historical links between Spain and Cuba explain the speed with which Castro found admirers and imitators in Iberian countries. On 26 and 27 June 1960, several bombs hidden in suitcases exploded in the Barcelona–Madrid train and in left-luggage offices in the stations of San Sebastian, Barcelona and Madrid. A girl was killed and a number of people injured. These incidents were the work of relatively insignificant groups, but they bear witness to the resolute anti-Francoism of a few. The regime reacted in two ways: it took advantage of this recrudescence of violence to provoke apprehension throughout the country, representing Franco as the sole bulwark of order; and it intensified repression. On 2 March 1960 Justiniano Álvarez Montero was given a life sentence and Antonio Abad Donoso condemned to death for their share in the Madrid outrages, which had merely damaged property. Donoso was executed on 8 March at dawn in the Carabanchel prison where so many others had already died. Official dispatches said he had been shot; other sources of information specify death by *garrote vil* (slow strangulation by the common garrote).

The 'Social Brigade' was untiringly active, and anarchists, *bandoleros* and *pistoleros* were not its only target. In 1960, in the fierce summer heat of Andalusia, huge operations were organized by the *Guardia Civil*. They combed the provinces of Cordoba and Seville. Interrogations and arrests took place in village after village. Over 400 persons were detained and, even if most of them were released, the figure shows that intimidation and surveillance were still the favourite methods of a police force that cared little about the *Fuero de los Españoles*.

Twenty-five persons were finally held under arrest at the close of the Andalusian operation for having collaborated with a *Front of anti-Francoist Resistance*. The total number of prisoners sentenced for political offences in 1960 amounted to at least 246, and their total sentences to 1,007 years in jail.

The determination to stifle any slight attempt at resistance was confirmed by the decree of 26 September 1960. Seventeen years after the law of 2 March 1943, twenty-three years after the Order in Council of 18 April 1937, it repeated the terms of these and even extended them: in a word, all those who opposed the regime were to be held guilty of *military rebellion*. This term covered such offences as 'spreading false and tendentious news ... injurious to the prestige of the State'. As for those who engaged in 'banditry or social subversion ... openly flouting social coexistence', their fate was the death penalty. Such vague definitions could be used to include any behaviour other than blind submission, absolute conformism or resigned acceptance. In 1960 the Spaniards were as fully *controlled* as they had been in 1937 or 1943, for the Caudillo and his men would tolerate no threat to their power. The successful development of the regime depended on their feeling secure. Franco, that prudent and experienced strategist, was clearly prepared to stamp out anything that caused him the least anxiety. He retained the means to enforce his sway, and he was prepared to use them coolly and unhesitatingly. The recourse to violence, abandoned by the majority of the opposition, thus remained a weapon in the hands of the government, which they were prepared, though not anxious, to use. The decree on military rebellion was, in the sense, an act of violence.

The opposition had only two alternatives: desperate actions which brought no result and were always severely punished, or cool caution, which meant impotence. At any moment violence might shatter attempts to act in a peaceable, restrained and rational fashion. For instance, the Communist Party issued fresh appeals for unity. Its Sixth Congress met in January 1960 in Prague, and declared itself ready 'to make all necessary concessions – without entailing any abandonment of principles – in order to reach an understanding, in one form or another, between all anti-Francoist forces, whether of the right or of the left'. The party's immediate objective was 'to bring to an end the Fascist dictatorship of General Franco so as to open the way for the democratic development of the country'. Santiago Carrillo even implied that 'this was an opportunity, unique in her history, for Spain to solve her problems' peacefully, thanks to the public-spiritedness of the Spanish people. Yet despite the coherence and prudence of this thesis the regime continued to keep the upper hand.

Many Communist delegates to the Prague Congress were arrested when they returned to Spain; the Madrid press denounced Communist subversion and published a letter of doubtful authenticity addressed by La Pasionaria to her Spanish comrades, urging them to conceal their party membership the better to infiltrate into various circles. The connivance between Liberals and Communists now seemed just another aspect of the offensive of international communism, initiated by the meeting in Paris between representatives of the French and Spanish Communist Parties.

The strength of Francoism was maintained not only through the all-important support of the army but also through the difficulty its opponents found in reaching agreement. Whereas the Spanish Communist Party reasserted its peaceable line, some of its militants had begun to denounce this as being defeatist and revisionist. Right-wing groups were reluctant to come to any agreement with what they still considered the extreme left, while new revolutionary groups moved on to direct action.

The Caudillo could go on playing his usual game. On 29 March he entertained the Pretender Don Juan at Cáceres, at the Palace of Las Cabezas. The two men lunched together, discussing the education of Don Juan Carlos, and 'questions of great importance for the life of the Nation' during a meeting which 'took place in an atmosphere of great cordiality'. Then the General returned to the Pardo Palace and Don Juan to his Estoril villa. The game went on. In Madrid, leaflets were circulated requesting Don Juan 'to state unequivocally whether he accepted the principles of the Franco regime'. Some clashes occurred between Falangists and Monarchists. At Estoril, Don Juan received delegates of the *Democracia Social Cristiana*. An imposing figure, with his deeply-lined face and his typical Bourbon nose, Don Juan heard Gil Robles declare on behalf of the delegates from the various Spanish provinces: 'We believe that it is our loyal duty to indicate to Your Highness, unequivocally, that the monarchy must adopt an essentially democratic foundation.'

As the years passed, the opposition had matured and spread to fresh groups, but it had not become more effective. In some cases, workers whose wages had dropped tried to force their employers to raise them: for instance, in April 4,000 workers at the Pegaso truck factory, in the suburbs of Madrid, refused to eat in the canteen or use the works trucks available to them for the seven-mile journey to the capital. Such resistance required a daily display of physical courage; the leaders were liable to be court-martialled. Elsewhere, intellectuals were arrested: Luis Goytisolo, poet and novelist, the painter Isidor Balaguer, the potter Godofredo Edo, imprisoned in Carabanchel, went on hunger strike on 2 April 1960; they were put in solitary confinement, but they held out for nine days. Elsewhere again, in the Basque country, when news came of the death in Paris on 22 March of José Antonio de Agurre, President of the Basque government in exile, masses were held everywhere in his memory: the Euzkadi (Basque) flag flew for a few moments at the top of Mount Urgull, overlooking San Sebastian, then the police broke up the religious ceremonies and made a number of arrests. When General Franco visited Barcelona in May the people's greeting was cool, in spite of police preparations. Worse still, an incident occurred at a concert given by the Catalan Orpheon; some students broke into the banned Catalan anthem, *Cant de la Señera*. The police immediately intervened and arrested the disturbers of the peace – some twenty of them – most of whom were soon released; however, they detained Dr Jorge Pujol, leader of the Catalan Catholic Youth Movement, and the printer Francisco Pizón. Jorge Pujol was handed over to the Social Brigade, and beaten by them for hours on end, on the soles of the feet and on the spine.[7] Finally, his strength exhausted, he admitted

[7] *Cahiers de Témoignage chrétien* (Paris, 1961),

being the author of a pamphlet entitled *Introducing General Franco*. Pizon admitted having printed it. For two consecutive nights some hundred young people demonstrated in front of the Archbishop's Palace, clamouring in vain to be heard. *Ecclesia* in its number of 15 June protested against the violence inflicted on the detainees, and in many churches sermons were preached denouncing the use of torture. Feelings ran high throughout Catalonia and in many Catholic circles. None the less Pujol was sentenced to seven years in jail.

Thus in 1960 inveterate hostility to Francoism was displayed in an impressive range which included Basques and Catalans, workers and intellectuals, Christian Democrats and Communists. It seemed as though the regime was cracking up on every side, now that stabilization had brought stagnation without any signs of recovery. Yet the opposition proved capable only of demonstrating; it was a huge advance on the past but insignificant in relation to what was needed to bring about a change of regime. The problem therefore remained intact: would the various forces of the opposition succeed in mobilizing the whole Spanish people so as to bring down the regime, while the latter retained all the resources of a totalitarian state, with none of the checks which in liberal democracies prevent a recourse to total and brutal violence, and while, thanks to the policy of the Opus Dei technocrats, Franco was about to superimpose on it the attractions of economic development and the consumer society?

To be sure, many facts bear witness to the people's hostile indifference to the regime, giving rise to a body of folklore, with popular songs parodying official anthems.[8] When a procession of personalities passed, the faces and glances of the spectators revealed mocking curiosity or resigned disdain, hardly ever enthusiasm. It was plain that the people felt remote and alien from the regime, but at the same time that with intuitive prudence, acquired through so many lost battles, they admitted its existence. A parody of *Cara al Sol*,[9] sung throughout Spain in the fifties, says:

> '*Cara al sol*
> *llevamos veinte años*
> *y estamos negros de aguantar*
> *militares, curas, falangistas,*
> *y esto se va acabar.*
> *Sin comer*
> *nos habeis mantenido*
> *sin hablar*
> *pues todo era prohibido.*
> *Imposible es aguantar*
> *ya más*
> *sin patria, justicia y pan.*'

[8] *Chansons de la nouvelle résistance espagnole*, collected by S. Liberovici and M. L. Straniero (Paris, 1963).

[9] Facing the Sun
   we've had enough of that for twenty years
   and we're furious at having to endure

This was only a song, an assertion, a wish, perhaps a conviction. The regime had other weapons with which to fight and resist, more powerful than ephemeral songs and assertions.

The Caudillo at Sixty-Eight

General Franco could celebrate his sixty-eighth birthday at the Pardo Palace without too much anxiety about his future. His photograph appeared on 4 December 1960, on the front page of every daily paper. He was smiling and relaxed, his scanty hair plastered down above his ears. His face had grown fleshy, his chin almost disappeared into his neck, deep lines were scored around his mouth and there was something absurd about the sparse pepper-and-salt moustache. The whole lower part of his face was insignificant. The eyes transformed it; his glance still retained its keenness and vivacity. At 68, Franco was ready to go on ruling Spain for a long time to come.

'One more year of patriotic devotion by the man who embodies the purest of our national virtues,' declared the newspapers. And the Caudillo gave his annual address to the country on 30 December:

'In the coming year', he said, 'the National Movement and the Regime born of the Crusade will attain fulfilment. . . . After a quarter of a century's march straight forward . . . a quarter of a century of permanent services rendered to the cause of the free world, services which are now recognized . . . a quarter of a century of manifest progress. . . .'

In this vision of things, everything falls into place: the way leads straight forward. He went on to speak of the help to be given to underdeveloped countries, ignoring the slums of La Chanca below the Alcabaza in Almería. 'We must remain unconditionally faithful to these permanent watchwords: religious, social and political unity.' The Caudillo's self-assurance was not that of a mountebank miming conviction. It was rooted in the heart of the discreet and tranquil man who had survived the storms of history.

His opponents had to contend with this smooth monolith; some of them seeking to unite or rouse the people, others appealing for help to the great powers. After John F. Kennedy's election on 8 November, Indalecio Prieto wrote him a moving appeal from Mexico. 'I am an old Spaniard, Sir, who, although nearing the end of my eighth decade of life, still have the courage to raise my voice in protest against injustice. . . .' and he asked Kennedy to bring pressure to bear on Franco to secure guarantees for the safety of the opposition. 'If I have some

---

soldiers, priests, Falangists,
all that's going to come to an end.
You have kept us without food
without speaking
since all that was forbidden.
It's impossible to hold out
any longer
without a fatherland, without justice and without bread.

faith in you, Mr Kennedy,' he wrote, 'it is not on account of your political tendencies but of your youth.' In this sad and dignified letter from an exile, weariness can be felt beneath the will to go on struggling. The victorious General, on the other hand, showed no trace of weariness. In his end-of-the-year speech he had already ensured the future of his regime for the duration of his own life. In his firm, quiet voice he told the Spanish people:

'Whoever has received the honour and the burden of being a nation's leader can at no moment lawfully accept relief or rest. He must spend his whole existence in the forefront of the fundamental undertaking to which he has been summoned by the votes and with the approval of his people, deepening the roots and bringing to perfection the system he has established.'

CHAPTER II

MAJOR CONFLICTS IN SPAIN
1961–JUNE 1962

During 1960, 1961 and the beginning of 1962 nothing important seemed to happen, and yet there was something in the air: changes were perceptible everywhere in Spain. A quarter of a century after the *Alzamiento* old Spain was disintegrating, and in every sphere new elements were to be found, mingled with, or side by side with, the past.

Changing Spain

In 1960 the population of Madrid was some 2,300,000. The villages on its periphery were lost in a sea of grey or yellowish buildings, cubic blocks huddled close together in the middle of fields. Sometimes the earth on which these new dwellings stood had been used to make the bricks for them, and the tall chimney of the brickworks was gradually surrounded and overtopped by their walls. Shanty towns, villages, blocks of cheap flats were dovetailed together in these muddy suburbs, from which silent streams of workers poured forth each morning. In certain sectors the population had grown fivefold in ten years. Spain was changing. The birth rate was falling regularly, coming closer to that of most European countries: 21·3 per 1,000 in 1961 as against 27·6 for the period 1930–4: an important sign that in the decisive field of demography Spain was once again following the path chosen by its rulers – integration into the Western bloc.

Spain was changing, and everyone could see it and experience it. From 1961 onwards the papers stressed these transformations, the credit for which they attributed to the regime. In 1961, the situation still reflected the results of the Stabilization Plan, but 1962 marked the 'take-off' of economic expansion. Spain's *milagro*, her miraculous recovery, following those of Germany, Japan and Italy, promised to ensure her access to the paradise of the consumer society.

The mystique of the *Desarrollo* (Development) Plan had formed part of government propaganda by 1962. On 26 January the Cabinet decided to create a planning commission, and it was Lopez Rodo, whose entry into the government as technical secretary to the President had heralded the new economic policy as early as 1956,[1] who was put at its head. This member of the Opus Dei, who was barely 41 years old, now held a key post. Since 1956 he had succeeded in making

[1] See above, Book III.

important contacts outside Spain; he had formed close links with the principal directors of the International Monetary Fund and of the World Bank, with leading American banks, and thus with the economic advisers to the White House. The words *Development, Planning, Miracle,* recur constantly during those years of transition; while a vast increase in the use of neon lighting and in the number of hotels, cars, asphalted roads, fast trains and television sets was either witnessed or promised.

These were not merely appearances: by 1964 the industrial index stood at 140·1 compared with 100 in 1961, setting Spain in the forefront for industrial progress, ahead of Japan (139·2), the United States (121·6) and the U.S.S.R. (121·1). Individual incomes also began to rise and, even more significantly, so did consumer spending. Spain was changing: the young men of 20 were born in 1942, and those who were born in 1936 were 26 already. From France and Switzerland and Germany came letters and news and money from workers who had emigrated, maintaining contact with Europe; while European tourists invaded the Spanish coast in ever-increasing numbers: 7,500,000 in 1961; 10,931,626 in 1963; 14,102,880 in 1964; 17,250,000 in 1966.

Things were stirring everywhere, as though the visible acceleration of these changes intensified the need for others in the field of politics or culture. Significantly, in May 1961 the most famous Spanish painters drew up and signed a manifesto criticizing the official commission for the *Biennales* of Venice, São-Paulo and Paris: 'We demand a free Spanish pavilion controlled and constituted by a committee of free men.'

Gradually, as consumer goods became available to fresh social strata, as propaganda in praise of development was intensified, as the fortunate few blatantly displayed a wealth which it was implied that the many would some day enjoy, and as, in the nearby countries where so many Spaniards worked, cars and television sets, homes and holidays were taken for granted by the majority of the population; above all, as the new generations – born after 1940 – became active, their *hunger* found expression throughout Spain. They wanted to improve their standard of living, they wanted to *have*, to possess, since this was the social law of the day and since the regime had adopted that law as its own, and offered it to the Spanish people as the aim of the incipient 'miracle'. Already the workers in certain foreign factories, Renault at Valladolid for instance, enjoyed good working and living conditions. By involving Spain (under pressure from necessity) in the process of economic development, the Franco regime had introduced the Spanish people to the habit of continuous economic demands. Franco's government had now to accept one of the laws of advanced capitalist societies, namely that the maintenance and above all the raising of the standard of living are necessary factors of economic and social stability.

Now in 1961 and at the beginning of 1962 there was a wide gap between the hopes of Spanish workers and the reality of their daily lives. Spain was changing, but the change had not yet affected those who were bringing it about (investments had never been so high in Spain as during 1960–1, the time when wages were frozen and then dropped). Early in 1962 the law fixed wages at 36 pesetas per day, which was scandalously inadequate. The Archbishop of Seville pointed out, on 3 March 1962, that a workman with a wife and two children could not live decently on a wage of less than 110 or 120 pesetas. On 12 February *Ecclesia* wrote:

'Recent statistics show that Spain is one of the countries with the lowest national income in Europe. On the other hand it ranks third as regards super-fluous expenses. The luxury and wastefulness of the wealthy classes are a provocation to those who lack the bare necessities to lead a life of human dignity, and they create a pathological condition within the body of society.'

This pathological condition could have been observed during the whole of 1961 and the opening months of 1962. Apparently ephemeral incidents accumulated in the most varied sectors of Spanish life, as its transformation became deeper and more rapid; tensions were sharpened between old traditions and new requirements and social categories. Wages remained frozen, while expansion had begun. Things seemed to be moving towards a crisis, towards a confrontation on the economic, social and political level which would represent the totality of the problems posed by the transformation going on in Spain. The Franco regime, which had *chosen* to promote this transformation and had abandoned none of its power to control,[2] was in a position to master this delicate situation. A historic situation is never totally determined, and the evolution of Spain was also dependent on the actions and intelligence of the men in power and those in opposition. All were making ready, because all could assess the slow and sure intensification of the conflict.

The Intensification of the Conflict (1961, March 1962)

The government's first concern was with the exploits of the D.R.I.L. When, during the night of 21 to 22 January 1961 a small commando group seized the Portuguese steamer *Santa María*, which Captain Henrique Galvão, who was responsible for the hijacking, promptly rechristened *Santa Liberdade*, and when it was learnt in Madrid that many of the commandos were Spaniards, real anxiety was felt. 'We don't know what will happen to Franco,' Galvão was said to have declared, 'but Salazar will soon be overthrown and the fall of one of these tyrants will bring the other toppling down into hell, where he ought to have been a long time ago.' Now the example of Cuba and the Algerian war had brought home the value of subversive warfare, and not only to the opposition. General Delgado, an unsuccessful candidate in the Portuguese elections, was said to have signed an agreement with the Spanish General Emilio Herrera, President of the Republican government in exile.

The violence of press reactions in Spain against the 'act of piracy' which had enabled 'Red propaganda to penetrate into the Western press' betrays Madrid's anxiety. Help to Portugal was immediately forthcoming: the cruiser *Canarias* hurried in pursuit of the steamer, and the Chiefs of Staff of the two armies met: 'The fraternal relations between the armies of Spain and Portugal have proved themselves stronger than ever.'

[2] On all these problems see above.

Madrid's fear of the D.R.I.L. was due to the recurrence of bomb attacks, testifying to the response aroused in Spain by revolutionary action. In the Basque country the unshakeable national feeling gave rise to a Basque Revolutionary Liberation movement, *Euzkadi Ta Azkatasuna* (E.T.A.), which demanded a representative democratic regime and showed its determination by attempts at sabotage (as on the railway near San Sebastian in July 1961) and by demonstrating on every occasion (for instance by producing Basque flags during religious ceremonies). Torture, heavy penalties and a large number of arrests were powerless to eradicate the E.T.A., which enjoyed the support of the whole Basque population.

The year 1961 even witnessed a recrudescence of *maquis* fighting. On 8 August *El Campesino*, with a band of thirteen men, attacked the electric power station of Irabia, at Orbaiceta; a civil guard was killed, and the *bandolero* escaped into France. *Paris-Match* published a long report on El Campesino, who declared that he had proclaimed the Third Spanish Republic and begun guerrilla warfare. The story ended, however, with his arrest by the French police. However limited such actions may have been, however diversely motivated, they all serve, like so many alarm signals, to show the rise of unease in Spain.

The universities, once again, became centres of unrest. At the Law Faculty in Barcelona, on 23 January 1963, at the Festival of San Raimondo de Penafort (the jurists' holiday) a band of commandos, consisting of members of the Opus Dei, armed with cudgels, attacked the students who, during a mock trial, had satirized the Opus and the advantages accruing to its members. After such incidents, during which many people were injured, a strike broke out which lasted over a week.

In Madrid, further incidents took place in March which also reveal hostility towards the Opus Dei. This is particularly understandable in that the Opus, in addition to its prominent role in the government, was acquiring fresh privileges in the academic world. The General Study Centre of Navarre, run by the Opus Dei, had ranked as a Church university since 6 August 1960. On 25 October of that year the solemn promulgation of Pope John XXIII's decree had taken place in the presence of the Minister of Justice and of Mgr Escriva de Balaguer, founder of the Opus. On 14 April 1962, the state recognized the diplomas conferred by the Catholic University of Navarre, thus giving up its own monopoly in this field. There was renewed agitation in the universities in protest against this decision, but in vain. They remained none the less, whatever the result of their demonstrations, the seat of covert hostility against the regime, against the rectors who were generally its devoted adherents, and against the Opus Dei. Lectures would be interrupted, brief speeches made, study groups formed; student strikes broke out, with demonstrations in the streets of Madrid (May 1961). Leaflets and wall inscriptions appeared everywhere. In Barcelona the anniversary of the disturbances of February 1951 provided the pretext for demonstrations. On each occasion students were arrested and sentenced.

However, they were no longer in isolation. Around them, the youngest and most dynamic elements of the Spanish intelligentsia (led by that of Catalonia) provided sympathetic support. Teachers often displayed their solidarity with the students; young writers, poets, painters – many with international reputations – unhesitatingly upheld their opposition and demanded the release of those imprisoned. They even faced trial, as when in March 1961 Tierno Calván, Antonio Menchaca, López Aparicio and Dioniso Ridruejo were brought to court. Ridruejo had in fact been moving steadily towards liberalism. His *Escrito en España*, published in 1962 in Buenos Aires by Losada (who published most of the Spanish authors banned in their own country) is an intellectual biography explaining the process which led him from falangism to unequivocal and radical opposition to Francoism. The book is evidence of the crisis facing the regime; so, too, are the many works that now appeared, displaying a clear critical intention: Goytisolo's stories about the impoverished south, novels by Armando López Salinas on miners' lives (*La Mina*) and plays by Alfredo Sastre (*En la red*). Living culture was developing outside Francoism, and in hostility to it. It openly retrieved the past, bringing back to light the Republican authors whom the regime had condemned: as for instance in José Maria Castellet's anthology, *Veinte años de poesía española* (*Twenty Years of Spanish Poetry*). It drew fresh strength from the vigorous upsurge of Catalan culture. In Barcelona an experimental theatre was set up in 1962, which put on Arnold Wesker's *Roots*; translations, of Camus's *La Peste* for example, appeared in Catalan, and there was also a renaissance of Catalan popular song, the first record being 'Espines sings Brassens'.

Moreover Spanish intellectuals were aware of European support. In the sixties, the publishers and the literary journals of Paris and Rome discovered the young intelligentsia of Madrid and Barcelona. Contact had become easy since mass tourism had abolished frontiers; and the revival of struggle within Spain, the rise of a dynamic generation of young writers and original painters, as well as the historic traditions of friendship, explain the strength of the bonds now formed between intellectual Spain and the rest of Europe. When leading publishers decided to found an international literary prize, Formentor was the place chosen for their meeting and the prize was awarded in 1961 to a Spanish writer, Juan García Hortelano, for his novel *Tormenta de Verano*, (*Summer Storm*) which uncompromisingly shows up the intrigues and the behaviour of high Spanish society.

Thus, when it opened its doors to Europe, the Franco regime found itself faced with new perils. On 25 and 26 March 1961 the Conference of Western Europe was held in Paris for the amnesty of Spanish political prisoners and exiles, demanding justice and freedom for all those who had been condemned, illustrating with precise data the situation in Spanish jails. In that of Burgos, for instance, at the end of 1960, 246 out of 393 political prisoners had been sentenced to over 30 years, 3 to 40 years, 7 to 60 years: 76 of them had already served more than 20 years, and 126 more than 15. On this occasion, student associations, *Cámaras Sindicales*, in certain faculties in Madrid and Barcelona, voted support for the Paris conference, sometimes with the approval of the Dean. Thus links were formed across the Pyrenees joining the younger generations to their seniors in exile.

At the end of 1961 a group of young intellectuals, in association with exiles living in other countries and with Spaniards in opposition at home, set up a publishing house abroad, *Ruedo Ibérico*, in order to issue in Spanish works that dealt with the country's problems from an angle other than the official Francoist one. Thus, they published books which were sometimes strictly historical accounts, but which would enable the younger generation to grasp and adopt a history of the Civil War which was new to them, since Francoist teaching had systematically distorted both the causes and the facts of the tragedy. The success of these books, introduced clandestinely into Spain and circulated there, was such that it led the Madrid authorities to modify the legends which had hitherto served as the history of the Civil War. Soon *Ruedo Ibérico* launched a review analysing Spain's contemporary problems, and these *Cuadernos de Ruedo Ibérico* became a focus for intellectuals in opposition. At the same time a picture of Franco Spain in the early sixties was presented in *España Hoy*.[3] The intellectuals living in Paris were in permanent contact with the Spanish poets, writers, teachers or painters who worked in their own country. Thus in February 1962 the *Ruedo Ibérico* prizes for fiction and poetry were awarded at Collioure by a jury including such men as Manuel Tuñon de Lara, Juan Goytisolo, Antonio Ferres and José María Castellet. Armando López Salina won the prize for his novel *Años tras años* (*Year After Year*), a realistic chronicle of life in Spain since the Civil War, which had been banned by the censor.[4]

Naturally the Francoist press reacted violently against the intellectual atmosphere in which, both in Spain and in the rest of Europe, the regime was denounced. Thus the Falangist journal *Arriba* commented on the amnesty conference (25 March):

'The signatories of the appeal in favour of the release of Spanish prisoners are a set of gentry some of whom call themselves French but who have very odd biographies. Madame Elsa Triolet, born in Russia, a Jewess and a member of the Communist Party: G. Gombault and Pierre Lazareff, both Jewish journalists. Alongside such members of the Jewish and Communist teams . . . Father Riquet, the first priest in more than a century and a half to have given a lecture in a freemasons' lodge.'

According to official Spain, the Paris conference was 'a cynical affair.'

The presence of many Catholics among the 500 delegates from seventeen countries aroused anxiety and indignation in Madrid, and resentment was felt at the repeated denunciation of social injustice by certain members of the Church hierarchy. The Twentieth 'Social Week of Spain' held in Granada from November from 27 November to 3 December 1961, after a study of the Encyclical *Mater et Magistra* of 15 May, uttered admonitions whose vigour astonished the secular authorities. Mgr Pablo Gurpide, Bishop of Bilbao, spoke of the lack of any strong

[3] *España Hoy*, compiled by Ignacio Fernández de Castro and Jose Martínez (Paris, 1963). An indispensable collection: text, drawings, photographs, detailed chronology.

[4] cf. above. The book has provided useful evidence. French version *Chaque jour compte en Espagne.*

Christian social consciousness in the society around him. Mgr Bueno Monreal, Cardinal Archbishop of Seville, was even more specific.

He wrote: 'When we consider the contrast between these rich estates and these sub-human slums, the terrible text of St James springs irresistibly to mind. "Your riches are corrupted". Too many industrial leaders are still a long way from the teachings of Christianity. . . . The Church demands that agricultural enterprise should be a community of persons.'

Such denunciations, new in their forthrightness, indicate the rise of a dissatisfaction of which the Church was all the more aware in that its ranks included militant members of the H.O.A.C., who were thereby spurred on to further action, resulting in the banning of their periodical *Juventud Obrera* (*Workers' Youth Movement*).

The working class, in fact, expressed itself directly through actions which became increasingly numerous as the economic revival got under way. Their aim was a strictly economic one: the unfreezing and readjustment of wages.

Social tension was felt everywhere by the autumn of 1961. Strikes had already broken out that spring in Granada and in Barcelona; now Madrid, Valencia, and Barcelona yet again were affected. The end of the year witnessed a sharpening of the conflict. Men from the Beasain works, which made railway material, wanted their new collective agreements concluded without delay. They clashed with the police and with the representatives of official unions, who were moreover quite incapable of controlling disturbances. In factories and workshops men began to appoint their own representatives, independently of the official union structure, and, reverting to a form of organization which had emerged in 1956 during the strikes in the Basque country, they created Workers' Commissions in a number of firms. At the end of 1961 and the beginning of 1962 these were already playing a considerable role. They were not yet permanent; they would come into being in order to promote a conflict or to represent the workers in some negotiation, then they would disappear. They were an original and spontaneous creation of the Spanish working class, born of its experience and bearing witness to its strong democratic traditions. Delegates elected at one meeting could be dismissed at the next. These committees were not the fruit of any one political trend, but naturally militants, whether Communist, Socialist or Catholic, were involved, and the Communist Party tried to establish them throughout the whole country. A force with which the Franco regime would have to reckon had arisen, providing a framework for the working class and succeeding, by dint of daily efforts and successive strikes, in reconstituting what the Nationalist victory of 1939 had annihilated by means of fire, prison, terror and banishment.

Such movements arose in quick succession at the beginning of 1962. In January one of the most important iron and steel works in Viscaya, the Basconia, was closed by order of the authorities following the strike of its 3,000 workers. In February, the workers of Guipuzcoa province demonstrated in the street; then the men of the arms and rolling-stock factories of Irún and Eibar went on strike, and the *Guardia Civil* had to drive them out of the buildings. There was renewed activity at Beasain: every evening some 3,000 workers marched past in the streets, either in silence or chanting the words: 'A minimum wage of a hundred a day.' In fact, 80 per cent of them earned less than 100 pesetas a day!

Aware that this accumulation of events revealed mounting tension, the opposition tried to control the situation and use it as a political weapon against the regime. In May 1961 the trade union organizations in exile, C.N.T., U.G.T., and the *Solidaridad de Trabajadores Vascos* (United Basque Workers (S.T.V.) united to form the *Alianza Sindical* (Syndicalist-Alliance). In June the parties of the non-Communist opposition, from the *Izquierda Demócrata Cristiana* to the U.G.T. and the P.S.O.E. and including the Basque groups, came together in a *Unión de Fuerzas democráticas* (Union of Democratic Forces) whose programme proposed a transitional regime which would finally take the shape either of a monarchy or a republic, as a result of elections. As for the Communists they issued an appeal for the organization of the *Huelga Nacional Pacífica*, then, as this met with no response, Santiago Carrillo made it clear in October that his party was prepared to come to a direct understanding with activists within the country, and to take the lead in the anti-Francoist movement. That same year 1961 witnessed the foundation of the *Movimiento Popular de Resistencia* (M.P.R. – People's Resistance Movement) which sought 'to go beyond those parties which have proved incapable of defeating Franco or organizing resistance', while such existing small groups as the F.L.P. acquired new recruits, feeling (as did the members of the D.R.I.L.) that traditional methods of action were no longer adequate.

Thus, as ever, the opposition lagged behind certain forms of working-class struggle (the Workers' Commissions went far beyond the *entente* reached by union leaders in exile with their *Alianza Sindical*) and it was, moreover, still divided. While it was aware of the growing crisis, it seemed unprepared to imagine an effective strategy capable of moving on from the partial economic struggle of the working class to directly political aims, and of unifying, to that end, the various efforts – those of students and of metal workers, of Basque priests and of poets. Even if all these forces were unified, the opposition would still have to contend with a state which still had power in its hands, which felt the crisis looming and was making ready to confront it.

The Caudillo and his Regime Face a Growing Threat

After a quarter of a century, Franco was still in power. Late in the afternoon of a stifling July day, he drove in an open car, accompanied by General Barroso, Minister of War, to the grandstand in the Paseo de la Castellan in Madrid. The avenue was bedecked with flags and lined with a cheering crowd, which included a large number of tourists. At seven o'clock the military march-past began: the motorized Jarama division, the armoured Brunete division, the Guadarrama division, with ultra-modern equipment adapted to atomic warfare. Then came 50,000 Falangist and *Requetés* veterans from all over Spain, and thousands of *Alféreces provisionales* (Temporary Subalterns): each group of a thousand ex-soldiers preceded by two rows of flags and a number of regular army officers. Overhead flew Sabre F 86 aircraft and also Messerschmitts and Junkers. In the other stands were former foreign volunteers of the Nationalist army:

Germans of the Condor Legion, Italians from the 'Black Arrows', Frenchmen, Belgians and Poles.

The regime thus regularly staged the great anniversary ceremonies which testified to its staying power and allowed it to display its military and political strength. In every town the same parades of well-armed soldiers and well-officered veterans took place: at Pampeluna, for instance, 20,000 Navarrese *Requetés* marched past. This twenty-fifth anniversary gave rise to an orgy of statistics, of balance-sheets proving that, as *Arriba* declared, 'the regime is 100 per cent constructive'. Its aim was to convince every Spaniard of the benefits of a perfect regime, or make him feel that every other Spaniard but himself was convinced of it. During this anniversary year 1961 the Caudillo made more speeches than ever before. In April he travelled through Andalusia, visiting Málaga, Almería, Granada, Córdoba, Jaen and Cadiz. Everywhere crowds gathered. 'Our democracy is sincere,' said the Caudillo. 'It turns to the people, it seeks to find out the people's will and wishes . . .' (25 April).

'¡ *Arriba España!*' he exclaimed each time, after extolling the achievements of his regime. At El Garrobo, a small village in the valley of the Guadalquivir, drawing a lesson from the military manoeuvres he had been watching, he praised the Spanish army for its loyalty to the regime in contrast with the French army, which was torn in two by the military *putsch* in Algiers. Amid cheering crowds he inaugurated barrages and housing blocks.

The poverty was so palpable, the social inequalities so glaring, the crisis so profound that in his speech at Cordoba, on the Plaza San Antonio, Franco was obliged to declare: 'I have realized the persistence of many social injustices and painful contrasts. . . .' The crowd interrupted him with enthusiastic cheers. 'And therefore,' he went on, 'I call upon the great landowners of Andalusia. I appeal to the generosity . . . of all those *whose property and possessions we have saved*, to the heads of firms' (here the crowd cheered and applauded once more) 'to collaborate in a Christian spirit to achieve social justice' (4 May). This was a promise of agrarian reform, the press declared. *Arriba*, voicing Falangist nostalgia, wrote: 'Franco is the people's leader. . . . He guides the Spanish people, but at the same time he takes his orders from them. . . . Franco can refuse them nothing.'

This important speech shows clearly that the Caudillo had assessed the gravity of the threatened crisis. The time had come to make a few concessions, and this was the meaning of his appeal to the big landowners, which further implied that the Caudillo was ensuring his personal popularity and strengthening his regime to the possible detriment of one particular category, the owners of *latifundia*. It was true, moreover, that the regime, having chosen the path of industrial development, the class of big landowners was doomed to submit to the requirements of the state as a whole, increasingly dominated by the specifically industrial interests of large-scale capitalism. The 'People's Leader' remained at the helm, and throughout his speeches that anniversary year there was never any reference to the problem of the succession. Prince Don Juan Carlos might entertain, in Barcelona, Catalan industrialists of every shade of opinion; his father might welcome to Estoril 250 officers of the *Tercios de Requetés*, come to render allegiance on the occasion of the festival of the 'traditional martyrs'; the Monarchist press might accumulate communiqués announcing the marriage of Juan Carlos with Sophia of Greece; yet the Caudillo kept the game in his own hands.

On 24 December it was learnt in Madrid that Franco had met with an accident; his gun had exploded while he was out shooting, his favourite sport, in the woods around the Pardo. However, all the confabulations, hopes and fears which this news had provoked in a few hours were dissipated with equal speed. The accident had indeed occurred: the Caudillo had fractured his left hand, and surgical help had been called in. However, on 27 December, at 1 p.m., the Generalísimo returned to his home, greeted by an enthusiastic crowd. On 31 December, in his end-of-the-year speech, he thanked the Spanish people for their demonstrations of affection towards him, and asserted in a tone of complete assurance: 'The Spanish crusade and the years that followed it are a proof of the favour and protection of Heaven. The blood of our heroes and martyrs has produced what the uninitiated call the Spanish miracle.'

A whole section of the Catholic hierarchy, moreover, was unsparing in its declarations of support for Franco and his regime. The encyclical *Mater et Magistra* was made out to be in complete agreement with the principles of the *Movimiento*; the Bishop of Málaga told the Caudillo: 'The services rendered by Your Excellency to the Church and to Spain are immense.' The Archbishop of Seville saw in Franco's presence a proof, blindingly evident to the whole world, of 'the exemplary concord existing between the Church and the civil power'.

Thus even though the Catholic hierarchy was outspoken in its indictment of social injustice, it did not deny its solidarity with the regime. Anxious about the unrest within the Church and the looming crisis, it denounced excesses, but acquitted the Caudillo and his regime of all responsibility for these. True, many Catholics went further than this, and joined in the political and trade union struggle; but they represented only one sector of the Church. Another sector, and a very powerful one, remained faithful to the regime, which had signed the Concordat, and to its head. The Caudillo missed no opportunity of repeating: 'We are a Catholic nation . . . we must see to it that the renaissance of our country conforms to the rules of religion.' And these words did not fall on deaf ears.

Franco thus retained his traditional props. While Martínez Barrio and Indalecio Prieto died in exile, after so many others, unskilful yet tenacious fighters in so many lost battles, the Caudillo was at the head of a state in process of transformation. The press still acclaimed him as successor to the Catholic kings, and as a final triumph he had now joined battle with Spain's feudal lords. 'Franco,' wrote *Arriba* on 6 May 1961, 'relying on the true Spanish people, is now waging a battle against capitalism, against a selfish and obstructive oligarchy.' What was actually happening was that within the Spanish government the 'Europeans', supporters of Spain's integration into the Common Market, led by the Minister of Trade, Alberto Ullastres, were pressing for a speedier modernization of the Spanish economy.

Concentration, rationalization, planning and pruning were the aims of the technocrats, and they presupposed the elimination of certain archaic features.

Thus the reform of agriculture was an essential factor in view of the export of high quality products to Western Europe, and this implied a transformation of the methods employed by the big landowners and a real improvement in working conditions. It was also essential to reform the banking system by means of an association of public and private banks to facilitate investment, and to modernize mines and industries. It was not a question of fighting capitalism, as *Arriba* had declared, but of effecting the transition to another form of capitalism, efficacious, dynamic and productive; the transition – which had already been begun – from an economy of penury and stagnation to one of abundance and development. The model for the government's technocratic economists, such as López Rodo, Planning Commissioner, or Ullastres, was obviously none of the under-developed countries still burdened by their latifundiary system of property, nor yet Greece, but Western Germany or, better still, as a long-term target, the United States. This presupposed integration into the Common Market and the association of the working class with the economic system, within the framework of a representative trade union movement, able – like American unions – to negotiate precise, limited and advantageous agreements: unions which would be pressure groups, elements within an economico-social machine, prepared to argue resolutely but having abandoned any prospect of revolution. Their existence would make it possible both to accelerate the process of modernization (by influencing cost prices and forcing firms to improve productivity) and to avoid the violent explosions that occur when the working class is inadequately represented, as for instance in the Falangist *sindicatos*; and above all, within the framework of a complex economy to *plan* a decisive element in the economic process by regulating wages and the claims of wage-earners. We can thus understand why the 'Europeans' within the Francoist government who had achieved stabilization and promoted the economic revival at the end of 1961 were concerned, at the start of 1962, with completing these next stages.

On the morning of Friday, 9 February 1962, Count de Casa-Miranda, Spanish Ambassador in Brussels, handed the Secretary-General of the ministers of the E.E.C. a letter from Castiella to M. Couve de Murville, acting President of the Council of Ministers of the Common Market.

'I have the honour,' the Spanish minister wrote, 'to ask in the name of my government for the opening of negotiations in order to examine the possible association of my country to the European Economic Community in the manner most befitting our mutual interests. . . . My government, being concerned with the task of accelerating the economic development of the country, is convinced that the requirements of this task will be duly appreciated by the Community. . . . The success of our Stabilization Plan, obtained with the collaboration of international organizations, constitutes an encouraging experience.'

The news provoked no surprise in Madrid. In fact it was the logical conclusion of a policy initiated *in 1957* with the entry of the Opus Dei members into the government, simultaneously with the signature of the Treaty of Rome on the Common Market.[5] Alberto Ullastres, commenting on Castiella's letter on 10

[5] See above, Book III.

February, declared: 'The request which has just been made by the Spanish government, at the direct instigation of the Caudillo, simply means that the time has come to do what was in all our minds, namely to take one further step towards the European and international integration of Spain.' The business world approved of the *démarche*: 'Spain could not adopt the strange attitude of an economic Crusoe,' wrote *A.B.C.* (10 February). Catholic circles were also in favour of it, although recommending gradual measures so as not to make things difficult for the Spanish economy.

Only a section of the Falange proved recalcitrant. Entry into the Common Market could in fact bring Spain's political evolution to a point which implied the death of the Falange and the transformation of 'vertical syndicates' into representative trade unions. The Falangists who were doing well in the union bureaucracy felt the threat the more in that certain European circles were demanding the transformation of Spanish trade unions as a prerequisite for Spain's entry into the Common Market. French and Belgian Socialist were supported on this issue by the powerful D.G.B., the Federation of German trade unions.

Now – and this could not be mere coincidence – the second Spanish Trade Union Congress opened on 5 March 1962, in Madrid, attended by 600 delegates and fifty foreign observers. It was a decisive event, revealing the importance of these turning-point years in which the regime asserted its will to control the transformation of Spain by taking successive steps, all tending towards that end: the Stabilization Plan, the creation of a Planning Commission, the reform of the banking and agrarian systems, the application to join the Common Market; and now the reform of the trade unions.

Within the Falange Jiménez Torres, Secretary-General of the trade union organization, supported by Solis Ruiz, Minister Secretary-General of the *Movimiento*, had drawn up a plan of reform, both men being 'Europeans'. A fortnight before the congress, Torres resigned, an indication that his project met with disapproval by the majority of the Falangist old guard. Fernández Cuesta led the attack, and at the last minute Solis Ruiz changed sides, abandoning all attempt at reform. On 10 March Franco presided over the ceremonial closing session of the congress. 'It is implied that we are a dictatorship,' he said amid applause, 'as though Spain could have lived twenty-five years under a dictatorship and as if Spaniards were not brave enough to repulse all dictatorships and all arbitrary power. . . . We are a new state, a new revolutionary state. . . . *¡ Arriba España!*'

'Franco, Franco, Franco,' chanted the assembled congress. Their clamour could not conceal the fact that an attempt to *democratize* Spanish unions, to make them part of a new economic system, had failed: rivalry between factions, and the interests of the Falangist group, had prevailed over the general interest of the Spanish regime. The Falange and the *Sindicatos* were thus an obstructive factor which showed that the government was not in a position to direct as it chose, rationally, all the aspects of its policy. Moreover, the members of the E.E.C. were not unanimous with respect to Spain's request. While Germany viewed it favourably, granting Madrid a long-term loan of $50 million, Belgium demanded

As Spain changes, new buildings arise . . . here, modern popular housing in a suburb of Madrid. *(Belga)*

A "normalized" Spain receives hordes of foreign tourists, some of whom are seen here at the Alhambra in Granada. *(Belga)*

The Caudillo in friendly conversation with Don Juan, Count of Barcelona, on the occasion of the christening of the Count's grandson, the first son of Don Juan Carlos (*Keystone*)

A manifestation by Carlists, partisans of Carlos-Hugo of Bourbon-Parma (*Belga*)

On 22 November 1966 the Chief of State unveiled his proposed Organic Law before the Cortes. *(Belga)*

The propaganda for the National Referendum of December 1966 was carried out by the Ministry of Information on a massive scale and was modern and effective. The opposition, legally, did not exist. *(Belga)*

Monarchist leader Gil Robles *(Keystone)*

Firemen voting in the National Referendum of December 1966. Since the urns were of glass, to keep one's vote secret was difficult. *(Belga)*

The years 1968 and 1969 were marked by renewed anti-Franco demonstrations in workers' and students' districts. Here students in Madrid flee before the *Policia Armada. (Belga)*

A unit of Spain's Civil Guard—80,000 men in permanent state of mobilization
(*Belga*)

Don Juan Carlos *(right)*, whom Franco designated on 22 July 1969 as his successor, with Admiral Carrero Blanco, *éminence grise* of the regime. Straw king and iron chancellor? *(Belga)*

that the question of Britain's entry be settled first. In short, in these two decisive fields (integration into Europe and transformation of the unions) which were the two aspects of the same endeavour to make Spain into an advanced capitalist country, the regime encountered difficulties due both to its own nature (the role of the Falange) and to the rivalries between great nations. These difficulties were also an inherent part of the crisis which was brewing, and which was to break out in the spring of 1962.

Conflicts During the Spring of 1962

Yet at the beginning of April the whole country had seemed undisturbed, and Spain's general situation favourable. Relations with the Kennedy administration, after a brief period of tension, were now good. Franco had appointed as Ambassador to Washington Antonio Garrigues, who was known to have connections with American banks. The twenty-third anniversary of victory had been duly celebrated on 1 April and the Minister of the Interior had represented Franco at the funeral of the financier Juan March Ordinas, who had played so important a role during the Civil War. Everything seemed calm.

It was learnt, however, that in the Canaries leaflets and inscriptions had appeared demanding '*Canarias libras*', and there were rowdy scenes at a football match on 25 March. The islands were in the throes of an economico-social crisis caused by drought, which partly accounted for the political unrest. Franco sent in ministers, reinforcements and men from the Social Brigade. This was only a warning sign. Soon there were student demonstrations in Madrid and Barcelona, protesting against the privileges granted to the Opus Dei; the police intervened and arrested a number of demonstrators. Gradually the atmosphere grew more tense. Intellectuals protested against the banning of Lauro Olmo's play *La Camisa*. In Asturias, the Workers' Commissions were demanding more pay. Abroad, the movement *España 59* organized a conference of youth organizations of the Democratic Opposition. An International Conference for the Liberty of the Spanish People was held in Rome.

Pietro Nenni and Jules Moch spoke, and hundreds of demonstrators gathered in the streets, calling for active opposition to Franco's regime and for solidarity with the Spanish people, 'whose only weapon is their anger'. Demonstrators marched past shouting: '*No al fascismo, no al O.A.S., no a la Falange*' (No to fascism, no to the O.A.S., no to the Falange). In Madrid itself, Gil Robles unhesitatingly declared during a public banquet that Spain could enter the Common Market only on condition of having a democratic regime.

Social tension was growing: in the Jerez region 10,000 agricultural workers were on strike. On 22 April the Cortes had voted the agrarian laws, one of which dealt with the inadequate cultivation of the latifundia; but in fact the regime was outpaced by the protests of workers in every sector.

In the first place by the Asturian miners. To begin with only 2,000 from the Nicolasa pit were involved, but before long 60,000 men were on strike. They demanded that their wage increases should come into force immediately. The strike spread quickly, and for the first time since the Civil War affected a whole branch of production in a given region. Metal workers from Beasaín and Bilbao joined the movement. In León, in Catalonia, in Madrid the repercussions of the strike gave rise to long-drawn-out conflicts. On 4 May Franco signed a decree declaring a state of emergency in the provinces of Asturias, Vizcaya and Guipuzcoa. On Monday, 7 May, however, the men had not resumed work; on the contrary, those of the rolling-stock works at Beasaín demonstrated at the factory gates and clashed with the police. Then the men of the Echevarria factory decided to join the strike. Thus, despite the state of emergency resistance increased, and the conflict, originally confined to economic matters, took on an openly political character. On 6 May leaflets calling for solidarity with the miners were distributed in the Basque provinces; this had already been done in Madrid and Barcelona, where from 5 to 11 May not a day passed without students, sometimes over a thousand of them, demonstrating in the streets, making for the centre of the city with shouts of *i Opus no, Asturias si, Opus no, mineros si*! They barricaded themselves into the faculty buildings and went on hunger strike to press for the release of those imprisoned. Their leaflets declared that 1962 was 'a critical year in the struggle against the Francoist dictatorship', and that 'the people and the university are united in the struggle'. On 9 May a public letter signed by twenty-three university teachers, academicians and artists, including Menéndez Pidal, José Bergamín, Gil Robles and Dioniso Ridruejo was addressed to the head of the state and to thousands of Spaniards. It called on the people to use the right of petition to demand 'freedom of information and the normalization of the economic system'.

On 9 May at least 100,000 were on strike, including 30,000 in Asturias. Many miners who had gone back to work on the 7th came out again during the next few days. By the 10th the strike had spread throughout the country, with active centres in León, in the mines of Puertollano, Penarroya in the region of Córdoba, Almadén, and Vizcaya where the situation was growing even more tense. On the 18th it spread to Barcelona, while leaflets were distributed in the suburbs of Madrid. No less than 300,000 workers were involved. In Europe, there were an increasing number of appeals for solidarity, and demonstrations took place. Naturally, the government reacted: several hundreds of arrests were made. Whole regions were occupied by the military, patrolled by troops, searched by Civil Guards. On 10 May Franco, in an interview with the United Press, denounced Communist activity; the Falange spoke of foreign conspiracy, and the journal *Madrid* accused Russia of organizing an economic battle against Europe.

Others, however, took a more balanced view. On Monday, 14 May, representatives of the Church and of the government met for discussions at the palace of Santa-Cruz and it is probable that Cardinal Pla y Daniel pleaded for conciliatory action. Four Catholic organizations (including the H.O.A.C.) declared that 'the workers have a right to fair wages ... that they must be able to set up and freely direct associations in defence of their legitimate interests'. Now the Workers' Commissions, which were illegal, had played an important part in the strikes. In several places they had opened negotiations with the employers over wage scales, and had won their case. The wage freeze which had been maintained since 1957 thus yielded under pressure from the strikers; in January 1963 the government raised the average daily wage from 30 to 60 pesetas. Moreover, the official *sindicatos* were now completely left behind; they had lost the game.

More serious still, during the night of 21 to 22 May four manifestoes from the underground opposition movement reached representatives of the foreign press. They came from the U.F.D., the *Izquierda Demócrata Cristiana*, the F.L.P. and the Communist Party. This marks the emergence into the open of political groups seeking to transform the strike by giving it a precise political objective: the overthrow of the Franco regime. An appeal for unity made by Santiago Carrillo in *L'Humanité* on 22 May concludes: 'What is happening now is a fore-taste of the mass movements which will destroy dictatorship in our country in a very short time. . . . Communists are aware that our party's forecasts are being realized. . . .' In spite of a statement issued by the *Izquierda Demócrata Cristiana* that it would never associate with the Communist Party, optimism prevailed generally throughout the opposition. Everywhere there was talk of a transitional government; and throughout Europe 'free' and Communist-dominated trade unions, as well as intellectuals, displayed their solidarity with the Spanish opposition. Santiago specifically declared (and this shows that the question seemed of some urgency) that 'the Spanish people will never consent to have a monarchy thrust upon them'.

In this atmosphere, which seemed to herald major political conflicts in the immediate future, came the sudden news that in Munich, at the Fourth Congress of the European Movement, on 5 to 6 June, eighty Spaniards from the opposi-tion within Spain and thirty-eight exiles had succeeded, after long labours by two parallel committees (one presided over by Salvador de Madariaga, the other by Gil Robles) in securing the unanimous adoption of a draft resolution, which was then approved by the congress on 7 and 8 June. It set forward the five condi-tions which Spain must fulfil before entering the Common Market: representa-tive institutions, guarantee of individual human rights and those of the various communities, trade union freedom, the right to strike, and the right to organize political parties.

The fact that Rodolfo Llopis had joined forces with Robles and with Ridruejo and voted for the same motion, as had representatives of the Liberal Mon-archists, and Christian-Democrats both left-wing and right-wing, was seen by the Francoists as 'a reconciliation between traitors' (*Arriba*, 10 June). It proved, in any case, the growing opposition to the regime from other quarters than the extreme left. At the same time it confirmed the divided character of the opposi-tion as a whole. The Communists had not been invited to Munich, and the meeting marked a setback for their policy of unification. They were isolated. Santiago Carrillo actually asserted in *Mundo Obrero* that Munich proved the success of his party's policy, of national reconciliation, but added immediately:

'A coalition of Socialists with the right lacks sufficient weight. It implies a highly dangerous venture. In a situation of the sort now facing Spain, any intelligent conservative must recognize that the guarantee of non-violent transition depends primarily on agreement with the Communist Party.'

Was this a kind of revolutionary blackmail? Would the Communist Party guarantee peaceful transition in exchange for political agreement. If this was refused, would it provoke a mass rising? A threat has no significance unless it is founded on reality. Now apart from certain small groups of the F.L.P. who considered it treachery to 'forgo the use of liberating violence as a weapon against oppressive violence', the P.O.U.M., the Anarchists and the D.R.I.L., all of which denounced the Munich agreement and were prepared to envisage direct revolutionary action, no plans for such a rising seem to have been envisaged by the Spanish Communist Party in 1962.

Moreover, by the end of May, following the wage increase and the rise in the price of coal, the Asturian miners went back into the pits, and the tide of industrial unrest seemed to be receding; while, on the contrary, political groups became active within Spain and in Munich. Three bomb explosions in Madrid on 5, 8 and 13 June gave the Seguridad the excuse for a series of arrests. Leaders of the F.L.P. and Communist militants were thrust into the Carabanchel jail. In spite of denials of responsibility by the F.L.P., the press and the police identified terrorism, political opposition, Christian progressivism (that twentieth-century heresy) and communism. Certain leaders, such as I. Fernández de Castra of the F.L.P., took refuge in foreign embassies, others were taken. In the countryside, opponents of the regime were pursued with equal severity and efficiency.

The authorities took advantage of the lull in the social movement to intensify repression and to launch a propaganda offensive through a series of parades, speeches and articles. Addressing a gathering of 15,000 *Alfereces Provisionales* at Garabitas, the Caudillo, amidst great applause, denounced 'Marxist infiltration into the organizations of the Church'; while Ullastres, in Barcelona, also inveighed against Catholics in the opposition: 'The Supreme Pontiff and the Church never intended the *Mater et Magistra* to be an instrument of class warfare.'

Meanwhile the personalities who had taken part in the Munich conference, particularly those of the Monarchist *Unión Española*, were put under house arrest immediately on their return; most of them were sent to the island of Fuertaventura in the Canaries. As for the Count of Barcelona, he hastened to declare that the Monarchists at Munich had spoken for nobody but themselves; his own attitude being that 'Spain's entry into the Common Market is a national duty which all Spaniards must defend unreservedly'. Gil Robles had no alternative but to resign from the Pretender's Privy Council on 17 June. Once more Franco had succeeded in splitting the Monarchists. It is true that the Spanish press, while the strikes were at their height, reported enthusiastically on the wedding of Juan Carlos with Sophia of Greece. On 3 June the young couple were received by Pope John XXIII; on the 6th the Air Minister welcomed them at Getafe airport, and on the 7th they were entertained by the Caudillo. Monarchist hopes rose again. During the whole of June, after the shock of the Munich meeting, while strikes were in abeyance, the regime pursued its advantages. Public meetings were organized in every town: attended by 10,000 at Guadalajara, and by several thousand at Logroño, Cadiz, Santander and Burgos. Everywhere the civil governors were loud in condemnation of 'the Munich conspirators', the 'bad Spaniards', the 'traitors', the 'pact of the defeated'

Pueblo wrote on 11 June: 'This gathering of the political dead is challenged by the daily plebiscite of all living Spaniards.'

The Caudillo appeared in person to crown his campaign. On 16 June, at 7 p.m., he arrived in Valencia, accompanied by Señora Carmen Polo de Franco. An excited crowd, officially estimated at 300,000, had gathered on the Plaza del Caudillo. They had come in truck-loads from all over the province. Franco drove through the outskirts in his old black Rolls-Royce, with an escort of motor-cyclists; women cheered: 'Franco, Franco!' but many onlookers, particularly among the younger men, stood silent with folded arms. Franco was beaming; in his white uniform, he stood up to greet the crowd. His wife sat smiling by his side. 'I am the captain of the ship," he said, 'and it's only natural that I should render you an account of the difficulties and accidents of the crossing. To navigate through this tormented world means waging a constant battle against the elements.' His speech was frequently interrupted by ovations. 'The sun is shining over Spain,' he concluded. '*¡Arriba España!*' There followed a visit to the Basilica of Our Lady into which the head of the state made a solemn entry under a canopy. After this he addressed the officers of the Third Military Region; in front of the rostrum stood Falangist veterans, wearing their decorations on their uniform shirts and flanked by their sons and their army Chaplains. They bore a banner inscribed '*La División Azul por la Justicia Social con Franco*'. Around the Caudillo on the rostrum were a crowd of dignitaries in white uniforms. Shouts of 'Franco, Franco, Franco' answered his cry of '*Arriba España*'; while above the crowd, advertisements for foodstuffs on the housefronts and television cameras on scaffolding represented the new face of Spain. The Caudillo quietened the applause with a wave of his hand: 'I wish the strangers who malign us could behold this instructive sight. I would tell them: This is where my power lies, in close union with my people.' And as the ovations died down a voice called out 'Hang the men of Munich'.

Now the Caudillo could return, in peace of mind, to his Pardo Palace.

CHAPTER III

LIBERALIZACIÓN.
DESARROLLO. GARROTE VIL
JULY 1962–1963

Every year in July General Franco took refuge from the heat of Madrid in his residence at Pazo de Meiras, at Coruña. The government moved to San Sebastian. During the height of summer Spain was handed over to tourists, while the Caudillo enjoyed deep-sea fishing off the coast. Only exceptionally did he grant an interview or entertain a diplomat. At the beginning of that summer everyone in Madrid was waiting anxiously to see whether Franco would reshuffle his Cabinet before or after his holidays. There could be no doubt that he intended to do so; after each crisis, the bucket-wheel began to turn again, bringing back forgotten figures while others disappeared, sometimes for good. Nobody was consulted; Franco alone decided. So one merely had to wait. By 10 July Franco had made his choice; on the 11th the *Boletín Official del Estado* issued the list of the new ministers.

The New Government Team and Its Significance

'By virtue of my powers, I appoint as Vice-President of the Government Captain-General of the Army Don Agustín Muñoz Grandes. . . .' The former head of the Division Azul, the highest-ranking officer in the Spanish army, who had been awarded the highest distinctions – the Iron Cross, the Silver Palm of the Falange, the Legion of Merit presented by President Eisenhower – seemed to be the heir apparent, since the office of Vice-President was thus created for the first time. As usual, Franco had made a judicious choice: Muñoz Grandes, a former pupil of the Military Academy of Toledo, who had fought in Morocco and on the Eastern front, enjoyed the confidence of the army and of the Falange. General Pablo Martín Alonso, former head of the *Guardia Civil*, became Minister of War; the navy was entrusted to Vice-Admiral Pedro Nieto Antúñez. He was a native of Ferrol, like the Caudillo; he had even commanded the Caudillo's yacht *Azor*: he was a favourite. Another general took over the air force: faithful General Camillo Alonso Vega was Minister for the Interior, and faithful Rear-Admiral Luis Carrero Blanco, discreet and powerful as ever, remained Minister-Secretary to the President. The army held seven posts, and was thus more than ever the backbone of the regime. Order would be maintained. At the same time

Ullastres retained the Ministry of Trade, while Industry was taken over by a brilliant 39-year-old engineer, López Bravo de Castro, and above all – an important innovation – the Ministry of Information and Tourism was entrusted to Manuel Fraga Iribarne. He was 40 years old but looked younger, with hooded eyes and a somewhat ironic smile: a professor at Madrid University, director of the Institute of Political Studies, delegate to UNESCO, deputy to the Cortes and author of several books. His predecessor Arias Salgado, whom he embraced fraternally beneath the portrait of Franco when the transfer of power took place, had held the post since 1951: a loyal Francoist but also a symbol of brutal intransigence. Iribarne's appointment meant the triumph of a new style, a blend of efficiency and shrewdness. The era of *liberalización* had begun. The technocrats of the Opus Dei were more firmly in the saddle than ever; Castiella was still Foreign Minister, and the military element, now reinforced, was ready to cope with things. The significance of the reshuffle was plain: Franco had chosen to continue the policy of *desarrollo* (development), to combine liberalization with repression.

On 14 July Manuel Fraga Iribarne made a statement to the press about the new government's intentions: 'One of the most important tasks to which the government must devote itself,' he said, 'is to get going the plan for the economic development of the nation ... as our economy develops the government will pay due attention to social progress and the general welfare.' Then came phrases that had a new ring: the government would encourage the trade union movement to perfect its organization, and at the same time it would pay due attention to the state of public opinion 'and to its legitimate expression by means of dialogue and information'. This, then, was liberalization: *within the framework of the regime*, which could not be contested, certain divergences would be tolerated, certain professional claims allowed. As Fraga Iribarne clearly stated: 'The government is convinced that its principles ... constitute a sure and definitive way forward, specifically Spanish and fundamentally Christian. ... The government will never accept anything that can imply retrogression.'

Thus the regime would permit opposition, provided it was never challenged or attacked. Anyone who sought to go further would soon be made to see reason, as in the past, by General Camillo Alonso Vega, Minister of the Gobernación, General Martín Alonso and his army, the *Guardia Civil* and the military tribunals. Manuel Fraga Iribarne and Muñoz Grandes did not represent contradictory sides of a regime hesitating between two paths, the old and the new, but complementary sides of an authority which, with consummate shrewdness and a sense of social and political realities, was prepared to make limited and controlled concessions, useful adaptations which it could annul and canalize at will.

The new style made itself felt by the end of July. While, by a symbolic coincidence, Arias Salgado met with a violent death, Fraga Iribarne was making speeches and appointments. His team consisted mainly of youngish men, in their early forties: able, with professional press experience as well as academic qualifications. They often came from Catholic journals or from the university, and they represented a new Francoist generation, technically superior to the old, more flexible but just as determined to maintain the regime, which promised them successful careers. They were the counterpart, in the field of information – of relations between political decisions and public opinion – of the already established young economists of the Opus Dei. Francoism proved its strength by associating these efficient personalities of a younger generation with a power still vested in the unchanging figure of the Caudillo and his team of old soldiers. These new men, who often concealed their personal ambitions behind a mask of disinterested technical efficiency, were the surest guarantee that the regime could find to ensure its continuity.

An examination of the appointments made to executive posts or under-secretaryships in various ministries (National Education, Labour, etc.), shows the prevalence of this new elite; which reflects the scale on which the regime was renewing its cadres. The myth of an ageing Franco, which misled many of his opponents, must therefore be corrected. Young men involved in the process of government would never willingly give up their power, since they felt themselves to be qualified heirs-apparent. Fraga Iribarne was one of the most active. He worked by means of personal contacts. On 15 November he opened an international Press Club in the Calle del Pinar: 'The Spanish authorities,' he stated, 'desire the fullest and most authentic information on affairs in Spain. . . . We keep our doors open.' When fresh strikes broke out in Asturias, affecting almost 15,000 miners, the papers reported these for the first time. True, news of the strike was relegated to inside pages, but in a country which had lacked all information the change was important, and readers appreciated it: the circulation of such a paper as *La Voz de Asturias* rose from 8,000 to 30,000 a day.[1]

Renewed Social Unrest; Opposition Activity; Repression

For the strikes had begun again. In the working-class bastion of Asturias, and also in Barcelona, disturbances broke out in August 1962. The workers sought to obtain collective contracts which would ensure not only an increase of wages but also control over such issues as bonuses, hours of work and so forth. They met with resistance from employers and ministries, and could scarcely count on support from the official unions. Nevertheless, owing to the strength of their pressure, and the possibilities of genuine concessions due to economic growth, the number of collective contracts signed rose from 412 in 1961 to 1,707 in 1962. This was an obvious success, particularly since the government was frequently forced to admit the *de facto* existence of the Workers' Commissions and to recognize that the unions should be represented by genuine workers elected by their fellows rather than by Falangist bureaucrats.

It was clear, however, that the strikes that took place during the autumn of 1962 were not on the same scale as those of the previous spring. The government was on a war footing: its strategy was now completely effective – limited concessions, but widespread repression. Moreover, the general atmosphere had changed. The Cuban crisis, the threat of world war affected Spain, both because of her Hispanic connections and because her soil provided American bases.

[1] Guy Hermet, La presse espagnole depuis la suppression de la censure, in *Revue française de Sciences politiques* (Paris, Feb. 1968).

Julián Grimau, a member of the Central Committee of the Spanish Communist Party, living in secrecy in Madrid, wrote thus to his party's leaders: 'What I have witnessed in streets and buses, and above all through direct contact with party committees, confirms what I told you previously about the anxiety and distress of the people of Madrid, in face of the gravity of the situation and its direct connection with Spain.' It was hardly a propitious moment for social protest. Furthermore, the end of 1962 marked the start of the public controversy between the U.S.S.R. and China, and this, through the rifts it caused, was inevitably damaging to the opposition; it caused great uneasiness among militant Communists, and thus weakened the fighting spirit of the whole working class.

Moreover, most Spaniards enjoyed a real rise in income during 1962 and 1963, as a result of the strikes, and consumer spending increased. All these factors contributed to limiting strike action. Differences of opinion reappeared: the *Alianza Sindical* (C.N.T., U.G.T. and S.T.V.) broke up, and an *Alianza Sindical Obrera de España* (A.S.O.) was formed, which included many Christian militants. From its foundation the A.S.O. specified: 'We assert clearly and honestly that we mistrust the Communists; our task is a different one, we aim at a social and economic democracy in the construction of which the trade unions must play a fundamental part without taking orders from anyone.'

Thus the opposition remained divided, and indeed split up even further. In September 1962, although the movement of resistance and protest was clearly on the ebb, the Communist Party proposed a *Huelga General Política*. Others hoped that by intensifying terrorist action they would show the way to revolution. A *Consejo Ibérico de Liberación* initiated operations known as *Justicia* and *Advertencia* (end of 1962 to the beginning of 1963); leaflets distributed in Madrid warned tourists against the dangers they ran in making use of Spanish or Portuguese conveyances or even in visiting Spain at all. In fact, in Geneva, Frankfurt, London and Madrid (June 1963) the police discovered explosive devices, often of a rudimentary character, among passengers' luggage in aircraft of the Iberia line. Naturally these actions were quite ineffective, as also was the Communist proposal.

On the other hand, the repression was formidably efficient. On 16 June, nine Communists were arrested in Vizcaya; they included Ramón Ormazábal, Gregorio Rodríguez and Agustín Ibarrola. Ormazábal proudly admitted being a member of the Central Committee of the Party. Ibarrola declared, during his court martial: 'For twenty-four days I have been subjected to incredible physical and moral torture in the cells of the Social Brigade of Bilbao.' In spite of international protest, the nine accused men received prison sentences ranging from four to twenty years. Elsewhere, militants of the F.L.P. were hunted and beaten up, as were also workers who, without belonging to any political organization, had taken an active or a leading part in the spring and autumn strikes. After being arrested and detained for a few days or a few weeks and, so they declared, beaten up, they were sometimes released without trial or put under house arrest, but invariably subjected to strict police surveillance. A young miner, César Rodríguez, for instance, was set free on condition of reporting at the police

303

station every afternoon at four o'clock, which in fact condemned him to unemployment.

The Ministries of the Interior, Information and Labour deliberately sought to identify strike movements, political opposition and anarchist activity as being three aspects of a single plot against Spain. 'Striking is a betrayal of Spain', declared the Minister of Labour, Romeo Gorria. In September 1962 the Ministry of the Interior announced the discovery of a terrorist organization and the arrest of its members. Frenchmen and Italians were involved as well as Spaniards, but in Barcelona the men arrested were all three Spaniards: Jorge Conill Vals, Marcelino Jiménez Cubas and Antonio Mur Peirón, militant members of a 'Libertarian Youth Movement'. At the court martial in Barcelona the public prosecutor demanded the death sentence. Their cause aroused wide sympathy in Europe. Cardinal Montini[2] sent the Caudillo a telegram pleading, in the name of the Catholic students of Milan, 'that human lives should be spared . . . so as to prove that in a Catholic nation public order can be defended otherwise than in countries without Christian faith and customs.'

It was in Milan, in fact, that some Italian students kidnapped the honorary Vice-Consul of Spain, announcing that he would not be released until Conill had been reprieved. Official Spain reacted violently. Castiella, the Foreign Minister, in a telegram to Mgr Montini, protested: 'It is deplorable that a scandal-mongering campaign should have misled your Most Reverend Eminence'. A.B.C. accused Montini of 'typical southern vehemence'; in the streets of Madrid groups of Falangists noisily displayed their hostility to the prelate. However, possibly as a result of these different actions, the authorities in Barcelona hesitated, and the court martial's sentence was not ratified by the Captain-General of Catalonia. Finally, on 9 October, the Ministry of Information announced that the Supreme Council of Military Justice had condemned Jorge Conill Vals to thirty years solitary confinement. He had escaped with his life.

Repression did not slacken its grip on the country. The workers of the Siemens factory at Cornella de Llobregat, near Barcelona, went on strike for a wage increase. It was clear by now that the government had the situation well in hand, and the employers sacked the forty leaders; when the strikers tried to extend their movement to the administrative staff, the police intervened vigorously. Workers were hunted down the streets of their suburb by the *Policía Armada*, and a priest who opened the door of his church to the fugitives was struck. Eventually, after throwing some stones at the police, the men went back to work. *Radio España Independiente*, broadcasting from Prague, which had played an important part in the strike movement that spring, referred to the immense solidarity of the working class and quoted some workers as asserting the need for a general strike. In fact circumstances were now all against any extension of social conflict. At the end of September torrential rain brought about serious flooding in the Barcelona region: 414 persons lost their lives, 200 were injured and almost 600 missing. The country was profoundly shaken. This natural disaster, with its toll of victims, appalled Spain and drove political and social problems into the back-

[2] He became Pope Paul VI in June 1963.

ground. The government stressed the scale of its help to the victims: Franco, Muñoz Grandes, Don Juan Carlos and his wife, and various ministers visited the stricken areas. The press spoke with one voice, and national mourning was officially decreed. The event served to show the unity prevailing among Spaniards, and made it easy to distinguish those who, in these difficult times, continued to disturb the peace by their actions. 'Catalans, Spaniards, all gathered together,' the Caudillo proclaimed in his speeches, '. . . we feel your grief in our own flesh. . . .' The crowd applauded the official cortège on its way to Barcelona Cathedral. At Tarrasa, the Caudillo concluded his report on the government's assistance on a political note: 'This is not the will of one man, it is the spirit of our Movement. . . . It is the efficiency of the National Movement, the Movement which unites us all . . . in a common historic destiny, which finds solutions for all social problems, which does not let itself be cast down by misfortune. . . .'

The regime was in a strong position: outside circumstances, the economic situation and the rifts within the opposition, everything was in its favour at the end of 1962. The *Desarrollo* plan had been actively prepared, the planning Commission organized. López Bravo was altering the structure of the Ministry of Industry so as to increase its efficiency by specializing the different departments. Banking reform, an essential factor in the process of industrialization and development, was being put into practice: the Cabinet, on 9 November 1962, created and organized special bank loans for construction, and authorized the creation of industrial and business banks in order to 'found industrial and agricultural firms and to finance them with . . . loans for up to three years.' A crucial decision, showing the part played by the State in setting up the legal and financial structures which prepared Spain for capitalistic development.

Thus the regime continued on its chosen path: *desarrollo, liberalización* (development, liberalization), greater flexibility of the news services – Fraga Iribarne excelled at emphasizing the help given to the victims of the Barcelona floods and denouncing the sinister machinations of international subversion. As the police, during the course of years, had perfected its methods, the regime scored further successes in the field of repression.

Julián Grimau

On 7 November 1961, at 4 p.m., Julián Grimau García, an active member of the Central Committee of the Communist Party, stood talking to another militant, Lara. He noticed the latter's nervousness with some surprise, but paid little heed to it; they soon parted, and Grimau took a bus for caution's sake, but noticing that he was being watched he was about to alight when several policemen surrounded him, seized him, stopped the bus and dragged Grimau into a small engineering workshop near by. He was presently taken in a big car to the Seguridad headquarters, through the Puerta de la Calle del Correo. He was not to escape alive from the hands of the police. They gave him a sheet of paper on which to make a statement. He simply wrote: 'I declare that I am a member of the Central Committee of the Spanish Communist Party, I am in Madrid to carry out my duties as a Communist.' It was a big catch for the police. Lara, who had been detained a few days earlier, had weakened and enabled them to arrest Grimau. On 9 November the Madrid papers announced that Grimau had thrown himself out of a window in the Seguridad and had been picked up seriously injured. Most of the world press was convinced that he had been tortured. Grimau was later to declare that he had been knocked down in the presence of a police doctor and kicked in the face. Then he lost consciousness, and only came to in hospital. The theory that the police had sought to conceal evidence of torture by throwing Grimau out of a window spread rapidly. Fraga Iribarne counterattacked: in a press conference on 6 December he declared that 'every time, after terrorist attempts, huge press campaigns are launched, particularly in Russia'. He indicated what were to be the prosecution's tactics against Grimau: 'We shall set forth the record of crimes and atrocities personally committed by him' during the Civil War.

World opinion was quickly mobilized. Evidence was produced, inquiries held, one in Spain itself by a team of French doctors, which showed the impossibility of an attempted suicide by Grimau; the many cases of ill treatment already noted before and after the arrest of Grimau made torture more than probable. The official publication of the Ministry of Information, *Julián Grimau or the Art of Manufacturing a Victim*, did not suffice to reverse the general opinion. On the contrary: Grimau, with his gentle face and that calm resoluteness which was the more striking because of his frail physique, Grimau with his two little girls and his wife, a simple woman whom her grief ennobled, with his whole past history of devotion to his cause, naturally became a symbol and a martyr. A trial of strength was on, now, between the Madrid government and those who, the world over, sought by their protests and pleas to save Grimau's life.

The trial opened at 8.20 a.m. on 18 April before the military court of Madrid. The crowded audience included foreign lawyers and plain-clothes police. Defending counsel was Captain Alejandro Rebello, a militant member of the Catholic Action group. The court was presided over by Colonel Valentino Bulnes, the military prosecutor was Major Enrique Amado. Without any verification by the defence, the prosecution had drawn up an overwhelming dossier against Grimau, stating that during the Civil War he had run a *Cheka* in the Calle Baranguer in Barcelona, where many people had been tortured and then executed. Grimau was accused of the 'continuous offence of military rebellion', and the prosecutor demanded the death sentence. Grimau denied all these accusations, admitting only that he was a Communist: 'I shall face death like a Communist, and as long as I live I shall behave like a Communist.' The defence lawyer objected to the concept of 'continuous offence'. He asked for acquittal for everything that concerned the period 1936–9 and suggested a three-year prison sentence for the current period. The court martial retired and deliberated in private. According to certain press agencies the sentence was discussed at the Cabinet meeting held on 19 April, at which Franco presided. It fell implacably: death.

Demonstrations followed throughout the world. Hundreds of telegrams reached Madrid. Khrushchev himself wrote to Franco: 'Moved by feelings of humanity, I appeal to you convinced that you will listen to the request to commute the sentence and spare the life of Julián Grimau.' The Caudillo refused, explaining in his reply that the 'horrible crimes committed' by Grimau made commutation impossible. Not even Pope John XXIII – who is said to have intervened – could alter the decision. Over and above the individual case of Grimau, the regime had to prove that it could still take harsh action against its enemies in the face of the whole world, if need be, and that it felt strong enough to do so. Grimau had to die, to remind the Spanish people, at a time when they had so often gone on strike and demonstrated, that they were liable to sudden violent reprisals and that the outside world could do nothing about it; that they were still in the power of those who had won the Civil War, and that those victors were the final judges of the rights and restrictions of Spaniards. Grimau had to die so that every Spaniard should know fear, fear of the death that might strike him suddenly, as in time of civil war, fear of a punishment from which nothing could save him except obedience to the regime and the magnanimity of his rulers.

In Madrid, on 19 April, a state of tension prevailed. The Cabinet meeting lasted over ten hours. The Ministers were divided: Generals Alonso Vega and Pablo Martín Alonso were said to have been in favour of immediate execution, while Muñoz Grandes had objections and Franco said nothing. The *Policía Armada* were reinforced at strategic points. Ruiz Jiménez, former Minister of National Education, called on Muñoz Grandes, Fraga Iribarne and Castiella, but got no precise answer. Then on 20 April, at 5.30 a.m., Grimau's lawyer announced that the sentence had been carried out. Grimau had died, officially, for things done at the time of the Civil War. As Antón Salamanca wrote, concentrating his powerless anger in sarcastic words:

> '*Que haya un cadáver mas, ¿ qué importa al mundo?*
> *Pero el mundo se agita y se remueve.*
> *En el mil novecientos treinta y nueve*
> *Se fusilaba más sin tanto in mundo*
> *Protestar de masones, liberales,*
> *Comunistas, social democristianos,*
> *Escritores borrachos, Italianos,*
> *Gente de mal vivir y radicales.*
> *Pero además, c qué pasa? ¿ Que presentas*
> *Mundo como protesta, inoportuno?*
> *¿ Te parece tan grave, pues, la cosa?*
> *¿ Tanta importancia tiene a fin de cuentas*
> *Que sean un millón o un millón y uno*
> *Los muertos de una guerra tan gloriosa?*'[3]

[3] What does one more corpse in the world matter?
And yet the world is astir, is moving.
In the year nineteen thirty-nine
More shooting went on without so many vile
Protests from freemasons and liberals,
Communists, Social-demo-Christians,
Drunken writers and Italians,
Malefactors and radicals.

Throughout the world, protests and indignant stupefaction were widespread after Grimau's execution. In most capital cities, impressive demonstrations were organized. From Harold Wilson to Giorgio la Pira, from Guy Mollet to Willy Brandt, those who protested were very different from the usual fellow-travellers of Communist parties. Aldo Moro, Secretary-General of the Italian Christian Democrats, expressed in a brief phrase what many people were feeling: 'This execution does not look like justice but like political vindictiveness.' In fact, as we have seen, it was something more than that: a clear warning to all those who, in Spain and elsewhere, forgot that Francoism still spelt strength. Grimau's death, recalling the Civil War, was a political action by present-day Spain. When Angela Grimau, her eyes brimming with tears, mastered her grief enough to say: '*que la sangre de Julián sea la última*' (may Julián's blood be the last shed), her wish was vain.

'*Garrote Vil*' for the Anarchists

Grimau's execution in the spring of 1963, a year after the great wave of strikes, also represented a form of self-defence against any renewed flare-up of social unrest. For this was an ever-present threat: there was fresh autonomist agitation in the Canaries, there were more strikes by the agricultural labourers of Andalusia and the factory workers of Barcelona. The mass of the working-class eluded control by the regime; only a minimum of votes were polled at the trade union elections held in April 1963; and there were fresh terrorist attempts.

On 29 July, at 5.45 p.m., a bomb suddenly exploded in the crowded passport office of the Seguridad headquarters. A desk was blown to fragments: the plastic bomb had been placed beneath it. Thirty-three people were injured. The same day, about midnight, there was another explosion in the trade union headquarters. The press waxed indignant: 'The Spanish people are victims of a new crime,' proclaimed *Arriba's* headlines. On Wednesday, 31 July (according to *A.B.C.*, 3 and 4 August) the police had a stroke of luck; they arrested two men who had been leaning over the balustrade overlooking the Campo del Moro, speaking to some young tourists. These two men, Francisco Grandado Cata and Joaquín Delgado Martínez (aged 28 and 30 respectively), were presumably the perpetrators of these outrages. They were unquestionably anarchists; it is more than doubtful whether they were guilty of the acts attributed to them. The trial was carried out at top speed on 13 August and ended with the death sentence; the Madrid court martial had never hesitated. Yet evidence from other sources indicated that these acts of violence had been committed by another rebel, having no connection with the two prisoners. These men, on the other hand, may have been reconnoitring with a view to a possible attempt on the Caudillo's life.

But what's happening? Why are you protesting,
Importunate world!
Does it matter so much in the long run
Whether a million people or a million and one
Have died in such a glorious war?

They had been tracked down from the frontier by the police and arrested, since somebody had to be found guilty of the explosion in the passport office. The press unanimously congratulated the police for 'the splendid service it had just rendered the population' (*Ya*, 31 July). World opinion was stirred once again. True, these were only a couple of anarchists, and they did not enjoy the international support afforded the cause of Julián Grimau. Meanwhile there was widespread excitement about the fate of two Spanish mountaineers who were attempting to climb the Eiger. None the less, strong feelings were aroused. Grimau was dead; the two anarchists were to die next. At dawn on Saturday, 17 August, in the Carabanchel prison, they were put to death by *garrote*, slow strangulation.

A few weeks later, on 18 October, three French students (Pecuina, Ferry and Batouz) were condemned to two, thirty and twenty years' imprisonment for having joined a commando group formed by the *Federación Ibérica de Juventudes Libertarias* (Iberian Federation of Youth for Freedom) and the United Socialist Party with a view to disturbing public order. This trial, too, was carried out before a special court martial. On 8 August, another police triumph: at dawn, close to the frontier zone of Tortello, they killed Ramón Vila Capdevila, known as Caraquemada, a 56-year-old anarchist who had belonged to Sabater's band and who had gone on organizing sabotage, particularly against high-tension pylons. Once again anarchist activity proved powerless against a regime which knew how to defend itself, and the attempts died out, without echo, in the general silence of the land. The further acts of terrorism that took place in September in various parts of Spain had no other effect than to enable the press to condemn the 'professional criminals' who were still at work, and the police to arrest young men who may or may not have been guilty. The *Unión Democrática Popular Española*, which claimed responsibility for these actions, did not succeed in really taking root in the country. The regime still remained in control of the situation.

The Regime's Successes: International Achievements and the Desarrollo

On the international plane, these executions by shooting or garrotting provoked a flare-up of anti-Francoist passion, but this soon died down except in circles which had been hostile to the regime ever since its victory. The crowds of tourists (several millions, remember!) returned to Spain in the spring, and while Grimau died, his body shattered by the bullets of the firing squad, while Granado and Delgado were inexorably choking in the iron collar, hundreds of thousands of European families were peacefully enjoying life on Spanish beaches or photographing the Holy Week ceremonies at Seville.

Governments, too, overlooking the internal vicissitudes of the Spanish situation, continued to improve relations with a regime which was inviting investment. Spanish planning experts took inspiration from French models and consulted their opposite numbers in Paris. The Minister of the Interior and the Chief of Staff of the French government visited Madrid (January–February 1963). Valéry Giscard d'Estaing, Minister of Finance, arrived in the Spanish capital on 19 April; the following day, Grimau was put to death. Of course, M. Giscard d'Estaing did not know this; the coincidence is none the less symbolic. It implies that realism and enduring strength are major components in political choice. The Caudillo never ignored this, and he was never short of credits.

While France considered granting a loan to Spain, the German Federal Republic had already done so, and expected to increase its exchanges; the visit of the German Minister of Agriculture to Madrid was followed by a visit from the Spanish Minister of Industry to Bonn.

Thus, systematically, the Madrid government pursued its policy of integration with Europe. In July 1963, moreover, Spain became a member of the G.A.T.T. (General Agreement on Tariffs and Trade). Its economic policy was clearly unaffected by the harshness of its repressive measures. The thirty commissions which were preparing the Development Plan had been at work for seventeen months, and on 16 November 1963 López Rodo was able to present for publication the first volume, 470 pages long, defining the aims of the plan and indicating the reasons for its priorities. The object was not only to increase the national revenue by 6 per cent annually, but equally, and fundamentally, to secure a better distribution of that revenue. López Rodo specified: 'The Plan has an indicative character as regards the private sector, which implies respect for free initiative, and an obligatory character as regards the public sector. It should affect employers chiefly by reducing uncertainty.' Stress was now laid, in all government speeches, on the necessary collaboration of all Spaniards in order to achieve the aims of the plan, while the Caudillo asserted his conviction that Spaniards would devote 'all their efforts and all their spirit of self-sacrifice' to that end. The mystique and the words were the same that the Caudillo had been proffering ever since 1936, and it was clear that whatever new directions were being taken the Generalissimo intended – and so, increasingly, did his supporters and advisers – to preserve the essential elements of power.

For the opposition, the continuity of this regime, which revolved on an immutable axis while showing different facets, and shed some of its appearances in order to maintain the essence of its strength, was in itself a setback. The year 1963 was thus for the opposition the trough after the wave of 1962: a period of dark depression, when its failure, its impotence, its impossible hopes were assessed, when past or lost illusions were measured by the yardstick of harsh reality, and when it listed fellow-fighters arrested or exiled. It was a year of fresh blows successively inflicted from outside. Thus on 25 January, on the occasion of the opening of the Pauline Year, the Papal Nuncio in Spain, Mgr Antonio Riberi, declared:

'Despite the iniquitous machinations and insidious campaigns conducted against this Catholic nation by those who pride themselves on denying God, the head of the state by his words, his wise decisions and his ever-edifying personal example still keeps her faithful to the doctrine bequeathed us by the Apostles St James and St Paul.'

On the same day came the announcement by the Madrid government of its official request for the revision of the Spanish–American defence agreements of 1953, and the understanding gradually reached with Kennedy's America, to which, once again, many of the opposition had pinned their hopes.

On 26 September 1963, the Madrid–Washington agreements were officially renewed for five years. At dawn on Friday the 27th Fraga Iribarne held a press conference in the Ministry, attended by over a hundred journalists, at which he commented with satisfaction on the new conditions, which were highly favourable to Spain: a system of mutual consultation was established, and above all the credits of the Export-Import Bank to the Spanish armed forces were raised to over $100 million. Aid for economic development was also increased. Franco awarded the Grand Cross of Carlos III to the Spanish Ambassador in Washington, Antonio Garrigues; the 1963 agreements, like those of 1953, marked a fresh success for his policy and consequently a fresh proof of the weakness of the opposition. The world situation, and the geopolitical position of Spain, were still a guarantee of inner security for the regime. When Dean Rusk, American Secretary of State, had exchanged a cordial handshake with Castiella at the headquarters of the American delegation to the United Nations in New York, he turned to General Curtis Lemay, chief of staff of the United States air force, with the revealing words: 'Your colleagues have helped to no small degree to make this agreement a reality.' The fact is that Franco's Spain with its air bases, its radar posts and its atomic stock-piles had become a decisive factor in the American strategic network. Naturally General Franco enjoyed the support of the military men in the Pentagon, and this contributed considerably to his strength.

When so many factors, both internal and external, made for the permanence of the regime, many of the opposition's efforts, viewed with hindsight, assume an aspect of hopeless impotence of which those who made them were to some extent aware. Sometimes, indeed, the circumstances of the struggle were merely the clever achievement of a pressure group favourable to the regime but anxious to secure certain advantages from it. Thus at the time of the Spanish–American agreement the miners of Asturias had been involved for weeks in a violent strike from which there seemed to be no way out.

The Strike in the Workers' Stronghold of Asturias (July–September 1963)

This fresh strike in the mining region of the Asturias had in fact broken out on Friday, 19 July. The men of the Minas Llanos pits had stopped work in protest against the behaviour of an engineer. Soon the strike spread, and by the beginning of August it affected some 10,000 workers. The mine-owners and the Civil Governor of Oviedo replied with lock-outs, and by their refusal to negotiate prevented any possibility of agreement. The fact was that while the miners' struggle was an essential part of their arduous day-to-day existence, of the long tradition which had made them, since the nineteenth century, the spearhead of the Spanish workers' movement, it was also connected with the particular circumstances of the coal-mining industry, which sought to obtain large state subsidies in view of its necessary technical renovation. By hardening their attitude, the mine-owners of Asturias forced the strikers into a long-drawn-out action which assumed a political character, and which necessitated state intervention; this was inevitably to the advantage of the employers, both from a financial and from a social point of view. In addition to this background, there were rivalries between those who, like Solis Ruiz and the Falangist trade unionists, wanted to find a solution to the conflict, and those who, like the Civil Governor and the Minister of the Interior, supported by the more conservative Asturian employers, sought to break the movement by force. In these circumstances the strike went on for over fifty days. Official data record that the workers of Asturias and León lost 48 million pesetas; and this, at a time when poverty was a constant factor in the lives of miners under normal conditions, meant destitution, hunger, almost unbearable privations.

Implacable repression followed. The Civil Guards invaded the streets where the miners lived, shooting and striking in the grey light of dawn; the uneven confrontation recalled, in 1963, the scenes that took place in Western industrial countries during the last third of the nineteenth century.

Indeed, such extreme violence was used that on 30 September 102 intellectuals sent a letter to the Minister of Information, Manuel Fraga Iribarne, asking for an explanation of certain specific cases of torture inflicted on miners by the Civil Guards. The signatories were outstanding men: the Catholic writer José Bergamín, the former university rector Pedro Laín Entralgo, the poet Vicente Alexandre, academics such as José Luis Aranguren, playwrights (Alfonso Sastre), critics (José María Moreno Galván and others). The entire younger generation of Spanish intellectuals were represented by the side of their elders – Bergamín and Entralgo – in a solid block determined to face repression openly; it was not the first time, in fact, that they had expressed their opinions publicly. The facts they advanced were sensational: at Sama de Langreo, for instance, on 3 September, the Civil Guards had castrated a miner and shorn his wife's head. Many other miners' wives had been treated in the same way; one miner had been tortured till he went out of his mind.

'We respectfully beg Your Excellency to demand from the competent authorities an inquiry into the activities of the Civil Guard Captain concerned ... which request we address to Your Excellency solely in our capacity as intellectuals concerned with the lives and sufferings of our people.'

Iribarne's reaction was typical of the flexible and efficient methods of the government's information policy during the period of *liberalización*. On 12 October, together with the Minister's reply the letter was published in the weekly *El Español*, the organ of the Ministry of Information, whose circulation was strictly limited. The era of impenetrable secrecy was thus definitely past. Fraga Iribarne addressed his reply personally to one of his correspondents, José Bergamín, the one who was most open to counterattack. It deserves study. According to Iribarne, these intellectuals were being 'used as mere pawns on the chequerboard of a political game, of whose tactics they were ignorant. ...' He pointed out that the facts reported had already been exploited by '*Pravda Ukraini* ... *l'Humanité*. ... Radio Belgrade, and the Free Spain broadcasting station in Prague.' Then came the decisive argument: Fraga Iribarne quoted Bergamín's preface to a book written in 1938 in which, he said; 'you actually gave your approval not only to crimes committed against Spanish Nationalists, but even ... to the repression of the Trotskyist group. ... Do you realize the mentality this preface reveals?' After thus casting aspersions on the authors of the protest, the minister could reject the essential part of their accusations. He concluded, admitting that two miners' wives might have had their heads shorn: 'You see how a couple of tonsures may be the sole basis on which this whole black legend has been built up.' The headlines in *El Español* ran: 'Bergamín, the defender of Stalin's crimes.' As for the fresh demand for an investigation made by some 200 intellectuals in another letter to him, Iribarne dismissed it as the result 'not of a sincere desire for information but of a wish to provoke scandal'. He thus considered 'the dialogue he had sought to engage with the intellectuals as broken off'. On 25 October it was learnt that the signatories of the letter had been charged with the offence of 'spreading false or tendentious news'. A special tribunal in charge of the affair proposed to indict the intellectuals for 'clandestine propaganda'. José Bergamín, aged 70, when summoned before the court, asked for right of asylum in Uruguay and took refuge in that country's embassy. The new path of *liberalización* led to the familiar ground of trial and exile; and the affair sheds light on many aspects and results of that policy. However, it had marked an important stage, and the Minister did not abandon it.

At Valladolid, on 30 October, Iribarne presided over the closing meeting of the Council of Spanish Festivals. The state was in fact increasing its efforts to attract tourists: new roads, hotels, development of building land, a whole programme of festivals for visitors to follow from one town to another, and general permissiveness. On Spanish beaches, all summer, French and English and German were spoken; shop signs were in all three languages; Spain was wide open, and this too proved the solidity of the regime. In his speech to the Council Iribarne stressed that 'there will be greater liberty every day as a natural consequence of the development of the principles of a political system which, believing firmly in spiritual values, is now firmly and surely constructing an order of coexistence befitting the Spanish people'. Giving further details about the policy of *liberalización*, Iribarne concluded: 'The vast majority of Spaniards have shown that they know how to use the liberty to which the law entitles them. ... This means that we can and must continue to advance. Our state must lead to ever clearer expressions of liberty.'

He's Going to Leave ...

Autumn 1963: the Asturian miners had gone back into the pits. Autumn 1963: the tourists were gradually leaving Spain, which had offered them such delights: *tertulias* (cafés), prawns, cheap wine, sun, corridas, flats or villas for the same price as some dark room in Paris or Cologne, dancing on the beaches, and 'the proud, dignified Spanish people, never fawning or grumbling, decent upright people who live like anyone else'.

Autumn 1963: millions of Europeans were convinced that they knew Spain, because they had seen it. University teachers were arrested in Barcelona and in Madrid; there was a strike in the Law Faculty of the capital.

According to statistics, in the past ten years, since the 1953 agreements, the United States had provided aid to Spain amounting to $1,154 million.

Autumn 1963: press agencies reported that eight members of Soviet trade unions would shortly visit Spain to study its 'vertical syndicalism . . . in whose achievements they were greatly interested'.

On 13 November the journal *Le Monde* published an interview with Dom Escarré, Abbot of the Benedictine monastery of Montserrat, who stated: 'The Spanish regime calls itself Christian but does not follow the basic principles of Christianity.' This called forth a severe reply from the Minister of Information, and some Falangists attacked the abbey.

Mgr Herrera Oria, in a commentary on the encyclical *Pacem in Terris*, wrote that 'the only wise revolution is from above, an intelligent, legal, guided' revolution, and added: 'The Parliamentary system does not seem to be adapted to the mentality of Latin peoples.'

Autumn 1963: one sign of Spain's apparently contradictory realities: on 24 October, *Cuadernos para el diálogo*, a journal edited by ex-Minister Joaquín Ruiz Jiménez, was on sale for the first time, while the journal of the Catholic workers' youth movement, *Juventud Obrera*, was seized by the police.

It might seem that the regime was hesitating, not knowing what to allow and what to censor, overwhelmed by the tide of new forces. On the one hand members of an opposition party, the *Izquierda Democrática Cristiana*, led by Giménez Fernández, could write openly, as members of that party, to Iribarne; on the other hand, trials and violent repression still went on.

In fact, nothing had changed; *liberalización* could coexist with the shooting of Grimau and the *garrote vil*. The contradiction was only apparent. The essential point was that by the end of 1963 the regime was still able to play almost at will on any part of the political keyboard.

Raimón, the young Catalan singer, was allowed to travel through town and country, performing to his own guitar accompaniment songs which were, as often as not, anti-Francoist; his audiences applauded him, and he won first prize at the Festival of Mediterranean Song with a song entitled 'He's going to leave', but all this did not deeply affect the regime, which had different foundations. All the courage, all the suffering of the opposition, its devotion, its hope were doomed, in 1963, to impotence and frustration.

BOOK V

THE FIRST *DESARROLLO* PLAN
1964–1968
SPAIN'S FUTURE IN QUESTION

CHAPTER I

DESARROLLO AND REFERENDUM
1964–1966

On 27 December 1963 a stream of official cars drew up before the palace of La Zarzuela, the home of Don Juan Carlos and Doña Sofía, for the christening of the young couple's first child. The baby's grandfather, Don Juan, Count of Barcelona, attended the ceremony and sat side by side with General Franco and Señora Carmen Polo de Franco. The Apostolic Nuncio performed the ceremony, with holy water from the Jordan. Next day the press published photographs of the Caudillo talking amicably to Don Juan. The regime thus seemed anxious to assert that Spain was a kingdom even if it had no king, or if its king had to wait until the Caudillo was kind enough to nominate him.

For when the christening party, with its smiles and cordial handshakes, was over, Don Juan, Count of Barcelona, had to go back to Portugal, to his Villa at Estoril. As for the Caudillo, when asked by a reporter from *Le Figaro*[1] when a possible transfer of powers might take place, and whether he foresaw the restoration of the monarchy in the person of the Count of Barcelona or in that of Prince Don Juan Carlos, he replied calmly that 'he would fix no time limits, and that the moment had not yet come for the choice to be made in either direction'. In a word, the problem of the succession was not of immediate urgency to the Caudillo.

Time Limits

Yet, whatever the Caudillo might think, time sets its own limits on a man's life. Nobody, except perhaps Franco himself, forgot this. In the mid-sixties, during all those celebrations of *Twenty-five years of peace* (since 1939) and thirty years of Francoism (since 1936) people were arguing, whispering, assessing the chances of such and such a man, or such and such a group. Would it be the Count of Barcelona or his son Don Juan Carlos, who in January 1968 would reach the age of 30 and thus be legally entitled to the succession? To be sure, he had often repeated: 'I shall never accept the crown while my father is alive', but at the same time he deliberately made his presence felt in Spain, appearing in uniform at official ceremonies, travelling through the land with his young wife, both busily shaking hands and greeting the children presented to them with the conventional smile assumed by royal persons who wish to become well-known

[1] Not reported in the Spanish press on 17 December.

317

and popular. Since May 1964 the Carlists had reasserted their claims. Prince Carlos-Hugo of Bourbon-Parma was back in the field. His wedding in Rome that April, in the church of Santa-Maria-Maggiore, was attended by a large delegation from the Carlist Party and was celebrated in noisy fashion by Carlist students in Barcelona. In May, at another Carlist demonstration, tens of thousands of men and women wearing red *boinas* assembled at Montejurra for an enthusiastic procession, concluding with an open-air mass on the mountain top. Carlist flags were flown and photographs of Carlos-Hugo displayed; the presence of such personalities as Fal Conde and Vázquez de Prada emphasized the political significance of the gathering. The Falangist press, moreover, gave great publicity to the event, proving yet again that the anti-Monarchist leaders of the *Movimiento* hoped to use Carlism as a weapon in their conflict with Don Juan and his son.

In other circles there was talk of a new regent: Muñoz Grandes or Carrero Blanco, the two important military men in the government, or else a man of the 'new right', such as López Bravo, whom some people thought of as a sort of Spanish Kennedy; others, again, hoped that by some unexplained process power would fall into the hands of a broad Christian-Democratic front, regrouping various trends from right to left, ranging from Martín Artajo, former Minister of Foreign Affairs, to Ruiz Jiménez, also a sometime Francoist minister and now the leading spirit of the *Cuadernos para el diálogo*, and to Giménez Fernández. Among members of the opposition there was much talk, too, of such Socialists as Professor Enrique Tierno Galván, dismissed in 1965 from his chair of law at Salamanca, whose brand of 'university socialism' conflicted with the aims of the P.S.O.E.

Thus plans were being laid for the succession. Many Monarchist circles, in order that the transition to a monarchy might take place naturally, wished to provide an institutional and juridical framework for the regime which, after its twenty-five years of peace, was still only Franco's regime. They would have liked to introduce a monarchy of modern type, with a strong executive and with popular representation, the Crown being the final arbiter. It was held in these circles that 'unconditional Francoism and pure anti-Francoism were emotional *a priori* attitudes and not serious political opinions. Their final quintessence amounts to nonsense.'[2]

All left-wing opposition groups were of course definitely anti-Francoist, but they were somewhat divided in their attitude towards the monarchy. Santiago Carrillo, speaking for the Communists, went so far as to argue:

'If the Pretender Don Juan is willing not to ascend the throne without the consent of the people, as he declared at Estoril, why should we refuse to allow his supporters to take part in the union which we Communists advocate between all parties and all groups seeking to establish in Spain a system of liberties?'

In June 1964, moreover, the Communist Party published a *Declaration* defining these liberties: it demanded (1) an amnesty, (2) the right to strike, (3) trade union freedom with independent unions, (4) the recognition of universal suffrage as the source of legitimate power, without however specifying the nature of that

[2] Antonio Forán.

power. The Communist Party's policy of peaceful unification was defined in a widely read book by Santiago Carrillo, *Después de Franco, ¿ qué?* (*After Franco, what?*) which offers far wider concessions; arguing against those who consider the army as a force irrevocably bound up with the regime, the general secretary of the Spanish Communist Party writes:

> 'There might arise a new possibility, unforeseeable a short while ago, of establishing collaboration between the people and the army, in an effort to establish political liberties and lift the heavy burden which the regime represents for Spain. . . . The Communist Party would be prepared to participate in such a movement with the people and the army.'

The time seemed ripe for an end to Francoism. During these years of anniversary celebrations the foreign press was full of reports with such significant titles as *L'Espagne à l'heure du dialogue*,[3] *L'Espagne de la succession, Le soleil se lève en Espagne*,[4] implying that the post-Franco era had begun.

The Caudillo

In such an atmosphere rumours of the Caudillo's ill health were rife. He would be 74 on 4 December 1966, having been in power for over thirty years. Some of his close acquaintances reported that he seemed frequently *distrait* and took ever greater care of his health, while his wife, thinner but still lively, kept a strict watch over his activities and shielded him from his ministers. He went hunting and fishing, played golf, took walks in the park of his Pardo Palace. He painted, too: seascapes in a highly conventional style depicting, for instance, a schooner wrecked on the rocks and partly submerged under the waves. He appeared less frequently in uniform, and when he posed proudly in front of his easel, palette in hand, he looked like the retired honorary chairman of a corporation. Whenever his birthday came round (in 1964 for instance) his doctor made a point of reassuring the press as to the excellent health of his patient. In fact Franco regularly attended the lengthy Cabinet meetings which took place every fortnight, and which went on for fifteen or twenty hours! He spoke little, some said he dozed off, but he would always intervene at the end of an argument, often to postpone the decision. Waiting was still the keynote of his policy.

As in the past, he made several public appearances each year: at ceremonies, at victory celebrations, at the National Congress of the *Movimiento*. However, he travelled less frequently about Spain, merely paying his annual summer visit to Coruña, where with a few guests, such as the Marquis of Villaverde and his wife, he would attend an occasional corrida. After this he would go and congratulate the toreros, Tinín or Antonete or El Cordobés; he let himself be photographed with the latter after a day's hunting. El Cordobés, who was a popular hero, is seen bowing to the Caudillo, and such a photograph, showing the supple, smiling torero side by side with the father-figure of Spain's ageing ruler, served a useful political purpose.

[3] *Esprit* (October 1965).
[4] French press, 1966.

In 1964, Irigarne's department made use of yet another medium to ensure the Caudillo's popularity: the cinema. Franco had always been a film enthusiast, and often watched full-length films at home in the Pardo. On 11 November 1964 a rather different show took place. During a reception at the Palace of Music in Madrid, attended by the Diplomatic Corps, by ministers and the nobility and gentry, there was shown a film by José Luis Saenz de Heredia entitled *Franco ese hombre* (Franco the Man),[5] in colour and in cinemascope, lasting a hundred minutes, which traced the life of the Caudillo from his childhood up till 1945. As *Arriba* wrote on 29 November, 'the little boy from Ferrol who looks out at us knows quite well what he wants to do: to serve Spain'. Scenes from the Second World War were not omitted: Franco was seen with Hitler, with Mussolini, Goering, Darlan and Pétain; but his meeting with Eisenhower was added. Such propaganda did not presage an imminent departure. Many Spaniards relished the story then current that Franco, playing with one of his grandsons as was his custom, asked him, like any other grandfather: 'What do you want to be when you grow up?' 'Caudillo of Spain, like you', the child replied. 'But that's not possible', says Franco. 'You know there cannot be two Caudillos in Spain at the same time.'[6]

The story shows that the Spanish people had few illusions as to the likelihood of the Caudillo's voluntary retirement.

Crisis in the opposition

Such a thing seemed all the more improbable in that despite the upsurge of opposition everywhere, and the unrest shown in hitherto submissive social strata, despite the quiet and resolute courage of men who risked their career and their freedom for the sake of a cause, the political groups of the opposition were undergoing a crisis.

Some moved further to the left. In October a militant section of the Communists formed a *Partido Comunista de España* which defined itself as Marxist-Leninist, that is to say associated on the international plane with Maoism. This new group, whose influence was very restricted and which was subjected to severe repression by the police, won some success in university circles in Madrid and in certain working-class districts of the capital; in its publications, published clandestinely by the *Ediciones Vanguardia Obrero*, it attacked the 'revisionist' line of the Communist Party. Pamphlets, appeals and denunciations came thick and fast, calling for a fight to the death – with arms if need be – against Franco-ism. The importance of this lies less in the response to these appeals, which was very slight, than in the problem that it reveals: the birth of a new extreme left, or the attempt to create one. Whereas Communist policy presupposed mastery of *all* social groups, the appearance of these nuclei hostile to it reveals the difficulty of controlling the opposition as a whole.

The Communist Party was moreover about to undergo another crisis. Within

[5] Produced by *Chapale Films*.

[6] Quoted by Marcel Niedergang in a report in *Le Monde, L'Espagne de la succession* (13–18 July 1966).

the Central Committee, a critical group forgathered around one of its most brilliant members, Fernando Claudín. He engaged in fierce controversy with Carrillo. Claudín, who was dismissed from the Central Committee, had criticized both the way the party functioned internally (the lack of opportunities for discussion, etc.) and the line that assumed the possibility of replacing Francoism by an advanced form of bourgeois democracy. In his view, in Spain, the only alternative to Francoism was Socialist revolution, not a bloc of Popular Front type. This was really the old conflict of 1936 revived on another level (for Spain had changed, and the world too): a reformist *Frente popular*, hoping to win the war with the aid of the middle class, or revolution as a necessary condition of victory? Attached to this controversy was the idea that the Communist Party had proved unable to analyse the changes that had taken place in Spain owing to its economic development and the social transformations resulting from this. According to Carrillo and the Central Committee, Claudín was a 'liquidator' who denied the importance of the party as advance-guard. *Después de Franco, ¿ qué?* was written as a consequence of this controversy, while Claudín set forth his position in *Horizonte Español 1966* (Two Ideas of the Spanish Road to Socialism), with a study entitled 'Dos Concepciones de la via española al socialisma'.[7] The controversy aroused echoes chiefly in intellectual circles. Claudín was soon joined by men like Jorge Semprun, who appealed to a wide audience. They expressed their views in the journal *Cuadernos de Ruedo Ibérico*,[8] which also published detailed studies of the real situation in contemporary Spain. When Claudín declared that

'in any case, the creation of a Marxist party of a new type – either by the renovation of the existing Communist Party and its fusion with other Marxist nuclei, or by some other means – is a historic necessity both in Spain and in other countries ... a party which would consider Marxism as a *problem*, as something constantly *in the making*, both in practice and in theory',

he was understood by a great many Spanish intellectuals. Here again, more than the ideas that seemed to Claudín and to such followers as Frederic Sánchez to promise a revival, what must be noted is the crisis within the Communist opposition that the controversy reveals.

There was another crisis in March 1965 within the *Frente de Liberación Popular* over the analysis of Spanish society in its new form and also over the types of oppositionist action to be taken and the possibility of creating a new revolutionary party. Here again we find dismissals, the formation of a breakaway group, a review – *Acción Communista* – and evidence of powerlessness. For these splinter groups, on whatever scale, prove that the failure of all the strategies hitherto attempted against Francoism had hit the opposition hard. It was unprepared, moreover, for the scale of the transformations affecting Spain. Skilful propaganda credited the regime with all this economic development, and the myths of *desarrollo*, planning, the 'miracle' were more widely broadcast than ever. While the opposition might criticize the regime's plan and the permanence

[7] *Horizonte Español 1966*, II (Ruedo Ibérico, 1966).
[8] No. 1 (June/July 1965).

of its structures, the fact remained that, thirty years after the outbreak of the Civil War, Spain was changing daily.

El Torero del Desarrollo. El Verdugo

On 20 May 1964: Manuel Benítez El Cordobés entered the bull ring of Madrid.[9] For this *torero* with the sharp teeth and long tangled hair, whose agility had become a legend, who had been a poor landless peasant and a petty thief, whom the Civil Guard had beaten up and imprisoned, for this sometime bricklayer whose father, an agricultural labourer, had died as a result of the Civil War, for this young man who had sacrificed everything to worldly success, there now came that moment of glory, the *alternativa* which might establish him as a great torero. He was injured in the fierce fight, against the enormous black beast that hurtled against him, but he survived to be admired by Spain. He was *el torero del desarrollo* because he had risen from extreme poverty like so many others, but now was wealthy and arrogantly happy; he could buy up hotels, he could do all the tricks expected of him. Prancing in the bull ring, acting the scenes of his wretched youth before the camera, he also let himself be used for political ends, posing with the self-satisfied smile of successful physical achievement for a poster, during the 1966 referendum, inscribed *Vote Yes like El Cordobés!*

For many a young Spaniard, for all those who in the back rooms of cafés practised bull-fighting with a pair of horns mounted on a stand, he symbolized possible triumph, the acquisition of those fabulous goods which, in industrial society, glitter in everyone's eyes but are granted only to a few. True, one must risk one's life to get them, but these Spaniards' hunger was boundless and many were prepared to sacrifice everything for the sake of *having*. El Cordobés was one of those, and that is why he became, like some football players (Pelé in Brazil) or boxers, the idol of the common people. True, the *aficionados* were quickly to discover that this torero who gambled with his life was not a classic fighter, that Paco Camino was a thousand times better, that his success was due primarily to clever publicity, to the intuition of a salesman who knows how to display himself, but this mattered little; just because he was the man who said 'I love money more than anyone else in the world', because his fortune was reckoned at some 55 million francs, he fascinated people; he was the embodiment of a whole side of Spanish life during the *desarrollo*.

He refused to take an interest in politics. When in 1967 a book was published telling his adventures, which inevitably revealed certain aspects of Francoist Spain, the CIFRA agency declared in his name (for he could barely read or write):

'The authors have taken unfair advantage of the cordial welcome I gave them, making use of my life and my name to give serious offence to Spain, her government and a host of Spaniards who deserve respect. I am a *torero* and not a

[9] Dominique Lapierre and Larry Collins, *Ou tu porteras mon deuil* (Laffont, Paris, 1967).

politician, but none the less I love my country deeply and I have the greatest respect for our government. I also have a great personal affection for our Caudillo who has proved able to preserve peace in Spain, to lead us through prosperous paths and to create conditions which will enable me to triumph in my profession as others have triumphed in theirs.'

Millions of other Spaniards, in that changing country, shared the hopes and desires of El Cordobés. They were indifferent to the world of politics; they knew they could not affect it and that it was dangerous to meddle with it. These millions of Spaniards were often neglected by the opposition, yet they had to be reckoned with; for they did exist, and the success of El Cordobés was not the only token of their presence. They are pitilessly indicted in Luis Berlanga's film *El Verdugo* (*The Executioner*), made in 1964, one of the most pessimistic and revealing works of *desarrollo* Spain. In a fable inspired by the whole Spanish tradition, it shows how a young man is forced, against his will – because he wants to get married and find a job and a flat in one of the new Madrid housing estates, and to enjoy holidays – to become an executioner like his father-in-law. Amidst the crowd of tourists and holiday-making Spaniards, he is summoned by the *Guardia Civil* to perform his duties. Escorted by guards, encouraged by the head warden of the prison, he proceeds to kill the condemned man by slow strangulation, *garrote vil*; executioner and victim being two identical figures walking at the same pace, flanked by the authorities, towards the place of death. What Berlanga denounced so violently was the forced complicity of the Spanish people with a pitiless society, the cruel hell of the *desarrollo*, the price to be paid for the scanty advantages it offered – a small flat, a holiday. The couples he shows quarrelling over a non-existent flat in an unfinished building amidst waste ground, and planning where to put the television set and the dining-table. are typical of that category of Spaniards who were escaping from hunger, showing that Spain – not all Spain, far from it – was now climbing out of the ranks of the underdeveloped countries and had reached the lowest rung of the ladder among European nations.

Six Hundred Dollars per Head

The evolution of the national income per head and per annum is convincing evidence, even if this reckoning disguises the rise in prices which affected the consumer's purchasing power: 281 dollars in 1958, 291 in 1960, then 332 by 1961, 380 by 1962, 497 by 1964 and 637 by 1966. The 500-dollar threshold had been crossed: Spain had 'taken off', she no longer formed part of the backward group that included Turkey and Greece. Naturally any such equal distribution of the national income between the 31 million inhabitants of Spain is purely illusory; for example, the Andalusians who crowded into the satellite towns around Barcelona, Hospitalet or Sabadell, formed a sub-proletariat compared with which the Catalan workers were a privileged class; not to mention the big bourgeoisie whose already considerable incomes had been swollen by expansion, and whose way of life was, definitively changing. In Madrid between 1964 and

1966 some 1,200 American-style bars had been opened, as well as innumerable night-clubs, where the bourgeois displayed their wealth and satisfied their thirst for pleasure in an atmosphere reminiscent of the French Second Empire, made more hectic by unbridled speculation. It must be remembered, too, that most Spanish workers did at least ten hours' work a day, often combining two jobs or working long overtime. In spite of these inequalities, and the price that some had to pay to live a decent life, the figure of 637 dollars *per capita* is an index to be noted. New Spain really existed, it was not merely a fiction of propaganda.

Its existence was apparent everywhere. In statistics: between 1963 and 1965 the consumption of sugar rose by 11 per cent, of meat by 3·23 per cent, of fish by 18 per cent. The production of television sets increased by 74·6 per cent (550,000), that of refrigerators by 146·91 per cent (600,000), that of washing-machines by 98·24 per cent; the number of private cars increased by 52·41 per cent to 807,317. Television aerials proliferated from end to end of the peninsula, sometimes ruining architectural prospects such as the Plaza Mayor in Madrid. There were building sites everywhere; squares (the Plaza Mayor again) were being turned into car parks. Here too the distribution was uneven: thirty television sets per thousand inhabitants in 1965; but an irreversible process had begun. A working class elite was acquiring the ways and standards of living of the middle class; the industrial workers were becoming the largest section of the working population. Meanwhile, ineluctably, the rural areas were being deserted and the rural sector, which in 1960 still represented 39·7 per cent of the working population, had dropped by 1965 to 31 per cent, and by 1966 to 28·9 per cent. Such figures, once again, are convincing evidence. Similarly the middle classes made swift progress because the tertiary sector, trade, the tourist industry and so forth, was developing so fast. Spanish families of the under-forty generation, satisfied with the Franco regime and with their own lives, could be seen everywhere, eating in restaurants, mingling with foreign tourists on the beaches or driving their small cars along the roads; they made up a petty bourgeoisie of wage-earning technicians, whose pride and self-confidence were enhanced by acquiring the visible signs (the car, the flat, the holidays) of their moderately privileged status. The political weight of these new strata was of course considerable. They were undoubtedly hostile to any disorder, anything that might endanger their standard of living and their position. The opposition would have to win them over, but would find it difficult. Francoism, with or without Franco, may perhaps have found in them a new group ready to support it: not in any return to a civil war situation but in the choice of a policy ensuring public peace and development. This was what they were offered by men like Fraga Iribarne, Ullastres and López Rodo.

The Spanish Boom

Spain's economic development was a fact, and propaganda helped to ensure that the credit went to Franco's regime and the *Desarrollo* Plan. This came into operation on 1 January 1964 for a period of three years: it provided for *poles of promotion* (Burgos and Huelva), *poles of development* (Coruña, Zaragoza,

Seville, Valladolid, Vigo) and *polygons of industrial decentralization* unlimited in number.

In fact between 1964 and 1966 spectacular transformations took place around these poles. Working-class housing estates and residential areas, topped by their forest of aerials, sprang up around Seville; Huelva became a capital of the chemical industry; Cáceres and Burgos were also surrounded by a network of council flats and new factories. Valladolid was the centre of the Renault assembly works and of more than seventy new industries; Pampeluna, Zaragoza and Vigo witnessed a similar expansion and transformation, as industrial growth modified the face of towns which for centuries had drowsed under the dust of tradition.

Everywhere there was speculation in land; tourists' villas went up along the coast, from the Costa Brava to the Costa del Sol; from Málaga to Gibraltar, at Marbela and at Carvajal; and they were rented or sold to people all over Europe. International financial firms provided customers from France and from all the wealthier countries. 'Your castle in Spain can come true,' promised the glossy brochures.

Meanwhile, Catalonia, covering 6 per cent of the nation's territory and providing 12 per cent of its population, still provided almost 25 per cent of its production. Catalonia had been slower to develop, but the standard of living there was considerably higher than in other parts of Spain, and Andalusians and Murcians came crowding into the suburbs of Barcelona, now a metropolis comprising 2·5 million inhabitants. A ten-year improvement plan, costing $20 million, had been set going over a 1,000-hectare area between Montjuich and Llobregat. Every day almost 300 young peasants came to settle there, while 500 more moved into Madrid.

The proud administrative capital of Spain had moreover become the leading industrial centre of the country, and with its 3 million inhabitants it displayed great vitality and some singular contrasts. With its crowded streets and underground trains, its traffic jams, its poorly clad workers, its roads cut up by heavy lorries, the capital gave the physical impression of the upheaval that was taking place. Everywhere road works and mechanical drills were in operation. In the suburbs, red brick buildings for the working class were hastily put up without regard for town planning. Sometimes the housefronts were less than a metre and a half apart. The whole Madrid region was changing; at Villaverde, where corn had been growing in 1965, the Barreiros factories now employed 26,000 hands on the mass production of cars (over 60,000 Simca 1000s). Orders poured in, and the great motor roads leading to Madrid, cut through the countryside, were already crowded on Sundays. The rate of increase in production – an average of 7·5 per cent for the years 1961 to 1966, and 9 per cent in 1965 – was the highest in all Europe.

Limited Freedom

The people of Spain witnessed and endured all these alterations. They had to give up all their time, their very existence to the task of production; the rhythm of their lives changed, the intensity of work increased, men had to get up early and go to bed earlier, hurry (if they lived in Madrid) to the Estación de Atocha or take the metro. Time was always short, and working overtime shortened it still further; this again made it harder to acquire the political education and the militancy which were needed for opposition to Francoism. That opposition, now, had to contend not only with fear of repression but with all the restrictions of life in a neo-capitalist society, that splitting-up of communities into individuals, living isolated from their neighbours, which characterizes modern urban life. Thus, while the opposition still had to fight on the traditional fronts – anti-Francoism, the right to freedom and so on – new fronts were opening up and the regime was launching counter-offensives in new sectors. Having failed to get rid of Francoism when it was an archaic political form, inherited from the days of fascism, the opposition was now confronted with a changed enemy, and it had to invent a modern form of strategy as yet unknown in France or in Italy. It was *inevitably behind time*.

The regime, moreover, yielded on secondary points, and this, although revealing its *relative* weakness – as the opposition did not fail to point out – also implied strength.

Under Fraga Iribarne's direction, the censorship relaxed. Translations of authors hitherto considered heretical – Marx, Engels, Castro – began to appear. On 23 April an annual Book Day was held in Barcelona, and Fraga Iribarne, speaking there in 1964, asserted that 'national unity was not threatened by the use of a provincial idiom'. So Sartre, Freud, Gramsci, Kafka, Pratolini and Brecht were translated into Catalan and widely read – as were also the James Bond novels.

In the field of religion Spain might be said to have been colonized by Europe: in 1950, 75 per cent of the works dealing with dogma were Spanish, by 1965 only 10 per cent, the rest being translations of foreign works. This implies that even the Church was changing, for the ideas that came across from Europe were those of the Vatican Council. Television followed the new trend, providing talks favourable to the ideas of Teilhard de Chardin. At the Council, it was a Spaniard, Mgr Guerra, auxiliary Bishop of Madrid and counsellor to the *Acción católica*, who asked for details about Marxist atheism, suggesting the desirability of an exchange of views with representatives of that philosophy. This gives some measure of the changes that had occurred.

One reason is that the Spanish Church, in its *demographic* structure, reflected the country's situation; 60 per cent of Spaniards, in 1966, were under 40 years of age and had not known the Civil War. The Spanish clergy was, in fact, the youngest in Europe (although its bishops were the oldest). In 1967, of Spain's 22,000 priests 9,000 (45 per cent) were under 40 and 2,889 between 40 and 49.[10] There was an increasing tendency among the younger clergy to demand the Church's total independence from the secular power. They had made deeper contact with the mass of the Spanish people, in whom they had discovered an underlying anti-clericalism: according to an investigation made by *Acción católica*, this affected 89·6 of the working class. They opened schools in the suburbs, such as the First of May school in Madrid, run by Father José María

[10] 3,440 were under 30: cf. *Vidanueva* 23 Dec. 1967).

Llanos, where each week some foreign flag was hoisted beside the Spanish and United Nations flags – even the red flag of the u.s.s.r. Certain priests in Barcelona even formed a *sindicato* which they hoped to extend throughout Spain, and which demanded increasing communication with unbelievers and a more open-minded attitude from the hierarchy.

This movement naturally met with resistance. The state confiscated an increasing number of Catholic publications. The hierarchy issued warnings and transferred defiant priests. The Archbishop of Madrid, Mgr Morcillo, went so far as to say that 'the Council's declaration involves more risks for Spain, perhaps, than for any other country'. Meanwhile the Opus Dei supported an integrist right wing which held progressivism to be 'the eighth deadly sin, quintessence of the other seven'.[11] Little reviews (*Cristiandad, El Cruzado Español, Qué Pasa*), virulent and clamorous, condemned the new tendencies of a section of the Church.

The important point, however, is the headway made by the progressive movement despite repression by the hierarchy and by the state, proving that a certain freedom was creeping in, in point of fact, within the new Spain.

Young academics, frequently economists such as Ramón Tamames and Alfonso Comín, openly criticized the Plan and its trends. Tamames' writings are particularly pertinent; they are based on a scientific analysis, but his conclusions have obvious political implications, whether he studies *Las estructuras económicas de España* (The Economic Structure of Spain)[12] or *Los monopolios en España* (Monopolies in Spain)[13], part of an even more significant work, *La lucha contra los monopolios* (*The Struggle Against the Monopolies*). His books were published in cheap paper-back editions; one of these, *Biblioteca Promoción del pueblo* (*People's Promotion Library*), introduced Tamames' work as a study of 'the financial and industrial oligarchy' which, if it played a part in the nation's development, represented only a minority. Such a comment would have been unthinkable a few years previously.

Books of this type were becoming ever more numerous, and publishers' production increased, between 1963 and 1965, by 28·2 per cent. The demand was growing, since illiteracy had dropped below 8 per cent of the population, while the number of those enjoying secondary and higher education had risen (between 1963 and 1965) by 45·12 per cent and 23·04 per cent respectively. Such books were on show in shop windows, they could be bought and read, and this is probably one of the keys to Fraga Iribarne's policy: by toleration, to neutralize. It was a dangerous game, for while force was on the side of the authorities, the opposition had another advantage, the strength of their ideas and of their needs.

In working-class milieux for instance, although there were noticeable improvements (skilled workers could now buy second-hand cars) indebtedness, overwork or work illegally undertaken were the general rule. On the basis of the people's needs, the Workers' Commissions formulated precise demands, here too with a certain degree of freedom. Ministers, representatives of the official *sindicatos*

[11] *Études: Où va le laïcat espagnol* (Sept. 1966).
[12] Madrid, 1964.
[13] Madrid, 1967.

327

and bosses held negotiations with delegates of the Commissions. The latter were illegal, of course, but bargaining went on. Thus the central committee of the 150,000 metal workers of Madrid drew up an eighteen-point programme, in January 1966, ranging from the demand for a minimum wage of 250 pesetas per day to the right to strike and to hold workers' meetings on the premises of factories and Unions. Four representatives of the Workers' Commissions even asked for an interview with the Minister of Labour (28 June); now they had no legal status and were even liable to prosecution for unlawful activities. The Minister, on this occasion, merely refused to see them, and had the Civil Guard disperse the small groups that stood waiting for their delegates. All this implies a certain degree of freedom, on this thirtieth anniversary of the *Alzamiento*.

On 15 July 1866, thirty years, almost to the day, since the cry *Arriba España* rang out, the first batch of Soviet tourists arrived in Barcelona. These were fourteen intellectuals, who paid an eighteen-day visit to the country; they included the novelist Konstantin Simonov and the film producer Roman Karmen, who in 1937 had shot some extremely exciting documentaries about the Civil War. Meanwhile trade relations between the Soviet Union and Franco Spain were growing, as well as exchanges in the field of sport.

La guerre est finie (*The War is Over*) was the title of a film made by Alain Resnais in 1966 from a scenario by Jorge Semprún; and it told the truth, to some extent, about this new Spain in ferment, where unfamiliar freedom seemed imminent, where a Jesuit father could hoist the Soviet flag one June morning in a school for workers' children. The anti-Francoist hero of *La guerre est finie*, before setting off for a mission in his own country where, no doubt, the police were in wait for him, also asserts that: 'action must go on, for this is a long stubborn work of construction whose end we cannot foresee.'

Action Must Go On

Not a month went by without some students demonstrating, some priests protesting, some workers striking. True, these movements were localized and impermanent, but activity would revive in another town, another factory, another university. Public protest – whether by strike action, by petition, or by demonstration in the street – had become once again, regardless of danger and legal prohibition, the means of action chosen by the most combative sections of the Spanish population. Undeniable victories were scored in the day-to-day struggle, but these were never definitive, and each time they required the unassuming courage of anonymous militants well aware that they were risking their liberty in these partial contests.

Workers, furthermore, risked losing their jobs, which was just as serious. None the less they became increasingly active; and the demand for freedom of association was inseparably linked with their material claims. The miners of Asturias, the metal workers of Bilbao, Barcelona and Madrid were in the vanguard of the struggle. In April 1964 strikes spread once more through Asturias, and in May the strikers at Mieres attacked a police station. Metal workers demonstrated in Madrid in November, demanding a minimum wage of 200 pesetas per day.

During the whole of 1965 and again in 1966 similar events took place: delegates from the Workers' Commissions presented their claims and organized demonstrations; they were arrested (February 1965, June 1966) and other demonstrations were held to secure their release. Charges might be dropped, but there were many dismissals. For at the same time that it was negotiating with the delegates of the Workers' Commissions, the government harried and persecuted them, and they would resist, backed by the solidarity of their fellow-workers. The vitality, the fighting spirit, the tenacity of the working class – on these limited issues – were such that the government was forced to make concessions: in December 1965 the final draft of Article 22 of the Penal Code, while authorizing severe sentences, distinguished between different types of strike. Collective stoppage of work was no longer automatically considered as an act of rebellion against the state. Similarly, in October 1965, a change was made in trade union organization, with the constitution, in Barcelona, of a *Consejo Nacional Empresarios* whereby the *vertical syndicate*, which ignored class divisions, was partially replaced by a *horizontal* structure which recognized the divergent interests of employers and workers. The strength of the workers' movement, parallel with this, made itself felt and at the official trade union elections (September 1966) the majority of delegates elected were from the Workers' Commissions. Yet the opposition had split once again: the Communist Party, the F.L.P., the Workers' Commissions wanted to work within the official *sindicatos*, while the Socialist Party, the *Alianza sindical* and the Catholic Organizations urged their members to boycott these. The appeal for participation carried the day. In Madrid, two well-known leaders from the Workers' Commissions, Camacho and Hernando, were elected by their fellow-workers, although the Ministry considered them ineligible.

Thus day by day the workers' movement acquired a wider scope and a firmer organization. Moreover, the social struggle spread outside the sectors traditionally involved. Housewives protested in the markets against the rise in prices (February 1965); in Barcelona, bank employees objected to their new work schedule (January 1965), while in April there were demonstrations on the Ramblas. In Asturias, small-scale dairy farmers clashed with wholesalers; they set up barriers on the roads and overturned lorries (June 1966). In Aragon a peasant conflict of traditional type broke out between a big landowner, the Conde de Sastago, and the farmers of the village. The incident was significant of the Spanish situation in 1966. The Supreme Court had just restored to the Count the 10,672 hectares he had given to the peasants in 1931, which had been his way of preserving his lands while avoiding the risk of agrarian reform, and furthermore of improving them, since, as the village priest pointed out, the peasants had made the soil arable by toiling for long days clearing away tons of stones. Now the Count got his lands back in good condition. The peasants' protests broke out. The government took action. Fraga Iribarne decreed that the authorities would 'intervene in the most appropriate manner'. A press campaign urged that the Count should make over his lands once more, and praised the government's actions. So the Conde de Sastago declared himself willing to recognize as landowners all non-tax-paying farmers of the locality. 'A victory for the government', boasted the press, but the 600 villagers were not taken in, and both the mayor and the priest pointed out that except for a few paupers everyone at Sastago (the village bore the Count's name) paid local taxes. The mayor declared: 'His pretended gift has been made in such a way that he keeps all his lands. He may perhaps deceive people outside, but here he deceives nobody.' The incident shows both the enduring power of the big landowners, the support given them by the legal and governmental authorities, and the impossibility of getting such practices accepted in timid silence as of old, whence the need for a tendentious news service to transform the facts that could no longer be concealed.

Government policy followed the same lines when dealing with the problems of the university.

Here, once again, the students' struggle was directed against the official *Sindicato Español Universitario*. The appointment of a Falangist, Heras, as delegate for the Madrid Law Faculty, set off a wave of strikes and violent demonstrations. These incidents continued throughout the beginning of 1965. In April, accordingly, the government altered the structure of the s.e.u. so as to satisfy certain of the students' demands. By now, in every faculty, the students were holding *free assemblies*: the police intervened, made arrests; names were taken and fines imposed. Some students were expelled from the university, and disciplinary measures were taken against junior staff who had supported the students (June 1966). The latter, rejecting the *Associaciones Profesionales de Estudiantes*, which was the new form assumed by the official union, drove its national president Luis Ortega Escos out of the University of Barcelona (in October 1966). New arrests followed.

Like the workers, the students now formed a *Free Union* and as in the Workers' Commissions, Catholics and Communists played a leading part in this. Indeed it was at the Capuchin Monastery at Sarria in the suburbs of Barcelona that the initial organization of the Free Union took place. This again is an event typical of Spain in 1966. The meeting had been announced throughout the university, but its place had been kept secret. At the last moment this was made known by telephone. By 4 p.m. the hall was full: 400 students and thirty-three guests (teachers, intellectuals including the painter Tapies, and the writers Joan Oliver and Salvador Espriu). At 5 p.m. the police surrounded the monastery and announced that the meeting was illegal and must be called off. As some students were leaving, the meeting being over, the police demanded to see their identity cards. The rest then ensconced themselves in the monastery and the Superior, asserting their right of asylum, refused to intervene. By 8 p.m. the news had been broadcast by foreign press agencies. The authorities were uncertain which way to act; they could not contact Franco, for his wife would not let him be disturbed, and it was only two days later, at the opening of the Cabinet meeting, that he was informed, and then gave orders for the affair to be 'liquidated': the police must lay siege to the monastery.

There were demonstrations of solidarity in the centre of Barcelona; arrests were made, fines totalling two and a half million pesetas imposed and eighty students deprived of their cards (April 1966). In spite of this, the Free Union of Students took root in most universities and free assemblies became increasingly frequent not only in Barcelona and Madrid but also in Bilbao and Pampeluna

(March–April 1966). The Rector of the University of Barcelona, who had not objected to the organization of a 'Week of University Renovation' (April 1966) now appealed to the police, who entered the campus and arrested many students attending the free assemblies; as unrest continued and similar movements arose in sympathy in other towns, the rector ordered the university to be closed down. This was a measure which the government, incapable of controlling the student body, was to take repeatedly in future.

The clash between police and clergy, as shown in the Sarrio monastery affair, was also to recur under different forms. The younger priests, particularly in Catalonia, were not afraid of committing themselves openly. Catalan particularism clearly contributed to the atmosphere of hostility towards the regime. The Abbot of Montserrat, moreover, had set an example when at a midnight mass he preached against the Law on Associations, recently voted by the Cortes, and made statements to the foreign press which obliged him to leave the country (March 1965). When the Church hierarchy and the secular power appointed as coadjutor to the Bishop of Barcelona one Marcelo González Martín, in March 1966, the Catholics of Barcelona protested because he was not a Catalan, and disturbances took place in the cathedral (May 1966).

Apart from catalanism, the political significance of their objection must be noted. In fact, a few days previously, 11 May, some hundred priests had demonstrated in the street in front of the *Dirección General de Policía* of Barcelona, seeking to convey to the authorities a letter of protest against the ill-treatment inflicted by the police on a student detainee. The police charged the peaceful demonstration brutally, injuring a number of priests: this was Spain in 1966. After this, clearly, by rejecting Mgr Martín they were displaying their hostility to the regime and to the Church hierarchy which often supported it.

It is in fact remarkable that the Spanish clergy no longer hesitated to voice its criticisms of the hierarchy. The latter discovered, in September 1966, that a large number of priests were secretly preparing *Operación Moisés*, a clandestine assembly for the discussion of problems raised by the relations between the Church and the Francoist state. A summons to the meeting was signed by several thousand priests. The hierarchy reacted strongly, condemning the organizers of the operation; meanwhile it sanctioned the seizure or prohibition of those publications which were the most actively committed to the defence of the working class and to hostility to the regime, such as *El Boletín de la H.O.A.C.* (June 1966) and *Juventud Obrera* (April 1966). The trend which led a large section of the clergy to break away from the regime was too powerful and too much in the spirit of the recent Vatican Council to be denied or annulled; the authorities could only try to contain and restrain it.

In the same way, the Madrid government gave up attempting to uproot particularist feelings. It tolerated, and even sought to make use of, the rising tide of catalanism, which was conquering new zones of influence towards the south;[14] it controlled this as best it could, exercising censorship – the singer Raimón, for instance, found most of his repertoire banned. He had sung to enthusiastic student audiences at the Free Assemblies, in natural amphitheatres improvised

[14] 'Littérature catalane', in *Europe* (Dec. 1967).

out of doors (to the students of the Institute of Chemistry of Sarria, for instance, in November 1966). He had sung verses by the Catalan poet Salvador Espriu; now he was silenced, and had to take his songs abroad; he performed them at the Sorbonne.

In the Basque country, where the particularist movement was all the stronger for being severely repressed, the Madrid government used force. It found itself confronted not merely with traditional nationalist organizations but also by the *Euzkadi Ta Askatasuna* (E.T.A.), which had taken root among the young, and whose theme *The Basque Country and Its Freedom* won secret support from most Basques and from the clergy. This was clearly seen when, in spite of preventive detention and the declaration of a state of martial law in their country, the Basques succeeded in celebrating both at Irun and at Vitoria their national festival, the *Aberri Eguna* (April 1966). People were held for questioning, and clashes with the police occurred, but the Basques assembled notwithstanding, thus proving their determination once again. Madrid, henceforward, had to maintain a considerable police force permanently in the Basque provinces, particularly in Guipuzcoa.

Thus, from Aragon to the Basque country, from Asturias to Barcelona, from faculty lecture-halls to Capuchin monasteries and from factories to villages, certain categories of Spaniards took action against the regime, at a given time, in a wide variety of ways. Beside these men – priests and workers, students and peasants, Catalans and Basques – Spain's 31 million inhabitants also included a vast mass who were indifferent to politics or collective action, concerned only with their daily affairs. The whole of the regime's propaganda, the whole way of life of society contributed to reinforce this apolitical attitude. It was because those in opposition forgot this other silent Spain that they so often deluded themselves as to their chances of success. In the same way, they tended to lose sight of the regime's unimpaired resources, its powers of revival. So, in spite of all these outbursts of activity, the political organizations of the opposition were either stagnating or in the throes of crisis.

The moderate programme of the Spanish Communist Party, drawn up to serve as a platform for the opposition, its call for a *Huelga General Pacífica* (March 1965) and the creation, by the former Republican Minister Álvarez del Vayo (in March 1964), of a *Frente de Liberación Nacional* open to all anti-Francoist parties, met with little response.

The P.S.O.E., at its ninth and tenth congresses (August 1964, August 1967), which still met at Toulouse, continued to appeal for the formation of a provisional government, for the bringing together of 'all authentically democratic political and trade union organizations'. It was poorly represented in the country, and these recommendations had no effect.

The only new factor was the foundation, in January 1965, of the *Union Democrática Cristiana*, which combined the *Izquierda Democrática Cristiana* (led by Gimenez Fernandez) and the *Unión de Juventudes Demócratas Cristianas*. This Christian-Democratic group was obviously well placed strategically; although in opposition, it was in contact with the authorities, if only through the past history of some of its members, such as Ruiz Jiménez. Although an illegal group, it could benefit from the existence of Catholic organizations and their press, and even from the protection of the Church. The courage and dedication of its militants, members of the H.O.A.C. or intellectuals (Comin, for instance) gave it deep roots in a country which was still preponderantly Catholic. The rival to this Christian-Democratic group was the Communist Party; the two had points of contact, and between them they gradually came to control the essential elements in the opposition.

The Communist Party continued to assert that it was possible, 'in view of the nation-wide character of the opposition to Francoism, to succeed in paralysing the country with the consensus and participation of the major social sectors' (June 1966). In fact, just because the militants of the Communist Party were involved in the mass of the working class, sharing its ambitions and its struggles, which were necessarily *partial*, their successes remained purely local and could not help towards paralysing the country. True, the Communist leaders could assert, on the basis of a formal analysis, that all these partial successes, these trade union liberties won, were cumulative in their effect, were so many steps leading to a national strike. In practice, it was still impossible to pass from limited achievements to attain the broader objective. Some oppositionists – the *Ruedo Ibérico* team – even considered that the Workers' Commissions were threatened by integration into the capitalist system, that they were bound to slip into reformist positions.

There was, in fact, a growing discrepancy between the character of anti-Francoist demonstrations and the organized political groups of the opposition. The latter lacked any real leaders; and such leaders could not emerge from obscurity and acquire national stature because the regime stifled their voices and concealed their faces. Outside a narrow circle, no one knew the names of Tierno Galván or Giménez Fernández; as for the leaders of the Workers' Commissions, they were indeed representative, but primarily of the industrial working class, which was not the whole of Spain. Once again it must be recognized that, thirty years after the onset of the Civil War, the political opposition was not equal to the tasks it had set itself and could not be, so long as the authorities still had the initiative in so many fields.

The Lost Bomb and the Press Law

On 17 January 1966, at an altitude of 9,000 metres, a B52 of the United States Strategic Air Command collided above the village of Palomares, in the province of Almeria, with a tanker aircraft KC135 which was refuelling it in flight. The two planes exploded, and three H-bombs fell to the ground. Two plunged into the earth and were soon recovered, a third, lost at sea, was not salvaged till 7 April, seventy-nine days later.[15] In spite of total censorship, the news gradually filtered through, and meanwhile Spain was in the throes of anxiety. Digging went on all around Palomares; anti-American leaflets were distributed throughout Madrid by the Communists, and the most popular song was one with the significant title: *La Bomba Perdida* (The Lost Bomb). To cope with the panic

[15] Christopher Morris, *The Big Catch* (London, 1967).

and silence alarmist rumours, to forestall the anxiety of tourists, the United States Ambassador and his family, with Fraga Iribarne and his children, went swimming at Palomares one March morning; and newspapers and television broadcast all over Spain the picture of the courageous minister plunging into the icy water.

This incident illustrates the new methods of Spain's information service, resolutely up to date and successfully concealing, by means of a spectacular news item, the true problem: the security of Spain and of all Europe at a time of nuclear peril.

A few days later, on 18 March 1966, the *Ley de Prensa e imprenta en España* laid down the rules which would henceforward govern the Spanish press. The censorship was abolished, *but* administrative powers of confiscation were maintained, and several copies of all dailies must be submitted to the authorities an hour before they were sent out. Courts could still prosecute journalists, indeed offences which were formerly subject only to administrative penalties were now punishable by fines and prison sentences. Meanwhile the Ministry boasted of its suppression of the censorship as a concrete measure of liberalization, whereas on 31 March 1966 a decree had established the system of *voluntary consultation*, whereby journalists and editors were asked to submit their texts beforehand to the Ministry of Information. Those who refused to follow this procedure were liable to confiscation: *Juventud Obrero, Serra d'Or* (the review published by the Abbey of Montserrat), *A.B.C.* itself, the *Diario de Las Palmas, Signo, Actualidad Española* and many more were seized and condemned for having published articles in favour of the Monarchists or of the workers on strike.

In other words, the law on the press brought about no change in the political content of the leading newspaper. As for the 'little reviews', often Catholic publications, they were hit harder than before, and in any case had only a limited circulation. The law drawn up by Fraga Iribarne was a clever one, revealing the limits and intentions of his *liberalización*. The main point was to alter the look of things (in this case by abolishing the censorship) and then to offer the petty and middle bourgeoisie, whom the *desarrollo* benefited, a greater freedom of expression, without allowing the slightest political argument. The law on the press was thus yet another sign of the regime's intention to satisfy the aspirations of new strata of the bourgeoisie, and enjoy their support: its liberalization was in fact technical and not political.[16]

Anniversary Celebration. Twenty-five Years of Peace. An Amnesty

The new style was also reflected in the celebration of anniversaries. Throughout Catalonia, for instance, there appeared huge posters in Catalan repeating the slogan which was to serve as leitmotiv for a whole series of ceremonies and speeches: *Twenty-five Years of Peace*. The Ministry of Information was responsible for organizing this campaign, and did so most effectively.

On Wednesday, 1 April 1964, which had been specially declared a public holiday, a solemn Te Deum was celebrated at the monastery of the Valley of the

[16] Guy Hermet, 'La presse espagnole. . . .'

Fallen. Franco stood beside Don Juan Carlos and Dona Sofía, and the Cardinal Primate Mgr Pla y Daniel officiated. In most places in Spain the year 1964 was marked by a succession of ceremonies: prizes were awarded to the works of art which best illustrated the achievements of the regime after its quarter-century in power. Television programmes were directed to the same end, quantities of books were published by the Ministry of Information, and for a fortnight, from 23 March to 6 April, the press devoted a large number of articles to the anniversary. On 24 May a big military parade took place in Madrid. Franco, in his Captain-General's uniform, clasped the hand of Don Juan Carlos, who figured increasingly as heir-apparent, and then came the march past of the troops, with their improved and increasingly mechanized arms. They were now equipped with quick-firing guns, *cetme* (600 shots a minute), produced by Spanish factories; the Civil Guards and the *Policia Armada*, which also took part in the parade, were also armed with this effective weapon.

Peace, strength, material improvements, liberalization within the limits of the Movement's principles, the development of Spain – such were the themes constantly reiterated between 1964 and 1966. Official texts rewrote the history of the past thirty years and at the same time the censorship allowed the sale, at newspaper kiosks, of a *History of the Spanish War* in a hundred instalments, *no apta para irreconciliables* (not intended for the irreconcilable) which represented an attempt at objectivity and which included a number of photographs illustrating the Republican side.

On 12 November, at the close of the Cabinet meeting held at the Pardo, Manuel Fraga Iribarne announced that the government had decided to grant a generous pardon in cases connected with the Civil War. He even implied that the special courts would be abolished. Following an earlier amnesty (in March 1964), the decree published on 15 November referred to 'total amnesty', and abroad it was assumed that all the exiled leaders and refugees would be able to go home. In Spain itself, two indomitable elderly brothers, one aged 62 and the other 57, who had spent the last twenty-seven years hidden in their farm, emerged to face the Court at Marbella. In Paris, *L'Humanité*'s headlines proclaimed: 'Fresh victory for the Spanish democratic forces,' while the Soviet Union recommended exiles to return to their country. A few days later, enthusiasm waned. This was no amnesty but an *indulto*, a limited pardon applying only to fines and confiscations ... while in virtue of the military code of justice, Republicans were still held guilty of the crime of military rebellion, or assistance to rebellion, and of treason. Military courts were not dissolved. The Ministry of Information had exaggerated the scope of a decree which introduced only a very slight alteration and left the basic legislation quite unaltered. A quarter of a century after its victory, the government still had discretionary power to decide whether a Republican should or should not be prosecuted for his attitude between 1936 and 1939. Exiles might indeed return to Spain, but at their own risk. The government might graciously forbear to prosecute them; but amnesty was denied them. Grimau had died barely three years before, and it was not surprising that Salvador de Madariaga and Llopis showed a certain caution.

Once again the Ministry of Information had displayed its efficiency, and *liberalización* its true limits; the event was a further proof of the regime's capacity to adapt itself to the changed conditions of Spain in 1966.

The time for shouting *Viva la Muerte* had passed, and that of Queipo de Llano's ruthless speeches. The watchword now was *amnesty* – even if it only meant pardon: the slogan was *Twenty-five Years of Peace*. The Ministry of Justice asserted unhesitatingly that no more political prisoners were now in jail on charges connected with the Civil War, and could disregard the statement of a Barcelona lawyer, Martín Fuste Salvatella, based on his own experience, that there were still people held in prison for their activities during the Civil War. The Minister's declaration, backed by the leading newspapers and by television, made far more impact on public opinion than its contradiction by a Catalan lawyer. The authorities had understood the power of the news media, and knew how to make use of them.

It still knew how to attract crowds, proving that, contrary to the hopes of the opposition, Francoism – in addition to its technical achievements – enjoyed a wide measure of support in the country. On 23 June Franco visited Catalonia; he was welcomed enthusiastically in Barcelona, with streamers flying and ships' hooters blowing in the harbour. True, the Abbot coadjutor of Montserrat stayed away so as not to have to receive the Caudillo, who entered the abbey church without a canopy for the first time since his victory. What did that matter? the tour was a spectacular one, and apart from a small hostile minority, nobody in Spain was aware of the incident.

The authorities now knew how to handle public opinion, and it had become part of their political strategy to reckon with it. From 1965 onwards the Ministries of Information and Foreign Affairs and the Caudillo himself reverted to the theme of Gibraltar. A Red Book was published in Madrid towards the end of 1965, which recalled Spanish rights over the Peñon (the Rock), denounced British encroachment on the north side of the Rock (some 900 yards), and stressed the risk to Spain of having the citadel used as an air base (here a wink to Moscow). On 31 December 1965 Franco demanded an end to 'the mutilation of Spain's territorial integrity for the benefit of certain foreign interests'. The press echoed all these arguments, mobilizing Spanish opinion; a land blockade of the Rock was instituted, an appeal made to the United Nations, which took note of the Spanish claim. In this struggle for Gibraltar, cleverly conducted in the diplomatic field and on the home ground, the regime displayed yet again its skill at using the international situation to its own advantage. The Spaniards, mobilized on behalf of Gibraltar, were in fact being called upon to rally round Franco as defender of their country's greatness, of peace and of *hispanidad*.

The Common Market. The Organic Law

Such nationalist enthusiasm was not incompatible with the wish, constantly reiterated by the Spanish rulers, to join the Common Market. The Six, however, delayed their reply to Madrid's official application, first in March 1964 and then, despite favourable arguments from France and Germany (October 1966), a second time in December 1966.

Great disappointment was felt in Madrid, where the technocrats had been gaining ground within the government: on 8 July 1965 a Cabinet reshuffle had promoted López Rodo (hitherto in charge of planning) to ministerial rank, thereby emphasizing the importance attached by Franco to economic co-ordination. The new Minister of Trade, Faustino García Monco, was a former director of the Bank of Bilbao and was only 49 years old; as for the Minister of Finance, Juan José Espinoza San Martín (aged 47) he had hitherto been Vice-President of the Bank of Industrial Credit, and the Minister of Public Works, Federico Silva Muñoz (aged 41) was a professor of political economy at Madrid University. Young, capable, members or close associates of the Opus Dei, concerned with economic development, these new men confirmed the direction followed by Francoist policy since 1957. Ullastres, former Minister of Trade, became Ambassador to the Common Market. At the end of December 1966 López Rodo declared in an interview with *Le Monde*:[17]

'The desire of the Spanish government is to obtain complete or almost complete integration with the Common Market. . . . The majority of Spanish employers are in agreement with the government; they are anxious for the fullest possible integration with Europe, and they would like this to take place by degrees and at suitable intervals. They do not wish to remain outside Europe, not merely for economic reasons but also for historic and cultural reasons.'

This openly proclaimed desire to join the six countries of Western Europe was also one of the causes of the evolution of the political structures of Franco Spain.

For if the problem of the succession, as we have seen, required the establishment of an institutional framework capable of ensuring the continuity of Francoism after Franco's death, it had also become necessary to give Spain the appearance of a democracy, to obliterate unpleasant memories, to provide the regime with that popular approval which would convince the European partnership of its legitimacy. Thus certain objections to Spain's entry into the European community would be dropped. Thirty years after the Alzamiento, the regime had to be normalized.

As early as 1965 the main concern of political circles in Madrid was the reform of the constitution, the establishment of an Organic Law, so as to safeguard the succession. On 20 November 1965 Fraga Iribarne gave an interview to *The Times* which called forth a storm of comments, protests and denials from Monarchist circles, so that it almost seemed as if that Minister, faithful to Francoist tactics, had sought to sow discord by his assertion. 'It is generally admitted today,' he declared, 'that when General Franco's rule comes to an end, Don Juan Carlos (son of the Count of Barcelona) will be King of Spain, and that General Franco's wishes concerning certain temporary changes will be followed. . . .' What commentators forgot to note was Fraga Iribarne's conclusion: 'Whatever happens, the armed forces will continue to stand surety for the situation, and no solution will be possible without their consent.'

[17] *Le Monde*, 26 Dec. 1966.

Arguments went on during the whole of 1966; then it was learnt that the Caudillo had decided to appear in person on 22 November at a special assembly of the Cortes to present the draft of an Organic Law. The Cortes had not the right to amend the text, but had simply to accept it or reject it as a whole. Franco was obviously taking no risks. Then the Spanish people would approve the project by means of a referendum. It was the first time the Caudillo had adopted this procedure; as was soon realized in Madrid, a political operation for internal and external purposes was being surrounded with an air of solemnity. Guesses were made as to the contents of the Law, but the request for silence was obeyed. Nothing leaked out about the meeting of the Council of the Realm, held on Saturday, 19 November. On the 22nd at 10 a.m. members of the *Consejo nacional del Movimiento*, assembled on the Plaza de Marina, learned nothing from their Minister, José Solis. The Caudillo himself was to reveal the text of his Law to the Cortes at five o'clock that afternoon. The assembly room had been redecorated for the occasion. A special armchair had been brought from the royal palace for Franco; a small lamp with a green shade stood on the rostrum, for the Caudillo clung to this old-fashioned form of lighting, whereas the glare of television lights filled the heavily decorated hall. At four-thirty the *Procuradores* arrived, wearing white coats, red sashes and decorations; bishops, army men, diplomats, deputies from Ifni and the Sahara and Guinea in their robes. Finally, flanked by his bodyguard of mounted lancers in spiked helmets, came the Caudillo's old armoured Rolls-Royce, unchanged, the visible sign, as it were, of his will to endure and to maintain. Some three thousand people, crowded behind a massive police guard and watched by sentinels posted on the roof tops, greeted him with applause. The country had been well prepared. *Radio Nacional de España* repeated that the law would be

'a triumph of peace, order, labour and strength for our society, whose ideals have been renovated during the past thirty years. . . . The man who has healed the wounds of war with a father's love and a surgeon's skill, who has faced the international giants resolutely in order to give Spain the rest needed for her convalescence, this man will crown his work with the new Organic Law.'

Of the law itself nothing was known. General Muñoz Grandes, Admiral Carrero Blanco, Solis, Fraga Iribarne, the President of the Cortes Antonio Iturmendi and the Minister of Justice Oriol, had all helped to work it out. What did it say? At home and abroad, people were waiting to know.

The gilt cornices and velvet seats in the hemicycle glittered under the lights. An ovation broke out as the Caudillo, wearing the full dress uniform of a Captain-General, mounted the platform and took his seat on the armchair from the throne room of the royal palace. Then in a low voice he read his speech, quietly, without raising his head, and looking in his rimless glasses every inch the wise old Chairman.

'The National Movement has become the locus where in future the different political opinions of the Spanish people can be expressed. . . . We are strong, we can do without antibiotics and allow ourselves certain daring liberties which at first sight might appear shocking: they give us the temperature of the nation and enable us to unmask the enemies of our internal peace.'

Such liberties were traps, some foreign journalists commented, but the Caudillo went on amid applause from the *Procuradores*: he vaunted 'the merits and the rights of the nation's cadres, consisting of those who have known and endured Red domination and those who have fought in the ranks of the Crusade'. Then Antonio Iturmendi read aloud the draft, which was unanimously accepted.

Now at last the documents in the case were available. In the first place, recognition was granted only to those Spaniards who accepted the principles of the National Movement, the ideals inspiring the crusade. Those who rejected these could play no part in the national life, and all the clandestine political trends existing in Spain in 1966 had to remain illegal. A few alterations were noted: General Franco was no longer National Chief of the F.E.T. and the J.O.N.S. . . . but he was appointed Leader of the *Movimiento* for life; the National Council of the Falange ceased to exist as such, but became a National Council with the functions of an upper chamber; the Cortes were to be more widely representative, with a hundred *Procuradores* elected by heads of households and married women. The Council of the Realm was increased from eleven to fourteen members, there would be a head of the government and a head of the state, but . . . in the meantime the Caudillo renounced none of his prerogatives, since a provisional clause in the new law left the presidency of the government in his hands.

A more immediately important aspect of the changes introduced by the Organic Law was first of all the *de facto* separation of the official *sindicatos* from the secretariat of the *Movimiento*, which aroused some protest within the ranks of the Falange; Solis, however, reassured the old guard – the *Movimiento* would stay. The law also altered Article 6 of the *Fuero de los Españoles*, and this was perhaps the most unexpected reform and the one whose effects were most directly felt: one small phrase, 'The state will assume the protection of religious freedom', replaced that which, since 1945, had specifically stated that only the Roman Catholic religion was tolerated. Now, although Catholicism was still 'the religion of the Spanish state', religious freedom was admitted. The efforts of Castiella and of Ruiz Jiménez, President of *Pax Romana*, who had attended the Vatican Council as a lay observer and was anxious to introduce its attitudes into Spanish life, combined with pressure from the United States, had won this result which made possible a revision of the Concordat.

Amid cheers, the Caudillo left the Cortes; in the cold night of a Madrid November he returned to his black Rolls under the glare of television projectors, while around him horses pranced, Civil Guards saluted, and *Requetés* officers in their red berets scurried about. The journalists were left to comment on the Law. Monarchist newspapers considered that henceforward the Monarchy was the obvious regime for Spain. 'This law,' according to *Vanguardia Española* (Barcelona, 24 November) 'confirms the reality of the Monarchy without any alternative being put forward.' The Falangist reactions were varied. *Arriba* noted that the law 'consecrated the Spanish people as heir and successor to the regime' (24 November). Emilio Romero, editor of the *sindicatos'* journal *Pueblo* and an intelligent political observer, wrote that 'the monarchy has scored some points, the regency has lost some, and the government of the state is no longer a drifting boat but a power that really exists'.

In fact hardly anything had changed. Franco had given up none of his powers and had appointed no successor. As Romero wrote, the law was typical of Franco, bearing his own political stamp, namely prudence and gradualism. The law sketched the outline of an authoritarian monarchy in which, thanks to the Council of the Realm, Franco would still play a part. So long as he lived everything remained ill defined. The law, Romero goes on, 'ought to solve the problem of two realities which for over a century have remained disunited: government and democracy, authority and liberty, these are like two toothed wheels turning in opposite directions, which have got to be engaged'.

The recent process of engagement may have been responsible for the death of such men as the Portuguese ex-General Humberto Delgado who, seeking to enter Portugal from Spain, had been found dead and hastily buried near Bajadoz in April 1965. Had this former leader of the Portuguese National Liberation Front been the victim of rivalries within his own movement or of efficient collaboration between the Spanish and Portuguese police? The problem was never solved. On the same day that the Law was put before the Cortes, five men and one woman appeared before the Court of Public Order in Madrid on charges of illegal propaganda and received sentences of from five to thirteen years' imprisonment. The Conservative *Daily Telegraph* might well comment that Spain was still confined within an authoritarian regime.

However, on 24 November the Caudillo's decree (No. 2930) was published. It announced:

'In order to serve the Spanish people better, and to enable it to give formal expression to its constituent will,

'Considering the transcendent importance of the proposed Organic Law of the State. . . .

'I have decided as follows:

'Article I: the draft of the Organic Law of the State . . . will be submitted to national referendum. . . .'

'Vote Yes for Spain's Progress'. The Referendum of 14 December 1966

The referendum was fixed for Wednesday, 14 December. There was little time for an electoral campaign, but the Ministry of Information's services were prepared. The referendum was to be the work of Fraga Iribarne, who was to display the full scope of the means at his disposal and the efficiency of his methods. Not that everything was in the bag, though; there might be abstentions. At the last municipal elections in November, organized by Alonso Vega, Minister of the Interior, the poll had been as low as 10 or 15 per cent. Such a result would be intolerable in a referendum.

On 24 November Fraga Iribarne launched the electoral campaign; the first words he spoke before the television cameras set the tone. 'To vote Yes means to vote for our Caudillo, to vote No means to follow the orders of Moscow or Prague.' During the same broadcast the head of the Institute of Political Studies added: 'To vote Yes means to vote for 18 July 1936.' Under the circumstances the referendum could only be a plebiscite for Franco; it had to be won.

Fraga Iribarne set off his campaign on a grand scale, with the aid of 2,000 giant posters each 40 feet square, 200,000 stickers and transfers, 250,000 photographs of the Caudillo, 50,000 of them in colour; a succession of television and radio broadcasts; continuous interruption of programmes on cinema and television screens; aeroplanes and helicopters scattering leaflets, and loud-speakers in the streets reiterating *Vote Yes, like El Cordobés*. All this, however merely created an atmosphere, and showed that the regime knew how to use the latest American-style campaigning methods. Fraga Iribarne was well aware that other pressures must be brought to bear on the electorate. Each of the 19,620,877 voters received, at his home, an envelope containing two voting papers, one blank, the other already inscribed by hand *Sí* (Yes), and three propaganda leaflets bearing slogans: 'You are Spain, her progress is your own. Vote Yes for the progress of Spain at the national referendum 1966.'

Faced with this intense and unilateral official propaganda, the opposition groups consulted together. On 29 November it was learnt that on the initiative of the Christian Democratic Union a clandestine meeting, lasting three days, had been held in the neighbourhood of Madrid. These united groups urged the electorate to abstain. At the end of November a document was sent to the head of the state, signed by 107 leading members of the opposition (among them Gil Robles, Dioniso Ridruejo, Tierno Galván, López Salinas and Alfonso Sastre) requesting a postponement of the referendum so as to allow the electorate to be more accurately informed, and also asking for a share of broadcasting time. Naturally, these requests were refused. Then on 2 December six personalities, including Ruiz Jiménez, addressed an open letter to the head of the state. They appealed to Franco to intervene personally to ensure that 'the referendum should not turn into a plebiscite', and that those who chose to vote No, 'which was as legal as Yes', should no longer be described as 'traitors, gangsters, mercenaries in the service of dark forces, emissaries of foreign powers or agents of international communism'.

The Church, meanwhile, declared on 8 December that it respected the legitimate opinions of all Spaniards, and that everyone must 'conscientiously assume responsibility for himself'. Eighty-three clerics in Barcelona added that in view of the one-sided character of the propaganda it was permissible to abstain. Thus, gradually, the atmosphere grew tense. On 6 December 4,000 people assembled in the centre of Madrid, answering the call of the Workers' Commissions, shouting 'Referendum No, democracy Yes'. At Tarrasa 2,000 forgathered with the same object. There were a large number of arrests, and government propaganda was intensified. Raimón's popular song *'Di que no'* (Say no) was banned over the air; hundreds of thousands of leaflets *in Catalan* were distributed in Barcelona: *'La libertat vol pau. La pau vol el teu vot. No l'hi neguis'* (Liberty needs peace. Peace needs your vote. Don't refuse it'). The government pointed out that by virtue of a law of 1908 voting was compulsory and that a note certifying that one had voted would be required by employers and administrations before the payment of wages. Pay would be docked from the wages of employees who had abstained, until the next referendum. 'If you do not vote you may be punishable by law', one leaflet said. 'You may have part of your wages kept back, you may lose your job.' It was also learnt that Spanish workers living abroad were not entitled to vote. While the tide of official propaganda flowed on, various authorities forecast an affirmative vote by all those under their administration, who naturally had not been consulted. Thus the directors of the Social Insurance Department in Barcelona 'anticipated' a *si* from their million contributors.

On the eve of the poll, propaganda redoubled; new leaflets were distributed. One of them declared in Catalan: '*Si dubtes, vota* SI. *La pace es el clima ideal per a poder dubtal tranquil*' (If you are in doubt, vote Yes. Peace is the ideal climate for doubting calmly). Another declared: 'The Pope has promised to pray for the success of the referendum. This is yet another token of the Pope's love for our country and its rulers. Spanish *caballeros*, don't disappoint the Pope. Vote Yes.' On Tuesday the 13th, the Caudillo spoke briefly over television. He stated clearly that the referendum was a favour granted by himself, General Franco, to the Spanish people; that the right he had earned by saving society and the power conferred on him by law entitled him to promulgate the organic law which was to procure such great benefits to the nation. 'But, thinking of the future, I wanted you to assume your share of responsibility by means of this referendum.'

Everything had been said. The voting could begin.

Wednesday, 14 December: workers had been given the morning off to vote. The weather was mild and sunny. The cafés were empty and there were few policemen in the streets. Long queues formed in front of the polling stations. The ballot boxes were made of glass: voting papers marked *Sí*, unfolded and without envelopes, piled up in the transparent containers. There was no violence, no pressure. In Barcelona, at Polling Station 35 in the second district, the acting supervisor was the Captain of the *Guardia Civil*. The opposition had no representatives at the polling stations; legally it did not exist. Papers marked *Sí* accumulated. Sometimes voters exchanged whispered jokes, particularly in the poorer districts. At San Andreu, a traditionally Anarchist and Communist district of Barcelona, the workers asked the Civil Guards which paper they should put in the box. Franco and his wife, who was presented with a bouquet, duly voted and so did Don Juan Carlos and his wife, Sophia of Greece. People on a visit – *transeuntes* – could vote wherever they happened to be; in Madrid, one foreign journalist succeeded in voting five times over in five different polling stations.[18] These transient voters obviously made any check impossible; in some polling stations they constituted 30 per cent of the poll, and in one place, Mostoles, they provided 700 out of the 1,900 Votes. In Málaga and Ciudad-Real, the number of voters was 15 per cent higher than the total number of registered electors.

On the evening of 14 December a sense of triumph, mingled with surprise,

[18] *Le Monde*, 1 February 1967.

prevailed in government circles. They had not dared hope for such a success. Franco and Francoism had won the battle of the referendum: 88·79 per cent of the population had voted; 95·6 per cent had said Yes, 1·81 No, with 2·33 per cent blank or spoiled papers.

Some ministers had feared that the number of abstentions might reach 30 per cent. In fact the number of votes cast was greatly in excess of the number of registered electors. In Bilbao, in Barcelona, in Guipuzcoa, the rate of abstention was higher, but the Caudillo had really won a 'plebiscitary vote', as *Ya* described it. Fraga Iribarne, who had organized the whole thing, commented on the result in a television interview on 15 December: 'Your *Sí*', he said, 'has increased our national credit . . . it constitutes a further attraction for tourists, since it is not only our sunshine but even more our exemplary peaceful and joyful way of life that attracts millions of visitors.' On 27 December, some days earlier than his usual date, the Caudillo spoke to the country: 'I was so anxious to thank you for the truly exemplary nobility with which you have consented to display, freely and wholeheartedly, your support and your trust.'

A Triumph?

It was a triumph. The opposition might denounce the absence of any check over the poll, the fact that there were nearly two million more voters than registered electors, the arrests made, the official propaganda; certain papers (*Vanguardia española* in Barcelona) might claim 14·2 per cent hostile votes, including abstentions and blank papers, yet it could not be denied that the regime had been successful in organizing this electoral triumph and that the opposition had been incapable of preventing it. The regime not only had might on its side, it knew how to use apparently democratic methods. It had kept pace with the times; it had proved itself able to bring a whole country to the polls (whatever the means employed), when it chose and as it chose, and yet, behind the triumph, the problems remained. After the results were announced, the men in power within the system were still at loggerheads as to the line to be followed, and as to Franco's successor; which implies that the Organic Law was merely a vague framework. Moreover, fresh disturbances broke out.

On 20 December 1966, cars driving at top speed scattered throughout the working-class districts of Madrid, Tetuan, Vallecas and Villaverde, leaflets appealing for 'unity in the struggle for an authentic peace to secure our children's future'. Social unrest increased at Bilbao and in Madrid, where 3,000 workers were laid off by the Barreiros company. The Spanish railwaymen of the RENFE were ready to go on strike.

Faced with these difficulties, which the plebiscitary *Sí* had been unable to suppress, the government took severe measures against the indomitable rebels who had rejected 'the great accolade of the whole great Spanish family' (Franco, 27 December 1966).

Leaders of the Workers' Commissions (including Ángel Rosas and Pedro Hernández) were arrested. The writer Miguel Sánchez Mazas was judged *in absentia* for having attacked General Franco in some articles published in

France, and sentenced to eighteen years in prison. The articles had appeared in 1957, nearly ten years previously. The press law, the organic law, the electoral triumph had not modified the meticulous watchfulness of Spanish justice. And 95·1 per cent of ayes did not prevent the arrest, all over Spain, of those who had appealed unsuccessfully for abstention. A ten-year prison sentence was imposed in February 1957 on Alfredo Fernández Antuna, charged with campaigning against the *Si*.

'We can do without antibiotics and allow ourselves certain daring liberties,' the Caudillo had told the Cortes on 22 November. Francoist justice, however, continued as before to use the surgeon's knife.

CHAPTER II

NOTHING IS SETTLED IN SPAIN

THE ANTI-FRANCOIST OFFENSIVE AND RENEWED REPRESSION

1967–1968

'The example we have set the working class of Vizcaya obliges us not to break faith.' Thus began a duplicated leaflet passed round from hand to hand in Basauri, a suburb of Bilbao. It came from the men of the Echevarri works; since 30 November 1966 they had been on strike in protest against a wage reduction resulting from the restriction of government credits. They had occupied the factory, then, on 2 December, had been driven out by Civil Guards armed with tommy-guns. The Echevarri bosses had then imposed a lockout, and laid off the 564 strikers, fifteen ringleaders being permanently dismissed. The workers demanded the reinstatement of the entire staff and claimed jurisdiction over all labour in Bilbao. Ruiz Jiménez spoke for the defence in this trial, which was without parallel in the history of the Franco regime: the strike, he said, was a professional one and therefore legal by virtue of the new Article 22 of the Penal Code. It was a political strike, retorted the Echevarri lawyers. On 30 January 1967 the court pronounced its verdict: the 564 workers could be laid off without compensation, but a leaflet was soon in circulation: 'Our lawyers are proud of us. For them, too, this was a historic trial. . . . The whole working class is being tried.' At Sestao and at Basauri there were demonstrations, followed by clashes with the Civil Guards.[1] That a former minister of Franco's, a president of *Pax Romana*, should defend determined strikers before a Francoist court shows that, despite the referendum, nothing was settled in Spain, and 1967 opened like so many other years with conflict and repression.

The Dark Side of the 'Desarrollo'

The year 1967 was also the end of the first Development Plan, and in January the Planning Commission submitted to the Bank of Spain, the Faculties of Economics and the National Economic Council the main lines of its policy for economic and social expansion for the next four years, 1968–71. Now while Spain's economic development between 1964 and 1967 had been unquestionable, it is also obvious that certain grave, and possibly decisive, weaknesses still

[1] *Nuestra Huelga. Editado por los trabajadores de laminación de bandas Echevarri* (IDES, Paris, 1968).

existed, and that they were responsible for the social tension which, from Viscaya to Catalonia, prevailed during the first months of 1967.

The fact is that since 1964 – and the end of the Stabilization Plan – prices and the cost of living had continued to rise, and inflationist tendencies had worsened, month after month. Between 1959 and 1965 the rise in the cost of living had reached 51 per cent, with an increase of at least 18 per cent during the first ten months of 1965. This went on during the next three years. There was an increase in speculation; in towns, the price of land rose and rents followed suit. Low-cost housing was naturally the first casualty from this trend. At Huelva, a development centre, 40,000 workers' dwellings were needed, but only 3,000 were being built, although the Plan foresaw an increase in the population. Inflation entailed a deficit in the balance of payments (at least $299 million in 1966). Gold reserves diminished steadily, by $976 million at the end of March 1968, and Spain's exports covered only 37 per cent of her imports – the lowest rate in Europe.

This unhealthy aspect of Spain's economic development obviously had its social repercussions: workers struck to obtain the improved wages that the rising cost of living made necessary. Inversely the government sought to check inflation by freezing wages in order to slow down consumption. Hence arose sharp conflicts, intensified by the fact that lowered consumption meant a slowing-down of production and the closing of certain factories. By the end of 1966, firms in Bilbao had done away with overtime; the same thing happened in Catalonia in the middle of 1967; while the blast furnaces of Sagunto asked for authorization to lay off a fifth of their personnel.

On Sunday, 19 November 1967, the Cabinet met in special session; it was decided to devalue the peseta by 16·6 per cent. Public opinion was surprised, but the measure reveals the gravity of the economic and financial situation. García Monco, Minister of Trade, made no secret of it; he declared the government's intention to encourage exports, to attract tourists who would bring in currency, to revalue the money sent into Spain by workers who had emigrated, and also to contend with 'the excessive growth of demand' by means of austerity measures.

It is true, of course, that consumption had increased: Spain produced almost 400,000 motor vehicles per year, and it was reckoned that one out of every twenty-five inhabitants owned a car. The roads to Madrid and Barcelona were crowded on Sunday evenings, and there were traffic jams on the *autopistas*. Statistics showed that in 1968 53 per cent of Spaniards owned their own apartments, 39 per cent had washing machines, 35 per cent refrigerators and 34 per cent television sets. There was a darker side: 23 per cent of urban families and 62 per cent of rural families lacked running water. In many regions of Spain the income per head was not more than $300, and the roots of inflation were to be sought not in consumer habits but in the economic structure of the country.

The agrarian reform had not been realized, and consequently productivity had not increased, because investors avoided a sector so rigidly bound by its own past. Development encouraged concentration into monopolies in many sectors, and particularly in the sphere of banking. The seven leading banks controlled over 70 per cent of the country's resources. Moreover, industrial monopolies and banks were closely interconnected, and they kept their full freedom of action, because the plan was only *indicative*. This monopolistic structure influenced the rise of prices. Moreover, economic development had not taken place in a balanced fashion either technically, geographically or socially. The tertiary sector (that of services) concentrated in urban agglomerations had grown out of all proportion: the parasitic character of many of its functions burdened the country's economic life at a time when the directly productive sector was diminishing. Urban development entailed new expenses, speculation was rife, while the fiscal system and the extremely unequal distribution of income enhanced the negative aspect of the country's economic expansion. Moreover, foreign investment (50 per cent American) now penetrated all sectors, making the Spanish economy dependent on other countries.

The plan now nearing completion had not succeeded in correcting these structural defects. According to certain economists, indeed, there were two realities: that of the Plan and that of the expansion which was taking place 'spontaneously'. Unquestionably, even in the public sector, where the Plan was theoretically imperative, the aims it had set itself had been only partially realized: 87 per cent as regards public investment, 64·1 per cent as regards social welfare.

The second plan, submitted to the Cortes by the Cabinet on 10 October 1968, provided for certain improvements with respect to the first: better co-ordination, a strictly controlled choice of investments. It proposed an increase of 24 per cent of the gross national production, the creation of a million new jobs and an increase in consumption of 19·3 per cent, 46·3 per cent of public investment was to be for social purposes. Nothing was said about the indispensable structural alterations: how to improve the country's low productivity, how to transform agriculture. In other respects, the Plan was still only indicative; but in a country where barely 6 per cent of the national income came from public enterprise, where the public sector provided less than 12 per cent of the gross national production, such an indicative plan could not be put into effect. So in 1967–8 the figures unquestionably reveal the recession that affected Spain's economy; in 1967 the annual increase in the gross national output fell from 11 per cent to 8·6 per cent; the index of industrial production, which had risen between 1962 and 1967 by 11 per cent on an average, was in 1967 only 4·1 per cent; and inflation continued. The plea of certain economists for radical transformations went unheard.

The fact is that political obstacles slowed down or prevented the necessary structural reforms: the government was still closely associated with the land-owning class; it refused to envisage fiscal reform; it rejected any restrictions on the private sector; it based its power both on the backwardness of the under-developed sections of the population and on the new urban bourgeoisie, which benefited by expansion. It is therefore not surprising that despite intense propaganda efforts the first Development Plan failed to convince the Spanish people; 43 per cent of them did not know of its existence, and of the remaining 57 per cent only 9 per cent were aware of its time limits.

A whole part of Spain thus remained outside the Plan, and the Francoist authorities were only to a very limited extent responsible for an economic development which took place largely outside their control and sometimes against their will, since they maintained an anachronistic structure which held expansion in check. Despite these weaknesses, development did take place, social reality was changing; in 1968 the upheaval was visible everywhere. The other Spain was alive, even if it was still burdened by the past and shackled by archaic economic structures.

In 1957 there had been only 1 tractor for every 169 Spanish farmers; by 1967 there was 1 for every 16. In 10 years (1955 to 1965) the number of telephones increased from 34 to 80 per thousand inhabitants; in 10 years (1950 to 1965) the percentage of women in the working population rose from 16 to 25 per cent; while 50 per cent of the Spanish people now lived in towns of more than 20,000 inhabitants.

This new Spain might be a source of strength to the Francoist authorities, whether because they took the credit for its creation, or because they sought support from new social strata, or because they hoped, thanks to increased consumption, to damp down political consciousness still further, if not to win definitive acceptance for the regime. In so far as economic development was held back by their inability to throw off the fetters (agrarian structure, monopolies, etc.) which caused the imbalance in the Spanish economy (inflation, rising prices, etc.), then the new Spain was a source of weakness to the regime; strikes broke out, and the conflict was renewed. Then Francoism had no alternative but to assume fully a role which it had seemed anxious to drop, at any rate superficially, during the period of *liberalización*, the role of a repressive power, threatening, imprisoning, controlling by force those whom it could not assimilate or accept in a freely functioning society.

The economic difficulties of the years 1967–8, which were connected with the general European situation and with the very nature of Francoist power, were thus the cause of a new flare-up of conflict in Spain and of renewed repression. Those who had looked forward to an era of mutual understanding in Spain, those who had assessed the progress made in the legislative field (press laws, modification of the penal code, etc.) or noted hopefully the unofficial talks held between representatives of the regime and members of the Workers' Commissions, or even former supporters of the C.N.T., now witnessed the reappearance, after a referendum which was to have established the normalization of the regime, of all the old violent conflicts, the arrests and trials, and the clash between large minorities against the background of an apolitical Spain.

Opposition on an Unprecedented Scale: Renewed Repression

During 1967 and 1968 the Francoist authorities were confronted with active opposition which despite repression quickly attained an unprecedented scale; its chief centres were factories and universities, the Basque provinces and the churches in which young priests deliberately joined in the activities of workers and students. Never since the Civil War had so many demonstrations been held, so much resolution displayed.

At the end of December 1966 the workers of Standard Electric demonstrated in the streets; the *Policía armada* had to intervene to disperse the compact, silent column of 8,000 metal workers; a few days later the truck drivers came out on strike, and a convoy of 400 trucks paralysed traffic in southern Madrid. They got their way: wages were increased by 25 per cent. At Palomares the inhabitants (and the Duchess of Medina Sidonia) began a march on Madrid in order to get $\$\frac{1}{2}$ million compensation from the United States. In Asturias there were strikes, lay-offs, demonstrations; at Bilbao workers clashed with the *Guardia Civil*. Everywhere in working-class districts the sight of calm, resolute men marching to join in demonstrations became a familiar one. Students, meanwhile, held their free assemblies. During the whole of January 1967 such actions accumulated, showing the scale of the people's discontent.

The Workers' Commissions decided to attempt a major coup. Thousands of leaflets were distributed, announcing a demonstration to be held in Madrid on 27 January, with five assembly points in the city. This was to be the trial of strength: the police made preliminary searches and arrests and threatened ruthless intervention, reinforcements of the Civil Guards were brought into the city and all leave was cancelled. In spite of this, on 27 January 1967, Madrid witnessed the greatest display of working-class protest since the end of the Civil War. There was a general boycott of transport, yet the workers succeeded in assembling at Cuatros Caminos, on the Plaza de Castilla, at Las Ventas and in the neighbourhood of Atocha, shouting '*Libertad*'. Students, barricaded into the faculties of Law and Philosophy, held out against a police siege. Conservative newspapers (*A.B.C., Ya* and *Madrid*, all connected with the Opus Dei) did not condemn the movement, and Calvo Serer wrote in *Madrid* that 'the heroic struggle of the workers' within their class unions had made possible a higher standard of living in Europe. In the Basque provinces, the demonstrations were on a considerable scale. A great many arrests were made, but the Franco regime had suffered a setback and as usual this strengthened the opposition.

In February strikes broke out in the universities of Valencia and Barcelona, and tension mounted when it was learnt that a young student, Rafael Guinarro, had committed suicide by throwing himself out of the window during a police search of his home. Laguna in the Canaries, Zaragoza, Oviedo and Bilbao were all affected by the student movement. The cry of '*Libertad, Libertad*' echoed increasingly in the streets. We hear of strikes and lock-outs, a factory occupied (the Barreiros company), sentences imposed (fines of 50,000 pesetas at Camacho). In Madrid University the police charged with tanker lorries, the students replied by throwing stones and, breaking the siege, succeeded in reaching the city centre with shouts of 'Workers and students for Liberty' (30 January 1967). The repression was intensified: some journalists were batoned, some writers arrested. The police had a new ally: the Casal de Montserrat, headquarters of the Spiritual League of the Virgin of Montserrat, was sacked by a dozen or so vandals apparently belonging to an extreme right-wing group; they attacked the monks, accusing them of having hidden leaflets in favour of workers' demonstrations.

Asturias (where the miners of Langreo and Mieres were on strike), Barcelona (where thirty-three textile works were paralysed), Madrid and Bilbao are regions and cities whose names recur constantly in the story of the workers' struggle; but gradually others appear – Seville, Valencia. In the Basque provinces, incessant activity took different forms: members of the E.T.A. sabotaged the television pylon of Olarizu, up in the mountains, in February 1967, during the retransmission of the football match between Madrid–Real and Milan–Inter. Throughout Spain the police were on a war footing: fifteen Catalan intellectuals were arrested for having tried to organize a 'Homage to Picasso'; searches were made in university faculties; 500 intellectuals signed a letter to Muñoz Grandes requesting the release of Camacho, who had been in Carabanchel jail since 1 March. A march on Carabanchel was organized; helmeted police charged and dispersed the demonstrators. Students from almost all Spain's universities sent delegates to Valencia for the first *National Congress of Democratic Student Unions*: the police intervened (3 February) and arrested a number of people, including an ecclesiastic representing the pontifical University of Salamanca. Lecturers were excluded from their universities, some faculties were threatened with closure, but for the first time the students gave the call for a general boycott of lectures; and those of the Opus Dei university at Navarre decided to join in the movement. Intellectuals petitioned for the dismissal of the Rector of Barcelona, García Valdecasas. It seemed that repression was powerless to break the movement.

In this tense atmosphere, it was learnt that the Communist Party had issued an appeal (April 1967) for 'all opposition forces to meet round a conference table and examine how to solve the Spanish political problem without violence and without civil war'. The aim was clear: the workers' and students' offensive had to be carried to a higher level at a time when signs of dissidence were appearing within the bloc that supported Franco. The authorities took vigorous repressive action: an increasing number of leaders of the Workers' Commissions were thrown into prison; heavy fines were imposed on students. The Penal Code was altered (February to April 1967) so as to restrict still further the freedom of the press. Journalists could be sentenced to six years' imprisonment for 'spreading false news or being disrespectful to institutions', and six to twelve years for 'calumniating, insulting or gravely threatening the Council of the Realm, the Government, the National Council of the *Movimiento*, or the Supreme Court of Justice'. At the same time it was widely rumoured that political detainees were no longer to be allowed conditional liberty. Editors of certain periodicals were suspended; these included *Signo*, the organ of Catholic youth. The government decided to suspend three articles of the *Fuero de los Españoles* in Vizcaya, where a *de facto* state of emergency was thus proclaimed.

All the potential developments promised by the Government's liberalizing policy were thus inhibited, and the few concessions it had granted were annulled. Some members of the Cortes asserted that religious unity was an indispensable factor in political unity, and the draft bill on religious freedom provided for by the Organic Law became merely a set of rules restricting tolerance. Protestants feared that it might even drive their communities underground. In May the government proposed before the Cortes a bill on *Secrets* which specified that everything concerning the head of state, the government, the Cortes, the army and police, etc., was covered by secrecy and to speak of such things meant breaking the law and risking punishment. The Catholic journal *Ya* declared that 'a new iron curtain has fallen over information in Spain, worsening the existing situation'. Protests were ignored: the Franco regime felt threatened, and it took stringent measures.

The Caudillo, moreover, did not forgo his usual propaganda methods. In April he spent six days in Andalusia, opening several new blocks of flats, and attended a Te Deum in Seville cathedral; it was clear, once again, that fighting Spain was not the whole of Spain. A crowd of 100,000 people gave Franco an enthusiastic welcome at the airport. Addressing a large crowd at Seville on 27 April he said: 'If those who speak of a diversity of opinions mean by that a return to political parties, let them know that this will never happen.' Once again, the boundaries were firmly fixed.

The disturbances continued, however. In April, prisoners in Carabanchel jail went on hunger strike. On 11 April students, using French passwords to confuse the police, marched through the streets of Madrid, clamouring for 'justice for workers and students'; in Calle Serrano, they held up the traffic. At El Ferrol, Franco's home town, workers who had been laid off clashed with the police. In Madrid on another occasion, students marched on the rector's residence; their column was stopped by mounted police with jeeps and fire hose. On Friday, 28 April, delegates of the Workers' Commissions were assembled in the Church of John XXIII in Madrid, a vast shed-like building in a shanty town. Standing on the altar, from which the Holy Sacrament had been removed, speakers harangued their comrades: a demonstration was planned for 1 May. As the meeting ended a voice rang out: *Viva Julián Grimau*. A new trial of strength was to be held with the regime.

The demonstrations of 1 May 1967 were impressive: in Asturias, in almost every large town, there were marches and meetings in the streets. Many priests joined the workers and students, and a large number of them were arrested. *But this was not the whole of Spain*: in Madrid itself, Franco attended the traditional gathering of the official *sindicatos*, at which some 100,000 people were present. Yet the success of this ceremony could not conceal that of the banned demonstrations, nor the violence that had followed. At San Sebastian the police had been attacked with stones, and had fired on the crowd; at Valencia, twenty-two people had been arrested and manhandled in their own homes. Here, the police had besieged the churches in which the demonstrators had taken refuge. Thus in spite of repression, in spite of anxious fears that the workers might take advantage of their three days' holiday to drive off into the country, 1 May was duly celebrated. Both sides were profoundly determined. The *Policía armada* had orders to fire; the Catholic sociologist Alfonso Comin was sentenced, in spite of protests (July 1967 to January 1968), while members of the Workers' Commissions, writers (Nestor Luján in August 1967) and painters (Agustín Ibarrola), as well as students, were prosecuted. Fernando Arrabal, accused of 'blasphemy against Spain' in a dedication, was arrested and subjected to a press campaign of vituperation. Juan Aparicio, former Director-General of the press, wrote in *Arriba* that Arrabal ought to be castrated so that he might not have children who denied their fatherland. The violence of this tone and indeed of all these happenings reflects the resurgence of an extremist Spain that many Spaniards had thought gone for ever.

Then came the third trial of strength within the space of a year: the Workers' Commissions decided to organize a national day of protest (27 October) against political repression and the rising cost of living. Arrests were now made daily: Julián Ariza, leader of the Commissions, was imprisoned with 250 other workers' leaders. Father Carlos Giménez de Parga, a worker priest belonging to a well-known family, who drove a taxi in Madrid, was also arrested. Seville, Bilbao, Granada and Málaga were affected because in these cities, too, preparations for 27 October had begun, with partial strikes and the distribution of leaflets. Prison sentences fell thick and fast: four years for having spoken at an illegal meeting, five for writing a letter justifying the right to strike, six for one young torero who had shouted, after a motor accident: 'Spaniards are cuckolds'. On 27 October the police occupied the larger towns; their orders were to put down all demonstrations. Civil Governors had warned workers that any stoppage of work would mean dismissal and the loss of the rights acquired. None the less, meetings were held in Madrid, in Barcelona and Asturias. In the capital, students started off the demonstration on the campus with shouts of *Franco no, Comisiones obreras sí*! Then, in the afternoon, thousands of workers from fifteen important works in the industrial suburbs downed tools and set off marching. The police intervened. They were now equipped with dogs; they fired into the air near Barajas airport in the suburbs of Barcelona, and in the Plaza d'Atocha there were repeated charges by mounted police. Meanwhile there was a general boycott of public transport, and stones were thrown at buses in the suburbs. Repression became fiercer, and affected fresh sectors: the former ambassador to Paris, the Conde de Motrico, a collaborator of Don Juan's, came under suspicion for 'collusion with the Workers' Commissions'; priests were flung into jail; at least 1,500 persons were arrested, and a large number of workers laid off.

After these months of conflict there came a lull on the industrial front, but unrest increased in the universities.

On 4 December 1967, the Caudillo celebrated his 75th birthday. The official press proclaimed his virtues. It was whispered that he had been taken seriously unwell during a hunting party, but the papers said nothing about that. On the contrary, *Hoja de lunes* pointed out that the Caudillo came from a long-lived family; his father had died at 82 and his maternal grandfather at 96. The Generalissimo still worked ten hours a day and was busy writing his memoirs. Several papers pointed out that while a cadet at the Military Academy he had already kept a journal, and when in Africa he had written a number of articles, that after the Civil War, under the pseudonym of Jaime de Andrade, he had prepared the scenario for the film *Raza*, and from 1940 to 1945 he had contributed a great many articles to the Falange journal *Arriba*, under the pseudonym of Hispanus. On 19 November the Caudillo spoke to the Cortes; he had aged noticeably, his voice was weaker and his speech halting; this did not mean that he was out of action or ready to give up the reins of power. 'I have devoted my whole life to the service of Spain and the Spaniards,' he said, adding immediately that he wished to prolong his achievement 'beyond his personal life'. There was much for him to do to ensure the succession.

The students of Madrid kept his 75th birthday in their own fashion: hundreds of them bearing placards inscribed 'Happy birthday, Murderer Franco', demon-strated with shouts of *Libertad*; newspapers were burnt. In Madrid on 7 December the police fired into the air to drive the students back into the univer-sity buildings, while shouts of hostility to Franco rang out everywhere. This was the first time in Spain that anyone had dared insult him personally, in public, braving the police. The demonstrators then broke out into 30-year-old Repub-lican songs, thereby displaying a definitely political intention which went far beyond the demands of the workers.

What is remarkable, however, is the convergence and similarity between the two movements, the workers' and the students'; both were on a national scale, seeking to co-ordinate their demands and the methods and times of their actions, and denouncing the obsolete character of official organizations; the Workers' Commissions and the s.d.e.u. (the Democratic Students' Union) seemed far more representative. What the Francoist government feared was the fusion and spread of the two movements. This was what the opposition sought to bring about. In Madrid, before several thousand students meeting in a 'free assembly', a letter was read aloud from the Socialist professor Tierno Galván, declaring: 'The important thing is the stimulating effect of your conscious actions for all of us who want the university to become a source of knowledge and moral strength in a regenerated Spanish society' (14 December 1967).

The government was once again driven to use harsh measures: twenty-two university leaders were arrested, and this set off fresh strikes. The importance of these is due not only to their political character but also to the fact that the number of students was growing seven times faster than the population, that 35 per cent of law graduates were unemployed, that out of 6,000 qualified veterinary surgeons 85 per cent had found no work in their profession. The solution of students' and workers' problems lay in the country's economic development and the transformation of the outdated structures of Spanish society, but, as we have seen, the question remained whether the Francoist regime was capable of achieving such radical transformations or whether its very nature precluded this: whether the economic archaism which generated these explosive social tensions, and which had originally given rise to Francoism, did not, perhaps, survive thanks to the existence of Francoism. *Could Francoism liquidate certain of the conditions which had brought it into being, and provide itself with other bases before it was too late?* The regime had shown its awareness of this necessity by includ-ing technocrats and 'Europeans' into the government, within the framework of a renovated Francoism. The hazards and difficulties of the operation are shown by the way in which, after certain steps towards liberalization had been taken, the renewal of conflict had been followed by a return to unconcealed repression.

Tension went on mounting during the whole of 1968. In January the govern-ment decided to close down the Centre of Advanced Studies and Research in Sociology. This was the only free institute in which intellectuals from the opposi-tion, high officials and foreign scholars could meet and exchange ideas. It was now no longer possible to study sociology in Spanish universities. More and more arrests were made: in Madrid the police refused to release sixteen students whom the judge of the Public Order Court had ordered to be set free. The strike now spread to most universities. On 21 January the students of Madrid published a *Declaration to the Spanish People* explaining the reasons for their actions.

The government reacted quickly: an increasing number of faculties were closed down. On 28 January, in a note published by the Ministry of National Education, it was stated that 'as from Monday, 29 January, a special squad of the secret police will be at the disposal of the Rector and deans of all departments of Madrid University'. Protests and demonstrations broke out with renewed violence: 'Down with the University Gestapo', the students shouted. In the vicinity of campuses, mounted police charged demonstrators and bludgeoned them ruthlessly. The political consciousness of the activist minority – some 20 per cent – of the student body was further increased; repression encouraged radicalization. Pro-Chinese, Marxist–Leninists and anarchist groups grew up side by side with Christian Democrats and with orthodox Communists, loyal to the line laid down by Carrillo. When Jean-Jacques Servan-Schreiber, editor of *L'Express*, introduced his book *Le défi américain* to a meeting of 4,000 students in Madrid, the hall was in a turmoil; there were shouts of 'Neither Franco nor the C.I.A., neither Franco nor Carrillo. A Socialist Europe' (March 1968).

On 18 May over 10,000 students and workers came together to hear Raimón sing. The recital turned into a political meeting: red flags were brandished for the first time, and portraits of Che Guevara. Five thousand students marched in procession to the centre of Madrid, shouting 'Workers and peasants against the oligarchy', 'popular democracy', 'socialist Spain'; they threw molotov cocktails at the police and stones at Princess Sofía's car, with cries of 'No monarchy', then entered the Calle Princesa in the heart of the city and flung chairs and tables on to the street. Similar incidents occurred day after day – strikes, campus barricades, sit-ins, boycotting of lectures (December 1968), violent affrays, 'free assemblies' and meetings.

On all other fronts the pattern of revolt and repression was repeated. The leaders of Workers' Commissions were condemned; the Asturian miners went on strike (January 1969); some newspapers (such as *El Alcázar*) were suspended, journalists prosecuted; in February the dockers of Las Palmas stopped work, in March 100 workers' leaders were arrested in Madrid; in April Camacho and Ariza were jailed for a year; while San Sebastian was put under martial law on the occasion of the Basque national day, *Aberri Eguna*.

A new national struggle broke out in the spring. On 30 April and on 1 and 2 May 1968 protest meetings organized by the Workers' Commissions entailed a series of skirmishes; in Madrid, the mounted police occupied the district round Atocha station; at Bilbao and in Seville, where traffic was held up for three hours in the city centre, there were many clashes with the police.

In the Basque country there was a notable increase of violence on both sides. In August the chief of the Special Brigade of police of Guipuzcoa was assassinated; a state of emergency was proclaimed throughout the province, while the police launched large-scale operations to break up the E.T.A.: militants, if caught, were liable to the death sentence.

Prisoners themselves demonstrated, with hunger strikes in December in the jails of Madrid and Soria; their womenfolk occupied the churches as a gesture of support. Strikes began again in Asturias. The authorities reacted by increasing the penalties for offences against public order, and reviving a decree of 1960 against terrorism: courts martial were given fresh powers, and a *summarísimo* procedure applied, by which civilian lawyers were forbidden to plead. At the same time a Cabinet meeting was held in the Caudillo's summer residence at Pazo de Meiras, at which it was decided to unfreeze wages. The strikes, however, still went on.

Los Encartelados (the Men with the Posters) and the Weaknesses of the Opposition

Sunday, 20 October 1968: for nine minutes a man walked through the streets of Madrid, duly observing red-light signals and pedestrian crossings; he carried a poster which read: 'In the name of the Spanish people, I respectfully request that free elections be organized to appoint the head of the state.' This was the writer Gonzalo Arias, a militant democrat, whose political novel, based on his own courageous experiences, describes an attempt at non-violent protest under a dictatorial regime.[2] A black limousine drew up beside Arias and policemen hurried him away; a few hours later another '*encartelado*', Professor Félix Villameriel, was arrested in his turn. The crowd looked on.

The actions of these two men were very different from those which during these two decisive years, 1967 and 1968, had daily disturbed the cities of Spain with growing violence and determination and an ever clearer political awareness. The police removed Arias, and the forces of order remained in control of the field; at the end of these two years of turmoil, when the conflict had reached a higher pitch than at any time since the Civil War, it must be admitted that the movement involved only a minority of the Spanish people. They never succeeded in paralysing the country, in involving the whole of Spain; they were still a long way from the *Huelga Nacional*, even though the movement was nation-wide; and a long way below the level needed to secure the overthrow of the Franco regime.

During the three days of conflict organized by the Workers' Commissions (30 April, 1 and 2 May 1968), public order was never seriously disturbed. In the side streets near the Gran Vía, strollers looked on while the police pursued some young men, and that was all. It was not a defeat, since thousands of men demonstrated in a score of places, but it was only a half-success. It was thus a half-success for the government too.

The truth is that the majority of the Spanish people turned their backs on political action, and this includes the majority of the proletariat. They were oppressed by unemployment (700,000 out of work in 1968) and knew that in a few weeks the price of meat had risen from 130 to 160 pesetas a kilo, that third-class railway fares had been abolished, which added further to the cost of living. They owed money, they were afraid of losing their jobs. Overtime had been cut down and officials had lost their bonuses. This did not necessarily lead to political consciousness, and the great mass of Spain's thirty-two millions remained unpolitical.

[2] Gonzalo Arias, *L'Homme à la pancarte* (Paris, 1968).

The middle and lower-middle classes were favourable, if not to the regime, at any rate to the maintenance of law and order. The strikes, the stone-throwing, the shots fired by the Civil Guards, the violent incidents in the Basque provinces and the red flags in lecture-halls revived their anxiety: they were haunted by memories of civil war and by the dread of its revival, while the birth of small revolutionary parties preaching armed conflict and guerrilla warfare fostered this latent fear, which in the long run was favourable to Francoism.

Less than ever, now, could the leaders of centre and left-wing opposition groups – moderate conservatives, liberals, Christian Democrats or socialists – have any real effect on the country's evolution. They might, like Ruiz Jiménez, defend strikers, speak to students (Tierno Galván, Dioniso Ridruejo), write articles (Gil Robles), but they had no power to influence decisions, and no followers; their voices, preaching clear-sightedness, common sense, provisional solutions, could be heard only by gracious permission of the regime. What such men, Ruiz Jiménez first and foremost, hoped for was that the government would recognize an opposition party; but the very circumstances under which the referendum and the subsequent repression took place had put an end to their hopes.

In short, the spectacular and unprecedented surge of the workers' and students' protest had called in question the policy of 'liberalization', and revealed, once more, its basic nature: it existed only in so far as the regime was not threatened, and it applied only to those who accepted the principles of Francoism. As soon as the regime was faced with opposition on a broad scale it cancelled all concessions, even superficial ones. This very fact intensified the resistance to Francoism of certain sectors. The non-violence preached by *los encartelados* was not a spontaneous answer to repression and political obstructiveness. In the Basque country some members of the E.T.A. declared: 'Here the revolution has begun, we shall be Europe's Cuba.' In Catalonia, Communists belonging to the P.S.U.C., hostile to the peaceful policy of Santiago Carrillo, decided (May 1967) to publish a Spanish edition of *Mundo Obrero* upholding a hard line whose aim was to prepare for a popular rising. Students' actions became increasingly violent, and naturally the emergence in several European countries of a new extreme left whose contours were ill defined and whose ideology was imprecise, but which was evidently in quest of a revolutionary type of action, could not fail to have repercussions in Spain. As for the Communists, they proposed and prepared for unifying actions in view of a *Huelga Nacional Pacífica*, whereas the other groups of the opposition – which apart from the Christian Democrats, were weak – withheld support from this programme, and meanwhile, to the left of the Communist Party, the new extremist groups arose.

The Contradictions of Francoism

Thus, at the end of two years of unprecedented struggle by Spanish workers and students, there was still no prospect of political success. From this point of view, there had been no radical change in the situation.

However, the mounting wave of strikes and demonstrations had forced the

Franco regime to drop its liberalizing policy; in order to succeed in its new line it had to break those elements which it had failed to integrate. These were only minorities, it is true, but economic development had brought into being new wage-earning classes on an ever-increasing scale, while the improvement in education had made culture more widely available to the young; the working class was growing and becoming organized, and as the population increased, the younger generation became more numerous. So that the Franco regime, while its policy involved harsh repression, had at the same time to pursue efforts at integration and seek to satisfy certain of the people's demands. Economic development and an increase in individual incomes were, in this sense, political imperatives. By the end of 1968, indeed, the adoption of the second Development Plan, and the part played in the government by López Rodo, clearly reveal the authorities' awareness of the need to speed up economic change. Was this possible under the Franco regime? Could it be achieved unless Spain were successful in her attempts to join the Common Market, which so far were still at the stage of talks?

Moreover, the economic development which had become a necessity produced in its turn a new type of society, and prosperity and full employment, although they created difficulties, did produce an atmosphere unfavourable to militancy. While in this sense a static policy was advantageous to Francoism, it was also dangerous, because at the point Spain had now reached, continuous development was essential on economic grounds. In short, the situation was fraught with contradictions for the Franco regime; *it was too late* to hold up the evolution of things completely and safely, but that evolution entailed potential dangers, implying a liberalization which the regime was not prepared to accept in view of the risk of things getting out of control.

The Problem of the Succession

The margin for manoeuvring was thus a narrow one, particularly since the Caudillo, who was still ruler of the regime, celebrated his 76th birthday on 4 December 1968. It was thus more than ever necessary for the Francoist team, which wished to remain in power, to prepare for his successor.

Now the organic law had settled nothing. On his 30th birthday, 5 January 1968, Don Juan Carlos had attained his constitutional majority. The Caudillo could now nominate him as future King of Spain. This tall, innocently smiling young man, who had been educated in the state's military academies, lived at the Zarzuela Palace and attended every official ceremony, seemed the ideal candidate for a Francoism without Franco, run by army men and such technocratic ministers as Fraga Iribarne, but his father Don Juan, Count of Barcelona, was still the official claimant, and from his residence at Estoril he kept an eye on Madrid, where his political secretariat was increasingly active under the leadership of the Count of Motrico. The Count of Barcelona was held to be a liberal, and he had always maintained contact, through intermediaries and without giving open approval, with opposition circles, even since the world war. Now he was in touch with men like Ruiz Jiménez and Tierno Galván, and to many in the opposition he seemed the man to bring about a transition, after the Caudillo's death, from Francoism to a democratic regime, without arousing the hostility of the army, since public order would be preserved.

Between father and son, under the mask of complete agreement, there existed a secret rivalry fostered by Francoist circles, which grew and finally came to light in 1968 on the day when Don Juan Carlos could lay claim to the throne of Spain.

On 30 January his third child and first son was born, and Queen Victoria Eugenia, widow of Alfonso XIII, returned to Spain for her great-grandson's christening, after thirty-seven years in exile. Her visit was boycotted by television and radio (controlled by Fraga Iribarne), but 10,000 gathered at the airport of Barajas to greet the last Spanish Queen. High-ranking officers, in uniform, and five ministers (including Castiella) were present. When the Queen appeared, on the arm of her son, the Count of Barcelona, cries of *Viva el rey* rang out; Don Juan Carlos was forgotten, lost in the crowd. In Madrid, all and sundry sought audience from Don Juan; ninety-four generals and army officers, political leaders and moderate oppositionists all paid tribute to the Pretender whom they had ignored two years previously. Franco himself attended the christening and entertained Don Juan on two occasions.

In Falangist circles and among the Carlists, supporters of the French Prince Xavier of Bourbon-Parma, as well as those (nicknamed Franco's Monarchists) who favoured Don Juan Carlos, disappointment and anger prevailed. They counter-attacked, and Franco was not the sort of man to forget the letters written to him by Don Juan after the war, inviting him to give up his office.

While the campaign in favour of Don Juan spread, and the famous writer José María Gironella published a small apologia, *Conversaciones con don Juan de Borbón* (which was soon out of print), it was learnt that the Franco government had banned all the ceremonies arranged for Monday, 24 June, St John's Day, in honour of Don Juan. The meaning of his measure was clear: the Caudillo and his supporters hoped to prevent Don Juan from appealing to a wider audience. In their eyes, the Count of Barcelona could not possibly become Franco's successor. So they openly encouraged Don Juan Carlos. He was at the Caudillo's side during the naval week which took place at Santander in July 1968; and a decree issued on 12 July proclaimed that in all official ceremonies, the heir to the throne was second only to the head of the state. Although no heir had been formally appointed, it was Don Juan Carlos who appeared on every rostrum beside the Generalissimo.

Another significant fact: on Friday, 20 December, at Zaragoza, police officers called at 8 a.m. on the Carlist pretender, Carlos-Hugo of Bourbon-Parma, informing him that he must leave Spanish territory. They escorted him to the frontier, and all observers noticed that the decision had been taken not at any Cabinet meeting but by the Caudillo himself. Franco thus eliminated the house of Bourbon-Parma from the line of succession to the throne. Its members had been useful for a time as a means of bringing pressure to bear on Don Juan, notably in order to persuade him to abdicate in favour of Juan Carlos. Prince Carlos-Hugo had addressed his supporters, standing on a chair: 'Our government speaks sword in hand. Such an attitude engenders irritation, fear and silence.' Franco had not forgiven him, and a meeting of Young Carlists at Pampeluna was broken up by the police. On 26 December it was the turn of Prince Xavier, Carlos-Hugo's father, to be expelled: 'We shall all continue to fight . . . for our regional liberties, our trade union rights and our freedom of political association,' he declared on arriving at Orly airport. In fact the services rendered by the 100,000 Carlists who had fought loyally for the Francoist cause during the Civil War were forgotten, and their candidates were definitively eliminated.

There remained Don Juan and his son. Would Franco go one step further and nominate Don Juan Carlos as his successor? That prince, promoted Captain on 1 January 1969, now broke openly with his father: in a statement to the E.F.E. press agency he asserted that to think in terms of a mere right was anachronistic and not realistic. This meant that he rejected the thesis of a *restoration* of the monarchy, after Franco: it would have to be *set up anew*, according to the institutional rules of the Franco regime. The king would be appointed by the head of state during his lifetime, or by the Council of the Realm in case of his death, and in either case the Cortes must ratify the appointment by a two-thirds majority. The Count of Barcelona protested indignantly in letters to José-María Pemán, head of his Privy Council, and to each of its ninety members (end of January 1969). He asserted the legitimacy of his claim; the councillors were loyal to him, but for how much longer? A reading of such monarchist papers as *A.B.C.* suggests that they would be ready to rally to Don Juan Carlos if the latter were chosen by Franco to reign over a Spain which had so few Monarchists. Would Franco nominate his heir before his death, or leave the Council of the Realm to decide, and would the latter and the Cortes (which included many Falangists) be willing to give themselves a sovereign, however docile?

The question was still unanswered at the beginning of 1969. And yet there was every indication that it would not remain so much longer.

A King of Straw and an Iron Chancellor?

Indeed, everything suggested that for years the Caudillo had been patiently and methodically preparing his succession, and the accession to the throne of Spain of Don Juan Carlos.

On 28 July 1967, a little phrase published in the official state bulletin had the effect of a bomb. It said that by virtue of certain juridical provisions the Caudillo 'thanked Captain-General Muñoz Grandes for services rendered', having decided 'that he would cease to exercise the function of Vice-President of the Government'. The former Chief of the Blue Division, who had been thought of as heir-apparent to the Caudillo, thus learnt through the press that he had been dismissed, and as a crowning irony, he, who had held the highest offices, was granted a minor decoration, the Order of the Yoke and Arrows.

Muñoz Grandes had undoubtedly been loyal to the Caudillo, but he was also hostile to the technocrats' policy and to a restoration of the monarchy, and moreover was closely associated with Solis Ruiz and the Falange. In a word, this old warrior from the Eastern front with his Iron Cross represented an outmoded

Francoism, that of the Second World War, and he might impede the manoeuvres necessary for the change-over. On 20 September 1967, the Caudillo appointed in his place Admiral Luis Carrero Blanco. This faithful companion of Franco's, his *éminence grise* who for years, it was said, had written his speeches, and who as Minister Secretary to the Presidency had lived in close association with him, now emerged from out of the shadows. Wearing white full-dress uniform, he took the oath, kneeling before the Caudillo with his hand laid on the Scriptures. In case of the power being in abeyance through the sickness or death of the Caudillo, he would assume the leadership.

Now this man who, for almost thirty years, had been working by Franco's side was connected with the Opus Dei. An unconditional supporter of the Caudillo's, he shared the latter's preoccupations, and apparently favoured the nomination of Juan Carlos as the best way of prolonging the power of the Francoist team after the Caudillo had gone. His scheme for securing a majority in the Cortes for Juan Carlos meant coming to terms with Solis Ruiz, who controlled almost half the *Procuradores*.

Thus the different trends within the regime, despite their rivalries, were all preparing for what should come after Franco. According to rumours current in Madrid, Carrero Blanco and many young technocratic ministers – the new-style Francoists – were in favour of a monarchy ruled by 'a king of straw and an iron chancellor'.

The various tendencies of Francoism were already represented in the National Council, whose members were appointed for life; in November 1968 the Council gave approval to a draft regulation for the *Movimiento* which perpetuated and strengthened the political monopoly of the bureaucracy which had originated with the Falange. Provincial Councils of the *Movimiento*, presided over by the Civil Governor of each region, would provide the framework for the whole political life of the country, and associations other than those of the Falange could play there only a subsidiary role: they must be authorized by the councils and would be allowed only eight representatives for fifty members.

Thus institutions and men were lined up ready for the day when the man who since 1936 had presented himself as Spain's guide should disappear from the scene. The authorities displayed confidence in the conditions of the succession, whether or not the Caudillo should appoint king or regent during his lifetime. While the opposition was so divided, its political leaders so few and its strategies so diverse, and while the government's repressive powers and control of the information media were so efficient, any risk of disturbances profound enough to threaten the structure of the Francoist regime could be set aside.

Yet, in contrast with this self-confidence, there were divisions between Francoist groups which could not always be solved by compromise, there was the growing pressure from workers and intellectuals, from that other indomitable Spain, and there was the inevitable element of uncertainty due in a large measure to the frenzied ambitions which sometimes blind men greedy for power. The death of Franco might inaugurate a dynamic period. Assessing all these factors which, seen during a moment's lull, assume the shape of a historic situation,

José Luis Aranguren writes in *Cuadernos para el Diálogo*: 'Everything is unforeseeable. One might say: *"Spain, or the story of insecurity"*.'[3]

Six Weeks of Continuous Fire

In point of fact Francoist circles were not as anxious as this Catholic professor. All of them, of whatever tendency, put their trust in the last resort in the Spanish army. The Communist Party, during the last few years, had sought in its appeals to drive a wedge between the generals, political figures deeply involved with Francoism, and professional soldiers and ordinary servicemen, belonging to the people. General Alfonso Vega, Minister of the Interior, Admiral Carrero Blanco, Fraga Iribarne and of course the Caudillo himself considered that the army would guarantee a peaceful handing-over of power within the order and framework of Francoism, even without Franco.

Protected by the army, the different trends of Francoism could find a compromise solution amongst themselves. If they should not succeed, the army would still be the last resort, since the Organic Law provided in Article 38 for the constitution of a Defence Junta which would comprise the ministers of service departments, the heads of the three forces and the head of the government. The latter, under these circumstances, would have little difficulty in imposing a political solution.

Thus, thirty years after the Civil War, the army was still, as it had so often been, the *Commendatore*'s statue of Spanish history.

Yet that army had changed.[4] Officers were no longer a privileged class: 80 per cent of them had civilian jobs outside their military careers, for pay was low and promotion slow in a country at peace. Technical developments had turned them into administrators or engineers; the army now was just a profession like any other, a way up the social ladder. If 70 per cent of soldiers were soldiers' sons, the great majority were sons of N.C.Os.; compared with 1950, the army had become democratic. Similarly, out of 20,000 officers only 150 had been in the Civil War, 3,500 were ex-cadets and the rest had been at military academies. The Spanish army had changed since the time of the Civil War, and had gradually turned away from active politics, concerned now with specifically military tasks.

It is true that only a few *azules* generals, former members of the Falangist Blueshirts, were directly connected with any particular faction within the regime, but the bulk of the army had a due respect for order and the hierarchy. Trained under Franco's authoritarian regime, it remained hostile to any activity which seemed as futile, and sometimes offensive to the country's honour, as was the challenge offered by the opposition. Now this opposition, because of the very nature of Francoism and its renewed repression, could only be a disturbing factor: strikes, street riots, student violence, red-flag-waving. What Spanish officer could fail to feel anxiety, confronted with such happenings, and how

[3] cf. Niedergang, 'L'Espagne ou la tentation des extrêmes', in *Le Monde*. 15–20 March 1968. Author's italics.

[4] Julio Busquets Bragulat, *El militar de carrera en España* (Barcelona, 1967).

could he not feel close to a power which embodied Spain's hierarchy and her traditions, but which at the same time proclaimed its *technocratic* character?

Now the technocratic viewpoint had gradually prevailed among middle-ranking army officers – the captains, majors and colonels – because, through contact with new weapons and with the American army, they had acquired an appreciation for efficiency and an awareness of the need for development, *but within a framework of order*. This was precisely the official programme of renovated Francoism: order, development, and the upholding of the nation's military values.

It is possible to envisage a situation in which, during a prolonged political crisis, one army clique, backed by a Francoist clique, might intervene directly, imposing its solution on another army clique: Republican versus Monarchist officers for instance, or colonels versus generals, taking advantage of Franco's death to act. In any case, this would be a solution *within* the regime, and the liberal opposition would not make itself heard.

In any case, the hypothesis is an unlikely one. For years now the Francoist regime had taken care not to involve the army directly in the country's affairs. It was on call in time of strikes, as a final resource, a sinister bogy with which Franco and Fraga Iribarne repeatedly threatened the country in their speeches. In fact it was their last reserve.

Year after year, day after day, when strikes broke out or students demonstrated, the various forces responsible for maintaining order were further strengthened: *Policia armada*, mounted police, units equipped with jeeps and with ever heavier weapons, increasingly adapted to repression. Although the army itself was not involved, these militarized forces had shown themselves effective and sufficient. Moreover, it must be repeated, the whole of Spain was not affected by unrest, but only an active, politically conscious minority of workers and students, who since the new wave of repression had not even had the opportunity to go out into the streets to demonstrate. Detectives from the politico-social brigade carried out preventive arrests, and courts martial pronounced summary judgements. When a demonstration was anticipated, the police were almost as numerous as the demonstrators, who sometimes lost heart as they were reduced to walking up and down amongst the crowds without daring to regroup themselves or even shout *Libertad*. Isolated groups of young men might fling a few stones or trip up an officer, but they paid dearly for it and the regime was none the worse off.

Out of Madrid's 3 million inhabitants, how many demonstrated? Out of Spain's 32 million, how many were prepared to take the risk of collective action in the interests of their trade union, or for a political aim? The country on the whole remained silent, and it was generally the same regions, the same towns, the same militants that took part in the struggle and paid the penalty.

Realizing these facts, the Francoist leaders hoped to survive Franco; during thirty years, they had organized power so as to keep it. The youngest of them had scarcely known the Civil War, but the bloody memories of it, which they revived from time to time, served to further their intentions.

They considered on the whole that the problem of the succession was something to be settled *between themselves*. The rest of Spain would have to accept their choice. Perhaps existing institutions would serve to put across whatever compromise they reached amongst themselves, probably the forces of order might have to intervene to break up demonstrations, possibly the army – or part of it – might be called in to decide between rival factions. In any case they, or a section of them, would still control Spain. They considered that they had the means to forestall, stifle, dominate or crush any attempt by the other Spain to influence the decisions that concerned its future.

They knew they had indomitable enemies, that young priests and prisoners on hunger-strike, the miners of Asturias, the metal workers of Madrid, the students of Barcelona, the Basque nationalists would never be convinced and that it would be hard to break them.

They knew too that the *Guardia Civil* was a force of 80,000 men, in a permanent state of mobilization, and that these men, who marched slowly and mechanically past to the sound of drums and castanets, had enough munitions to fire unremittingly for a month and a half.

Thirty years after the Civil War, the Spanish people knew this too.

CHAPTER III

AN OPEN QUESTION

FROM FRANCO TO JUAN CARLOS

1936–1969

1939–1969. Thirty years of Franco's rule. On 21 July 1969 Fraga Iribarne declared, at the close of the Cabinet meeting at which Franco announced that he was about to nominate Juan Carlos as his successor: 'In one and the same year we shall have buried for ever the memory of our old divisions, put a full stop to our last civil war and, now, blazed the trail to a future full of certainty and hope.'

Thirty years: other men, a new Spain, and yet the interaction between past and present was still keenly felt.

January 1936: Franco's troops launched their assault on Barcelona.

January 1969: on the 17th 1,000 students gathered in the great amphitheatre of the University of Barcelona to discuss the attitude they should adopt towards the new liberal rector, Albadalejo. A group of extremists marched on the Rector's residence, broke furniture, flung a bust of Franco into the street and burned the crimson and gold flag of the Spanish monarchy. On the 18th some fifty students stopped the official car taking Vice-Admiral Antonio González Aller past the University City in Madrid and insulted him.

January 1936: Catalan refugees fled in bitter weather towards the French frontier.

January 1969: On the 20th, following a demand from the lawyers of Madrid for an alteration of the Penal Code, those of Barcelona requested the promulgation of a statute for political prisoners. In the capital, the student Enrique Ruano Casanova committed suicide by throwing himself out of a seventh-floor window after forty-eight hours in the hands of the police. Fifteen hundred leading personalities, including many priests, addressed a petition to the government denouncing police brutality. Thousands of students demonstrated in Madrid.

24 January 1969: The Madrid government, 'in order to combat the systematic efforts of a minority to disturb the peace of Spain . . . and to plunge its youth into an orgy of nihilism and anarchy' (Fraga Iribarne), decreed for the first time since the end of the Civil War a state of emergency throughout the country. The guarantees granted by the *Fuero de los Españoles* were suspended. Then the series of strikes, arrests, petitions, sentences and protests was accelerated:

young workers and students distributing leaflets were prosecuted. The repression, ruthless and widespread, affected Christian Democrats (such as Comín), left-wing students, Basques, Communists and members of the Workers' Commissions. It was even thought at one point that Ruiz Jiménez might be arrested. The press proclaimed that the Caudillo had 'an iron constitution' and Fraga Iribarne announced that 'General Franco is in better health than ever and has no intention of retiring next April'. The decisive pressure for the proclamation of a state of emergency must have come from military men.

26 January 1939: Barcelona capitulated and Franco's troops entered the city.

26 January 1969: General Alfonso Pérez Vineta, former secretary of Falangist Youth, Captain-General of Catalonia, organized an impressive ceremony in the Plaza de l'Universitad to redress the insult paid on the 17th to the Caudillo and the Spanish flag. The Rector himself hoisted the flag in front of a crowd of officials present by order, soldiers in mufti also present by order, and all the supporters of Francoism that the town could muster. Part of the audience gave the Fascist salute.

January 1939: After the fall of Barcelona, Franco's victory was only a matter of weeks.

January 1969: From all parts of Spain ex-servicemen from the Civil War, the *Alfereces provisionales* and the *División azul* sent laudatory messages to the Caudillo. 'The army and the people must unite against injustice and tyranny,' asserted the Communist Party. 'The state of emergency is the gravest mistake the regime has made in the past thirty years,' declared Tierco Galván. Hundreds of persons – intellectuals, students, priests, union officials – were seized and placed under house arrest in Southern villages.

25 March 1969: End of the state of emergency. Arrests still went on.

Thirty years after the Civil War, fear and anxiety and violence still prevailed, if not for the entire Spanish people at any rate for a large section of them. 'We are ready to defend our country by *all legal means* and for as long as is necessary,' Fraga Iribarne had said. The warning was clear: the state of emergency was the proof that the men who had linked their destinies with Francoism were determined to preserve their power 'by all legal means'. It must be remembered that they made the laws themselves. Thus thirty years after the Civil War – and whether or not they had fought in those battles matters little – they were equally resolute, equally convinced that what they thought and chose must be the right road for Spain, for the whole of Spain. In July 1936 they had imposed their policy by force of arms. It had taken them three years of bloodshed to triumph, but they had won, and they had punished. Thirty years later they gave proof of the same determination. This iron will, this ruthlessness about the methods used constituted the basic unity of those thirty years of Francoism. The people of Spain had to accept, and follow, or yield, or disappear. Or keep silence.

Their decision was supreme. 'Normalization', a term which Fraga Iribarne preferred to 'liberalization', had been only partly initiated, thirty years after the Civil War. 'The state of emergency will not arrest this process,' the Minister of Information declared, 'it will merely constitute a warning and a slight pause.'

The Caudillo, in his opening speech to the Cortes on 17 November 1967, defined the direction of his country's policy for the years to come.

'In thirty years', he said, 'the face of Spanish society has changed considerably. The task before us is a heavy one: for long years our country will need to be governed with infinite prudence, and also with understanding and love. Above all, it will be necessary to avoid the luxury of light-hearted and impulsive improvisation, of freedom to turn against oneself and break up into mutually hostile factions. Your health, so newly restored, would not resist such an ordeal.'

Order, Authority, Acceptance

On the twentieth anniversary of his victory, the Caudillo had inaugurated the memorial of the *Valley of the Fallen*, where those who had fallen in the Civil War were brought together. On the thirtieth anniversary, a state of emergency prevailed, and the Cabinet had even, at one point, considered proclaiming a *state of war* which would justify the replacement of civilian by military governors.

Thus, from one anniversary to the next, the Civil War, of which the Caudillo was still the embodiment, was painfully revived. For even if the war had ended long since, if new generations had sprung up all over Spain, the root of violence was still deeply implanted in the country's soil. It survived because the very principles of the *Movimiento* and the organic law precluded the possibility of power changing hands. The most that the regime would tolerate was, as the Caudillo said on 17 November 1967, 'a criticism of the administration, a change of personnel' among those in power: Admiral Carrero Blanco instead of General Muñoz Grandes.

Methodically Franco and his advisers (Carrero Blanco, López Rodo, General Juan Castañón) applied their plan for prolonging Francoism when Franco should be no more. On 22 July 1969, the Cortes met for the official nomination of the Caudillo's successor. A scarlet 'E' adorned the facade of the building where the 519 *Procuradores* welcomed the Caudillo with enthusiastic applause.

Franco spoke in a voice choked with sobs, the voice of an old man who could scarcely restrain his emotion but whose mind was still clear. 'Conscious of my responsibility before God and before History,' he said, 'and having weighed with due objectivity the qualities united in the person of Prince Juan Carlos de Borbón, I have decided to propose him to the nation as my successor.'

So there was to be no surprise: the new Francoists of the Caudillo's entourage had prevailed over the rival factions (old Falangists, partisans of Don Juan, Carlists). Would this successor in fact be able to reign? They were sure of it, and we have seen why.

'When, by the laws of nature,' Franco went on, 'I shall no longer be able to steer the ship of state, which must inexorably happen, the decision we are to take today will prove to have been a wise one.' Indubitably the monarchy which the Caudillo willed into existence that day was a Francoist monarchy, a new institution rather than a restoration, which would satisfy those supporters of the regime who wished to prolong its existence beyond the Caudillo's death. Franco went on to emphasize that this new monarchy, set up with the approval of the nation, owed nothing to the past; that it was born on 18 July 1936, 'a transcendental fact admitting neither pacts nor conditions'.

Eleven times over, the *Procuradores* applauded. Then they gave approval to Franco's choice by 491 votes to 19, with 9 abstentions.

Madrid and Spain seemed little concerned, that day, by the decisions taken on their behalf by this group of men in uniform or in formal dress. Apollo XI, carrying astronauts who had walked on the moon, was making its way back to earth; but this fact, which measures the distance travelled by mankind between July 1936 and July 1969, did not disturb the man who, born before the beginning of the century, had remained faithful to himself, to his ideas and his beliefs. As for the decision for which he had just won approval, he was well aware that his authority and that of the men associated with him could find the means to enforce it: means which had originated with the Civil War of 1936, strengthened by an authoritarian government and used without hesitation.

Franco had thus chosen for Spain's Francoist king Don Juan Carlos, born in 1938 in Fascist Rome and coeval with the regime.

Thirty years of power, innumerable external events, profound scientific, social and economic developments had taken place, while the same calm, impassive man endeavoured amid a changing world, despite the weight of his years, to decide his country's fate.

Francoist Spain from this point of view seems an exceptional state, surviving, prolonging itself in the midst of difficulties and yet stable, perhaps simply because thirty years earlier hundreds of thousands of men had died, and so deep a wound, such long-drawn-out bloodshed had left its mark on every Spaniard.

This period of peace, constructed on a charnel-house, enabled the Francoist regime to endure, and Spain to change its aspect, perhaps even to skip a stage, passing from economic and social backwardness to the threshold of a society – to which it did not yet fully belong – in which power is wielded not by guns but by other means. As López Rodo said when proposing the second Development Plan in February 1969: 'The plan is eminently social. Its aim is not to create a richer state with poor citizens but a society of free men, bound together not in aggressive opposition but in order, not in constraint but in well-being.'

Had not one of the future king's advisers written a book entitled *The Twilight of Ideologies*? The objective of the neo-Francoists who supported Juan Carlos was a state which would not need to crush its opponents because the whole social structure would have rendered them powerless.

Francoism would thus have enabled Spain to pass, thanks to its costly victory in 1939, from a society pregnant with social revolution (of the October 1917 type) to a society of order and well-being, skipping the stage of democratic freedom and a liberal parliamentary regime.

This social pattern, planned by the neo-Francoists, would make Spain not the exception but the rule, since parliamentary regimes everywhere seemed shaky or distorted; and yet the transition has by no means been achieved. There are threats of retrogression. Spain is not Sweden or Denmark. New problems arise:

that economic development must be achieved which is, for the neo-Francoist regime, what the enlightenment was for eighteenth-century despots.

The truth is that under enlightened despots nations are not called upon to choose the path they are forced to follow. The same is true of Francoist Spain. 'When a country is going through difficult stages in its economic and social development,' Franco said on 17 November 1969, 'it would be suicidal to waste its best men on dialectical argument instead of using them as planners and efficient executives.'

The efficient execution of plans drawn up by a minority in power is the fate in store, perhaps, for most men of our time, and undoubtedly for Spaniards under the rule of Franco or his successor Juan Carlos, should the latter come to power. The exceptional measures taken, the state of emergency, show clearly by what means the regime is prepared to uphold its decisions against those who question them. Henceforward, taking into account the relation between forces which we have repeatedly analysed in the course of this study, and unless there should arise a profound political and social crisis, an upheaval affecting all the great European countries, the fate of Spain, Francoist and post-Francoist Spain, will be confined within the narrow limits we have sketched.

Here history overflows from the present on to the future, which is never merely a prolongation of past or present data but also a new creation, marked by the will and intelligence of men resolutely determined to construct, and to invent, their own epoch.

Paris–Madrid–Nice
1966–August 1969

ABBREVIATIONS

(An approximate English translation has been given of the names of the different groups.)

A.S.O.   *Alianza Sindical Obrera de España,* Syndical Alliance of Spanish Workers: an association of workers of socialist tendency, often Catholic, mistrustful of communism.

A.S.U.   *Agrupación Socialista Universitaria,* University Socialist Association: formed in 1957–8 by young Socialists anxious to go further than the traditional parties and organizations.

C.E.D.A.   *Confederación Española de Derechas Autónomas,* National Confederation of autonomous right-wing groups: a pre-Civil War party led by Gil Robles.

C.N.T.   *Confederación Nacional del Trabajo,* National Confederation of Labour: anarchist in tendency, highly influential before the Civil War; its importance subsequently decreased.

D.R.I.L.   *Directorio Revolucionario Ibérico de Liberación,* Iberian Revolutionary Liberation Council: an anti-Fascist fighting front which sought to unite men of widely differing outlook in order to overthrow the regimes of Franco and Salazar.

E.T.A.   *Euzkadi Ta Azkatasuna,* The Basque Country and its Freedom: a Basque revolutionary movement for national liberation, demanding respect for the individuality of the Basque people and using forms of direct action.

F.A.I.   *Federación Anarquista Ibérica,* Iberian Anarchist Federation: very influential before and during the Civil War.

F.L.P.   *Frente de Liberación Popular,* People's Liberation Front: considering that the situation in Spain was a revolutionary one but that the traditional parties are incapable of turning it to account, the F.L.P., whose aim is socialist revolution, seeks to unite, irrespective of party, all those who envisage the seizure of power to overthrow capitalism.

F.U.D.E.   *Federación Universitaria Democrática Española,* Spanish Democratic University Federation: its statutes lay down the principle that the student is an intellectual worker who is entitled to a truly representative and democratic union system.

F.U.E.   *Federación Universitaria Escolar,* University Student Federation: a clandestine student union.

H.O.A.C.   *Hermandades Obreras de Acción Católica,* Workers' Brotherhoods of Catholic Action: groups belonging to the Catholic Action movement, in close contact with the working class, determined to detach the Church from the Franco regime.

I.D.C.   *Izquierda Democrática Cristiana,* Christian Democratic Left: a movement seeking to ensure the peaceful displacement of Francoism by discarding the oppositions born of the Civil War, and to abide by Christian and democratic principles.

369

J.O.C.   *Juventud Obrera Católica*, Catholic Workers' Youth movement: committed to awakening the Church to social problems.

J.O.N.S.   F.E.T. y de la J.O.N.S. *Falange Española Tradicionalista y de las Juntas de ofensivas nacional-sindicalista*: the *Falange*, inaugurated by José Antonio Primo de Rivera (29 October 1933), joined up with the *National-Syndicalist Offensive Junta* (February 1934) and then with the *Traditionalist Communion* (April 1937) to constitute the single party.

P.C.E.   *Partido Comunista de España*, Spanish Communist Party: led in 1969 by Santiago Carrillo. One of the broadest of Western Communist Parties. Favouring a peaceful national road to socialism, the P.C.E. adopted a strategy centred round the project of a *Huelga Nacional Pacífica*, a peaceful national strike, and of social reconciliation.

P.C.E. (M.L.)   *Partido Comunista de España (marxisto-leninista)*: this small pro-Chinese group is characteristic of the new tendencies which reject the P.C.E.'s peaceful line as 'revisionist'.

P.O.U.M.   *Partido Obrero de Unificación Marxista*, Workers' Party of Marxist Unification: a group of Trotskyist tendency, influential during the Civil War and still in being.

P.S.U.C.   *Partit Socialista Unificat de Catalunya*, Unified Socialist Party of Catalonia: a formally autonomous branch of the Spanish Communist Party.

P.S.O.E.   *Partido Socialista Obrero Español*, Spanish Workers' Socialist Party: a 'social-democratic' group which has always been very anti-Communist. Its influence in Spain has decreased considerably since the Second World War.

S.E.U.   *Sindicato Español Universitario*, Spanish University Syndicate: this official and unrepresentative union, after being challenged by the students, was eventually transformed by the government itself, so feeble had its influence become.

U.D.E.   *Unión Democrática de Estudiantes*, Democratic Students' Union: one of the organizations set up by students to represent them truly, in opposition to the S.E.U. The U.D.E. later dissolved itself voluntarily and was replaced by the F.U.D.E.

U.F.D.   *Unión de Fuerzas Democráticas*, Union of Democratic Forces: constituted to ensure a democratic succession to the Franco regime by means of elections, this Union combines the principal parties, excluding the Communists.

U.G.T.   *Unión General de Trabajadores de España*, General Union of Spanish Workers: a trade union federation of Socialist inspiration, gradually outstripped by the workers' committees in which Catholics and Communists play a preponderant role.

GENEALOGICAL TABLE

FROM LOUIS XIV TO JUAN CARLOS

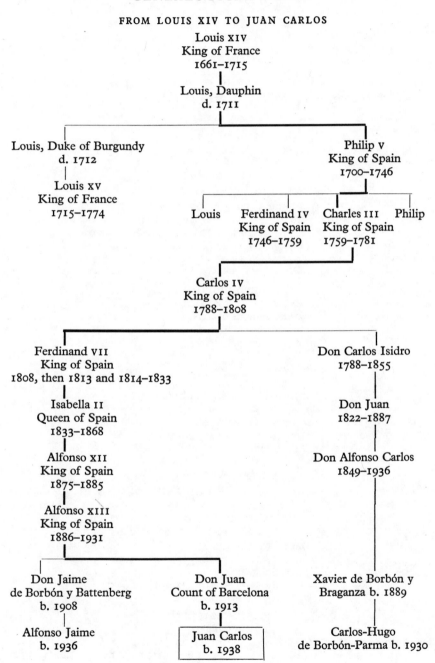

Louis XIV
King of France
1661–1715

Louis, Dauphin
d. 1711

Louis, Duke of Burgundy
d. 1712

Louis XV
King of France
1715–1774

Philip V
King of Spain
1700–1746

Louis

Ferdinand IV
King of Spain
1746–1759

Charles III
King of Spain
1759–1781

Philip

Carlos IV
King of Spain
1788–1808

Ferdinand VII
King of Spain
1808, then 1813 and 1814–1833

Isabella II
Queen of Spain
1833–1868

Alfonso XII
King of Spain
1875–1885

Alfonso XIII
King of Spain
1886–1931

Don Carlos Isidro
1788–1855

Don Juan
1822–1887

Don Alfonso Carlos
1849–1936

Don Jaime
de Borbón y Battenberg
b. 1908

Alfonso Jaime
b. 1936

Don Juan
Count of Barcelona
b. 1913

Juan Carlos
b. 1938

Xavier de Borbón y
Braganza b. 1889

Carlos-Hugo
de Borbón-Parma b. 1930

STATISTICS

Area of Spain: 197,000 sq. miles; density (1966): 170 per sq. mile

1. POPULATION
(in millions)

c. 1900	1930	1966	1969
19	23·5	31·8	33

2. BIRTH RATE
(per annum and per 1,000 inhabitants)

1910	1925	1938	1946	1955	1966
33·2	29·8	20·1	21·6	20·6	20·9

DEATH RATE (idem)

24·0	20·2	19·3	13·0	9·4	8·6

3. SOME PRODUCTION FIGURES

1938	1946	1955	1966	1968

Wheat (in millions of tons)

4·3	3·6	4·0	4·8	

Cattle (in millions)

3·7	3·8	3·0	3·6	

Sheep (idem)

24		16	17	

Electricity (in thousands of kWh)

2·7	5·4	11·9	36·7	

Coal (in millions of tons)

5·6	10·7	12·4	12·7	

Steel (in millions)

0·5	0·6	1·2	3·6	

Motors (in thousands)

		14·5	250·5	350

4. POPULATION

1930	1940	1950	1960	1968

of Madrid (in thousands)

950	1,040	1,618	2,260	3,000

of Barcelona (idem)

1,005	1,081	1,280	1,558	2,000

5. TOURISTS
(in millions)

1953	1955	1959	1960	1961	1962	1963	1964	1965	1966
0·9	1·4	4·1	6·1	7·5	8·6	10·9	14·1	14·2	17·2

6. INDICES OF INDUSTRIAL PRODUCTION
(per cent of 1942)

1940	1942	1945	1950	1953	1955	1957	1959	1961	1963	1965	1966
97	100	97	123	153	186	216	298	388	441	546	669

7. RISE OF INDIVIDUAL INCOME PER HEAD
(in dollars)

1958	1959	1960	1961	1962	1963	1964	1965	1966
281	282	291	332	380	448	497	594	637

COST OF LIVING (per cent of 1958)

100	107	109·6	111	117	128	137	156	165

8. DISTRIBUTION OF THE WORKING POPULATION
IN SECTORS PER CENT OF TOTAL

Years	Agriculture	Industry	Services
1940	50·52	22·13	27·35
1950	47·57	26·55	25·88
1960	39·70	32·98	27·32
1965	34·30	35·20	31·20
1967	27·90	38·20	34·00

BIBLIOGRAPHY

I. WORKS OF GENERAL INTEREST
providing a historical and cultural background to the present study.

Aubier, D. and Tunon de Lara, M., *Espagne*, Paris, 1956.
Brenan, Gerald, *The Spanish Labyrinth*, New York and Cambridge, 1943.
Bruguera, F. G., *Histoire contemporaine d'Espagne, 1789–1950*, Gap, 1953.
Carr, Raymond, *Spain, 1808–1939*, Oxford, 1966.
Castro, Americo, *Réalité de l'Espagne, Histoire et valeur*, Paris, 1963.
De Castro, Ignacio Fernandez, *De las Cortes de Cadiz al Plan de Desarrollo (1808–1966)*, Paris, 1968.
Chastenet, Jacques, *Histoire de l'Espagne*, Paris, 1968.
Descola, Jean, *Histoire d'Espagne*, Paris, 1959.
Payne, Stanley G., *Falange, a history of Spanish Fascism*, Stanford, California, 1962: *Los militares y la política en la España moderna*, Paris, 1967.
Rama, Carlos M., *La crise espagnole au XXe siècle*, Paris, 1962; *Ideologia, clases y regiones en España contemporánea*, Montevideo, 1956.
Seco, Carlos, *Historia de España, Epoca contemporánea*, Barcelona, 1966.
Souchère, Elena de la, *Explication de l'Espagne*, Paris, 1962.
Tuñón de Lara, Manuel, *Historia y realidad del Poder*, Madrid, 1967.
Tuñón de Lara, Manuel, *La España del Siglo XX, 1917–1939*, Paris, 1966.
Ubieto, Regla, Jover, Seco, *Introducción a la Historia de España*, Barcelona, 1966.
Vilar, Pierre, *Histoire d'Espagne*, Paris, 1965; *La Catalogne dans l'Espagne moderne*, Paris, 1960.

II. ON FRANCO

A. TEXTS

Discursas y mensajes del Jefe del Estado, Madrid, appeared regularly from 1951 onward.
Franco ha dicho (1936–1942), Madrid, 1947.
Palabras del Caudillo, Madrid, 1943.
Recopilación de las mas importantes declaraciones, Madrid, 1947.

B. BIOGRAPHIES

Arraras, Joaquín, *El general Franco*, San Sebastian, 1937.
Coles, S. F. A., *Franco of Spain*, London, 1955.
Crozier, Brian, *Franco, a Biographical History*, London and Boston, 1967.
Galinsoga, Luis de, *Centinela de Occidente, Semblenza biográfica de Francisco*, Madrid, 1958.
Hills, George, *Franco, the Man and his Nation*, London and New York, 1967.

374

Martin, Claude, *Franco, Soldat et Chef d'Etat*, Paris, 1959.
Ramírez, Luis, *Vie de Francisco Franco*, Paris, 1965.
Salva, Miguel F., *Francisco Franco*, Barcelona, 1959.

III. THE CIVIL WAR

This list comprises only a few works indispensable for the understanding of subsequent events.

A. DOCUMENTS (see also V)

Archives secrètes de la Wilhelmstrasse, vol. III, *L'Allemagne et la guerre civile espagnole*, Paris, 1952.
Documents on German Foreign Policy, series D, London, 1951.
Documents secrets du ministère des Affaires étrangères d'Allemagne (1936–1943), vol. III, *Espagne*, Paris, 1946.
Gallo, Max, *Contribution à l'étude des méthodes et des résultats de la propagande fasciste dans l'immédiat avant-guerre (1930–1940)*, duplicated thesis, Nice, 1968.

B. STUDIES

Aznar, Manuel, *Historia militar de la guerra de España (1936–1939)*, Madrid, 1940; *Guerra y victoria de Espana*, Madrid, 1942.
Broue, Pierre and Temime, E., *La Révolution et la Guerre d'Espagne*, Paris, 1961.
Jackson, Gabriel, *The Spanish Republic and the Civil War (1931–1939)*, Princeton, 1965.
London, Arthur G., *Espagne*, Paris, 1966.
Peter, Jean Pierre, 'L'Histoire à l'épreuve de la Guerre d'Espagne', in *Annales, Economies, Sociétés* . . . Paris, Jan./Feb. 1964.
Ricardo de la Cierva, *Historia de la guerra civil española*, I, Madrid, 1969.
Southworth, Herbert R., *Le mythe de la Croisade de Franco*, Paris, 1964; *Antifalange : estudio critico de Falange en la guerra de España de M. G. Venero*, Paris, 1967.
Thomas, Hugh, *The Spanish Civil War*, London and New York, 1961.
Venero, M. Garcia, *Falange en la guerra de España; la unificación y Hedilla*, Paris, 1967.

C. ON JOSÉ ANTONIO PRIMO DE RIVERA

Nellesen, B., *J. A. Primo de Rivera, der troubadour der spanischen Falange*, Stuttgart, 1965.
Primo de Rivera, José Antonio, *Obras completas*, Madrid, 1952; *Textos inéditos y epistolarios*, Madrid, 1956.
Thomas, Hugh, 'The Hero in the Empty Room, José Antonio and Spanish Fascism', in the *Journal of Contemporary History*, no. 1, London, 1966.
Ximénez de Sandoval, Felipe, *José Antonio, biográfica apasionada*, Barcelona, 1941.
cf. Southworth, García Venero, Payne, etc., op. cit. above. Cf. also documents in Max Gallo, op. cit., below.

D. OTHER ACCOUNTS

Bowers, Claude, *My Mission to Spain*, New York and London, 1954.
Casado, *Asi cayó Madrid*, Madrid, 1968.
Churchill, Winston, *Step by Step, 1936–1939*, London and New York, 1939.
Hernández, Jesús, *La grande trahison*, Paris, 1947.
Ibarruri, Dolors, *Mémoires de la Pasionaria*, Paris, 1964.
Koltsov, Mijail, *Diario de la guerra de España*, Paris, 1966.
Nenni, Pietro, *La guerre d'Espagne*, Paris, 1959.
Rossif, F., and Chapsal, M., *Mourir à Madrid*, Marabout University no. 40, Verviers, 1963.

IV. FRANCO'S VICTORY

Aparicio, Juan, *El Estado nacional*, Madrid, 1943.
Corthis, A., *L'Espagne de la victoire*, Paris, 1941.
Gimenez, Caballero E., *España nuestra, el libro de las Juventudes Españolas*, Madrid, 1943.
Marcotte, V. A., *L'Espagne Nationale-syndicaliste*, Brussels, 1943.
Maurras, Charles, *Vers l'Espagne de Franco*, Paris, 1943.
Solmi, Arrigo, *Lo stato nuovo nella Spagna di Franco*, Milan, 1940.

V. SPAIN IN THE SECOND WORLD WAR

A. DOCUMENTS

Archives secrètes de la Wilhelmstrasse, vols VIII and IX, Paris, 1954–5.
Ciano, G., *Diplomatic Papers* (ed. Malcolm Muggeridge), London, 1948; *Journal politique, 1939–1943*, Geneva, 1948, English versions London, 1947 (ed. Malcolm Muggeridge), and New York, 1947 (ed. Hugh Gibson) (page references in footnotes are to Geneva edn.).
Documents on German Foreign Policy, series D, London, 1951.
Documents secrets du ministère des Affaires étrangères d'Allemagne (1936–1943), vol. III, *Espagne*, Paris, 1946.
Franco's Neutrality and British Policy, London, 1944. Cf. also works cited above in III.
The Spanish Government and the Axis, Documents (1940–1943), Washington, 1946.

B. STUDIES

Allison, Peers, E., *Spain in Eclipse*, London, 1945.
de la Baume, R., *L'Espagne non belligérante*, in *Revue d'Histoire diplomatique*, Paris, April/June 1955.
Doussinague, Teixidor J. Maria, *España tenía razón*, Madrid, 1949.
Dzelepy, E. N., *Franco, Hitler et les alliés*, Brussels, 1961.
'L'Espagne pendant la guerre', in *Revue d'histoire de la deuxième guerre mondiale*, no. 5, Paris, Jan. 1952.
Fernández, Alberto E., *La España de los maquis*, Milan, 1967.
Puzzo, Dante A., *Spain and the Great Powers (1936–1941)*, New York, 1962.
Villanova, Antonio, *Los Olvidados*, Paris, 1968.
Villegas, Diaz de, *La División Azul en linea*, Barcelona, 1967.

C. MEMOIRS

Anfuso, *Roma–Berlino–Salo*, Milan, 1955.
Churchill, Winston, *The Second World War*, London and New York, 1960–5.
Eden, Anthony (Lord Avon), *Memoirs*, London and Boston, 1960–5.
de Gaulle, Charles, *Discours* (June 1940–Sept. 1945), Paris, 1945; *War Memoirs*, London, 1959.
Hayes, Carlton J. H., *Wartime Mission in Spain*, New York, 1946.
Hoare, Samuel (Lord Templewood), *Ambassador on Special Mission*, London, 1946, published as *The Complacent Dictator*, New York, 1947.
Pietri, F., *Mes années d'Espagne*, Paris, 1954.
Schmidt, P., *Sur la scène internationale. Ma figuration auprès d'Hitler*, Paris, 1953.
Suñer, Serrano R., *Entre les Pyrénées et Gibraltar*, Geneva, 1947.

VI. IMMEDIATE POST-WAR PERIOD. CONSEQUENCES OF THE WORLD WAR

A. DOCUMENTS

U.N.O., *Security Council of the U.N.: The Spanish Question*, 1946.

B. STUDIES

'L'Espagne 1950' in *Les Temps Modernes*, Paris, May 1950.
Francotte, R. A., *L'heure de l'Espagne*, Brussels, 1947.
Hughes, J., *L'Espagne de Franco*, Paris, 1948.

C. ACCOUNTS

Alba, Victor, *Insomnie espagnole*, Paris, 1946.
Ansaldo, Juan Antonio, *Mémoires d'un monarchiste*, Monaco, 1954.
Bost, J. L., *L'Espagne au jour le jour*, Paris, 1950.
Hermanos, Juan, *La fin de l'espoir*, Paris, 1950.
Izcaray, J., *Las guerrillas de Levante*, Paris, 1949.
Ramírez, Luis, *Nuestros primeros veinticinco años*, Paris, 1964.

VII. SPAIN FROM 1950 TO THE PRESENT DAY

A. DOCUMENTS

El nuevo Estado español (1936–1961), Madrid, 1961.
España en su prensa, Madrid, published annually since 1963.
Fundamental Laws of the State: the Spanish Constitution, Madrid, 1968.
Instituto de Estudios políticos: *Leyes políticas de España*, Madrid, 1956.

B. STUDIES AND INVESTIGATIONS

'Analyse de l'Espagne', in *La Table Ronde*, Paris, Oct. 1968.
Del Boca, Angelo, *L'altra Spagna*, Milan, 1961.
Bourdarias, J., *L'Espagne nouvelle*, Paris, 1969.

De Castro, Ignacio Fernández y Martínez, José, *España hoy*, Paris, 1963.
Clark, C. L., *The Evolution of the Franco Regime*, 3 vols, Washington, n.d.
Conférence d'Europe Occidentale pour l'amnistie aux emprisonnés et exilés politiques espagnols, Paris, 1961.
Il Contemporaneo, number devoted to Spain, Rome, July/Aug. 1961.
Crozier, Brian, 'Spain after Franco', in *The Times*, London, 10–11 July 1967.
'Espagne 1939–1959', in *La Nouvelle Critique*, Paris, April 1959.
'Espagne 1967', in *Partisans*, Paris, Dec. 1966/Jan. 1967.
'L'Espagne à l'heure du dialogue', in *Esprit*, Paris, Oct. 1965.
L'Espagne et la primauté du droit, Geneva, 1962.
'Espagnols sans baillon, documents 1958–1961', in *Cahiers de Témoignage Chrétien*, Paris, 1961.
Horizonte español 1966, vols I and II, Paris, 1966.
Meyriat, Jean, *L'Espagne*, Paris, 1961–2.
Niedergang, M., 'L'Espagne de la succession', in *Le Monde*, Paris, 13–18 July 1966.
Niedergang, M., 'L'Espagne en exception', in *Le Monde*, Paris, no. 9, March 1969; 'L'Espagne ou la tentation des extrêmes', in *Le Monde*, Paris, 15–20 March 1968.
Pattee, R., *This is Spain*, Milwaukee, 1951.
Valera, F., 'Evolution de l'Espagne', in *Revue socialiste*, no. 204, June 1967.

C. SPECIAL POINTS

(i) *The Church*

Artigues, Daniel, *L'Opus Dei en Espagne*, vol. I, 1928–57, Paris, 1968.
Doncastella, R., *Análisis sociológico del catolicismo español*, Barcelona, 1967.
Drochon, P., *Le cléricalisme dans l'Espagne franquiste*, thesis, Poitiers, 1961.
Langlois, Noël, 'Le drame du clergé espagnol', in *Etudes*, Paris, April 1968.
Raymat, A., 'Où va le laïcat espagnol', in *Etudes*, Paris, Sept. 1966.
Vasquez, Jesús Maria, *Realidades socio-religiosas de España*, Madrid, 1967.

(ii) *The Army*

Busquets Bragulat, Julio, *El militar de carrera en España*, Barcelona, 1967.

(iii) *Trade Unions*

Iglesias Selgas, Carlos, *Los sindicatos en España*, Madrid, 1966.
Nuestra huelga, leaflet published by the Echevarri workers, IDES, Paris, 1968.
'Presente y futuro de las Comisiones obreras', in *Cuadernos de ruedo ibérico*, Paris, Aug./Sept. 1968.

(iv) *Politics*

Duenas, Gonzalo, *La ley de prensa de Manuel Fraga*, Paris, 1968.
Hermet, Guy, 'La presse espagnole depuis la suppression de la censure', in *Revue française de Science politique*, Paris, Feb. 1968.
Julián Grimau, el hombre, el crimen, la protesta, Paris, 1963.
Los nuevos liberales, Madrid, 1966.
Vilar, Sergio, *Protagonistas de la España democrática. La oposición a la dictadura (1939–1969)*, Paris, 1969.

(v) *Gibraltar*
Documents on Gibraltar presented before the Spanish Cortes, Madrid, 1965.

D. POINTS OF VIEW AND ACCOUNTS

Adulteraciones del equipo de Santiago Carrillo, Madrid, n.d.
Le bilan de vingt ans de dictature fasciste (the balance-sheet of twenty years of Fascist dictatorship), the Spanish Communist Party, 1 April 1969.
Carrillo, Santiago, *Après Franco quoi?* Paris, 1966; *Nuevos enfoques a problema de hoy*, Paris, 1967; 'Problems of Socialism Today', London, 1970.
Claudín, Fernando, 'Dos concepciones de la vía española al socialismo', in *Horizonte espanol*, vol. II, Paris, 1966.
Creach, Jean, *Le coeur et l'épée*, Paris, 1958.
Iribarne, Fraga Manuel, *Como está gobernada España*, Madrid, 1950.
Ridruejo, Dioniso, *Escrito en España*, Buenos Aires, 1962.
Romero, Emilio, *El futuro de España nace un poco todos los días*, Madrid, 1959.
Saint Paulien, *J'ai vu vivre l'Espagne*, Paris, 1958.
Serer, Calvo Rafael, *España sin problema*, Madrid, 1949.
Yglesia, José, *The Goodbye Land*, New York, 1966.

VIII. SPAIN'S ECONOMY

A. SOURCES

Etudes économiques de l'O.C.D.E. Paris, regularly since 1959.
Images économiques du monde, Paris, annually.
Spanish Statistics.

B. GENERAL PROBLEMS

Drain, Michel, *Géographie de la péninsule ibérique*, Paris, 1964.
Fuertes, J. V., *Sobre la decadencia económica de España*, Madrid, 1967.
Problèmes du développement économique dans les pays méditerranéens, Paris, 1963.
Tamames, Ramón, *Estructura económica de España*, Madrid, 1960; *Lucha contro los monopolios en España*, Madrid, 1964; *Los monopolios en España*, Madrid, 1967; *Introducción a la economía española*, Madrid, 1967.
Tuñón de Lara, Manuel, *Panorama de la economía española*, Madrid, 1962; *Variaciones del nivel de vida en España*, Madrid, 1965.
Vila, Valenti Juan, *La Péninsule ibérique*, Paris, 1968.

C. AGRICULTURE AND UNDERDEVELOPMENT IN THE SOUTH

Baade, F., *La agricultura española y el comercio exterior*, Madrid, 1967.
Canovas, Garcia C., *Agricultura española (1957–65)*, Madrid, 1966.
Comín, Alfonso, *España del Sur. Aspectos económicos y sociales del desarrollo industrial de Andalucía*, Madrid, 1965.
Hermet, Guy, *Le Problème méridional de l'Espagne*, Paris, 1965.
Martínez Alier, Juan, *La estabilidad del latifundismo*, Paris, 1967.
'Tres estudios sobre el campo español', in *Cuadernos de Ruedo ibérico*, Paris, June/Sept. 1967.

D. IMMIGRATION

Hermet, Guy, *Les Espagnols en France*, Paris, 1967.
J'ai quitté l'Espagne . . . Les prolétaires du Marché commun, Lausanne, 1963.
García, Fernández Jesús, *La emigración exterior de España*, Barcelona, 1965.

E. COMMON MARKET: DEVELOPMENT PLAN

Beltrán, Luca, *La integración económica européa y la posición de España*, Madrid, 1966.
L'Espagne à l'heure du développement, special issue of the review *Tiers Monde*, Paris, Oct./Dec. 1967.
Fontela, Montes E., *Commerce extérieur et développement économique : l'Espagne*, Geneva–Paris, 1962.
Rudel, Christian, *L'Espagne du Plan ou la succession ouverte*, Paris, 1966.
Tamames, Ramón, *Espanya : Segon pla de desenvolupment?* Barcelona, 1967.

IX. HISTORY REFLECTED IN LITERATURE
(the new movement in poetry and fiction)

Arias, Gonzalo, *L'homme à la pancarte*, Paris, 1968.
Auclair, Marcelle, *Enfance et mort de García Lorca*, Paris, 1968.
Darmangeat, P., *La poésie espagnole : anthologie des origines à nos jours*, Paris, 1963.
Espriu, Salvador, *La peau du taureau*, Paris, 1968.
Ferres, Antonio, *Les vaincus*, Paris, 1964.
Gironella, J. M., *Les cyprès croient en Dieu*; *Un million de morts*; *Quand la paix éclata*; *La grande déception*, Paris, 1964–9.
Goytisolo, Juan, *Jeux de mains*; *Fiestas*; *Chronique d'une île*; *Pour vivre ici*; *Terres de Nijar*; *La Chanca*; *Pièces d'identité*; Paris, 1956–60–61–62–64–68.
Guerena, J.-L., *Anthologie bilingue de la poésie espagnole contemporaine*, Verviers, 1969.
Liberovici, S., and Straniero, M. L., *Chansons de la nouvelle résistance espagnole*, Paris, 1963.
'Littérature catalane', in *Europe*, Paris, Dec. 1967.
'La littérature de l'Espagne', in *Europe*, Paris, Jan./Feb. 1958.
López, Salinas, Armando, *Chaque jour compte en Espagne*, Paris, 1965.
López, F., and Marrast, R., *La poésie ibérique de combat*, Paris, 1966.
'Miguel Hernández', in *Europe*, Paris, Sept./Oct. 1962.
Puccini, D., *Romancero de la résistance espagnole*, 2 vols. Paris, 1967.

X. SPECIAL POINTS

Cau, Jean, *Les oreilles et la queue*, Paris, 1961.
Lapierre, Dominique, and Collins, Larry, *. . . Ou tu porteras mon deuil*, Paris, 1967.
Morris, Christopher, *The Big Catch* (Palomares), London, 1967.
Saint Paulien, *Histoire de la corrida*, Paris, 1968.
t'Serstevens, A., *Itinéraire espagnol*, Paris, 1963.

XI. DOCUMENTATION: THE PRESS

It is impossible to cite all the newspapers and periodicals consulted. However the immense task of abstracting achieved by *Documentation française* has made research easier. The following must be mentioned:

Le Bulletin de presse étrangère, Les chroniques étrangères (Espagne) from 1949 to Dec. 1967, *Les Problèmes économiques, Notes et études documentaires, Articles et documents,* all in *Documentation française,* Paris.

I have made use of the following periodicals: *Cuadernos de Ruedo Ibérico, Cuadernos para el diálogo, Les Temps Modernes, Esprit, Europe, Lo spettatore internazionale, La nouvelle revue internationale, La Table Ronde, La Revue d'histoire de la deuxième guerre mondiale, Etudes,* etc.

From the newspapers (*Le Monde, The Times, A.B.C., Ya, Arriba, Mundo Obrero, La Batalla, L'Humanité,* etc.) I have been able to glean many facts and discover points of view, as also from weekly and monthly journals such as *Le Monde diplomatique, L'Express, L'Observateur* and its successors, *Les Lettres françaises,* etc., and, for an earlier period, *L'Illustration.*

XII. FILM

A. DOCUMENTARY FILMS

Buñuel, Luis, *Land without Bread,* 1932.
Malraux, André, *L'Espoir,* 1939–45.
Rossif, Frédéric, *Mourir à Madrid,* 1963.
Saenz de Heredia, José Luis, *Franco ese hombre,* 1964.

B. FILMS REVEALING THE TRUTH ABOUT SPAIN

Bardem, J. A., *Muerte de un ciclista,* 1955; *Calle Mayor,* 1956; *A las cinco de la tarde,* 1960.
Berlanga, Luis García, *El Verdugo,* 1964.
Berlanga, Luis García, and Bardem, J. A., *Benvenida Mr Marshall,* 1952.
Ferreri, Mario, *El Cochecito,* 1961.
Resnais, Alain, *La Guerre est finie,* 1965–6 (scenario J. Semprún).
Rosi, Francesco, *The Moment of Truth,* 1965.

C. ON THE SPANISH CINEMA

Annuario de Cine español, Madrid, regularly.
García Escudero, J., *La historia en cien palabras del Cine español,* Salamanca, 1954.
Vizcaíno Casas, Fernando, *Diccionario del cine español,* Madrid, 1966.

INDEX

ABOUT THE AUTHOR

Max Gallo was born in 1932 at Nice. Awarded the degree of Doctor of Letters for studies of Italian Fascism and other totalitarian governments, he is now a member of the faculty of the Institute of Political Studies in Paris. In addition to *Spain Under Franco,* Dr. Gallo is the author of *Robespierre the Incorruptible: A Psycho-Biography* and of *The Night of the Long Knives,* both of which books have been translated into English. His many other books include a novel, *La Grande Peur de 1989.* Max Gallo also writes regularly for the newspaper *L'Express.* His home is in Paris.